How to
Make It in the
New Music
Business

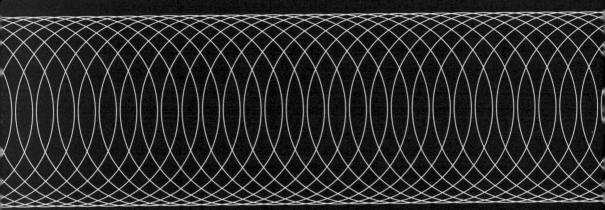

How to Make It in the

Lessons, Tips, and Inspiration from

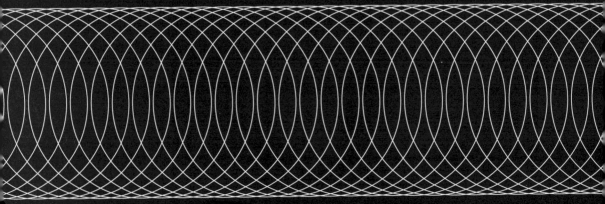

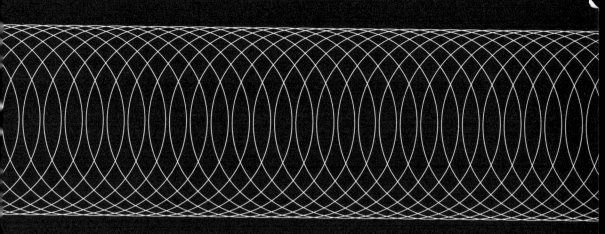

New Music Business

Music's Biggest and Best

Robert Wolff

Billboard Books

An Imprint of Watson-Guptill Publications • New York

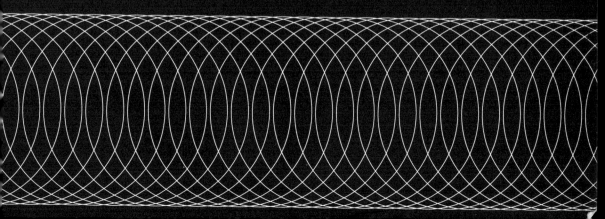

Dedication

This book is dedicated to
my parents, Adam and Mary Wolff.
Thank you for everything.

Executive Editor: Bob Nirkind

Editor: Sylvia Warren

Production Manager: Hector Campbell

Cover design: Derek Bacchus

Interior design: Leah Lococo

First published in 2004 by

Billboard Books

An imprint of Watson-Guptill Publications,

a division of VNU Business Media, Inc.,

770 Broadway, New York, NY 10003

www.watsonguptill.com

Library of Congress Cataloging-in-Publication Data for this title may be obtained
from the Library of Congress Library of Congress Card Number: 2003116048

ISBN-13: 978-0-8230-7954-4
ISBN: 0-8230-7954-6

Printed in the United States

First printing, 2004

2 3 4 5 6 7 8 / 10 09 08 07 06

Acknowledgments

There are some very special people that I'd like to thank for making this book a reality.

To Bob Nirkind: Without a doubt, you are the finest editor I've ever worked with. Your advice and direction on how to turn my vision into reality has been instrumental in making this book what it is and one I'm so very proud of. Thank you Bob.

To Bob Bradshaw: When I called you years ago to build my dream guitar rig, I never knew I'd be getting a great friend to go along with it. Thank you Bob for that friendship and all your help.

To Steve Lukather: You're an amazing person, Steve. Over the years, your playing has been such an inspiration. I want to thank you for all of your help with this book and count myself fortunate as now having the privilege to be your friend.

To Bob Ludwig: Thank you Bob for being a part of this book. I always knew there was a reason why you and your work are so respected. Spending time with you proved it.

To Diane Warren: Diane, I'll admit it: I've been a fan of your music for a long time. You always find the right things to say and how to say them and for this book, it was no exception. Thank you for being part of it.

To Bob Clearmountain: Thank you for inviting me to your home and studio and for taking the time to share your wealth of knowledge. I know readers of this book will be helped and inspired in ways you may never imagine.

To Larry Cohen: To a good friend and trusted advisor. Thanks for always being there and thank you for being part of this book.

Special thanks also go to:

My developmental editor, Sylvia Warren

Billboard Books and Watson-Guptill

Julie Horton, Becca Gilbert, and Realsongs

Christine Wilhemy and Emagic

Eric Persing and Spectrasonics

Paul Lefebvre, Rolf Hartley, and Sonic Solutions

Jim Cooper and MOTU

Michael Logue and Antares

Andy Broadaway and Hamilton Domains

Steve Chang and Live365

Brian McConnon and Steinberg

Peter Maund and Sibelius

Didi Dori, Bob Reardon, and Waves

Marsha Vdovon and Ableton, Cycling '74, and Propellerhead

Bela Canhoto and Native Instruments

Karen Lange and The Company Corporation

Eric Newbauer, Gary Holiday, and Studio Network Solutions

Peter Snell and Tascam

Dave Kerzner, Gary Kerzner, and IK Multimedia

Chandra Lynn and Digidesign

Larry Crane and TapeOp magazine

Adrienne Crew and Salon.com

Peter Glanville, Jennifer Wolfe, and Glyph

Mark Altekruse, Melissa Horn, Nathalie Welch, and Apple

Table of Contents

Introduction **13**

Part 1: Welcome to the New Music Business 21

Lesson 1: Old School vs. New Reality: The Digital Revolution Levels the Playing Field **22**

Welcome to the Old School Music Business:
What Your Record Earns and What You Get to Keep **23**

Start with the Royalty Rate **23**　　*Here Come the Deductions* **24**

What's Left? **27**　　*Now Consider an Even Worse Scenario* **28**

Welcome to the New Reality **29**

New School vs. Old School: Your Decisions vs. Corporate Structures **29**

New School vs. Old School: Home Studio vs. Big Studio **30**

New School vs. Old School: Internet Radio vs. Traditional Radio **31**

New School vs. Old School: Your Label vs. Their Label **32**

New School vs. Old School: Your Marketing vs. Their Marketing **32**

New School vs. Old School: Your Profits vs. Their Profits **33**

New School vs. Old School: Your Control vs. Their Control **33**

Lesson 2: Radio and Records: How to Play the Game **35**

The Radio/Record Company Dance **35**

Making Radio Work for You **40**

Pay-for-Play **41**　　*Basic Calls to Action* **42**

Another Call to Action: The Power of 200 Letter and Request **43**

Create the Right Ad and Start Small **44**

Lesson 3: The Illusion of Needing a Record Deal: Courtney Love's Real-World Wake-Up Call **47**

Courtney Does the Math on Record Contracts **48**

Artists, Copyright Law, and the RIAA **50**

Technology Is Not Piracy **52**

Artists Have Options **54**

Equity for Artists **56**

Music Is a Service to Its Customers **57**

New Models for the Record Business **58**

An Open Letter to Steve Case **58**

Corporate Sponsorships **59**

Money as Incentive **60**

In Conclusion **66**

**Lesson 4: A View from Both Sides of the Fence: Steve Lukather on
What's Right and What's Wrong with the Music Business** **63**

Lukather on the Music Business, Yesterday and Today **64**

Musicians and Their Craft **69**

Signing with a Major Label or an Independent **71**

Keeping It Real **72**

Making a Hit Record **73**

Enjoying Your Gift of Music **74**

**Lesson 5: Building Your A-Team:
Who You Need and Who You Don't** **75**

Attorneys **75**

It's All about Billable Hours **76**   *Finding and Hiring the Right Attorney* **78**

Get It in Writing **79**   *Negotiating a Fee* **81**

Setting Deal Parameters **82**   *When You Need an Attorney—And When You Don't* **83**

Great Advice and Free Stuff You Can Get in Seconds **85**

Good CPAs: Worth Their Weight in Gold **87**

A Cautionary Tale **87**   *Tracking Expenses on Your Own* **90**

Agents: Do You Really Need One? **91**

*Part 2: Writing Your Songs, Getting Your Sound, and
Mixing, Mastering, and Recording Your Music* **95**

**Lesson 6: It's All About the Song: Advice and
Inspiration from Diane Warren** **96**

Diane on Starting Out **97**

The Big Break **99**
The Learning That'll Never End **99**
The Diane Warren Songwriting Process **100**
Protect Yourself and Your Music **101**
Radio and the Music Business Today **102**
A Song Is a Part of Who You Are **103**

Lesson 7: Developing Your Sound: Advice from Bob Bradshaw 105
Bob Bradshaw on Starting Out **106**
Great Combinations = Great Sounds **108**
The Bob Bradshaw Sound Philosophy **108**
Getting a Great Sound **111**
Amps and Speakers: The Keys to a Great Sound **112**
Getting a Professional Sound on a Modest Budget **116**
Going the Custom Route **116**
Twenty Ways to Get Great Sounds **117**

**Lesson 8: Finding the Best Recording and Creating Platform:
Using What the Pros Use 122**
Your Computer: The Hub of Your System **123**
Your Computer/Audio Interface **124**
Digital Audio Workstations (DAWs) **126**
Digidesign Pro Tools **127**   *MOTU Digital Performer* **131**
Emagic Logic **135**   *Steinberg* **138**

Plug-ins **144**
Ableton Live **145**   *Antares* **147**   *Cycling '74 pluggo 3* **150**
IK Multimedia **151**   *MOTU MachFive* **153**   *Native Instruments* **155**
Propellerhead **160**   *Sibelius* **163**   *Sonic Solutions* **167**
Spectrasonics **169**   *Steinberg* **172**   *TASCAM GigaStudio* **174**   *Waves* **176**

Outboard Gear, Sound Controllers, and Mixers **177**
Sound Controllers **178**   *Mixers* **178**

Storage Systems **179**
Tape Storage **179**   *Hard Disk Storage* **180**

Lesson 9: Mixing Your Music: Advice from Bob Clearmountain 184

Bob on Starting Out 185

Being Successful in Music Is Doing the Best You Can 187

A Constantly Changing Approach to Recording and Mixing Music 188

The Bob Clearmountain Mixing Process 190

It Doesn't Take a Lot of Money to Mix Great-Sounding Records 192

Bob Clearmountain's Mix This! Studio Equipment List 197

On How Long It Should Take to Make a Record 201

How Making Music and Records Has Changed 201

Lesson 10: Mastering Your Music: Advice from Bob Ludwig 203

Bob on Starting Out 204

The Music Business, Yesterday and Today 205

The Importance of Mixing in the Recording Process 206

The Importance of Mastering in the Recording Process 207

The Biggest Mistakes People Make in Recording 210

Tips on Setting Up a Recording Studio Workstation
and Recording Platform 211

Some Advice on Internet and Remote Broadcasting 212

The Future of Recording 213

Part 3: Your Business in the New Music Business 215

**Lesson 11: Launching the Business of You, Inc.:
Five Steps to Incorporation 216**

The Benefits of Incorporation 216

Tax Advantages 217   *Other Advantages* 219

Step One: Determine the Type of Business You Want 221

Step Two: Choose a Business Name 222

Step Three: Get Good Advice 222

Step Four: File with the IRS 224

Form SS-4 224   *Form 2553* 225

Step Five: File a Business in My State 225

After Incorporating 226

Lesson 12: Real-World New Music Business Boot Camp: What You Need to Know about Copyrights, Music Publishing, and Licensing 227

The Get Smart Quick Guide to Copyrights **228**

Your Copyright Is All Yours **229**   *How to Copyright Your Work in Three Easy Steps* **230**

Copyright Issues Regarding Employment **231**

The Basic Ins and Outs of Music Publishing **232**

How Music Publishers Generate Revenue **233**   *Writer–Publisher Relationships* **235**

How Your Publisher Works for You **236**   *Administrative Agreements* **238**

Negotiating the Best Agreement **239**

Forming Your Own Music Publishing Company **240**

Joining the Right Organizations **241**

Licensing and Protecting Your Work **242**

Key Points in a Licensing Agreement **243**

Part 4: Marketing, Selling, and Distributing Your Music All Over the World: Tapping into the Big Money Potential of Niche Markets, the Internet, and Webcasting 247

Lesson 13: Premiering Your Music: Three Steps to Broadcasting and Selling Your Music to a Global Audience 248

Step One: Get a Domain Name **249**

Step Two: Get a Web Site **253**

Decide on the Basics: Size and Layout **254**   *Personalizing Your Site* **254**   *Go Global* **255**

Step Three: Begin Broadcasting Your Music **255**

Personalize Your Music and Message **257**   *Know Who's Listening to Your Music* **258**

Learn How to Promote Your Music **259**   *Select the Broadcast Package Best Suited to Your Needs* **259**

Create Your Internet Radio Station **260**   *Questions about Internet Broadcasting* **260**

Promoting and Selling Your Music and Web Site 264

Use Search Engines and Metatags to Direct Traffic to Your Site 264

Create Tie-ins with Other Sites and Companies 265

Associate Yourself with a Powerful Brand 265   *Do Deals with Other Web Sites 265*

Sell Your Music on the Internet 265   *Sell All Forms of Your Music on Your Site 266*

**Cool Ways to Record, Send, and Receive Music from
Anyone, Anywhere, Anytime 266**

Lessons of Inspiration 269

Learning from Greatness: The Tommy Tedesco Story 269

On Selling Your Creative Ideas to Noncreative People 272

On How to Make Yourself Wanted 273

Shattering the Myth of the Must-Have Music Town:
The Studio on Music Row 275

On What Inspires Greatness 276

On Getting to Where You Want to Go and Suprising Ways
It Can Inspire You 278

Index 282

A Word from the Author

This book is more than advice, tips, and information put to ink and paper. It's a lifetime of friends, influences, and experiences that have touched my heart in some special way. Along the road in my musical journey, I've learned a lot—sometimes the hard way—about why doors open to some people and not to others. I've also learned a lot about how to open them. This book is a distillation of my experience and understanding, told in a straightforward, direct way—with a minimum of legalese. I know it will help you get where you want to go. I hope it will also inspire you to create the music that is in your heart, on *your* terms.

For more information on music business tips, advice, individual and business plans and success strategies, latest news, global message board, resources and links, to contact the author, and much more, please visit www.RobertWolff.com.

Introduction

*I*t's funny how life works. Just when you think you've got things all figured out, boom. . . . Things change. Along comes something new, and it's time to learn all over again.

Take music. Before the digital revolution, unless you had a major label record deal, access to huge piles of cash (courtesy of your record label, to whom you had to pay it all back), a big-name producer (who got a cut of whatever money your record *might* make), a decent studio (cheap at $2,000 a day), and talented musicians (double and triple scale pay), your chances of making serious money in the music business, even if you sold over a half a million copies of your record, were slim to none.

But then the digital revolution hit. Almost overnight, the way that music was created, recorded, distributed, marketed, and sold was changed forever. The digital revolution has changed something else as well. It has pretty well leveled the playing field for you, for me, and for everyone else. It allows us to make our music, our way.

As my former mentor, the legendary magazine and fitness icon Joe Weider, always said, "You'll never get rich working for anyone else. You've got to do your own thing and be an owner." In music, this means having complete control over your music, your product, and your dream.

So in this book we're going to go to school. I'm going to teach you the lessons of how to achieve this control in today's and tomorrow's digital world. And you're going to learn tips and secrets from many of music's primo players—the people who get paid huge major record label dollars to make the hits. My lessons and their wisdom will help you to get *your* signature sound. We'll teach you how you can create a business— no, make that an empire, if you like—called You, Inc. And you'll be able to use today's and tomorrow's technology to make it all happen right from your own home.

It's conventional wisdom that musicians can spend countless years becoming good players and singers, but very rarely do they become good businesspeople too. Unfortunately, this has all too often been true, from the brilliant Mozart, who struggled financially and was known for his lack of business acumen, to today's artists, most of whom constantly carp that they need to play out more regularly and wonder why there is always too much month left at the end of the check. That's all about to change.

The idea that there are only a few ways to make money with your music (e.g., perform in clubs, get signed to a record deal, or play on records) has for years been accepted as the gospel truth, but that "truth" is false. There are lots of ways to make money in music, and I'm going to show you some good ones.

I'm also going to teach you how to do what you do now, but better. I think many people would agree that creativity is stifled by pressure—especially when that pressure is financial. It's hard to come up with a great new song when the rent is due tomorrow and your credit cards are maxed out. Follow the strategies in this book and you're going to get some major breathing room in a hurry.

A very rich man once told me, "It's not how much you make, but how much you keep that counts." With the strategies I'm going to teach you, you're going to learn the very things that successful businesspeople do to create wealth and keep it.

I'm going to teach you how to play the major record label game as well, but on your own terms. Let me warn you, though: Many highly respected record business insiders have told me that the record business as we know it is dead. Its years of excess, its lack of creative vision, its inability to promote new sounds and develop enduring artists, and its unwillingness to change, adapt, and ride the Internet/distribution revolution have cut off its lifeline. So far gone is the old record business, my sources say, that in 5 years, the new record business will be composed of independent labels doing distribution deals with key distributors who will get their product to the public.

That said, it must be admitted that there can be benefits to being signed to a major label. However, for every musician who snags a major label deal, there are tens of thousands who don't. And of those who do make the majors, 90 percent of them will never sell more than 10,000 copies of their recordings. Think about it: So many musicians will spend untold precious years of their lives chasing the major label rainbow only to find that at the end of it there's no pot of gold.

Forget those visions of stardom and riches that would be yours if you could only have a gold record (RIAA certified sales of 500,000 units). The old record business reality is that, after all expenses are recouped by your label, you'll be lucky to clear $50,000. Make that *very* lucky. As many who've had huge major label deals have told me, even after selling a million records, you can *still* owe the record company money.

But don't worry about it. As promised, I'm going to teach you how to create your business—You, Inc.—and as you learn, you're going to get the smarts and the knowledge to take your music as far as you'd like, with or without the support of a major label.

So how am I going to do all this? I'm going to give you specific steps to follow that will give you your best chance for success. We all know that there are no guarantees in life—especially in the music business. Not only are you dealing with fickle public tastes that bend with the wind, as well as a volatile economy that affects individuals' and businesses' spending and saving, but also with a tough career path that can come to a dead end in a heartbeat. Yet if you stick with the plan and follow the steps, you're going to have a great shot at music success.

The first part of this book is all about the new music business. And make no mistake; it is the *new* music business. As Lesson One says, it's old school vs. new reality. For those who think they've got to keep doing things the same old way, the new reality is that it's time for a change.

Take the radio/record label playlist game. Once you learn about how that game is played—Lesson 2—and how incredibly much money it takes to become a player, you'll quickly realize just what little chance you have to win *if* you play by their rules. But not to worry: I've got a few strategies to get your music on the radio—just like the record companies do—and one of them is going to get you there for a fraction of the old school price.

Ah, I can hear some of you saying, "But, I'd really like to get a major label deal." Just wait until you read Lesson 3, "The Illusion of Needing a Record Deal," and then tell me how badly you want that major label deal. If that doesn't get your attention, then Lesson 4 will. It's a view from both sides of the fence from 12-time Grammy nominee and 5-time Grammy winner Steve Lukather. Luke's no-holds-barred tell-it-like-it-is view of the music business—and why it's not just record labels that have caused its demise—is riveting.

After *that* wake-up call you'll be ready to make your first move: getting the right people to help you. It all begins with Lesson 5, "Building Your A-Team." For years, musicians have made huge mistakes by giving away too much of the income and ownership from their music to people undeserving of it. They've signed bad deals with the wrong people that ceded too much control, and they've overpaid for services that yielded too few results. You're going to find out who you need and who you don't, learn strategies that can save you tens of thousands, if not more, in taxes, and discover how to create your own A-Team without giving away your life, your rights, and your money.

The second part of this book teaches you how to get your music together. It focuses on how the new music business has changed the way music is written and recorded. In order for people to remember you, in order for people to call you and want what you have to offer, you've got to give them something unique. You can either play the music that other people write or you can write the music that other people play. I think you can figure out which has the greatest potential for bringing you the life that you want.

To help you to create your song and develop your sound, I've asked the biggest and best names in music to give you their advice. My basic criterion was simple: Each person chosen had to have been in the music business for a minimum of 20 years and still be at the top of the profession. This was a tough standard to meet. The music business is filled with talented people who were on the scene for only a short while before dropping off the radar screen. I wanted people who had really impacted me and countless others over the years—the ones who, as musical tastes changed, stayed at the top. The individuals you're about to learn from were and still are. We're talking Grammy winners and nominees, industry award winners, and people who still command the utmost respect from the music industry's best.

The first is Diane Warren. In the world of contemporary music and songwriting, Diane is a giant. Her songs have been recorded by the biggest stars in music, and are instantly recognizable and loved by millions of fans all over the world. Diane leads off Part 2 of our book with Lesson 6, "It's All About the Song." Get ready, because I'm taking you into the private songwriting world of the woman many have called "the premier songwriter of our generation," and whether you write lyrics, music, or both, Diane Warren's words of advice will inspire you.

There's no doubt that with a great song you can go far. But if you also have a great sound, then the chances of your musical success can skyrocket. So how do you get a great sound? There are three steps to developing your own sound. The first is to develop your playing and/or singing ability. When you hear B.B. King, you know it's B.B. King. When you hear Bruce Springsteen, you know it's Bruce Springsteen. If you've already put many years into your music, there's a good chance you're already well on your way to this. If not, you'll find out how to get there.

So the second step is to create your own individual sound, a sound that identifies you. And to help you to create that sound and learn how to use it, Bob Bradshaw, sound designer to the biggest stars in music, gives you advice, tips, and studio tricks people pay big money for. That's Lesson Seven.

Once you have your sound, you need to record it. . . and that's the third step. There are many, many recording platforms to choose from, and Lesson 8 narrows things down for you. Lesson 8 gives a rundown of the equipment and software that are firmly established and used by the record industry's biggest and best producers, artists, and engineers, plus some tried-and-true quickie how-to's on how to use them.

So now that you have your song, have your sound and mastered a few cool tricks on how to use it, and chosen the right recording platform and tools, how do you make your best recording? You wouldn't believe how many demos and potentially great songs and ideas get tossed in the wastebasket each day by people who can give you opportunities, yet are completely turned off by the quality of the recording.

As many record industry people have told me, "There are a lot of s*#t songs out there." While it's up to you to make your song the best it can be, you can use some help on the philosophy and mechanics of recording your music. It all starts with the mix, and Lesson 9 gives you mixing advice from one of the world's best: Bob Clearmountain.

You can walk into any major recording studio anywhere in the world and ask if they've heard of Bob Clearmountain, and you'll hear what a recording genius he is. From Bruce Springsteen to The Rolling Stones to Bryan Adams and Def Leppard, to your personal who's-who of major recording artists who have moved you, Bob Clearmountain is their go-to guy for mixing music. Bob has plenty to say that's going to help you record your best mix and music.

Having your sound and knowing how to mix your recording are only two of the three components needed to having a great sounding record. You also need to master it—the last and crucially important step that most people forget.

If there is one guy who's done it all, and with almost every major artist in the business—from The Beatles to Hendrix to Jim Morrison to Joplin to Frank Sinatra to Phish to Mariah Carey, Whitney Houston, Norah Jones, and Celine Dion, to the best artists of any music genre—it's got to be mastering guru Bob Ludwig. In Lesson 10, he shares his philosophy and some tips that are going to give you a great finished product.

The third part of this book is concerned with the *business* of the new music business. It begins in Lesson 11, "Launching the Business of You, Inc." Without a doubt, this is one of my favorite lessons. It's full of some of the most powerful strategies you'll ever need for protecting you and your business. It gives you a number of options to make, keep, and leverage wealth, and to legally put you on the same playing field as the major labels.

It's vitally important that, once you have your music ready but before you release it for the world to hear, you protect yourself. I'm talking about being armed with weapons that successful businesses use to protect their company and their assets from people who are ready to rip them off. I'm talking about strategies that'll help you keep more of your hard-earned money. This means having your own business. That's right. It's time for you to get serious about your music and your life, and to become the owner of your own business. It's not as mysterious as it sounds. Think about it: You're already running your own business when you're selling your music, your talents, and your skills to the right buyer. I'm going to teach you how to be *legally* protected, and along with that how to take advantage of the tremendous tax deductions and investment and saving opportunities unavailable to others who don't use these legal entities. In fact, I'm going to teach you how to form your own corporation or other legal entity of your choosing, over the Internet or over the phone, in 10 minutes or less!

Lesson 12 takes you to boot camp: real-world new music business boot camp, that is. And I've got three subjects to cover: copyrights, protecting your licensing, and protecting your royalties. You're going to learn quickly that getting rich is not about how many gigs you play or hours you work. It's about you creating, owning, licensing, and distributing the intellectual property and copyrights from *your* music.

The fourth and final section of this book takes a new music business approach to marketing, selling, and distributing your music. It begins in Lesson 13 with how to premier your masterpiece to tens of millions all over the world—which starts with having your own Web site. Every serious business has one, and your name, time, talent, and music are too valuable for you not to have one, too. And is it ever easy and cheap to do it! I'll teach you some great ways to have your own Web site up and on the Internet in less than 30 minutes, and all for under $25 a month.

But let's not stop there. Once your Web site is up, I'll teach you how to Webcast and have your own Internet radio station playing your music 24/7/365 to a global audience of over 500 million people. Imagine the possibilities. And if you've ever dreamed of recording and mixing records with different musicians in another state or country—without having to be there—I'm going to show you how you can do it while sitting in your bedroom.

On the musical road I've traveled, I've had incredible ups and downs. I've toured, lived out of a van, played night-after-thankless-night for not much more money than I could've earned flippin' burgers at McDonald's. As a teenager, I knew the adrenaline and excitement of hearing my first record played on the radio. I know what it's like to be nearly broke, to not have money for food and rent, and to have to pawn my guitars just to survive. Yet I also know what it's like to write and produce award-winning music for a major movie studio—Warner Bros.—and to do it in the bedroom studio in my little house in Idaho. So much for having to live in a city where music is made.

I've been employed by a major record label and have met and worked with many of music's biggest stars and hit makers. I've worked for a major market radio station and have seen first-hand how radio really works. I've been involved in many recording sessions as a musician, and I've had my jingle work played on national television. I've lived in and near the three biggest music cities in the United States—Los Angeles, New York, and Nashville—and include among my friends many of the very music stars I grew up reading about.

I tell you these things not to brag or go off on some ego trip. Life's too short for that. I tell you these things because I think I just might be able to relate to where you're coming from.

You see, where I came from is a little Midwestern town and I was given no silver spoon or special favors. My parents, grandparents, aunts, uncles, and cousins weren't musicians. What I've learned—be it how to play an instrument or the real world of people and how business is done—I've learned through many lessons of trial and error, lots of time and money spent, and the amazing predictability of just how wonderfully life can work, how it can open doors and put the right people in your path, at just the right time, when you know what you want and are focused, resilient, and steadfast until you get it.

I came up the hard way, probably just like you, following a dream—a "calling" if you will—that keeps pulling at the heartstrings and says, "Follow your gift wherever and however it leads you and don't be afraid." And you know what else it says? "And don't you dare give up or lose the music—the gift—inside your soul."

With all the experiences I've had during the last few years—the people I've met and the musical awakening I've experienced as to how music is created, made, distributed, and sold—I knew I had to write a book about it. This is that book. It's the book I would've rushed to the bookstore to buy if it had only been there. In a sense, it's the book I always wanted, always needed, but could never find.

Of course, this book shouldn't be the only one in your musical library. The more knowledge you have about the things that you love, the wiser and better off you'll be. There are many other music books out there—*This Business of Music, What They'll Never Tell You about the Music Business, All You Need to Know about the Music Business, Everything You Better Know about the Record Industry, Start and Run Your Own Record Label,* and *How I Make $100,000/Year in the Music Business—Without a Record Label, Manager or Booking Agent,* to name a few—and those books have solid information on the business and legal aspects of the music industry. But first, you've got to get from dream to reality, and this is the book that's going to take you there.

This is the book that will give you the very tools and knowledge that have helped me and countless others to see the light and that will help you once and for all, as Henry David Thoreau said, to "Live the life you imagine."

Here's to your amazing success!

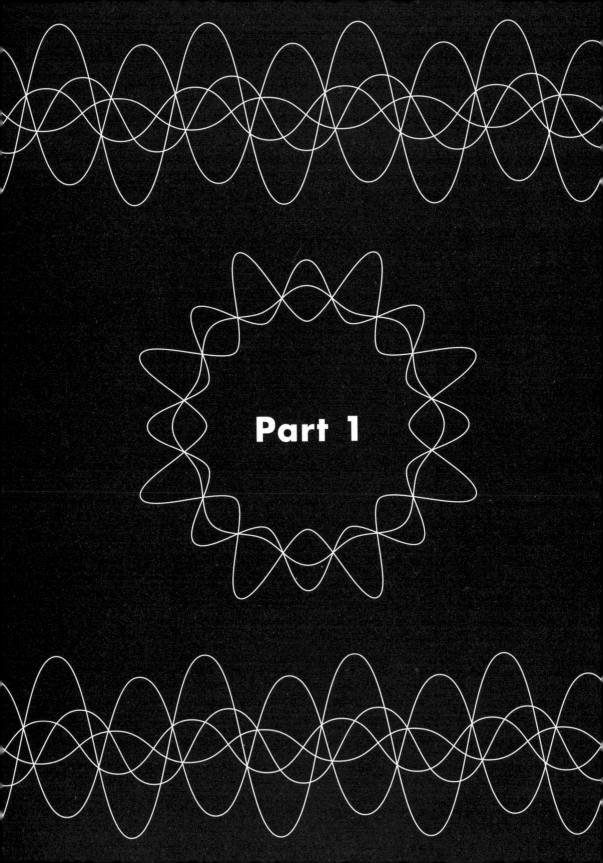

Part 1

Welcome to
the New Music
Business

Old School vs. New Reality:

The Digital Revolution Levels

the Playing Field

It's time for a wake-up call. You are one lucky person because you couldn't have picked a better time to follow your musical, singer/songwriting, or recording dreams. The information, new technology, Internet power, untapped markets, and huge potential audience that await your efforts give you more power than ever before to create music in your own way and on your own terms.

Until very recently, songwriters and composers—not just the great classical composers but also the immortal Broadway tunesmiths—had to spend untold hours writing out their music by hand, note by note. No longer. Today, we have music software that notates and automatically scores your music for you, either as you're playing it or after you've recorded it. All you need to do is click on the "print" icon on your computer and voilá, your music is transcribed.

In the days of the Sun, Motown, and Stax sessions, all those immortal record labels had was tape, a limited number of tracks, and a small arsenal of outboard processing gear. And with those tools at their disposal, they made incredible recordings. But today we have over 60 tracks, higher sampling and recording rates, higher fidelity, and amazing editing, processing, and mastering capabilities, and they're all inside that computer, waiting for you to tap into their power.

To make music in the '70s, '80s, and '90s, you needed a major recording studio, a roomful of studio musicians with numerous instruments and racks filled with gear, and a control room with a million or more dollars in consoles, recorders, and processing equipment. Today, you have plug-in capabilities that create and re-create classic models of keyboards, synthesizers, guitars, effects, basses, drums, percussion, horns, orchestras of strings, samplers, and mixers at a touch, generating the same kinds of sounds achieved in those high-priced studios, but now available via computer software, with many in the $200 to $500 price range.

And it doesn't stop there. You can get software that adds vocal harmonies to your song, software that keeps your pitch automatically in tune, software that models classic amps and equipment, and even software that changes the sound of that cheap microphone you love using into the sound of a mic costing thousands of dollars. On a laptop, you can access everything you need to record, mix, and master your music: at home, on a plane, sitting on a boat, or on the beach.

And that's just the beginning.

So why on earth would anyone want a major label deal today? Well, if you are one of the rare few who have the looks, the talent, and the charisma that says star quality, *and* if a major label is willing to commit big bucks to your promotion and "long-term" success, then maybe that's an opportunity too good to pass up. If you're among the rest of us, then you and I need to talk.

Welcome to the Old School Music Business: What Your Record Earns and What You Get to Keep

Let's begin by talking money. As I mentioned in my Introduction, 90 percent of artists with record deals never sell more than 10,000 records. And the big dollars you end up paying back (the label says they pay for it, but at least 50 percent of the cost, if not more, comes out of your royalty) for a chance to be played on the radio could leave you in debt for the rest of your major label life.

So, what if you *do* get signed and what if you *do* have a record that starts making money? How much do you think you'll make? Honestly, do you have a clue? Very few people do. Let's do a little real-world record royalty calculation.

Start with the Royalty Rate

Let's say you've signed a standard record deal with standard terms. For the most part, this will be a one-record deal that gives your label first options for perhaps another two or three follow-up albums. Your royalty rate, also known as "points" (a point is a percentage, with 1 point being equal to 1 percent), might be a 10- to 14-point deal. It might be based on the retail selling price of your record. It might also be based on the wholesale price or the price to dealer/price to distributor (a better deal for the label and not a good deal for you, since the royalty is now paid on a lower sales price).

Let's say your royalty is 13 percent based on the retail price of your record, which is $12.98. (Some CDs are priced higher, but there's a lot of consumer pressure on the labels to lower their prices, so $12.98 puts us in the ballpark.) If there weren't any deductions (dream on), you would make approximately $1.69 per record sold. So if you sold 50,000 records, you'd make $84,500, right? Wrong.

Here Come the Deductions

For money earned on each record sold there are deductions, and lots of them. Based on the standard and accepted terms of your record contract, your label can, and most likely will, deduct *all* of the following.

Recording Costs. All expenses having to do with the recording of your record must be paid back by you to your record label. Albums can easily cost $125,000 and up, so those "let's do another take's" end up costing you big time. And these costs are not recouped by the *gross* money your label receives from your total sales, which would repay your label debt quicker. They are paid back to the label at *your* royalty rate, which, as you'll recall, is 13 percent. In other words, for every sale of your record, 13 percent (or whatever your royalty rate is) is paid back to the label until your debt is paid off. What about that other 87 percent of the money the label has received that could be used to pay off your debt? The label gets to keep it.

Producer Points. Your producer also gets royalties. How much depends on how much in demand he or she is. Producer points range from 2 to 5. These royalties begin with the first record sold and are paid to the producer after your record has recouped its costs. This is not the same deal that you, the artist, receive. You only start receiving royalties on records sold after your debts are recouped. This means that over 100,000 records need to be sold before you're entitled to start receiving any money. Yet while *you* don't receive any money from those first 100,000 records sold, your producer does. He or she receives a royalty check for every one of those 100,000 records, and for every record sold thereafter as well. Producer royalties are either paid by the label directly to the producer or are paid by you to the producer. They are always paid, though, and they always come from your royalties.

Mixer Points. If you use the services of a record mixer, he or she is often offered points from the sale of your music as well. It's not uncommon for good mixers to ask for 1 to 2 points. What *is* common is that you pay for them.

A&R Points. The person at the label who discovers and signs you can also be entitled to a percentage (typically between 1 to 2 percent) of the money that your label makes from your records. Be aware: These "bonuses" can come out of the artist's royalty, and not from the label's portion.

Breakage. Remember the days of vinyl albums and singles? Because a certain percentage of them would be damaged or broken en route to distributors and stores, and thus couldn't be sold, record labels decided to pay royalties on only 90 percent of records sold to offset this potential loss. The 10 percent had nothing to do with how many records were actually broken; it was simply an arbitrary percentage the labels agreed on to give them a cushion against any returns damage. And if you think the breakage deduction went out with vinyl, you're wrong. In effect, it means that the total number of records you sell is automatically decreased by 10 percent right from the start. If you sell 1 million records, your label doesn't have to pay you for the first 100,000.

Foreign Sales. Because it takes more time, effort, and expense to promote and distribute your record outside the United States, your record label can reduce your royalty rate for any sales made outside the United States (or outside whatever country where your label is based). The percentages can vary with each country and market. Record companies may accept less of a deduction in countries and territories where they have some ownership in the foreign distributor. In the bigger global markets (also known as "major territories"), the discount can be in the range of 25 to 40 percent. For the rest of the world (R.O.W.), deductions may be as high as 40 to 50 percent.

Record Clubs. Who hasn't received those enticing notices from record clubs offering lots of CDs for the price of one? This is a good deal for the consumer, but not for the artist. In addition to having a term in your contract that allows your label to pay you, for record club sales, a royalty rate of half of what you'd normally get, the label also gets to give away (such as when they offer a certain number of free CDs if you buy one) as many of your records for free as it sells. Hence, the bigger artists (those who are often chosen as the free product selections) help sell the lesser artists' (the CD you buy) music. Sell 50,000 and the label can give away 50,000. Good deal?

Singles. Singles used to be big movers until some labels decided to limit their releases so that fans would buy the album first—not a popular move with music buyers. If your label does release a single from your record, don't be surprised if your royalty rate is cut in half.

Free Product. In the record business, every record a record company sells is discounted. The size of the discount depends on the merchant. Record labels can offer retailers free product as an incentive to carry more of that label's artists. They might give free product to a new retailer with whom they're seeking to establish a relationship. They can use free product as an incentive/reward to retailers for selling x number of records. Retailers like free product because they can sell it at a discount without having to pay the record label a dime; this increases overall sales numbers and drives additional traffic into their stores. The record companies like it because they don't have to pay you royalties on free product sales and they keep their retailers smiling. However, you're probably not smiling about the 10 to 20 percent (15 percent is about average) that is automatically taken off the top for free product that you'll never get paid for.

New Technology. Many label contracts have provisions that allow them to reduce your royalty rate by up to 50 percent should they use a "new technology" (i.e., one they theoretically might have to invest R&D money in, such as digital delivery) to get your music to consumers. However, while record companies will fight to keep this clause in, it can be negotiated. One way is by having the label reduce the deducted amount slightly during the first few years of the exploitation of the new technology, with the proviso that the full new technology royalty rate deduction will not kick in until at least 50 percent of your sales are made as a direct result of that new technology.

Promotion. Any promotional expense (e.g., independent radio promotions, music videos, television and radio campaigns, record store appearances, etc.) can be fully recouped by your label from your sales. Not only that, if you're doing a television promotional tour, the label can reduce your royalty during the 6-month period that your promotional tour takes place by as much as 50 percent.

Tour Support. Sending you and the band on the road is expensive, especially if you need to buy music equipment. And while your label has a vested interest in seeing you build a fan base (read: potential record buyers), all this comes at a price—to you. Some labels split some of the costs with you, thereby reducing the amount you'll have to pay back to them. Others will pay the up-front costs only if 100 percent of those expenses are recoupable.

Packaging. Who doesn't enjoy seeing great CD covers and reading all the cool little tidbits in the liner notes? The labels know this and they make you, the artist, pay big time for it. How much? You would think it wouldn't be too much, since CD jewel cases are fairly inexpensive (especially if you're buying them in the quantity the label does). And for goodness sakes, cover art and design can't cost that much, can they? The record labels think so, and they have happily put a clause in contracts for a packaging deduction, typically 20 to 25 percent, which is subtracted from your record's agreed-upon selling price regardless of whether it's wholesale or retail. On your $12.98 retail-priced record, you've just lost anywhere from $2.60 to $3.25.

Other Deductions. There are too many other possible deductions to list here. I highly recommend Peter M. Thall's book *What They'll Never Tell You about the Music Business* for more on this.

What's Left?

Okay, now let's do a little math to see what you're left with after calculating only *some* of the deductions I've just mentioned.

First, let's recap the price of your CD, your royalty rate, and the first deduction, producer points.

* You have a record that has a $12.98 retail price.
* You have a record deal that pays you a 13 percent royalty on the retail price of your record.
* You must pay 2 percent in producer points, which is deducted from your 13 percent royalty rate up front, giving you a royalty rate of 11 percent. Now let's start with the $12.98 retail price and figure in the free product, packaging, breakage, and new technology deductions:
* $12.98 x 85% = $11.03 (what's left after subtracting the free product deduction)
* $11.03 x 75% = $8.27 (what's left after subtracting the packaging deduction)
* $8.27 x 90% = $7.44 (what's left after including the breakage deduction)
* $7.44 x 75% = $5.58 (what's left after taking the technology deduction)

You might be thinking "Geez, that's a bunch taken off, but I can live with $5.58 per record." But, hold on! I don't recall saying we were finished yet. Now it's time to calculate what percentage of that $5.58 you will actually get. Remember, your royalty rate is 11 percent. At that rate you get a whopping $5.58 x 11 percent = $0.61 cents for every record you sell *after all costs are recouped by your label.* And let's not forget that the label credits your account (to pay them back) at *your* royalty rate, not from the *total* monies it receives.

So how much has your label made on all this? Well, if the label sells your record to retailers at $9.00, it receives $900,000 if all 100,000 records were paid for. Even if you're recouped (all debts paid off) and the label now owes you royalty money, after all the deductions you only get paid on 25,000 of the 100,000 records sold. (Remember, all the deductions total up to 75 percent, leaving you 25 percent.) Multiply 25,000 times $0.61, and you get $15,250 for selling 100,000 records. Yippee! Factor in all the time you've invested and all the money you've spent to get yourself this far, and you're losing money big time.

If that doesn't have you reeling, then perhaps this might. Of the 61 cents per record you're now getting (I'm being generous here and not deducting everything that could be deducted), you *still* have to pay your attorney (if he or she gets a cut of what you make), your manager (if he or she gets a cut of what you make), and your agent (if he or she gets a cut of what you make). After those fine folks get paid, you *might* be left with little more than 50 cents per record sold. Fifty cents!

Now, factor in how much your time is worth. Do you know? You should, because when you include all the hours, days, months, and perhaps years you've put in to becoming a professional musician and to getting a label deal, plus the time you put into making your record and all the touring and promotional appearances you did to sell it, plus the amount of time you've had to wait to collect your measly 50 cents per record, and then add to your expenses all the taxes you'll have to pay whatever the total turns out to be, the reality is, you're working for free. Sure hope you really love the record business.

And that scenario, ugly as it is, can only happen if the record label decides to actually release your record. They don't have to do that, you know. Even if you've got a major label deal, the record company isn't obligated to release your recording. Let me explain.

Now Consider an Even Worse Scenario

Record labels have clauses in their contracts that give them the option, if they so choose, to release your recording. You'd think that if they've gone to all the trouble of signing you and perhaps paying you a little signing advance, they'd be in a hurry to get your music out and sold. But that's not always the case.

If a new act or singer comes along (after you've been signed) and the label believes that they are, as they say, "the bomb," then guess where those limited new artist development dollars are now going? You guessed it, and sorry Mr. or Ms. Thang, but you've been officially put on hold (Aimee Mann can speak from experience about this).

With few exceptions, this is not a good move for your career. The record business is such that listeners want the newest and hippest sounds (and this changes quickly), and labels are focused on how this artist or the next one can increase next quarter's profits. The days of slowly building and breaking an artist's career over multiple years and albums are pretty much over. For you, the signed major label artist, whose career and life have now been put on hold, that can mean huge frustration and seeing your window of opportunity to make it in the music business slam shut.

You see, when you signed that record deal, you also signed away your option to quickly terminate your agreement if the label didn't release your record within a specified time (unless you had your attorney put in a weasel-out clause that allows you to terminate the agreement without penalty). The record company is likely to have language in their agreement that basically says that, at their discretion, they have the option to record and release your recording within the next 12, 18, 24, or 36 months, and if they don't, then your agreement with them can be terminated.

However, keep in mind that during those 1 to 3 years that they haven't recorded or released anything on you, you are still *exclusively* bound to them. You read it right. You're exclusively theirs, and they don't need to do anything more with you if they don't want to. Meanwhile, as you're waiting, and with each passing day you're not on radio, the Internet, or in record stores, your career, and the audience for your music, are going bye-bye.

Let's change all that.

Welcome to the New Reality

The new music business says it's time for you to be in charge of your musical destiny and life. The new music business says those who embrace change and technology and ride its wave will be greatly rewarded. The new music business says no one can write, record, perform, and promote your music better than you. The new music business says the more time you spend playing other people's music, the less time you'll have to create your own. And the new music business says you don't need to pay people who simply see you as another number that exists only to generate profit for them.

I've often wondered why some major label stars don't do more things on their own. With all the money they've made, with all the great contacts and millions of fans they have, they no longer need the power of major label dollars to jump-start a beginning career or carry on a successful one.

What if they realized how much freedom and financial reward they could gain by having their own label and doing music on their own terms, without having a company tell them what kind of music they can record and when they can release it. What a different world they would experience. Yes, all of them—creators, owners, and visionaries in a world called the new music business.

To them, and to you, I say, Welcome to the new reality.

New School vs. Old School: Your Decisions vs. Corporate Structures

In the old school corporate record world, decisions are often made by committees and can take weeks; this is quickly apparent when you're the party on the other end of the line or e-mail who's been waiting for a response. Now throw in office politics, be it people constantly jockeying for position over one another, or supposed deal makers not going after an artist because they don't want to take the risk of losing whatever power and position they currently have. The fact is, when you deal with an old school label, you are dealing with a hierarchy and structure (often with a limited creative vision) that must operate within the walls, dictates, and beliefs of "the company."

In complete contrast, as an owner in the new music business, you have free rein—in wide-open fields with no fences—to be both maverick and visionary. The only limit to your dreams and decisions about your music is what you believe about them. As Master P, independent hip-hop record mogul and impresario, always believed about his dreams, there are no limits and he named his company and empire just that, No Limit Records. His attitude and belief were that he was going to grow something. He did, others wanted to help grow it with him, and his phenomenal success is proof you can do it, too.

Master P started out on his own; he owned his masters and copyrights, and used the major labels only to distribute his records. Yes, the labels may have made a little money, but P made an empire. He promoted his artists anywhere and everywhere. He personally financed each record and video. And he always controlled the bank. His bank. More than four hundred million dollars later, he hasn't done too badly for a guy from the projects in Louisiana who started with $10,000 and sold records out of the trunk of his car.

The major labels aren't going away anytime soon. Perhaps the old business model they've used for so long will change, but there will always be some type of major record label. Learn from them. Study what you think they do right and wrong. Continuously adjust your label and new music business model so you can capitalize on what's good about today's music business, but never stop thinking ahead about what tomorrow's hits will sound like—and then create them. And use the distribution services of a major label as *one* of the many ways that will help you distribute them. That's having your cake and eating it, too. That's the new music business.

New School vs. Old School: Home Studio vs. Big Studio

The new music business has seen a paradigm shift from large studios to home studio recording. The old school belief was that if you wanted major label/hit radio sound and quality, you needed to record your music in a big studio, an undertaking that often required weeks and months of planning financing equivalent to taking out a second mortgage on your home.

The digital revolution and new music business have changed all that. Never again do you have to put your inspiration on hold until a studio has an open calendar.

As muses in the arts go, music is a quirky one whose inspiration and creative ideas can come to you in the strangest of places and at the oddest times—often in the middle of the night. In the new music business, that's plenty of time for you to turn on the computer and begin recording.

And that's the beauty of today's technology. You buy it once, use it however long or often you want, and most likely that's the biggest expense you'll have. Old school big recording studios charge you by the hour, day, week, or month. You must turn on your creative juices according to *their* schedules. And there's also the time and expense of travel, meals, lodging (if you don't live near the studio), lugging equipment and setting it up, and the discomfort of being in a strange place, with people you don't know staring at you through the control room glass as you "perform."

This is not the greatest environment for the artist who needs to go at his or her own pace, not force the flow, and experiment with the infinite palette of sounds and textures that can produce an amazing piece of work.

Your business in the new music business allows you that expression and that freedom, and so much more. Just as the major labels won't all disappear, there'll always be big studios and they'll have their purpose and place. But in your new music world, the most important place will be yours. And the beauty of it is, with the digital revolution your recording studio will be any place you want it to be.

New School vs. Old School: Internet Radio vs. Traditional Radio

Old school says traditional radio will always be important in breaking and promoting artists and music. New school says Internet radio can be used for a fraction of the entry fee you'd need to sit at the "good ol' boys" poker table because you don't need the chips to wager big dollars on old school's traditional, and risky, radio bets.

Old school says that radio is so powerful because it's a passive medium. You don't need to do anything but listen to it once you've turned it on. Not entirely true, because you still need to change the stations and hit the buttons if don't like what they're playing. New school says that's about to change.

Streaming audio is one of the Internet's terrific technologies; it allows you to listen to your favorite Internet radio station(s) while you're busy surfing, researching, e-mailing, or doing anything else on the Web, be it on your home computer, laptop and Wi-Fi, or even PDA. And with DSL or cable that always keeps you connected to the Internet, you don't even need to be in front of your computer screen to have Internet radio playing 24/7 throughout the house. All you have to do, just like old school radio, is simply turn it on and listen. With Internet radio scanning technology, you can have the same features of traditional radio (i.e., like scanning until you find the right music station and clicking your mouse to select the station to stop scanning) all with the click of your mouse.

The key to making new school Internet radio work is how you promote it. Like old school radio, promotions drive artist, music, and station popularity. Old school radio likes contests, remotes, and giveaways. New school Internet radio can do the same, and from anywhere you choose to do your remote/on location broadcast. Traditional radio is limited to what they say, what they play, and how long they can say and play it. You are not.

The Internet is one of the last bastions of interstate communications freedom because its content is not regulated by the FCC (Federal Communication Commission) in the same way that old school radio is, and you don't have to play by old school radio rules to achieve new music business rewards. Your creative potential is unlimited, and so can be your possibilities for success in the new school Internet radio world, that is, if you give listeners the music and entertainment content they can't get anywhere else. Always think in terms of "what kind of experience would this be for me?" If it's one that excites you, chances are, it's going to do the same for all those people out there who are your potential listeners.

New School vs. Old School: Your Label vs. Their Label

Old school says you need a major record label to make major things happen with your music. New school says, not so fast. New school says, let's make it that you need *your* label.

The old and new reality is, and will be, regardless of who owns the label, the artist needs to be unique and have the sound and the song that'll translate to hit quality and potential. If you can provide that, major labels will be interested. And that's what you want—interest. You want them to make money by helping you distribute your dreams, but in the new music business, you want the Wells Fargo truck pulling up to your door and not theirs. You don't want them to own you.

Despite what they say, major labels like distribution deals. Think about it: They don't have to go to all the "expense" of finding, developing, and recording a new artist (read: throwing huge major label money out for projects), and since they already have their well-oiled and constantly flowing distribution pipeline in place, it's easy to add another CD/artist to the mix. And for just saying yes to distributing your music or artist on your label, they get a cut of the profits and they're not out a dime.

Ah, but new school says, you don't stop there. If your label's music and talent are strong enough with huge upside potential, you can cut a deal with the major label whereby they agree to help promote the music, too. Shoot for the best deal you can, but focus on at least a 75/25 split, with your label receiving the 75 percent. Depending on what kinds of things old school label will kick into the pot, new school label may decide to give up a little more, but for doing so could realize a lot more on the back end. End result: old school helps new school and both are smiling.

New School vs. Old School: Your Marketing vs. Their Marketing

The new music business says take a look at the kinds of music marketing that's been done in the past to determine the kinds of new marketing to do for the future. Old school likes to dole out dollars for things that cost lots of them. Radio promotion and concert tours (all that you, as an old school artist, pay for) are high on the list. But new school asks why so much emphasis there and not in other, often-neglected avenues?

Take, for example, school promotions. The biggest audience of record buyers remains those who are school age—from elementary school through college. The amazing success of the movie *The Blair Witch Project* proves that a low-budget project can make major studio dollars when the power of buzz is added to the mystique of an underground movement that's promoted by word of mouth. The same can happen with your music.

College radio is and will continue to be one of the best oases for artists who don't fit the old school corporate label and playlist rosters. Yes, it's regulated by the FCC. Yes, many of the FM college stations are in big cities and are 100,000-watt full-power stations (just like the commercial ones). But no, they don't accept independent promotional "consideration" (if you know what I mean) and they aren't influenced by the corporate owners and higher-ups who tell them which artists and songs to play. The students decide, and if you've got a great song you think they'll like, the next song they play could be yours.

The Internet has made it easy to locate directories, addresses, and contacts of all the high schools and colleges that have radio stations, so finding the right people and places to send your CD and promo package to has never been easier. Old school believes there are only a limited number of promotional avenues for music that can recoup their huge investments quickly. New school says it likes building an audience in places where old school pays little attention, for little money, and watching the power of word of mouth create behind-the-scenes momentum that builds an audience base that can sustain an empire—a new music business empire.

New School vs. Old School: Your Profits vs. Their Profits

Old school believes that even though you create and perform the songs, *they* should make the majority of the money. Old school knows the power and attraction of being able to say, "I've just been signed to a major label." Old school knows that once their artists learn how the game is played, many will wish they could "resign" from the major label. But they also know that by then it'll be too late.

New school asks what will a major label do for me that I can't do on my own? Do I need to pay inflated recording costs when, thanks to the digital revolution, I can get hit quality music for a fraction of the price? Do I need to pay for radio promotion at a major label price when I can get both traditional and Internet radio promotion for a fraction of the price? Can a label that doesn't know me or my music promote me better than I can promote myself?

And new school also asks, Why am I giving away roughly 90 cents of every dollar in profit my music makes to an old school label, when that label is basically a lending institution, advancing me money which I'm contractually bound to pay back but keeping almost 100 percent of everything I make?

New School vs. Old School: Your Control vs. Their Control

Old school likes structure and control. New school likes freedom and unlimited opportunity. Old school has rules that anyone who enters its doors (i.e., signs a contract) must play by or they're either ostracized, neglected, or forgotten. New school says I make my own rules and even those rules are made to be broken—by me!

Old school has a catalog and roster of artists and dates for release that are followed slavishly. Old school constantly seeks new artists to create magic, while old artists are given one more chance to spin the profit wheel. Old school label decision makers decide which new album cuts will get released and which ones won't. And when it comes to artists and their music, old school decides when, where, and how they'll be released.

The new music business says it's time to change that. New school knows that many times an artist's best work is passed on by the old school decision committee that believes it knows the artist's music and fans better than the artist. Old school will often chose unflattering album covers and photos and fill those CDs with one, maybe two strong songs, with the rest being filler. They'll then overprice the CD, do little, if any, promotion for a few weeks, and then blame the artist for the lack of sales.

The new music business says that's a failing business model and one we will not follow. In the new music business, the artist picks his or her own songs and decides which ones should be on that life work called their album. The artist is the one who says "Let's give listeners a CD full of my best work, let's give them more tracks than they'll get from CDs from old school, and let's price our CD below all the others." The new school dictum is: *Let's give 'em more than they paid for and let's make it better than they ever expected.* Follow that model, and in the new music business you will succeed.

Lesson 2

Radio and Records:

How to Play the Game

During the California Gold Rush of the late 1800s, people had dreams of a new life and new prosperity and a desire to follow their adventurous spirit to virgin territory where untold opportunities and possibilities awaited. It was a heady time when folks like you and me could strike it rich overnight. All one needed was an opportunity and a willingness to try.

Radio in its infancy was much like that. And back in the '40s, '50s, and '60s, radio was the first place that people who sang or played music went to for their big break. Disc jockeys were mavericks, and stations were often mom-and-pop operations that got just as much of a kick discovering new artists as the DJs who played their records.

Then it all changed. Not suddenly, mind you, but station by station, and under the radar. Corporations began buying up radio stations ("business units" as they call them), and each time they gobbled up a station, another piece of the great American dream was taken away. Untold numbers of artists and their music were silenced—many before anyone had the opportunity to hear their first note.

The *business* of radio has a long, checkered past, from the famous payola scandal of 1960, when disc jockeys like Alan Freed actually *admitted* taking money from record companies to play their artists, to today, where many say it's still done, only now through the back door. It may have a new spin, a new name, and a new set of players, but if you're an artist, you'd better have a *lot* of money if you want to get your song heard on the airwaves.

The Radio/Record Company Dance

I have many friends who work in radio, and they and many others in the music business completely agree on one thing: *Radio is the ruler and the record companies are the servants.* Let me give you an example. Did you know that, depending on the station and the market, a radio station only plays 15 to 30 *different* songs a day? Which songs do you think they keep recycling throughout each 24-hour period? You guessed it: the songs performed by stars on major record labels. When it comes to radio, however, things aren't all a bed of roses, even for the stars. A music industry insider revealed to me the little-known (and even less admitted-to) practice involving what is known as the "26-week cycle." Twenty-six weeks is the time it usually takes for a record label or independent promoter to get a new single pitched, placed on stations, and played regularly. Once placed on the rotation, the song will be played until the promotional money dwindles and/or the song loses chart position. Once either of those things happens, the song will be replaced on the station's playlist by the next potential hit. The typical cycle usually ends up taking about 26 weeks. The only way to keep a song on the playlist beyond that 26 weeks is to spend big-time promotional dollars.

Let's call our artist Superstar. Radio networks (i.e., companies and stations) tell Superstar's record company that they expect the label to commit major marketing dollars to promote Superstar's single. The more money Superstar's record company is willing to spend, the more buzz and enthusiasm for Superstar's record it'll likely create. The more buzz and enthusiasm that's created, the more people will listen to the song and request it on radio. The more people who listen to that station, the more money the station can charge per 30- or 60-second spot for advertising. (Never forget: Radio, like television, is in business to sell ads. Ads pay the bills and generate hefty profits for owners and shareholders. Music or talk is simply the product the companies use to sell ads.) Ah, but woe to the artist whose record company won't commit major marketing dollars to a new recording. Unless radio gets the dollar commitment it wants from Superstar's record label, Superstar's new single won't get much airplay. Of course, according to radio, the lack of airplay has nothing to do with the movement of promotional dollars from record label to radio. It's because focus group feedback and nonexistent call-in response have made it clear that audience interest is falling off. Get it?

And what happens if radio decides early on to stop playing Superstar's new single? Do you remember that "26-week cycle" I mentioned? Well, two of those 26-week periods equals one year (52 weeks), and it doesn't take a college degree to figure out that Superstar could very well have to wait until the next "26-week cycle" before radio is willing to consider his or her next single.

When I first heard people talk about this, I was shocked. Obviously it's inherently unfair to an artist whose song deserves a shot at being successful. But what's more, even for those who have sold gold or platinum and have come out with a new album filled with great songs, under this system, few Superstars will get the opportunity to have more than two or three hits a year.

One of my friends, a top-rated disc jockey in a major east coast market, has said to me, "I can't even begin to tell you how much I want to play new songs, but I can't. I get new songs sent to me all the time from unknown artists. I hear great new songs (that never get played) from known artists, but it does little good, because I'm *told* what to play and what to say."

At the same time that the mechanics of how network radio operates have stayed the same—that is, they work to limit the opportunities for new artists as well as superstars with new releases to get their music heard—the *business* of radio has changed. The majority of all the radio stations in this country are owned by *only a small number of corporations*—Clear Channel, Infinity, ABC Radio, Cox, Entercom, Radio One, Emmis, Citadel, Univision Communications, and Cumulus. The largest of these corporations, Clear Channel, has approximately 1200 stations. And these companies all operate very much the same way.

Many big city stations owned by one of these corporations are run by computer-automated systems. Many of them use something called "voice tracking." Suppose you're listening to WWWW, Your City. You might hear the announcer say, "You're listening to the best of the '80s, '90s, and today on WWWW." However, there's a good chance that what you've just heard is a taped loop, and the announcer doesn't even live in Your City. Listeners in numerous cities and states may be listening to the same announcer at the same time you are! Everything you've heard has been planned, programmed, and produced in a city and state many miles away. Ever wonder why you don't hear those listener request lines anymore?

These corporations have program directors (PDs) who do lots of research. Some stations and markets do research and focus group testing locally; others do it nationally, and the results can impact the corporation's other stations in other cities, depending on station format. The radio corporations brag that decisions on what to play are not made at the top, and that the corporate office regularly has conference calls with its PDs across the country who tell them who's hot and who's not. But industry insiders tell me not to put too much stock in that. The big decisions—on what to play and when to play it—continue to be made at the top by the Chiefs, with the Indians, as always, simply following orders.

According to music industry insiders I've spoken with, the stations do *too much* research. Based on their "research," stations choose the playlists for their formats. Unless an artist is well known, with a sound that fits ideally into the demographic of their audience, his or her music will not be heard on these stations.

And good luck trying to break in a new artist. Even if you're a big name producer, you're all too likely to be told something like this: "Sorry, Mr. Famous Producer. Unless your new artist is male, has this type of sound and look, and can appeal to women in the 28 to 34 age group, we're not interested."

Radio stations speak of their research and audience feedback in terms of such things as "percentage of burn." One hundred percent burn, for example, would mean that 100 percent of listeners are tired of hearing a particular song. If Superstar's record test results in a 20, 25, or even 33 percent burn, that means that one-fifth to one-third of that station's listeners are not interested in hearing the song anymore. And not surprisingly, the station soon pulls the song off the playlist. Often this happens very quickly, certainly way before the artist and song have enough time to create significant listening impressions and get any "traction."

With ad rates skyrocketing beyond what many markets will bear, and with radio's corporate owners wanting more and more stations, all in the belief it'll create more revenue and save a business facing diminishing listeners and revenue, they don't see that the solution to their problems is staring them right in the face. To see this, they'd have to spend less time being bean counters and focus on the answer to the age-old marketing paradox question, "Are your actions dictated by what the numbers do, or do your actions dictate what the numbers do?"

Much like the magazine business, radio and record companies give listeners what they—a handful of people—"think" listeners want. Having few options to choose from, listeners can only pick the best of what they're given. And you'd better believe that radio and record labels support their actions by telling us, "See. We know what our listeners want. We've tested and these are the numbers that prove it." Duh.

What many listeners want radio and record companies to understand is that, given a broader choice of artists and music, they would be very likely not to choose those same old 15 to 30 songs that air each day. Could it be that capturing a larger audience of listeners is not as complicated as radio and record businesses say? Maybe it's as simple as this: By giving listeners more variety, you broaden your market and appeal, and by broadening your appeal, you increase your audience, which brings you more sales, and—this will get 'em listening—more profits?

I remember when I worked for a major FM radio station in Nashville. One day I was having a conversation with an artist whose independent label had invested over $250,000 in him (in recording and promotion costs) and was trying to get him a major record label deal. This artist had a terrific voice, good looks, and the right attitude, and his single had reached the 30s on the Billboard Country charts. Not too shabby for an independent release. When the artist's indy label pitched his package to a major label, one of the major label execs told them, "There's no audience on radio for this guy, and if there is I seriously question their taste." The indy label was shocked. However, the major record label exec knew how the radio game was played, and Mr. "I Cracked the Billboard Top 50" didn't fit into the pigeonhole. "Next."

Let's talk money. Don't worry. With this book, you're not going to need a fraction of the numbers I'm about to give you.

In today's radio, with few exceptions, it takes big money for the opportunity to get big results. How does $1 million to promote that new album grab you? But maybe you only have a single you want to get on the air. You better figure on setting aside about $200,000—per record you want played—just to get *access* to the airwaves. Here's how you get that access. You're going to hire an independent promoter.

The cost? Well, a good independent promoter's time and access channels don't come cheap. Some records cost less and some cost more, but the $200,000 number should put you in the ballpark. But before I hear you say, "OK, let's play ball," wait.

Like radio station corporations, there are only a handful of independent promoters who do the majority of the work. Their job is to get you access to the radio stations, provided that you have the look, the sound, and the demographic audience appeal the radio stations want. Independent promoters have great contacts with the stations and program directors throughout the country, and when you hire them, you're essentially buying the use of their Rolodex and time. Here's how they do it.

Years ago, the record companies created the independent record promotion business not only to free up their in-house staff from doing that work, but to circumvent the federal payola law which essentially states that it's illegal for radio station personnel to accept money for playing a song if that station does not tell its listeners it has accepted some sort of financial compensation to do so. It's the "independent promotions person," not the station, who gets paid by the label to promote its music on each radio station. And note the word "promote." It's by *promoting* the label's music, and not any specific song or artist, that the independent—and thereby the label and the radio station—get around the letter of the payola law.

Think of the independent record promoter as an exclusive gatekeeper without whom you can't enter radio's doors. The independent pays radio stations (fees can range from $50,000 for a smaller station to more than $350,000 for a major station in a big city) to be the exclusive facilitator between a record label and a radio station. The independent then becomes the one and only person the record label deals with to get its new songs and artists on the radio stations the independent has access to.

Whenever the independent promoter gets a song added to a radio station's playlist, depending on the size of market, an invoice is sent to the label for $500 or more. If a station picks up 100 new songs a year (a very conservative number), the independent promoter has made at least $50,000, and that's just for one station out of many that he or she may have on the roster. Add to that the extra money that the independent promoter makes by billing the label for "spins" (extra plays of a song), and "adds" (having a song added to a station's playlist), and you can see that the amounts paid out by labels are enormous. One estimate puts the money paid to independent promoters at more than $100 million a year—that's roughly $2 million a week.

Depending on how big a radio breakout the label has planned for an artist's new record, it can conservatively pay independent promoters from $150,000 to over a million dollars—per single—just to get it on the air. And keep in mind that the money the labels pay to independent promoters comes with a *no money back/no results* (read: even if I don't get results, you don't get your money back) guarantee. Sound like a good investment to you? If you're signed to a major label, you might not think so, since the independent promoter's cost (or at least 50 percent of it) comes out of your pocket (i.e., your royalty) and is recouped by the label.

The music industry sources I've talked to know that the independent promoter/record label relationship is not a good deal for them, but say they have little choice. The promoters have just become too powerful to avoid dealing with. The radio stations have gotten too accustomed to receiving all these wonderful windfall payments (which they say they use to buy much-needed station equipment like promo remote broadcast vans and the like. Sure they do.). The result is a system that's broken and needs a major fix—in a hurry.

Making Radio Work for You

I'm going to show you a strategy that'll let you use radio—even old-school radio—to your own advantage—and you'll be spending a lot less than $200,000 per song.

The key to making your music any sort of commercial success is to get it out there and into people's cars, stereos, Walkmans, MP3s, and other digital storage players. Music fans need to hear you. One of the biggest obstacles for any new artist attempting to get a record deal is generating enough interest, or buzz. Buzz is the feedback that gives record companies the confidence that there is an audience for your music that will pay money for it. The more buzz you have, the safer the record label feels in taking a chance on being able to recoup its investment in you.

So, how can you create that buzz and, perhaps, even get your music played on radio without a record deal? Let's begin by reviewing what makes radio work. Radio stations make money by selling airtime to advertisers. But radio stations can't get and keep listeners, or stay in business, if all they broadcast are commercials, so they have two products that they use to fill the time between commercials: talk and music. The more listeners a radio station attracts, the more money it can charge advertisers for airtime, and thus the more money it makes.

Now let's see what action you can take to make radio work for *you*.

Pay-for-Play

No radio station is able to sell every commercial time slot that it has available in a day. Airtime is like hotel rooms. Rarely does any hotel sell out every night of the week, and on any given night, the empty rooms represent potential profits the hotel has missed for that night. In radio, empty time slots that are not filled with an ad to play represent missed profits.

Keep that in mind as we talk about how to get your song played on the radio without your label—or you—paying $200,000 to an independent promoter who might succeed in getting you airtime *if* you had a record deal and *if* you fit all those guidelines that the record labels, independent promoters, and radio stations have.

But what if you bought your own airtime? That's right. What if you became an advertiser? What if you were to buy a 30-second or 60-second spot on a radio station, and the product that you were selling was you and your music? Can you do it? You bet you can, and it's cheaper and easier than you think.

Remember years ago when infomercials hit cable television? First there were just a handful that you'd see over and over again late at night. It was perfect for the cable companies, since they had all of this unused airtime to sell and they could generate some profit where there wasn't any before. For the infomercial product company, it was perfect, too, since it had access to a potentially huge market and was able to buy airtime to reach that huge audience dirt cheap. As the number of infomercials proliferated, the time slots that the stations allotted to infomercial broadcasting expanded, and now you see them all hours of the day and night, on hundreds of channels, selling everything from computers to exercise equipment. By the way, they also sell music.

Using the same strategy, we're going to have you putting together *your* product commercial and buying select airtime on the radio station to play your ads. Here are some basic ground rules.

* Figure out what you can comfortably afford and stay within your budget.
* The rates for a 30- or 60-second spot vary with the station and time
  of day it airs, so while we'd like to get on the top station in your city at the
  best time slot, for now let's start generating some buzz (and money for you)
  by hooking you up with one of the stations that plays music similar to yours
  and sells spots at a price you can afford.
* The late night/early morning time slots are cheapest, so to begin, you'll
  probably want to buy ads that air during those time slots. When I was selling
  airtime for a major FM station on Music Row in Nashville, I was able to sell
  some ads for as little as $10 per 30-second spot (late nights and weekends)
  as an incentive to get advertisers to buy a block of ads or a package.

* Stations will give you a better deal if you buy a block of time rather than just buying one ad every one or two weeks. Besides, people need to hear your music repeatedly before any kind of impression can be made.
* Stations traditionally give a 10 to 20 percent discount off their normal book rate to agencies that buy airtime for their clients. So before you negotiate with a station, think up a name for *your* agency and ask the station to give you the agency rate. They will if you ask, but they won't if you don't.
* Next comes deciding what music you're going to use. If you have a new CD, choose "stingers" (a few seconds of music—the "hooks") from two to three of your songs with the most commercial appeal. Get opinions from friends and associates as to which songs you should use. Many times we think we know which songs other people will like best, but in the end they choose something completely different.
* Be sure to create your ad to fit the station's policies as to content and what you can and cannot say or sell.

Basic Calls to Action

Once you've picked out a station and a time slot, negotiated a rate, and know what you're going to use, you need to decide what you want people to *do* who hear your commercial. Paying for airtime to get your song on the radio is a start, but it doesn't put money in your pocket or build the business of You, Inc. It's also not what a smart businessperson does. You need to figure out a *call to action,* an end result that you want to achieve.

Here are two simple calls to action.

1. Have a toll-free 800 number in your ad that listeners can call to order your CD.

2. Ask listeners to request your CD at their favorite record store.
Even if a store has turned down your CDs in the past, if people start asking for them—and they will when they hear your radio ads—it will be calling you to supply the store.

Here's what this strategy—buying airtime plus having a call to action—does for you. It:
* Immediately starts creating buzz, because now you're on the air and being heard by *lots* of people
* Begins building an audience, and that audience can only grow the more your music is heard.

* Puts you in control of your music and your message. You created your music, and you can create *any* message that you want to help promote you and your music to the world.
* Gives you a major calling card to an open-ended number of radio stations that might have been reluctant in the past to air your ads, because now you're being heard, you're a paying advertiser, and you have an audience, and that audience will follow you to whatever station plays your music. Remember what I told you: The more listeners a station gets, the higher their ratings, and the higher the ad rates they can charge for airtime.
* Provides you with a major calling card to the record labels—should you ever decide you need one—since now you will have created the buzz they want. You have an audience, a fan base, and a following, representing big numbers and profits if the company decided to put major label marketing money behind you (which they would of course *always* recoup).

Another Call to Action: The Power of 200 Letter and Request

Have you ever wondered how some special interest groups—people who vocally and physically rally behind a cause—manage to create such a stir and get so much attention when the silent majority is just sitting on their hands and watching? The fact is that successful special interest groups *know* that the silent majority is watching, and they give them something to watch. They know that public actions produce results, and they use such things as the media, protest demonstrations, public meetings, phone calls, and letters to achieve the results they want. Since this strategy is so effective, why don't we use it to generate even more buzz for you. Here's how.

It's all about impressions—having people hear your music and message enough times that they remember it. The road to making an impression that gets results goes like this:

Stage 1: No interest

Stage 2: Some interest

Stage 3: Acceptance

Stage 4: Embracing

Stage 5: Desire

Each time your ad is heard, your music and message moves one step closer to Stage 5, people's desire to hear them. Once you've reached Stage 5, then you've made a powerful impression, and it's that type of impression that will get people calling a station. If enough people call, believe me, the station will listen.

How many calls are enough? You'd be surprised. Radio industry people tell me that if a station gets a few calls a day requesting a song, it takes notice. And when people keep calling, if the local program director doesn't have the power to insert a new song that's generating local buzz, he or she passes the word to the corporate programming director(s) who does have that power. It all goes back to understanding how the radio game is played. Radio's audience is listeners, and those listeners buy advertisers' products. If those listeners and advertisers don't get what they want, they get upset.

Now it takes only a few listeners to write letters and make phone calls to complain to the advertisers on that station that the station is not playing what they—the listeners (read: potential customers) want to hear. When listeners complain, advertisers become unhappy, not only because of the negative feedback they're receiving from customers (listeners), but from the lack of positive results they're getting from the money they're spending on ads on that radio station. When advertisers become unhappy, they let the station know. People are given new directives, and things are changed. And it doesn't take much to accomplish this. Both Senator Orrin Hatch (R-Utah) and former House Minority leader Richard Gephardt (D-Missouri) have told me that the power that letters from constituents have in influencing laws and actions in this country is significant. They also said that although it's amazing how few people actually take the time to write those letters, those who do, however, get listened to. Advertisers listen, too, especially if you put everything I've told you behind the Power of 200.

It's been said that when we add up our friends, their friends, and the friends of their friends, etc., each of us has potential access to roughly 200 people, give or take a few either way. It's also been said that if someone is happy with a service, they'll tell two people, but if they're unhappy, they'll tell ten.

I'm going to teach a strategy that can help you get your music heard on radio, and all you'll need is a few friends who will write letters and make calls to radio stations in your city requesting that your music be played. It's called the Letter and Request Strategy, and you'll be amazed at how little work it can take to get results. Just remember that few people write or call, and those that do, get listened to. It all begins with having the right commercial with your music, message, and call to action for people to hear.

Create the Right Ad and Start Small

If you're buying airtime at a radio station, one of the little known services many of these stations will offer you, the advertiser, is to help you physically create and record your ad. When I worked in radio, I helped create and produce an ad with a business owner who had a single tire store. Hey, I don't know about you, but selling tires on the radio is not the most exciting kind of ad I want to hear. To top it off, this guy wasn't flashy or full of hype.

The tire store owner had never recorded his own ad before, so I invited him into the radio station. I worked with him on an ad concept and script, but instead of using a professional announcer, I had him read his own ad, in his own voice, in his own way. He was 100 percent down to earth, laid back, and believable, and people loved him. The response he got was fantastic. People were not only buying his tires left and right, but also brakes, alignments, and other services he offered.

The bigger stations typically reserve their ad production service for their best-paying clients, so you may have to get help on your first ad at a smaller station. But that's okay, too, since once you get a great ad recorded—and all it takes is one—you can take that ad to any station anywhere you want and have them play it whenever you decide you want to buy more airtime.

The strategy here is to start off small, get on the air, and see what kind of response you get. Buy a few ads during the cheapest times in a station's schedule (along with "the agency rate," always ask for their "best package deal"). It may take a few weeks of people hearing your ad and music at, say, every Saturday night at 1:30 a.m., but they will respond. And each time they hear your ad, you'll make an *impression,* and the more impressions you make, the greater the probability they will act.

But don't stop there. Keep the momentum going, because as tough as it is to get started, once you do, it only takes a little action to keep it flowing. It's a lot like priming the pump. It takes a lot of pumping the well handle up and down to get anything to come out of the spout, but once it starts flowing, then all it takes is a little pump every now and then to keep it flowing.

Once the money starts coming in from people buying your product, I want you to earmark a portion of that money (10 to 30 percent) to buy airtime on another station in town. Go a step up in station rank and audience size. The ads will most likely cost more, but you'll be hitting a bigger audience for those higher dollars, with the potential for bigger results. I also want you to use a portion of that money to buy ads on the station you started with, but in earlier time slots and on different days and watch what happens.

Once you've done this, I want you to test your ad, music, and message (the "call to action") by looking at how many responses you received for the number of ad(s) and the time periods they played. If listeners have ordered CDs from your 800 number, how many did they order, and how many ads did they need to hear before they bought? If one of your ads asked them to request your CD at ABC record store (the "call to action"), how many ads had to play before ABC contacted you to order product? Always know how many ads need to be aired before action is taken, what the best times for them to play are, and what stations produce the best results for the money.

Do sequential tests, with clearly defined, simple parameters. For example, try looking at one month of ads playing on just one station at one time period. Then look at another month on that same station but in a different time period or perhaps a combination of time periods. If you find that a particular time period or combination of time periods is getting good results, stick with it until it stops getting results. When it does, you can either change your ad or try a different station. Start off slowly and find out what works and what doesn't. Refine your marketing plan using the tips I just gave you, and you'll be amazed at how quickly you and your music take off.

Stop and think about what you've done by using this strategy. By buying airtime on that first station, you *instantly* had access to the same station and the same potential audience that Superstar and his or her record label paid dearly for (did you write that $200,000 check yet?), and you've done it for a fraction of the cost.

To repeat: Always know your market and spend only the amount necessary to give you the results you want. Be smart. Be wise. Treat people right. Be a person of your word. Stay in control of your market, your image, and your music, and the rest will take care of itself.

Lesson 3

The Illusion of Needing a Record Deal:

Courtney Love's Real-World Wake-up Call

*I*f you ever thought you needed to have a record deal in place before being able to make your mark in the music business, you need to think again. The media love to regale us with stories about how much money this artist or that artist has made. Yet what we're not told is how few musicians make it to the level of financial success, or who actually keeps the majority of Mr. or Ms. Superstar's hard-earned money. In case you've been on vacation, it's the record company.

Courtney Love may be known as an actor, a singer, songwriter, and perhaps a bit of a lightning rod for controversy, but no one can ever say she doesn't tell it like it is. Especially when it comes to the record business and where all the money goes. The musical lineage of Courtney Love is one that brought her fame in her first group, the Minneapolis-based all-female punk band Babes in Toyland, and ultimately the recognition of being one of the most famous people in alternative rock.

Love, the singer and guitarist, started the band Hole in 1989, and in 1991 the band released its debut album, *Pretty on the Inside.* Its follow-up *Live Through This* hit platinum. However, things suddenly changed. Tragedy struck when the band's bassist Kristen Pfaff died from a heroin overdose.

Perhaps most people know Courtney Love for her now-famous relationship and marriage to the late Nirvana singer/songwriter/guitarist Kurt Cobain. Despite the downs of losing husband Kurt (who committed suicide) and bassist Pfaff, Love has always emerged as a fighter and has been able to reinvent herself (her image and appearance) whenever the situation called for it.

To this day, rumors about her drug use and her relationship with Cobain continue to swirl in gossip circles, but one thing is indisputable: Love's talent. Her first movie, *Sid & Nancy* (the story of Sex Pistols bassist Sid Vicious and lover Nancy Spungen), wasn't a big box office success, nor was her other film *Straight to Hell,* which was more like straight to video. But things would soon change.

Courtney received critical praise for her roles in such movies as *Man on the Moon* with Jim Carrey and *Feeling Minnesota* with Keanu Reeves and Cameron Diaz, and in 1999 she was nominated for a Golden Globe for her performance in the movie *The People Vs. Larry Flynt.* Since then, she's continued to be outspoken in her support for the causes she believes in, and the rights of artists in the music business is one of the causes she believes in most deeply.

In May 2000, at the Digital Hollywood Online Entertainment Conference, an annual conference that brings together many of the biggest stars and players in entertainment, Love gave a speech that was quickly recognized as a devastating expose of the record business, Napster, and the Record Industry Association of America (RIAA). It was a time of huge popularity for Napster, unlimited downloads, and a music business desperately looking for a new way to do business. The speech pulls no punches. What Courtney Love has to say is about to open your eyes to the real world of the music business and how the math is done. What follows is an unedited transcript of Love's speech, reprinted with the permission of Salon.com.

Courtney Does the Math on Record Contracts

Today I want to talk about piracy and music. What is piracy? Piracy is the act of stealing an artist's work without any intention of paying for it. I'm not talking about Napster-type software. I'm talking about major label recording contracts.

I want to start with a story about rock bands and record companies, and do some recording-contract math: This story is about a bidding-war band that gets a huge deal with a 20 percent royalty rate and a million-dollar advance. (No bidding-war band ever got a 20 percent royalty, but whatever.)

This is my "funny" math based on some reality and I just want to qualify it by saying I'm positive it's better math than what Edgar Bronfman Jr. [president and CEO of Seagram, which owns Polygram] would provide. What happens to that million dollars?

They spend half a million to record their album. That leaves the band with $500,000. They pay $100,000 to their manager for 20 percent commission. They pay $25,000 each to their lawyer and business manager. That leaves $350,000 for the four band members to split. After $170,000 in taxes, there's $180,000 left. That comes out to $45,000 per person. That's $45,000 to live on for a year until the record gets released.

The record is a big hit and sells a million copies. (How a bidding-war band sells a million copies of its debut record is another rant entirely, but it's based on any basic civics-class knowledge that any of us have about cartels. Put simply, the antitrust laws in this country are basically a joke, protecting us just enough to not have to re-name our park service the Phillip Morris National Park Service.)

So, this band releases two singles and makes two videos. The two videos cost a million dollars to make and 50 percent of the video production costs are recouped out of the band's royalties. The band gets $200,000 in tour support, which is 100 percent recoupable. The record company spends $300,000 on independent radio promotion. You have to pay independent promotion to get your song on the radio; independent promotion is a system where the record companies use middlemen so they can pretend not to know that radio stations—the unified broadcast system—are getting paid to play their records. All of those independent promotion costs are charged to the band.

Since the original million-dollar advance is also recoupable, the band owes $2 million to the record company. If all of the million records are sold at full price with no discounts or record clubs, the band earns $2 million in royalties, since their 20 percent royalty works out to $2 a record. Two million dollars in royalties minus $2 million in recoupable expenses equals . . . zero! How much does the record company make? They grossed $11 million.

It costs $500,000 to manufacture the CDs and they advanced the band $1 million. Plus there were $1 million in video costs, $300,000 in radio promotion, and $200,000 in tour support. The company also paid $750,000 in music publishing royalties. They spent $2.2 million on marketing. That's mostly retail advertising, but marketing also pays for those huge posters of Marilyn Manson in Times Square and the street scouts who drive around in vans handing out black Korn T-shirts and backwards baseball caps. Not to mention trips to Scores and cash for tips for all and sundry. Add it up and the record company has spent about $4.4 million. So their profit is $6.6 million; the band may as well be working at a 7-Eleven.

Of course, they had fun. Hearing yourself on the radio, selling records, getting new fans, and being on TV is great, but now the band doesn't have enough money to pay the rent and nobody has any credit. Worst of all, after all this, the band owns none of its work. They can pay the mortgage forever, but they'll never own the house.

Like I said: Sharecropping. Our media says, "Boo hoo, poor pop stars, they had a nice ride. Fuck them for speaking up"; but I say this dialogue is imperative. And cynical media people, who are more fascinated with celebrity than most celebrities, need to reacquaint themselves with their value systems.

When you look at the legal line on a CD, it says copyright 1976 Atlantic Records or copyright 1996 RCA Records. When you look at a book, though, it'll say something like copyright 1999 Susan Faludi, or David Foster Wallace. Authors own their books and license them to publishers. When the contract runs out, writers get their books back. But record companies own our copyrights forever. The system's set up so almost nobody gets paid.

Artists, Copyright Law, and the RIAA

Last November, a Congressional aide named Mitch Glazier, with the support of the RIAA, added a "technical amendment" to a bill that defined recorded music as "works for hire" under the 1978 Copyright Act.

He did this after all the hearings on the bill were over. By the time artists found out about the change, it was too late. The bill was on its way to the White House for the president's signature. That subtle change in copyright law will add billions of dollars to record company bank accounts over the next few years—billions of dollars that rightfully should have been paid to artists. A work for hire is now owned in perpetuity by the record company.

Under the 1978 Copyright Act, artists could reclaim the copyrights on their work after 35 years. If you wrote and recorded "Everybody Hurts," you at least got it back as a family legacy after 35 years. But now, because of this corrupt little pisher, "Everybody Hurts" never gets returned to your family, and can now be sold to the highest bidder.

Over the years, record companies have tried to put work-for-hire provisions in their contracts, and Mr. Glazier claims that the "work for hire" only "codified" a standard industry practice. But copyright laws didn't identify sound recordings as being eligible to be called works for hire, so those contracts didn't mean anything. Until now.

Writing and recording "Hey Jude" is now the same thing as writing an English textbook, writing standardized tests, translating a novel from one language to another, or making a map. These are the types of things addressed in the work-for-hire act. And writing a standardized test is a work for hire. Not making a record.

So an assistant substantially altered a major law when he only had the authority to make spelling corrections. That's not what I learned about how government works in my high school civics class. Three months later, the RIAA hired Mr. Glazier to become its top lobbyist at a salary that was obviously much greater than the one he had as the spelling corrector guy.

The RIAA tries to argue that this change was necessary because of a provision in the bill that musicians supported. That provision prevents anyone from registering a famous person's name as a Web address without that person's permission. That's great. I own my name, and should be able to do what I want with my name.

But the bill also created an exception that allows a company to take a person's name for a Web address if they create a work for hire. Which means a record company would be allowed to own your Web site when you record your work-for-hire album. Like I said: Sharecropping.

Although I've never met anyone at a record company who "believed in the Internet," they've all been trying to cover their asses by securing everyone's digital rights. Not that they know what to do with them. Go to a major label–owned band site. Give me a dollar for every time you see an annoying "under construction" sign. I used to pester Geffen (when it was a label) to do a better job. I was totally ignored for two years, until I got my band name back. The Goo Goo Dolls are struggling to gain control of their domain name from Warner Bros., who claim they own the name because they set up a shitty promotional Web site for the band.

Orrin Hatch, songwriter and Republican senator from Utah, seems to be the only person in Washington with a progressive view of copyright law. One lobbyist says that there's no one in the House with a similar view and that "this would have never happened if Sonny Bono was still alive."

By the way, which bill do you think the recording industry used for this amendment? The Record Company Redefinition Act? No. The Music Copyright Act? No. The Work for Hire Authorship Act? No. How about the Satellite Home Viewing Act of 1999? Stealing our copyright reversions in the dead of night while no one was looking, and with no hearings held, is piracy.

It's piracy when the RIAA lobbies to change the bankruptcy law to make it more difficult for musicians to declare bankruptcy. Some musicians have declared bankruptcy to free themselves from truly evil contracts. TLC declared bankruptcy after they received less than 2 percent of the $175 million earned by their CD sales. That was about 40 times less than the profit that was divided among their management, production, and record companies.

Toni Braxton also declared bankruptcy in 1998. She sold $188 million worth of CDs, but she was broke because of a terrible recording contract that paid her less than 35 cents per album. Bankruptcy can be an artist's only defense against a truly horrible deal and the RIAA wants to take it away.

Artists want to believe that we can make lots of money if we're successful. But there are hundreds of stories about artists in their sixties and seventies who are broke because they never made a dime from their hit records. And real success is still a long shot for a new artist today. Of the 32,000 new releases each year, only 250 sell more than 10,000 copies. And less than 30 go platinum.

The four major record corporations fund the RIAA. These companies are rich and obviously well-represented. Recording artists and musicians don't really have the money to compete. The 273,000 working musicians in America make about $30,000 a year. Only 15 percent of American Federation of Musicians members work steadily in music.

But the music industry is a $40 billion-a-year business. One-third of that revenue comes from the United States. The annual sales of cassettes, CDs, and video are larger than the gross national product of 80 countries. Americans have more CD players, radios, and VCRs than we have bathtubs.

Story after story gets told about artists—some of them in their 60s and 70s, some of them authors of huge successful songs that we all enjoy, use, and sing—living in total poverty, never having been paid anything. Not even having access to a union or to basic health care. Artists who have generated billions of dollars for an industry die broke and un-cared for. And they're not actors or participators. They're the rightful owners, originators, and performers of original compositions. This is piracy.

Technology Is Not Piracy

This opinion is one I really haven't formed yet, so as I speak about Napster now, please understand that I'm not totally informed. I will be the first in line to file a class action suit to protect my copyrights if Napster or even the far more advanced Gnutella doesn't work with us to protect us. I'm on [Metallica drummer] Lars Ulrich's side, in other words, and I feel really badly for him that he doesn't know how to condense his case down to a sound-bite that sounds more reasonable than the one I saw today.

I also think Metallica is being given too much grief. It's anti-artist, for one thing. An artist speaks up and the artist gets squashed: Sharecropping. Don't get above your station, kid. It's not piracy when kids swap music over the Internet using Napster or Gnutella or Freenet or iMesh or beaming their CDs into a My.MP3.com or MyPlay.com music locker. It's piracy when those guys that run those companies make side deals with the cartel lawyers and label heads so that they can be "the labels' friend," and not the artists'.

Recording artists have essentially been giving their music away for free under the old system, so new technology that exposes our music to a larger audience can only be a good thing. Why aren't these companies working with us to create some peace?

There were a billion music downloads last year, but music sales are up. Where's the evidence that downloads hurt business? Downloads are creating more demand. Why aren't record companies embracing this great opportunity? Why aren't they trying to talk to the kids passing compilations around to learn what they like? Why is the RIAA suing the companies that are stimulating this new demand? What's the point of going after people swapping cruddy-sounding MP3s? Cash! Cash they have no intention of passing on to us, the writers of their profits.

At this point the "record collector" geniuses who use Napster don't have the coolest, most arcane selection anyway, unless you're into techno. Hardly any pre-1982 REM fans, no '60s punk, even the Alan Parsons Project was underrepresented when I tried to find some Napster buddies. For the most part, it was college boy rawk without a lot of imagination. Maybe that's the demographic that cares—and in that case, My Bloody Valentine and Bert Jansch aren't going to get screwed just yet. There's still time to negotiate.

Somewhere along the way, record companies figured out that it's a lot more profitable to control the distribution system than it is to nurture artists. And since the companies didn't have any real competition, artists had no other place to go. Record companies controlled the promotion and marketing; only they had the ability to get lots of radio play, and get records into all the big chain stores. That power put them above both the artists and the audience. They own the plantation.

Being the gatekeeper was the most profitable place to be, but now we're in a world half without gates. The Internet allows artists to communicate directly with their audiences; we don't have to depend solely on an inefficient system where the record company promotes our records to radio, press, or retail and then sits back and hopes fans find out about our music.

Record companies don't understand the intimacy between artists and their fans. They put records on the radio and buy some advertising and hope for the best. Digital distribution gives everyone worldwide, instant access to music.

And filters are replacing gatekeepers. In a world where we can get anything we want, whenever we want it, how does a company create value? By filtering. In a world without friction, the only friction people value is editing. A filter is valuable when it understands the needs of both artists and the public. New companies should be conduits between musicians and their fans.

Right now the only way you can get music is by shelling out $17. In a world where music costs a nickel, an artist can "sell" 100 million copies instead of just a million. The present system keeps artists from finding an audience because it has too many artificial scarcities: limited radio promotion, limited bin space in stores, and a limited number of spots on the record company roster. The digital world has no scarcities. There are countless ways to reach an audience. Radio is no longer the only place to hear a new song. And tiny mall record stores aren't the only place to buy a new CD.

Artists Have Options

Now artists have options. We don't have to work with major labels anymore, because the digital economy is creating new ways to distribute and market music. And the free ones amongst us aren't going to. That means the slave class, which I represent, has to find ways to get out of our deals. This didn't really matter before, and that's why we all stayed.

I want my 7-year contract law California labor code case to mean something to other artists. (Universal Records sues me because I leave because my employment is up, but they say a recording contract is not a personal contract; because the recording industry—who, we have established, are excellent lobbyists, getting, as they did, a clerk to disallow Don Henley or Tom Petty the right to give their copyrights to their families—in California, in 1987, lobbied to pass an amendment that nullified recording contracts as personal contracts, sort of. Maybe. Kind of. A little bit. And again, in the dead of night, succeeded.)

That's why I'm willing to do it with a sword in my teeth. I expect I'll be ignored or ostracized following this lawsuit. I expect that the treatment you're seeing Lars Ulrich get now will quadruple for me. Cool. At least I'll serve a purpose. I'm an artist, and a good artist, I think, but I'm not that artist that has to play all the time, and thus has to get fucked. Maybe my laziness and self-destructive streak will finally pay off and serve a community desperately in need of it. They can't torture me like they could Lucinda Williams.

I want to work with people who believe in music and art and passion. And I'm just the tip of the iceberg. I'm leaving the major label system, and there are hundreds of artists who are going to follow me. There's an unbelievable opportunity for new companies that dare to get it right.

How can anyone defend the current system when it fails to deliver music to so many potential fans? That only expects of itself a "5 percent success rate" a year? The status quo gives us a boring culture. In a society of over 300 million people, only 30 new artists a year sell a million records. By any measure, that's a huge failure.

Maybe each fan will spend less money, but maybe each artist will have a better chance of making a living. Maybe our culture will get more interesting than the one currently owned by Time-Warner. I'm not crazy. Ask yourself, are any of you somehow connected to Time-Warner media? I think there are a lot of yes's to that, and I'd have to say that in that case President McKinley truly failed to bust any trusts. Maybe we can remedy that now.

Artists will make that compromise if it means we can connect with hundreds of millions of fans instead of the hundreds of thousands that we have now. Especially if we lose all the crap that goes with success under the current system. I'm willing, right now, to leave half of these trappings—fuck it, all these trappings—at the door to have a pure artist experience. They cosset us with trappings to shut us up. That way when we say "sharecropper!" you can point to my free suit and say "Shut up, pop star."

Here, take my Prada pants. Fuck it. Let us do our real jobs. And those of us addicted to celebrity because we have nothing else to give will fade away. And those of us addicted to celebrity because it was there will find a better, purer way to live.

Since I've basically been giving my music away for free under the old system, I'm not afraid of wireless, MP3 files, or any of the other threats to my copyrights. Anything that makes my music more available to more people is great. MP3 files sound cruddy, but a well-made album sounds great. And I don't care what anyone says about digital recordings. At this point they are good for dance music, but try listening to a warm guitar tone on them. They suck for what I do.

Record companies are terrified of anything that challenges their control of distribution. This is the business that insisted that CDs be sold in incredibly wasteful 6-by-12 inch long boxes just because no one thought you could change the bins in a record store.

Let's not call the major labels "labels." Let's call them by their real names: They are the distributors. They're the only distributors and they exist because of scarcity. Artists pay 95 percent of whatever we make to gatekeepers because we used to need gatekeepers to get our music heard. Because they have a system, and when they decide to spend enough money—all of it recoupable, all of it owed by me—they can occasionally shove things through this system, depending on a lot of arbitrary factors.

The corporate filtering system, which is the system that brought you (in my humble opinion) a piece of crap like "Mambo No. 5" and didn't let you hear the brilliant Cat Power record or the amazing new Sleater Kinney record, obviously doesn't have good taste anyway. But we've never paid major label/distributors for their good taste. They've never been like Yahoo and provided a filter service.

There were a lot of factors that made a distributor decide to push a recording through the system:

* How powerful is management?
* Who owes whom a favor?
* What independent promoter's cousin is the drummer?
* What part of the fiscal year is the company putting out the record?
* Is the royalty rate for the artist so obscenely bad that it's almost 100 percent profit instead of just 95 percent so that if the record sells, it's literally a steal?
* How much bin space is left over this year?
* Was the record already a hit in Europe so that there's corporate pressure to make it work?
* Will the band screw up its live career to play free shows for radio stations?

* Does the artist's song sound enough like someone else that radio stations will play it because it fits the sound of the month?
* Did the artist get the song on a film soundtrack so that the movie studio will pay for the video?

These factors affect the decisions that go into the system. Not public taste. All these things are becoming eradicated now. They are gone or on their way out. We don't need the gatekeepers anymore. We just don't need them.

And if they aren't going to do for me what I can do for myself with my 19-year-old Webmistress on my own Web site, then they need to get the hell out of my way. [I will] allow millions of people to get my music for nothing if they want and hopefully they'll be kind enough to leave a tip if they like it.

I still need the old stuff. I still need a producer in the creation of a recording, I still need to get on the radio (which costs a lot of money), I still need bin space for hardware CDs, I still need to provide an opportunity for people without computers to buy the hardware that I make. I still need a lot of this stuff, but I can get these things from a joint venture with a company that serves as a conduit and knows its place. Serving the artist and serving the public: That's its place.

Equity for Artists

A new company that gives artists true equity in their work can take over the world, kick ass, and make a lot of money. We're inspired by how people get paid in the new economy. Many visual artists and software and hardware designers have real ownership of their work.

I have a 14-year-old niece. She used to want to be a rock star. Before that she wanted to be an actress. As of 6 months ago, what do you think she wants to be when she grows up? What's the glamorous, emancipating career of choice? Of course, she wants to be a Web designer. It's such a glamorous business!

When you people do business with artists, you have to take a different view of things. We want to be treated with the respect that now goes to Web designers. We're not Dockers-wearing Intel workers from Portland who know how to "manage our stress." We don't understand or want to understand corporate culture.

I feel this obscene gold rush greed . . . greed . . . greed . . . vibe that bothers me a lot when I talk to dot-com people about all this. You guys can't hustle artists that well. At least slick A&R guys know the buzzwords. Don't try to compete with them. I just laugh at you when you do! Maybe you could a year ago when anything dot-com sounded smarter than the rest of us, but the scam has been uncovered.

The celebrity-for-sale business is about to crash, I hope, and the idea of a sucker VC gifting some company with four floors just because they can "do" "chats" with "Christina" once or twice is ridiculous. I did a chat today, twice. Big damn deal.

200 bucks for the software and some elbow grease and a good back-end coder. Wow. That's not worth 150 million bucks.

I mean, yeah, sure it is if you'd like to give it to me.

Music Is a Service to Its Customers

I know my place. I'm a waiter. I'm in the service industry. I live on tips. Occasionally, I'm going to get stiffed, but that's OK. If I work hard and I'm doing good work, I believe that the people who enjoy it are going to want to come directly to me and get my music because it sounds better, since it's mastered and packaged by me personally. I'm providing an honest, real experience. Period.

When people buy the bootleg T-shirt in the concert parking lot and not the more expensive T-shirt inside the venue, it isn't to save money. The T-shirt in the parking lot is cheap and badly made, but it's easier to buy. The bootleggers have a better distribution system. There's no waiting in line and it only takes 2 minutes to buy one.

I know that if I can provide my own T-shirt that I designed, that I made, and provide it as quickly or quicker than the bootleggers, people who've enjoyed the experience I've provided will be happy to shell out a little more money to cover my costs. Especially if they understand this context, and aren't being shoveled a load of shit about "uppity" artists.

It's exactly the same with recorded music. The real thing to fear from Napster is its simple and excellent distribution system. No one really prefers a cruddy-sounding Napster MP3 file to the real thing. But it's really easy to get an MP3 file; and in the middle of Kansas you may never see my record because major distribution is really bad if your record's not in the charts this week, and even then it takes a couple of weeks to restock the one copy they usually keep on hand.

I also know how many times I have heard a song on the radio that I loved only to buy the record and have the album be a piece of crap. If you're afraid of your own filler, then I bet you're afraid of Napster. I'm afraid of Napster because I think the major label cartel will get to them before I do.

I've made three records. I like them all. I haven't made filler and they're all committed pieces of work. I'm not scared of you previewing my record. If you like it enough to have it be a part of your life, I know you'll come to me to get it, as long as I show you how to get to me, and as long as you know that it's out.

Most people don't go into restaurants and stiff waiters, but record labels represent the restaurant that forces the waiters to live on, and sometimes pool, their tips. And they even fight for a bit of their tips. Music is a service to its consumers, not a product. I live on tips. Giving music away for free is what artists have been doing naturally all their lives.

New Models for the Record Business

Record companies stand between artists and their fans. We signed terrible deals with them because they controlled our access to the public. But in a world of total connectivity, record companies lose that control. With unlimited bin space and intelligent search engines, fans will have no trouble finding the music they know they want. They have to know they want it, and that needs to be a marketing business that takes a fee.

If a record company has a reason to exist, it has to bring an artist's music to more fans and it has to deliver more and better music to the audience. You bring me a bigger audience or a better relationship with my audience or get the fuck out of my way. Next time I release a record, I'll be able to go directly to my fans and let them hear it before anyone else.

We'll still have to use radio and traditional CD distribution. Record stores aren't going away any time soon and radio is still the most important part of record promotion. Major labels are freaking out because they have no control in this new world. Artists can sell CDs directly to fans. We can make direct deals with thousands of other Web sites and promote our music to millions of people that old record companies never touch. We're about to have lots of new ways to sell our music: downloads, hardware bundles, memory sticks, live Webcasts, and lots of other things that aren't even invented yet.

An Open Letter to Steve Case

But there's something you guys have to figure out. Here's my open letter to Steve Case:

> Avatars don't talk back! But what are you going to do with real live artists? Artists aren't like you. We go through a creative process that's demented and crazy. There's a lot of soul-searching and turning ourselves inside-out and all kinds of gross stuff that ends up on Behind the Music.
>
> A lot of people who haven't been around artists very much get really weird when they sit down to lunch with us. So I want to give you some advice: Learn to speak our language. Talk about songs and melody and hooks and art and beauty and soul. Not sleazy record-guy crap, where you're in a cashmere sweater murmuring that the perfect deal really is perfect, Courtney. Yuck. Honestly hire honestly committed people. We're in a "new economy," right? You can afford to do that. But don't talk to me about "content."
>
> I get really freaked out when I meet someone and they start telling me that I should record 34 songs in the next 6 months so that we have enough content for my site. Defining artistic expression as content is anathema to me.
>
> What the hell is content? Nobody buys content. Real people pay money for music because it means something to them. A great song is not just something to take up space on a Web site next to stock market quotes and baseball scores. DEN tried to build a site with artist-free content and I'm not sorry to see it fail.

The DEN shows look like art if you're not paying attention, but they forgot to hire anyone to be creative. So they ended up with a lot of content nobody wants to see because they thought they could avoid dealing with defiant and moody personalities. Because they were arrogant. And because they were conformists. Artists have to deal with businesspeople and businesspeople have to deal with artists. We hate each other. Let's create companies of mediators.

Every single artist who makes records believes and hopes that they give you something that will transform your life. If you're really just interested in data mining or selling banner ads, stick with those "artists" willing to call themselves content providers.

I don't know if an artist can last by meeting the current public taste, the taste from the last quarterly report. I don't think you can last by following demographics and carefully meeting expectations. I don't know many lasting works of art that are condescending or deliberately stupid or were created as content.

Don't tell me I'm a brand. I'm famous and people recognize me, but I can't look in the mirror and see my brand identity. Keep talking about brands and you know what you'll get? Bad clothes. Bad hair. Bad books. Bad movies. And bad records. And bankrupt businesses. Rides that were fun for a year with no employee loyalty but everyone got rich fucking you. Who wants that? The answer is purity. We can afford it. Let's go find it again while we can.

I also feel filthy trying to call my music a product. It's not a thing that I test-market like toothpaste or a new car. Music is personal and mysterious. Being a "content provider" is prostitution work that devalues our art and doesn't satisfy our spirits. Artistic expression has to be provocative. The problem with artists and the Internet: Once their art is reduced to content, they may never have the opportunity to retrieve their souls. When you form your business for creative people, with creative people, come at us with some thought. Everybody's process is different. And remember that it's art. We're not craftspeople.

Corporate Sponsorships

I don't know what a good sponsorship would be for me or for other artists I respect. People bring up sponsorships a lot as a way for artists to get our music paid for up-front and for us to earn a fee. I've dealt with large corporations for long enough to know that any alliance where I'm an owned service is going to be doomed.

When I agreed to allow a large cola company to promote a live show, I couldn't have been more miserable. They screwed up every single thing imaginable. The venue was empty but sold out. There were thousands of people outside who wanted to be there, trying to get tickets. And there were the empty seats the company had purchased for a lump sum and failed to market because they were clueless about music. It was really dumb. You had to buy the cola. You had to dial a number. You had to press a bunch of buttons. You had to do all this crap that nobody wanted to do. Why not just bring a can to the door?

On top of all this, I felt embarrassed to be an advertising agent for a product that I'd never let my daughter use. Plus they were a condescending bunch of little guys. They treated me like I was an ungrateful little bitch who should be groveling for the experience to play for their damn soda. I ended up playing without my shirt on and ordering a six-pack of the rival cola onstage. Also lots of unwholesome cursing and nudity occurred. This way I knew that no matter how tempting the cash was, they'd never do business with me again.

If you want some little obedient slave content provider, then fine. But I think most musicians don't want to be responsible for your clean-cut, wholesome, all-American, sugar-corrosive cancer-causing, all-white-people, no-women-allowed sodapop images.

Nor, on the converse, do we want to be responsible for your vice-inducing, liver-rotting, child-labor-law-violating, all-white-people, no-women-allowed booze images. So as a defiant moody artist worth my salt, I've got to think of something else. Tampax, maybe.

Money as Incentive

As a user, I love Napster. It carries some risk. I hear idealistic business people talk about how people that are musicians would be musicians no matter what and that we're already doing it for free, so what about copyright?

Please. It's incredibly easy not to be a musician. It's always a struggle and a dangerous career choice. We are motivated by passion and by money. That's not a dirty little secret. It's a fact. Take away the incentive for major or minor financial reward and you dilute the pool of musicians. I am not saying that only pure artists will survive. Like a few of the more utopian people who discuss this, I don't want just pure artists to survive.

Where would we all be without the trash? We need the trash to cover up our national depression. The utopians also say that because in their minds "pure" artists are all Ani DiFranco and don't demand a lot of money. Why are the utopians all entertainment lawyers and major label workers anyway?

I demand a lot of money if I do a big huge worthwhile job and millions of people like it, don't kid yourself. In economic terms, you've got an industry that's loathsome and outmoded, but when it works it creates some incentive and some efficiency even though absolutely no one gets paid. We suffer as a society and a culture when we don't pay the true value of goods and services delivered. We create a lack of production. Less good music is recorded if we remove the incentive to create it.

Music is intellectual property with full cash and opportunity costs required to create, polish, and record a finished product. If I invest money and time into my business, I should be reasonably protected from the theft of my goods and services.

When the judgment came against MP3.com, the RIAA sought damages of $150,000 for each major-label-"owned" musical track in MP3's database. Multiply by 80,000 CDs, and MP3.com could owe the gatekeepers $120 billion.

But what about the Plimsouls? Why can't MP3.com pay each artist a fixed amount based on the number of their downloads? Why on earth should MP3.com pay $120 billion to four distribution companies, who in most cases won't have to pay a nickel to the artists whose copyrights they've stolen through their system of organized theft?

It's a ridiculous judgment. I believe if evidence had been entered that ultimately it's just shuffling big cash around two or three corporations, I can only pray that the judge in the MP3.com case would have seen the RIAA's case for the joke that it was.

I'd rather work out a deal with MP3.com myself, and force them to be artist-friendly, instead of being laughed at and having my money hidden by a major label as they sell my records out the back door, behind everyone's back.

How dare they behave in such a horrified manner in regards to copyright law when their entire industry is based on piracy? When Mister Label Head Guy, whom my lawyer yelled at me not to name, got caught last year selling millions of "cleans" out the back door, "cleans" being the records that aren't for marketing but are to be sold. Who the fuck is this guy? He wants to save a little cash so he fucks the artist and goes home? Do they fire him? Does Chuck Phillips of the *LA Times* say anything? No way! This guy's a source! He throws awesome dinner parties! Why fuck with the status quo? Let's pick on Lars Ulrich instead because he brought up an interesting point!

In Conclusion

I'm looking for people to help connect me to more fans, because I believe fans will leave a tip based on the enjoyment and service I provide. I'm not scared of them getting a preview. It really is going to be a global village where a billion people have access to one artist and a billion people can leave a tip if they want to.

It's a radical democratization. Every artist has access to every fan and every fan has access to every artist and to the people who direct fans to those artists. People that give advice and technical value are the people we need. People crowding the distribution pipe and trying to ignore fans and artists have no value. This is a perfect system.

If you're going to start a company that deals with musicians, please do it because you like music. Offer some control and equity to the artists and try to give us some creative guidance. If music and art and passion are important to you, there are hundreds of artists who are ready to rewrite the rules.

In the last few years, business pulled our culture away from the idea that music is important and emotional and sacred. But new technology has brought a real opportunity for change; we can break down the old system and give musicians real freedom and choice.

A great writer named Neal Stephenson said that America does four things better than any other country in the world: rock music, movies, software, and high-speed pizza delivery. All of these are sacred American art forms. Let's return to our purity and our idealism while we have this shot. Warren Beatty once said: "The greatest gift God gives us is to enjoy the sound of our own voice. And the second greatest gift is to get somebody to listen to it." And for that, I humbly thank you.

Lesson 4

A View from Both Sides of the Fence:

Steve Lukather on What's Right and What's Wrong with the Music Business

Steve Lukather. Where do I begin to tell you about this guy? As a guitar player, there's no denying the inspiration and soul that pours from his fingers to the six strings of his instrument. His playing has influenced and will go on influencing untold numbers of people all over the world. Yet, if you ask Luke, as friends call him, he'll tell you he's not that good and he's one lucky mutha to earn a living—albeit a good one—at playing the guitar for people.

Luke, of course, is a cofounding member of the band Toto, which sold over 27 million records. As a solo artist, he's sold many more records on his own.

Then there's that little thing he did in his life called doing sessions. In the course of Luke's studio journeys, he's played on over 1,000 records, including hits by almost every major musical artist in the last 30 years. He's been nominated for a Grammy 12 times, and has won 5 of those little prized statues.

But all of this means little to a man who values family and friends above all, is thankful every day for the Gift of Life, and whose philosophy encompasses such feelings as "Live for today," "Enjoy every moment," "Deny yourself nothing," "Have a great time," "Try to be nice to people," and always "Try to leave a little love behind."

Luke is a guy who's been around the block a time or two. He also has a unique perspective on the music business, since he has been a successful recording artist on both sides of the fence, winning Grammys both as an independent and as a major label artist. He also knows how to put things in perspective on how the old music business works—or doesn't—why music is where it is today, and, most importantly, why you need to be thinking and doing things differently in today's new music business.

As Luke likes to say, "I'm old school," and it's his old school education that's about to teach you some new school lessons on becoming the success you were meant to be.

Lukather on the Music Business, Yesterday and Today

When I was first starting to play music, it used to be that people practiced and tried to get really good at whatever instrument they played. Nowadays, it seems most people could give a rat's ass. All my peers—Van Halen, Satriani, Vai, Landau, all the A-level cats—practiced their asses off to get really good, and today, hardly anyone cares about being a great musician anymore. I wish someone would've told me this 25 years ago so I could've stopped all the hours of practice and had more fun (laughs).

Right now, I still get up and practice everyday because I still care and it's because I love playing the guitar and what I do. I mean, I do it because first and foremost I care about it for myself. I don't care how many years I'll play the guitar, I'll never have it all figured out. Not even close. And that's what I like about it because it's always a challenge to see if I can become just a little better today than yesterday. God gave me whatever talent I have—and thank God it was playing the guitar because I ain't the prettiest mutha you've ever seen—and I try each day to make the most of it.

I have a recording studio where major record producers work, and would you believe that the most important person on the gig is not the musicians? It's the Pro Tools guy. These young muthas come into the studio with the attitude that "I'm all this or that" and yet they can't play four bars in time. And when it ain't working on the session, they'll say, "Screw it. Go ahead and Pro Tool it and it'll be cool." That's their excuse for not becoming a good player.

When I was a kid, I spent 10 hours a day trying to get my shit together just so I could be good enough to get asked to play on one record, which maybe might get me a second record. And now, people who practice, people who truly care about the music and less about technology, are considered a bunch of old assholes.

Let me tell you something. I was in Toronto jamming with an old pal named Jeff Healy and I got invited to a Rolling Stones rehearsal. These 60-year-old players started their rehearsal at midnight and there I was sitting there watching them like a kid with cotton candy and a hard-on (laughs). When I heard them play "Satisfaction" and "Start Me Up," those 60-year-old guys sounded better than anything I've heard in the last 20 years. They had the fire, they had the attitude, they were laughing, they were partying, they were just groovin'.

Say what you will about my man Keith, but he was playing his ass off. And when Mick sang, I actually called my home answering machine and held up my cell phone to record how great they sounded, to have a memory of being there and inspired.

I've been doing sessions since I was 17 years old. Back in the old days, they didn't have machines that did everything, like they do today, and you actually had demo sessions. There'd be singers, songwriters, piano players, acoustic guitar players who were trying to get record deals, and there were lots of demos going on. I was making 25 dollars a tune and that was great money then.

That was where we all got our practical knowledge about how you play on sessions, how you get your sound, and all that good stuff. There was a wealth of work back in those days from 1975 to 1985. During that 10-year period, I played on over 1,000 records.

When I was doing sessions, each day that I'd come into the studio was always a surprise. I'd ask, "So who's playing on the record today? Steve Gadd is playing drums. Awesome! Anthony Jackson on bass. Who's on keyboards? David Paich. David Foster. Incredible. Lenny Castro is playing percussion and me and Ray Parker or Dean Parks or Jay Graydon or Larry Carlton is playing guitar? Excellent." The exciting question each day I walked into any studio was always, "Who am I playing with today?"

And it was fantastic, as many, many times, we'd immediately begin writing this record for whoever singer/songwriter we were working with who came into the session with three chords on a piece of paper and no demo and we'd all write and rewrite the song just like that. We were arranging and rewriting this guy or gal's material every day. That was what we got hired to do. And even though being a studio musician was a thankless gig, it was still fun.

I played on records of every musical hero in my life, from the lamest singer/songwriters to Miles Davis to Paul McCartney and every major artist that's been on the music scene in the last 30 years. And you know how it all started? I began doing those 25-dollar-a-song demos and those led to a bigger gig which led to a bigger gig and it just sort of snowballed from there. It was word of mouth.

I was lucky enough to grow up with the Porcaro brothers, and Jeff Porcaro (the late legendary drummer) was doing Steely Dan sessions when I was in high school. Guys I grew up with and began playing gigs with, like David Paichs and Jeff Porcaro's fathers, were A-level studio musicians, and that was a powerful influence and inspiration. That inspired me to learn to read music and do whatever I needed to do so I could play on everybody's records.

I could go on and on about the incredible experiences I've had playing on records. I remember one record date with Elton John where Elton and I are sitting at the piano drinking cognac and there he was playing "Levon" for me. I was 20 years old and having the time of my life, and you know, I'm still having the time of my life playing music.

Early on, I got hooked up with some great people like Boz Scaggs, and did his world tour and all the records that followed. Of course, there were many times in the studio when we were tested when the unexpected happened. Like the time when we played on Michael Jackson's "Beat It" and Eddie Van Halen had come in and cut the tape and screwed up the whole SMPTE code and Jeff Porcaro and I had to put the whole record together without producer Quincy Jones (a guy I truly love working with) in the room, and would you believe, that record ended up winning record of the year.

I can't even begin to tell you how many times we pulled producers' asses out of the fire. So many times we were doing all this arranging—and not getting credit or money for it—while this or that friggin' producer was in the bathroom snortin' blow or taking Quaaludes or passed out on the studio couch.

Or . . . guys who will remain nameless—who were the head of record labels for the biggest record companies in the world—didn't even show up to their own sessions when they were producing. They'd walk into the studio when we were finished and say, "Wow, that sounds great. Where do you want to go for dinner?"

Many, many times they'd come into the session early or late and after one or two takes, they'd say, "Great, that sounds perfect . . . next" when in fact, we were just getting things started and could've given them far better takes. Meanwhile, they're up there on the stage accepting their Grammy awards with the attitude "I'd like to thank no one because I'm a genius."

These are the same people whose asses we'd pull out of the fire time and time again. Guys who never gave us any extra taste—i.e., money—or credit for what we did. I'm talking about guys who are heads of major record companies right now, that if you put a gun to their friggin' head and told them, "You play me a C scale right now or you're dead," you'd have a bunch of dead record company people, because they couldn't do it. And these are the people who are in charge of the music business and the music that gets made today, and we wonder why the record business is so screwed up.

Think of it: If you're the head of all the doctors in a hospital, chances are you're going to be one of the best doctors. You're the go-to guy. But if you're the head of a record label, chances are you're not only one lucky bastard, but you're also not the best guy for the job, you're also not a musician, you also don't have much of a musical background, and your typical plan of action is "Let's fire 5,000 people, so we can show shareholders great numbers and a profit and while we're at it, why don't we give ourselves millions of dollars as a bonus."

I'm old school. I mean I was crushed when I found out the Monkeys didn't play on their own records. That's when I found out about studio guys like Tommy Tedesco and all the others who played on those records. Then I found out about the Motown guys. Do you know who played on all those records? Those Motown session guys and they got 25 bucks a tune!

I mean c'mon, where do you want to start with the Motown shit? There were 25 guys in the studio and everything was going down live. It was when music was real, instead of today of "Let's Pro Tools everything into oblivion."

You can hear Pro Tools on the radio today. I can hear the shit. I mean they auto-tune this or that to the point as soon as you hear some dude singing, you know that mutha couldn't sing "Happy Birthday" in tune if his friggin' life depended on it. What the hell is that all about?

I keep going back to the old school because that's where the inspiration and soul still is. Listen to The Beatles and The Rolling Stones. They're playing live. Those records are what happened when they pressed the red button and heard "One, two, three, four." Compare that to today. You go and see those artists on MTV live and few of them can play. I'm talking about "play" their instrument. My kids and their friends come back from these concerts and say, "Dad, it was weak."

Today, there is no session scene. It's dead, it's gone. Today, all you need is Pro Tools in your house and if you can't play it, no problem we'll fix it. We'll tune it. We'll make it in time and we'll cut and paste your parts so you don't have to play them again and possibly mess things up.

The day of the session player is gone. Bye-bye, nice talking to you. Unless you're doing TV and film, you can forget about all those big recording dates like we used to do not too many years ago. Even top call A-list players are not making a living being session players. They're taking high-paying road gigs.

People often ask me how has music changed and I tell them that it's no longer necessary to become a good musician anymore. Seems like some people who are making music today will accidentally trip and fall down on a sound, and if that sound turns into a hit record, then you're labeled a genius.

Whereas, with the people I grew up with, we actually sat in a room for hours at a time—with fingers numb and bleeding—as we took vinyl LPs and lifted the needle off the record to learn Eric Clapton solos from "Crossroads," all the while driving our parents crazy from lifting it (the needle) up and down just so we could learn every freakin' lick.

Today, people who do that kind of shit are considered pompous old pricks because the attitude of today's musicians is that all that shit really doesn't matter 'cause you don't need to do it to create a hit. Technology and not talent is their crutch and solution.

It is getting so hard to find good musicians anymore. It really is. Perhaps that's why I have more affinity for jazz musicians than I do rock musicians, even though I'm not a jazz musician because I'm not good enough. Call me a rock guy with jazz aspirations.

I look up to cats like Pat Metheny, Mike Stern, Scott Henderson, Michael Landau, and these kinds of great players who set the bar a little higher, but aren't household names because we live in an Eminem world. Jazz guys may not make a million dollars or sell a million records but they can inspire you. For jazz, it's always been the old joke, How do you make a million dollars playing jazz? Start with five million.

For years, people have believed that if only you could have a hit record, then life would be wonderful, but thinking like that is going to get you in big trouble. You see, it's not as hard as people think to have a one-hit record. But let me tell something, having a one-hit record is not going to make you a millionaire, and you're still going to be in debt to the record company. And even if your record hits gold (sale of 500,000 units), you're still in debt to the record company. Make that deep in debt.

To give you an idea of how things work, let's go back to "old school." Old school in my day is when they had big budgets for records. They'd give you half a million dollars to make a record. That's when we used to play on sessions and when they used to hire human beings to make music instead of computers to play on records.

We used to get double-scale rates to be in the studio and come up with ideas while the drummer took 2 or 3 days to get a great drum sound. It was a shameless display of wealth, the total opposite end of the spectrum, whereby there was too much money to make records. Nowadays, people do records in their house for one hundredth of the budget.

However, even though the way music is made has greatly changed and the pendulum has swung from excess money to do it, to now doing it on a budget in your house, what cats today are missing is the human element and soul in their music and creation.

That's what's going on right now. Record companies are dying and it's a dead scene. And you know what? They [the record labels] deserve to go out of business because they make too much friggin' money for doing friggin' nothing and promoting the mediocrity that we call "music" these days.

And the negative influence of many of the magazine music critics on promoting the music we have today isn't any better. I ask you, why does it seem that the magazine music critics seem to like the music of artists that they can play themselves, which is why they almost always critique the lyrics, as opposed to the musicality or musicianship of the records they review?

I can say this shit now, because I've been in the game close to 30 years and the critics already hate me for telling it like it is, so what am I going to do, piss them off? Who cares? If they'd be honest and tell things like they were, then you wouldn't be hearing me rant.

But it's not just me, some old school geezer, that knows the story. You should hear my teenage kids and their friends. They read so many of the bullshit magazine music reviews about this or that artist and where time and time again they say, "Man, that magazine and the artists they promote are so lame." They know the difference between who sounds good and who doesn't and they know the reality of what's happening in music right now, and let me tell you, it ain't pretty.

People today don't have an idea of how the music business works. All they see on TV is reality shows where people are turned into stars in weeks and given million-dollar recording deals if they win the show. They see other music stars display excesses of wealth and think the music business is the easy road to big money. My friend, it ain't true.

Let me give you an example. I love this MTV show called *Cribs*. Let me just say that I don't like MTV, as I think it's one of the big reasons for music's downfall, but the show *Cribs* is a powerful wake-up call for musicians who want to be stars.

First of all, I would bet you that half the people featured on *Cribs* rent the fabulous house for the day to show off their shameless grotesque show of wealth. Then, after the cameras are packed up and gone, these "stars" go back to their two-bedroom apartment and wonder why they aren't making any money from the record label.

And I'll go a step further. I'd also be willing to bet that most of those "stars" have yet to see the bank statement from the record label that says you're making money. For the handful of them that are making money, I've heard story after story of them living the good life for a few years and a few years later, they're friggin' broke, they're back in their little apartments and people saying, "Who the hell were you?"

Musicians and Their Craft

Let me give you a little advice: As soon as you have a little success, get ready for people to start bashing you and your music. It happens to anyone. But always stay true to your music and your art and you'll be fine. Over the years, the press hated our group, Toto. They'd make up stories about the band that weren't true and they were gunning for us.

Maybe it was the name, who knows? The reality is, between 1980–84, our band Toto was the house band that won the album, song, and producer of the year at the Grammys. We also played on more than 100 of the records that were nominated for Grammys within those 3 years. We were the go-to band to hate. I laugh at the shit now because even though people hated us, we were good enough to play with Paul

McCartney, George Harrison, and Miles Davis and had a discography that people tell us is staggering.

And even with all the press and critic bashing, talk about musicians who loved their craft. Even all these years after his passing, there isn't a day that goes by that I don't think of my buddy, Jeff Porcaro.

Not only was his charisma so deep that people would call him "God's drummer," he would walk into the room and the room would light up and everything got better. He always had the coolest clothes, the coolest music, he was always the guy that found the newest shit to listen to.

His groove was so deep. He could take a piece of shit tune on a session and turn it into something you could really groove with. And he could turn something that was great into something that was *really* great. He was just special in that way.

Everyone looked to Jeff for the okay and direction. I mean the biggest friggin' record producers in the world would look to Jeff and ask, "Is that the take?" and he'd say, "Yeah, that's the one, man."

I'm telling you, we'd be on sessions playing some suck ass tune that wasn't going anywhere, with all of us just wanting to leave, and we'd look over at Jeff and he'd get a groove going and get that big smile on his face and wink at me and say, "We're out of here in like 10 minutes" and we'd know he would always find the right groove that everyone loved.

I've worked with a lot of really great famous people, yet I still get giddy like a kid when I see and hear greatness. I mean, I was once sitting next to Miles Davis and he was playing one of my songs and my weenie was so hard I could cut diamonds with it [laughs]. I was listening to greatness.

But today, thanks to the record labels and who they and radio promote, we have rock stars and wannabe rock stars, who, if they're lucky, will have 5 years of fame. Check back in 5 years, when there's a good chance you'll see them down at the club or bar, drinking to forget their problems and telling anyone who'll listen, "Yeah, my wife took all the money and I'm not really good enough to play with other musicians and I used to be a rock star, so screw you all." None of them are good enough to make a career as a musician, but they're rock stars.

Anyone can be a rock star. In one day, I taught my son how to play the guitar. Gave him a drop D tuning, plugged him into a little mini Marshall amp, gave him some distortion, showed him a few chords and one riff, and an hour later, he was playing everything he was listening to on MTV. He's a rock star I tell ya.

I gave a clinic at MIT [Musician's Institute of Technology] and I asked the people there, how many of you want to be rock stars? They all raised their hands. Then I asked them, how many of you want to be working musicians who do studio gigs, play Bar Mitzvahs, weddings, club dates, and everything else that blue-collar musicians play? Would you believe only two of them raised their hands?

I never wanted to be a rock star or some guitar guy that people put on a pedestal. All I ever wanted to be—and still want to be—is a working musician. I'll play on anybody's record. Call me up, pay me, I'm there.

Signing with a Major Label or an Independent

People often ask me what's the difference between being signed on a major label or doing the independent label thing? First of all, if you are signed to a major label, they will bleed you big time. If you sell 2 million records, you'll still be in debt to them for 3 million dollars, because you have to pay for the record, pay for the producer, pay for the rehearsal time, pay for the musicians, pay for the video, pay for tour support, and pay, pay, pay.

The testimony that Courtney Love gave about the record business [Lesson Three, pages 48 to 62] is absolutely a fact, and she spoke for a lot of people. Hey, a platinum record [sales of 1 million units] means nothing. It's like a friggin' bowling trophy.

I know because I've lived it. I've sold over 27 million records in my life and the only thing I can say about that is "Show me the money! Where's all the friggin' money?" People think that by selling that many records I should be wiping my arse with hundred dollar bills, but I'm still waiting for that day to happen.

People mistakenly believe that if they can have a one-hit record and sell a million copies, then they're going to have money and the good life and I'm here to tell you, if you're playing the major label game, it ain't going to happen. It's a lie, and anybody that buys into that is a fool.

Don't tell me there's no payola out there when it costs you a million dollars to get on the radio. The record business is the most corrupt business—next to politics—in the world. C'mon, cats that are running the business can't play music, yet they think they know better than anyone else how to sell music!

They actually believe they know what's going on and they buy into their genius. Yet, look what all that genius has done to the record and music business. Guys that know nothing about the music business are getting promoted onward and upward. It's because of them that music sucks now, and the record business is in the shitter and my prediction is, in 5 years, the record business as we know it today will not be around.

Look at what happened with recording artist Robbie Williams, where they paid him in the neighborhood of 80 million dollars. His record label fired more than 1,000 people, yet the record executives gave themselves a bonus. Meanwhile, their quarterly profits are down and their losses are in the tens of millions of dollars.

The artists never see the money. Robbie Williams means nothing to them except over in Europe where he's a big name. They can't give the shit away in Asia and the

United States, but that 80-million-dollar deal to sign him and fire all those people and have the company willing to go bankrupt because of this guy was deemed a good deal? Who made that decision? I want that guy to manage my career, that is, if I'm looking to quickly run it into the ground. The whole friggin' record business is smoke and mirrors.

Anyone who is signed to a major label right now is a fool. What you need to do right now is become independent. You make your record and then you license it to a major company who can help you get it into the stores. You will make 10 times the royalty rate doing it the independent way and you own it at the end of 7 years.

I was signed to Sony Records for 25 years, and I had a 1977 royalty rate when records cost 7 dollars. When record prices bumped up to 15 dollars, guess what? Our royalty rate didn't get bumped up. We were still making the 1977 royalty rate of 1 dollar 20 cents a record.

And we still owed money for all those videos the record company made us shoot and pay for that no one would ever see. All that shit still had to be recouped from any record sales. And we had to do it and we had to pay for it because the record company was afraid of not having a video they hoped MTV *might* play.

If you're a musician and you want control of your career and your life, then you need to make sure you own everything you do. You mark my words that 5 years from now, major record companies will not exist anymore. They will become major distribution outlets for independent music.

All these rap guys got it right a long time ago. Guys like Master P own their shit and they're making 5 bucks a record. They sell 100,000 units and they make $500,000. They make enough money so they'll have the money to promote themselves and their artists so that people you've never heard of can enter the charts at number one.

These guys are smart. My respect, my thumbs up, goes to all these cats, these rappers, who said, "Screw the white man and his record company games. Why is that mutha making more money than me?"

These guys figured it out and they took their music and message to the streets where they were telling everyone, "Hey, dig this new record." By the time the record hit the stores, all these people were already hip to it and were already playing it in their cars. These rappers gave the shit away just to get the word out. Now that's smart. They know how to promote. They know how to work it. They are the really smart ones and I have so much respect for them.

Keeping It Real

Whatever you do, however you want to create, record, and promote your music, always keep it real. I love the underdog story. Take Norah Jones. You gotta love this chick. A few years ago she was an unknown and she's still living in the same apartment, yet she's a real musician. Same with Diana Krall. She's great. She's a schooled musician who loves playing music.

I'm a Grammy-voting member and I left half the voting ballot blank this year because I never heard of some of these people. I mean, c'mon. Are the people who made the ballot list the best we've got? I wanna see real shit. Norah Jones. *Real.* Bruce Springsteen. *Real.* Arif Marden. *Real.* I've worked with him for years. He's real, he's a genius, and he's a guy that knows how to put it all together.

Friend, how fast or slow or how technical or nontechnical you can play means nothing. Whether you can read music or not doesn't matter. I don't care if you can only play three notes. All that matters is how you *play* those three notes and if it's real and if they come from deep inside your heart and soul.

It's all about your soul, your sound, your aura, your heart, your spirit, and your touch coming out through your music. It's not about the gear. It's not about the latest technology. It's not about being signed to a major record label. It's all about letting "you" come through in your music. When you do that, you will be in the company of the greats, and you're going to be someone I'm going to dig listening to.

Making a Hit Record

If I knew what makes a record a hit, I'd be writing this to you from my yacht taking a colonic, but the truth is no one knows for sure. Half the hit records I've played on—and there have been a lot—I'd think they sucked, but lo and behold they'd become hits. Who knew?

You don't have to be on a major label to have a big hit. I'd say, do it with your own independent label, because you're going to have complete control of your music, you'll own your creation, and you'll make a boatload more money.

And you need to realize that you don't even need a hit record to be a musical success. If you're doing what you love to do, perhaps able to make a little money at it, and you're loving your life, then in my book, you're already a great success.

By all means, use technology to help you create your own "real" music, but don't get hung up on technology and worrying about what kind of guitar, amp, or little blue wire Mr. Rockstar has in the back of his effects rack. All of that shit means absolutely nothing and almost everyone could care less.

It's all about the song. Some of the greatest songs the world has ever heard and are still timeless (like Motown or any of The Beatles's work) were done without all the high-tech computers and software you have today. It's not about the technology. It's all about the song. It's about the music. It's about your soul. It's about keeping it real.

Enjoying Your Gift of Music

The musical road you travel down always turns out to be way different from the one you originally thought you'd take. And in the end, it's all good, even though at the time, you could be going through some experiences that really suck.

Over the years, I've had many great successes and many great disappointments, yet through them all, I've always kept a few things about life in perspective: Live for today. Enjoy every moment. Deny yourself nothing. Have a great time. Try to be nice to people. Try to leave a little love behind. Small little gestures make you feel good inside. Respect others. My friend, all the fame and fortune don't matter. It's about caring for the people who care about you.

My parents thought I was insane in 1967 when I was 10 years old and announced I wanted to be a musician, as I held up Jimi's [Hendrix] album *Are You Experienced* in my hand. I've never wanted to be a rock star, but always wanted to be a lifer who played music from that magical day until the day I die.

I'll be the first to admit that I'm an overpaid guitar player who's a happy guy that's mystified by my own success and is grateful to any and everyone who has been and will be important in my musical road and this journey and experience called Life.

In the big picture of life, what I do is insignificant. It really is. I mean, c'mon. We don't know if we'll be here tomorrow, and a long time ago I stopped caring about the little stupid things that used to upset me. Really, what we've got to do is enjoy the moment.

I care nothing about material things. What matters to me is not how many Grammys or awards I get or what the critics say. What matters most is my family, my wife, my children, and my friends. Everything else is expendable. That's my philosophy: Everything in life is fleeting except the people I truly love and care about. I love my wife. I love my family. I love my friends and everything else is just bullshit.

I know I'm blessed and so lucky to do what I do. I mean for heaven's sakes, I'm a guitar player and able to earn a good living at what I love to do. What more do I need?

Web sites: www.toto99.com and www.stevelukather.net

Lesson 5

Building Your A-Team:
Who You Need and Who You Don't

If you want to take your music out of the bars and into a bigger market, you need a good team behind you. A good attorney and CPA can save your money and maybe even your hide. Along with an attorney and CPA, you may think that you need a manager or an agent. But as you read through this lesson, you'll be surprised how many doors you can open by yourself—and save some money to boot.

So who do you really need and how do you find "the good ones" for your team? The road to success in the music business is littered with bad experiences, broken promises, and a lot of money gone up in smoke chasing the "You're really going to make it, kiddo" come-ons tossed out each day to the wanting to believe by the conniving.

Attorneys

We live in a litigious society. No longer are the courts viewed as a place where big corporations battle big corporations. If two people can't resolve a dispute to both parties' satisfaction, then civil court is often the next place they'll meet.

Thank goodness for attorneys! While there's plenty to *not* thank them for (e.g., huge damage awards that have helped drive insurance costs through the roof), when it comes to having the law on your side, it's tough to do without a good attorney. That's why you need the right attorney on your team, one who can make sure you're legally protected, both personally and professionally. He or she can help you structure and negotiate good deals and prevent you from getting into bad ones.

There are some first-class attorneys who do great work and truly care about helping their clients succeed. Of this, I am absolutely sure, and in a moment I'll tell you how to find them. You also need to be aware that there are some attorneys you should absolutely stay away from, and you need to know how to differentiate between the two. You need to know how the legal game is played as well.

The first must-have member of your A-team is going to be an attorney, but not just any attorney. You want what is known as an entertainment attorney, one whose specialty is music, media, and entertainment. As you'll soon read, lots of lawyers call themselves entertainment attorneys, but only a handful are both true specialists in the field and also of the caliber you want on your team. But first, you should understand how attorneys operate and how they charge for their time. Attorneys either charge a flat fee (say, $500 to draw up a simple agreement), or a commission or percentage (if they think you've got serious star power potential), or on an as needed/per hour basis, or a combination of any or all of them. It's the as needed/per hour basis I want to tell you about first.

It's All about Billable Hours

If your attorney is charging you by billable hours, it means that every time you call him or her, the clock is ticking—just like a cab driver who turns on the meter as soon as you get in the cab. You're being charged for every minute of your attorney's time, and it goes something like this:

Attorney: Hi Matt (20 dollars). How have you been? (25 dollars).

Matt: I've been good, thanks. I just wanted to see if you heard from that record label about our demo we sent to them?

Attorney: Well, Matt (30 dollars), I put in a few calls to them and the A&R's assistant told me (35 dollars) they were out of town this week, but they'd be back in touch next week and let us know (40 dollars) what they think.

Before you've spent 60 cents on your call, you've just racked up 40 bucks worth of attorney charges you could've used for 2 months of Webcasting access or new gear.

You see, attorneys (especially the ones who work for the big firms with prestigious addresses, great-looking offices, and lots of attorney names printed on their letterhead) have a huge monthly nut. As much as they come across as wanting to be your buddy, they are paid to do one thing, and that's produce income for the firm. And unless they're in litigation, winning lawsuits and jury awards, or on retainer doing work for big companies, they're watching the clock and billing—big time—for every minute they're working for you. A lot of them have a quota they've got to meet of billing x number of hours for the firm, and if they don't meet it, they're out on the street looking for another job.

Music is a big money business, and the major players want to deal with those who already have deals, will soon be getting deals, or need help getting out of deals. Rarely will the handful of "My Calls Get Taken by Record Label Presidents Every Time" attorneys ever get back to you unless you can make the cash register ring (for them and the record company executives who'll take their calls) in a big way.

Many firms ask for an up-front advance fee for work they are promising to do. You have to be very wary about agreeing to such a fee, especially if it is preceded by promises of a big financial return for you. The following story illustrates what can happen if you are not careful.

One of my companies owns some rare video footage of a very famous person, and at some point we found out it had been pirated and copies were being sold all over the country by some of the biggest retailers out there. I called one of the largest music and entertainment law firms in Los Angeles and asked about handling our case. Their response was classic. Here's how it went:

RW: Hi, my name is Robert Wolff. My company owns Famous Person video and we have gathered evidence from a number of sources that such and such and so and so have been illegally manufacturing, distributing, and selling our intellectual property. I'd like to discuss the merits of our case with you.

Big Name Law Firm: We've got you on speakerphone Mr. Wolff, and we have (attorneys) Mr. X, Mr. Y, and Ms. Z here. We'd like to know how long this has been going on and how much money you estimate this has cost you.

RW: We just found out about it a few months ago, and based on the preliminary research we've been able to do, they've been illegally selling our property for over a year. Until we can find out the full extent of the piracy, it's going to be difficult to come up with a figure of damages.

BNLF: Well, based on what you've told us thus far, it sounds like you've got a strong case. You could be entitled to anywhere from x to x^2 for damages for violation of this copyright statute, along with y to y^2 for damages for that copyright infringement, plus other damages.

RW: Well, that's interesting. What do you suggest as the best way for us to proceed?

BNLF: We think the award for damages if a suit is filed and it goes to court—but it most likely won't and would be settled out of court—could be quite significant, and possibly much more than the figures we just quoted you. We'll do a search within the firm to make sure there is no conflict of interest and that we do not have the companies you named as our clients. If we don't, then we'd need you to send us $5,000 to get started.

RW: And what will that $5,000 cover?

BNLF: Probably a couple of calls and a couple of letters to "cease and desist" to the people who are infringing your copyrights and illegally selling your property.

RW: What if we find that there are more people involved in illegally selling our property than we know about now?

BNLF: That would obviously cost more. But you would also have excellent potential to collect even more money in the settlement.

RW: Tell you what. The more I think about this, sure, we can pay you $5,000 now, and perhaps another $5,000 a little later, but it's really unfair to you guys.

BNLF: What do you mean?

RW: Well, think about it. If you took our case on a contingency basis, you'd get a percentage—say one-third—of any damages and money we recovered, and with the numbers you just quoted, your firm stands to make far more money than if we just pay you $5,000 or $10,000. This is a real win-win for our company and your firm.

BNLF: [After a long silence] We'll have to talk about it and get back to you. What are your telephone and fax numbers?

The next day, I received a fax from Big Name Law Firm saying that they had to devote their resources to cases they were already busy with, so "regrettably" they could take our case only if we paid them a flat fee up front. So much for having a strong case with a big money pay-off potential.

Finding and Hiring the Right Attorney

The point of the story I just told is that *before* you enter into any agreement with an attorney, you've got to weed out the fast talkers, quick promisers, and "I can do it for you's." The first step is to compile a list of likely candidates. Then you've got to put each one through your own Pass This Test before you trust them with your time, talent, and money.

There are a number of ways that people in the music business find others in the business:

* Friends, referrals, and contacts in the business. If they're in music, they either have an attorney or know someone who does and can get that attorney's name for you.
* Trade publication stories naming attorneys involved in deals made or cases won.
* Mainstream media news or feature stories that involve attorneys.
* The Internet. Check out two sites in particular: Lawyers.com is a Web site devoted to helping you find attorneys anywhere in the United States. It lists those who specialize in various aspects of the law, including entertainment and music. The site has a search engine that lets you choose the type of

attorney you need, and once you type in the city where you'd like to find one, it gives you a listing in that area and information about each. The second good Internet source is on abanet.org, the official Web site of the American Bar Association (the granddaddy organization to which all legit lawyers belong). It's easy to find lots of references for your area or for any area you wish. Go to the organization's home page, point and click on General Public Resources, click on Find Legal Help, and you'll be directed to their Help page, which will offer Hiring a Lawyer, Online Lawyer Referral, Handling Legal Matters Yourself, Legal Information Services, and more.

Once you've got a list of attorneys who advertise themselves as music/entertainment attorneys, you need to narrow it down. Here's how you need to deal with anyone who's a potential candidate to be your attorney:

* Make sure they are not a music/entertainment firm in name only. Ask how *long* the firm has specialized in music/entertainment law and ask to see their client list.

* Check out their client list. Make sure it's current. I know some "music/ entertainment" attorneys who proudly list the names of clients on their Web sites who haven't been clients of theirs for many years. Believe me, there's a reason why these people aren't their clients anymore. Find out why. Be alert.

* Ask them for references. Specifically, ask them for names of *three* people or companies who are *current* clients whom you can contact to get feedback about the work their firm did for those clients.

* Ask them to tell you about *three* of the most recent deals they've made. Who were they with, and for what? A reputable attorney (while being ever mindful of attorney/client privilege and privacy) won't mind telling you about recent success stories that he or she is proud of. They don't need to divulge dollar amounts and deal details. Those should remain private. The good ones will have a file full of successes. The turkey attorneys? Well, they'll have a file full of "that deal almost happened."

Get It in Writing

Some attorneys do not like putting things in writing because written agreements can come back and bite them on the ass. You need to get attorneys to make a written, signed commitment to you that they can be held to. The good ones won't have a problem with this. The ones who do should be immediately crossed off your list.

The first thing you need to get in writing is the basis of your agreement. Ask them to put the following five things in writing:

* What specifically they will do for you.
* How long it will take and when they will begin. Put a completion deadline on it.
* How they will do it.
* What they will need from you in order to do the things they're promising they'll do.
* How much *everything* will cost. There should be no surprises, or "Oh, by the way's," or "I forgot to tell you's" coming back at you.

Let me tell you another quick story—another one involving piracy—from my company's personal files about how not getting things in writing can end up costing you big money.

We were referred to a "great attorney" by a friend (usually, but unfortunately not always, referrals by friends are good starting points in finding someone) who told us Mr. Attorney was a specialist in the entertainment field. We called him at his swanky law firm in Los Angeles and told him that we had discovered that a group of infringers was ripping us off and we wanted him to go after them.

Oh, man, after we filled him in about our case, this guy came on like a tiger with big teeth, ready to go after those bad people and get us the lost income we deserved. We were stoked! He said he would look over our files as well and register whatever additional papers needed to be filed in order to bring us up to date and totally protected. He also said to send him a check for $3,000. So we did.

After weeks of Mr. Attorney's calls and letter writing to the infringing party, he bluntly told us that they were digging their feet in the sand and were not going to budge anymore on their offer of restitution. All this after telling us that, based on his *years of experience with similar cases,* he believed we could expect to receive an amount five times greater than the amount he said they were now being very firm on. Imagine our surprise. When we asked him how things were going regarding the papers he said he was filing for us, he assured us everything was on track.

So another month goes by and nothing's happening, and this guy is asking us to send more money so he can continue! We thought, continue what? His time and money-wasting with no results? So we fired him. Canned him that day. We told him to send all our files back, along with the confirmation of the papers he had filed for us, and to stop his "negotiations" with the infringing party.

The next day, I contacted the infringing party's attorney directly and informed her that we had fired our attorney and that all negotiations were to be done between her, myself, and my partner. Within a week, we had settled out of court for more than three times the money and "best deal" Mr. Attorney said he had been able to get. My dealing with the other attorney was smooth, and based on what she told me, far more enjoyable for her than dealing with the abrasive and seemingly incompetent goofball we had just fired.

This got us thinking: If one attorney is being so negative about another attorney (and usually attorneys don't talk crap about other attorneys unless there is something *really* wrong), just how competent had this guy been in carrying out our instructions to him to file the papers we asked him—and paid him (up front)—to file? As it turned out, not very.

After nearly three months of letters, calls, e-mails, and faxes demanding the return of our files, Mr. Attorney finally did send them back (after we had to provide our FedEx number so that he wouldn't have to pay for it). It wasn't until two years later that we discovered that he hadn't filed the papers correctly. In the end, his errors and incompetence ended up costing us tens of thousands of dollars in recoverable damages from future copyright infringers.

Needless to say, since that time we've hired a group of top-notch entertainment attorneys (not based in Los Angeles, thank you) who have us protected six ways to Sunday and they are worth every cent we pay them. The best ones always are. Never forget that.

Negotiating a Fee

You've located a good attorney, so now what? When you're first starting out—perhaps you haven't lost enough money yet or been stung enough times through other people's lies, or you've fallen for the pompous windbags who love to tell you what you want to hear—any kind of negotiation may seem overwhelming. But don't worry. It's a piece of cake, especially if you understand a big factor that motivates attorneys, and everyone else in business—making money.

If you can make an attorney some money, then you've got a listening ear and a new best friend who'll have you wondering where in the world they've been hiding all these years. You want your attorney to make money. This is only fair and right. They have dreams. They have a family. They have a business, and they should be paid for helping you. However, you don't want to give away the farm.

If you've traveled to a foreign country and shopped in the stores and outdoor markets, you know how the negotiation game is played. You see something you like, ask the owner how much, and they give you a price. You tell them the price is too high, and then they tell you they will lower it. This back-and-forth bargaining goes on for a while, until the owner says that his or her last price is the lowest they can go. If it's still not the price you want, you begin to walk out of the store. However, just as you *almost* reach the door, they yell at you to come back and—big surprise—they can go a little lower.

It's all about testing limits: theirs and yours. Their job is to sell you their services at the highest price, and your job is to buy it at the lowest price. The middle point is where they've come down low enough and you've raised your offer high enough so that both of you can walk away happy.

In the business of You, Inc., regardless of whether you're shopping for an attorney, a CPA, an agent, or anyone else you'll either be making money for or giving money to, always remember that *you don't get what you want; you get what you negotiate.* And the better your negotiation skills, the more value you'll receive, and the wiser businessperson you'll become.

Almost every negotiation involves some trade-off. If you're in negotiations to use an attorney's services, the attorney may say he or she is quoting a "firm" price, but nearly everyone will negotiate from that price. He or she may say, "We charge $200 an hour and we need you to pay us a starting retainer of $1000 within 30 days," to which you might counter, "I can pay you $175 an hour and a $500 starting retainer *today*." That's *today* money, that's a done deal, and don't be at all surprised when they say, "Okay, when can you come in?"

It's all about give and take: You give a little, they give a little. Anytime anyone wants something from you, don't just give it to them. It's a fact of human nature that things quickly and easily gotten are likely to be less appreciated and more quickly taken for granted—like your music and your life. It's also a fact of human nature that the more we have to work for things, the more we appreciate and value them.

So make your attorney work for whatever he or she's getting from you. After all, you've had to work your butt off many long years and long hours to get to where you are right now. Chances are slim that anyone, anywhere, will ever call you or knock on your door one day and say, "Gee, you're so talented. We'd like to give you money and opportunities just for being you." Be sure to write me if that happens.

Setting Deal Parameters

Being the wise businessperson you're now becoming, you already know what kind of deal you want and don't want. You want the best terms, you want the most money for your services and product, and you want to give up the least amount necessary to make the deal happen. You also want to feed your attorney a script that he or she should follow. Understand that no one knows, wants, or understands your dreams better than you. And no one can sell you better than you. This is your life. Don't give the keys to your future to anyone for any reason.

Never give a blank check to an attorney—or to a CPA, manager, agent, or anyone else who's "going to be looking after you." Whenever an attorney is negotiating something for you, be absolutely certain that he or she knows what you want and don't want in your deal. Make sure that everyone who works for you understands that unless you're happy, they don't get paid.

For any deal you're thinking of getting into, tell your attorney your must-haves as well as your would-like-to-haves. The must-haves are points you will not and cannot budge on. If you don't get those must-haves—if the deal is asking too much from you, doesn't feel right anymore, or is no longer keeping you excited and happy—you won't make the deal.

The would-like-to-haves are negotiable points that would be great if you can get them but it won't be a deal killer if you don't. This is ammunition that your attorney needs for those give-and-take negotiations with the other party. Just like our street vendor in that foreign country, the seller is the party with whom your attorney will be negotiating, and you are the customer who walked in. Always remember that you can just as quickly walk out the door if the price and deal are not right.

Giving your attorney your deal makers and breakers also saves you a wad of cash. No longer will you be paying for their "get me up to speed" educational lesson at $200 or more per hour. He or she will have a specific understanding of what must be negotiated, and the results that must be achieved, and won't be charging you for chit-chat/feel-good calls back and forth with the other party "to see what they are offering."

Good attorneys know that time is money, and the more time they take with you, the less time they have to spend with their other clients who are bigger, richer, and more famous (for now) and can bring in more money. Do yourself and your attorney a favor: Know exactly what you want, write it down, explain it in precise detail, reach a mutually acceptable fee and performance arrangement, and let him or her help get you that deal.

When You Need an Attorney—And When You Don't

Have you ever heard the story of an artist or band who decided that they didn't need an attorney when they signed their music and lives away, and for the next 20 or so years they were stuck with such a bummer of a deal that their attorney, manager, agent, and practically everyone else they dealt with made more money than they did? Better get out your calculator, because you don't have enough fingers and toes to count how many times this has happened in the music business.

Stories like this used to be more common than they are today, but they still happen. In the past, artists' contracts and deals were closed books that only the privileged few were privy to, so you just needed to trust that your attorney, agent, and manager were getting you the best deal possible.

Thank goodness that's not the case anymore. Now, if you want to see what a record contract, management deal, or other legal document looks like, you can go to the Internet and do a search on Google. In a matter of seconds, you'll have your pick from hundreds, if not thousands, of them to look over and learn from. This brings me to a subject many have asked me about: What *should* I use an attorney for and what can I do on my own?

Think of attorneys as people who protect you. They are the guard dogs who stand at the gate of your future, and anyone who wishes to enter has to first get past the guard dog. Guard dogs protect you and keep people from taking things from you, unless of course you knowingly or unknowingly neutralize your guard dog and give something away.

In addition to offering guard dog services, legit music and entertainment attorneys will have a Rolodex of names and contacts that can be worth far more than the hourly fee they charge. Music, like any business, is all about networking and contacts, and the more people you know who know people who know people, the better chance you have of getting what you want and making your dreams come true.

Here's a list of areas in which you may or may not need the services of an attorney, depending on the circumstances.

Copyrights. You can always register your own copyrights. Any music you create will be a copyright intellectual property that is yours, and there's a good chance that someone, somewhere down the road will rip you off. It happens every day, so get used to it. But you can protect yourself and your composition from the get-go by having it formally registered, in writing, with the copyright office. It's quick, it's cheap, it's easy, and in Lesson 12, I'll show you how to do it. In the meantime, keep this in mind:

* After you receive your "filed" copyright papers back from the copyright office, you need to file those copyright papers away in a safe place.
* Make at least two copies that you can keep in different locations. If you ever need them, you'll have them, and it'll be just the evidence and protection you'll need to protect your songs and your income and to recover damages from those who need a big bank-account-draining lesson should they or anyone else ever rip you off.
* Down the road, if despite your meticulous registration procedures people are stealing your property, you *will* need an attorney to take charge of going after them.

Goods and Services. When you're making minor purchases, like supplies and gear, obviously you don't need an attorney holding your hand and running "the meter." For those types of purchases, save your money and negotiate the best deals by yourself. Likewise, for simple equipment repairs, there's no need for an attorney to be standing next to you. However, if you're thinking of signing any kind of contract, including leasing a car, equipment, an office, or a home for your business, you want your CPA (more about them in a moment) and your attorney looking things over and making absolutely certain you're not locked into something that can come back to bite you in the ass down the road.

For services beyond straightforward repairs—such as a photographer shooting photos for your album cover or an engineer who's mastering your record—you can use a standard release and work-for-hire agreement. You can also have your attorney write one for you which you can use anytime in the future, saving yourself fees down the road. Another source for useful agreements is legal forms books, which you can find online or in your local bookstore. My advice is that if your budget allows, go the attorney route. You can probably get an attorney to provide you with a release and work-for-hire agreement specific to your needs for a couple of hundred dollars. If you prefer DIY, look at several of the online or in-print forms and check to see whether they cover all the bases. Bottom line: Always seek competent legal counsel before *signing* any legal forms.

Deal Negotiation. This is the area where too many people spend too much money needlessly bringing in an attorney too quickly. The "let's get things started" call they're making on your behalf could just as easily be made by you, saving yourself a few hundred dollars. At $200 or more an hour, that gets to be expensive chit-chat.

The bottom line is, make the calls and talk to the people who are interested in doing business with you yourself. Keep those conversations going between you and them until you reach the point where you no longer feel comfortable doing it on your own, where the conversation and deal are now above your head and beyond your level of understanding. *That* is the ideal place to bring in an attorney. And for heaven sakes, *do not* orally promise or sign anything unless and until an attorney has looked everything over and given you the legal okay to proceed.

Great Advice and Free Stuff You Can Get in Seconds

The Internet makes it easy for you to do many things you used to need an attorney for, such as getting answers to legal questions. You can also get tons of information and downloadable agreements and contracts for free. Check out the following four sites before you go spending hundreds of dollars in attorney fees for answers you might get for nothing.

* **www.Nolo.com.** This is an excellent site with loads of information on a variety of legal topics. It includes a reference library of articles, free legal forms, dictionaries and encyclopedias, and answers to over 400 of your legal questions.
* **www.Legaldocs.com.** I'm all for saving you lots of money, so if you're looking for a terrific place to find legal documents that you can simply download, print out, and complete yourself, look no further than Legaldocs.com. You'll find plenty of free legal documents along with others that can be downloaded for a very small fee.
* **www.Law.com.** If you're looking for a Web site that can give you a quick and very basic understanding of the law, your rights, self-representation, and a host of other topics, then check out this site. It has just about everything you could ask for (easy topic menus, links to lots of other law-related sites and information) to get you up to speed in a hurry.
* **www.Lawinfo.com.** Let's say that after you've created your music, filed your copyright registration, and done all the right things (that I just told you about), you find someone or some company ripping you off. They've sold your song all over the place without asking or telling you, and now you need an expert to tell you what that song is worth, and to put a figure on how much they've damaged you. Would you know where to look? Your attorney most likely will (the great ones always do), but how about you? Click on this site and you'll find all the legal expertise you'll need.

For more information, answers to questions, resources, documents and links about copyrights and U.S. Copyright Laws, check out the following five sites:
* **www.law.cornell.edu.** This site is maintained by the Legal Information Institute of Cornell Law School. You'll find lots of full-text documents, including the U.S. Code; U.S. Constitution; the Code of Federal Regulations; federal, state, and international laws; and directories of lawyers, organizations, and journals.
* **www.loc.gov.** This is the main site of the United States Library of Congress. There's plenty of information on this site, including an exhaustive database on U.S. copyright law.
* **www.copyright.iupui.edu.** This site, the Copyright Management Center from Indiana University, has lots of good copyright information, including a Copyright Quickguide with basic information on protection, registration, rights, ownership, and duration.

* **www.benedict.com.** This Web site covers some of the same ground as the Cornell and Indiana sites, but it also has interesting cases of copyright use and infringement involving celebrities.
* **www.weblawresources.com.** This Web site features information on protecting your copyrighted works on the Internet. It offers packages (some with more than 50 legal form documents for the Web, copyrights, etc.) that you can purchase for a fraction of what it would cost to have them each created by attorneys. However, the site advises that you secure competent legal counsel to review your documents prior to use.

Good CPAs: Worth Their Weight in Gold

The second must-have member of your A-team is a good (emphasis on *good*) accountant. For the sake of keeping things simple, I recommend that you find a CPA (certified public accountant), as CPA experience, training, and certification are the skills you want when it comes to keeping your taxes at a minimum and the records of your money coming in and going out up-to-date and precise.

A good CPA can offer advice and services that can help you become and remain wealthy. All CPAs deal with numbers, and in your world that means income and expenses. The more money you make and the less money you spend, the wealthier you become. It's that simple.

But knowing what to do with your expenses and how to treat your income can make all the difference in just how much money you keep and how quickly you'll reach financial independence. A good CPA knows this. A good CPA also knows the latest tax laws and deductions (which change all the time), and how those laws and changes will affect you and your business. If you would rather spend your time making music rather than studying tax code, the fees you pay to your CPA are a wise investment.

Over the years, I've met many people who fill out their own tax returns. They think they're saving money, but when they add up the cost of their time to learn the newest tax laws; the number of hours they spend going over all the previous years' records of income, expenses, and deductions; the frustration of not knowing whether they took the right deduction and filled out the forms correctly (and then sometimes having the IRS send back the return because it was filled out incorrectly)—when all is said and done, they're losing money big time. This is money and time that could've been saved (with the difference invested!) by letting a CPA do it. Not just any CPA. As you're about to read, the *right* CPA.

A Cautionary Tale

The music business of a friend of mine had enjoyed a blockbuster year. It took him years of struggle and small paydays before his name and his business finally paid off and his phone was beginning to ring off the hook. Although he knew he had the makings of a good year, it wasn't until its end, when he finally got a breather and had an opportunity to sit down and look at his bank account, that he nearly fell out of his chair—he had had a *great* year. He had made more money in that one year than in the previous 8 years combined.

My friend needed some help, though. Not in spending his money, mind you— he was already great at that—but taking advantage of all his expenses and deductions to minimize his taxes. Because he was now in a new city and devoting his business to music, he believed he needed someone who specialized in *music* business.

One day, during a phone call to a friend also involved in music, he mentioned that he needed to find a CPA who was a music specialist. Without hesitation, his friend gave him the name of someone he had heard was excellent. My friend called Mr. New CPA. Everything sounded great. The CPA specialized in the music business, had a large staff, and had lots of industry clients. New CPA told my friend that his firm would be perfect for what he was looking for, as it was "right down our alley" and "the very thing we do each day."

Within a few weeks, my friend had gathered all his papers, invoices, check stubs, bank statements, and records and sent them to New CPA, along with a detailed letter explaining his business and his purchases and expenses for the year. He called New CPA's office and told them that everything was on the way. "Perfect" he was told; they'd get back to him soon.

Weeks went by. No call. No letter. No e-mail. No fax. My friend started getting concerned, so he called them. He was told that New CPA was "out of town," but he'd be given the message. My friend sent e-mails, then more e-mails. Still, no reply. After two more weeks, he received a reply from New CPA apologizing for the delay in getting back to him as "things have been just crazy this time of year." Another two weeks went by and he received a call and message from New CPA with news that he had my friend's taxes ready and wanted to go over the numbers with him. He quickly called New CPA and the conversation went like this:

F: Hi. This is Friend. I got your message that you wanted to go over my tax returns and some numbers with me.

NCPA: Hey, How's it going? Sorry for not getting back to you sooner. Things have just been such a &!$#*! around here. We've been swamped.

F: No problem. What did you come up with?

NCPA [sound of fumbling through papers]: Just a second. I thought I had your returns right in front of me. Damn. Where in the heck are those. [long pause] Ah . . . there they are. Okay, here are the numbers. Your company made *x* dollars last year. You had *x* in expenses and you owe *x* (here gives a number in the tens of thousands] dollars to the IRS and *x* [thousands of dollars] to the state."

F: You can't be serious!

NCPA: Yeah, man, I'm sorry but that's the way the numbers came out.

F [still in shock]: What about all the expenses I had? The equipment I bought?

NCPA: Sorry. I took everything you sent me and that's what came out. Hey, look at the bright side; you've just had your best year ever and with your income, it'll be easy for you to get a mortgage. I'll go ahead and put everything in the mail to you. Oh, and I'll also send you my invoice and would appreciate if you could pay it as soon as you can. Talk to you soon. By the way, start getting this year's tax receipts together and send those to me so we can get started on those.

Friend: Yeah, sure. Talk to you later.

After he hung up with New CPA, my friend felt really angry—both with the numbers he had just heard and with the whole experience of trusting his business and financial (and dare I say, emotional) life to a firm that had more clients than they had time for and treated their new client like the number he certainly felt he had become.

When the "taxes due" forms arrived a week later, instead of signing and mailing them, my friend decided to get a second opinion. He called a CPA he knew who had done his taxes in the past but wasn't a "music CPA" and told his tale of woe. "Old" CPA told my friend to send him everything and let him take a look at it.

About two weeks later he got a phone call, and it went like this:

OCPA: Hi. I've had a chance to go over everything. Are you sitting down?

F [thinking he's going to owe even more money]: Yes.

OCPA: First I'd like you to verify that you had major equipment purchases [names them], laid out major dollars for business-related travel [names a big number], and had *x* [another big number] business expenses last year.

F: Yes. All of that.

OCPA: Well, New CPA failed to record *any* of those in the categories they needed to go in.

F: How could that be?

OCPA: It looks to me like he just didn't spend the time to give you the attention your business—and you—deserve.

F: Geez, I knew there was something wrong.

OCPA: I hope you're still sitting down, because you owe $40,000 less than New CPA said you did.

F: Are you sure?

OCPA: Absolutely.

F: You are the best. Wow! Thank you a million times!

OCPA: Not a problem. But I do have one piece of advice. Keep your old CPA.

That's a happy ending to what could have been a very sad story. Unfortunately, for every great story like that, there are countless others that aren't so great. Too many of us spend too many of our waking hours thinking of all the ways to *create* money and too few thinking about ways to keep what we make. Having a great CPA, one who knows his or her business, and truly cares about your business and about you as a person, is one of the most effective ways for you to keep most of your money, pay in taxes no more than you honestly need to pay, and invest the rest.

One of the best CPAs I've met is a man named Larry Cohen (LMCohen@msn.com). He's also the Old CPA in the story you just read who saved my friend over $40,000. He doesn't work for a firm that has hundreds of CPAs and accountants. He doesn't drive a flashy car. And he doesn't talk about all the *big deals* he's working on. He simply happens to be one of the best CPAs you'll find anywhere—not only for his knowledge of money, taxes, and accounting, but because he truly cares about his clients and about helping them become successful. Larry has this to say about why it's a good idea to have a CPA on your team.

> People ask me which is better when it comes to handling their business and personal taxes: a CPA or non-CPA accountant? Even before I became one, I've always felt CPAs were the best choice. First, they go through a more extensive educational process than non-CPAs. Second, they must be accredited and have passed numerous tests. Finally, there are only three people who can represent you in front of the IRS should you or your business ever get called before them for an audit. The first is an attorney. The second is an Enrolled Agent. The third is a CPA.

Tracking Expenses on Your Own

Many years ago, when I first started my own business, I came up with a simple way to keep track of my cash expenses. I do use a corporate charge card for most of my travel and business-related expenses, but I sometimes also pay cash. Charge card statements provide plenty of information on what, when, and where a business expense occurred. Here's an easy way to record cash business expenses.

* Get a small spiral-bound notebook, and at the top of each page you use write the words "Cash Business Expenses for Year 2xxx."
* Whenever you have a cash business expense, write down on each line what the expense is, when and where the expense occurred, the date of the expense, who (if anyone) you were with and the amount.

* On the front of a letter-size envelope, write "Cash Business Expense Receipts for ____ (month), ____ (year)." You can use a new envelope for each month, or do what I do and make each envelope cover a 2-month period.
* Each time you create a cash business expense, record the expense in your journal notebook and place the receipt in the envelope.
* At the end of your tax year, simply remove the pages from that year's Cash Business Expense notebook and record the totals for each category of expense you had.
* Send copies of those pages and your year-end summary of expenses in their categories, with total amounts for each category, to the accountant or CPA who is doing your taxes.

Agents: Do You Really Need One?

It's been said that agents (also known as managers) are more interested in your numbers than in your potential. Perhaps. Yet if they're smart, and if you've got potential, they'll definitely see how the two can become one. Many of the people I've spoken with have mixed feelings about needing an agent. This is especially true for an artist whose real-world ability to become a commercial success may not yet warrant having an agent.

Regardless of where you currently stand on the agent/no agent question, if you *do* decide you need one, you need to make your choice on the basis of the same kind of test you would give to a prospective attorney. Do not sign with an agent just because he or she is telling you all the things you want to hear. Time and time again I see and hear the stories of smart and talented people signing over their talent to people who don't have any talent of their own for making things happen. Here's just one among many that I could tell.

A singer I know who writes his own songs and has a unique voice was part of a band that had opened for some once-famous name acts, but, it seemed to the singer/songwriter, wasn't going much of anywhere. So he called a friend of mine who runs a very successful music business in a major music city and told him that while it would be great to get some big things happening with the band, he would like to see what could happen for him as a solo artist. My friend told the singer to send him a demo. He'd listen to it and let his other music friends (who are in the studios on a daily basis producing and playing on major label records) listen to it, and he'd get back to him with their honest opinions. No promises. Just a "let's see what happens" kind of thing.

The singer sent the demo out, and after a few weeks my friend called the singer back to give him the promised feedback. He began by saying that while there were many good points about his demo, the people who heard it agreed that it didn't stand out enough to make a major label want to offer a development, demo, or record deal. My friend also explained that what he was telling him was simply *their* opinions and that someone else could have a very different opinion.

A few weeks later, my friend found out that the singer who had sent him the demo, and his band, were seriously considering signing with an "entertainment attorney" who is also an "agent/manager" and who was "really interested" in "doing big things" for the singer and his band. Out of curiosity, my friend checked around and found out that this "entertainment attorney" was fresh out of college, had just passed the bar exam, and had no other clients. But he's really interested in doing big things for this guy and his band.

Sadly, the singer and his band bit. They signed an agreement with this attorney that had ridiculously low performance guarantees; exclusivity clauses that locked them up for multiple years; too broad a control of the use of their names, likeness, and image; and way too much in out-of-pocket expenses that they (the band), and not the attorney, would be responsible for. Feels good to have a deal, eh?

Don't get me wrong. There are good deals and good agents. But you need to know why you need one and when. Like attorneys, there are some terrific agents who really know this business. Yet there are only a small number who have the creative genius to know how to create the next stars. And not all of these people have years of experience or Rolodexes full of contacts.

Remember that all those great and high-priced people you hear or read about who are at the top right now all started at the same place—the bottom. It was through effective work, personality, and great ideas that these people quickly rose to the top. And it's the best ones who've stayed there.

Go after the ones at the top first. If they can't take you on right now (once your star rises, you'll be surprised at how many people who wouldn't give you the time of day suddenly have an opening for you), have them refer you to a few people they admire who *can* take you on. I've done this for many other aspects of the music and publishing business a number of times.

Case in point: I needed to have some photos shot for a book project we were working on, so I found out who was the best photographer in town for the cover shoot we were doing. The photographer also turned out to be one of the best album cover photographers in the world, who works with the major record labels photographing their artists.

I called him, and after we talked and he told me his fee began at $20,000, I asked if he could recommend someone who could do the project within our budget.

He said he'd be happy to, and referred me to one of his assistants, who, by the way, was great to work with and did the entire project for a fraction of the price. Don't be shy. Ask . . . Ask . . . Ask!

When it comes to hiring an agent, you should really give some serious thought to how great you could be at being your own agent. As I've said time and again, nobody, but nobody, can sell you to the world better than you.

Throughout my publishing career, I have pitched my book ideas to major publishers—this one included—by myself. When agents find out that I have sold all of my books without help, they ask, "How in the world do you do it?" "Well," I answer, "I identify an editor at a publishing house that does books like the one I am working on. I pick up the phone, call the editor, and give him or her a rundown of my ideas and ask if they would be interested in seeing more specifics. When the answer is 'yes' (and you'd be surprised at how often it is), I send an e-mail with details of the proposal. That's the beginning, but I do all follow-up calls and e-mails myself, and the publishers make their offers to me, not to some agent." It isn't such a complicated process, is it? So why would I want to give up 15 percent to someone who could've done the same thing?

When it comes to needing or getting an agent, my advice is simple: Unless this individual can bring big things to the table that will significantly help you and your career, keep control and do it yourself. If you meet someone you think can truly help your career rise and you don't mind giving a percentage of royalties and money to that person, then consider it. Until that time—until you are sure the person you are signing with can contribute something to whatever it is you are doing that you could not do on your own—don't give away the keys to your life or music to anyone, for any reason.

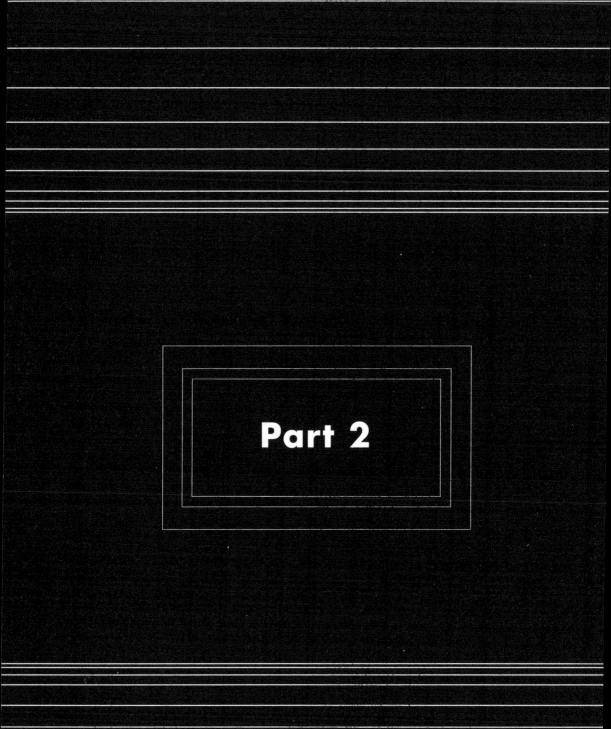

Part 2

Writing Your Songs, Getting Your Sound, and Mixing, Mastering, and Recording Your Music

It's All about the Song:

Advice and Inspiration

from Diane Warren

Where were you when you heard DeBarge's "Rhythm of the Night"? Diane Warren could tell you where she was. Driving down Sunset Boulevard in Los Angeles with the radio blasting, the windows down, and the biggest smile you could imagine on anyone's face.

Who could blame her? She's the one who wrote it. That and over 800 other songs, including such hits as Aerosmith's "I Don't Want to Miss a Thing," Faith Hill's "There You'll Be," Celine Dion's "Because You Loved Me," Toni Braxton's "Unbreak My Heart," Starship's "Nothing's Gonna Stop Us Now," Belinda Carlisle's "I Get Weak," Heart's "Who Will You Run To?" Chicago's "I Don't Want to Live Without Your Love," Cher's "If I Could Turn Back Time," Bad English's "When I See You Smile," Taylor Dayne's "Love Will Lead You Back," Michael Bolton's "How Can We Be Lovers?" and Trisha Yearwood and LeAnn Rimes' "How Do I Live," which became the longest-running song in the history of *Billboard*'s Hot 100 and Country Singles charts. And that's only the beginning.

Diane's songs have been sung by Elton John, Tina Turner, Barbra Streisand, Aretha Franklin, Patti LaBelle, Roberta Flack, Roy Orbison, *NSYNC, Gloria Estefan, Britney Spears, Christina Aguilera, Reba McEntire, Whitney Houston, Enrique Iglesias, Ricky Martin, Mary J. Blige, and many, many others. Diane's music has been heard in over 80 movies from *Mannequin* to *Coyote Ugly, Armageddon* to *Moulin Rouge, Gone in Sixty Seconds* to *Pearl Harbor.* And her first television theme for *ENTERPRISE* was also the first theme song for the *Star Trek* series.

Okay, let's forget the hits. What about the awards? Diane has done what no one else has ever done; she's had her songs on seven different *Billboard* music charts at the same time. She has won the coveted ASCAP Songwriter of the Year six times and *Billboard*'s Songwriter of the Year four times. Diane has also won a Grammy award and a NARAS Governor's Award. She's been nominated for four Golden Globes and six Academy Awards. In 2001 she got her own star on the Hollywood Walk of Fame and was inducted into the National Academy of Music/Songwriters Hall of Fame. Whew!

Diane's publishing company, Realsongs, is considered one of the most successful publishing companies in music. It has won walls full of awards, including being named *Billboard*'s Number 1 Singles Publisher and Top 10 Publishing Corporation and *American Songwriter*'s Number 1 Pop Publisher. Quite a feat when you consider that her publishing company only has one songwriter: Diane Warren.

Realsongs is the name of her publishing company, and make no mistake about it; when it comes to songwriting, Diane Warren is the Real Deal. Word has it that record mogul and legend Clive Davis has a standing appointment with her each month when he visits Los Angeles. As famed Hollywood film director and producer Jerry Bruckheimer says, "I think she is on the top of her game. Where she goes, the public goes."

The life of Diane Warren is one of intense focus. It's an inspiring example of truly following your muse. She writes the hits that touch millions of people's hearts. With such a consuming passion and zeal for what she does, and so much time and attention devoted to her craft, she rarely has the opportunity to fully appreciate the impact of her gift on the millions who are touched by it. But you won't hear any complaints, for Diane Warren is one of those truly rare people who loves what she does and lives for each moment she's able to do it.

As you're about to read, Diane's life was changed forever when as a young girl she heard the magic of music speak to her from the speakers of the radio. Her destiny would be to hone and develop her gift and calling—despite incredible rejection from the music meisters who "knew" music and the audience they said "listened" to it—to become the premier contemporary songwriter of our time.

With the world's biggest music stars ringing her phone each day for just one more magical Diane Warren song, life is indeed very good for the songwriter whose words may inspire you to follow your passion and gift for a song, wherever it may lead you.

Diane on Starting Out

I started out just wanting to be a songwriter, even when I was little. One of my earliest memories of wanting to be a songwriter was when my two sisters—one being 11 years and the other 14 years older—had lots of 45s, and for some reason I always wanted to know who wrote the songs. I didn't really care who sang them. I just wanted to know who wrote them. Perhaps it was some sort of psychic thing that at that early age I just knew one day I would be a songwriter.

When I was growing up, probably around the age of 9, a bunch of us girls in the neighborhood wanted to start a band. One friend wanted to play the drums, another wanted to play the guitar, but I wanted to be the songwriter. I just wanted to write the songs. The band never happened, but the dream of becoming a songwriter did.

As I look back on it, I guess you could say I was one of those kids who loved listening to the radio and would spend hours upon hours each day doing it. I loved listening to songs and escaping into the music. I'd imagine if you'd talk to Steven Spielberg he'd probably say he lived in movies when he was a kid. It was the same thing for me. My world was the song and radio was my escape into it.

People ask me what kind of music has had the most influence on me, and I must say it was pop music and hit records. Back when I began listening to radio, the hits of the day were everything because radio was so different than it is today. It wasn't fragmented and formatted, and you were getting the best of everything. I grew up loving Top 40, and Top 40 back then was a lot of different kinds of music—great songs, and great artists.

I was influenced by lots of artists and different kinds of music, but The Beatles were up there at the top. The songs really hooked me, and to this day those songs are still great. It's always been about the songs for me, and that's never changed.

As I look back on things, I realize I was very lucky when I was growing up to have so much support from my family. When I was 14, my father got me a subscription to *Billboard* magazine and I would study each issue from first page to last. I knew who wrote everything, who produced everything, and who sang everything. Forget school textbooks. Music and *Billboard* magazine became the only subjects I was interested in.

My father recognized my love for music from the start and encouraged me so much. The first guitar I got was this real piece of junk 6-string from Tijuana, and I was just dying to have a 12-string. So my dad made a deal with me. If I could get all A's and B's for one semester, he would buy me a brand-new Martin 12-string. For the first time in my life, I didn't get D's and F's. I was a terrible student because I just didn't care about school. Music was all I was interested in. For that one little brief semester, I got a lot of A's and B's and dad paid $500—a lot of money at that time—for my new Martin 12-string. Next semester, my grades slid right back down, but hey, at least I got the guitar [laughs]!

My mother was supportive of my music dreams. She wanted me to be happy and follow my heart's desire, but she thought the music business was a very tough business to make it in. And she was right. Understandably, she was always a bit reserved in her support. She only wanted the best for me and I knew her concern came from love.

My dad was a dreamer and he saw the same thing in me. It was his encouragement I knew I could count on that helped me through those struggling early years of my songwriting career.

The Big Break

My big break came in 1985, shortly after I began working for Jack White, who produced Laura Branigan. Laura had cut a few of my songs with some success, but it wasn't until someone at Arista Publishing, who administered my early songs, gave my song "Rhythm of the Night" to DeBarge to do for the movie *The Last Dragon* that things started to happen.

DeBarge recorded the song and it became a huge hit. I was 28 years old at the time. That song was my first *big* hit, and the one I had written by myself. I did have a Top 10 record with the song "Solitaire," but that was a song I had only written lyrics to. "Rhythm of the Night" was the song that got things started for me as a songwriter of *both* music and lyrics.

I remember the first time I heard my song on the radio. I was driving down Sunset Boulevard in Los Angeles and heard "Rhythm of the Night" playing on two radio stations. I was just freaking out in excitement. People must've thought I was crazy when they heard me yelling "Oh my God, that's my song! That's my song!" Heaven knows how I didn't hit anybody [laughs]. To this day, I still get excited and love hearing my songs on the radio. I'm such a kid when it comes to that kind of stuff.

The Learning That'll Never End

I can honestly say that even though I've had wonderful success as a songwriter—which I'm so incredibly thankful for—I still don't know if I've learned *how* to be a songwriter. That may sound a bit strange, but with every new song I write, I learn something. It could be about me, about others, about music, about life, about writing, and the magical creative process that it is so hard to describe. Perhaps I've gotten better at what I do, yet, it's just so hard to explain to anyone how to become a songwriter. I just do it. I just write. I just create, and the end result happens to be a song.

It seems that for so many things in life, we want to have specific answers and the how-to's. Yet what I have discovered about songwriting is that it cannot be described like "Put six words here for the first bar, then four words on the second bar, then pause . . ." or anything like that. Songs have to come from inside, at their own time, in their own way, and they can't be forced. Coaxed, yes, and a great way to do that is by writing a little bit each day. But forcing a song to happen today or three hours from now, has never worked for me.

The Diane Warren Songwriting Process

I love to work and come up with concepts, ideas, melodies, and lyrics. I'll sit at the keyboard and play around with different ideas. I might turn on the drum machine and find a good groove and build some music around it. I might get out the guitar and play some chords and see if anything flows.

When writing a song, I gravitate towards *ideas* that interest me first. I'm inspired by everything, everywhere, and have notebook after notebook filled with ideas. An idea could come to me when I'm playing chords or driving my car. I just never know when or where it'll happen.

I always like to write about *something.* It needs to have a *meaning* for me. I like interesting key changes, and you'll hear them in a lot of my songs. Strange rhythmic things are interesting to me. Shifting keys and awkward bars and measures are fun. I like making my songs deceptively simple when you hear them, but when you sing them, you realize they aren't. I think that's cool. I laugh when I hear artists or producers who get my songs say "There are too many words here. How do I sing this?" All those words and weird rhythmic things I put in my songs sometimes throws them a curve ball, but I like that [laughs].

The way I write songs today is the way I've always written songs. Technology may make things like the demo and recording process easier, but it doesn't change the process of how I write a song. I still use my old piece of junk cassette player—that's broken—that sits next to me on my seat when I'm writing. I have nice keyboards with great sounds and have drum machines with lots of different beats, but that's about it. Don't know much about technology and don't really care. I just write songs.

People have asked if my environment plays a big part in influencing how I write a song. Honestly, I don't pay attention to the environment or scenery around me. I haven't cleaned my writing room in 18 years. The scenery won't change what I write. I write every day, but I don't write a song every day. I just feel compelled, perhaps pulled, to write a little something each day.

Writing is so magical for me that I don't like to talk about it, because it takes away the magic of how it happens. I love to write songs and I don't know how you learn, except by just doing it. It's a lot like being an athlete. You work out. You practice. You get good at it. You just do it, and you learn by doing it. As a songwriter, you leave your antennas up for inspiration, because each day, no matter where you live, or what you do, you're going to find it. Inspiration is everywhere you look, and it's just waiting for you to discover and make it your own.

When I write a song, every note has a reason. Every word, every "and" and "though," has a meaning. To me, a powerful song should contain great words and a great melody that work beautifully with each other and almost cannot work without each other. They're just meant to be together. A powerful song has to touch you and make you feel something. Whether it makes you cry or get up and dance, a powerful song needs to move you inside.

Some people are inspired to write from either a painful or pleasurable experience or event. I'm one of those people who believe you don't need to feel miserable to write a great song, and I've discovered that while I've written some of my songs at times when I wasn't feeling good, or at trying times in my life, most of my songs have been written when I feel good about myself and life. The better I feel, the better I write.

Protect Yourself and Your Music

Besides following inspiration wherever it leads you, and writing it down in a song, the one piece of advice I give to people who want to be songwriters is to protect your music. That means not signing away all your publishing to anyone or any company.

Granted, when you're first starting out, you don't have the stature to get The Deal you want, and you may need to take the best publishing deal you're offered. But you need to hold on to as much of your publishing as possible, and have whatever publishing rights you do give up revert back to you at some time in the near future.

My advice is that before you sign anything, to make sure you have a good music/entertainment attorney look things over to ensure that you're protected. If you need help finding one, just call ASCAP or BMI and have them give you a list of attorneys to choose from.

When I got my first publishing deal, I didn't own 100 percent of my songs. But as soon as I was able, I started my own publishing company, which began as a one-person business—me—in my home. From day one, that company, Realsongs, has and still publishes only one person, and it's me. Once it makes sense businesswise and financially, I think having your own publishing company is a good idea for any songwriter who wants to keep control of their music.

If you're an unknown songwriter, and you want to get your music recorded by artists and heard on the radio, the most important thing you can do to get your foot in the door—besides writing great songs—is to get hooked up with a music publisher. Bring them your *best* songs and try and get a publishing deal. Try to get anything you can at the beginning, because you don't yet have the clout to ask for a lot of money or any crazy kind of terms. I've seen more potentially great careers stopped right at the beginning because some artist or songwriter asked for too much too soon. Be smart. Be patient. If you're writing good stuff, you'll get your big break.

You just need to find the right person who'll believe in you and your music. When I started, I had meetings with, and got my music out to, as many publishers as I could, just to find the right one who believed in my ability and me. They're out there. You'll get rejected a lot—I certainly did—but you're going to find the right one if only you don't quit too soon and give up on your dream.

Think of joining a performance rights organization like ASCAP or BMI. You'll need them when your songs get recorded and played. They essentially do the same thing—collect money—so the choice of which organization feels best to you is a personal thing. I've been with ASCAP since day one and I always liked the fact that the great old-time songwriters, like Irving Berlin, were also ASCAP writers. You can't go wrong with either organization.

Radio and the Music Business Today

As I look back on what radio was when I was growing up, to what it has become today, it's changed so much. It's so corporate and rigidly formatted now. Years ago, a radio station program director in a city could pick up on a record and break it and the artist in that city. Things like that don't happen as much now.

The stations of today do so much research and focus group things, that if a song doesn't research well at one station, it might go through the corporation's whole system of stations and not get played in other cities as well. I think that's one of the reasons why so many records get dropped so quickly from airplay. I've always thought that was a bit unfair, since some records do take a while to break, and perhaps, just in that one city, it might not be working, but in another city, it could work great.

The music business has changed in a big way, too. I think there are two big reasons: downloading and corporate buyouts and mergers. The record companies are shrinking to the point where there might be as few as four major companies. To a songwriter, that can be frustrating, especially if it means that with so few companies, if they turn down that individual's music, does that also close the door to their music in the future?

Yet, I think there could be some great news in all of this. I think the way the music business is changing will mean it's going to be good for independent labels again. There's going to be a lot of great talent out there that some smart person is going to sign. I get a sense the music business is going full circle and is going back to the way it started: Lots of indy labels and great artists making great music. That's exciting for everyone, especially for songwriters. The new music business will be such that while the distribution, promotion, and delivery of music may change, people will never stop loving songs.

I really believe that one of the ways the record companies have hurt themselves is when they cut out the singles market. When I was a kid, I wanted to buy artists' singles and if that single interested me enough, I'd want to buy the whole album. Singles were like an appetizer, and more times than not, after having the appetizer, I wanted the whole meal—the album.

Yet record labels began changing things, and many times they wouldn't put out a single because they wanted people to buy the whole album. But I ask you, why would anyone go out and pay all that money for an album, only to get one or two great songs, and the rest of the album would be crap? That kind of thinking really turned people off to music and to the record labels in a big way. And wouldn't you know that not too long after that, the Internet thing and Napster happened, and it forever changed how music will be distributed.

I think the great record legend Clive Davis said it best when he was asked about technology and how it will change music. Clive told the interviewer that while he didn't know too much about technology, he simply wanted to create the kinds of artists and great music people will *want* to steal. For Clive, it's all about the artist, the music, and the song. Ah, once a music person, always a music person.

The record business has changed so much, to the point where there are now more suits and bean counters in positions of power than those like my dear friend Clive Davis, who is the last of the dying breed of record visionaries and music mavericks. Clive is the man who keeps reinventing himself with great new music and artists—even after more than 40 years in the business.

A Song Is a Part of Who You Are

I'll be the first to admit that I'm a bit of a control freak when it comes to my music. Songs are so personal. They're almost like little children you've created, and it can sometimes be difficult to let them go. But you've got to let them go. Once my song gets into the artist's hands, they take my creation, put their own unique spin on it, and that song becomes their own. Which is as it should be. But I'll admit that when it does leave my hands, I always hope the melody is sung right and that too many things aren't changed around. Over the years, I've been very lucky that the artists who record my songs have kept them close to the way I originally wrote them.

Sometimes I do enjoy being in the studio when an artist is recording my song, especially when I'm working with a great producer like David Foster. The process of watching and hearing the song come alive is exciting. For me, it's always been that as long as an artist respects my song, then I'm okay with what they do to it.

For me, being a songwriter is the only thing I know how to do. It's so powerful of a passion for me that I have no choice *but* to be a songwriter. *To choose not to do this, for me, would be like deciding not to breathe.* Each day, I just want to get better and better at it. I want to keep writing songs that people want to take into their hearts and into their lives. It's that much a part of who I am. I don't have time for any other kind of life and probably wouldn't know what to do with it if I did [laughs].

The power of words and music can be so intense. For some people, finding the words to express their feelings and emotions can be tough. But a song can express those things in ways unlike anything else. A song with the perfect words and melody can be as true to revealing the soul and essence of who we are as anything else we may say or do.

I've always thought of my songs as my little creations that I want to be everywhere bringing a smile to someone's face and a good feeling inside someone's heart. I want my music to make them happy. So many times in life we get so caught up in what we're doing that we don't stop often and long enough to see just how much who we are and what we do impacts others.

Heaven knows I'm guilty of being a workaholic, and being so focused and caught up in what I do, often, make that *too* often, I don't stop long enough to realize many things. Yet the way life can get our attention can be so amazingly wonderful. Sometimes, all it takes is a smile, perhaps a good word at the right time, or something as unexpected as reading the inside of a fortune cookie that says, "*You'll never know just how much you touch other people's lives.*"

Web sites: www.realsongs.com and www.dianewarren.com

Developing Your Sound:
Advice from Bob Bradshaw

When it comes to music, the greatest thing you can give to someone is *your* sound. Sure, all of us start out learning and copying music from those we admire, be they composers, singers, or musicians, but for many of us, that's a phase we soon outgrow. As we all know, cover bands are everywhere, but very few, if any, are ever remembered except for sounding "like so-and-so (fill in the blank famous artist)."

There comes a time in your journey when you have to decide which road you want to take. Do you want to be a copy or do you want to be an original? You see, when it comes to music, you have two choices: *either play the music other people write or write the music other people play.* The choice you make can change your life.

I'm betting you choose to follow your passion, your calling, and your desire to compose and perform the music that's inside of you. After all, no one but you has the distinct abilities, the combination of influences, and the experiences to compose, sing, and/or play in your own way. Friend, you were born an original so don't die a copy.

Now that it's been decided you're going to write and play *your* music, you're going to need your sound. Just as singers like Mariah Carey, Bono, Whitney Houston, Bruce Springsteen, Bob Dylan, and Celine Dion have their own signature vocal sound, you, too, as a singer or musician, need to possess your own voice.

How you sing and how you play are only one part of getting your sound. The other part is in the equipment you use or don't use. Some musicians, like U2's The Edge, use technology as an important element of their sound. Just listen to all those layered delays in his guitar work and you'll hear what I'm talking about. Other musicians like the raw sound of an acoustic guitar or prefer one cable going straight from guitar to amp or microphone to mixing board and recorder.

Whichever equipment path you choose, you'll save lots of time and money if you know how to get the sound you want. To help you learn how to get the sounds that you hear on radio and on records, though, you'd need the guidance of a handful of people with the experience to teach you the tricks of the trade. Among this handful of people is Bob Bradshaw, the granddaddy and king of Custom Audio Electronics.

To the guitar world, Bob Bradshaw is the Einstein of sound. His work and sound architectures are legendary. They've been heard on countless hit records and in concerts all over the world. His clients include—and this is the short list—Trey Anastasio [Phish], Babyface, Walter Becker [Steely Dan], George Benson, Vivian Campbell [Def Leppard], Bill Champlin [Chicago], Kyle Cook & Adam Gaynor [matchbox 20], Tom Delonge [Blink 182], The Edge [U2], Peter Frampton, Sammy Hagar, Warren Haynes [Gov't Mule], Lenny Kravitz, Steve Lukather [Toto], Yngie Malmsteen, John Mayer, Steve Miller, Dave Mustaine [Megadeth], Dean Parks [studio legend], Joe Perry and Brad Whitford [Aerosmith], Tom Petty, Prince, Nigel Pulsford, and Gavin Rossdale [Bush], Lee Ritenour, Richie Sambora [Bon Jovi], Neil Schon [Journey and Bad English], Seal, Franz Stahl [Foo Fighters], Johnny Rzeznik [Goo Goo Dolls], Steve Vai, Edward Van Halen.

Although much of his work has been for guitarists, Bob's advice is going to be a real godsend to you whether you're a keyboard player, drummer, a percussionist, singer, etc. He's about to teach you the secrets to discovering and achieving your sound, and doing it cheaper and easier than you may have thought possible.

Bob Bradshaw on Starting Out

I started out loving music. It all began when I was just a kid. I'm going to have to blame my sister for this, because as soon as she started playing all the Beatles and Motown stuff in our house, I was hooked. It was a love of music that blossomed into a curiosity about how it was made.

I always loved sounds. I was the kid in school who had the biggest stereo and the first guy to have an 8-track recorder. I would record everything from records to bands, and loved pretending I was the recording and sound engineer for big concerts.

I was fascinated by sonics and sounds. What can I say: Turning all those knobs was really cool. Yet I never played an instrument. I had a guitar and fiddled with it a bit, and I can even play a few things, but I'd consider myself a guitar owner and not a play-er. However, knowing how to get great guitar sounds was the big thing for me.

The first audio project I built was a 2-12 speaker cabinet. I was 14 years old. I grew up in Florida, and since I didn't grow up with musicians or knew anyone who was, I knew I had to get whatever sound knowledge I wanted on my own. Let me tell you, I read and experimented with anything and everything I could to get what I was imagining in my head out into the real world. But there remained one problem: I didn't know enough about how electronic things worked.

One day in the mail, I received something about electronics from DeVry Institute [a technical school] and it caught my attention. I realized that school could be my chance to learn about electronics and I hoped, how sounds were made. The school was located in Atlanta. A friend and I enrolled and off to Atlanta we went. While there, and for the first time in my life, I applied myself to studying and quickly found how easy the electronics stuff came to me. Also for the first time in my life, something else happened: I graduated at the top of my class with a 4.0 grade average. I was hooked.

Yet there was still one problem: Here I was, a young kid with all this technical knowledge, but no practical hands-on knowledge of how to apply what I knew in the real world of music and audio. I knew I had to get out to Los Angeles and be where all the music was being made, but there was one big obstacle: I needed a way to get out there. As fortune would have it, Hughes Aircraft hired me as an electronics technician and they paid for my move. Bingo!

Not long after my arrival in Los Angeles, I went to work for Musicians Service Center. This was a place that repaired music equipment, and it wasn't long before I was meeting lots of musicians and studio players. There were guys in L.A., one in particular named Paul Rivera, building pedalboards for players. While his [Rivera's] designs were good and players liked them, I was thinking of going in an entirely different direction. Inspired by Craig Anderton's *Guitar Player* magazine column, I wanted to create a switching system—with the effects into loops—that could give someone immediate access to multiple pieces of gear with a remote control foot switcher.

I began building a prototype switching system. The first prototype consisted of a rack mount unit whereby all the pedals would be on a sliding tray connected to a floorboard controller which would offer a uniform way to select various effects. Keep in mind, this was years before MIDI.

I wanted an individual switch and a light for every effect in the rack which would tell me when an effect was off or on, and also keep everything in the rack to take the place of having all those pedals on the floor that people were having to dance around and stomp on to either turn them off or on. I wanted a system whereby I wasn't modifying any effects but, rather, could interchange effects whenever I wanted simply by unplugging the old effect and plugging a new one in its place. Would you believe the basic prototype model I developed in 1980 is the same one I use today? Hey, if it ain't broke, don't fix it.

Great Combinations = Great Sounds

An important lesson I've learned over the years is that to get the greatest combinations and types of sounds in any system, it's all about instant individual direct access to any piece of gear you have—that is, using that gear in any way you want simply by use of multiple footswitches, and then being able to create individual presets and/or combinations, with one, two, three, or all the pieces of gear in your system. Truly amazing sounds can be created in this way.

To me, it's always been about allowing musicians the ability to choose whatever kind of gear they want to use in order to make their system and sound unique, regardless of the kind of equipment or manufacturer. If you plug your instrument directly into your amplifier, great. But as soon as you put something between that instrument and your amplifier, then I can help you. Even your cable is an effect, because different kinds of cables can color your sound due to their capacitive quality. Yes, even something so simple as a cable can make a big difference in your sound.

The Bob Bradshaw Sound Philosophy

Much of my sound philosophy revolves around how things would be configured in a studio. Such as taking a dry [no effects] amplifier, mic it up, then process, blend, and mix it through the studio's effects to create lots of great sound combinations. That's why I make the line mixer an important part of many sound system setups I build.

Whether a player is well-known or not known, people looking for their own sounds come to me for the same thing. Typically, a player will call me and say they've got this kind of delay, that kind of reverb, this kind of overdrive pedal, that kind of amp, or any other pieces of gear and/or amps, and they'll want to put them in some kind of system that will allow them to use all the gear they've got, but in an easy way, and with the most options for sounds.

For me, it's always been about working with the players directly. I'm hands-on, and sound design is my forte. When people in Los Angeles started hearing about my work, some didn't know what to think. I was the guy wanting to change the way things were being done, and some people shied away from me. However, there were a few forward-thinking folks who wanted to see and hear what I was all about. That's when things started to happen. I was dealing with studio players and it was all word of mouth. It was, as they say, "the best advertising."

I began designing sound rigs for studio players like Buzzy Feiten, Michael Landau, Steve Lukather, Dean Parks, Paul Jackson, Jr., Grant Geisman, and many others. Word quickly got back to me that because of this new-found power of creating sounds like never before, arrangers were writing more complex parts just to take advantage of what the studio players who were using my rigs could now do. That was really cool.

Over the years, I've learned from the top players in the world—those whose career depends on their sound—that a great guitar, bass, or keyboard sound is one that has feeling behind it, is unique, and grabs you. It can be anything from thin and tinny sounding to big and in your face. Anything goes and it's all cool, as long as it works for you. A favorite kind of sound is such a subjective thing. There's no such thing as "the best" sound. One person will totally dig a sound while another will totally hate it. The bottom line is, if it's your sound, if it's what you like, then that's all that matters. It's all good, so don't limit yourself.

Years ago, it used to be that people took the time to really learn their instrument and craft. They took lessons, they studied, copied licks from great records, and all of these things helped develop their style. Today, and with technology the way it is, I see too many people using that technology and effects as a crutch to cover up bad playing, laziness, lack of ability, or musicianship.

In the past, the kind of effort you needed to put into your chosen instrument was enormous compared to what people can get away with now. Today, anybody can buy a drum/beat box, keyboards that have all of these sounds and instruments in them that are immediately accessed at the touch of a button or piano key, sequencers and samplers that make it so much easier to create music without having to be a good player in order to do it. But what kinds of great music are being created? Of course, music is all in the ears of the listener. However, when you see the decline of the record labels, radio stations, and the kind of stuff that gets made and played, it really makes you wonder where it's going.

People tell me they think the same is true of Pro Tools and other digital-do-everything-on-a-computer ways of recording and mixing music. If someone is singing or playing off key or not in time, it's not a problem; they just put it through the auto tune, timing device, other software program, and everything's fine. It's almost as if cut 'n paste has become the must-have solution to making records. All of that may make things quicker and easier, but it doesn't help one become a better singer or player. I think for too many people, it's become a crutch they can't or won't do without.

Whether it's old classic analog gear or the newest digital whiz-bang in a box, the sound is everything. Yet, when you go back and listen to older records, the records I and so many of the pros I work with grew up on, there's something to be said about those analog recordings. In my mind, there's nothing like having an analog signal path you're recording into for sonics, then using the ease of editing in the digital realm. It's the best of both the analog and digital worlds and it's a combination that's tough to beat.

I read a letter in a magazine called *Tape Op* [for a free subscription go to www.tapeop.com] that really caught my attention. It talked about how we've stopped listening to the music and have instead become computer screen watchers when making music. It's a fascinating account by a reader that proves the stimulus of the visual takes precedent over the audio in the processing by the brain. Here's what it said:

> I made the switch about a year ago to hard disk computer recording. Since the switch and move of home and studio, I've had some major problems in monitoring—hearing properly. I have my computer monitor set up in front of me with the audio monitors off to each side about six feet apart. The speakers have been shielded so no interference can come from the computer monitor. I'm using Event 20/20's and EV 100A's. My console is at the side of me because I can really mix mainly in the computer itself.
>
> I thought the room was causing problems and needed tuning. I had it checked and done. No help. Then one fine day about a week ago, I was experiencing eye strain from looking at the computer monitor for so long. I said "Screw it. I'll just shut it off and listen to give my eyes a break."
>
> Well, lo and behold, I could hear again. I could sit back and gaze into each audio monitor and hear like I used to. I could almost see where the musician was standing in the audio field! The apparent volume seemed louder and the field was wider, just like it's supposed to be. Now, I know you may think it's because of some humming or masking of sound from the monitor/video itself. Not so.
>
> I tested the theory by leaving [the monitor] on and covering it with a towel. Same result. And this listening test was confirmed by every client who passed through the studio that week: about nine musicians and three engineers. Many a mouth flew open. The only down side is now I have to rewire and reconfigure the damn studio.
>
> The reason for the more accurate listening with the computer monitor off seems to be the battle between audio and visual. Visual, being a stronger medium, seems to win out when the monitor is on. Attention is diverted away from the listening so I can watch a stupid wave file and general scrolling go by. That also explains what happened to music because of MTV. Hope this helps some readers.

When searching for your sound, be patient. You'll try some things that sound good and others that don't. You'll buy the hottest piece of gear today and two months from now, you could be selling it because it no longer sounds good to you. It's all a growing, experimenting, and learning process that never ends.

Whether you choose to plug your instrument straight into your amp or recording console, or choose to use effects to color and embellish your sound, just remember they are *choices* and *tools* to help *you* get whatever sound *you* want. Each is valid and each is good and there's not one way better than another. It's all up to you because in the end, you and your sound are all that matter.

Getting a Great Sound

I have people ask me what the must-have elements are to getting a great sound. To them I answer, a well-tuned and well-maintained instrument. After that, anything goes. Your instrument is the first and most important thing you make music with, so you need to have one that feels good in your hands and fingers. Your instrument is the first step in your music, and your style, and your sound, and all else follows from there.

I tell people don't get caught up in thinking you need to have every new piece of gear that comes out. Technology and gear change so fast. Build your sound around two key pieces of equipment first—your instrument and amplifier—then add whatever kinds of effects sound good to you. Effects will change, but a good-sounding instrument and amp won't. And everything is good. Even a crappy-sounding piece of gear can be a great-sounding piece of gear, if it has the sound you like.

As much as we like new and modern sounding stuff, players will always go back to the old and vintage pieces of gear because they have a vibe and sound uniquely their own. My advice is, if you have a good mix of pedals and rack gear, you won't go wrong.

I've never been the guy who tells people what kinds of sounds they should use. It's not my music and style. It's theirs, and they need to listen to the records and things they like that will help them put together elements that will create their sound.

Many times, people will tell me that they want to get Van Halen or some other rock star's sound and I'll ask them, "Do you play like them?" Also, what you hear on a CD and how the musician got that sound in the studio can be *very* different than a live rig. People need to be realistic, know their ability and needs, and think more about creating something unique to them instead of trying to copy someone else and simply becoming known as another copycat. There's so much great gear, options, and possibilities for creating your own unique sound that you don't need to sound like someone else.

Over the years people have also asked me for a Bob Bradshaw sound. I tell them there isn't one and there can't be. You see, I help people get *their* sounds by using whatever kinds of gear *they* want, and then putting all that gear together for them in ways that'll give them the widest possibilities for any kinds of sounds *they* wish to create.

Having said that, I do, however, have certain ideas about sound that I apply to how things are ordered in the signal path. For example, I like to put my delays after the reverbs, whereas a lot of people will put the reverb at the end of the line. To my ears, I like the delay after the reverb because of the distinctness of the decay.

When looking for your sound and access to lots of sounds, the first thing I want to know is what's the purpose of your rig? Do you need it for the studio? The road?

You need to know why you need the sounds you're seeking. Next would be, what kind of effects do you need and why? Unless a piece of gear has its own unique sound or thing it can do that cannot be duplicated by anything else, I say keep the duplication of gear to a minimum. Ultimately, it all comes down to getting the equipment that you like and that sounds good to you.

You need to keep in mind that, for example, guitar gear is built for guitar, and there can be problems between one manufacturer and another as to how well different types and brands of gear interface with each other. You also need to keep in mind as you design a sound system that what you are putting in it today could be very different a year from now, when new gear comes out or when you're at a different place musically and looking for a different kind of sound. This happens all the time. Be flexible and open so that you can easily change things should you ever want to.

A big decision you'll need to make is whether your sound system will be a pedal-based rig that you'll put between your instrument and your amp or whether it will be a preamp/power amp type configuration, where there are effects between the preamp and power amp. Will it be a rack-mount gear-based system or a combination?

Some people's needs are pretty simple. Once they know what kinds of effects they want, they can go the off-the-store-shelf route and they're fine. Others need more versatility and options. They want to be able to create a set of sounds they can't get with off-the-store-shelf gear. For them, my switching system is unlike anything else they'll find anywhere and it's perfect for their needs.

Amps and Speakers: The Keys to a Great Sound

I think it helps when people understand sound from the perspective of how the amp and speaker work with or against each other. For example, with an amplifier, you have an output transformer and with a speaker you have a coil. When the amp sends its signal to the speaker, that speaker is loaded in a cabinet and its resonance depends on the damping and its cabinet and, along with that, the resonance within the cabinet itself. And as that speaker pushes back at the amplifier, it creates a reactive load.

Of the amps we first experimented with, Marshall's were much more sensitive to having a reactive load and the sound difference was immediately apparent. In comparison, Mesa Boogies were more forgiving. So, even though an amp can be the same wattage or use the same kinds of tubes, there can be big differences in how they'll react to your gear, your system, or ways you'd like to use it to record.

Years ago, when we were interfacing effects to amps, there weren't effects loops, so all of the effects went right into the front [into the inputs] of amps. And we weren't using preamps either. We were using regular amplifiers. A good example of that setup was the early Michael Landau rigs.

We designed a rack of effects and pedals that went right into the front end [the inputs] of the amps. There would be two amps and two cabinets for the clean sound and another pair of amps and cabinets for the dirty [overdriven] sound. The effects were smacking the front ends of these two setups of four amps all at the same time, so he could get a clean and dirty sound both at once. And that was a cool thing at the time.

Then I had a revelation of sorts. I began thinking about using load resistors along with speakers within the signal chain. A load resistor is a fixed impedance and not a reactive impedance like a speaker, meaning that depending upon the frequency the amp is trying to reproduce, a speaker will give and take from the amplifier's damping and reactance from the coils. A load resistor won't, but using the two together could create some interesting results.

I wanted to know what would happen if we just took one amplifier and put a load resistor on it so it could be turned all the way up to give the whole sound of the amp and without needing a speaker. I also wanted to find out what would happen if we also used a speaker to give us the wet/dry [speaker/no speaker] sound, along with the amp's slave out, which would allow us to take a portion of the signal and then re-amp it any way we wanted. In essence, what would happen if we used the load resistor, padded the signal down to line level, then through the effects, and we took the signal out through power amps and into the speakers, or a direct out into a mixing board?

I tried it and a whole new set of sound possibilities opened up. Now the effects had that whole amp sound they were processing, whereas before, when an effect, like an echo, hit the front end of the amplifiers, the repeats and decay died off because of their lower output levels. Those effects weren't hitting the amp as hard, and the result was a thinner sound.

However, with this new way of routing things—having the amp first with the gain cranked up and *then* processing the echoes—the sound you'd get was this great overdriven/distortion sound with the echoes on it. And along with it, as the over-driven/distortion sounds died off, so did the echoes at the same time. A way thicker sound.

And that brings up a good point about using and recording speakers: A 16-ohm single speaker in a single-speaker cabinet will act as a different load than four 16-ohm speakers placed in a 4-12 cabinet. The same is true for single-speaker cabinets versus double-speaker cabinets. Keep that in mind when recording or playing live and you're wanting a tighter vs. more open sound.

Let me tell you a great story about Van Halen. For years, Ed always felt a 16-ohm load was the way to go, for example, a 4-12 16-ohm Marshall cabinet that had two sets of two 12-inch speakers wired in series with all the speakers connected together in parallel. When we built the first rig for Van Halen back in 1986 for his 5150

Tour, I built this elaborate load box that allowed him to switch amplifiers and a bank of load resistors simply by turning a knob on the front of the box.

When Ed came to check out the rig for the first time, I had this thing set up with a 4-ohm load and not 16 ohms like he always liked, and he freaked out. "Oh no, it won't sound good on 4 ohms and we've gotta set it back to 16" were the first words from his mouth. I told him that there wouldn't be any problems and all he had to do was set his amplifier for 4 ohms instead of 16 and everything would sound great. But no, he wanted it 16 ohms, so I went back into his system and rewired everything to 16.

Ed goes out and does the tour with his favorite hallowed Marshall Plexi amp head now being plugged into a static load box and not going directly from there into a speaker. Instead, we took that loaded signal through his effects, and then into his power amps, and then into just two speakers, and not all those speaker cabinets people would see on stage. He had the dry sound and the effects sound coming out in stereo. It was a big huge sound and Ed loved it.

Then one year later, in 1987, he's getting ready to do another tour, and in the meantime we come across the wonderful revelation that this static load resistor thing isn't happening anymore, especially on a Marshall. Sound from the amp needed to be heard on a reactive load. So one day I'm with him at a rehearsal and I'm coming to him with this amazing sound revelation. I was thinking to myself, Ed, you're going to be amazed at how unbelievable this is going to sound. This is it, pal. Now, it's *really* going to sound like the amp. I go in there and hook this up for him and I'm all excited and he hates it! Didn't like it at all. I was crushed. I was thinking, are you nuts and out of your friggin' mind! Just listen to how this sounds!

But I learned a powerful lesson that day and it was, he was used to the other sound and in his mind, that was the only sound there was. It wasn't until a year or two later that we finally convinced him to use our new setup. And when he did, and when we brought out that other speaker that had the effects coming out in stereo on either side of it, Ed realized he had the wet/dry approach and his new sound system was really happening. He was hooked.

Regardless of how much or little you spend, or how famous or not famous you are, getting a great sound is not having Ed Van Halen's or anyone else's setup. It all goes back to plugging your instrument into your amp. After that, the possibilities are unlimited, be they as simple as miking the speaker cabinet(s) and having that sound go into the studio mixing board and through the studio's effects units or anything else. It's how and where you use your effects, amps, preamps, and anything else that can give you lots of possibilities for recording your own cool sound.

Over 20 years ago, I started out interfacing pedals with high-end studio-quality rack-mount gear, like Steve Lukather using API EQs, which were right from the studio and very pricey. My clients back then—again, Ed Van Halen comes to mind—

weren't into MIDI program changes. Ed simply wanted combinations of gear to come on and off and he used my foot controller with four presets to get his great sound. The sound that people today still want to get.

And you don't need a lot of amps to get a great sound. Ed used lots of amps for years before I started working with him, and the inconsistencies of sound and power from multiple amps and from stage to stage weren't worth it. With Ed's rig, I got him into using one amp that we would take a signal from, then run the signal into the effects, from which [it] would go into a power amp—in Ed's rig, they were HH V800 solid-state MOSFET power amps—and then line out into a cabinet. It's the wet/dry approach. Keep in mind that it takes a doubling of power [e.g., going from 100 watts to 200 watts] just to get 3 decibels more loudness, so you might want to save your money next time you think you need to have all these amps and power. Look at what Ed Van Halen did with just one amp. It's how you use your gear that makes all the difference.

Years ago, when I was touring with Steve Lukather and Toto, he was using a Mesa amp for a clean sound, a Marshall amp for a crunch sound, and a Soldano SLO-100 for the lead sound, and all of these amps were on load resistors. The freight costs of taking all those amps, cabinets, and effects racks overseas were outrageous.

There had to be a way to get a Fender clean sound—which was what we were using the Boogie for—a Marshall crunch sound, and the SLO sound, but in one unit. Make that a double rack space unit that had individual gain, EQs, and individual output levels for each channel that would offer three totally independent amplifiers. Working with Mike Soldano, we built the first prototype of that very thing into one of my switching system chassis.

One day, I brought the prototype into the studio for Steve to play and told him to check this out. There were all the amp sounds he was using, but in a double rack space! He loved it. We then began using this new prototype along with flat frequency-response Mesa M-180 tube power amps. Yet, it still wasn't there in terms of the sound I wanted. We still needed to beef it up and EQ it, because we weren't using guitar-voiced power stages.

Then came the proliferation of guitar preamps. Bogner made one. Soldano took my prototype and design and turned it into the X-88R. But as good as all these sounded, there was still work to do for the sounds I was looking to get. That led to my collaboration with famed guitar maker John Suhr to build the Custom Audio Electronics 3+SE preamp. It became the preamp that took things further and just sounded right to us. It had more tone, more output drive capability, a more balanced sound between all three channels, and a switchable tube stage EQ that gave players plenty of low and top end.

I've always believed that a good preamp is 80 percent of your tone with the other

20 percent coming from your power amp when the power amps are 100 watts or more. I prefer using lower-wattage power amps since you can really crank them up and allow their voicing to be more a part of your overall sound.

Getting a Professional Sound on a Modest Budget

Each week I get calls from all over the world from people who are planning to get one of our pro systems built for them, but, in the meantime, would like to know if they can get a good-sounding system without spending a lot of money. I tell them yes, if they know what to look for.

The more effects a piece of gear has inside of it and the more effects it can do simultaneously, the better chance the quality and/or options on how to use that effect will be limiting—*unless* that multieffects unit is a high-end product that'll cost you top dollar.

You need to know that when you put all your eggs in one basket for your sound—like having only one piece of gear that you want to do everything—you're also at the mercy of two things out of your control: the possibility of something going wrong with that piece of gear, and getting that gear manufacturer's idea of what they think a chorus or a delay should sound like. As many people have found, it may be very different from what your ears tell you sounds better.

If a company is selling a unit that'll do 10 effects at once and it's priced at 200 dollars, for the most part you're simply not going to get the best-quality and realistic-sounding effect. The company has to cut costs somewhere in the manufacturing to be able to give you all those goodies at such a low price. And many of them cut costs in the processing system—the very thing you don't want to be compromised.

If you're looking to go the cheaper route, I say stick to the basic sound groups—delay, reverb, compressor, chorus, vibrato, flanger, overdrive—and get a unit, from a good company, that does these things well. You might want to add a wah-wah pedal and another distortion/overdrive pedal. That should give you the basic tools to get you on the road to getting your sound. And remember: Nobody says you have to turn everything on at once. Pick and choose what sounds best to you and focus your sound around those effects [or no effects].

Going the Custom Route

If you go the custom route, that is, having us design your sound system, the kind of service you'll get will be the same, regardless of whether you spend a little money or a lot. The only differences are the size of the system, how elaborate it is, and what kind of tools it's going to take to realize the sounds you need to get. When we're building your system, you're talking directly to me and not to anyone else, and you and I will be the only ones who'll design your system.

For example, I'll build the hardware components, such as a rack-mount audio router/controller and the foot controller that controls it, and all of your effects and amps plug into this audio router—or several audio routers, depending upon the size of the system. This would be the basic building blocks from which we would create your rig.

Now you can take all of that hardware home with you and wire it up yourself, but no one does it better than us when it comes to designing, wiring, and interfacing all the various products you have, because this is all we do. That's why the pro players come to us and stay with us.

Back in the '80s, we were building giant rigs for pro players because there were certain kinds of gear that only did one thing and the player had to have that piece of gear. As you can imagine, putting all those unique pieces of gear into a system required a big system.

Things have changed. While we still build elaborate rigs for people who use them as their "A rig," we'll also build them a smaller version of that huge system for fly dates and road gigs. The cartage and freight of shipping these monsters around the world can be costly, and having a smaller, lighter, and more portable version is the ideal solution for a lot of people.

When it comes to sound, keep in mind that you're dealing with little input signals [i.e., -20 decibels or less from a guitar). You have to amplify it through screaming amps with tons of gain, and it's all an unbalanced circuit, which means there's all kinds of room for noise and other things you don't want to have going on.

Everything you get from us is hand-built and made to order.

Although we do have off-the-shelf products, such as the RS-10 MIDI foot controllers, most switching systems and products are built on a per-order basis. Each piece is built for each player and the player's needs. One of the things we do is take the music gear you have, go inside of it, and configure and program things to help you get your sound. When your rig leaves our shop, it will be a one-of-a-kind unique piece of gear that you will own, built entirely to your specifications, based on our circuit designs. We build tools; we don't build toys.

Twenty Great Ways to Get Great Sounds

I did sound system variations for Andy Summers [guitarist for The Police], whereby we designed a looping system when he toured by himself. Since it was only Andy, he needed to create real-time loops on stage by using his effects and then playing against them. And we didn't do it with loop devices, but by using infinite holds on delays. Today, there are lots of looping effect devices—Boomerang, Lexicon Jam Man, Oberheim Echoplex, Electrix Repeater, and others—that can do Andy's looping sounds.

For years, the pros had monitors on stage and that was their only way of hearing the sound and the band mix. Today, that's changed. With the advent of in-ear monitors, the pro players are very meticulous about being able to play on stage the sounds they used on every one of their records. And the guy who is taking creating record sounds live further than most is The Edge from U2. Every sound he has played, on every record he's ever done, needs to be recreated live on stage. Let me tell you how tough this can be.

We're talking about being able to create sounds, on records, with equipment he used 20 or more years ago [like a Korg SDD-3000] that spans U2's entire career. Lots of loops [more than 24 in a series chain], lots of programming, lots of effects, buffers in the signal path to keep the guitar signal sounding its best, a sound that must be quiet when switched off, and it's got to sound like he had plugged straight into his amp, with all of it going through a signal path that takes everything into the front end of a Vox AC-30 amp. We're talking 2-hour sound checks here.

Before in-ear monitors, there were lots of monitor/speaker sweet spots depending upon where you were standing or sitting when you played. Now you can't escape your sound and there are no sweet spots. What's coming out of your amp is what you hear in your ears and there's no running away from it like when they used to move away from a screaming Marshall stack. That's why it's important that you have the best-quality effects you can afford—effects that are quiet, switchable, programmable, and will give you the greatest possibilities for using combinations of those effects to create your sound.

Here's a list of 20 tips for getting your own great sound.

1. Use the highest-quality cable you can afford, because cable can make a big difference in your sound. Cabling is the pipeline from your instrument of music creation to recording or amplification.

2. Always use some type of buffering in the signal path if your cable coming from your instrument is more than 20 feet long. It will help preserve the instrument's original tone before it gets to the amplifier.

3. Keep the signal path as short as possible, with the least amount of effects in between your instrument and the amp. The most critical link in the sound system is between your instrument and the input of the amp, whether it's a power amp, preamp, or an instrument into an amp with pedals. There's nothing more pure than to be able to put your effects into a looping system that allows you to get them out of the signal path whenever you desire. The way we design our systems, not only do we bypass the effects, we also bypass the cabling connected to the effects, which allows us to take a lot more than just the effects out of the signal path. And everything you take out of the signal path helps to eliminate yet another connection that could create noise and/or problems.

4. When miking speaker cabinets, you can't go wrong with a Shure SM-57 up against the grill, although there are many other choices available. However, having a little "air" on things, giving the sound some room to "breathe," and keeping the mics not so close to the speakers also works great.

5. Multiple miking [i.e., close/off-axis/back of the cabinet], using different kinds of mics—that create phase shifting—can either be a good thing or a not so good thing, depending on what sounds good to your music.

6. Listen to the sound source and put your head and ears near the speaker [not when playing at loud volumes] where the sound is going to come out. When you find a "sweet spot" on that speaker that sounds good, put a mic there. Same thing when using a room mic. Get on a ladder and put your head where the microphone is going to go. Once you find a great-sounding place, put a mic there. Experiment with different mics, distances, angles, and positions. I've never heard any direct recording music that sounded convincing to me. There's nothing better than miked speakers to faithfully reproduce sounds, especially your sound.

7. If you're new to multiple effects and/or pedals, or combining things, remember that anything goes. When using a single effect, the order isn't an issue, but when you combine other pedals and multiple effects, where they are placed does become important. Give the following a try.

8. Put envelope filters and octave boxes first, because they work best when they receive a good, clean, pure signal. Then add overdrives and distortion boxes. Now add wah pedals, phasers, chorus, and tremelo. Finally, add in reverbs and delays.

9. If a volume pedal is used, I typically place it as far down the effects chain as possible, but just prior to the reverbs and delays. The reason? When you pull your volume back, the reverbs and delays will naturally decay.

10. This order holds true regardless of whether you're using pedals into an amplifier or rack-mount gear-type configuration with preamps and power amps and effects in between them.

11. When it's a preamp/power amp type configuration, and if there is compression and such involved as well, I like to keep the volume pedals as far down the path as possible, but just prior to the reverbs and delays, so that things that may be threshold-sensitive [like compressors, gates, and noise-reduction units], aren't affected by the volume fluctuation.

12. If you're using pedals, I like the wah and volume pedals to come after the distortions. Here's why. Let's say you've got an amplifier and you've got it set for a certain amount of crunch, but you like your volume pedal to clean that up a little bit, since by pulling your volume back, you're essentially using the volume pedal like an extension of the volume knob on your guitar.

13. If you put the volume pedal a little further down the effects chain, but after the distortions, now you've got another level in which you can help create your crunch. In other words, if your guitar signal comes out full volume and hits your distortion boxes, the distortion boxes then hit your volume pedal, the volume pedal then hits your amplifier, you've now got a wide range of adjustments in being able to control the amount of gain stages going to end the result—the input of your amplifier. The end result is you've got a healthy signal hitting your distortion boxes with your guitar wide open, your volume pedal will pull that amount of crunch back hitting the input of your amplifier, and if the distortions are not on, then the volume pedal can be used the same way to help clean up the sound of the amplifier.

14. Typically, people who wire their pedal boards do so in the most convenient fashion, such as plugging into a wah pedal first and then adding the rest of the effects from there. However, if you move the wah pedal and let your distortion boxes come first, and you combine the distortions with the wah, it gives the wah a thicker and more harmonically rich signal to filter. To me, the wahs sound better when they're hit by a distorted signal, rather than a clean one. Again, anything goes, and all these tips are just my personal preferences.

15. It's important to have some form of buffering/impedance matching on your pedal board, even if your pedal board has true-bypass switching. Regardless if all your pedals have true-bypass switching and you're playing a passive instrument [like a guitar], a cumulative capacitive buildup is going to occur. The flow of your signal from guitar to amp still passes through every cable, every effect and its switches, and the end result is it's going to suck your tone just like it would if you were using a 100-foot cable.

16. Find out what devices in your signal path are sensitive to any low-impedence buffer output. Often, discrete and germanium transistor—type fuzz boxes don't like to use a buffered signal. They work better with the high-output impedence of the instrument. One solution to try is to use any active pedal as a good buffer and put any active pedals—like any of the BOSS pedals including the BOSS TU-12 Tuner or Ibanez TS-9 Tube Screamer type pedals, since they are buffered and are active bypass—after these distortion boxes, and let your high-impedance instrument, like a guitar, feed the inputs.

17. To find out if any of your pedals has a hardwire bypass [not true 100 percent bypass], plug your guitar into the pedal and plug the pedal into an amp. Then pull out the pedal battery. If you have no sound, then you've got an active bypass pedal. If it does have sound when it's in the bypass mode, it's at least a hardwire bypass.

18. If you have a rack-type system, be aware of the placement of certain types of gear. Keep the more sensitive high-gain-type devices—like preamps or low-level signal devices—away from other devices that have power transformers in them that could radiate hum fields and magnetic interference. I like to keep preamps away from power amps because a power amp often generates more hum than practically any other piece of equipment due to its large power transformers.

19. Take note of which side of the effects box the internal power transformer is on by looking at which side the power cable comes out. For example, you wouldn't want to put a preamp that has its input on the left side next to or close to any effects devices that has its power cable coming out the same side. The idea is to keep them physically apart, with the transformer of one and the input of the other on opposite sides.

20. Try using isolation transformers [available from companies like Furman or Custom Audio Electronics] to break ground loops rather than AC ground lifting devices. It's okay to use an AC ground lifting device in a multicomponent system as long as one device in the rack is grounded to ensure safety and proper shielding.

Website: www.customaudioelectronics.com

Finding the Best Recording and Creating Platform:

Using What the Pros Use

I think you're going to like this lesson because it's going to give you lots of information about great recording tools that can do more to put you on the same playing field as the music industry pros than anything else. In essence, you're going to be using many of the same tools they're using. It's *how* you use them that'll help you to create your signature sound (along with, of course, the tips you received from Bob Bradshaw) and perhaps open doors for you in the business.

This is a big lesson, and we're going to cover it by breaking the discussion down into six sections:

1. The system hub: Your computer

2. The computer–audio interface

3. Digital audio workstations (DAWs)

4. Plug-ins

5. Outboard gear, controllers, and mixers

6. Storage systems

Please keep in mind that it's important for you not to get locked into thinking there's only one or a few ways of using all of the equipment I'll be telling you about. The ideal way to use any technology—old or new technology—is to pick and choose from among them carefully. Use analog hardware equipment in tandem with digital audio equipment to create something that says, "This is me. This is my sound."

And by all means, don't think that once you get any (or all) of these great tools you must become an island unto yourself, with no outside involvement, influence, or inspiration. Most of the producers and musicians I know use their home studios to work on new ideas, which includes having others send them hard disks of music projects so that they can lay down guitar, percussion, key and synth parts, produce remixes, add sound textures, and do anything else needed to help create the finished product. I like to think of it as the great hard disk swap and it makes collaborating with others lots of fun.

Along with that, many of these studio pros will take their hard disk(s) with all their digital audio workstation (DAW) and plug-in data on them to a bigger studio that has compatible equipment and finish overdubbing and mixing before the final product is ready to be mastered.

Your Computer: The Hub of Your System

In the new music business, the brains, hub, and centerpiece of your recording studio is your computer. Creating, recording, editing, and mixing with a computer is the way a lot of music is made today. While big studios, big consoles, bulky tape machines, and racks of analog and digital outboard gear were once the key, today's key—and probably tomorrow's as well—is a personal computer. You can simply do more things musically with a computer than you can without one.

We're about to get into debatable territory here. That is, which computer should you use for recording? Both platforms (Mac and Windows-based PCs) have their die-hard devotees, and I'll tell you about great music software along with ways you can use both. And if you really want to know which platform more music pros use, I have the answer for you.

For years, I've been a PC/Windows kind of guy. It was the first operating system I learned on, and it's been what I've used to write all of my books, including this one. I still think my PC is great. However, the operating system of choice of serious professionals who make their living and reputation creating music is the Mac (at least for music production).

The PC is still the most popular consumer computer; it outsells Mac by a wide margin. But you'll find Macs being used in very demanding environments. When I was the editor of a major health and fitness magazine, all of the layout designers and creatives used a Mac. For high-demand processing power applications, a Mac can do everything your PC does and better.

The Mac has always had plenty of loyal fans who love its innovations and user-friendly operating system. In the music world, third-party developers typically create innovative state-of-the-art software technologies for the Mac before creating them for any other type of computer platform. Why? Because when it comes to music, the majority of people who create the hits use Macs. Also, you can run Windows on a Mac, as well as share files between a Mac and a Windows-based PC.

In the years I've been in the music business and around those who produce music and artists for major labels, I've found that the Mac is either the main computer system that their studio is built around, or is part of their Pro Tools and other computer recording workstation rack rigs, or is their laptop portable studio. These people get paid big money to make records. They also pay big money to the studios and musicians for sessions. And when there's so much money involved, the people and equipment (especially the often-joked-about "fickle computer") have got to be rock-solid and reliable. While no computer platform or manufacturer can claim 100 percent reliability, the Mac comes awfully close.

The digital revolution has changed the way the music business operates. Who would've thought that the computer would become such an important piece of equipment for musicians creating music? Lots of artists and musicians use a Mac onstage to run their rigs, trigger sounds, or create amazing music live and on the fly. Some call it their second instrument. But while guitarists are likely to have lots of back-up guitars in the event their strings break or something else goes wrong, you don't see many musicians with back-up Mac iBooks or Powerbooks. There's got to be a good reason for this.

Now I'm not going to tell you that the Mac is the only computer you should have. I have both a Mac and a Windows-based PC. In fact, a couple of key pieces of amazing software technology I'll recommend in this lesson (e.g., TASCAM's GigaStudio and Sonic's DVD Producer and ReelDVD) are on Windows/PC platforms, not to mention the many plug-ins, virtual instruments, samplers, and DAWs that can be used on both Windows-based PCs and Macs.

I'm simply saying that if you want to get smart about creating and recording in the new music business, you need to be thinking about using *both* the PC and the Mac. Having those two will allow you to maximize your possibilities and abilities to create in ways you may never have imagined possible. If it's not in your budget right now to have both a Mac and PC, my recommendation is to start with a Mac. Once you have it, we need to take you to the next step, and that's hooking you up with a computer-audio interface.

Your Computer-Audio Interface

Think of your computer-audio interface as the terminal where the outside world of audio meets the inside world of recording and processing. For example, audio interfaces allow you to take the analog signal from a guitar or from effects and then convert that analog signal to digital (A/D) and vice versa, from digital to analog (D/A), so it can be used by your computer's music software (DAWs, plug-ins, etc.) and hardware. There are lots of companies that make interfaces, ranging from those that cost a couple of hundred dollars to the higher-end gear (such as Apogee) that can cost $2,000 and up.

I'm assuming you want to keep costs to a minimum and features to a maximum, so in continuing our biggest bang for the buck musical crusade, let me tell you about one interface that'll be terrific for your music projects—both in the studio and out on the road: the 828mkII, made by MOTU (Mark of the Unicorn). The 828mkII gives you what you need to turn your computer into a powerful 24-bit 96-kHz DAW. As a computer interface, it provides 20 separate inputs and 22 outputs, including 10 channels of pristine 96-kHz analog recording and playback, combined with eight channels of ADAT digital input/output (I/O) and stereo S/PDIF (Sony/Phillips digital interface format), and separate main outs and headphone out. (Alesis's ADAT, which is the industry standard interface for multichannel audio, allows transfer of 8 channels of digital audio over one fiber-optic cable. S/PDIF links digital audio equipment together by using fiber-optic, unbalanced, or high-impedance coaxial cables.) The two mic/guitar/instrument inputs feature analog, preamplified sends which allow you to insert your outboard EQ, compressor, guitar amp, reverb, or other effects processor before the signal goes digital. You have the choice of using any of its inputs as a return.

You can add additional send/return loops using its CueMix DSP on-board mixing feature, which is a digital signal processing (DSP)–driven 20-input 8-bus mixing and monitoring matrix that eliminates the need for an external mixer or patchbay. This means you can connect all your studio gear, including microphones, guitars, synths, keyboards, drum machines, and even effects processors. You can then monitor all of these live inputs via the 828mkII's main outs, headphone jack, or any other output, with virtually no monitoring latency and no processor drain on your computer. You can create separate monitor mixes for the main outs, headphones, and other outputs, and then control everything from the CueMix Console software (which is included) or directly from the 828mkII's front panel.

Many musicians take this piece of gear on the road because it can also function as a stand-alone mixer with no computer required. You can tweak your mix by using the 828mkII's backlit LCD and front-panel controls. Every 828mkII setting can be accessed from the front panel.

For your studio needs, the 828mkII comes with eight channels of ADAT optical digital I/O, plus stereo S/PDIF, and its all-digital I/O connections support standard sample rates up to 96 kHz. The 828mkII includes 16 channels of MIDI input and output via the FireWire connection to the computer. Setup is easy: Simply plug in your FireWire cable and both MIDI and audio are ready to go. (FireWire was developed by Apple as a cross-platform implementation of three IEEE standards covering high-speed data transfer between computers and peripheral devices. For more on FireWire, see page 180) You can connect any MIDI device, such as a controller keyboard, synth module, automated control surface, or drum machine. And timing is sample-accurate with supporting software.

The 828mkII is compatible with Mac OS 9, Mac OS X (version 10.2 or later),

Windows Me/2000/XP, and your favorite audio software and host-based effects via WDM/ASIO/Core Audio/Sound Manager drivers. You can even use the included AudioDesk workstation software for Macintosh, with 24-bit recording/editing and 32-bit mixing/processing/mastering.

For more information on the 828mkII go to www.motu.com.

Digital Audio Workstations (DAWs)

How should I record my music? Boy, has that question been asked untold number of times. It used to be that you needed the services of a recording studio to do it. Those $250,000 multitrack recorders and half-million-dollar recording consoles sure sounded good, but the hefty price tags put them way beyond many musicians' budgets.

Along came the personal computer. The first personal computers were expensive and lacked power and features. But, like all emerging technology, they soon became faster, better, and cheaper. And so did the software and hardware from the companies who created products for them. Music recording is a prime example.

Pro Tools and MOTU Performer were among the first major products embraced by the professional music community. Both offered sophisticated recording, mixing, and editing capabilities, as well as an alternative to outboard gear, large studio consoles, and analog and digital tape. As far as digital tape recording goes, Alesis's ADAT was a major innovation, but it was simply a cheaper way to record to digital tape, and it offered no extensive effects, composing, and editing capabilities.

Since then, much has changed—and for the better. The kinds of music you can create; the myriad ways you can create, mix, master, and edit it; the surround sound capabilities; the seamless merging of audio to video; and the vast number and types of plug-in effects and instruments, all controlled through your home computer and accessed by the click of a mouse, are astonishing. Never in the history of music making have you been able to do so much for so little.

If you want to get serious about your music, you need to start using the DAW platforms that the pros use in almost every major studio in the world. They've been extensively tested, they're reliable, and they produce outstanding results.

To make things simple, I've asked the recording software companies I'm featuring in this lesson for the features of their products. Why features? Because whenever I look for new gear, I want to first know about its features. The more features a product has that fit with your musical goals, needs, and budget, the more benefits you'll be able to reap from using it. While software versions can and do change, key features for the most part do not.

When deciding on which DAWs to use, my advice is to give the following a good read, then click on the Web site of the company whose product interests you most.

There you'll find more in-depth information about the product, who uses it and how, helpful tips on how you can use it, and much more. Follow up by going to the nearest music store that carries the DAW that interests you and get some hands-on experience by trying it out. And always get the recording and creating platform that's right for *your* needs, without regard as to which hot star is using it.

Digidesign Pro Tools

Look in the liner notes of many of your favorite albums and there's a good chance you'll see credits for Pro Tools. For many years now, Pro Tools systems have been used by top producers and in studios everywhere. The higher-end Pro Tools HD systems are very expensive, but there are three much lower-priced alternatives, Digi 002, the Digi 002 Rack, and the Mbox (for mobile recording).

All three feature the essentials of Pro Tools software, but are stripped down a tad from their higher-priced cousins. And, once you've mastered one of them you can either move up to the higher-end products yourself or take the Pro Tools sessions you've recorded and go into any major recording studio that has one of the Pro Tools HD systems and transfer your work for more recording, mixing, effects, editing, and mastering options—a good idea if you're wanting to use all that great expensive gear without having to dish out the bucks to buy it.

Digi 002. Working with your computer through a single FireWire connection, Digi 002 pairs Pro Tools LE software with an integrated control surface. You can record, edit, process, mix, and master your projects, and then take Digi 002 to a gig and use it as an 8x4x2 digital mixer complete with EQ, dynamics, delay, and reverb with snapshots. Getting a Digi 002 system up and running involves a straightforward five-step process:

1. Load the Pro Tools LE software onto your computer.
2. If you have a Mac, connect the computer to the Digi 002 unit with the included FireWire cable. (PC users first need to purchase a compatible FireWire card.)
3. Power up Digi 002.
4. Connect your signal sources (mics, instrument cables, patch cords, etc.) to the I/O on the back of Digi 002.
5. Launch Pro Tools LE software. At this point, you're ready to go. Your audio and MIDI information travel back and forth between your computer and Digi 002 via the FireWire cable, along with information generated by or returned to the Digi 002 control surface. Any changes you make via your Pro Tools software interface are reflected on the control surface and vice versa.

Digi 002 includes two modes of operation: Pro Tools mode and Standalone mode. With the push of a button, the Digi 002 unit enters Standalone mode and becomes an 8x2 digital mixer, complete with four effects sends (two internal, two external), EQ, dynamics, effects, and snapshots. Pro Tools LE is disabled in this mode, and your computer is no longer needed for Digi 002 to operate.

Once you've routed your audio and MIDI signals via Digi 002's I/O, and created a session to build and manage your project, you can create from beginning to end in a fully self-contained environment. The Digi 002 workstation has the following features:

* FireWire connectivity (no PCI card required)
* Eight touch-sensitive, motorized faders
* Eight motion-sensitive rotary encoders used for pan/send/meter/ plug-in control
* Ten scribble strips for track name, pan, send, fader, plug-in values, and time-line position
* Eight analog inputs, eight analog outputs
* Four mic preamps with individual gain and high-pass filter; 48-V phantom power enabled on channel pairs
* Eight channels of ADAT optical I/O, two channels of S/PDIF I/O
* Outputs 1 and 2 mirrored on $\frac{1}{4}$-inch TRS monitor output (with dedicated volume control) and RCA-based—10-dBV fixed output
* MIDI I/O: 1 IN port, 2 OUT ports (16 channels IN/32 channels OUT)
* 24-bit 96-kHz A/D and D/A converters
* Standalone mode: 8x4x2 digital mixer with EQ, dynamics, effects
* Alternate source input for direct monitoring of 10-dBV audio equipment (tape players, CD players, etc.)
* Headphone output with dedicated volume-control knob included
* Transport control

Digi 002's Pro Tools LE software enables you to record and play back up to 32 tracks of audio at sample rates of up to 96 kHz. As soon as audio enters Pro Tools, it's in a 24-bit signal path. Coming or going, the sound involved with your sessions goes through high-quality signal converters (A/D and D/A). You can also determine the bit rate and sample resolution quality of your audio.

You can use either Digi 002's control surface or the Pro Tools LE software interface to tweak every component of your mix. They share information, so what you do on one is instantly reflected on the other. As your computer's processor crunches mixing data, you guide the mixing process via either the Pro Tools LE user interface, the Digi 002 control surface, or both. However you choose to operate,

Digi 002 and Pro Tools LE software give you a variety of methods to control and automate your mix, all within a nondestructive, recovery-friendly environment.

Pro Tools LE's MIDI environment gives you full and simple control over the MIDI components of your projects. It supports the import, creation, and export of MIDI data, as well as extensive MIDI editing and manipulation capabilities. The software gives you full integration of Mac OS X's Core MIDI Services as well as MIDI Time Stamping, Groove Quantize, Restore Performance, and many others.

Many people swear by Pro Tools' editing capabilities, and just as with Pro Tools TDM software (the kind used in the higher-end Pro Tools HD systems), a single screen within the Pro Tools LE interface—the Edit window—enables you to adjust literally every aspect of both audio and MIDI data at sample-level resolution. You can trim waveforms, reprocess regions of audio, pitch-correct a compromised performance, replace drum sounds, and rearrange song sections, and Pro Tools' nonlinear approach to editing enables you to try your choices without having to commit to them.

Plug-ins, those add-on software-based tools that work in conjunction with Pro Tools, are the key to the effectiveness of the platform. Plug-ins facilitate and embody everything from dynamics to effects to sound design, often improving upon the hardware counterparts and equivalents that many emulate. To use plug-ins, you simply activate them within the Pro Tools interface. At that point, you are free to employ presets, customize settings, and/or automate a given plug-in's activity within a mix. Unlike outboard gear, you can use your plug-ins on multiple tracks, with multiple settings.

Pro Tools LE-compatible plug-ins take two forms: Real-Time AudioSuite (RTAS) plug-ins and AudioSuite plug-ins. The former are host-based processors, using the computer's processing power to do their job. Functionally, RTAS plug-ins offer many of the real-time benefits of TDM plug-ins. They are fully automatable, their parameters can change in real time, and their effects are not permanently written to the audio file. Since they are host-based, RTAS plug-ins require trade-offs between track and plug-in count, edit density, and amount of mix automation in a session.

AudioSuite plug-ins provide file-based processing; that is, they process or alter the sound file and create a new file with the processed sound. The resulting effect is applied to the entire file. AudioSuite plug-ins are great for conserving DSP power and certain types of processing where there is no real-time benefit or application, such as normalization and noise reduction.

In addition to providing an excellent recording, editing, and mixing environment, Digi 002 also affords you the opportunity to add the finishing touches to your projects through mastering. Editing capabilities and plug-ins used in conjunction with the Pro Tools LE software interface enable you to make the necessary fine adjustments to your final mix to achieve the right combination of warmth, presence, and balance. Alternatively, there are many off-the-shelf options available for producing Red Book–compatible CDs from final Pro Tools mixes.

Digi 002 Rack. Digi 002 Rack is a FireWire-based Pro Tools solution that gives you all the features of Digi 002 (minus the control surface) in a portable 2U rack-mountable unit.

It's a single-box design that includes a single FireWire (or 1394) connection to handle the exchange of information to and from your computer, so you just plug in and go. Along with the included Pro Tools LE software, Digi 002 Rack provides the means to create your music with 24-bit clarity and up to 96-kHz sample-rate support. Digi 002 Rack's analog, digital, and MIDI capabilities enable it to handle a wide variety of I/O configurations, while dedicated monitor and headphone outputs allow you to hear how everything is sounding. The Digi 002 Rack has the following features:

* FireWire connectivity
* Eight analog inputs, eight analog outputs
* Four mic preamps with individual gain and high-pass filter; 48-V phantom power enabled on channel pairs
* Eight channels of ADAT optical I/O or two channels of S/PDIF I/O
* Outputs 1 and 2 mirrored on ¼-inch TRS monitor output (with dedicated volume control) and RCA-based—10-dBV fixed output
* MIDI I/O: 1 IN port, 2 OUT ports (16 channels IN/32 channels OUT)
* 24-bit 96-kHz A/D and D/A converters
* Alternate source input for direct monitoring of 10-dBV audio equipment (tape players, CD players, etc.)
* Headphone output with dedicated volume-control knob included
* Footswitch for QuickPunch control
* 2U rack-mountable chassis

Digi 002 Rack with Pro Tools LE software supports RTAS and AudioSuite plug-in formats on Windows XP and Mac OS.

Mbox. Mbox, Pro Tools' mobile recording solution for those on the go, is a two-channel universal serial bus (USB) audio peripheral specifically engineered to give you precision sound in a very small, portable package. Powered by Pro Tools LE software, Mbox integrates audio and MIDI recording, editing, and real-time mixing. The USB connection both powers your Mbox and manages audio data transactions between Mbox and your computer.

Mbox's Pro Tools LE software enables you to simultaneously record and play backup to 32 tracks of audio at sample rates of up to 48 kHz. As soon as your audio enters Pro Tools, it provides a 24-bit signal path until it leaves via your Mbox. Coming or going, the sound involved with your sessions also benefits from high-quality A/D and D/A signal converters.

As with the Digi 002, getting your Mbox system up and running is quick and easy. First, you load your Pro Tools LE software onto your computer, then you connect your Mbox to the computer with the provided USB cable. After you connect signal sources (mics, instrument cables, patch cords, etc.) to your Mbox, you launch Pro Tools LE software and you're ready to go.

The hardware features of the Mbox, which are designed for high-quality mobile recording, include:

* Two analog inputs and outputs, featuring Focusrite mic preamps
* 24-bit signal path from input to output
* 24-bit stereo S/PDIF digital I/O (RCA)
* Separate source selection (MIC/LINE/INST) and gain control per channel
* 48-V phantom power
* Hi-Z input for instrument pickup
* Two analog TRS inserts
* Zero-latency monitoring
* Balanced/unbalanced connections
* Headphone output with dedicated volume control
* 100 percent USB-powered (passive USB hubs not supported)
* Pro Tools LE software (supporting DigiStudio)

Mbox system with Pro Tools LE currently supports RTAS and AudioSuite plug-in formats on Windows XP and Mac OS.

For more information on Digi 002 and Mbox go to www.digidesign.com.

MOTU Digital Performer

Mark of the Unicorn, Inc., now called MOTU, was one of the first big players to hit the computer recording scene. MOTU's Digital Performer is an integrated digital audio and MIDI sequencing production system for Mac that provides a comprehensive environment for editing, arranging, mixing, processing, and mastering multitrack audio projects for a wide variety of applications.

Digital Performer allows you to simultaneously record and play back multiple tracks of digital audio and MIDI data in a totally integrated environment. Its sequencer and nondestructive digital audio editing capabilities provide you with lots of flexibility and control over the audio you create. Digital Performer does not place restrictions on the number of audio and MIDI tracks you can work with; that number is limited only by what your computer can handle. Digital Performer supports a wide range of audio hardware including TDM (Pro Tools), Direct I/O, ASIO, Sound Manager, and MOTU audio interfaces, all in high-resolution 24-bit 192-kHz audio.

Digital Performer provides mono, stereo, and surround (n-channel) tracks. The maximum number of tracks you can play back at a time depends primarily on the speed of your hard drive and the amount of RAM you have. For example, 64 megabytes and a reasonably fast hard drive should provide 16 to 20 independent tracks of audio. The Bounce to Disk feature gives you an unlimited number of audio tracks by letting you nondestructively combine them into a single track or stereo track pair. Even if you need to hear 100 audio tracks at one time, it's no problem.

Digital Performer allows you to view your MIDI and audio tracks in a single, unified mixer. You can configure up to 20 effects inserts per audio channel and 32 stereo busses. Everything is automatable, including effects parameters with five advanced automation modes, beat-synchronized effects, and sample-accurate editing of automation data. The automation system features a set of user interface technologies, such as event flags for discrete events and spline tools for manipulating control points. Automation parameters are displayed in meaningful real-world values such as decibels and milliseconds, and not arbitrary values like 0—127.

Digital Performer's Mixing Board window gives you a virtual mixing console on your computer screen. You can ride faders and knobs during playback to record automated mixes. You can create snapshots of the entire mixer—or any portion of it—anywhere in your sequence with the click of a button. You can save your fully automated mixdown for instant recall at any time and then create an unlimited number of alternative mixdowns, all of which are then also available from the Mixing Board menu for instant recall. And you can create fader automation groups with any fader as the master.

Each track has its own solo, mute, and automation enable/disable buttons, allowing you to instantly create customized board layouts, such as drag track strips anywhere you like, and show or hide any combination of tracks (or even mixer sections, for example, inserts), all with the click of a mouse. You can save and recall any number of custom Mixing Board configurations—for example, assigning tracks to plug-ins and MOTU MIDI effects processors for real-time output processing. Faders can respond to control surfaces or any MIDI controller, such as a volume slider or pedal, modulation wheel, or any data slider—even the physical sliders already on your synths.

Digital Performer includes dozens of real-time DSP effects with graphical controls and complete automation. You'll find 2-, 4-, and 8-band EQ; tube simulation and distortion effects; three reverbs; two noise gates, including one with real-time look-ahead gating; two compressors; a synthesizer-style multimode filter; echo and delay effects, including a surround delay, chorus, phaser, flanger, Sonic Modulator; and more.

Digital Performer also supports multiple processors (e.g., Mac G4 and G5), so if you have a dual-processor CPU, you can get nearly twice as much processing power as you could with a single processor. Digital Performer's multiple-processor engine is fully compatible with all MOTU audio system plug-ins, as well as those from third-party vendors.

Also included are dozens of real-time automatable 32-bit plug-ins, with graphical control, including reverb, dynamics processors, and EQ. Use the effects as an insert, on a single channel, or via a send/receive bus. The number of effects you can apply at any one time is limited only by the speed of your computer.

Digital Performer supports mono, stereo, and surround tracks. MOTU Audio System allows for effects with mono, stereo, or surround (n-channel) inputs and mono, stereo, or surround (n-channel) outputs. This enables the plug-in to do things like intelligent mono to stereo or surround effects, or to efficiently process power-hungry surround input to surround output configurations.

The editing features found on Digital Performer include a 24-bit waveform editor that allows you to zoom in to the sample level to see exactly what's going on in your audio. You can use the pencil tool to permanently remove clicks and pops from your audio files and edit sound-bite boundaries with single-sample accuracy. You have the option of viewing mono or stereo sound bites at any zoom setting you like. You can view and edit all your digital audio tracks in a single window.

Digital Performer can automatically apply cross-fades of any length you specify any time you cut, copy, paste, splice, or otherwise edit your audio files. It allows you to make edits quickly and efficiently without having to tediously return to each edit boundary and check for pops and clicks. You can graphically draw volume automation curves or pan sounds left to right. You can even do loop recordings as your music plays. It's simple to copy and paste regions to repeat verses or sound effects by dragging and dropping audio regions from the Soundbites window to any editing window for placement. All of these operations are nondestructive, so you can always revert back to your original recording should you change your mind.

Anyone who has used a destructive editor knows that at least 50 percent of your time is spent navigating and locating the part you want to edit. Digital Performer's waveform editor provides tools like scrubbing, jumping to selection or loop boundaries, and user-definable zoom levels. You can define a region of audio from your

Digital Performer project, edit it, trim the edges with sample-level precision, specify loop points, normalize, fade in and fade out, and send it to your sampler without ever leaving Digital Performer. All audio editing is accurate to a single sample. Edit MIDI with a resolution of 1/10,000,000 ppq (pulses per quarter). When used with a USB MOTU MIDI interface, Digital Performer provides MIDI timing resolution to within a single MIDI byte—under 0.33 millisecond.

For MIDI, multiple tracks can be edited and displayed in one window. The notes for each track are displayed in the track's color, and a track selector list is provided along the left edge of the window to show or hide tracks as desired. Some of MOTU's other MIDI features include:

* *Side-by-side display of MIDI and audio tracks.* The Sequence Editor window provides combined viewing and editing of MIDI notes, audio sound bites, audio automation, and MIDI controller data in one window along a single timeline.

* *Independent vertical zooming.* Both MIDI and audio tracks can be independently resized vertically. Many zoom shortcuts are provided, including the ability to enlarge one track and automatically scale all other tracks to fit in the window.

* *Movie track.* Digital Performer's Sequence Editor includes a QuickTime movie track that displays movie frames side by side with MIDI and audio data. More frames are displayed as you zoom in and fewer frames when you zoom out, so frames are never obscured by overlapping one another.

* *Complete MIDI graphic editing.* The Sequence Editor provides complete MIDI graphic editing in the same window with audio tracks. You can scale the vertical resolution and track height of each MIDI track on a per-track basis. For consistency, you can choose the break-point display of MIDI controller data to match the breakpoint automation in adjacent audio tracks.

With Multirecord MIDI recording, you can record on an unlimited number of MIDI tracks simultaneously. With three continuous controller editing modes, creating continuous controller streams for the automation of your MIDI instruments is flexible and intuitive. Movie track and Quicktime support integrates Digital Performer with the video world, enabling you to see instantly how your edits relate to the video images. Individually zoomable tracks, flexible window arrangement, and navigation tools allow for trouble-free manipulation within even the largest projects.

Digital Performer provides many flexible editors, including Sequence Editor, Graphic Editor, Event List, Drum Editor, and QuickScribe (notation). Whether you prefer list-editing or graphical style display; score layout or extensive drum programming; fine-tuning of single MIDI events or massive changes of entire sections, Digital Performer has an editor that will do what you need.

Its sampler integration allows you to transfer audio from your project to your sampler with a simple drag-and-drop operation. Because your sampler appears as a device inside Digital Performer, you can seamlessly share data. Digital Performer's PureDSP functions provide independent control over the duration and pitch of audio files with exceptional sound quality. You can tempo-conform drum loops, add vocal harmony, or even gender-bend vocal tracks.

Digital Performer offers a QuickScribe notation window that allows you to print out the whole score or individual parts. To help you follow the flow of your music, continuous scrolling moves the music under the wiper which stays fixed to the center of the window. The Adjust Beats feature lets you graphically drag beats and bar lines to line them up with MIDI note data—without changing how it plays back. The result is readable notation and time rulers that match your music.

Other QuickScribe features allow you to print individual parts and separately print each track by itself and choose a specific instrument transposition as well as a score transposition for each instrument. The QuickScribe notation window provides multistaff notation transcription of MIDI tracks for viewing, editing, and WYSIWYG printing.

When working with surround-sound applications, a single type of surround panner may not be appropriate for every application. Digital Performer provides a choice of four panner plug-ins, including a localizing room simulator. Each audio track can be assigned to any surround-sound format, from LCRS up to 10.2. Sophisticated panning movements can be automated using Digital Performer's automation system. You can also include complete surround submixes or record the output of a surround reverb with surround tracks.

Digital Performer's Audio Bundles window allows you to create "bundles" of inputs, outputs, and busses. For each bundle, you choose a name and a set of physical inputs or outputs on your audio interface, or a series of busses within Digital Performer's virtual mixing environment. Then the bundle appears by name throughout Digital Performer wherever I/O or bus assignments are made.

Bundles allows you to quickly rewire the internal routings of a project with a few mouse clicks, regardless of how many surround formats or other routing scenarios you use. You can create multiple output setups—from a simple, tape-deck-style "direct line out" mode to advanced surround configurations.

For more information on Digital Performer go to www.motu.com.

Emagic Logic

In the early 1990s, a German company, Emagic, developed a Mac-based computerized music production system called Logic, and it's been a hit ever since. At last count, it was in more than 250,000 commercial and private studios and that number keeps growing.

Emagic is now a part of the Apple computer family, and its innovative Logic continues to get glowing reviews for its user-friendliness, freely configurable interface, comprehensive MIDI and audio editing possibilities, and easy-to-use film and synch features.

Like Digital Performer, Logic offers superb sound quality with 32-bit signal processing, along with surround-sound digital mixer (up to 7.1), sample-accurate automation, and over 50 high-quality audio effect plug-ins. Logic can also be used with the higher-end Pro Tools HD systems with sample rates up to 192 kHz and 24-bit resolution.

Some of its features include QuickTime movie synchronization and DV Movie playback via FireWire. Along with that, you get a Video Thumbnail Track that you watch in the Arrange window as you're creating. You can utilize a virtually unlimited number of MIDI tracks. Logic gives you a Professional Score Editor that allows you to display your music notation in real time and easily create professional-looking score printouts.

You can also time-stretch audio and MIDI. Logic gives you Markers so that you can quickly jump to any location in your song, and it's capable of handling up to 255 stereo tracks, with 64 busses and 64 auxiliary tracks. You get 15 inserts, 8 sends per input, Audio Track, Aux Track, and Audio Instrument. A wide range of synchronization options allows Logic to connect easily to both the digital and analog worlds.

One of the many things people like about Logic is its ability to use lots of different audio interface hardware and software, like Core Audio, AV (SoundManager), EASI, ASIO, Digidesign DirectI/O and Audiowerk on Mac OS, and Digidesign's TDM system for ProTools hardware, including Surround. Logic incorporates a proprietary Emagic technology called AMT (Active MIDI Transmission). This ensures that MIDI timing is precise across all ports, even in the largest of MIDI systems. Literally hundreds of MIDI ports can be addressed, with MIDI data arriving simultaneously at each, no matter how dense the MIDI arrangement. For synchronization purposes, Logic will send and receive MIDI Clock, MTC, MMC, and word clock signals, making it a good choice for film, television, and postproduction facilities.

The Arrange window is Logic's primary workspace. Individual MIDI sequences and audio regions can be recorded, arranged, and edited, with audio and MIDI data handled in a virtually identical fashion. These audio and MIDI "objects" can be packed into nested folders for quick and easy song arrangement.

Tracks can be individually zoomed, soloed, or muted, and mixing of audio and

MIDI data is handled by its automation system. Markers can be created and recalled to quickly "jump" to any location in your songs, complete with production notes. Audio regions can be flexibly and easily managed. MIDI edits such as quantization, transposition, note length changes, and more are calculated in real time. Audio and MIDI objects can be resized, soloed, muted, looped, and mixed in the Arrange window in real time without stopping the sequencer. Logic features a track-based automation system found in the Arrange window. Automated parameters are displayed with full names and values for fast and optimal control over even complex automation tasks.

Logic's Score window is a MIDI editor that displays traditional music notation. It also provides layout functions which make it possible to create professional-quality score printouts quickly and easily. Logic's interpretation converts MIDI recordings to clear and legible sheet music in real time, without changing the original performance.

Notation can be edited with or without affecting the MIDI data. Score Styles offers immediate changes to the display of each sequence according to preset or user-defined staff formats. Note colors make parts in polyphonic score styles more legible. Instrument Sets allows you to save and print the entire score, individual parts, or any desired combination of instruments used in the composition. The Step input allows the computer keyboard to be used as a note typewriter.

Logic features a vast range of notation symbols, with optional use of third-party fonts (Sonata, Jazz, Swing fonts), fast lyric input aligned to notes, voice separation tool for polyphonic parts, graphic export of any desired part of a page, automatic guitar tab and drum notation, individual editing of note-head size and stem length, individual staff indents, cross-staff beaming, notation of alias sequences, and more.

Logic has a feature called The Environment that is your on-screen "flowchart" of the connected MIDI equipment, providing many creative options for visually combining software-based processing devices such as faders, arpeggiators, delays, and more. You can build remote controls for your MIDI gear, use a Mod Wheel to cross-fade between audio tracks, or create real-time instruments like step sequencers and rhythm generators.

Every song you create with Logic gives you up to 90 Screensets, which are customized combinations of edit windows. Each Screenset recalls the type of window(s) opened plus size, position, and zoom settings within each. Logic also features over 800 user-definable Key Commands. These are computer or MIDI keyboard shortcuts accessing almost every program function.

Logic is built for plug-ins. Its fully automated effects system offers the extensive Channel EQ, 8 sends and 8 inserts to 64 busses per audio track, with inserts and sends also available for audio instruments and live inputs. Insert effects to be used in inputs, tracks, instruments, busses, and outputs include Audio Units (AU) and Virtual Studio Technology (VST) (Mac OS 9), as well as over 50 built-in effects. These range from the traditional (e.g., dynamics, reverbs, and EQs) to unique sound sculpting tools (e.g., Autofilter or Spectral Gate) to mastering processors (e.g., the Multiband Compressor and Limiter). The optional EVOC20 provides vocoding and filter bank effects. All plug-ins operate at 32-bit resolution, making signal overloads virtually impossible and providing superb audio quality.

Logic also works well in the front end of a Pro Tools TDM-based system. It even includes surround capabilities. Depending on the configuration, up to 64 audio tracks and 64 busses are available. TDM plug-ins from all major developers can be used and fully automated. I/O inserts even allow the integration of external audio effect processors.

With Logic's Audio Instrument channels, you can use up to 64 software-based synthesizers and samplers, such as the Emagic ES1, ES2, EVP88, EXS24, Audio Unit, or VST2 instruments. You also get three audio instruments for basses, pads, and polyphonic sounds. Playback timing is sample-accurate. The audio output of external software instrument applications, such as Propellerhead's Rebirth and Reason, can be streamed into Logic's mixer via Propellerhead's ReWire, which gives you full access to Logic's effects and mixing facilities.

So you can really fine-tune your music, Logic offers linked editors. With them, you can view a composition in its entirety or select and make changes to the smallest detail with the Matrix, Event List, or Hyper Editors. The Stereo Sample Editor offers destructive manipulation of audio recordings, plus many DSP tools for creation, including time stretching and pitch shifting with formant correction. (*Formant* refers to any of several frequency regions of relatively high intensity in a sound spectrum, which together determine the characteristic quality of a vowel sound.)

For more information on Logic go to www.emagic.de.

Steinberg

Another German company, Steinberg, started making waves in the music world when they released Cubase and Nuendo. Their VST (Virtual Studio Technology) has revolutionized and simplified how music making is done. Although both Nuendo and Cubase can do many things, it might be helpful to think of Cubase as software for your basic recording, editing, and mastering needs and Nuendo as the go-to software for film, television, surround recording, editing, mixing, and mastering.

Nuendo. Nuendo, which works on both Mac and Windows platforms, is the DAW of choice for many in the music and media industry. It shines in audio production, composition, film, broadcast, music, postproduction, surround, game sound, and multimedia.

To start with, Nuendo lets you set up a project the way you want it. All program menus are user-configurable, enabling you to hide all features you seldom use or currently do not need for a specific kind of production. If you don't need MIDI functions for a 10.2 surround mix, you can hide all MIDI menu entries, disable the corresponding key commands, and assign these preferences to a template. If you're doing music production, but don't need video-related menu entries, you can hide them and design the interface that you need. All hidden features are still waiting in the background in case you need them in the future.

You can also configure the controls for each track to suit your personal way of working. If you are engaged in audio recordings, Nuendo can instantly be adapted as a pure audio tracker with only a record and a monitoring button on each track. After finishing your recordings, you can "unhide" additional functionality as it is needed or switch to a template which gives you immediate access to all track controls again.

Adding processing power to your project can easily be achieved with VST System Link. This technology is based on transmission of synch and transport commands via simple digital audio connections. It allows multiple computers to run in sample-accurate synch without the need for additional hardware. CPU-intensive tasks of larger projects, such as effect processing, video, or virtual instruments playback, can be outsourced to selected exclusive computers. Large projects can also be allocated to various computers in order to permit simultaneous playback of hundreds of audio and MIDI tracks from a range of different computers in sample-accurate synchronization.

Nuendo's networking capabilities allow teamwork on any kind of project, from postproduction to music, from multimedia to game sound design. This networking technology supports the full range of editing tools, over a network, on projects, audio, MIDI, and even video tracks. It allows users to connect multiple Nuendo workstation computers via standard LAN network cards. The system supports simple and fast connection of several stand-alone computers.

Complete management of access rights and user groups makes it simple to collaborate on large-scale projects. An entire project or selected tracks can be opened on multiple computers for other members of the network to access and edit. For example, after the first video copy has been placed in a master project template location, the sound editor and sound designers can begin preparing their tracks for mixing while additional recordings (such as music and dialog) are still being made. Once these are completed, additional editors can hook up to the same project template and add their work to it.

Throughout the entire course of building the final mix, the project owner has the ability to monitor the work in process and evaluate the quality of the sound. In a bigger production facility, Nuendo allows for central data management on a server. This enables multiple Nuendo workstations to access several projects, including all audio and video files and the company sound library. Editors can be freed from the process of data backup, which can instead be initiated by the system administrator. In a world of high-speed Internet connections, Nuendo workstations can even join a project via the Internet. It's perfect for the new music business.

One of the big reasons the pros love Nuendo is that from input to final mix, it's all about surround, with multichannel architecture through the entire signal path. Every input, audio track, effect, group, and output now offers up to 12 discrete channels, ready for full-scale 5.1, 7.1, or even 10.2 productions. To make routing in the project even more transparent, Nuendo organizes inputs and outputs, allowing the user to customize multichannel I/O configurations and switch between them with a single keystroke.

Several input and output busses can also be utilized at the same time, with any type of configuration possible—mono, stereo, or any of a wide range of surround formats—and any track can be routed to and from any of these busses. Nuendo even allows switching between multiple monitoring configurations (speaker arrangements) and can simulate a wide variety of end-user monitoring environments.

Nuendo offers a 32-bit floating-point mixer and features multiple multichannel I/O busses. This allows for recording in either split or interleaved surround audio file formats and makes managing a surround project easy, as Nuendo always keeps track of which part of the signal chain is multichannel and which is simply stereo or mono.

The mixer itself is user-configurable, allowing you to choose between a variety of display options. Above the normal mixer with the fader section you can display either insert effects, effects sends, EQs, or an additional view with I/O settings including gain change and phase shift per channel. In addition, the mixer is available in a narrow view for simultaneous display of many channels.

Unlimited processing of audio files is one of the greatest advantages of digital audio environments. Nuendo offers a huge list of audio processes, and it supplies you with a large collection of virtual effect processors, ranging from standard dynamic processing and filtering to creative modulation effects or restoration processors. If your project needs anything exotic or special, you can choose from a wide range of VST or DirectX plug-ins available from well-known manufacturers like TC, Native Instruments, or Waves. Of course, all of these plug-ins can be used both online or off-line. And you're able to load and use them as many times as your computer can handle.

If you are using MIDI, Nuendo allows you to create some truly unique sounds. Arpeggiators, chord processors, and many other plug-ins are included that manipulate the dynamics, pitch, and time elements of MIDI events. There are also three unique virtual instruments for creating warm analog layers or playing back powerful drum samples. The integration of the VST interface opens Nuendo up for additional software samplers like HALion Sampler, synthesizers like PLEX or D'cota, or other virtual instruments by third-party manufacturers.

Nuendo also features extensive MIDI capabilities. The large range of MIDI editors (e.g., Drum, Logical, SysEx, List) make editing MIDI information in Nuendo quite intuitive. The MIDI plug-ins are all directly reachable from the Project window. The Nuendo automation system extends to all MIDI parameters, letting you draw MIDI automation data with any of the mathematical shape tools. Multiple controller lanes within the editors give you a clear oversight over your MIDI data, as all data can now be displayed on the same page.

Many consider editing to be the backbone of any digital workstation, and Nuendo has a powerful editing engine, with unlimited undo/redo as a standard asset. You can undo cuts, fades, and other basic edits; bouncing and off-line processing can be undone; and complete tracks can be removed. The Edit History window lists all actions made on your project down to every single event, ready to undo or redo by moving a handle to the point where you want to work from.

Every single audio file listed in the pool or used in the Project window has its own off-line process history. All processing carried out on a file can be removed, changed, or replaced by another audio process or plug-in, no matter how much processing has taken place in the meantime. All later processes are reprocessed automatically for you. These lists of off-line processes can be stored as a batch, enabling you to apply the exact same process batch to any file you need to process later. This batch capability allows for adjustments of the parameters and easy storing of the altered batch settings.

Nuendo also supports various kinds of editing styles. Traditional cuts, nudging, trims, and fades can be made using a variety of object-based or range-based tools or using a jog wheel from any of the supported remote controllers. Mouse, keyboard, and remote control can be used separately or combined.

Nuendo allows scrubbing of all audio at the same time, as well as video-track scrubbing. Various forward and backward scrubbing speeds are supported, and can be executed from a specific wheel on the Nuendo transport bar or by the jog or shuttle wheel of a supported remote controller or mixing desk.

You can do all of the editing of your project in the sample-accurate Project window, which has a set of zooming features, or you can do it within the integrated sample editor. This opens an additional range of features permitting faster work flow, for example, easy creation of regions, bouncing regions into a library, creating processed regions, or tuning synch points by scrubbing the audio with them. Nuendo also features hit-point detection for fast locating of audio peaks, for adapting grooves, and for creating groove templates in the sample editor, which supports full drag and drop to tie up with the Project window.

Cubase SX. Musicians have told me that one of the many things they like about Cubase SX is that it has the ability to do off-line processing of individual audio files, which allows effects to be "stamped" onto them layer after layer. The off-line process history lets you jump back to any individual process, such as a reverb, and edit it, remove it, or replace it with any other effect you desire. Musicians also like the adaptive track mixer with automation that provides flexible routing options for surround-sound mixing and panning controls that allow them to mix any project to 5.1 surround format for DVD productions.

Perhaps the most popular feature of Cubase is its VST System Link. This feature allows you to use the power of several computers simultaneously regardless of platform, thereby giving you more recording power and options. As plug-ins get more complex and advanced in their abilities to create amazing sounds and effects, so do their demands for RAM and processing power. Many pros use two or more computers in their studios, with each being assigned a specific set of tasks and functions in the recording process. Here's how it works.

VST System Link is a system for networking computers using Steinberg VST software and Digidesign's Audio Stream Input Output (ASIO) hardware. VST System Link enables the transfer of synchronization, transport, and audio data between two or more workstations equipped with compatible software and hardware over standard digital audio cabling systems such as ADAT, TDIF (TASCAM Digital Interface), AES/EBU (Audio Engineering Society/European Broadcasting System) digital audio transfer standard, S/PDIF, etc. And because it uses the audio stream itself, synchronization is completely sample-accurate, even across multiple workstation configurations.

VST System Link uses a single bit of the audio stream as a carrier for transport and synchronization information, plus (optionally) other bits of the audio stream for MIDI information. Several computers can be linked in a daisy-chain configuration, each one passing on the accumulated information to the next via standard digital audio cables, with routing to the various systems controlled by a master software patchbay running on the first computer in the chain.

VST System Link can carry literally hundreds of MIDI channels down the one channel of a digital audio cable. Once you hook up your keyboard to the computer system via a standard MIDI interface, you won't need to use MIDI cables again. Any computer in a VST System Link network can be accessed from any other, so one keyboard can play any VST instrument loaded on to any of the other computers on the network. Don't have enough power to run eight synths on one computer? Then run some of them on another machine and access them just as if you had a hardware synth rack in your studio. Also, VST MIDI doesn't suffer from the same timing and bandwidth problems of traditional MIDI because VST MIDI has sample-accurate timing.

Since any audio stream can be sent to any machine, you can configure audio routing and processing in an almost infinite number of ways. This means you can run audio tracks on one computer, run virtual instruments on a second computer, do virtual effects processing on another computer, and mix it on a fourth computer. All you have to do is link their ASIO sound cards with the appropriate digital audio cables.

Cubase is simple to use on either Mac and Windows platforms, and you can easily network both Windows and Macintosh machines with VST System Link. The VST engine doesn't care which operating system is running; it just sends data via the cross-platform ASIO protocol. In addition, Nuendo and Cubase can be networked seamlessly together as one system.

If your laptop has some kind of digital I/O, you can network it transparently with your desktop computer. Someone using a Mac Titanium PowerBook for field recording can bring the machine into the studio, link it with the Windows machine there, and start working immediately, without needing to wait to transfer files or burn a CD. The two systems will automatically coexist as one.

The great thing about VST System Link is that it gets rid of the limitations of computer-based recording. It allows you to have and use unlimited numbers of simultaneous tracks and enormous amounts of virtual effects, as well as create incredible polyphony on virtual instruments. It also allows you to get around the "one person in front of the keyboard at a time" syndrome. Now several people can work on the same project at the same time, each in front of his or her own computer.

There are a number of ways you can use VST System Link and Cubase SX.

Music and audio postproduction is one of them. Several engineers and producers can work on different areas of the same project. One workstation can be configured to do sound effects, another can be doing dialogue editing, and another can be working on background music. Each machine can stream its output to the master mixing console, with all the streams being time-locked by VST System Link's synch protocol. Or they can all stream to yet another computer for virtual mixdown. Of course yet another machine can be used to run digital video in perfect synchronization too, with a lockup time of only a few milliseconds.

For recording music, one workstation can be the virtual tape machine and another can be dedicated to running virtual instruments. This allows the keyboard player to layer up huge synth sounds and samples on his or her own computer without affecting the tracking engineer's ability to record lots of audio tracks quickly. All the data from both of them can be locked together instantly, without having to run mounds of audio cables around the studio. One digital audio cable handles it all.

For mixing, one computer can be used as a virtual mixer and one as an effects rack, and a third can be running virtual instruments. The mixer station handles audio playback with lots of EQ and dynamics processing, virtual instruments run on a second machine, and then both audio and virtual synth tracks run together to the third computer for adding reverbs, flangers, etc. For huge mixes with lots of audio tracks, tracks can be split across computers to give a pseudo RAID (redundant array of independent/inexpensive disks) effect. Note that in this scenario there is no latency in mixing the virtual instruments, nor is there any timing fluctuation (both of which can be major headaches if locking computers together with MIDI), and the full 32-bit resolution of the virtual synths and the effects outputs is passed directly to the mixing computer.

For the project studio, using Cubase and your old computer can give you more sound options. How about making it another processor in your system? Use it as a dedicated keyboard rack full of virtual synths, use it as a powerful sampler, or add that new surround reverb effects processor without having to worry about it hogging your main machine's processor. An old computer can be invisibly hooked into a project system with very little effort and cost, and give great results in whatever capacity you need. Or you can rack-mount a bunch of machines for the ultimate in tracks and effects capability.

For more information on Nuendo and Cubase SX go to www.steinbergusa.net.

Plug-Ins

The world of digital technology changes incredibly fast. Almost as quickly as you learn the latest version of that hot new software, a new and improved version comes along, and this is certainly true for recording and music software and hardware.

In the world of computer-recorded music, one of the most-talked-about evolving technologies is that of plug-ins. Through a complex process involving mathematical algorithms, computer code, and amazing human ingenuity, today's plug-ins can virtually recreate (many times with breathtaking realism) instruments and effects.

There are software and hardware sound samplers that'll give you a studio full of symphony orchestra instruments, the baddest (read: great) sounding hip-hop beats and rhythms you can imagine, all at the touch of your computer mouse, keypad, or keyboard. There is software that'll allow you to create racks of studio equipment and instruments, patch them in any configurations you want, and adjust any of the knobs and controls. You can see all of this on your computer screen. You don't even have to have any real instruments in your home.

For many of us, the days of locating vintage gear or buying expensive outboard processing equipment—like a $30,000 Fairchild tube limiter—are over, as plug-ins come so very close to emulating the real thing. With many plug-ins priced in the neighborhood of $150 to $600, you can get software filled with instruments, effects, and recording capabilities unimaginable only a few years ago. Computer software plug-ins have become *the* way to create hit-quality music on a tight budget.

As plug-in technology is changing so rapidly, more and more companies are offering products with more features and for less money. Whether you're using a Mac or a Windows-based PC, plug-in music software essentially does one thing: It turns your computer into a recording studio filled with effects and instruments. All you need to add are talent and creativity.

In keeping with what the pros use, I've chosen a handful of products (from many) that folks have been raving about. Composers, artists, producers, remixers, and players (live and in studio) all use these powerful tools in their creative musical toolbox. I'm going to give you a brief overview of each. If you find something that interests you, go to the company's Web site, where you'll find loads of great information on the product, including who's using it and how, as well as tips on how to get the most from it. You can't go wrong with any of these products. You do, however, need to make sure that what you're buying will work with your computer's operating system and your DAW software.

You may be asking, "Can a software program (effects, instruments, etc.) actually sound as good as the original hardware versions?" In many instances, the answer is "yes." And plug-ins can be even better than hardware when you consider all the additional capabilities, like improved audio specs, sound quality, and new options for use, to name a few, that they offer. As you go through the following list of some of the very best plug-ins out there, prepare to be amazed.

Ableton Live

Your home and studio recording world can change for the better once you use the power of a DAW to create and record your music. And having the ability to use that workstation audio in a live situation can change how you'll think about live performance. How would you like to play your studio recordings live on stage or record your live performances and then edit them in the studio? One plug-in gives you that power: Ableton Live.

Live changes how audio is created, recorded, and used. In the context of a multitrack recording system, this means you can change your tempo, pitch, and groove at any time. You can combine loops, phrases, and songs from many origins and Live plays them all in synch with your chosen tempo.

Think of Live as a sequencer that becomes your instrument. You can launch loops or sound effects on the fly. It has automatic beat matching and real-time quantization. You can easily improvise song arrangements, instantly drop samples on cue, or interact with other performers, musicians, or DJs.

Live lets you bend sampled grooves, correct timing problems in your recordings, and create new sounds by restructuring existing sounds. It will time-align tracks for remixes and fit your music to film cues—all in real time and with excellent sound quality.

Live lets you drag samples from the built-in browser into a time line, and with its Time-Warping Engine you don't need to worry about their original tempo or key. You can prelisten to samples in synch with your song before actually putting them in, or apply tempo changes and manipulate the key of your samples any time you like.

In the studio, Live's real-time song arrangement allows you to create rough layouts of samples and jam with them to get ideas. Live gives you the ability to create music on the fly, without being bound to a fixed time line or tempo. People who use it say it has changed the way they can use their computers on stage. For those who are into DJ'ing and remixing, Live lets you combine any style of music—automatically in synch and in real time—with the press of a button.

In addition to the basic multitrack functions such as recording, monitoring, and punch-in/punch-out takes, Live lets you tap to set a tempo for a take, slow it down to record a difficult part, then speed it up after the take. You can then combine that take with a slower one from any previous session.

And here's one for you. Let's say you're having band practice, writing songs, or just jamming with some friends. Live's instant recording capabilities allow you to capture loops on the fly and then go directly from recording into loop playback without interrupting the flow. You can create beat-matched loops directly out of Propellerhead's Reason or any other ReWire slave program, or resample Live's own output.

Live comes with lots of the effects goodies, like parametric EQ, chorus, compressor, delay, vinyl distortion simulator, and analog synth filter emulation. When you add VST plug-ins, you've got a lot of power under the hood of that computer. You can insert, chain, and reorder the effects using drag and drop without interrupting the music. And all Live effects and VST plug-ins can be fully automated and remote-controlled via MIDI.

Finally, the answer to "Do I need a mouse to play this?" is, "No." Nearly every one of Live's functions (e.g., launching of sound files, transport functions, tempo and tap button, mixer and effects controls) can be arbitrarily assigned to computer keys, MIDI notes, and MIDI controllers.

Ableton Live runs on both Macs and PCs. It follows MIDI synch signals from your hardware sequencer and connects to Pro Tools, Logic, Cubase, Nuendo, Digital Performer, Sonar, Reason, MAX/MSP, or any other ReWire-compatible application.

For more information on Ableton Live go to www.ableton.com.

Antares

Antares turned the plug-in software effects world on its ear when it introduced its Mic Modeler and Auto-Tune. I'm also going to tell you about those as well as two other unique plug-ins called Tube and kantos.

Mic Modeler. Imagine what it would be like if you could record your vocal with your trusty SM-57 mic, then with the click of a mouse change the sound to emulate one recorded with a Neumann, AKG, Beyer, or . . . well, you get the picture. What Mic Modeler does is give you the ability to take music recorded with one type of microphone and change the sound of it as if it was recorded with any other kind of microphone you like. Now the microphones you own can sound like the microphones you wished you owned.

Antares's Spectral Shaping Tool technology allows them to create digital models of a wide variety of microphones, from historical classics to modern exotics, as well as a selection of industry-standard workhorses. You simply tell the Microphone Modeler what microphone you are actually using and what microphone you'd like it to sound like. It's as simple as that. Not only do the models reproduce sonic characteristics that make each microphone unique, but they also give you control of each mic's specific options. Does the mic have a low-cut filter? If so, it's in the model. Wind screen on or off? Close or far placement? Each option results in the same sonic effect that it would have with the actual modeled mic. And you can even add some good old-fashioned tube saturation.

One of the cool things about Microphone Modeler is that you can record every track through a model of the specific mic that produces the ideal sound you're looking for. Or you can use it in live performance to get the sound of rare or hugely expensive mics you'd never be able to bring on stage. You can even use it during mixdown to effectively change the mic on an already recorded track. And with the ability to download new models from Antares's Web site, Microphone Modeler will keep your studio full of state-of-the-art mics without shelling out the big bucks for them.

The Microphone Modeler is available as a plug-in for TDM, MAS Mac VST, RTAS, and DirectX.

Auto-Tune 3. This amazing technology from Antares can make your performing and recording life easier and more enjoyable. There are so many producers and artists who use Auto-Tune that I sometimes wonder if there is anyone who doesn't. Auto-Tune is all about pitch correction. In the days before its development, if you sang a take that had all the emotional energy you could ask for, but some of the parts were off key, you only had two choices: You could either punch in and out overdubs to correct the off-pitch parts or you could scrap the track and cut a fresh one. But I think we all know how difficult it can be to recapture a once-in-a-lifetime performance.

With Auto-Tune 3, all you need to do is run the track through its software and, voilá, pitch problems are automatically and instantly corrected. It can be used for live performance too. Auto-Tune uses source-specific pitch detection and correction algorithms and allows you to choose which source you want it to detect (e.g., soprano voice, alto/tenor voice, low male voice, instrument, and bass instrument).

Another of its features is a Bass Mode that lowers the lowest detectable frequency by about one octave to 25 Hz. Since the lowest E string on a bass guitar is approximately 41 Hz, Bass Mode allows the user to apply pitch correction to fretless bass lines as well as other low-bass-range instruments.

Auto-Tune 3 gives you a Make Scale From MIDI function for occasions when it's not clear exactly what key a melody line is in, or when the line has too many accidentals to fit comfortably into a conventional scale. For those occasions, the Make Scale From MIDI function allows you to simply play the line from a MIDI keyboard or sequencer and let Auto-Tune 3 construct a custom scale containing only those notes that appear in the line.

Auto-Tune 3's audio quality is superb, with high sample rate (88.2 and 96 kHz) compatibility, all of which, of course, depends upon your host application and audio hardware support. It supports Mac TDM and RTAS versions compatible with Pro Tools HD (OS 9 and OS X) and Pro Tools 6 (OS X), and AudioSuite in TDM and RTAS.

Tube. People love the warm sound of analog tube gear. Of course, not all tube gear is great-sounding, but if you want to add some nice-sounding tube warmth and even a bit of distortion (the good kind), then you should give Tube a look.

Antares's Tube plug-in gives you lots of options to create a wide range of modeled analog tube effects. It's based on technology from the company's Microphone Modeler plug-in. Tube is easy to use and very DSP-efficient, so even a modest native system will support dozens of tracks' worth (in some of their tests, over 40).

Choosing the Blue Tube adds the warmth of a classic tube preamp to vocals, acoustic guitar, horns, strings, synth pads, or anything else you can imagine. The Orange Tube gives your tracks the deep, warm distortion of an overdriven tube amplifier. You can use it in moderation to impart a subtle (or not-so-subtle) effect to almost any track. Or crank it up on electric guitar, bass, synths, even voice. The Drive control lets you select the degree of dynamic saturation.

In addition to the tube models, Tube includes an OmniTube function. Without OmniTube engaged, Tube functions exactly like a tube preamp: Only the regions of the input signal that exceed the clipping level—typically transients—are affected; all other regions are passed with no change. With OmniTube on, a compressor is inserted into the signal path before the tube model. This compressor is set to compress the signal and then apply sufficient makeup gain to ensure that Tube's drive control can drive the signal above the clipping level. After the tube effect is applied to the entire signal, an inverse gain function restores the signal's original dynamics.

Tube is available for RTAS (Mac and PC), VST (Mac and PC), MAS, and DirectX.

kantos. kantos is a unique software-based synthesizer. Unlike conventional MIDI synthesizers, kantos is controlled by audio. You can use any pitched monophonic audio, for example, your voice or a musical instrument, and do it live and in real time. Kantos analyzes incoming audio and instantaneously extracts pitch, dynamics, harmonic content, and formant characteristics. This information is then used to control the kantos sound engine in ways unlike a conventional MIDI synth.

Kantos's input signal need not be a solo voice or instrument, but for reliable pitch detection, the input *does* have to be monophonic. Unlike most pitch-detection algorithms, kantos works well with unison sections (i.e., multiple singers or instrumentalists playing the same pitch). As kantos is not polyphonic in the traditional sense, you can create melodic lines, but you get one line per instance. If you want harmony, you can create multiple lines one at a time or instantiate kantos on as many individual tracks as your processing system will allow.

Kantos provides a combination of traditional synthesizer functions and new functions unique to audio control. They include two wave-table oscillators, pitch constraint and quantization control, noise source, three resonant multimode filters, two chorus generators, a timbral articulator, two envelope generators, two low-frequency oscillators (LFOs), modulation matrix, gate generator, noise gate, delay line, and mixers.

Kantos's articulator is a unique module that takes the harmonic content and formant information from the input signal and dynamically applies it to the synthesized signal. It can either reproduce the input signal's formant and harmonic characteristics with uncanny accuracy or, through the use of its formant offset and resonance controls, warp them into a variety of mutant forms. In addition, you can add new wave tables to its oscillators by downloading them from the Antares Web site.

For more information on Mic Modeler, Auto-Tune 3, Tube, and kantos go to www.antarestech.com.

Cycling '74 pluggo 3

In the realm of most plug-ins in one software program and biggest bang for the buck, it would be hard to beat Cycling '74's pluggo 3 collection. It costs under $200, and has more than 100 audio plug-ins that work with Mac OS sequencers and audio applications that support Steinberg's VST plug-in format, the MOTU Audio System (MAS) format used by Digital Performer, and Digidesign's RTAS plug-in format.

This audio plug-in offers real-time interactive audio processing, modulation, and synthesis environment that works right inside your favorite audio application. Effects categories include delays, filters, pitch effects, distortion, granulation, spectral effects, modulators, multichannel effects, synthesizers, audio routing, reverb and dynamics, and visual display. Also included are the pluggo legendary Feedback Network, Tapped Delay, and Swish. Plus there are more than 19 Essential Instruments that work with your RTAS, MAS, or VST applications.

These instruments were created by eowave, the developers of the iSynth, and use the Max4/MSP2 audio programming environment. They include the Pretty Good Synth, additive synths, analog-modeling drum and percussion synths, theremins, sampling, granular synthesis, FM synthesis, wave-table synthesis, and sonic waveshaping.

You can seamlessly combine these exciting new instruments with pluggo effects plug-ins and modulator plug-ins for a world of sonic possibilities you'll be hard-pressed to exhaust.

Cycling '74's Max/MSP audio processing system allows its plug-ins to run within the same environment, allowing them to work together behind the back of your sequencer. The number of plug-ins that you can use simultaneously depends on your computer's processing speed and available memory.

The PluggoSynch plug-in listens to an audio click track, then tells other plug-ins where the beat is. The PluggoBus system lets plug-ins send up to 8 channels of audio to each other, removing the limitation of one or two outputs per plug-in in audio sequencers. Pluggo also offers a set of modulators, which are plug-ins that allow you to change the parameters of other plug-ins in different and unusual ways. VST and MAS users can even modulate the parameters of VST plug-ins that are not part of pluggo.

Here's how the creators of pluggo describe their product:

[We took] a breathtakingly simple yet radical concept: lots of interesting plug-ins for a modest price. We wanted people who would never consider paying hundreds of dollars for a single plug-in to find the pluggo deal impossible to resist. Since Max/MSP allows you to make so much cool audio

stuff so quickly, we could prototype an effect in minutes and then ask, "Would we pay a buck or two for this?" The result is that ideas that would been rejected by other plug-in developers have become the stars of the parade. Raindrops? Sine Bank? Phone Filter? Then there's the stuff that is simply unlike anything you've ever plugged in, like Spectral Filter, Feedback Network, Granular-to-Go, and Noyzckippr.

Pluggo includes MIDI support when used with VST, MAS, and RTAS host applications. Its plug-ins can send and receive MIDI information, and Max/MSP developers can now develop their own MIDI processor plug-ins and virtual MIDI instruments. It also offers a plug-in that converts MIDI information into modulation data to change the parameters of other plug-ins.

In addition, pluggo 3 includes support for host synchronization for VST and MAS users. Its plug-ins support beat-synchronized parameter changes, sample-accurate tempo synch for a plug-in's modulating LFOs, and tempo-relative settings for plug-in parameters such as delay time. And pluggo isn't limited to the assortment of plug-ins that is available today. If you want to tweak your own plug-ins, you might want to consider Cycling 74's Max/MSP, which includes everything you need. And the pluggo Run-time System allows you to give your own plug-ins to everyone, regardless of whether they own pluggo or not.

With so many plug-ins to use, Cycling'74 offers Plug-in Manager, which is an easy-to-use application that lets you keep track of your plug-ins just as you do for system extensions and control panels with the Mac Extensions Manager. The Plug-in Manager is included free with pluggo, and while it was originally intended for use only with audio plug-ins, you can use it for any application that gets its plug-ins from a specific folder.

For more information on pluggo 3 go to www.cycling74.com.

IK Multimedia

Whenever I've asked producers, artists, and engineers to name their favorite plug-ins, IK Multimedia is always mentioned. IK is all about quality and innovation, and the four plug-ins I'm going to tell you about are all wise choices for your computer studio/live rig.

T-RackS. Think of this plug-in as the one you'll want to use to make warm-sounding tube-toned masters with your sequencer. Its algorithms are based on true analog circuitry and it emulates the sounds of many types of tube and analog audio hardware. Its interface, resembling a typical rack of studio hardware gear with analog controls, gives you five processors: EQ, compressor, limiter, soft-clipping output stage, and a complete mastering suite.

AmpliTube. As a guitarist, with racks of studio gear, amps, and preamps, AmpliTube is something that caught my attention in a big way. Here's just some of what you can do with it.

The sought-after tones from modern and vintage amp emulations (both solid-state and tube) are all built in, and AmpliTube makes it easy to create as many as 1,260 different configurations with combinations of any of these settings. You also get tremolo and spring reverb. You'll be tweaking for days! You can combine amp models and, let's say, blend a Fender Super Reverb's preamp and EQ with a VOX AC30 amp and a Marshall 4x12 cabinet to create a unique amp combination for "your" sound. The Amp module lets you combine seven different preamp models, five EQs, four power amps, nine cabinets, and two mic models to get your favorite amp sounds.

The axis and placement of recording mics are critical in tailoring final amp sounds. AmpliTube allows you to select the type (condenser/dynamic), axis, and placement of the recording mics for maximum sonic quality and flexibility.

AmpliTube features 10 classic analog stomp and rack-style effects, including wah-wah, delay, chorus, flanger, and overdrive. The Post FX module includes three stereo posteffects with 3-band parametric equalizer, stereo delay, and stereo reverb with more than 200 fully editable presets allowing you to create a sound, save it, and get it back with a single click.

AmpliTube can also be used to tailor the sound of vocals, keyboards, and synths, thereby giving your music a whole different kind of dimension and sound.

Amplitude's 32-bit processing provides excellent sound quality, and it is compatible with all major recording platforms.

AmpliTube Live. Okay, now let's give you something you can use live without needing a tractor trailer full of amps and roadies to set everything up. It's called AmpliTube Live, and this Mac-based software gives you the power of a big stack of amps. AmpliTube Live allows you to combine three different preamp models and related EQs with three accurately emulated cabinets to precisely craft a wide palette of guitar sounds ranging from clean to crunch to lead. It gives you a set of four classic effects, including spring reverb, wah-wah, delay, and overdrive. You also get a chromatic tuner.

The Mac OS X Core Audio features are fully exploited by AmpliTube Live, which plays without any perceivable latency (delay). This means that what you play sounds like there's a hard-wired amp at the other end of your cord. It needs no special hardware or software (it works with built-in Mac audio cards) and no special setup or configuration.

And by using a MIDI foot controller, you can call up to 128 presets (64 factory-installed and 64 user-controlled).

SampleTank 2. If you have the need for a very different kind of sampler, this could be the one for you. Its three synth engines can be switched on the fly to give you traditional resampling and pitch shift/time stretch, and its STRETCH (SampleTank Time REsyn TeCHnology) engine gives you loads of control over tempo, tune, and harmonics.

Lots of folks have a rack full of sound modules, but with SampleTank 2 you get more than 5,000 native sounds and you can import unlimited sounds. This means you can import your own WAV, AIFF (Audio Interchange File Format), and SDII (Sound Designer II) files, for loops and multisampled banks, plus read thousands of high-quality libraries in AKAI and SampleCell formats directly from the plug-in.

You get more than 50 synth-engine parameters, including filters, envelopes, LFOs, and velocity, and the Switchable Engines function lets you fine-tune and tweak sounds. You can use 16 layerable parts with full mix control.

SampleTank 2's Loop Synch feature lets you synchronize any loop to the sequencer tempo with a single click and synchronize various loops together with ease. Loops can be stretched using one of the three available synth engines: Resampling, Pitch Shift/Time Stretch or STRETCH, for everything from rich natural sounds to unique experimental sonic textures.

SampleTank 2 comes with 32 DSP effects to choose from (you can use up to five effects per instrument). You get amp and cabinet simulators, analog phaser, parametric EQ, compressor, limiter, and others. Storing and recalling your sounds is simple with its Preset and Module Save and Back Up functions. You can even back up your session with one click for fast file exchange. SampleTank 2 files can also be transparently swapped among different platforms using a sequencer or operating system.

Any of SampleTank 2's controls can be associated with any MIDI source with just one click. You can control all features on the fly, including STRETCH, for live performances. Every SampleTank 2 sound module can play up to 256 polyphonic notes with per-instrument polyphony management.

The SampleTank 2 sample-based sound workstation supports all platforms in all operating systems, including Pro Tools, VST, AU, Dxi, and MAS in Mac OS 9 and Mac OS X and Windows 98SE/ME/2000/XP.

For more information on T-RackS, AmpliTube, AmpliTube Live, and SampleTank 2 go to www.ikmultimedia.com. As a bonus, IK has free demo versions online of all their products. At the home page, click on Download Demos.

MOTU MachFive

The main thing musicians want from a sampler is easy access to their sounds, and MOTU's MachFive provides just that. It remembers where your sounds are located, and even multigigabyte libraries are quickly and efficiently scanned. It's also a true plug-in. You can save any project using your own workstation software and everything about MachFive is saved with it, allowing you to manage everything in the same environment. MachFive's single window allows you to see all editing and performance parameters in one glance, making for lots of speed and flexibility.

MachFive supports every major audio production platform on both Macintosh and Windows (e.g., MAS, VST, AudioUnits, HTDM, RTAS, and DXi.), thereby allowing you to move from one platform to another or even collaborate with colleagues who use different audio software. For example, you might write and track a project in Digital Performer or Logic, and then move to Pro Tools for mixing. All you need to do is save a MachFive performance in Digital Performer or Logic, then load it into Pro Tools along with your MIDI tracks, and you're ready to go.

MachFive's UVI-Xtract feature allows you to audition and load programs and samples from every major sampler format, such as Akai, SampleCell, EXS24, and even Gigasampler. Legacy formats are also supported. Simply insert your Kurzweil, E-mu, or Roland CD-ROMs and convert programs, or even the entire disc, in just a few clicks.

Each MachFive multitimbral performance (Multi) includes 16 parts, each with a choice of audio outputs, volume, pan, etc., and each part can receive MIDI data from any channel (for instant stacks) and send its output to unique audio outputs (depending on your host audio software). Multi is also the place where MachFive's Expert mode allows you to use keys to open and close multiparts in real time, mix several parts in real time using any MIDI controller, and create splits with cross-fades between keys.

The visuals on this sampler are clear and easy to understand. The central section of the MachFive window shows the filter, three envelopes, and every modulation tool. Eight filter algorithms are provided, and crucial parameters, such as filter resonance, cutoff frequency, and overdrive, can be controlled and automated by MIDI. Modulation options are provided at every stage of the synth section. The UVI-Engine that powers MachFive gives you unlimited polyphony and ultra-low latency.

In keeping with the theme of cross-platform compatibility and use, MachFive accepts audio samples in all formats from mono to 5.1. The waveform display allows truncating, normalizing, fading, and many other destructive DSP audio manipulations—all in real time. If desired, you can cross-fade a loop in real time while listening to your full sequence and listen to your edits on the fly in the full context of your mix.

As audio production moves into higher fidelity, MachFive lets you use high-definition audio interfaces. You no longer need to keep low-res "draft" versions of the same samples, either. High-resolution samples can be used at lower sample rates, making it easy to sample and use everything—whether it's 96 or 192 kHz.

Besides using the higher sampling rates, more and more music production is moving into surround sound and MachFive helps you jump right into it by giving you the ability to play and transpose 5.1 audio files in real time, add multichannel effects, and route the multichannel preset to your host software's mixer with multiple outputs (if your host software supports these surround features).

The drag-and-drop feature on MachFive allows you to drag samples from your desktop or host application to the MachFive keyboard. You can drag multiple samples in one step to map chromatically, on white keys only, or by pitch according to their name. You can also audition samples when importing them, listening to each note as you stretch a key map over a range of keys.

MachFive gives you loads of processing power too. Each multitimbral part can have up to four insert effects plus four preset effects. You can add four global aux effects and four master effects, all operating simultaneously, thereby giving you 136 total effects slots and 85 separate effects chains per instance with instant recall.

Included are dozens of effects, each with dozens of presets, such as reverb, tempo-synched delay, tremolo, chorus, filter, bit crusher, and many others. Four LFOs are available per preset. Each LFO can be routed to an assortment of destinations, including filter frequency, filter resonance, drive, pitch, pan, and amplitude. MachFive can synch both the LFO and effects parameters to sequence tempo. All settings are saved with the Multi for total recall. You can also save effects with each preset to build your own sound library. The Effects section allows you to leave one part's effects in place while you audition other parts.

For more on MachFive go to www.motu.com.

Native Instruments

One company that has passed the litmus test of legitimacy—the software and plug-in products it makes have been embraced by the people who create the music we want to listen to—is Native Instruments, which has successfully marketed numerous amazing products, including ABSYNTH 2, REAKTOR SESSION, B4, KONTAKT, AND TRAKTOR DJ STUDIO.

ABSYNTH 2. Many film composers use this synth/sampling software to create some very unique sounds. Check out the soundtrack to the movie *Matrix Reloaded* and you'll hear ABSYNTH 2 all over it. ABSYNTH 2 uses a combination of multiple synthesis techniques, granular sampling, and flexible envelope control to create everything from organic textures to rhythmic madness, from time-evolving soundscapes to vintage sounds. ABSYNTH 2 includes more than 800 evocative, expressive, and musical presets that cover an amazing range.

ABSYNTH 2's patch window makes it easy to mix sampling, granular sampling, subtractive, wave table, FM, AM, ring modulation, and waveshaping synthesis. Each voice has six synth oscillators (or three sampling oscillators), four filters, three ring modulators, and a waveshaping distortion function. Waveforms can be drawn by hand or created by sketching harmonics. A built-in context-menu library of waveforms, envelopes, and even entire oscillator channels enables the quick construction of complex, evolving sounds with just a few clicks.

Nearly every synthesis, sampling, and effects parameter can be controlled by ABSYNTH's envelopes. Each envelope can contain up to 68 break points and can be synched to the tempo, making it possible to dynamically control an envelope (or a group of envelopes) with a MIDI controller to morph and twist the sound with a single gesture (e.g., a mouse click or a keyboard MIDI controller keystroke). Each envelope can be modulated with its own graphically displayed variable-speed LFO for creating very lifelike sounds. A Link mode allows multiple envelopes to be chained together, with adjustable time, amplitude, and slope scaling—ideal for detuned chords or phasing filters or for mirroring the sample playback position with filter resonance.

Aliasing occurs when numerous continuous different signals become indistinguishable when sampled. Anti-aliasing limits that and helps remove unwanted high-frequency noise. With ABSYNTH 2, anti-aliasing can be switched on or off on a per-oscillator basis, allowing you to choose between smooth analog highs to cool digital jitter (an abrupt and unwanted variation of one or multiple signal characteristics like pulses and cycles).

ABSYNTH 2 runs completely in stereo, and each oscillator can be dynamically panned by its powerful envelopes. You'll also find several different filters, including a four-pole low-pass filter and a multipole all-pass filter for phasing and resonant effects. Plug-in operation is simple, as each plug-in can open its own bank, and the ABSYNTH engine is no longer needed to play sounds.

ABSYNTH 2 works on both Mac and Windows platforms and with nearly every plug-in format.

REAKTOR SESSION. If you have the time and desire to construct your own software audio instruments, then Native Instrument's REAKTOR is for you. For those who'd rather jump right in and start making music with some terrific-sounding instruments and effects with presets all ready to go, you need to check out REAKTOR SESSION.

With over 30 instruments—from synths to analog basses to leads to sequenced percussion and exotic sounds—REAKTOR SESSION can be an ideal place to begin when the urge to create strikes. The pros rave about the quality of the effects, which they say sound just as good as expensive hardware synths. Among REAKTOR

SESSION's features are multiband compressors, rich filters, vocoder, delays, beat loopers, groove and drum machines, samplers, granular resynthesis capability, spring reverbs, surround effects, live performance tools, and much more.

REAKTOR SESSION can load and use any instrument made with REAKTOR. In addition to the sound library included with REAKTOR SESSION, over 1,000 unique REAKTOR creations are available for free download from Native Instrument's online User Library. And the number of free samples continues to grow as instrument creators from all over the world regularly contribute sounds for others to use.

REAKTOR SESSION allows you to create, edit, and save your own sounds. Its integrated randomizer makes it possible to randomly create and change presets, and the morphing function enables dynamic transitions between two presets for getting unique sound combinations.

All user interface objects can be fully controlled over MIDI with the built-in MIDI Learn function. After activating the MIDI Learn function for the desired parameter, you can simply move any hardware controller, such as a knob on a MIDI controller, and it is automatically assigned to the desired parameter. All MIDI settings are saved with the instrument.

REAKTOR SESSION's sound quality, with its 32-bit floating audio and sample-rate support of up to 192 kHz, is excellent. It supports nearly every native plug-in interface and works with both Mac and Windows platforms.

B4 Organ. Native Instruments boasts that its B4 software instrument is the "perfect emulation of the most legendary organ of all time." If the trade reviews are any indication, this may very well be true. B4 Organ is a complete virtual tonewheel organ (with a full set of 91 tonewheels), capable of reproducing in authentic detail the sound of the legendary B3 organ and rotating speaker cabinet. It is a tonewheel organ combo for stand-alone or plug-in use. It can also be used as an insert plug-in, making it easy to run vocals, guitar, or anything else through the guitar and Leslie tube amp simulators.

Unlike a sample-based instrument, the B4 accurately models subtle details of the old B3, such as harmonic fold-back, drawbar cross-talk, and loudness robbing. The result is a very warm and powerful sound over the entire range of the keyboard, complete with subtle tonal shades. The realistic on-screen graphics offer two views. One shows the two manuals, bass pedals, and other knobs; the other view omits the manuals and knobs but allows access to the B4's extended settings.

The B4 recaptures and recreates the many variations from this type of organ. For years, people have used it on all kinds of music including rock, jazz, or even house music. The B4 rear panel gives you access to numerous adjustment parameters which allow the sound to be tailored for particular applications. You can even use the B4 to process other sounds. Just plug it in as a VST Insert Effect and apply any combination of Scanner Vibrato, Tube Overdrive, and Rotating Speaker effect to your audio tracks.

You can add new sounds by replacing the tonewheels that can transform the B4 into a Vox Continental, Farsifa, or even an Indian Harmonium. The Tonewheel-Sets function permits the master tuning to be altered and allows you to "age" the sound at six different levels, from "well matured" to "far beyond repair." B4 users can purchase the Tonewheel-Sets from Native Instruments via its Web site.

The B4 works on both Mac and Windows platforms.

KONTAKT. This powerful sampler loads *all* popular sample libraries. In addition to supporting all the standard sample-playback and manipulation abilities of its hardware and software predecessors, KONTAKT adds several technologies to give sampling a new dimension. Real-time time stretching and pitch shifting allow you to manipulate length and pitch. It has drag and drop of samples and instruments. And its resynthesis, graphical break-point envelopes, integrated loop editor, analog-modeled filters, and visually displayed modulation together make up a sample library containing more than 3 gigabytes of sounds in various styles and categories.

On a standard computer, KONTAKT's audio engine allows up to 256 stereo voices, 16 multitimbral parts, and 32 outputs per instance (i.e., per use or per application). The semimodular architecture of KONTAKT's audio engine corresponds exactly to its on-screen layout. Filters, effects, and modulations can easily be added with one click. If an audio process is not active, it is neither displayed on the screen nor calculated by the computer's CPU.

Unlike a conventional sampler, where pitch and length are always linked, KONTAKT's integrated granular resynthesis engine frees you to compose with pitch and time stretch independently. KONTAKT can play back each sample in one of three modes: Classic, Time Machine, or Tone Machine mode. Time Machine allows real-time manipulation of length, pitch, and formant and Tone Machine imprints a playable pitch onto the sample and maintains the same length across the keyboard.

The comprehensive filter section offers 17 varieties of filters ranging from analog low-pass and high-pass to exotic sound-design filters. A broad range of insert and send effects, including EQs, waveshapers, delays, and reverbs, are available to position the instruments in the mix. All effects are inherent parts of the instrument, regardless of how many instruments are playing at once. Nearly all of KONTAKT's parameters can be dynamically modulated by LFOs, break-point envelopes, or step modulators, or via MIDI velocity or controller. All time-based modulation can be synched to song tempo. Nothing is hidden behind the scenes, since all modulation is shown graphically. For instance, if a filter cutoff is modulated by a step modulator, the filter cutoff knob displays the modulation movements as well as the current value.

KONTAKT's user interface is easy to learn, yet is very flexible during the creative process. An integrated file browser supporting drag and drop makes setting up multisamples quick and easy. Samples can be trimmed and looped within the main sampler window. The built-in graphical loop editor features seamless looping with advanced autocorrelation algorithms and supports up to 8 loops per sample.

More than 3 gigabytes of top-quality samples are included, ranging from acoustic pianos, drums, percussion, basses, and guitars to vintage instruments. The library, produced by YellowTools and Native Instruments, makes extensive use of KONTAKT's modulation abilities. KONTAKT ships with five sample CDs, each focusing on a different musical category. It can also import AKAI CDs and many other common formats, providing immediate access to an immense library.

KONTAKT'S Direct From Disk feature enables it to play samples directly from the hard drive, so sample size is no longer limited by the amount of available RAM. KONTAKT is able to load nearly any sample library format: AKAI S-1000/S-3000, Gigasampler, SF2, HAlion, EXS, SDII, BATTERY, REAKTOR Map, LM4, AIFF, and WAV files up to 32 bit and 192 kHz.

KONTAKT supports every professional native interface and seamlessly fits into all computer-based studios. It can be used as a plug-in with VST 2.0, DXi, DirectConnect, and MAS. In the studio or during a live performance, it can be used with less latency than a hardware sampler with ASIO offering 32 outputs and up to 256 stereo voices. It works on both Mac and Windows platforms.

TRAKTOR DJ STUDIO. TRAKTOR DJ STUDIO is a powerful software solution for professional DJ mixing, live remixing, and mix recording using tracks in MP3, WAV, AIFF, and Audio CD format.

Native Instruments says that functions and features of TRAKTOR DJ STUDIO were developed in cooperation with professional DJs and include extended mixer, tempo-synched loop and cue functions, filters, over 400 remote controllable functions and actions, and a fast search function. The tracks are graphically shown as waveform displays, with the sound in two frequency bands for visual control of beats, breaks, and instrumentation. The waveform can be stopped and accurately cued like a record.

TRAKTOR DJ STUDIO's tempo detection uses complex algorithms for reliable beat alignment of two tracks on the fly. You can perceive beats, breaks, and instrumentation ahead of time, regardless of whether an MP3, WAV, or Audio CD format is being used. Tempo reading for complex beats can be improved by additional user tapping. You can use up to 10 cue points and loops per track for live remixing. Cue points can be beat-quantized and loops can be set accurately on the bar, resized, or moved, all without losing the groove. Its filters and equalizers can be used to radically transform the sound of the tracks.

The track database provides a tree navigator, quick search, MP3 browser, and automatic playlist icons that keep track of the set and direct prelistening of tracks. The full automation of functions and actions allows recording of all user actions so that mixing sessions, editing, and redubbing can be seamlessly resumed at any time and the session exported as WAV or AIFF files.

All of TRAKTOR's more than 400 functions and actions can be operated by mouse, user-programmed keyboard shortcuts, MIDI controllers, or MIDI note events. TRAKTOR DJ STUDIO runs on both Mac and Windows platforms.

For more information on ABSYNTH 2, REAKTOR SESSION, B4, KONTAKT, AND TRAKTOR DJ STUDIO, go to www.native-instruments.com.

Propellerhead

Founded in 1994, the Swedish company Propellerhead has rapidly grown into one of the leading forces in music and audio software.

Reason. Propellerhead turned a computer into an all-in-one music production studio when it came out with Reason. Think of Reason as the studio equipment rack of your dreams. How would you like to add as many pieces of rack gear as your computer can handle? Do you want four separate delays? No problem. One drum machine not enough? Then add two, three, or four more. Want more than one reverb? Simply click on another one and you've got it.

Reason is loaded with synthesizers, samplers, drum machine, ReCycle-based loop player, mixer, effects, pattern sequencer, and more—and as many of each as your computer can handle. Reason is an infinitely expandable music workstation on a CD-ROM, complete with its own real-time sequencer.

One of the things that makes Reason so popular is its ease of use. There are no confusing connections. Reason's cables don't tangle. Forget about steep learning curves and menus within menus. No need to gather all those different disks and sound banks required to load up a song. This is a program you'll learn how to use in minutes.

With so many instruments and possibilities, you might think you'd need to remember all your settings whenever you come back to a song again. Not so. When you save your music, your whole studio setup is stored along with it. You can even include your samples, loops, and drum kits in the Reason file for easy Web publishing or e-mail distribution to other Reason users. Everything can be totally recalled.

Each unit in Reason's virtual rack is edited from its own on-screen front panel.

All the sliders, knobs, buttons, and functions are right in front of you and can be tweaked, turned, and twisted in real time. Plus all your front-panel actions, such as filter adjustments, pitch bending, and gain riding or panning, can be recorded and automated in the Reason sequencer.

Reason allows you to add instruments and change control parameters by showing you the front face plates and controls for everything you're using. By simply pressing one key, you can flip the entire rack around to reveal the back of all the rack units, thereby allowing you to patch them in any combination you want. Very cool.

It's easy to add more instruments whenever you need them. You can choose a synth, a drum machine, a loop player, or any device from the Create menu, and it instantly appears in your rack, logically patched into the signal chain. If you ever wished you had 11 samplers and 10 compressors, Reason is definitely for you. And if you have created more machines than you have mixer channels, just create another mixer.

Reason is a self-contained synth studio system. Everything you need is there, including a fast and flexible sequencer with powerful, dedicated event editors for each type of device. And you can use it with your audio sequencer, too, by processing Reason's audio output with plug-in effects and then mixing it with your hard disk tracks. In ReWire mode, its instruments are automatically and seamlessly patched into the mixer in any other ReWire-compatible application. Reason can be used as a virtual synth rack with your MIDI sequencer, but you don't need a MIDI sequencer to do this. Reason's devices can be handled in exactly the same way as hardware.

With Reason, you'll never run out of rack space. A partial list of what's available includes 512-band vocoder, 64-channel audio interface, mixer, multieffects, RV7000 Advanced reverb, Subtractor polyphonic synth, Scream 4 sound destruction unit, Spider audio and CV merger and splitters, digital sampler, Dr. Rex loop player, Unison effect, Graintable synth, Matrix pattern sequencer, NN-XT Advanced sampler, Redrum drum machine, ReBirth input machine, and Reason sequencer. Reason works on both Mac and Windows platforms and offers 32-bit floating-point audio, 24-bit playback, and sample rates up to 96 kHz.

ReBirth. If you're into techno music, you know how great those old bass synth and drum machines like the Roland TB-303, TR-808, and TR-909 sounded. Today, those cool pieces of gear are quite pricey and hard to find. To solve this problem, Propellerhead came out with a stunningly accurate reproduction of the bare essentials of techno music making—all the way down to the interactive screens of those classic silver boxes, blinking LEDs, and a myriad of knobs.

ReBirth is the software reincarnation of two analog bass-line synths and two classic drum machines. It includes a digital delay, a quad-input distortion unit, a compressor, and an analog filter emulation unit, the PCF (Pattern Controlled Filter). You get those great little quirks and subtle qualities of analog, combined with the convenience of modern computers (a minimum of cables, integration with your sequencer software, complete front-panel automation, real-time audio streaming, and much more).

Instead of sampling the sound, Propellerhead "sampled" the actual synth hardware. They analyzed the inner workings of the analog design and created a mathematical model of it, incorporating practically every nuance. They then converted this theoretical model into lightning-fast computer code, so that it runs on the computer you already have, with no need to get customized cards, DSP chips, or other expensive accessories.

ReCycle. Now let's talk loops, grooves, and samples. ReCycle lets you do with sampled loops what you can do with beats programmed from individual drum sounds, such as alter the tempo or replace sounds and process them individually. ReCycle turns concrete-rigid loops into something more musical sounding, thereby giving you lots of room for creative expression.

Here's how it works. You start out with a regular audio file or a sample in your sampler, preferably one of a groovy nature. You then load the groove into ReCycle; the program "looks" at the groove, analyzes it, and breaks it up into its rhythmic components.

Each part of the groove is called a "slice." The process itself is fully automated, but once the slices are there, they are yours to move, monitor, or delete, using the program's on-screen tools and controls. Other tools allow you to set the length, attack, and decay of the slices, and to change your grooves' overall tempo or pitch, without having a change in one affect the other.

The procedures for bringing your groove into one of your songs differ depending on your equipment and preferred working method. If you like, you can use ReCycle simply as a problem solver for loops. Load a drum loop into ReCycle, set a new tempo or pitch, and save the results as a new file. Or load up any groove, and use ReCycle's on-screen signal processors—Compressor, EQ, and Transient Designer—to give it some punch and distinction. Anything you choose to do in ReCycle can be applied to your loop and saved as a new file.

To use your loop directly in Propellerhead Reason, Steinberg Cubase VST, or other programs supporting REX2 files, all you need to do is save your sliced-up loop as a REX2 file and import it onto an Audio Track in your sequencer. The imported loop plays back like the original, but you can change the tempo freely, and you have full control over the original slices. You can even silence, move, or replace individual hits, and change volume and panning.

If you're using a sampler, ReCycle creates a sound bank containing the samples and slices and transmits it to your sampler. ReCycle then creates a MIDI file based on the timing of the original groove. You can import the MIDI file into your sequencer, and it triggers the slices in your sampler, playing back the groove you started out with. This time, however, you can change it any way you like, be it a tempo change, a retuning, or replacing the sounds.

For more information on Reason, ReBirth, and ReCycle go to www.propeller-heads.se.

Sibelius

Many people who make great music don't have the ability to create a written copy of it. Yet written copies are a good thing to have if you ever need to take your music into studios for session players to read or anyone else to perform. And let's not forget that you'll be able to generate more money from the sale of your written music via mail order, retail distribution, or over the Internet.

Before music notation software was developed, you typically needed the services of someone with music scoring expertise to listen to your tape or CD, then transpose it to written notes and notations on paper. Not anymore. I want to tell you about some innovative music scoring software programs developed by a company named Sibelius.

Sibelius 3. Sibelius 3 is a complete software package that scores and prints your music. What it can do is simply amazing. Sibelius:

* Automatically writes your music at the speed at which you play it.
* Plays back your scores with realistic instrument sounds using the new sample library from Native Instruments.
* Saves your scores as audio files directly to CD-ROM.
* Gives you improved playback of repeats including DC, DS, Codas, multiple endings, and more.
* Plays live and accurately transcribes your playing, even using multiple voices when necessary.
* Makes MIDI file import accurate and notation cleaner.
* Gives you the option of listening to the transcribed notation or the original version using Live Playback.
* Lets you view and edit the entire score or individual parts, or choose any number of staves you wish to view and/or edit using the Focus on Staves feature.
* Automatically creates any scale or arpeggio you need and prints out exercises in a few seconds.

* Scans in sheet music with PhotoScore Lite 3 for improved accuracy.
* Allows you to write music for nearly 300 different instruments and use an unlimited number of instruments in your score. The instruments are automatically arranged into correct order, bracketed and bar-lined into groups, and given correct names, abbreviations, clefs, transpositions, and playback sounds.
* Gives you 25 types of clef, covering standard notation, avant garde music, early music, percussion, and guitar tab. Your music automatically shifts to maintain sounding pitch when clef is inserted or moved.
* Automatically positions notes, rests, accidentals, articulation marks, clefs, key signatures, beams, time signatures, bar lines, etc., to standard music engraving rules (with alternative rules available as House Style options). Layout is entirely automated. You can choose from over 130 ready-made "manuscript papers" (templates) for standard instrumentations and page sizes. It automatically reformats the whole score (in about 0.1 second) whenever you make any change to it.
* Provides automatic page numbers in any position on the page.
* Automatically arranges (with over 130 styles) and orchestrates music, choosing appropriate instruments and doublings (e.g., Piccolo an octave above Flute) and making adjustments to suit instrument ranges.
* Automatically positions and spaces lyrics according to standard engraving rules.
* Lets you copy lyrics from/to word processors.
* Copies any selected object(s) with one click and transposes a whole score or any passage of music in less than 1 second.
* Automatically understands all standard markings, including instrument names, articulations, ties, trills, slurs, hairpins, fermatas (pauses), repeats, first/second endings (first/second time bars), rits, accels, pedaling, transposing instruments, tremolos, glissandos (continuous/chromatic/white note/black note), percussion and drum sets, and guitar tab.
* Provides comprehensive guitar tab notations including bends, quarter-tone and microtone bends, prebends, slides, hammer-on, pull-off, vibrato bar scoop/dip/dive and return, bracketed notes, vibrato and wide vibrato, stem-less grace notes, palm mute, rake, etc. It easily converts notation to tab and back, and offers an almost unlimited range of fret instruments and tunings support that includes mandolin, lute, banjo, dobro, etc. It can even create custom fret instruments and tunings.

* Creates guitar frames automatically for over 50 chord types with any key note, bass note, stretch and tuning, along with optional chord symbols with guitar frames.
* Provides simple scoring for jazz, commercial, and rock music with chord symbols with automatic superscripts/subscripts that can be automatically transposed from Nashville chord numbering, jazz chord slashes, lifts and falls, etc., to drum set notation (based on recommendations of the U.S. Percussive Arts Society).
* Plays back in real time while screen follows the music and plays back text (e.g., mezzo-forte, mute, allegro, change to piccolo, etc.) using a customizable dictionary of musical terms in several languages.
* Provides fast-forward, rewind, and pause buttons and real-time tempo slider and tempo display. It offers Espressivo (five levels) natural-sounding expression, with independent phrasing for each instrument; Rubato (six levels), which has subtle variations of tempo that emulate a human performer; Rhythmic Feel, which modifies the rhythm and/or beat accents for 16 styles of music, including swing, funk, Viennese waltz, and notes inégales. Its SoundStage reproduces the real-world positioning of orchestral and band instruments.
* Supports a wide range of standard sound cards, keyboards, and sound modules, making it easy to add MIDI messages (e.g., control changes, SYSEX messages) and export MIDI files, incorporating all playback features into MIDI files (e.g., Espressivo, SoundStage, swing, interpretation of musical words, etc.).
* Calculates the duration of your score and displays time code above bar lines as a digital clock during playback.
* Allows seamless transfers of Sibelius files between Macs and PCs.
* Preserves your 40 most recently saved files with an auto-backup feature.
* Converts other music notation software from Finale 98 / 2000 / 2001 (.etf) / 2002 (.etf), SCORE, Allegro, PrintMusic, Acorn Sibelius, and MIDI (type 0 and 1) files in seconds.
* Prints music with exceptional quality based on the stringent printing requirements of the world's top music publishers. It also offers a wide array of printing options.
* Allows you to place your Sibelius scores on the Internet so that people can access, transpose, play, print, and save them from Web sites. The free Scorch Web browser (see below) plug-in allows the Web viewer to get the

same playback and print quality as the original Sibelius score. Using the Save as Scorch Web Page feature you can automatically create a Web page containing your score.

* You can click on a button that allows you to upload your music to Sibelius-Music.com (the largest sheet music self-publishing site on the Internet), where other people can purchase your music score. You also have the option of saving it to disc or CD-ROM.

Scorch. Scorch is a free download from Sibelius that allows people anywhere in the world to view, play, and print scores instantly and securely from your Web site, and even change the key and instrumentation of the music.

Many people save and send their music scores online in PDF, TIFF, GIFF, BMP, or JPEG file format. However, those kinds of files don't play back, they can't be transposed, you can't change the instruments, they are tens or hundreds of times larger than Sibelius files (so they take far longer to download, compared to the 2 seconds it takes a Sibelius file to be downloaded), and they are insecure (they can easily be copied without authorization). Even MIDI files, which do play online, can't be viewed, transposed, or printed unless the customer has a program which can turn them into notation and even then the notation produced is crude and omits many musical markings.

You can launch Scorch from your Web site and sell your music there or you can sell it on SibeliusMusic.com. If you choose to sell from the Sibelius Web site, they will handle all the transactions, and in return, you share 50/50 any money generated from Web site sales. This is another good way to get your music out there, in a different format, and generate some extra money.

G7. Yes, G7 is the name of a chord, but it's also the name of software that's billed as "the ultimate software for creating and playing guitar TAB." G7 can turn tab into notation and create lead sheets. It reads and plays tab from other people, allowing you to learn new songs quickly. You can add chord diagrams, symbols, and lyrics.

G7 plays back everything you create, including bends, slides, and other guitar techniques. You can hear how it sounds instantly, and if you need to learn to play it fast, simply watch the interactive fretboard play the music and follow along. G7 can create drum parts in seconds. You simply pick the style and G7's pattern generator writes out the entire drum part.

G7 also allows you to market your music to a worldwide audience via the Web and provides you with a free Web page to place your photo and bio. You can send your music (in tab format) to others by e-mail in the G7/Scorch format, where they can see it, print it, and play it using their browser.

The G7 software comes with a Guitar Guide, an encyclopedia of guitars, styles, and techniques that makes it easy to learn guitar skills and techniques. Plus it allows you to write tab faster and quicker with a feature called Fretboard Entry.

For more information on Sibelius 2, Scorch, and G7, go to www.sibelius.com.

Sonic Solutions

To take maximum advantage of digital audio technology in the new music business, you need to be thinking beyond the world of CDs. The worldwide video format is now DVD, and new markets can open for you and your music if you successfully merge the visual with the musical on DVD.

One company on the cutting edge of DVD-producing technology is Sonic Solutions, which was started by some of the folks who worked for legendary director George Lucas and his LucasFilms division. Sonic has brought powerful DVD-producing capabilities—which not too long ago would have cost tens of hundreds or even thousands of dollars—within the reach of anyone who uses a Mac or PC.

When mixing your music in 5.1 surround with DAWs like Nuendo, and then merging it into your own DVD (read: get a digital video camera and go out and start shooting bands or your own music videos), you'll be getting in the feature and function neighborhood of what the big DVD studios offer, and you can quickly add another title and business to your media empire—director of your own film production company.

ReelDVD. If you've always wanted a simple way to make pro-quality DVDs, then you need to check out ReelDVD. Indie filmmakers and producers use it, and it may be an ideal way for you to jump into music and film (on the cheap) and see where it takes you. Lots of would-be composers and musicians also have film aspirations, but in the past have been turned off by the steep learning curve and prohibitive costs. If you're looking for easy, ReelDVD is about as close to one-click DVD creation as you're likely to find.

ReelDVD comes with an interactive storyboard layout editor that provides a complete overview of your project. Along with that, you get an interactive time line, where you can add chapter marks, audio tracks, and subtitles.

Since DVD is the universal video standard, you have the ability to add up to 8 audio and 32 subtitle tracks alongside your video. If you're in a group that has a great sound with potential international appeal, you can shoot a video of the band, put a surround audio track of the music on the DVD, and then add foreign-language subtitles so your fans in Germany, Russia, Japan, or wherever can follow the lyrics and sing along.

To keep things simple, ReelDVD gives you an integrated project preview.

This feature allows you to play back your project directly from the hard drive so you can double-check every aspect of the kinds of interactivity you want your DVD to have *before* you replicate or burn to DVD-R.

You also get a subtitle editor that lets you quickly and easily add subtitles on the fly. Simply move the cursor to the time-line position for the subtitle, and enter the text. You get motion menus that let you interact with the video content by adding button links on top of video, and slide shows that'll let you take those digital and regular camera prints of the band, the gig, or whatever else, and put your music behind it and create a DVD.

Let's talk audio. ReelDVD automatically converts your audio to stereo Dolby Digital for professional set-top playback. This is a must-have if you don't want your music to sound cheesy or cheaply produced. It'll let you record your DVDs to DVD-R, DVD+R, DVD-RW, DVD+RW, DVD-RAM, CD-R, CD-RW, and DLT (digital linear tape) formats.

Sonic runs on the Windows platform.

DVD Producer. Let's say that Sonic sounds great to you, but you'd like to step up a notch to something with more features. Then check out Sonic DVD Producer. Sonic says DVD Producer is *the* DVD standard for multimedia professionals on Windows, and when you read what it can do on that Windows PC of yours you just might agree.

First, Sonic developed a feature called JumpAnywhere. This technology enables you to execute complex navigation sequences using simple drop-down menus and check boxes. This means you can author complex titles the day you load the software into your computer without having to learn the ins and outs of in-depth DVD production. DVD Producer automatically allows you to mix and match 4:3 and 16:9 video footage anywhere on the same disc. For those of you who may be new to DVD production, this is a function that used to take lots of time and a thorough understanding of how to do it—or megabucks to pay someone else to do it.

Okay, time for the cool stuff. With traditional DVDs, once you created the DVD, that was it. Changing things later was difficult and time-consuming. With OpenDVD, it is possible to open and re-edit your DVD discs across different applications. DVD Producer can both write to and read OpenDVD-compliant files, which will save you time and money any time you want to change your DVD project.

OpenDVD enables you to make changes to your DVD projects by simply reopening the project from the finished disc, making the requested changes, and then reburning. It's that simple. And you can do it as many times as you want.

Another of its features is a built-in menu compositor that lets you compile a range of DVD menus within the application. You can start with any generic still image or moving background, and then add graphics, text, and animated buttons. DVD Producer's animated menu compositor is able to extract any length of imported video, resize it, and then combine it with other text and graphic elements into a single MPEG file for use as a motion menu. It's a huge time-saver.

Ever see those still-image screen savers on your DVD when it's in the pause or stop mode? DVD Producer lets you create those same kinds of screen savers on your DVD; they're displayed whenever the disc is loaded and the DVD player is in the pause or stop mode.

DVD Producer's WriteDirect technology gives you a fast way to create a DVD-R or DLT from a finished project: The system writes directly to the DVD-R or DLT using the elements (e.g., pics, video, music) you used for your DVD. By eliminating the intermediate step of writing data to your computer's hard drive, WriteDirect can save hours of production time.

DVD Producer integrates the entire DVD production process—encoding, authoring, and writing DVD data to any medium—into a single application.

It has all the goodies of ReelDVD, including 8 audio streams and 32 subtitle streams (and each audio stream can be up to 5.1 surround sound) and real-time proofing that allows you to preview your DVD project at any time during assembly, or after the disc has been formatted, prior to replication. Its unlimited undo function allows you to experiment and change music and images as many times as you want and to return to a previous state quickly and easily—a feature quite similar to using a DAW's nondestructive editing capabilities.

DVD Producer lets you create visual and audio content with full D1-resolution video so your DVD has the same kind of surround sound and playback that the big studios use.

For more information on ReelDVD and DVD Producer go to www.sonic.com.

Spectrasonics

In the world of virtual instruments, one company is always mentioned for its innovation, great sounds, and powerful capabilities and that's Spectrasonics. The company was founded in 1994 by Eric Persing, composer/producer/chief sound designer for Roland. Persing's sounds on such Roland classics as the D-50, XV, and Variphrase instruments have been heard on countless hits, and it's no accident that this guy had what it took to come up with powerful music creation tools.

Professionals throughout the entertainment industry—from artists to producers to remixers to motion picture composers—use Spectrasonics products. Not surprisingly, you'll hear its samples on television, radio, and in hundreds of motion pictures. Its cross-platform plug-in compatibility makes it easy to use them with any DAW platform or Mac or PC. I'm going to tell you about three Spectrasonic plug-ins that will definitely take care of your bass, keys, synth, and drum and percussion needs: Trilogy, Atmosphere, and Styles.

Trilogy. Trilogy is a programmable sample-based sound-module plug-in that integrates a massive 3-gigabyte core library of hundreds of truly terrific bass sounds and, along with it, a powerful user interface for creating your own unique patches.

The real power of Trilogy lies within its layering concept. Beyond the core library are hundreds of basses, and every patch in Trilogy has two layers that you can tweak individually. You can also immediately mix and match any of the layers in the core library, and you can edit each one independently. You can easily combine the sound of a real Minimoog with a fretless bass, or a Virus with a TB-303, or even add a Juno suboscillator to an upright bass. There are thousands of combinations and it's safe to say you'll never run out of options. There are three parts to Trilogy: Acoustic Bass, Electric Bass, and Synth Bass.

Acoustic Bass. The highly detailed acoustic upright bass is one of the highlights of this instrument. Due to Trilogy's unique interface, you can get a wide variety of tones. This is made possible because the interface has separate control of the Neumann U-47 tube microphone signal and the direct pickup signal, which was sampled through a vintage Neve 1083 Console. This acoustic is chromatically sampled, with multidynamic velocity switching. The hardest velocity in every bass patch in Trilogy brings in real bass glisses, similar in concept to the idea Spectrasonics pioneered on the Hans Zimmer Guitar libraries. An acoustic Martin dreadnought bass guitar is also available in the Acoustic section, which can be perfect for those "unplugged" sessions.

Trilogy even features something called True Staccato technique, which lets you play repeated notes on the acoustic and electric basses in real time with a whole new level of realistic phrasing, and allows for repeated notes that sound completely natural.

Electric Bass. The huge selection of electric basses feature classic four-, five-, and six-string models, performed in fingered, picked, muted, rock and roll, slapping, ballad, fretless, and R&B techniques through rare, custom-made tube preamps. Special variations are presented that include harmonics, glisses, fuzz, trills, FX, and thousands of slides. Both modern and vintage old-school electrics are available, providing a wide array of tones for different musical settings. All the patches are mapped the same way, so that one sequence will work with any bass you select.

There are thousands of samples used in these instruments, mapped with multiple dynamics for expression. You don't have to "assemble" bass parts with Trilogy, as it's extremely playable as a highly expressive real-time instrument too. Every acoustic and electric bass has a special Finger Noise layer with release triggering that gives the basses realism that accurately simulates the fretboard response of the real bass.

When a note is released, the Finger Noise layer triggers an appropriate noise sample from among hundreds of tiny fret noises, subtle string scrapes, squeeks, x-notes, taps, and mutes, adding a user-controllable "human" imperfection element to your performance. You can easily control how much of this effect you want, since the noise effect is on its own layer, which is controlled from the Trilogy Mixer.

Synth Bass. The synth bass is built around high-resolution core samples from legendary analog bass synths like the Minimoog, Roland Juno 60, Roland TB-303, Roland SH-101, Oberheim SEM, Moog Taurus, OSCar, Virus, Yamaha CS-80, Arp Odyssey and 2600, Studio Electronics SE-1, Omega and ATC Tone Chameleon, Sequential Circuits Pro One, Moog Voyager, and many others. Trilogy's multimode resonant filters retain the original character and power of the classic analog instruments but still give you total control over the sound.

Each fully programmable layer has its own multimode resonant filters, four LFOs, three envelopes, adjustable sample start, and matrix modulation. There's also an additional master filter for quick tone shaping. In addition to gigabytes of high-resolution sampled vintage synth waveforms, Trilogy features smooth analog synth-style legato triggering and glide. This capability allows for synth bass sounds that truly play like a vintage analog synth. This feature can also be used with any of the electric or acoustic basses for unique hybrid bass sounds that may sound new to you.

Atmosphere. Atmosphere features a 3-gigabyte core library of over 1,000 unique sounds and layer elements, along with an intuitive interface for shaping new textures. Atmosphere works as a native plug-in instrument in all major hosts: Logic, Digital Performer, Cubase, Nuendo, Pro Tools, etc.

The Atmosphere custom core library offers a massive variety of tonal textures, especially when compared to standard soft synths, and includes over a hundred sound-design devices and nearly every conceivable synthesis method, including granular, additive, wave table, waves canning, grain table, neural processing, vintage analog, vector, virtual analog, FM, and plug-in manipulations, as well as unusual acoustic sources.

The sound quality is superb, and people who use this plug-in rave about the range of sounds Atmosphere is capable of, from lush ethereal pads to powerful leads, from crystalline glass swells to dark brooding atonal clouds, as well as unusual synth basses, evocative ambiences, deep drones, complex textures, vintage analog sounds, disturbing noise FX, europhasers, gorgeous ambient string ensembles, thick trance/techno sounds, wave-table sweeps, vocoded choirs, dense vocal washes, transparent evolutions, and shimmering prisms of harmonic convergence.

When you utilize Atmosphere's dual-layer feature (as with Trilogy, each layer has its own multimode resonant filters, four LFOs, and three envelopes, plus matrix modulation, etc.) you can mix and match the layers of any of the 1,000 patches and tweak each layer fully independently, giving you over 1 million possible sound combinations.

Stylus. A lot of people are into loops, samples, and grooves, and if you're one of them then check this out. It's called Stylus, and it features thousands of cutting-edge groove elements, loops, and samples, all with a powerful user interface for creating your own grooves. Stylus can be used as a native plug-in instrument in hosts like Logic, Digital Performer, Cubase VST, Nuendo, and Pro Tools, and no sampler is necessary

The 3-gigabyte core library of Stylus has over 3,000 patches and 38,000 samples with break-beat remix loops and a huge variety of remix genres including R&B, two-step, trip-hop, chemical, epic house, underground hip-hop, UK garage, down-tempo dub, nu-skool, acid jazz, trance, funk, alternative, progressive, rap, abstract, urban neo-soul, big beat, slo-jamz, drum 'n bass, and many others. It has 1,000 kicks, 1,000 snares, and 500 hi-hats, so there's little chance you'll be running out of choices anytime soon.

Each groove is presented in a Groove Control—activated version that allows you to change the pitch, tempo, feel, and pattern independently and without using any DSP. Since every groove can be mixed and matched at any tempo or feel, there are almost limitless combination possibilities. You can also program your own grooves from scratch with thousands of drum samples. In addition, Groove Menus lets you remix loops in real time at every tempo from 50 to 180 beats per minute in both straight and swing feels. It's as simple as selecting a patch and playing your keyboard.

Over a thousand wild turntable FX and DJ tricks are included, as well as a live percussion loop section that includes congas, bongos, djembes, shakers, triangles, agogos, and tambourines, all of which can be mixed into any groove separately. Groove Control also allows you to randomize the accents of a loop, turn a conga loop into a melodic part, do radical filter sequencing, and tweak the tuning of just the snare or filter just the kicks, panning each slice in a different part of the stereo field, each inside the loop. Each sample and slice has its own adjustable synth parameters, and selecting the samples is as simple as playing the sample from your keyboard.

For more information on Trilogy, Atmosphere, and Stylus go to www.spectra-sonics.net.

Steinberg

It didn't take the creator of Nuendo, Cubase, and VST long to become a major player in the virtual instrument field. The three Steinberg products I want to tell you about are Virtual Guitarist, Groove Agent, and XPhrase.

Virtual Guitarist. Have you ever wanted to play guitar? If you already play, have you ever wished you had more guitars (don't worry, all guitarists do)? How about being able to create great sounding guitar parts with your computer? If you answered "Yes" to any one of the above, Virtual Guitarist (VG) could be your answer. Designed to be used within any VST-compatible host application on both Mac and PC, here's how it works.

Virtual Guitarist comes with two VST instruments: electric and acoustic. You get 27 different players, and each has its own variety of guitars, sounds, and phrasing styles. Each of those 27 players can create 8 parts (variations) in real time. You can choose from loads of styles, be it Spanish to steel string to resonator to clean strat to wah to power chord to heavy metal.

You simply choose which guitar you want (acoustic or electric) and select a player from the 27 choices. You can use a single key, play whole chords, or use a MIDI track to create your music. Virtual Guitarist gives lots of control over shuffle (groove), dynamics, timing (tight or loose), syncopated rhythms, and long chords.

Included are effects that let you double-track and affect stereo width. You can do low cut and enhance for acoustic, and it gives you a pickup selector and presence control for electric. You can make sound changes in real time by using a keyboard or mod-wheel, after-touch, or velocity controls.

Groove Agent. Now that we've taken care of your virtual guitar needs, it's time for a virtual drummer with a plug-in called Groove Agent. Like Virtual Guitarist, this too is a VST-compatible host application for both Mac and PC. With only a few mouse clicks, you can have a studio drummer at your fingertips ready to play the hottest, most popular, and influential musical styles from the past 50 years.

Here's how it works. Simply choose a music style (there are over 50) and a drum kit (you get four drum kits plus percussion and lots of electronic sounds), and you're ready to go. You can tweak the drum rhythms and sounds over such parameters as drum room ambience (wet and dry), fills, and half-time breaks. You can choose from over 25 complexity levels simply by moving a slider, and you can combine each playing style with any other drum kit to get lots of cool grooves and sound combinations.

In addition, you can replace any of the preprogrammed instruments with your live playing from your keyboard, and adjust volume, ambience, decay, tuning, and velocity response individually for each instrument. And if you use Groove Agent with Cubase SX/SL or Nuendo, you can record its beats to a MIDI track and then edit them manually. Most of the sounds contained on Groove Agent were recorded on analog tape and all are in 24-bit.

Xphraze. This phrase synthesizer brings together unlimited sound creation, real-time polyphonic phrase creation, and intuitive live remixing functions. What does all that mean? It means you can create riffs, effects, arpeggios, morphs, pads, leads, and even 4-track songs quickly. But that's not all.

The power behind this VST-based plug-in is a multitimbral synth engine that lets you create a variety of rhythmical phrases, such as polyphonic chord patterns, drum grooves, bass lines, lead riffs, and tempo-synched sound effects. To use it, simply drag a phrase from the sound pool, tweak the groove and sound any way you want, play a note or chord, and then listen as Xphraze creates sound textures perfectly in synch with your song. You can even drag your own sounds into Xphraze.

Its Xmix function lets you use its live sound creation and remix of entire tracks using MIDI keys. You get controllable stereo insert effects for each timbre from 24 effects types, plus 4 master effects from 11 types. The Wave ROM gives you more than 200 waveforms, plus an import function for AIFF and WAV samples. The sound quality is superb. It offers 32-bit floating-point resolution and a 192-kHz sample rate, and it offers 1,024 voice/notes (256 per timbre).

For more information on Virtual Guitarist, Groove Agent, and Xphraze, go to www.steinberg.net.

TASCAM GigaStudio

Many musicians absolutely love, and wouldn't be caught making music without, their samplers. And for many of them, the samplers they've used have been hardware-based. However, while they're able to store, use, and create great sounds, the hardware-based samplers have limits, most notably sample size and polyphony (number of voices you can simultaneously play).

For some time now, one of the secret weapons found in the studios of many top film composers is TASCAM's GigaStudio. Even the name sounds huge. It's a complete sample playback system that uses the power of your Windows PC to create audio productions, complete with mixing and effects.

Many of the composers, artists, and producers who use Macs as their main music computers also have a Windows-based PC that runs GigaStudio. Using both Mac and PC with Giga is simple. You connect the PC with Giga software on it to a Mac and a DAW using any of the recommended interfaces listed on the GigaStudio Web site, and you've got a software sampler that acts like a hardware sample module, only with far more power and capabilities. And here's another secret: To get those amazing-sounding movie soundtracks, many composers are using *multiple* GigaStudio setups. Here's the lowdown on Giga.

GigaStudio is based on TASCAM's GigaSampler and its Endless Wave technology, a patented system that allows samples to be streamed off the hard drive instead of taking up RAM like many of the other samplers. Unlike the smaller-capacity samplers, which can handle only relatively small sample sizes that need to be looped, the Giga platform lets you work with huge sample sizes—up to 4.3 gigabytes—with low latency.

TASCAM's GigaStudio 160 delivers 64 MIDI channels over four unique ports. It has dedicated MIDI input for real-time effects and mixer automation, allowing the creation of massive performances with dynamically controllable effects. And GigaStudio 3 provides 24-bit 96-kHz audio and VST effects capabilities, and can be used with Propellerhead's ReWire.

GigaStudio provides up to 160 disk-based, streaming voices of polyphony in real time. In combination with your MIDI sequencer, you can create anything from a simple pop tune to an advanced, fully-orchestrated film score with sound quality that has been praised as indistinguishable from live recordings of performed instruments. You can also use 32-bit effects with it. The NFX real-time signal processing series includes the NFX1 Reverb/Multi-Effects, the NFX2 Chorus/Flanger, the NFX3 Tap Delay/Auto Pan, and the NFX4 EQ. And the NFX series operates with true zero-latency performance with GigaStudio.

GigaStudio has lots of sample libraries that have been specifically developed for the Giga platform (be sure to check out the Vienna Symphonic Orchestra Strings). GigaStudio is compatible with CD-ROM libraries, as well as with WAVE format samples. It comes with a DSP Station Mixing Console that includes Volume, Pan, Effect Sends, and Insert points that enable professional-quality mixing without the need for additional plug-ins or hardware. All parameters can be automated via MIDI and employ a 32-bit signal path for terrific sound quality.

GigaStudio features QuickSound technology that enables instant locating and previewing of samples, waves, and instruments in real time via an intuitive, database-assisted technology for cataloging instruments and sound samples using plain language. Just type in the type of sound you need (piano, drums, French horn, etc.) and QuickSound pulls up all the samples that fit the description. Plus, Giga-compatible instruments don't have to be resident on the client hard drive. Users of 100-baseT or better networks can easily access mapped drives in real time, allowing instant access to Giga-compatible systems and instruments via standard LAN connectivity.

GigaStudio includes a capture-to-wave feature which records entire performances, including effects, faders, pan, and MIDI automation, directly to disk. It supports 24-bit 96-kHz hardware, and has plenty of embedded help tools, an instrument editor which features advanced synthesis tools like multimode resonant filters, multiple envelopes and LFOs, drag-and-drop sample assignment, and up to 32 samples per key.

For more information on GigaStudio go to www.nemesysmusic.com.

Waves

You need to get turned on to a company whose audio plug-in products I've seen (and heard) used by more producers, artists, and engineers than any other. The company is called Waves, and its technology is top-notch. You know you are dealing with some serious tools when you get an endorsement like this from mastering guru Bob Ludwig: "The (Waves) Renaissance Vox is of one the easiest ways to get great-sounding vocals in your mix. One knob sets the amount of compression and automatic gain makeup, another knob sets a fabulous sounding gate for noise suppression. Two knobs. Waves does everything else for you!"

I'm going to tell you about three Waves audio bundles, any one of which might be just what you need.

Platinum Bundle. Platinum Bundle includes 25 processors that combine the Waves Gold, Masters, and Renaissance Collection 2 bundles all in one. It has over 300 setups and processors providing the highest-resolution tools for mastering, remix, restoration, multimedia, film, Web, games, and everything audio. Some of the audio tools included in this bundle are:

C4 Multiband Parametric EQ	MondoMod
Renaissance Reverberator	Doppler
Renaissance Compressor	UltraPitch
Renaissance EQ	MetaFlanger
L1 Ultramaximizer	TrueVerb Room Emulator
MaxxBass	DeEsser
Q10 Paragraphic	AudioTrack
S1 Stereo Imager	PAZ Psychoacoustic Analyzer
C1 Parametric Compander	Linear Phase Equalizer
Enigma	Linear Phase Multiband
Supertap	L2 Ultramaximizer

Broadcast and Production Bundle. The Waves Broadcast and Production Bundle is a great choice if you're doing work in television, film, or other media. It features the Renaissance Maxx, Masters, and Restoration processors (see below) and includes limiters, compressors, EQs, filters, noise removal, reverb, bass enhancement, de-essing, and voice processing. You'll be able to clean up audio, create superb voiceovers, quickly create both common and signature audio effects, fatten the sound, maintain complete level control, and create high-quality feeds and mixes. These are the same world-class standard processors used in Hollywood and in audio and music production all over the world.

Renaissance Maxx. This includes Renaissance EQ, Renaissance Compressor, Renaissance Reverberator, Renaissance Bass, Renaissance VOX, Renaissance De-Esser, and Renaissance Channel, allowing you to create common, signature, or special audio effects, enhance room simulations and reverberations, and generate a full-body sound on any consumer playback system.

For all-around sound shaping, this bundle is hard to beat. It features emulation of classic vintage analog equalization, dynamics, and reverb, plus a powerful vocal processor, a de-esser offering adaptive threshold for natural-sounding de-essing, Renaissance Bass, and Renaissance Channel that handles EQ, compression, gating, and limiting.

The Renaissance Compressor uses vintage Opto modeling and an L1-style limiter. It is not only a great compressor, limiter, and gate, but allows you to increase perceived volume and stability for vocal and solo instruments, and lets you bring vocals to the front of the mix with ease. You'll also use Renaissance Bass to add some big-time subsonic to your music tracks, and Renaissance DeEsser to clean up those vocal hisses and esses for a more natural-sounding result.

Restoration. This includes X-Noise, X-Click, X-Hum, and X-Crackle, offering a powerful (and largely self-explanatory) group of noise-cleaning and noise-removal tools. You'll be able to clean up location and production audio, salvage previously unusable audio, quickly solve special audio problems (such as rumble, hiss, bad mic placement, noisy environment, and poor tone), and make old recordings worthy of today's broadcasting standards.

Masters. This includes Linear Phase EQ and 5-band Multi-band dynamics processor, plus the L2, offering tools for precision content preparation for transmission and broadcast dynamics control, phase distortion and coloration eliminator, transparent and precise dynamics and filtering control, multiband dynamics control, and an EQ that has to be heard to be believed.

For more information on the Platinum, Broadcast and Production, and Renaissance Maxx bundles, go to www.waves.com.

Outboard Gear, Sound Controllers, and Mixers

We've talked a lot about computers, DAWs, and software plug-ins that recreate real instruments and many great effects. However, lots of artists, engineers, and producers also use outboard effects gear. Some use them for signal processing prior to voice and music recording, others to process recorded tracks and give them effects. There isn't any "right" or "wrong" when it comes to choosing equipment. Great joy and inspiration can be found when you come up with your own combinations and create your sound in your own way. This section covers—briefly—some of the outboard gear and sound modules you might want to check out.

Sound Controllers

In addition to outboard gear, it's smart to have a sound controller (or two or three) that allows you to access sounds from a keyboard and not just from a computer keyboard or mouse. Some MIDI controllers are just that—a keyboard that is used to control, patch, or program sounds from your plug-ins and outboard sound module gear.

While other MIDI controllers have sounds (some of them, lots of sounds), you'll pay more for the added features. You can choose anything from a small, inexpensive Edirol or M-Audio MIDI controller, to a classic MIDI controller like the Roland A-70, A-80, or A-90, to a fully loaded Kurzweil. The best advice I can give you is go to a music store and have them demo MIDI controllers (even those with sound capabilities), then go with what works best for your needs and your budget.

Some of my musician/producer friends have racks of outboard gear and sound modules, and/or keyboards of classic gear like the Nord rack, Korg Triton Studio keyboard/rack, Roland XV series rack, E-MU sound modules, Access Virus, Waldorf, Kurzweil keys/rack, Parametric EQs, and others that they'll use along with plug-ins. Many of them also use the Electrix rack gear (cheaply priced, good quality, out of production, though still easy to find on eBay or Harmony-Central.com) to shape music and vocals either before or after tracks are recorded, or during recording.

Ask others what they are using. Log in to a few of the gear chatrooms and don't be shy about asking lots of questions. Musicians like to help other musicians.

Mixers

If you've ever played live or been in a recording studio, you know what the recording console/mixer does. While the DAWs featured in this book allow you to use your computer screen, keyboard, and mouse as your mixer, you might want to give some thought to getting a dedicated mixer that's compatible with the DAW you have (or will soon be getting), as well as your outboard gear and keyboard/MIDI controller.

Many digital mixers (also known as DAW controllers or DAW control surfaces) are completely compatible with your DAW applications software and include lots of shortcuts for many DAW program tasks—a huge time-saver. Having a dedicated mixer also means that you don't have to be in the computer realm all the time. You can turn real knobs and move real faders—the kind of thing that makes it feel like you're recording and mixing music in a professional studio.

My advice here is to begin your search for a good digital mixer/control surface from companies like Yamaha, Mackie, Emagic, Mixed Logic, Digidesign, Sony, and TASCAM. Demo them. Get a good feel for how they work. Discuss your current and future needs with a pro audio person, and then pick the mixer that best fits those needs and your budget.

Storage Systems

As I said way back at the beginning of this lesson, there are six components to your recording studio setup: your computer; your computer/audio interface; DAWs; plug-ins; outboard gear, controllers, and mixers; and storage systems. It's the last one that I want to talk to you about now. It makes no sense to spend money on the first five if you don't cover yourself by having a bullet-proof number six.

Storage. I know, it's boring, it just sits there, and it doesn't make any cool sounds. It's usually the last thing people think about while they're recording. But it's the first thing they think about if something goes wrong with it. Great sessions and ideas—great music—can be lost forever if you don't have a backup storage medium that *safely and reliably* records them.

Before going into the different backup storage options, let me emphasize an important point. Far too many people rely on a single internal hard drive as a storage medium. But as we all know, computers (and hard drives) can crash. If your computer crashes, and the only place you have stored your work is on that computer's hard drive, everything you've done can be gone in an instant. Retrieving data (if it's even possible) from a crashed hard drive can be very expensive. That's why you need an external storage medium (or even two) to archive your masterpieces.

Tape Storage

As Bob Clearmountain tells you in the next chapter, he uses a Sony 3348 digital tape machine for backup storage for several reasons: It's a good interface for his SSL console; the music can be played back without the need for a particular edition of a music editing program; and it allows him to mix right off the tape. I'd like to suggest that the 3348 is a good choice for you also. If the price of the 3348 puts it beyond your reach right now, you can still use a tape backup. There are plenty of great used 24- to 48-track tape machines out there. Check out the Internet for used analog and digital tape machines made by Ampex, MCI, Otari, Revox, Sony, and Studer. Read the reviews and note the prices, and as soon as your budget allows, pick one up. It'll be a smart move.

Hard Disk Storage

Before going into specific hard disk storage options, I'd like to review some facts about recording in the new music business. The following "primer" is based on material prepared by the folks at Glyph, a company that has built its reputation on making storage systems for music applications.

As you know, DAWs are computer-based systems that facilitate digital audio recording. They bring the power of random access (nonlinear), nondestructive editing and excellent signal-to-noise ratios to home studios as well as to the world's elite professional studios.

In multitrack audio there are generally numerous data files for each track, especially with punch-ins and edits. The time it takes a computer drive to find and process files depends both on the number and size of the files and several hardware-related factors: the rotational speed of the platters that make up the hard disk, expressed in revolutions per minue; the time it takes the drive's read/write heads to find the physical location of a piece of data, expressed in milliseconds; and the media rate (the speed at which data is transferred to and from the platters), expressed in megabytes per second.

Because of the time it takes for the data to pass underneath the heads, drives with slower spindle speeds, like 7,200 rpm, take longer to access each file than drives with speeds of 10,000 and 15,000 rpm. Audio applications are very demanding on drives, since small delays in the delivery of requested files results in playback errors. Faster spindle speeds yield extra audio tracks with more edits. This is the reason that a bargain-price 5,400-rpm drive is useless for your DAW.

The switch from analog recording tape to digital storage media has built an insatiable demand for higher capacities and increased performance from disk drives. At the same time, it is vital to be able to create digital backup copies of sessions and masters. Historically, the dominant interface for connecting storage media devices to a DAW has been small computer system interface (SCSI).

Macintosh computers don't ship with an integrated SCSI bus anymore, so a host bus adapter is needed when connecting any SCSI device to a newer Mac. Over the past few years, SCSI's domination has been challenged, especially in home and project studios. FireWire is usually sufficient for the needs of home-studio digital audio. Only at the very high end of computer-based audio production, when it's important to run extremely large sessions on one drive, is SCSI absolutely necessary.

If audio tracks are spread across multiple FireWire drives, the user can effectively get the same or better performance than SCSI. For this reason, it's now possible to have a totally FireWire studio. One of the advantages to FireWire is that you no longer need a SCSI host bus adapter card for your Mac.

One thing all DAWs have in common is that the digital audio data must be stored, edited, and backed up for archival purposes. In the past, a fixed hard disk drive was the most common device used for storing data from a DAW. Today, hot swapping allows you to remove one hard drive while the computer is still running and insert another for immediate use. Hot swapping is tricky, but if done right it is efficient and cost-effective. It is also expandable. When you need more storage, just add more drives.

The audio/music sampler market is very mature, with multiple generations of samplers in the field from many manufacturers. Fortunately, most of the sampling units available today have SCSI interfaces to allow the user to connect CD-ROM drives and hard disk drives. Users should beware, though, as most samplers are quite specific as to what storage devices are compatible.

While audio and video are often thought of together ("A/V" this and "A/V" that), they are actually quite different animals. Audio and video have different data transaction requirements, and therefore each has its own storage needs. Due to the relatively small size and large number of files that must be pushed through the system in many audio applications, processing digital audio is transaction-intensive. In contrast, video applications usually involve a constant demand for huge files, but a smaller number of them. Capturing a half hour of DV-quality footage takes up over 6 gigabytes of disk space, and that's with compressed files. If you are working with uncompressed files, to get the same quality you could expect to use over 40 gigabytes for a half hour. Nonlinear editors trying to record and play back such files need sufficient bandwidth to do the job. (*Bandwidth* refers to the amount of data that can be transmitted in a fixed amount of time, and it is often expressed in megabytes per second.) Nonlinear editors create large files comprised of detailed pixel and color information. If the data is not transferred quickly enough for the application to process it—that is, if there is insufficient bandwidth—frames will be dropped. Achieving relatively high bandwidths can be done with consistent use of high-speed interfaces such as FireWire, SCSI, or Fibre Channel. In addition, the drives on these interfaces can be configured in a redundant array of independent disks (RAIDs), which spreads the I/O load over several drives, improving access time and reducing the risk of losing data if one drive fails. With RAID, the multiple drives are striped, or partitioned, then arranged as if they were one storage unit. More disks yield greater bandwidth up to the limits of the interface. For example, the FireWire limit is 50 megabytes per second, whereas the 2-Gbit Fibre Channel limit is 200 megabytes per second.

As stated above, audio files tend to be smaller than video files, but there are more of them, and the time it would take for multiple drive heads to synchronize an audio project's files would negate any bandwidth gains. The only time to consider using RAID in audio is when you intend to mirror your data to safeguard it.

With all that in mind, and with the emergence of FireWire-based connections and its ability to carry lots of bandwidth quickly, I'm going to suggest that FireWire be a starting point for your hard disk music storage. All you need to do is plug in the FireWire connection from your computer into the FireWire storage drive and you're ready to record and play back.

In the digital storage world, FireWire and hot swapping can make your music recording way easier and enjoyable. FireWire allows you to:

✽ Record in the studio, pulling the FireWire drive and taking it home to mix the record there

✽ Move projects from one room to another, allowing you to track directly to it or use a different drive for each client's work

✽ Send a drive home with anyone on the session or use one drive to back up the data on another one

Glyph Technologies. Here are two Glyph storage drives I'd like you to check out.

GT 051. Glyph's GT 051 (FireWire Tabletop) is a good starting point for your hard disk music storage. GT 051 is a tabletop hot-swap single-space three-bay enclosure. It comes in a sturdy steel case, and includes a built-in power supply and a standard dual 6-pin FireWire interface. It can be combined with GT Key drives that are available in 80-, 120- and 180-gigabyte capacities so you can organize projects on one or multiple drives and manage them through the single tabletop enclosure. You can even rack-mount the GT 051.

One of the big benefits of FireWire is hot-swappability, which lets you remove or insert the drive tray at the FireWire interface level. Another cool thing about Glyph's storage systems is that the hard drives and fans are mounted on Glyph's QuietMetal, which is a composite metal technology that keeps things very quiet in the studio. Lots of storage drives are noisy. These aren't. The GT 051 can handle high-definition sample rates, and includes the Glyph Audio Storage Toolkit formatting and partitioning software.

GT 103. Equipment in the audio world just keeps getting smaller, better, faster, and cheaper. If you're looking for lots of storage in a small space, then what you can accomplish with this one-space rack-mounted unit is noteworthy. For example, you can configure any combination of up to three fixed-mount or GT Key hot-swappable drives. It has a 7,200-rpm hard drive and uses the same QuietMetal trilaminate technology found in the GT 051. It also has 80-, 120-, and 180-gigabyte hard drive storage capacities in each storage drive bay. Imagine having three 180-gig drives in just one rack space. That's room for lots of music.

For more information go to www.glyphtech.com.

Studio Network Solutions. I first got turned on to Studio Network Solutions after I saw their storage systems being used by producers and engineers in high-end Pro Tools studio rigs.

Be forewarned: These are pro-level systems for pro-level applications (but you're a pro, so relax), and the people who use them swear by them. The innovative Studio Network Solutions technology is built around two things: fiber-channel storage and multiple-user storage networking. Here's the idea behind it.

Within traditional local storage systems—for example, SCSI or integrated data electronics (IDE)—a single computer has one or more internal or external dedicated drives which can't be easily shared at the same time by other computers without the help of networking software. With a storage area network (SAN), each computer in your studio can be connected directly, or through a fiber-channel switch or hub, to an array of hard drives. And multiple users, with multiple computers, can work on the same song (or do live recording, tracking, mixing, and video capture and playback), at the same time, and it doesn't matter whether the computers being used are Macs or PCs.

With a SAN system, you can simultaneously connect a storage drive with as many as 20 other storage drives, as well as record or play back as many as 128 tracks at 48 kHz or 64 tracks of 24-bit 96-kHz audio at once. Two SAN products developed by Studio Network Solutions are Fibredrive and A/V SAN.

Fibredrive: Fibredrive is an entry-level one-user system that's ideal for a single DAW. It's easy to hook up and, once you've installed it, the system appears to your DAW as a local drive. This means that it can be used with virtually any audio, video, or digital imaging application, and on either Mac or Windows platforms.

A/V SAN. A/V SAN is a step up from Fibredrive, and it's a great solution for your studio if you have two workstations. It offers a Second User option that gives simultaneous access to its storage. The benefit of adding a second workstation to your studio (having both a Mac and a Windows-based PC) is that it allows two separate control rooms or suites to collaborate on projects. Each workstation connects to the centralized storage unit optical cable, so there's no longer the need to physically move hard drives from one workstation to another.

With its SANmp Management Software, the A/V SAN allows you to configure shared storage any way you'd like. You can secure certain portions of it so that only authorized people (like engineers, editors, or clients) can access the stored data. You can also specify which users are to have read-only access and which will be able to edit files and record content. A/V SAN is easily upgradable as your music projects grow and your workstation needs increase.

For more information on Fibredrive and A/V SAN go to www.studionetworksolutions.com.

Mixing Your Music:

Advice from Bob Clearmountain

I'll admit it: At times, I can be a liner note reader. You know, someone who picks up a CD and goes right to the inside liner to find out who engineered and mixed the songs. And wouldn't you know, on many of my favorite songs and albums, the name that has popped up over and over again is Bob Clearmountain.

Although I heard the magic that Bob Clearmountain worked on records in the 1980s, I think the first time I really stopped to give a good listen to what this guy did was when I played Bryan Adams's 1993 greatest hits album *So Far So Good.* The production and mix of those hits would make even the lamest of stereo systems sound terrific. It's how a great rock album should sound. And perhaps the greatest compliment is that it *still* doesn't sound dated today.

Now add to that his work on Simple Minds' *Once Upon a Time* and Hall & Oates' *Big Bam Boom* and INXS's *Kick* and Bruce Springsteen's *Born in the USA,* as well as records by Aerosmith, Bon Jovi, David Bowie, Jackson Browne, The Clash, Shawn Colvin, The Corrs, Crowded House, The Cure, Dire Straits, Melissa Etheridge, Goo Goo Dolls, The Kinks, King Crimson, Kiss, Huey Lewis & the News, Elton John, Edwin McCain, Paul McCartney, Willie Nelson, The Pretenders, The Rolling Stones, Carly Simon, Sister Sledge, Ringo Starr, Tears For Fears, Toto, Tina Turner, The Who, and many others, and you'll get a good idea of what this guy is capable of.

But don't stop there. Bob's also done the music for movies like *9 1/2 Weeks, Ace Ventura, Bridget Jones's Diary, Four Weddings and a Funeral, Philadelphia,* and *Stuart Little 2.* And add to the mix such special projects as Bruce Springsteen & the E-Street Band in *Live in New York* [HBO Special], *Live Aid* (live worldwide TV and radio), *Saturday Night Live: 25 Years* [NBC], *The Concert for Nelson Mandela* [live worldwide TV and renamed *Freedom Fest* in the United States on Fox TV Network], *The Concert for New York City* [VH-1], *Woodstock '94* [live pay-per-view cablecast], *The Rolling Stones and The Who* [live pay-per-view and Fox TV], and you have an amazing body of work that has defined a man, a genre, and an approach to mixing music and records that people will be going back to years from now.

To meet Clearmountain, as he often signs his e-mails, is to get a quick lesson in humbleness and not letting a name, a reputation, or even vast amounts of success go to your head. There's nothing pretentious about Bob or his work. What you see is what you get, and what you hear is what so many people would like to get.

I had the opportunity to sit down with Bob at his home studio in Pacific Palisades, California, and for the next few hours he gave me tape after tape of inspiring advice. In this lesson Bob offers a gold mine of information that's bound to help anyone wanting to produce and mix music in today's new music business.

Bob on Starting Out

I grew up in Greenwich, Connecticut, and was an amateur musician, playing bass in a couple of different local bar bands there and in Westchester County in New York. The last band was doing a couple of demos in a studio in New York City called Media Sound with an engineer named Michael Delugg. In the middle of doing that, the band split up.

So, I started coming into New York and hanging around the studio, bugging them to hire me. In fact, the first time I had ever been in a studio was with my band when we were doing those demos. I was 19 years old.

The studio experience was fascinating to me. I was always the guy in the band who was recording the rehearsals and the gigs. I was kind of the producer, too, who was telling everybody what to play and doing the arranging. The first time I walked into the studio, I knew I could spend all my time there. It had everything I wanted.

The studio experience was a real turning point for me. For one thing, I really didn't feel I could depend on other musicians for my living, which is what you have to do when you're in a band. And bands had let me down so many other times that I thought, okay, maybe it's time for a real job.

I never went to recording school or had any specific training to do what I do. I was in high school bands and in choirs and took a few electronics classes, but no formal music or recording training to speak of. It was just something I loved doing and I was always wanting to learn as much as I could on my own.

I even skipped college. My parents were just retiring at the time I was finishing high school and they told me to either go to state college or be on my own and pay for college myself. And at the time, I really didn't know what I wanted to go to college for, because what I really wanted to do was be in a recording studio. And since there weren't any college courses at that time for recording, I just went right to work. What I did was an old time hands-on apprenticeship in the studio.

So I started learning more about recording and what the studio did until the folks at Media finally hired me after bugging them over and over again. I was an assistant for a few years, but pretty early on, I got to do some recording sessions myself.

In those days, studios would assign staff engineers to sessions. One day I was assisting on a Kool & the Gang session with an engineer who was mainly a jingle guy and he said to me, "Hey, why don't you go ahead and do this session?" As he just sat there and read the paper, I did overdubs and mixed a couple of songs. That happened only after three months of working there, so I was pretty lucky.

About six months later, Kool & the Gang was working on its next album and I was the assistant once again. However, the engineer was sick this time and I recorded basic tracks for them for two nights. The two songs I engineered ended up being hits. One was called "Hollywood Swinging" and the other was called "Funky Stuff." I think "Hollywood Swinging" reached number six on the charts. It was the first song I actually ever recorded from scratch.

I ended up doing a lot of R&B records and I worked on a lot of things like jingles and movies. Media did most of the music for *Sesame Street* as well.

Then, in 1977, two guys from Media Sound opened a studio called Power Station in New York. I went over to work at Power Station for a few years and helped design that studio, which is now called Avatar. Once I started working at Power Station, I began producing. At first, it was some punk rock bands for Sire Records. Soon thereafter, I began producing Bryan Adams and lots of others. The mixing thing quickly followed.

The first client at Power Station was a band called Chic. It was a big disco act at the time. I got a reputation at Atlantic Records for the work I did with them because Chic was quite successful. The Rolling Stones were on Atlantic at the time and so was Roxy Music.

The Rolling Stones were looking to do a dance mix of a song called "Miss You," and someone from Atlantic Records recommended me. I mixed the 12-inch of that song and got to mix the single as well. That was sort of my introduction to big-time rock music. After that, I started doing some stuff for Bruce Springsteen, because the E-Street Band played on an Ian Hunter album called *You're Never Alone with a Schizophrenic* that I had engineered. I also did more things with the Stones and with Roxy Music, whose song "Dance Away" and album *Avalon* were big records for them.

Things just picked up from there. I was doing more mixing, I became independent, and began producing and mixing in other studios in New York, London, San Francisco, and Sydney. I eventually moved to Los Angeles, where I built my own home studio from which I work out of today.

Early on in my musical career, I was really influenced by The Beatles,

The Rolling Stones, the Who, Traffic, and Led Zeppelin. Hendrix was a big thing for me in terms of influencing my producing and mixing.

When I was a kid listening to Hendrix records, I didn't know anything about recording, but I noticed he would do wacky things like crazy panning and flanging effects. The environment of the records always managed to match his incredible lyrics. I wondered what that was and how they were doing it. I knew somebody, besides the musicians, was in the picture, and I wanted to be that guy.

To this day, Beatles records still amaze me. It's almost depressing, because with such basic tools they got amazing sounds that we still can't get—even today. Geoff Emerick, George Martin, and The Beatles were one of those rare combinations of talent with the unbelievable creativity to come up with many of the best pop records ever made. Everyone should listen to those records carefully if they're wanting to be inspired and learn a powerful lesson: Modern technology can be great, but you don't need it to create brilliant records.

Being Successful in Music Is Doing the Best You Can

My philosophy about being successful in music is just simply to do what you do and do it the best you can. I was never much of a schmoozer, and I don't hang out with people and try and sell myself to them and explain to them why they should be working with me. I'm terrible at those kinds of things.

All I do is mix records the best way I can, and if people hear them and like what I do, hopefully they'll ask me to mix their record. I mean, I don't even have a manager going out getting me gigs, whereas a lot of other mixers and producers have managers that are always in the faces of record labels.

My manager, Dan Crewe, is off the beaten path and lives up in Maine. In fact, in the 1980s I had to *talk him* into managing me. He had managed his brother, Bob Crewe, who was a big record producer in the 1960s, and Dan had had it with the record business. But he was the only one I knew that *knew* anything about the business. He was a down-to-earth guy. He wasn't a hustler, which I liked. And it's worked great. He does the deals and makes sure I don't get ripped off.

I've always told people, whether you're a composer, musician, engineer, producer or anything in-between, just enjoy what you're doing. I always have and I was pretty amazed that I could make a nice comfortable living doing what I do. Years ago, it never occurred to me that I could make money doing what I do. I would've done it anyway, regardless of whether I made a little or a lot of money. The only thing I ever wanted to do was make records for the rest of my life. And if I could do that and earn a living, even live in a little studio apartment somewhere, then I'd be totally happy.

A Constantly Changing Approach
to Recording and Mixing Music

You never know what song or record you're working on will become a hit or not become a hit, and which ones will still be touching people's lives 20 years from now. Chic had a record called "Good Times" and it was obvious it was going to be a hit. I knew for sure that Bruce Springsteen's *Dancing in the Dark* would be a hit. Yet for the most part, you just never know.

The album *Avalon* from Roxy Music that I mixed in the '80s is a good example of how a record has a big impact on a lot of people and I wouldn't realize it until many years later. It wasn't until a few years ago that it went platinum, and surprisingly it's been the record that I get the most compliments about. I mean, people tell me that their child was conceived to that record [laughs]. You just never know.

I remember when we mixed Shawn Colvin's "Sunny Came Home." As soon as I heard it I thought, wow, that's a great song. In my opinion, it was the best song on the album. Then the record company released "Get Out of This House" as the first single and it did absolutely nothing. They finally came out with "Sunny Came Home" and it was a big hit. Go figure!

There have been plenty of other times I thought songs would be hits and nothing happened. And a lot of times it was because they weren't promoted and the label didn't do anything to get the record out there. Yet who's to say whether they weren't hits because nobody heard them or possibly because the songs weren't actually good enough?

My philosophy about mixing records has gone through many changes over the years. Even though a hit song is a hit song, I like to look at it as an evolving process, because music and styles are always changing. My criterion for a well-engineered, mixed, or recorded song is simple: Does the song come through? If everything in the mix and the music enhances the feeling and the thought behind the lyric, melody, and music, then I'm doing my job.

It isn't the best drum sound or guitar sound that makes a great recording. It's all about how everything fits into the mix. If you're doing a rock record, you're looking for a certain kind of excitement. If you're doing a dance or hip-hop record, you're looking for something that's going to make you dance, get up, and move around.

If it's a Springsteen song, you want something that's going to make you think and not take away from the power of the song's lyrics. You want it to make you think about what is the state of the character in the lyric. You don't want your mix to get in the way of that, and you want everything in your mix to enhance those qualities.

When I was producing, it was all about being transparent and enhancing each of the song's most important qualities, bringing them to the surface for everyone to hear, so the message was easy to get at by the listener.

I go back and listen to stuff I mixed in the '80s and it all sounds like there's way too much reverb and delay. Nowadays, I mix a lot drier. I'm always learning so much from working with many different producers, artists, and kinds of music.

People like Bryan Adams and Bruce Springsteen taught me about how important the *song* is. It doesn't matter if you're playing, mixing, or recording. The song is the most important thing, and nothing should ever get in the way of that. It's an important lesson I've learned and I hope it's been reflected in everything I've done since then.

Whenever I listen to a new song on the radio, my ears go to the melody first and the way the melody relates to the chords. After that, I'll listen to how the words work with the melody and what it's about. The production and the mix are the last things I listen to. On a lot of pop records, what the words are saying really doesn't matter that much. But it is really nice when you hear a hit record and the words actually mean something.

I think that's what's so powerful about someone like Eminem. Even though a lot of what he's saying is irritating to a lot of people, whether you like it or not, you immediately get exactly what he's talking about—the songs are actually *about* something. For a lot of records, you don't know or don't care what they're saying, but with Eminem, there are two listeners: those who are pissed off at what he's saying and those who agree with him. He's making a statement and it's very powerful. That's the kind of thing that makes a hit record.

Some people have asked me if I think less is more when it comes to mixing and recording music, and I say *sometimes,* but not always. A philosophy I've always had is that there aren't any real rules about recording and mixing music.

I noticed that whenever I've done lectures or seminars and tell people, okay, in that kind of situation you want to do this and in this kind of situation you want to do that, there's always the exception where you do just the opposite. Never get locked into thinking you must always do something a certain way, because you'll find a situation where that's completely wrong and you need to go the other direction.

There are some things that I find myself preferring when I mix a record in regards to vocal and instrument placing. However, pop music styles have changed and the emphasis on even those things shifts over the years. I'll give you a couple of examples.

In the 1970s and '80s, emphasis on the drums and bass was the big thing. Then, when we got into the '90s, the drums weren't that important. In fact, it sounded stupid to have big overpowering drums. Rhythm has always been important, but the rhythm now comes from other things and not necessarily just the drums.

Along with that, my tastes change as well, and I think that has to be if I'm wanting to stay current and a little ahead of the curve. I'll hear stuff on the radio that I like and I might take some of that inspiration and use it on a project where it could be just what the record needed. I think it's a good thing that one's taste changes over time. You can't keep making the same kind of records you made in 1979 or else nobody's going to hire you, not to mention boring yourself to death. As John Lennon once said, "So who says I have to be consistent?"

I've had people ask me over the years if I have a signature sound and I tell them, I hope not. I don't think I do and I try not to, because to me, the signature should be the artist and whatever the project is I'm mixing. I try not to impose any signature of mine on what they do. The only thing I want to give them is a great record that's fun and enjoyable for the listener. Hopefully, that's my signature. There are records that I hear and I can tell who mixed them. For me, I just hope people can't tell I'm the one mixing the records. I really do not want to have that sort of identity. I just want the records to be great.

Always remember that there really is no right or wrong way to record music. It's all a matter of perspective and taste. The way I record and mix records could be very different than someone else. That's what makes records interesting and hopefully enjoyable. We all have different styles, as we all like different types of music. If I turned on the radio to find every record sounded like one of mine, I'd just switch to the news station!

I think a mixer or producer should approach each record as if it's the only one he'll ever do. Give it all you've got, and you'll always be able to say you gave it your best. Where it goes from there, only time will tell and the listeners, or the label, will decide.

The Bob Clearmountain Mixing Process

One of my biggest pet peeves is a rhythm track that's mixed really dry—where the drums and the guitar are right up front and in your face—and then the vocals are swimming in reverb way off in the back. I just don't understand that. The mental picture gets very confused, or is simply nonexistent. The band sounds like it's in this little anechoic chamber, but the singer is in the Grand Canyon or Carnegie Hall— it doesn't make sense. It's usually much easier to picture the vocalist up close to the listener and fairly dry, with the band behind him or her.

It's as if the engineer soloed the drums and said "Oh, this sounds good" and soloed the guitars and said "This sounds good" and then soloed the voice with a lot of reverb and said "That sounds nice," then put it all together and didn't bother to really pay attention to hear if it all *worked* together.

It's really obvious to me that you would want everybody to sound like they're coming from basically the same place. Of course quite often you'll use a unique massive 'verb on an element of the mix simply for contrast. See, I told you there are no hard and fast rules about mixing. When it's done *purposefully* to be interesting, that can work. It's when it doesn't make any sense, and when it's all thrown together without much thought, that I have a problem with it.

I think you need to be careful about using too much compression. Yet for some records and styles of music, it can work, especially modern rock records where maximum excitement is the goal. So many of these songs are mixed for hit radio where they're trying to make things as loud as they possibly can to grab your attention and using lots of compression can help do that. Unfortunately, using too much compression tends to homogenize everything and when you lose the dynamics—particularly on records with more dynamically open arrangements—you can suck the life out of what could have been a great-sounding mix. For some records, lots of compression does work really well. However for others, you want to hear less compression, you want to hear the dynamics, and you want to let the record breathe. You want to hear the space between the instruments instead of having every moment constantly filled.

Nowadays, almost every project we get comes in on hard drives or CD-ROM instead of tape. And there's a lot of bad editing from people who don't know how to use the music software, were very rushed to finish the project, or are just lazy. On a lot of projects, we'll spend several hours just fixing pops and clicks, redoing crossfades, and things like that. The other problem we see is tracks not labeled correctly, so working out what's what can take a lot of time.

Once the tracks in the DAW session are reorganized and all the edits are cleaned, we'll digitally transfer everything over to my Sony 3348 HR, which is a 24-bit 48-track digital tape recorder. They don't get used much anymore since most people mix directly off of their digital workstation. I like using the 3348 because it interfaces well with my SSL console and it also gives me another degree of safety. I now have another backup to what's on the hard disk. Not to mention, the record labels like that there's a safety master and it's on a format that's easy for them to deal with in the future, without needing the right version of some music editing software in order to play it back.

Another bonus in having the tape backup is that it allows me to mix off the tape, while my assistant can work on doing some additional editing, such as moving vocals around or adding a bass drum sample if needed.

As I start mixing, typically the artist, the producer, or both will come into the studio in the morning and give me a rundown on what's on the tape and what I should be watching out for. They'll also tell me what the thought was behind the recording. I'll take some notes and ask questions about the song and what's important to them about the track.

What the artist and producer say is the important thing to me. I try to think like they're thinking. Once I get a good idea of where they're coming from, I'll then spend a few hours and give them my interpretation. If theirs is different, they'll tell me "No, this is the kind of thing we were thinking about," and I'll change it to give them the record they're wanting.

To me, what I think about the record is just a suggestion. Take it or leave it. If they see it differently, that's what's most important. I'll never get married to an idea unless it's the right one for the artist and producer.

After our meeting, they'll usually leave for a while, or just go outside and hang by the pool, and I'll begin the mix. At first I'll spend a couple of hours just getting to learn what's on the tracks. I'll do a quick rough mix and try to get what the song is all about while really listening closely to the vocal. I'll then spend a good amount of time soloing or featuring individual tracks, learning what each instrument or vocal contributes to the overall picture. If it's a song with only 20 tracks, then it goes pretty quickly, but some songs will have 80 tracks, which might take a bit longer.

Next, I begin working on sounds and perspectives, such as panning, EQ, compression, effects, and figure out what sort of environment the song should be in, what sort of reverbs, if any, I should be using, or maybe adding some effects, such as a delay on a voice.

As far as sounds go, sounds are sounds, and rarely are things good or bad. It's bad if it's totally the opposite sound of what the producer had in mind. Yet a "bad" sound can be a good sound if it works in the record and it's what the producer and artist want.

The other day, a project came into the studio that was based on a bunch of loops that were all distorted and filtered. Fifteen years ago I would've thought "What the hell is that?" Nowadays, that's a really hip sound, so the sound of records is always changing.

Once I get a mix that I'm generally happy with, I'll fire up the automation and do rides to get the elements in perspective for each section of the tune. I'll then play it down a number of times with the automation in "trim" or "relative" mode, usually carefully riding the vocal to keep it properly focused and featuring melodic moments from various instruments.

Later, the producer and/or artist will come back and I'll play them what I've done. They'll either say, "Wow, that's great. Just put it down" or "No, that completely sucks. Start over! (laughs)." What usually happens is that they'll like the mix, but perhaps would like a few things emphasized or de-emphasized.

It Doesn't Take a Lot of Money to Mix Great-Sounding Records

You can make records on just about anything these days, so don't think you need to spend a lot of money to make a good-sounding record. And while the SSL G Series mixing table is what I would call "my axe," I've made good records on equipment that was far less expensive. Remember, it's all about the song and the way you record that brings out the best of that song, and you can pretty much use any kind of equipment to do that.

If I was starting out today and wanting to record my own music, chances are I'd be going the DAW route, like Nuendo, Logic Audio, or maybe even Pro Tools, since they're the formats so many people are using right now. You see Pro Tools rigs in nearly every major studio these days. But that format could change. The way technology changes today, it's tough for anyone to say this or that's going to be the recording format for the next 10, 15, or even 2 years. Formats come and go, and chances are in a few years it'll be something else.

As far as the recording medium goes, it's probably going to stay in the digital domain from this point forward. As good as analog can sound, there's just certain advantages that you can't deny about digital. Even a lot of the old analog die-hards aren't using analog anymore; they're doing most of their work digitally. With the converters always getting better with higher bit and sample rates, this stuff keeps sounding better all the time.

I think things will always be digital but not necessarily Pro Tools, because there are other systems around that are getting to be better now. Like Nuendo or Logic Audio. Here at Mix This! we have them all and can use everything that's brought to us, whether it's Nuendo, Logic, Cubase, Soundscape, Pro Tools, or even ADAT and DTRS.

Most sessions come in on Pro Tools, which I transfer to the Sony 3348HR and then I mix them down to Nuendo at 88.2 kHz. I like Nuendo a lot, because it's got great editing facilities. It records broadcast WAV files, which is perfect since that's becoming the standard delivery format. Nuendo also interfaces directly to my Apogee converters, which I feel are the best on the market.

I'm also mixing to surround along with stereo, even when people don't ask me for it. I'm doing the surround mix simultaneously so, via the Apogee AD-16, I can record eight tracks at a time, ending up with multiple groups of eight. For example, if I have to do an edit for a single, there's always the choice—a vocal up-mix, a vocal down-mix, a TV backing track with just backing vocals and an instrumental—all mixed in both stereo and surround. I'll always have a minimum of five mixes—five groups of eight tracks. And because they're all locked to time code from the multitrack, if need be I can do an edit on all of them at once in Nuendo, which is quite convenient and saves time.

Not too long ago, I was mixing a pop record in stereo and it sounded good. Then I did the surround mix, where I broke things out a bit and put strings and horns in the back, and so on. When I heard the surround mix, it gave me goose bumps. It sounded that good! I mean, it was like a whole different record that really sounded amazing. For years I kinda thought it was a novelty, but it's not anymore. The surround sound thing—if it's set up properly—can be an amazing experience.

Although having said that, until the home surround systems get easier to set up and use, it'll probably remain a novelty.

Whether or not I chose Pro Tools, Nuendo, Logic, Cubase, Performer, or any other kind of computer recording platform, I'd still go with some kind of tape-based recorder/playback system in addition to the computer stuff I'm recording into. I like the idea of having a backup and the option to use either one. I really don't trust any hard disk system by itself, and people who do are really taking a risk, especially if they're paying musicians when they're recording.

I heard about some sessions that went down in London where they had a whole orchestra and it was all going to Pro Tools and the thing crashed. The engineer just about lost his mind. When I heard that, I thought why was he even bothering with Pro Tools only because at AIR Studios [in London], they have 3348's that never crash. I don't think any computer—MAC or PC—can say that.

My computer of choice would be a Mac, because it's been my experience that Macs are way more stable than Windows-based machines. When we first got Nuendo [Steinberg] recommended we use PCs. But for us, every few minutes the PC just crashed. We had three PCs. We had one we had bought and one Steinberg had recommended and had set up for us—which crashed big time. We also had a PC whiz at Apogee bring over his hand-built PC that he used for Cubase. While his PC was better than the others, it still crashed. We needed the PC to lock up to the SMPTE. None of them would do it reliably.

Once we got on the Mac, it never crashed and it locked up perfectly to SMPTE. The only thing we wish would be a little better is the software. That can be a little sluggish when you're zooming in and out on the waveform, but other than that, Macs are really reliable.

If I was going portable and wanted a music computer I could take anywhere, I'd go with a Mac Powerbook. Along with the Mac, I'd have a bunch of Apogee AD-16s [analog-to-digital converters], depending on how many channels I needed. Just for recording, I probably wouldn't need a D/A converter, so I wouldn't worry about getting one of those.

In my portable rig, I'd want to have some great sounding mic preamps like the Apogee Trak-2, which is an amazing pair of stereo mic pre's, or the Apogee Mini-Me, that I really love the sound of, or perhaps some Avalons, that are really good mic preamps. I'd probably want some good compressors, like a couple of Avalons or a couple of the Urei LA-3A's, and perhaps a Pultec EQ.

For people who are wanting to get into Webcasting, one option I'd recommend would be the Apogee stuff. We did some experiments not too long ago by trying to make Web streaming digital audio sound better. We found that using Apogee UV-22 in the mastering stage to get from 24 to 16 bits first makes the after-effects of digitally compressed sounds much less irritating. It sounds clearer, more realistic, and a lot less of that swishy top-end stuff that you typically get from Webcasting audio. That's a big advantage.

Another option would be checking out some other compressors and processors on the market that are specifically built for Webcasting audio. Check out the Aphex 2020 Mk. II. Pieces of gear like this really do enhance Webcasting because they do a certain type of processing—like taking a digital signal and processing it in analog and then converting it back again to digital before it's Webcast—that makes the Webcast sound better. It's amazing what damage Webcasting can do—depending on the bit rate, of course—and how it can mangle your sound unless you're mixing your music specifically for it.

As far as plug-ins go, I'm not really excited about a lot of them. I do use the Mac DSP EQ and Compression, which sounds amazing and the realest to me of any of the other ones I've heard. And it looks kind of normal. Some of these plug-ins make me wonder why they spent so much time graphically duplicating the look of the front panel of a piece of gear the plug-in is trying to duplicate, instead of making it sound better.

My preference is more on the analog side of things, whereas, even though I use digital for storage, I like the hands-on feel of creating and mixing music from a mixing console and not a computer keyboard and mouse.

Sonically, I can't tell the difference between something recorded into Pro Tools or on digital tape, because all my gear has the same kinds of converters and that's the thing that makes the difference. As long as the clocking is really good, since it's all transferred digitally, I don't think most people will be able to tell any difference.

And don't get hung up on all the things people say about technology and recording. For example, a lot of people today say the recording standard is 24 bit—96 kHz and to me, I don't really understand where that's all coming from.

CDs are still recorded at 44.1 kHz and that's still what sells, right? Well, 96k isn't compatible in any way with a CD. We'll either record the multitrack at 44.1k or 48k and then we mix to 88.2, which is compatible with CDs because it's a multiple of 44.1 and a simple division by two gets you there. As a result, there's a lot less signal degradation. Whereas going from 96k to 44.1 is a very complex process and you can lose sound quality by doing it. If you're mastering analog, it doesn't really matter because you're converting it back to analog and then reconverting it to digital anyway.

And the big question if you're sending your music out to be mastered is, will the equipment they'll use be compatible with how your music was recorded and mixed? Bob Ludwig at Gateway Mastering usually does my stuff digitally, so I do everything at 88.2 and it works out great.

I challenge anybody on this planet to be able to tell the difference between something recorded at 88.2 and something recorded at 96k. The difference is so minute that it's just not audible.

If you're mixing for film work and DVD, then 24 bit/48k is the standard, because the video format for digital audio is 48k. On a video DVD, there's usually no room for audio sampled higher than 48k. Occasionally, they'll just want 16 bits on some of these DVDs, simply because if there's so much video content, the audio gets squeezed, and there's not enough room to put 24 bits on them. In these situations, I'll sometimes get asked for a 16-bit DAT [digital audio tape] recorded at 48k for DVD.

A lot of people see the latest gear that's getting all written up and talked about everywhere and think they've got to get rid of their "old" equipment and get the latest stuff that comes out. For example, getting rid of their older Pro Tools rigs and getting the Pro Tools HD system with the 192k sample rate or something like that. My question to them is, why?

First of all, do you realize how much disk space you'll need for a 192k system? It's incredible. Just shuffling that amount of data around and backing it all up can be a nightmare. Not only that, you better get ready to spend a lot of money for more tracks, because Pro Tools HD does 128 channels at 48k, 64 channels at 96k, and 32 channels at 192k. So now what do you do if you need more tracks? Link up multiple Pro Tools HD systems?

Think about it: You're going to spend more time just getting all of that to work and synched and you're going to have to have extra people just to deal with all that. Talk about a big distraction and taking away from the recording process. I mean, what are we doing here: recording for technology tweak heads or making records for humans? It's meaningless and it doesn't add to the music, not to mention it's a whole lot of grief, distraction, and expense.

Anything that people use that distracts from the actual musical recording process is what I don't get. Some of my friends do it and I've heard nightmares about their sessions. My advice is to keep things simple.

In today's digital world, there are some key pieces of gear I think people should have if they're wanting to make really good sounding records. Besides the digital converters—that I've probably mentioned too many times—there comes the regular toolbox of effects that people like to use such as reverbs, compressors, and delays. I've heard some good sounding units that weren't that expensive. I've also heard some bad sounding units that were, so instead of me recommending a certain brand and model, my suggestion is to go to a music store or studio, hear lots of different ones for yourself, and see which ones sound best to your ears.

When I make and mix records, I don't use anything that fancy. I don't need a ton of tube gear. There's a lot of people who think that just because something's got a tube in it, it's going to make it better. But there's a lot of really crappy sounding tube gear too. In fact, I think I have some of it (laughs).

BOB CLEARMOUNTAIN'S
MIX THIS! STUDIO EQUIPMENT LIST

Dynamic Processing

UREI 1178 Stereo Compressor—Fantastic, but old and cranky; difficult to recall.

Focusrite Red 3 Stereo Compressor—Sounds and looks good but noisy and hard to recall; could use control markings.

UREI LA-3A Compressor—Classic and transparent on vocals; modified for low noise.

Empirical Labs Distressor—Excellent on acoustic guitars and many other things; great knobs!

SSL FXG384 Outboard Stereo Compressor—Same as in the G-Series Console; great for piano or submixed drums.

Avalon AD2044 Stereo Compressor—Great on bass and guitars; difficult to recall.

BSS DPR-901 Dynamic Equalizer—For vocals, it's like cheating!

DBX 902 De-Esser—Quite handy, but not for lead vocals.

Drawmer DS-201 Dual Gate—Great problem-solvers.

Equalizers

Pultec EQP-1A3—The best then, now, and always will be.

Avalon AD2055, Stereo—Excellent alternative EQ; extremely posh sound.

Digital Signal Processors—Reverbs, delays, and so on

Yamaha SPX-990 Multieffects Processor—Not well-known, but versatile and sounds great.

Yamaha Pro-R3 Reverb—Very smooth and rich for long reverbs.

Yamaha SPX-90 Multieffects Processor—Not used much anymore.

Eventide H-3000 Multieffects/Harmonizer—The old standby; lots of cool stuff in there—when it's working; great sampling.

Eventide H-3500 Multieffects/Harmonizer—Pretty much same as above.

Eventide DSP-4000 Multieffects/Harmonizer—Excellent for tuning vocals, "tape" flanging, and many other things.

Yamaha D5000 Digital Delay—The best DDL ever made.

Roland SDE-3000 Digital Delay—The second-best DDL ever made.

AMS DMX 15-80S Digital Delay—Vintage '80s DDL; I still use it every day.

AMS RMX 16 Reverb—Classic digital verb, a bit grainy and dark; used occasionally.

Lexicon PCM-70 Multi-effects Processor—"Concert Hall" with some mods is the bomb on piano.

Lexicon 480L Multi-effects Processor—Not my favorite, but very expensive.

Antares AMM-1 Mic Modeler—Makes most any mic sound better, or worse, which sometimes is better. . . .or not.

Ursa Major SST-282 Space Station—Disgusting, grungy early digital reverb, for a raggedy garage band sound.

MXR Phaser/Flanger Rack (two of each in four-unit rack)—Classic analog effects from the '70s; quite rare these days.

Analog Signal Processors

Sans Amp guitar amp simulator—The old, nonmemory type; great!

Roland Space Echo 201—Great classic analog tape delay effects — until the tape jams.

Live Echo Chambers—You don't come across these much anymore; kinda like Motown verb.

UREI Filter Set—Great for removing hums or feedback. Mix this! would be a lame studio without this device.

Funk Logic Valvecaster 1960—This box makes everything better; very transparent, subtle effect; looks great!

Funk Logic Digilog Dynamicator—Of all the pieces of gear in the room, this is definitely one of 'em!

Tape Recorders

Studer A-800 Mk.I, modified to chase code—Classic analog!

Sony PCM-3348HR 48 Trk. Digital w/remote meter—The best multitrack recorder ever made; even better with Apogee converters!

Sony 7030 DAT—The best DAT machine; chases timecode; not easy to operate.

Sony 7010 DAT—Looks like the 7030, but is very different; records code but won't chase.

TASCAM DA-88 Digital 8-Track w/timecode—Used with the PSX-100 for "bit-split" 88.2-kHz stereo mix safeties.

TASCAM DA-38 Digital 8-Track—Used for L-C-R stems for movies, but not much anymore.

ADAT XT Digital 8-Track w/BRC—I'm glad this spends most of its time in the closet nowadays!

TASCAM DA-302 Dual DAT Recorder—Great for double-speed DAT copies.

TASCAM 122 Mk. III Cassette—The best cassette machine, but hardly used anymore.

Digital Converters

Apogee AD-8000SE 8-Channel A/D, D/A Converter—Don't even mention anything else; perfect for the front end of Pro Tools.

Apogee Trak 2 Stereo Mic Pre & A/D Converter—The best mic pre going, with the best 2-channel A/D, 8-channel D/A and AMBus.

Apogee PSX-100 Stereo AD-D/A Converter—Great for mixing double-wide 88.2/96-kHz stereo to Pro Tools or a DA-88.

Apogee AD-16, 16-channel A/D Converter—On the front end of the Nuendo system.

Apogee DA-16, 16-channel D/A Converter—On the back end of the Nuendo system.

Apogee AD-1000 Stereo A/D Converter—That classic Apogee digital sound.

Apogee AD-500 Stereo A/D Converter—Even more classic Apogee digital sound, with "Soft Saturate."

Apogee DA-1000 Stereo D/A Converter—The old standby D to A.

Apogee DA-2000 Stereo D/A Converter—Cello used to sell this great box for about six grand.

Apogee FC-8 ADAT/TDIF Format Converter—They won a TEC award for a format converter!

Microphone Preamps and DIs

Apogee Trak 2 Stereo Mic Pre and A/D Converter—An amazing mic preamp that happens to have an Apogee A/D attached.

Avalon M5 Mic Preamplifier—Great classic-sounding mic pre.

Avalon U5 Active/Passive Direct Box—Perfect for bass and electric guitars.

Microphones

Neumann M-49 Multipattern Condenser—Great vintage tube vocal mics.

AKG C24 Stereo Multipattern Condenser—Excellent on the Boesendorfer.

Royer R-21 Ribbon—Very warm and smooth.

Royer SF-12 Stereo Ribbon—The best for the top of the Leslie; works well with the Trak 2.

Mojave Multipattern Condenser, David Royer Custom—Hand-made by D.R.; the power supply is in an ammo case.

AKG C460 B Condenser—Two of these live in the live chambers.

AKG 414 Condenser—Not thrilling, but OK on the piano.

Octavia MC 012 Condenser—Good, strong Russian sound.

Shure SM-98 Condenser—Great mic for toms.

Shure SM 58 Dynamic—The most versatile mic ever created.

Sennheiser MD-421 Dynamic—The classic tom or bass drum mic.

Speakers

KRK E7 Self-powered—The bomb for 5-channel [5.1] monitoring.

KRK S-12 Self-powered Subwoofer—Ditto for the 5.1.

Audix N5—Really nice!

Yamaha NS-10M Studio—The old standard.

Monitor Audio—In the Lounge; the best, inexpensive hi-fi speakers I've ever heard.

Mackie HR-824 Self-powered—These make the live chambers sing.

Amplifiers

Hafler Trans-Nova 9500—Excellent with the Audix N5s.

Yamaha P-2700—Standing by for whatever.

Yamaha P-3200—Perfect for the NS-10Ms.

Sony ES-444 Surround Receiver—Fantastic surround receiver; would be much better without all the DSP.

Computers, DAWs, and Software

Macintosh G4 733 MHz—For Pro Tools and Logic.

Macintosh G4 933 MHz—For Nuendo [see below].

Steinberg's Nuendo Digital Audio Workstation—I'm mixing to stereo and 5.1 to this on the G4 with the Apogee 16s; sounds excellent!

Macintosh 9600 w/ Newer G4 400 MHz upgrade—Retired to the machine room for playing Quicktime movies, doing soundfile backups and making CDs.

Apple Macintosh G3 Powerbook—The original; runs SessionTools—among many other things—in the control room.

Apple Orange iMac—Prints SessionTools J-cards, labels, and CDs in the Lounge; client's Web access.

Apple Macintosh Beige G3—Server for SessionTools, e-mail router; Now Up-To-Date and remote file transfers.

Digidesign ProTools Mix Plus—On the 733 G4 and uses an AD-8000SE and the two Trak 2s for interfaces.

E-Magic Logic Audio—Uses the DAE and Apogees, if someone needs it.

Mackie HDR-24 24-track Hard Disk Recorder—Very stable, reliable recorder; however, the editing software isn't quite there yet.

Digidesign Universal Slave Driver—Great synchronizer, but only Pro Tools can use it.

Opcode Studio 3 SMPTE/MIDI Interface—Not used much anymore, but did serve us well.

Microboards DSR 8800 CD Duplicator, plus five slaves—Everyone in the band gets a CD in a few minutes; runs off the Mac 9600.

Yamaha CDR 1000 CD/CD-RW Recorder—Great for one-offs from the desk or DAT safeties.

Glyph Hard Disk/DDS3 Tape Drive Combo—For backing up without that beeping noise; rather unreliable.

Kensington Data Express Hotswap Drive Bay—For when we need more disk space . . . NOW!

VXA Tape Backup Drive—Faster backups, and less expensive than AIT.

Aurora Fuse Video PCI Card—For getting Quicktime out of the Mac 9600 to the Video Projector.

Other Studio Gear Goodies

Dolby "Dolbyfax" ISDN AC-2 encoder/decoder—Incredibly handy when the client can't be here for the mix.

TimeLine Lynx Synchronizer Module—Still the standard.

Brainstorm Timecode Destripalyzer—Lets you know what you've got—but not what to do with it.

Brainstorm Dual Timecode Distribution Amplifier—Makes sure there's enough code to go around.

Grass Valley Video Sync Generator—NTSC house synch.

Sigma Electronics Blackburst Video Sync Generator—PAL house synch.

Little Labs Sample Switcher—Jonathan Little did this one up for me special.

Russian Dragon—Tells you if you're rushing or dragging.

DTS CAD-4 Decoder—For checking surround CD refs; it'd be nice if it had alternate output configs.

Studio Technologies StudioCom 5.1 Monitor Control—Crank up all those six speakers at once; needed a mod for a prefade line out to connect to the Lounge 5.1 hi-fi system for alternate listening. "We've actually done that mod with some help from Lucas Van Der Mee at Apogee—*works great!*"

Mitsubishi X500-U Professional Video Projector—We show synched Quicktime movies with this when mixing to picture.

On How Long It Should Take to Make a Record

I've had people ask me how long should it take to make a record. I tell them as long as you need to make the record sound the best it can. I've done records that only took a couple of weeks and I've done some that have taken a couple of years.

When we did David Bowie's *Let's Dance* record that my old friend Nile Rogers produced, it took us 3 weeks from start to finish to record and mix, and it was a huge hit album. Whereas John Fogerty's *Blue Moon Swamp* took 5 years. I mean, it only took us two-and-a-half weeks to mix it, but he took a really long time to record it. He probably went through every drummer he could get ahold of to try new arrangements for every song. I think Def Leppard's *Pyromania* record took a couple of years.

I would say the normal amount of time to record and mix a record would be 2 to 3 months. As far as cost goes, if you're not engineering or mixing the record yourself, I tell people to plan on spending anywhere from $50 to $75 an hour for the engineer. For mixing, figure on anywhere from $1,000 to $5,000 a song, with the higher end mixers also getting points [a percentage royalty] of record sales. Typically, their fee becomes an advance against their royalty.

Having said that, I do believe fees are coming down, as the market and budgets are getting tighter and people have to adjust to stay competitive and working. So it doesn't hurt to negotiate a fair rate for you and them.

And if you don't have a lot of money, don't be shy about asking a producer, engineer, or mixer to defer their fees in exchange for a small percentage or royalty on your record. If you've got the right song, sound, and potential to make something happen, I know many people who'll do just that.

How Making Music and Records Has Changed

When I started recording it was really exciting, because it was always with live musicians and that's what I enjoyed the most. Early on, I thought mixing records was boring because you're just sitting there in this room with one other guy pushing faders.

I always liked having a whole band out in the studio where you're running around plugging in mics and getting the headphones to work. Then, when everything is all hooked up and working, and they start playing and you start recording, you'd get a great take and everyone would say "Wow, what was that!" That was exciting.

Nowadays, that so rarely happens. Today, most records are made by someone sitting in front of a computer with a mouse. That's not exciting at all. In fact, it's kinda dull and I'm amazed people put up with it. How does making records like that actually interest anyone at all? I couldn't do it.

We have a guy here at the studio who runs our DAW system and luckily, he likes it, whereas, even though I know how to work the thing, I can't do it because I don't have the patience. At least when I'm mixing, I'm turning knobs and pressing buttons and stuff and I get to slide back and forth in front of a big mixing console!

New Thinking for a New Music Business

People often ask me what I would do today if I was just starting out. To tell you the truth, I don't know what I'd do nowadays, because the record business is in such a mess. It's dying because of downloads and people copying. It's literally getting sucked down the Internet! If I were starting out today, I'd probably get more into mixing music for films, television, and things like that. Perhaps I'd go into mixing live sound.

It just doesn't seem as much fun to make records as it did not too long ago. The fact that the record business seems to be disappearing now has really affected a lot of people who are serious about making records.

There's all these people who download and copy music who think music should be free. Yet, I just wonder what they're going to be thinking a few years from now, when there'll be a lack of new music because the record companies have shut down from people not paying for the records. Of course, it doesn't help that record prices are kept so high because of the astronomical costs of radio and other types of promotion. The creeps running Clear Channel will probably wonder why their thousand or so radio stations have no new music to play after they helped put the nails in the record business's coffin by demanding huge payments for record spins!

Whether or not that actually happens is one of the scenarios for the future of the record business. I mean, who's to say, but you've got to be thinking where is it all going to go if people keep doing what they're doing? To me, it's all leading in that direction.

Hopefully, there's still going to be enough people who don't steal and actually understand that downloading free music is stealing not only from the record company, but more importantly, from the artists who creates the music they are downloading, and whom they're supposedly fans of. Make no mistake, the record business has been overinflated for years. And like the stock market, maybe the record business will take a correction and come back down to normal again. We'll all just have to drive cheaper cars. I'm in—it's worth it!

Web site: www.mixthis.com

Lesson 10

Mastering Your Music:

Advice from Bob Ludwig

I n the world of mastering engineers, none is as sought after as Bob Ludwig. Bob is to mastering what Enzo Ferrari is to cars. Mastering is that oft-heard term that few people really understand. Perhaps its obfuscation is deliberate. It is the mastering engineers who bring out the best in recorded audio, but few are willing to reveal their methods and trade secrets to those seeking but a taste of technique to help them create better recordings.

Consider yourself one of the fortunate few, because Bob is about to impart advice that's bound to help you think differently when it comes to that final—and many say crucial—component of your music.

I went to Portland, Maine, to interview Bob, and what I discovered was eye-opening, to say the least. Despite having mastered the recordings of music's greatest stars and legends, he still has the twinkle in his eye of a young boy who's met the love of his life—music—for the first time. Bob loves his artists and his music, and everything he does is done with a zeal and zest that any of us would do well to emulate.

Ludwig's Gateway Mastering studio is a sight to behold. From the album-lined walls and award-filled shelves to rooms packed with equipment and people who know how to work its magic, Bob's paradise is contained in the two stories he calls home.

Walk into his traffic control room—the room with a wall-sized bulletin board filled with client names in time slots of days and hours—and on any day of the week, you'll find names like Beck, Mariah Carey, Celine Dion, Faith Hill, John Mellencamp, Natalie Merchant, Bruce Springsteen, and the hottest new group and artist climbing the Billboard charts, booked to have their record mastered by Bob Ludwig.

Over the years, Bob has mastered thousands upon thousands of records for such artists as Bryan Adams, Rush, Dire Straits, The Bee Gees, Eric Clapton, The Band, Elvis Costello, Gloria Estefan, Bryan Ferry, Foo Fighters, Jimi Hendrix, Journey, Nirvana, Radiohead, Pearl Jam, Rage Against the Machine, The Police, REM, Lou Reed, The Rolling Stones (almost every album!), Paul Simon, Carly Simon, Peter

Wolf, ZZ Top, Led Zeppelin, and . . . well, you get the picture. (For a more complete listing go to www.allmusic.com or www.gatewaymastering.com.)

A classically trained and inspired trumpet virtuoso who found his love in many kinds of music, Bob's enthusiasm for the song and the artist has never wavered. And his advice has never been more timely for anyone ready to make their mark in the new music business.

Bob on Starting Out

My music recording career started in the late 1960s. I received my Master of Music degree from the Eastman School of Music in Rochester, New York. Many wonderful things happened when I was at Eastman. I played trumpet for the Utica Symphony Orchestra, which was an amazing experience, and I received lots of great hands-on recording experience while working in Eastman's recording department.

About the time I was finishing up my master's degree, Phil Ramone came to teach the first recording workshop at the school. At the end of his workshop program, he asked me if I wanted to come work for him at A&R Recording in New York. How could I refuse?

When Phil arrived on campus to teach his workshop, I was working in the recording department, and while he was there I became his de facto assistant, which led to his job offer. Little did I know what I was about to get into. Even though I had already recorded thousands of student and faculty recitals and concerts prior to Phil's arrival at Eastman, once I was introduced to the pop music recording world it was surprising in ways I never imagined.

When I began my musical career, I never wanted to do anything other than be a professional symphonic player. And once it happened, it was tremendously fulfilling. The thrill of playing solo trumpet and performing many of the great works was immensely enjoyable. However, it wasn't too long before I had experienced enough of the symphony to realize it wasn't quite what I was looking for. And much to my parents' chagrin (they wanted me to be a music teacher), I decided to go to New York and work with Phil.

From the first time I had a tape recorder when I was eight years old, I had always loved recording. All those concerts, orchestral, recital, and symphonic recordings I had done at Eastman were priceless experiences. However, working with Phil would be a learning experience like no other. And I would be in good company.

Although I originally wanted to be a mix and remix engineer while at A&R, I learned the art of mastering, which I found I had an affinity for. Every recording engineer at A&R was an apprentice; some have gone on to become legends in the business, like Eliot Scheiner [who worked with Aerosmith, Eagles, Steely Dan] and Shelly Yakus [who worked with B.B. King, Tom Petty, U2].

Working with Phil at A&R was a great training ground. I learned disk cutting, which for some genetic reason (laughs) came easy. It really was an art; either you got it or you didn't. There's also the patience that a disk cutter needs. There were many times when I'd be 23 minutes into cutting a 24-minute side and something would go wrong with the disk cutting lathe vacuum, and I'd have to start all over again. Sometimes it would happen four or five times in a row.

In addition to disk cutting, A&R kept me busy assisting on many recording and mixing sessions. And because I read music scores, I did a lot of work for many classical clients, including Nonesuch Records, who is still my oldest client to this day.

After working at A&R for a couple of years, Neumann had developed a highly advanced disk cutting system that was a major leap from anything we had seen or heard. Though management at A&R didn't want to buy the new gear at the time, I knew it would be impossible to compete against this gear, because it was just that good.

Right about the same time as the Neumann equipment was coming out, a new recording and mastering company called Sterling Sound was starting in New York. The buzz surrounding Sterling was exciting, and most exciting for me was the fact that they already had Neumann, Studer, and Telefunken gear. After much thought, I left A&R and went to work for Sterling.

It didn't take long for things to start happening. I cut *Led Zeppelin II* after just joining Sterling and things just snowballed from there. Some of the first hits I cut were Neil Diamond's "Kentucky Woman" along with albums from artists like Jimi Hendrix and The Doors.

Early on in my career, I was fortunate to have worked on some masterpiece records with some musical legends. The Led Zeppelin records were unique in their time, and have held up all these years as timeless recordings. When I started out there were no oldies radio stations. The songs those stations would play years later were the ones we were creating.

It was a time when I was mastering records for Janis Joplin, Jim Morrison, and Jimi Hendrix—all at the same time! And talk about a scary moment. I was working on each one's record when they died. I thought, my gosh, I'm jinxed [laughs].

The Music Business, Yesterday and Today

When rock and roll was being created, practically all artists were on independent record labels, with the exception of a few artists like The Beatles who were on the huge record label EMI. Back then, the majority of the labels were independent. None of the conglomerates and corporate takeover of the labels and radio had happened yet.

Elektra was independent. So were Atlantic, Warner Bros., and Columbia. The music business was filled full of great independents, from large to small.

Since that time music has changed, and not always for the better. We've gone from an era when there were only independent record labels and radio stations to today, where we have five major labels and three corporations that own most of the radio stations in America—radio stations that are programmed by a handful of people, and it's horrible. Number one records are bought now and not created.

Years ago, before the conglomerates took over the record labels and business, I used to easily be able to pick out a number one hit record. It's different now. The first time I listened to Hall and Oates's "Private Eyes" or "Your Kiss Is on My List" it was immediately clear to me that what I was hearing would become a hit. Same thing happened for ZZ Tops's "Legs." I couldn't believe what was coming off the tape. It was just magic.

Working on those records and with those artists was a thrill from the first day I did it, and still continues to be to this day. Even after all these years, it's just as fresh for me to work on music today as it was when I first started. Each day is exciting. I never know whose record will come in for me to master or what great song I might hear. What better job can I have than working on a daily basis with such artists as Faith Hill, Beck, and Bruce Springsteen?

While the ownership and business of today's record labels have changed, when it comes to a record's success, two things have not: a great hook and a great performance. That's it. All you need is one microphone in a studio, and if it's a great song with a great performance, it will probably sell—even today.

Years ago, some record label did a survey to find out how much quality influenced the sales of a record. The number they found was something like five percent. The other ninety-five percent was the artist, the song, the publicity, the price, and other factors.

The Importance of Mixing in the Recording Process

When I look at the three parts of the recording process—recording, mixing, and mastering—without a doubt I think the mix is the most important part. The top mixers, if they're good enough, will actually get a royalty percentage of the record. That's how important they and the mix are to a record. The mix can make or break a record—no matter how well it's recorded.

There's nothing sadder to see than an engineer who's recorded great-sounding tracks coming into our studio and listening for the first time to someone's poor mix on them. Watching the devastation on the face of an engineer who's hearing how his work was trashed is tough. On the other hand, if the mixing is done by someone great, it can be an entirely different story. I've seen Bob Clearmountain rescue terrible recordings and make these amazing mixes out of them—mixes so good, you just can't believe anyone could be capable of pulling that off.

Some recordings have the same people record and mix their music, while others have a separate engineer and mixer. There are pros and cons to both. From a mastering point of view it doesn't impact me at all, since I work with the final product that I'm given, regardless of how many people worked on the recording.

The point can be made that the person who engineered the project is the best person to mix the project. He or she know all the tapes, all the overdubs, and everything that happened on the session. The counterpoint to that would be the case of a record that's taken a long time to finish. Some records I've mastered took a year or more to record. In those situations, the engineer can be so close to the project that the perspective has been lost on what's good and bad, what the record needs or doesn't. When that happens, taking the record to a separate mixer can be a good idea.

The mixer is hearing the record for the first time, and he or she will have a vision of the many ways they can make it sound like what they're hearing in their heads. Many times, the mixer will come up with a whole different musical context of great ideas that the artist and producer never dreamed of.

I think the ideal recording/engineering/mixing situation is really quite simple. Bruce Springsteen comes to mind here. For his Grammy-winning album *The Rising*, the whole record was recorded in just a matter of weeks, which was the shortest time he ever took to cut an album. To put recording a complete album that quickly in some context, years ago I mastered a record for James Brown. When I received the tapes, James called me and said, "We really care about this record Bob, and I want you to know that we spent a *week* on it." That was recording *and* mixing it (laughs)!

For *The Rising*, Bruce was working with Brendan O'Brien, who is one of the most successful musical producers today, as well as being a great engineer. As Bruce was recording, Brendan was also mixing the record. So every time Bruce was working on the record, he was also hearing a mix that was becoming more finely honed. Then, when it came time to do the final mix, all it needed was basically just a few slight adjustments to what he had been hearing over those last few weeks. To me, that's an ideal recording, engineering, and mixing situation.

Taking a long time to record a record, hearing the same thing over and over, and then hearing how that record can sound with a fresh new mix can be a bit traumatic to some. Whereas, doing everything in a shorter period of time, like Bruce did for *The Rising*, can be a very gratifying and enjoyable way to make a record.

The Importance of Mastering in the Recording Process

With so many people doing home and project studio recordings, mastering is more important now than it's ever been. Mastering is the last creative step, where the final sound of the record will be determined. In many instances, when costs may have been cut during some part of the recording process, people are amazed at how poorly recorded music can be made to at least sound normal through excellent mastering. Many times, it can sound better than ever imagined. Mastering can make that big a difference.

Sometimes our job as mastering engineers is to take a really bad-sounding tape and make it sound normal. On the other hand, when we get a tape to master from one of these really great mixers—like Tom Lord-Alge, Jack Joseph Puig, Andy Wallace, Eliot Scheiner, Bob Clearmountain, and others like them—the mixes are so good that simply adding a small amount of mastering in a certain place will make it sound like you've made huge sonic changes. The extraordinary mixing work these great mixers do before their music comes to me is so carefully balanced that, many times, the slightest adjustment will make a radical change to it.

Recording has changed so much and so fast in just a brief period of time. Years ago, we used to be able to pick out all digital recordings very easily. They were brittle sounding and a bit one-dimensional. As time has gone on, and as the quality of analog-to-digital converters has gotten so much better, some of the best-sounding music now is completely digital. Again, regardless if you're using analog or digital, it all depends on how it's mixed.

The first commandment in the mastering bible is to do no harm to the sound. I think any gifted mastering engineer has the ability to hear a raw tape and imagine in their head how it could sound, and then know what kinds of gear to use and what buttons to move to make it sound like it does in their head.

The first time I hear new music from a client, my goal is to listen to the tape to hear what's really in there. After that, my job is to bring out and maximize the most musicality that's inherent in their music and on that tape. Having the ability to hear the raw tape and imagining in my head how it can sound, and then knowing what equipment to use and knobs to move to make it sound that way, is the essence of what I do.

My speakers are able to reveal things that people have never heard—even after they've been working on an album for months. There have been times when we've found ticks and defects on an album, and the studio where it came from can't hear them—even after they've been told where they are. Great speakers can reveal those kinds of things and are critically important to your music.

As a mastering engineer perhaps I'm like a painter, and the things that I use in order for me to get the sounds I do are the different colors in the palette. Those different colors could be the many different kinds of analog and digital equalizers, because they each have different colors, or capabilities to shape or paint the soundscape. Some of them are extremely clinical and pristine, and others have a very musical color that can add a lot of life to the music.

The other colors I use may be the many different compressors we have, each having different sounds and arrangements in the signal path. Colors can also include the choices for the playback medium—whether it's going to be digital or analog—that influences the final sound.

We have five different kinds of analog tape playback here at the studio. We have Studer and Ampex stock machines. We have Ampex machines with discrete class A electronics. We have two different kinds of tube playback systems for the machines. And every one of those machines sounds distinctly different from every other one. Just to be able to choose the most appropriate playback for whatever kind of music comes through our doors makes a *huge* impact on the mastering and music.

And people can hear the difference. Sometimes a tape will come through the door, from a group I've never heard before, and I need to get acclimated to where they are coming from with their music. My goal as a mastering engineer is to make the musicality that they put into their project come through to the listener as much as possible. I want to get in tune with where they are, so I can forward their vision. One way we do that is by playing the artist's music on solid state versus tube playback electronics to see which they prefer. Some will say they like tube because it's so warm. Then when they hear solid state they understand what the trade-off might be, and they might not want their music to sound so warm.

When new music comes in, the first thing we do if it's analog is to align it to calibration tones that have been made for that particular project. We obviously won't know if the song has any sonic problems such as ticks and defects, etc., until we listen to it. The time it takes to master an album can vary, but for the most part, I'll typically begin mastering an album at 10:00 a.m. and will have it finished, edited, and deticked if needed by 7 p.m.

The first song usually takes the longest, I'd say roughly ninety minutes, since, before I work on the first song, I'll listen to certain parts of the entire album to get an idea where the band or artist is coming from. After the first song, the other songs may take a half hour or so, per song, to master.

These days, when working with a new artist or group, some A&R people will stack the majority of strong songs up front on the recording. Unless you spot-check the entire album first, you might think the first few songs are what the band and album are all about, only to find something different a few more cuts down the line.

After giving the entire recording a good spot check, I then set the bearings for the album. This is where I'll decide how much compression it does or doesn't need, along with making lots of decisions about the first song that will apply to the rest of the album. Mastering is the last chance to give your recording any of the elements it needs before the public hears it. And if you do it right, the results can be astounding.

I tell people if you want to record multitrack digital, then try mixing down into analog. It'll make a huge difference on how your record sounds. If you can mix down to $^1/_2$-inch analog tape running at 30 ips [inches per second], it can really help gel a poor mix into a much better-sounding mix.

With digital-only, the highest-quality and best-sounding product you'll be able to achieve and say, is that it sounds exactly like it came off the console. With analog tape, many times, especially if you're not the world's greatest mixer, it sounds *better* than what came off the console. Why? Because analog tends to very musically *glue* the elements together in a way that's very satisfying to our ears. Even if you can't buy a $^1/_2$-inch analog machine, I recommend renting one when it comes time to mix down your music.

People at the top of the mastering heap like Doug Sax, Stephen Marcussen, George Marino, and Greg Calbi will often get tapes from people who trust them completely to do whatever they want to their music. A good mastering engineer will have a vision and can give the client a finished product that will truly blow their mind.

I must say that even if you're a well-known mastering engineer, getting projects coming in from great mixers can be very daunting. At times, we'll get projects in from the best mixers on the planet, from people who will have worked on a record as long as they needed to—many times with little or no budget limits—in order to get the record as perfect as possible, and we are expected to make the record sound even better.

There's no question that a great mix locks in how great the final record will be. Good mastering is simply the icing on the cake. It makes a good record sound better. When it comes to mastering your music, paying someone else to do it for you is well worth the time and money spent.

The Biggest Mistakes People Make in Recording

Probably the biggest mistake I hear people making is using too much compression. Listen, you don't even want to get me going on the state of compression these days. It's one of the things that's hurting the music business. Artists and A&R people insist on having their music squashed way beyond anything they should. It only hurts the music and ruins its longevity.

If the digital compressors people use today had been invented and used at the time of The Beatles, their music would not have near the longevity to it. It absolutely makes that big a difference. Too much compression on music fatigues listeners' ears. You simply don't feel like hearing the music again.

Yet today it's a catch-22, because the music business is so highly competitive, with records competing against each other for chart position and sales. A program director, an A&R person, or even an artist will listen to one version of their record and then listen to the same record that's slightly louder—not better, just louder—

from added compression, and the overly compressed record seems to have that much more impact. The extra loudness seems more attractive, so when you listen to the louder one for eight bars it does seem to sound better. Yet if you listen to the record from beginning to end, that same record now assaults and tires the ears, and you won't want to listen to it or put it on again until some time has passed.

Compare this to the original Beatles records. The only compression they used back then was during recording and mixing. Those Beatles records still have superb dynamic range, and that's critically important. When it comes to using compression, always remember that less is more. And keep in mind that when you're recording into the digital domain, using processing once is much better than using processing twice. And with cheaper digital gear, it doesn't like to be processed too much.

Tips on Setting Up a Recording Studio Workstation and Recording Platform

Pro Tools is a ubiquitous workstation for a good reason; it's fabulous. When compared to the older Pro Tools systems, the newer HD systems are, in my opinion, better for recording and mixing. And while there are many plug-ins to choose from, one of my favorites is the Waves plug-ins. The good news about plug-ins and digital recording is that things keep sounding better and getting cheaper.

Today you can literally replace a 250,000-dollar, forty-eight-track digital open-reel tape machine with an Apple iBook and a FireWire I/O box for a fraction of the price. I have clients who will come into the studio with Pro Tools loaded into an iBook and they can play forty-eight tracks simultaneously off their iBook's internal hard drive. With a great song and performance, making great music has never been easier or cheaper, regardless of where you do it. It *does* help if you know what you are doing with it all!

We have nine different digital audio workstations at Gateway—Pro Tools Mix 24, Pro Tools HD, classic Sonic, Sonic HD, SADIE, Nuendo, Wave Lab, Pyramix, and the direct stream digital Sony Sonoma workstation—so we're able to handle most any digital audio workstation format that comes in.

A lot of clients will use Pro Tools in their main studio and use Pro Tools LE when they're on the road. We run Pro Tools and Sonic Solutions software on Mac computers. We run Nuendo, Wave Lab, Sonoma, and Pyramix on PCs. All of the software recording platforms work great. It all comes down to what works best for you.

When it comes to deciding whether you should spend extra money for software and equipment that can handle the higher sampling rates, such as 192 kHz, it's all dependent on how important sound accuracy is to you. The higher sampling rates for a given converter will yield a better sound.

Which format to choose and what kind of gear to buy are always complicated questions. There's no single answer, because what you choose must take into account your budget compared to your needs. For example, great older equipment can sometimes blow the doors off many new pieces of gear with the latest technology. There's no question that a Pacific Microsonics Model One digital-to-analog converter running at 44.1 kHz at 16 bits will blow away a five-dollar 192-kHz 24-bit computer chip.

My advice to people who may not have the money for a high-end workstation system right now is to buy the best digital audio workstation you can afford, and spend the extra money on A/D and D/A converters. Get the very best you can, because excellent converters are crucial to making high-quality recordings.

Keep in mind that when you digitize your music, any distortions or jitter that are put into the analog-to-digital part of it cannot be removed in any fashion by anything further down the recording, mixing, editing, and mastering line. If your analog-to-digital conversion is no good, then the rest of the recording processing chain can't possibly help it.

Some Advice on Internet and Remote Broadcasting

With regard to Internet broadcasting, we use a dedicated FTP [file transfer protocol] system that allows our clients to send their music via the Internet to transfer non-data-compressed files. If we're doing a music project with a 100-megabyte song recorded at 88.2 kHz and 24 bits, it's completely lossless—no data changed or lost in the transfer process—when the other person receives it.

Broadcasting music works in a different way than FTP, since the method that it's broadcast by is streaming; it's received only bits at a time and not as a complete file all at once. As such, streaming requires mega data reduction on the order of something like 40 kbits per second, which is similar to what is used for satellite radio broadcasts. They use severely data-compressed signals, and some people under certain conditions, like using headphones while listening to classical music, will find that sound unacceptable.

On rare occasions we're asked to make an MP3 for use on the Internet. Sometimes we'll try different techniques to see if we can make it sound better for that kind of broadcast, but on the whole you're still pretty much beholden to the companies that make the software and hardware for Internet broadcast conversion. While MP3s can sound good, especially given the process they must go through before the listener hears them, many of the subtleties of the music are still lost.

With most codecs—code-decode, which is the process of coding your files for sending and decoding the files when received—we've found that if we do an FFT [fast Fourier transform] of the music with and without the codec in the circuit, store each in the analyzer, and subtract them from each other, the resulting frequency response ends up being about the same.

There is no EQ one can use to "correct" the codec. You might make a copy, hear it, and think it sounds brittle, but once it goes through these codecs—necessary for delivery of Internet broadcast files—and you try to change things and pre-EQ for it, you usually end up hurting some other part of the sound.

The high-quality codecs handle music with a lot of dynamics in it very well. However, most codecs do strange things to music files. It's tough to have some sort of global setting or fix that will work for all of them. My advice is to record your music at the highest sampling rate you can.

The Future of Recording

What I do is a lot like being a doctor. For one, you need to have a lot of dedication and love for what you do. There are always manuals to read, things to study, new technology and gear to learn. Over the years I've found that keeping up with changing technology is really important.

One of the things that has helped our business is that when a new technology is emerging, people usually knock on our door and tell us about it. Many times they get us involved before the technology or equipment is established. We're able to work with designers and manufacturers of these new technologies and understand and use them sometimes months before they hit the market.

For example, Sony came to us when they were developing the Super Audio CD. A team of Sony engineers from Tokyo came to visit Gateway Mastering twice during the development process for our evaluation. We were able to start working with SACD in the very early stages of its development, which helped both us and Sony a lot.

I think the future of recorded music is moving in the direction of SACD, DVD Audio, and surround. In automobiles, surround sound has the potential to be a big thing. A car is a very compelling place to listen to surround audio. Often I'll have record-label A&R people ask me how they can hear the surround mix in their cars. Whether it's in a car, studio, or home, when people hear 5.1 surround sound done correctly, most people don't want to go back to stereo. You can't go wrong by moving more of your music and recording work in the direction of these formats. In the case of surround, it's simply that good.

Web site: www.gatewaymastering.com

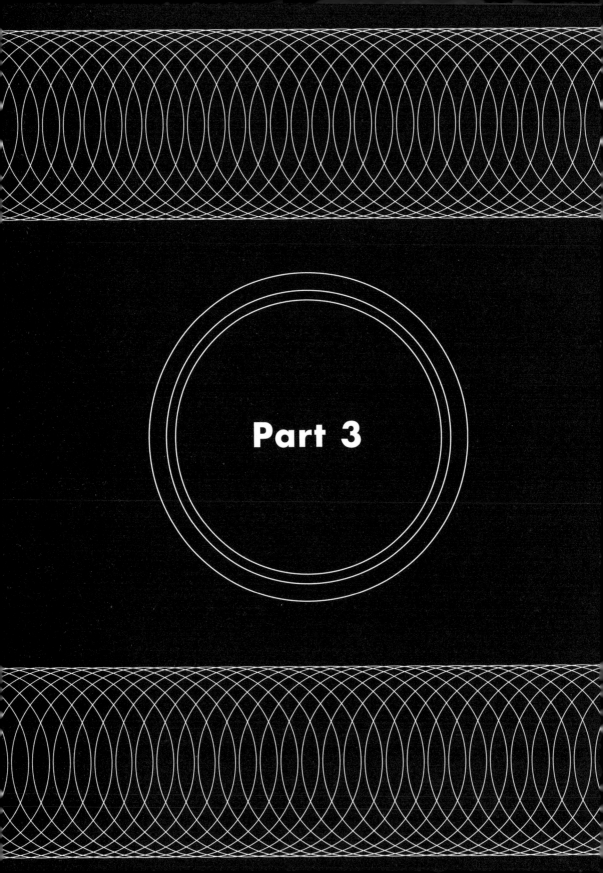

Part 3

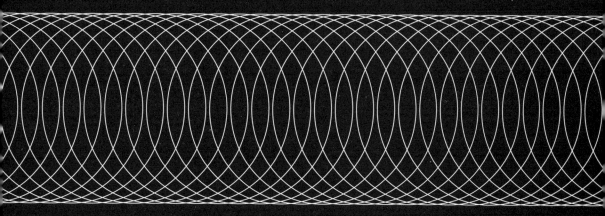

Your Business
in the New
Music Business

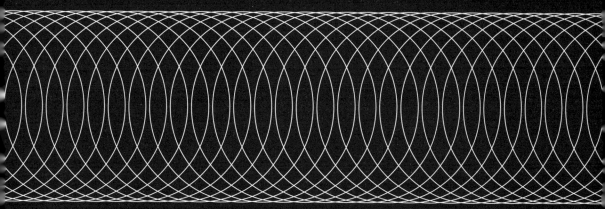

Launching the Business
of You, Inc.:

Five Steps to Incorporation

*I*t's time you become a "real" businessperson. It's time you get smart about protecting your assets, deducting all the business expenses you're entitled to, taking advantage of the immense saving and investment opportunities awaiting you and, finally, using the power of owning your own business to give you the clout that will change the way other businesses and people will see you from this point on. It's time for you to learn how to incorporate.

The Benefits of Incorporation

Why incorporate? In Lesson 5, "Building Your A-Team," I introduced you to Larry Cohen, one of the best CPAs in the business, who helped a friend of mine save $40,000 on his tax return. Larry strongly believes that the benefits of incorporation far outweigh any slight disadvantages. Here is some of what he has to say on the subject.

Let me ask you a question: Would you spend $500 to save $50,000? I'm imagining your answer will be yes. One of the best things anyone can do is to start a business. And over the life of your corporate entity, you will easily save thousands (perhaps tens of thousands) or more in tax deductions and saving benefits. This is a country built on small businesses, and so important are they that the government created all kinds of wonderful benefits designed to help small businesses get started and grow.

Many musicians simply start their business as a sole proprietorship. This is a simple and easy way to begin taking advantage of the tax deductions available for businesses, since the IRS acknowledges sole proprietorships as long as there is an intent by the business to make a profit within a specified period (i.e., the "ruling period").

However, many musicians find it more desirable to form a corporate entity. Some form limited liability companies (LLCs), and LLCs have their plusses and minuses. Here are a few things to keep in mind regarding an LLC:

* An LLC can be taxed as a partnership for federal income tax purposes. However, most of the time the profit or loss is reported on the "members'" individual income tax returns.
* The LLC is state-registered. California, for example, taxes the LLC on gross receipts plus a minimum tax of $800.
* "Members" are not personally liable for the LLC's debts and liabilities.
* "Members" may participate in management without risking personal liability. No limitations are placed on the number of owners.
* LLCs have the ability to make disproportionate allocations and distributions.

For most of his clients, Larry recommends forming an S Corporation. For information on the advantages of forming an S corporation, see below, pages 221 to 226.

Tax Advantages

One of the major tax advantages to having a corporation is the ability to invest up to 25 percent of your earnings or $30,000, whichever is less, into a SEP-IRA. Compare that to the $3,000 a year limit with regular or Roth IRAs. It's a no-brainer as to which is the better deal for you.

Then there are the deductions. The IRS makes it simple for you as the owner of your business—be it a sole proprietorship, LLC, or S corporation—to deduct *necessary* and *ordinary* business expenses. Necessary expenses—those that are crucial to your business—include office supplies, professional membership fees (e.g., musician's union dues), magazine and book purchases, and the like. Ordinary expenses are any kind of equipment and gear you need to make music, like keyboards, drums, mics, speakers, effects, amps, guitars, and so on.

* *Business formation.* You can deduct the costs of creating your corporate entity.
* *Business use of car.* If you need a car to help you get to and from your business, to your practices, to the music store or studio, or in any other way for your business, the cost of purchase or leasing can be deducted.
* *Gas, insurance, and car repairs.* The business portion of anything your car needs to keep it running and insured is deductible.
* *Music equipment.* If you're a musician and you're making money by playing, writing, creating, or the like in the music business, you can deduct that amp, those strings, that new CD, your guitar, microphones, and any other music supplies or equipment from your taxes.
* *Leasing.* Your vehicle, an office, or any other equipment leased for your business can be a big tax deduction.
* *Insurances.* Health insurance, car insurance, equipment insurance, home insurance, and the like are all legit business deductions.

* *Services.* Repairs on your equipment including regular maintenance for your instruments and hiring others to perform work for your business can also be a deduction.

* *Business loan interest.* Unlike personal credit card interest, business loan interest charges can be a tax deduction as well.

* *Internet and its services.* If you use the Internet to inform yourself about and find the latest gear, to keep up with music news that can help your business, or to stay in touch via e-mail with other musicians, then you can deduct your monthly access fee and other costs.

* *Web site.* If you've got a Web site or are thinking of putting one up for your business, those costs are tax-deductible.

* *Computer and office equipment.* If you are using your computer and office equipment in your business, then those expenses can be deducted.

* *Computer software and supplies.* The latest plug-ins, as well as peripherals, disks, cables, and extra storage drives, can be a big deduction.

* *Clothes and shoes.* If you're a performer and your clothes are required for your gig, then you've got a deduction.

* *Books, magazines, other publications, and CDs.* If you need print media or music on disc to help you in your business, then they're deductible.

* *Moving.* If you relocate to a new town for a new job, a better job, or a different job, and it's related to your business, the entire cost of your move is deductible, including the costs of hiring a mover, as well as your gas, meals, lodging, flights, car rentals, etc.

* *Printing, advertising, and marketing.* If you had flyers printed to promote your band or music, bought advertising (print, television, radio, Internet, etc.), and paid for any other kinds of marketing to help you and your music business, then you've got deductions coming.

* *Continuing education.* If you want to take that latest Pro Tools class or go to recording school, or perhaps take a few classes at your local college to learn more about international business, go ahead and take them and keep your receipts. Continuing education is a tax deduction.

* *Food.* If you have lunch or dinner with a potential business client, or talk business with other people who could get you work or other business opportunities, then a portion of those expenses are deductible.

* *Travel.* If you travel anywhere on business, the cost of your trip is deductible, including flights, rental car, hotel, food, entertainment (that new show with great music and lighting that may help you create something good for your business), and other out-of-pocket expenses. Save all receipts.

* *Home.* If you use your home or apartment to conduct business, a portion

of that residence is deductible. This means that a portion of what you pay in either rent or mortgage payments can be deducted, over and above your mortgage interest. A double benefit. The deduction is based on how much space and how many rooms you are using for your business, with a percentage formula applied to arrive at your total deduction.

* *Home utilities and insurance.* That same percentage formula can be applied to your home's utilities and insurance required for the areas you use for your home business.
* *Phone.* Your home and cell phone charges can be deductible if they are used for your business.
* *Parking.* Business-related parking is deductible.
* *Postage and shipping.* Any time you use any mail service—U.S. Post Office or private services—to send letters or packages for your business, those expenses are tax-deductible.
* *Office supplies.* Envelopes, printer paper, staples, pens, paper, etc., are tax deductions if you need them for your business.
* *Research.* If you write movie scripts and you go to the movie theater to see the newest film, your ticket is deductible since it's research that can give you new ideas for plots, characters, story, setting, and the like. And don't forget to keep your receipt for the Diet Coke and popcorn, too. Likewise, if you're a musician and you're looking for some great new ideas for songs and you want to check out the latest solo artist or group at a club or concert venue in town, go ahead and enjoy yourself. Just keep your receipts.
* *CPA and attorney fees.* The costs of professional services that your company uses are tax-deductible as well. Get the double benefit of using these services to help you, and then deduct the cost to help you reduce your tax liability.
* And there are many more.

Other Advantages

As Larry told you, having a corporate legal business entity can also protect your personal assets as well as your business. If your business is a sole proprietorship, partnership, or, even worse, has no formal business structure at all, you (or you and your partners) are personally liable if someone sues you as well as for any debts your business incurs.

However, if your business is set up as a corporation or LLC, it is the legal entity (and not you) that is responsible for the debts it incurs. While there are cases of illegalities of corporate malfeasance where both the corporation and principals can be liable, sued, and fined, these are the exception and not the rule. Having a legal corporate entity provides you (and your assets) maximum protections under the law.

Yes, incorporating does cost money, though not much as you may think, and it does take a little extra time (probably less than one hour a year) to fill out the yearly updates and corporation compliance forms that'll be sent to you, but I'm absolutely convinced that the benefits far exceed any cost and time.

When I first began my business, I did so as a sole proprietor. I didn't have any kind of corporate legal structure. I had a name for my business and kept good records of my expenses and income. When my taxes were filed, my CPA simply noted my sole proprietorship on them and that was that.

However, as I began to do more business with incorporated businesses, they would often ask me if I was incorporated. Often, when I answered that I wasn't, it was like bingo, the light went on for them that my business was a one-person, small-potatoes operation, and the way they treated me from that point on changed. You wouldn't think it would—after all, I was still the same person offering the same kind of service they enjoyed receiving—but in the real world of business, perception is reality. If you're perceived as operating out of your garage or bedroom, then more often than you may think, you're not given the same respect and treatment as someone who represents a larger company.

Once I figured out how that aspect of the business game is played, I decided to change my sole proprietorship to a corporation, and when I moved to California, I did just that. And sure enough, when people I was doing business with read the "Inc." after my company's name, they had no idea if I was working out of a home office or had a penthouse office suite and a huge staff. In a way, it leveled the playing field, giving me greater opportunities for good business deals.

That's why, even though you can do the sole proprietor thing, to save time, protect your assets, minimize taxes, and maximize wealth, opportunities, and deals, I want you to *seriously* think of incorporation. I'm about to show you how to save lots of money when you do it yourself and how quick and easy it is to accomplish.

Some years ago while traveling, I kept seeing a little ad in the pages of in-flight airline magazines for an outfit called The Company Corporation. The company promised that anyone could incorporate a business "over the phone," "in any state," "in as little as 10 minutes," and for under $500.

This caught my attention for a couple of reasons. One reason was the cost. At the time I was living in Los Angeles, and a partner and I had just set up a media/publishing company. To incorporate we used an attorney. The cost: $2,000.

There was another reason: aside from the promised ease, speed, and convenience, I definitely wanted to investigate the options of incorporating in states that could be more favorable (business and taxwise) than California.

I did more research on The Company Corporation and the legality of what they offered, and everything checked out. After speaking with my CPA about the best type of corporate entity for me (S corporation, C corporation, or LLC), I made the call, and the cost, the time it took, the services they offered, and the business entity I was able to set up were exactly as the ad promised. Since then, it's been the only company I've used to set up other businesses, and it's the one I recommend you use, too. They've been around since 1899, over 100 years, so there's a good chance they're not going anywhere. Incorporating businesses is all they do, so they know their field and no, they aren't paying me any money to tell you so. In my opinion, I simply think they're the best for the money.

To show you just how easy it was to set up my own business, I'm going to walk you step by step through everything I did. Keep in mind that this was the first time I had ever done it on my own. Believe me, if I can do it, so can you.

Step One: Determine the Type of Business You Want

I knew I wanted to create another business that would be used for all my publishing, music, and entertainment business ventures. I wanted to be the sole owner and I wanted the business structure to offer maximum protection and great tax benefits for my personal income, too.

After discussing my needs with my CPA, he suggested forming an S Corporation and basing it in a state with very favorable tax laws for business. Two states came to mind: Delaware and Nevada. I liked Delaware for these reasons:

* Anyone may form a corporation in Delaware without ever having to visit the state.
* Delaware has kept its fees low and is one of the friendliest states to corporations. Over 50 percent of all companies listed on the New York Stock Exchange are Delaware Corporations.
* The names and addresses of initial directors need not be listed in public records.
* The cost of forming a Delaware corporation is among the lowest in the nation.
* The annual $50 Franchise Tax compares favorably with that of most other states.
* Delaware maintains a separate court system for business, called the Court of Chancery, so if legal matters involving a trial arise in Delaware, there is an established record of pertinent business decisions.
* No minimum capital is required to organize the corporation, and there is no need to have a bank account in Delaware. Just one person can hold all the offices of the corporation: President, Vice President, Secretary, and Treasurer.

* There is no state corporate income tax on Delaware corporations that do not operate within the state.
* Shares of stock owned by persons outside of Delaware are not subject to Delaware personal income tax.
* There is no Delaware inheritance tax levied on stock held by nonresidents.
* A Delaware corporation can be formed quickly and easily by phone in under 5 minutes. Nevada has similar favorable business tax and corporate laws, but since my former magazine publisher had his publications business as a Delaware corporation, and knowing the owner to be a very shrewd and very wealthy businessman, I felt I couldn't go wrong doing the same.

So a Delaware corporation it would be. Then came the next step.

Step Two: Choose a Business Name

Choosing a name for my new business took a little time. I came up with lots of names, but most didn't have a good ring to them. Many people believe that using your own name as the brand name for your company is a good idea. For many, it is. Others prefer using something a bit catchier, like Google.

I came up with three names I liked and ranked them in order of my first, second, and third choices. I figured there was always the possibility that one of the names would have already been taken, so it was better to have some options if I couldn't use my first choice. I was ready for the next step.

Step Three: Get Good Advice

I then called The Company Corporation's toll-free number (their Web site is www.corporate.com) and in less than 15 minutes, an associate and I had gone through the following process.

First, I told him I wanted to form a Delaware S Corporation and asked him to explain the benefits (my CPA had already told me, but it never hurts to double-check). He told me the following:

* A Subchapter S Corporation is a general corporation that has elected a special tax status with the IRS after formation. Subchapter S corporations are most appropriate for small business owners and entrepreneurs who prefer to be taxed as if they were still sole proprietors or partners.
* When a general corporation makes a profit, it pays a federal corporate income tax on the profit. If the company also declares a dividend, the stockholders must report the dividend as personal income and pay more taxes. S Corporations avoid this "double taxation" (once at the corporate level and again at the personal level), because all income or loss is reported only once on the personal tax returns of the stockholders. For many small

businesses, the S Corporation offers the best of both worlds, combining the tax advantages of a sole proprietorship or partnership with the limited liability and enduring life of a corporate structure.

* If you choose an S Corporation, your corporation must meet specific guidelines. They are:

   1. All stockholders must be U.S. citizens or permanent residents.

   2. The maximum number of stockholders for an S Corporation is 75.

   3. If an S Corporation is held by an "electing small business trust," then all beneficiaries of the trust must be individuals, estates, or charitable organizations. Interests in the trust cannot be purchased.

   4. S Corporations may only issue one class of stock.

   5. No more than 25 percent of the gross corporate income may be derived from passive income (money received from business and real estate investment deals in which the person receiving the money is not actively involved).

   6. Not all domestic general business corporations are eligible for S Corporation status. The exclusions are a financial institution that is a bank, an insurance company taxed under Subchapter L, a Domestic International Sales Corporation (DISC), and certain affiliated groups of corporations.

I then asked him to explain what kinds of corporation-forming packages they offered and the costs. The prices ranged from about $200 to $500, depending on services and features. The more services The Company Corporation performed for you, the higher the cost.

The associate asked where the business would be based and its address. I told him that I lived in Idaho, but wanted a Delaware corporation. He said that would be no problem, and if I wanted to do business in my home state of Idaho, all I would need to do is simply obtain a Letter of Good Standing from the Delaware Secretary of State and then file it (along with payment of the Idaho state fee) with the Idaho Secretary of State office as a Foreign Corporation (i.e., a business registered in one state that wants to do business in another state.) More on this in a moment.

He asked me for the name and address of the person who would be in charge of the corporation and I told him it would be myself. He asked how many shares of stock I wanted issued (in the event I ever wanted shareholders) and I said 20 would be fine.

He asked me what name I wanted for my corporation and I told him. He put me on hold for about a minute while he checked the Delaware Corporation name database. He came back online, told me that my first name choice was available, and asked whether I would like to register it. I told him I would and it was done.

The associate asked whom I wanted to use as my Registered Agent. For any corporation that is filed in a state outside the one you live in, you need to have a person or company with a physical address in that state who can receive official mail and notifications, should there ever be any sent. Since I didn't live in Delaware or know anyone who did, I chose to use The Company Corporation. The fee they charged for this service (which includes sending you advance notices of the annual $50 Delaware Franchise Tax due date) was $175, tax-deductible.

I picked a corporate package and he asked how I would like to pay for it. I put it on my corporate American Express card. It, too, was tax-deductible.

That was it. I had given him all the information he needed. He said my new corporation package would arrive within 14 days and provided a toll-free number and Web address, should I have any questions.

Within 10 days, the package arrived and inside of it were

* *Articles of incorporation.* Official documents from Delaware that say I own my own corporation.
* *Bylaws.* The rules and procedures I need to follow for my corporation.
* *Minutes.* The written record of actions taken or authorized by me.
* *Stock certificates.* The evidence of ownership of shares in my corporation.
* *Transfer ledger.* The record of people to whom I've issued shares of my corporation's stock.
* *Year in review.* The detailed summary of my corporation's state of compliance for the fiscal year.
* *Tax returns.* The file where I can keep copies of my federal, state, and local tax returns.
* *Miscellaneous.* The file where I keep forms and permits, leases, business licenses, and financial statements.
* *An official metal stamp.* A stamp like the kind a notary public uses, with my corporation's name on it. Cool.

Step Four: File with the IRS

Also included in the package were two forms I needed to file with the Internal Revenue Service, Form SS-4 and Form 2553.

Form SS-4

Form SS-4 is the Application for Employer Identification Number. Think of an employee identification number as a social security number for your business. In business it's known as your Tax I.D. Number. It's easy to get. The form took less than 5 minutes to fill out, I signed it, and faxed it to my regional IRS office. A few days later the IRS faxed me a copy of it back with the official IRS stamp showing date registered along with my new Tax ID Number.

Form 2553

Form 2553 is the Election by a Small Business Corporation form. The IRS required me to fill out this form to officially register my business as an S corporation. After filling out the form in under 5 minutes, I sent it to the same IRS Regional Headquarters fax number I had used for the SS-4. So simple, and I just saved myself a bunch of money doing it myself. And don't worry; if you've accidentally made a mistake, the IRS won't knock on your door to hassle you. They'll simply return your form (by fax or mail) with instructions on what they need corrected. All you need to do is make the corrections and send it back. Done deal.

So, in less than 30 minutes, I had successfully completed—for the very first time!—all the paperwork the IRS requires for having a 100 percent legally official and protected business.

Step Five: File a Business in My State

After I had filed all the necessary paperwork with the IRS and received my official federal Tax ID Number, I needed to do one more thing: Get a Letter of Good Standing (that says my new company has paid its registration dues and is officially recognized by the state of Delaware as a Delaware Corporation) from the Delaware Secretary of State. This was easy, too. I simply phoned their office (you can now go online and do it) and requested the letter so that I could register my business in my home state of Idaho.

The Delaware Secretary of State's Division of Corporations office told me to send them a formal request by mail and to include the name of my company, the Delaware corporate number listed at the top right-hand corner of my Certificate of Incorporation, and a check for the small fee (I believe it was something like $20 at that time). I did, and 2 weeks later I received the Letter of Good Standing.

The day I received the letter, I went to the Idaho State Capitol in downtown Boise (I lived only 15 minutes away) and found the Secretary of State's office. If you live in a city outside your state's capitol, you can send your application and check via mail, FedEx, UPS, or any other overnight delivery service. I told them I had a Delaware corporation and that I wanted to file as a Foreign (a state other than the one you're in) Corporation so I could also do business in Idaho.

They asked for a copy of my Delaware Certificate of Incorporation and a copy of my IRS Form SS-4 with my IRS Tax ID Number. They had me fill out a simple Application for Certificate of Authority (for Profit), which took all of 3 minutes. I paid them $120 and my application was filed and stamped. I was now an official Idaho business!

After Incorporating

With documents in hand, I left the State Capitol building and headed for the bank to open my new business checking account. The process took less than 20 minutes, and 7 days later, I had a box delivered to me with my company's checks and deposit slips inside. I was ready for business!

I'll be the first to admit that math wasn't my favorite subject in school, and I did not want to spend endless hours doing balances and ledgers and all that accounting stuff. So after talking things over with my CPA, we decided that I'd keep track of my payables and receivables through the company checkbook ledger.

I'd simply send him my check ledgers, bank statements, and cancelled checks every quarter (though sometimes he doesn't get them until the end of the year. . . oops), along with a synopsis of what kinds of activities the business had for that period (deals made, money received, gear bought and sold, etc.). Everything has worked beautifully. And I made things even easier with a business accounting software package, Quick Books.

Having my own business has given me freedom, independence, and many financial and personal rewards. I can't say enough good things about the considerable benefits of having incorporated. Over the years, many of my friends and associates have said, "I need to ask you about how to do that corporation thing." *You* don't even have to ask. Follow the steps in this chapter, and you'll be on your way in a hurry. I believe you'll find it to be one of the best business decisions you'll ever make. Here's a final suggestion: Go to www.corporate.com. There you'll find answers to any other questions you might have about incorporation as well as lots of helpful information that'll guide you as to what kind of corporation might be best for you.

Real-World New Music Business Boot Camp:

What You Need to Know about Copyrights, Music Publishing, and Licensing

All right, listen up. It's time for you to get in shape. I'm talking music business shape. It's time you entered boot camp. While this boot camp won't demand any tough physical challenges or make you physically fit, it will make you more business savvy and fiscally fit. Our boot camp is only going to talk about three things—copyrights, music publishing, and licensing—but those three things can help you to create a protected and enduring music empire.

The foundation of your music empire is copyrights. Copyrights are like a bank full of money. If you control the copyrights, you own the bank. Far too many people give away potentially valuable copyrights for the promise of great things to come. Rarely are they pleased with the results. You've got to run the bank.

Many of us were taught by well-intentioned family members, business associates, and friends that if only you worked hard and long enough, success in life would be yours. But how many people do you know who've gotten rich working at their jobs? The real secret to wealth (if there is one) is to make one effort pay multiple times. And when you have copyrights that can be licensed, then you have something that can pay you time and time again. In this lesson, I'll give you the basics of copyright law—how it works, your rights, and three easy steps to registering your work.

The second part of our boot camp is the music publishing business. In the music world, you need to have copyrights in order for a music publishing company (yours or someone else's) to license them. As music publishing is quite a different animal from other kinds of publishing, I'll give you the basics of how the music publishing business works, as well as tips and advice that you can use as you decide to work with a publisher or form your own company. If having your own music publishing company sounds good to you, I'll show you the simple steps to do it and also give you the music publishing vocabulary and lingo guide so you'll sound like you've been doing it for years.

Finally, we'll focus on licensing your work. You need to have a solid understanding of key points you want included in all your agreements. Far too many people don't read or include the fine points in their contracts, only to find out too late that they've given up too much or will receive too little. I'll also give you tips that'll help you get the best licensing deal possible. And I promise to make it all as simple as possible.

Boot camp has officially begun!

The Get Smart Quick Guide to Copyrights

Copyrights. I know you've heard about them, but do you know what they are and where they came from? American copyright law goes all the way back to late fifteenth-century England and the printing press. Back then, as the number of printing presses increased, authorities wanted to control the publication of books. So they gave printers what we would consider today to be a monopoly on publishing.

The Licensing Act of 1662 established that a register of licensed books was to be administered by the Stationers' Company, which was a group of printers with the authority to censor publications. A few years later, the Act did relax government censorship, but it wasn't until 1710 that English Parliament enacted the Statute of Anne that has essentially become the basic principles of our copyright law today.

The statute provided for an author's ownership of copyright and a fixed term of protection of copyrighted works (14 years with a provision to renew another 14 years if the author was still living). At that time, while this may have sounded like a big win for the creators of a copyright, it really wasn't. If authors wanted to be paid for their work, they had to assign it to a publisher or bookseller. In addition, the statute broke up the monopoly by printing press owners and established a public domain for literary works by limiting copyright terms. It also made clear that if a work was sold, then the previous owner of that work could not control how it was used.

Since then, much has changed (and for the better) for those who create copyrights. Instead of 14 years of protection, you now get the life of the copyright creator plus 70 years. Instead of formally needing to register a copyright work, it's no longer mandatory (although it's still a wise idea so that you're afforded the maximum protections under the law).

Today's copyright law gives the creator of a work the exclusive right to control who can make copies, or make works derived from the original work, along with full rights to license and sell the copyright. For a work to be copyrightable, it needs to be in tangible form. This means it needs to be recorded (words and/or music), written, painted, sculpted, or photographed, giving your copyrighted work some tangible form. It just can't be some brilliant idea floating around in your head. Under the Berne Copyright Convention of 1989 (a treaty to which nearly all major nations are signatories), every creative work is copyrighted the moment it is fixed in tangible form. No notice or registration is necessary, although registration can be greatly beneficial in the event of litigation, awarding of damages, settlement, etc. But keep in mind that ideas and facts can't be copyrighted. Your creative expression—in whatever tangible form you choose to express it in—can.

When it comes to music, the first thing for you to know is that as soon as you've written your lyrics or your song, it's copyrighted. You are considered the "author" of the lyrics and/or music, and as the creator of that work, or *intellectual property,* you are entitled to the ownership of its copyright and all copyright protections under the law.

Now, let's talk about those protections. As I just told you, the work you create is legally protected for the life of the creator (that's you) plus 70 years. That's right. Whether you're 25, 45, or 65 when you create your masterpiece, your creation is exclusively yours for as long as you live *plus* 70 more years! There is no automatic renewal once that term expires, but if you've got a younger brother, sister, cousin, friend, or you have children (even a baby), you can extend your copyright term by naming one or more of them as a coauthor on your copyright. Once you include a younger coauthor, the entire protection is extended to the life of the youngest author on the copyright, plus 70 years. You've got automatic pass-through protection with nothing more that you need to do. Be sure, however, that when assigning a copyright or any portion thereof you put everything in writing: the percentage of copyright ownership, percentage of income derived from exploiting the copyright, effective date of assignment (e.g., your son/daughter will be assigned 100 percent ownership upon your death).

But let's not stop there. We want to protect your assets, and this involves officially registering what you've created with the Copyright Office. I'll show you how in just a minute. You'll find it to be something so quick and easy to do that you'll want to do it every time another masterpiece falls from your lips or fingers.

Your Copyright Is All Yours

How would it feel to create anything you want and then have the full power of the U.S. government (as well as the governments of many other countries) to protect you from anyone else stealing, copying, or using your creation without your permission? Once you create your song and music, you will have that power.

Your work is your exclusive creation, and this means you can sell, lease, distribute, or rent your creation to anyone you want. It means you make derivative works of your creation or take bits and pieces of it to do with as you please. It means you can make copies and reproduce your creation as often and as much as you like. It means you own it and you can do anything with it that you please. Pretty cool, eh?

But what if someone else decides they want to use your creation and not tell you about it or pay you for it? Uh-oh, it's bad news for the other person. Remember what I told you earlier in the book about dealing with pirates and copyright infringers who take advantage of others by not getting permission or paying for using things that don't belong to them? Having your creation "officially" registered gives you added protection, and if you decide to take them to court, you have the potential to make a lot of money.

I'm talking statutory damages that can be anywhere from $500 to $20,000 for each infringement, and up to $100,000 if the infringement was willful. And, if the actual damages and profits you've lost because of the infringement would be greater than statutory damages, you have the option to go after those instead. In addition, the guilty party (the infringer) may be required to pay your attorney's fees. All of this is courtesy of, and enforced on your behalf by, Uncle Sam.

With Webcasting and Internet radio, which I'll be telling you about in Lesson 13, you should also know about a copyright law called the Digital Millennium Copyright Act (DMCA). The what-you-need-to-know lesson here is that if anyone steals, borrows, or uses your music from your Web site or any other Web site that you've given permission to use, or licensed your creation to, the person using it without your permission is in violation of this statute, and most likely, other copyright laws. The same goes for you. Note to self: Never record or use something that you don't have permission to use—free music downloads included. Check out www.loc.copyright/ legislation/dmca/ for more in-depth information about the DMCA.

How to Copyright Your Work in Three Easy Steps

The U.S. Copyright Office makes it easy to copyright your sound recordings in three easy steps. Here they are:

Step One: Make Sure Your Work is a Sound Recording. First, your work needs to be a sound recording. That is, "works that result from the fixation of a series of musical, spoken, or other sounds, but not including the sounds accompanying a motion picture or other audiovisual work."

A copyright registration for a sound recording alone is neither the same as, nor can it substitute for, registration for the musical, dramatic, or literary work recorded. The underlying work may be registered in its own right apart from any recording of the performance, or in certain cases, the underlying work may be registered together with the sound recording.

Step Two: Mail the Necessary Materials. Here's what you need to put into one package.
* A completed application: Form SR
* A $30 payment to the Register of Copyrights
* Nonreturnable copy(ies) of the material to be registered

Step Three: Send Your Package to the Library of Congress. Mail your package to the following address:

Library of Congress
Copyright Office
101 Independence Avenue, S.E.
Washington, D.C. 20559-6000

Your registration becomes effective the day that the Copyright Office receives your application, payment, and copy(ies) in acceptable form. If your submission is in order, you will receive a certificate of registration in 4 to 5 months.

Copyright Issues Regarding Employment

On the journey down your musical road, there's a good chance that you will need and want to use the services and talents of other people, or that others will want to hire you. But as the creator of your own work, you always want to keep your copyrights. However, there may be times when you want to sell your music for other people to use (e.g., creating jingle music for ad agencies), and other times when you want to hire people to create music. So, here's what you need to know.

Independent Contractor. If you are the person being asked/paid to create music, you want to perform your work as an *independent contractor,* which allows you to retain all copyrights. The person who hires you only gets the rights to use your creation for a specific purpose and in a specific way (that you'll make sure is specifically stated in any agreement you have your attorney agree to before you sign).

Works for Hire. If you are the person who is paying someone else to create music for you, you want the other person to perform their work as a *work for hire,* which allows you to retain all copyrights and use their services however and whenever you wish. The person you hire only gets paid once for the work he or she creates for you.

The 1976 Copyright Act says that a work for hire is a work prepared by an employee within the scope of his/her employment, or a work specially ordered or commissioned for use by another person in accordance with a written document as a contribution to a collective work, motion picture, audio/visual, and other certain types of works, the nature of which is specifically defined in Section 101 of the Copyright Act. For more on this subject, read Courtney Love's advice, in Lesson 3, page 50.

Remember: If you hire someone to perform any work for you, under the Copyright Act you, as the employer, are considered the author, and as such, own all the rights in and to the work.

The Basic Ins and Outs of Music Publishing

Over the years, I've heard many of the wisest and richest people in the music business say that the only people who make *big* money in music are the record companies, songwriters, and music publishers. What about the superstar artists and all their tens of millions of dollars the media loves telling us about? The artist only gets a small piece of the bigger split between the music publisher, songwriter, and record label.

My hat goes off to people like Shania Twain and her husband/producer Mutt Lange. Even though they don't operate their own label (yet), they wisely work the music business. Shania is the artist, Mutt is the producer, and it's only the two of them who write every song on her records. As such, they receive royalties from many different sources, but they only created the work (song/album) once. This is true whether they had their own label or signed to a major. Very smart.

Music publishers are important in the music business. In the early days before the various ways to carry sounds were invented, the business centered on publishing sheet music. While that's still an important part of what music publishers do today, it's just one piece of a much larger and more lucrative business.

In today's music world, music publishers bring songwriters and recording artists together. They exploit songs for the songwriter and publisher's benefit. They also administer, manage, and protect music copyrights.

During the 1920s to the 1950s, artists sang and played songs written by professional songwriters. In fact, this is where the term A&R (artists and repertoire) originated. Record labels would find the right songs from a songwriter's repertoire and match them with the right artist.

Today, that's changed. Although there are still label A&R departments, artists are increasingly writing or cowriting their material. For those who do, owning a share of the publishing pie can mean huge financial rewards *if* they have a good understanding of just how the music publishing business works.

When people think of songs, many believe that the music and lyrics constitute the song. But that's not always true. A song often has three components: the lyrics, the music, and the arrangement. Songs are also different from a sound recording.

A song can be recorded by 50 or more other artists and each of them can arrange it and record it differently, thereby creating 50 different recordings of that one song. As the creator and copyright owner, songwriters are the ones who grant permission for use of their songs. And the terms of the permission can be as limited or unlimited as the copyright owner wishes. While songs can be copyrighted separately from sound recordings, until a song is made into some kind of tangible form (remember our copyright lesson?), it is not a physical entity like a record. This separation of song from recording gives songwriters a potentially very lucrative source of income: publishing agreements with publishers who will, hopefully, have their songs placed with artists who will record them.

So how is this done? One of the many avenues that music publishers use is their relationship with record labels. They must get the songs they represent (e.g., their catalog) into the hands of any of a label's upper-level staff, such as A&R. This may be accomplished directly, through the publisher's relationships with the artist, the artist's management, or his or her attorney. In other instances an artist or record label may call the music publisher looking for a certain kind of song.

The biggest publishers—like EMI Music, Universal Music, Warner Chappell Music, Sony/ATV Music, and BMG Music—are typically the first call and go-to source for the best songs (since they have the biggest stable of writers and track record of hits). These publishers have lots of contacts in the music business and know whom to go to and how to get songs placed.

How Music Publishers Generate Revenue

The ultimate goal in music publishing is to generate revenue for both the author of the work and the music publisher. There are a number of ways that this can be accomplished.

Sheet Music. The sale of sheet music, songbooks, and reproduction rights for a song's lyrics in books, magazines, and CD jackets was the foundation of music publishing and it continues to be a big part of the business.

Broadcast and Performance. Each time an artist's song is broadcast, that artist (and the publisher) must be paid. Publishers, along with performing rights organizations like ASCAP (American Society of Composers, Authors and Publishers), BMI (Broadcast Music Incorporated), SESAC (Society of European Stage Authors and Composers) make sure of it. A common way to cover performance of music is by issuing a *blanket license*. The venue—restaurant, broadcast or cable television company, programmed music company, etc.—pays a fee to the performing rights organization that represents the songwriter and publisher in return for which they have unlimited use of the music for a specified time. The blanket license income that the performance rights organizations collect is distributed to songwriters and publishers based on specific formulas, which are different depending on which organization represents the copyright owner. The performing rights organizations use various means of determining how often a song has been played and charge stations a set per minute rate. After deducting their administration commission, the organizations pay out the money collected to songwriters and publishers. (Visit the ASCAP, BMI, and SESAC Web sites for more information about rates and services.)

Mechanical License Fees. Under copyright law, once a phonorecord of a non-dramatic composition has been distributed to the public with authorization of the copyright owner ("voluntarily and permanently parted with"), any other person may record and distribute phonorecords of the work after paying a mechanical license fee to the copyright owner. For example, an artist does not have to obtain permission to make a cover record of a song once it has been distributed, but will have to pay the requisite mechanical license fees to the copyright owner(s). The amount of the fee depends on the current minimum statutory rate. As of January 1, 2004, that rate became 8.5 cents per copy for songs under 5 minutes or 1.65 cents per minute, whichever is greater. In January 2006 it will go up to 9.10 cents per copy or 1.75 cents per minute. Payment of this fee is required for anyone who includes a copyrighted song on any physical product (including those designer cell phone ring tones). Most of the work of collecting and distributing mechanical license fees in the United States is handled by the Harry Fox Agency, Inc.

Controlled Compositions. Record agreements include a provision that allows record companies to license your songs—the songs you write, own, or control in whole or in part—at three-fourths the statutory rate. In addition, the agreements usually say that the company will only pay 10 times the minimum rate for a CD even if the CD contains more than 10 songs. Using the current minimum statutory rate, that means that for a 12-song album (with each song under 5 minutes in length) that sells 500,000 copies, you, the artist (or you the artist and your publisher), has lost $127,000, which the record label keeps. Perhaps you should also think of owning your own label, too!

Other License Income. Other sources of revenue from licensing include:
* Commercial use (e.g., use of music in an advertisement)
* Grand rights (use of music in dramatic performance of a ballet, operetta, opera, musical comedy, etc.)

* Nondramatic performance (use of music in a public performance of a song on radio, TV, cabaret, hotel, concert, etc.)
* Synchronization (use of music on the soundtrack of an audiovisual work, e.g., background music on a television show, film soundtrack, multimedia work such as a video game, or a Web site)

Sampling. Whenever anyone records and uses sound samples from another artist's recording, regardless of length, the person using the sample must have written permission from the copyright owner, and permission is usually not granted for free.

Writer-Publisher Relationships

If you're a new writer and don't have a name, following, or catalog (a collection of songs) yet, you need to find an outlet for your work to be placed with artists who will record it. Most songwriters use a music publisher.

Establishing the Nature of the Agreement. If you're fortunate enough to capture the interest of a publisher who likes your songs and music, that publisher may want to enter into a publishing deal with you. This is where negotiations begin on how much of your song's copyright the publisher wants you to assign to them, and how much money you want them to pay you in exchange for it.

From the publisher's perspective, they would like you to assign them the largest percentage of your song's copyright, for the longest term, in exchange for paying you the least amount of money. From your perspective, you want to assign the smallest percentage possible, for the briefest term, and have them pay you the most money up front. The final deal usually ends up being someplace in the middle.

It is a big advantage for you, the songwriter (as opposed to a recording artist), to include in your *written* publishing agreement a provision that states that when the term of the deal expires, the copyright ownership reverts back to you, at which time you would be free to sign a different publishing deal with a different publishing company.

Once you've got a publishing deal, chances are that the publisher is going to have to spend time and money to promote you and your material to people who'll want to "cut" one of your songs. You could get lucky and get a cut quickly. More often than not, this process takes time. Publishers realize this, and they realize that you need to eat, pay the bills, and keep the creative juices flowing. The solution? A publishing advance.

Much like a book advance, a publishing advance can be a few thousand dollars to tens of thousands of dollars. Typically, it's nonrefundable. This means that if a publisher pays you an advance and then decides to do nothing with your song, you don't have to give the money back.

If, on the other hand, you sign exclusively with one music publisher (e.g., to be a staff writer), you will most likely be paid on a bi-weekly or monthly basis. A staff writer typically agrees to write a certain number of songs per month, year, or whatever the length of his or her contract is. The publisher has the exclusive rights to all the writer's songs written during the contract period, and in return for paying the writer an advance, the publisher gets a percentage of any royalty income received.

If you are not a staff writer and you have a nonexclusive publishing agreement (for example, a single-song one-off deal, a multiple-song agreement, or an administrative deal where the publisher gets a certain percentage of your songs' income for taking care of the administrative, royalty collection, monitoring, and registration work), you may get an advance based on a specified number of songs you've agreed to write. This advance will, of course, be recouped by your publisher from any royalties generated from your music.

Because the publishing business is so lucrative, there are lots of . . . shall I say, less than reputable publishers who not only promise aspiring songwriters the moon and then some, but will charge them for the experience. I'm referring to the song-sharks who charge fees to hear and shop your music. The biggest and most reputable publishers don't do this. If you find a publisher who does, head the other direction.

In return for paying you up-front money and/or being assigned a percentage ownership of your song(s') copyrights, the publisher will exploit your material and get it out to as many people and places as possible in order to recoup their investment. Once you sign your rights over to the publisher, where and how your songs will be used will be at the discretion of the publisher, and not you.

How Your Publisher Works for You

There are a number of ways in which publishers say they will work for you.

Song Plugging. In addition to the recorded demos of the songs a publisher will have in its catalog, some publishers will also have the songwriter perform the song in front of the interested party. Some songwriters I've talked to don't mind this, because it gets their names and faces in front of people who may be able to help them in a big way down the road. Others tell a different story; they felt paraded around town in front of many people who were simply "tire kickers" and not serious buyers and placers. It's always a good idea to know up front what will be expected of you.

Writing Sessions. Sometimes publishers will pair two or more writers together to see what kind of magic it creates. This can be a good idea if one is a strong lyric writer and the other's strength is writing music. Some of these collaborations can be amazing, as in the case of Elton John and Bernie Taupin, so keep an open mind.

Divided Publishing. Suppose you have a great song that would be perfect for a country artist but your publisher specializes in R&B (your usual genre). To get the song placed with a top country artist, the publisher may enter into a copublishing deal with a publisher who does specialize in country music. Large publishing companies are often able to make copublishing deals with multiple publishers. In addition, music publishers, like book publishers, have agreements with foreign publishers to exploit their songs in overseas markets. For a fee or percentage, these foreign publishers collect royalties and handle all licensing matters in their territory or country. However, be careful. With both your domestic copublishers and foreign subpublishers taking a share of your revenue, the amounts can add up quickly. To maximize your income and minimize double or more commissions, make sure all of your publisher's subpublishing deals include a provision that states you are to be paid your full royalty percentage rate "at source" from each publisher and subpublisher, territory, and deal, which means that you will receive the same percentage regardless of where the money was earned. For example, if you have a 50/50 publishing deal, you will get 50 percent of every dollar your song earns "at the source" of wherever it is earned.

Demo Sessions. In some cities, publishers have their own recording studios and have a staff that specializes in cutting demos for its writers. Most publishers encourage their writers to demo their songs at their home studios, however, and if the material is strong enough, they'll record a master quality demo in one of the big studios in the city of the publisher. This more elaborate demo will often be the one the publisher will shop around, pitch, and plug to try to get a cut or placement. It's also the one that many times can make it on an artist's record—even in demo form.

If You're on the A List. . . . Publishers know that the big money is made when major artists cut their clients' songs. Even though they seldom admit that they have A-list or B-list songs, they do, and they set aside the real jewels in their publishing catalog and vault for the A-list artists and their producers, or their "people," who come in looking for material for their new album. Get a few moneymaking cuts under your belt and watch how quickly you graduate to A-cut status.

The Hold. In the music world, making decisions is often a long-drawn-out process. With so much money involved and so many people reluctant to part with it, getting commitments can be like pulling teeth. However, publishers will sometimes allow A-list artists, producers, or labels to put a "hold" on a song. The way this works is that if an artist, producer, or label likes a publisher's song, they'll ask the publisher to put a hold on it so that they'll have exclusive right to use it. This does not *obligate* them to use the song, but as long as the hold is on, the song is effectively tied up so that no one else can use it.

Of course, publishers know that many of the songs that have holds placed on them are never used, and while they are just sitting there, the publisher is missing out on potential song placement opportunities. Therefore, some publishers have policies that put a time limit on those holds, but they may find themselves walking a fine line between wanting to move on with a song and keeping the hold on it in the hopes that the A-list artist will use it, generating major revenue.

For this reason, publishers will let other interested parties hear the song as well and place a second, third, or fourth hold on it. In the event that the party who placed the first hold doesn't use it, the song will be offered to the next artist on the hold list.

As you might imagine, this can be both exciting and frustrating for a songwriter. If a writer gets word that a major artist has put a hold on one of his or her songs, visions of mega success and big royalty bank deposits can be very heady stuff. Yet when the reality sets in as 1, 2, or 3 months pass and still no word has been received, excitement turns to disappointment. Have this happen to you a couple times and you'll better understand the adage "I'll get excited once the check clears the bank."

Administrative Agreements

Administrative agreements are different from agreements in which you agree to share ownership of your copyrights with a publisher. In administrative agreements, the administrative publisher—usually a publisher with offices and agents around the world—takes care of collecting royalties and other payments and handling legal documents and paperwork for you in return for a percentage of all income collected. The percentage varies depending on the nature of the services performed and on the bargaining clout of the songwriter. If the administrative publisher only does registration of songs with performance and mechanical rights organizations, the percentage is generally low, in the neighborhood of 10 to 15 percent. If, however, the administrative publisher provides a full range of services, including promotional efforts, recording demos and tapes, drafting agreements, etc., they may get up to 50 percent of all income collected.

Note that many administrative agreements stipulate that if the administrative publisher obtains a new recording (cover version) of a song or a lucrative audiovisual use (a major motion picture or TV program), the percentage paid to the publisher will be increased. Increases may also be contingent on a cover version reaching a certain level on the charts.

Negotiating the Best Agreement

If you're ready to jump in headfirst and start your own company, you can skip this section and go straight to "Forming Your Own Music Publishing Company," on page 240. If you're not, one option that may cross your mind is to sign a music publishing deal, learn the publishing business a bit better, and then go off on your own. If signing with a music publisher is the direction you're leaning toward, you'll find the following information helpful.

* First and foremost, *everything possible needs to be spelled out in the agreement.* Always remember that one's assumptions are usually the cause of one's screw-ups. Make sure that your attorney has looked over the agreement carefully and, where necessary, made changes and inserted important clauses in your agreement that give you the best possible terms in the areas of advances, royalties, copyright assignment, territories, accounting and statements, governing laws, warranties, and subpublishing deals.

* If you're entering into a copublishing deal rather than an administrative deal, don't sign away all your rights. Go for a 75/25 deal, whereby you control 75 percent of your publishing and the publisher gets 25 percent. If the publisher refuses, propose a 50/50 split. Under no circumstances should you take any deal that asks you to give up more.

* If you are signing away a portion of your publishing rights to your publisher, be sure they will revert back to you in a short period of time. Some publishing deals are based on a two-tier arrangement, whereby one tier is the initial songwriting time period (e.g., 3, 5, or 7 years.), and the second tier is a longer retention period, whereby the publisher controls your songs for more than 10 years. Negotiate to keep both periods as short as possible.

* Have your attorney include a performance clause in your publishing agreement stating that you'll agree to write *x* number of songs in a specified period and that the publisher agrees to shop/place/promote that number of songs in that same period. If the publisher fails to abide by the terms of this clause, you can cancel the agreement ("without penalty," which means that no interest or additional funds are to be repaid to you beyond what was originally received) and all your rights immediately revert back to you.

* Your agreement should state that there will be an automatic reversion of your copyrights if the publisher goes into bankruptcy or is liquidated. Plus you should have the option of canceling the agreement if the publisher sells the business or new management takes over.

* In fairness to both parties, the agreement should state that if you breach the terms of the agreement, any advance monies paid to you shall be paid back by you to the publisher without penalty. If the publisher breaches the agreement, any advance monies paid to you by the publisher shall be kept by you without repayment or penalty.

* Make sure the agreement gives you the right to audit the publisher's books. One audit per year should be enough, but if you can get two times per any 12-month period, all the better. One caveat: My advice is to not use this clause *unless* your songs are earning decent royalties ("decent" would be any amount over and above what it would cost to hire an independent CPA or auditor) and you have *good reason* to believe you are being cheated. In most cases, quarterly or semiannual accountings are sufficient.

Forming Your Own Music Publishing Company

As Diane Warren told you, when you're first starting out as a songwriter, it can be a good idea to hook up with a major publisher in order to get your songs recorded, placed, and administered. That's what she did, but only until she began experiencing success as a songwriter and making a name in the business. Once that happened, she quickly formed her own company, *Realsongs.* Her meteoric success is a powerful lesson that you can do it too.

Of course, many people dream of having their own music publishing company. But for this to make sense, you've got to be the right kind of person. By that, I mean a person who is disciplined and organized, enjoys taking care of business and details, and doesn't mind going after people, companies, and deals.

If you don't want to give up a percentage of your copyrights to a company to have them chase down royalties and the people who owe them to you, read on. Keep in mind as you read, however, that even if you're a songwriter who has no music publishing deal and you don't have any ambition to have your own music publishing company, you can still join organizations like ASCAP, BMI, or SESAC and the Harry Fox Agency and take advantage of their services.

If the idea of having your own music publishing company sounds good to you, there are some things you need to consider:

* All successful music publishers have a catalog of songs they can exploit for commercial gain. If you don't have enough of your own songs (many people say you should have at least 20) and/or access to songs from other songwriters, you might not be ready to form your own music publishing company.

* Let's say you've decided that you want to have your own publishing company. How do you form it? A company is a company, right? It's just the name and nature of the business that differentiates one company from

another. And since what you'll be creating is a company, follow the advice in Lesson 11, "Launching the Business of You, Inc," and you will have completed the first step. You will have all the legal protections afforded to a corporation.

* Music publishing is all about the exploitation of copyrights, and your corporation will need to have access to a team of legal advisers who thoroughly understand copyright law, can negotiate contracts, and take care of litigation should the need ever arise.

* You'll also need to have a top-notch accounting system and people in place who understand music royalties and publishing. Registering copyrights, contracts, licenses, royalties, compliance issues, and the like can be very time-consuming and costly if you're not properly prepared to deal with them.

* Finally, you'll need to have the financial resources necessary for the successful promotion of your music—recording demos, creating promo packages, printing and distributing sheet music, etc.—all the things that will get you, your company, and your songs promoted and in the hands of those who can record and use them.

* Down the road, you'll probably want to be able to sign new songwriters, which can be costly, so plan ahead.

Joining the Right Organizations

Let's say you've formed your company and are ready for business. One of the first things you need to do is establish the right professional connections. As a songwriter you of course need to be affiliated with one of the top three performing rights organizations: ASCAP, BMI, or SESAC. Each offers a slightly different package, but all of them essentially do one thing: collect royalties for the performances of your songs. These organizations also offer publishers a similar service, so it might make sense for you to have an affiliation with one organization to handle both your songwriting and publishing collections.

Many songwriters who have their own publishing companies choose ASCAP, BMI, or SESAC for their songwriting and the Harry Fox Agency for their publishing. The Harry Fox Agency represents publishers and licensees and, like the other performance rights organizations, it also collects royalties in many markets and countries all over the world. If you're a publisher with a song that'll be recorded by another party, then you're eligible for Harry Fox Agency representation. Go to their Web site (www.HarryFoxAgency.com) for more information, as well as commission rates.

Now, to help get your name out there as well as getting access to potentially beneficial new contacts, you might want to consider joining the National Music

Publishers Association (NMPA.org), the trade group that represents more than 800 music publishers. One of its missions is to protect the rights of music copyright owners and it's been successful on many fronts to help change and enact legislation to do so.

Another good organization to join is the Alliance of Artists and Recording Companies (AARC), which is a nonprofit entity formed to distribute Audio Home Recording Act of 1992 (AHRA) royalties. The essence of the AHRA legislation is that it requires the manufacturers of digital audio recorders and blank digital discs and tapes to pay royalties to the U.S. Copyright Office for the benefit of, and distribution to, eligible artists and sound recording copyright owners. This law was enacted as a way to compensate artists and copyright owners for lost revenue due to loss of sales caused by home recording. The Alliance of Artists and Recording Companies represents over 20,000 artists and record companies.

The Recording Industry Association of America (RIAA) is a good organization to consider joining as well. Despite what you may have heard about the RIAA being the villain in the file-sharing controversy, the truth is that the organization's main purpose is to protect artists and others in the music business from people who choose not to pay for music, services, and rights that are protected under the law. Its Web site and its Sound Exchange offer a lot of good information about licensing, copyrights, the industry, and the law.

Joining these organizations and gaining additional exposure is important whether you're an artist or starting your music publishing company. All of them can help get your name out there where people can see it. And the more people who see it, the better your chances of some of those people contacting you and using your songs.

Licensing and Protecting Your Work

To make money from your copyrighted masterpiece, you'll need to exploit it. This means getting it out and having it performed in public. No, I'm not just talking about someone else singing your song in a coffeehouse or bar. I'm talking about any kind of performance that requires a license for its use.

Along with licensing your work, you want you and your work to be protected. This means having the teeth in your licensing agreements to enforce your copyright and make as certain as you possibly can that anyone to whom your copyright is licensed complies with the terms. Be forewarned: With so many copyright pirates and infringers, for a new publisher, this can be expensive, unless you know a few tricks. Here are a couple that might be helpful.

* Whenever you do any kind of licensing deal, always ask for an advance against royalties and make sure the advance is large enough to ensure that in the event the license deal doesn't pay any royalties down the road, you

can be happy with just the advance. Many times, that advance is the only money you'll see.

* For license agreements with royalties, always have your attorney approve any legal agreements before you sign them. For advances, accountings, and royalties, I suggest that you make sure your agreements include such clauses as quarterly accountings with statements sent to you, and reversion of all rights and loss of all advance money paid to you by the party that doesn't live up to the terms of the license agreement and fails to cure (make good within a specified period of days) any breach of that agreement.

Key Points in a Licensing Agreement

Now let's run through some key points to include in your license agreement. First, of course, any license agreement must include the clearly stated Licensor (you/your company) and Licensee (the party who will be receiving the license from you); the date of the agreement; the name of the property (your copyrighted material/song) being licensed; and the purpose of the license being granted. The stated terms of the license agreement must include the following:

* A description of the licensed material.
* The specific grant of rights you will be giving to the licensee for its use.
* The name of the production that will be using your copyrighted material.
* The type of media in which your copyrighted material will be used.
* The license period you are granting to the Licensee.
* The day, month, and year the license begins.
* The day, month, and year the license ends.
* The territory in which the copyrighted property will be used.
* The length of the amount of material that will be used, which could be as little as a few seconds of music (for sampling) or an entire song.
* The production use, stating that your copyrighted material can be used solely within the production of the licensee and stipulating what the licensee can and cannot do with your property during the license term.
* The license fee you have agreed to accept.
* The license fee payment instructions that define when, how, and to whom the license fee will be paid.
* The license materials' effective date of use, indicating that the agreement becomes effective upon receipt of the agreed-upon license fee.
* The license warranty of rights that states that you, as the copyright owner/ holder, have full power and permission to exclusively grant all rights contained in the license agreement.

* You may also want to include some kind of language (lawyer-approved, of course) that you, the licensor, will indemnify (i.e., protect against loss, damage, and injury) the licensee from any breach of warranty (i.e., this license agreement and the words contained in it) during the term of the agreement.
* The termination of agreement that gives the right to cancel the agreement in the event that a licensee breaches the agreement and fails to correct the breach within a specified time period (typically 10 days to 2 weeks).

The last page of the agreement must include spaces that indicate where you (the copyright owner/Licensor) and the Licensee (person/company obtaining the license) will sign, date, and agree to all the terms contained in the license agreement.

Always keep in mind that based on your own unique needs and copyrighted properties, your attorney will most likely want to add more contract language to these points. Keeping things simple and being protected is not as difficult as it may seem.

Finally, despite how much legal language and teeth your legal license agreements may have, someone, somewhere, will some day most likely rip you off. When it comes to copyrighted property, that is simply the cost of doing business in the entertainment world.

So what can you do? You can try and find them, and once you do, you can spend lots of money, hours, and emotional energy taking them to court and trying to shut them down. But that can be a never-ending cycle. Sure, you've got to protect your copyrights and assert your legal ownership whenever and wherever you find someone ripping you off, but you've got to be smart and pick your court battles carefully.

The vice-president of legal affairs at one of the world's biggest movie studios told me once that every day, someone, somewhere, is ripping off the studio's films and bootlegging them. I asked her what they did about it. She said that even for a company like hers, with billions of dollars in assets and a huge legal team (both in-house and outside), it's simply not worth the time and expense to go after every little mom-and-pop operation that puts up a dummy address and runs duplicators in the back room of an office.

Her advice was to go after the biggest fish first—those who are the biggest infringers, and those who have the deepest pockets and have the ability to pay big damages, regardless of whether settlement occurs inside or outside the courtroom. Because the entertainment business is such a small, interconnected world, word can travel fast once it gets out that not only are you going after, suing, and shutting down infringers, but those found guilty must pay heavy damages. And once the word is out, many would-be copyright infringers will think twice about stealing from you.

Yes, having the law on your side is a good thing. And for many of you, so will having your own publishing and licensing business. But like all good things in life, it comes with a price. First, you've got to be disciplined enough to take care of the details when it comes to the business of You, Inc. You've got to have a good team. You need to be on solid ground financially with sufficient money that can sustain your new business. You need to be protected with the right kinds of agreements that allow you to seek out and enter into the best deals you can, all the while being mindful that people who use your copyrighted property must abide by the terms of your agreements or else you're going after them.

Whatever your publishing and licensing goals may be, if you follow the guidelines in this chapter, you'll always be one step ahead and smiling all the way to the bank.

Part 4

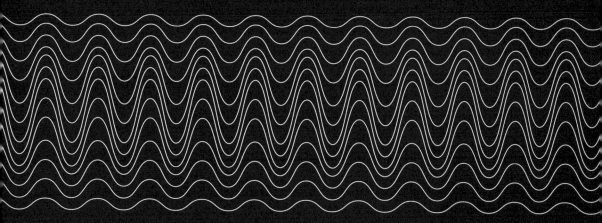

Marketing, Selling, and Distributing Your Music All Over the World:

Tapping into the Big Money Potential of Niche

Markets, the Internet, and Webcasting

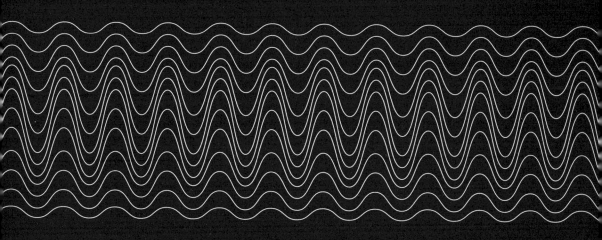

Premiering Your Music:

Three Steps to Broadcasting and Selling

Your Music to a Global Audience

Now it's time to have some fun. I'm going to tell you what you need to do to get on the same Internet playing field as the major labels. And here's how we level that playing field. They've got a domain name. You'll have a domain name. They've got a Web site. You'll have a Web site. They use the Internet to broadcast their music. You'll use the Internet to broadcast your music. Follow the three steps in this lesson and you can be up and running before you know it, getting your music to listeners all over the world.

For now, let's talk about how the labels use the Internet to broadcast music. It's well known just how slow the labels were to jump into Internet music distribution. Piracy and downloads really caught them off guard. One of the first ways labels began using the Web was by putting bios, photos, and tour information for their artists on the label's main Web site, with links (where applicable) to each artist's own Web site. Many also included links to legitimate (read: *not* prelegit Napster) music download sites.

Today, the world of downloadable music sites is so rapidly that it is not useful to try and list the different players and the download options/prices they offer. In the fall of 2003, MusicNet, Pressplay, BuyMusic.com, Apple's iTunes, MusicNow, and Rhapsody (Listen.com) were among the sites vying with one another to gain market share. For current information, check out their Web sites.

As mentioned in Lesson 2, some artists and bands are using the Internet to create an audience, interest, and buzz (perhaps even worldwide) by allowing free downloads of their music. If you were to go this route, you could, for example, send MP3s of your music to Web radio stations (go to any search engine and type in "Internet radio stations" for a listing of sites). Once you get your music to chart on such sites as MP3.com and Amp3.com, you can see what kind of global audience could build from such exposure. However, be sure to have a link to your own Web site (which we're going to show you how to set up) and make sure CDs are available for those new listeners who'd like to buy them.

David Bowie was one of the first established artists to embrace the Internet and its power for music distribution big time. Besides offering his music for sale on his Web site, Bowie has offered free songs online from his live shows and sneak previews of upcoming albums. He has even run a contest giving fans the opportunity to write lyrics for his songs.

And make no mistake. The enormous potential of the Internet for promoting and distributing music is just beginning to be tapped. So what *you* need to do is get your name and your music out there by choosing a cool domain name, setting up your own site, and, ultimately, broadcasting your music to listeners all over the world.

Step One: Get a Domain Name

Before you create your Web site, you're going to need an address. In the world of the Internet, this address is called a domain name. Each day, thousands of domain names are registered all over the world. The good names—maybe the very one you'd like—are going quickly.

Many businesses use their business names as their domain names because the name recognition makes them easy for people to remember. If you're a solo artist or in a band, you might want to try using your name or the band's name for your Web site address. The bad news is that if you haven't already registered your domain name, it may already be taken. The good news is that even though the .com-ending addresses were gobbled up quickly, under the appropriate circumstances, you can now register your favorite name with a different ending. In fact, getting a domain name has never been easier. Type in the words "domain name" into any search engine and you'll get hundreds, if not thousands, of results. The process is pretty much the same from site to site. Here's how it works.

When you type in the name you want in the site's domain name search box, it searches its database to see if the name's available. The search results also indicate the different dot endings available for that name. Once you find a name that's available, you choose which available dot ending you'd like (org, biz, com, etc.). There are over a hundred possibilities, but some are restricted, as discussed below.

After you've chosen your domain name and dot endings, you then choose how long you want the registration of that name to be in effect. Some people opt for only a 1- or 2-year term because they aren't sure that, down the road, they'll want to keep the name they've chosen. I suggest that if you're lucky enough to find that your name or names of choice are available, you'd be wise to lock it in for as long as you can. When I found that my name was available, I initially registered it for 1 year. But before the registration expired, I took advantage of a bargain-price package deal that allowed me to lock up my name for another 9 years before I would have to renew the registration.

After you choose your domain name, dot endings, and length of term, you fill out a registration that asks for your name, address, contact information, etc. Easy stuff. The final step is payment, and a credit card is the way to go. You can register a domain name for as little as $10 (less if you choose more than one). You should do all this quickly because the name you want can be snatched up by someone else in an instant.

Over the years, I've tried a few different domain name service companies, all with good results. If you've found one you like, stick with it. Otherwise, check out www.hamiltondomains.com or www.10buckdomains.com. I've been using them for the past few years and recommend them both.

I've just walked you through the process of finding and registering a domain name. If you're like me, though, you probably have a few questions. I asked Andy Broadaway at Hamilton Domains (www.hamiltondomains.com) to give you some answers.

What exactly is a domain name?

To understand what a domain name is you need to know some basic World Wide Web—Internet terminology. A domain name is part of the Internet *domain name system,* which is the system that assigns a 32-bit number, or Internet Protocol (IP) address, to every computer logging on to the Internet. If you are simply using your computer to browse the Web or to access your e-mail service, your computer probably does not have a static (permanent) IP. The IPs of most host computers are static. Obviously, it would be ridiculously unwieldy to require you to store and/or remember numerical IPs for Web sites you want to access, so every host computer's IP is mapped to a *domain name,* the more or less user-friendly string of letters and dots you type in when you want to go to a site. All domain names have a TLD (top-level domain) part and an SLD (second-level domain) part.

What do you mean by "host" computer?

The definition of "host" varies depending on the circumstances, but for our purposes, a host computer is any computer that houses, serves, and maintains one or more Web sites.

What is a TLD?

A TLD is that part of the domain name that identifies the *type* of entity being named. There are some restrictions on the use of certain TLDs. There are also ccTLDs (country-code TLDs), which indicate the country in which that entity is located, for example, .bz (Belize),.ca (Canada), .dk (Denmark), .ec (Ecuador), .ie (Republic of Ireland), .uk (United Kingdom), .us (United States), and .zw (Zimbabwe). The number of TLDs available is limited (currently about 100). A few of the most well-known unrestricted TLDs are as follows:

* .com ("commercial") is the most common extension for domain names; it often represents companies or for-profit organizations. Most personal Web sites also use this extension.
* .net generally represents Internet Service Providers (ISPs).
* .org usually represents nonprofit organizations or groups.
* .biz ("business") is reserved for use by businesses.
* .info can be for either businesses or individuals. Usage is unrestricted, but an .info TLD indicates that the Web site primarily is informative.
* .ws (Web site) is an all-around, universally available top-level domain.

Some restricted TLDs—meaning that you cannot choose one of them unless you can prove you have the right to it—are .aero, .biz, .edu, .mil, .museum, .name, and .pro. The .name TLD is available strictly for use by individuals, .edu is reserved for educational entities such as universities or high schools, .mil can be used only by the U.S. military, and .pro is currently reserved for certified doctors, lawyers, and accountants.

What is an SLD?
Located immediately after www. or http://, the SLD is the "readable" part of the domain name. A second-level domain name is entirely defined by the registrant, and may or may not be some form of an organization's or businesses' brand name. For example, in www.cnn.com "cnn" (Cable News Networks) is an SLD. There can be more than one part to an SLD, for example, www.sportsillustrated.cnn.com, where "sportsillustrated" is a subdomain.

What does it mean to register a domain name?
The Internet domain name system consists of a directory, organized hierarchically, of all the IP/domain names and their corresponding computers registered to particular companies and persons using the Internet. When you register a domain name *and* designate an Internet host (whether it is your own computer or one of the many, many host computers out there), that name will be associated with the host during the period the registration is in effect.

What if I haven't designated a host?
You can register as many names as you like without designating a host. However, you

cannot build a Web site around any of those names. They are considered "parked." If you aren't yet ready to go to the expense of setting up and maintaining a Web site, but don't want anyone else out there to register the name you want, go ahead and register and park the name or names you have in mind. For the same reason, many people also register and park several variations of their company names, effectively preventing anyone else from using them. If this option is chosen, users typing in the name will be directed to a temporary one-page site that says "under construction," "coming soon," or "for sale," according to circumstances.

What can I do if the domain name I want is unavailable?
If the domain name you requested is already taken, you will be presented with reasonable alternatives that *are* available. If you have requested the name www.mybusinessname.com, and that name is already taken, you might be offered the alternatives www.mybusinessname.info or www.mybusinessname.ws. Or you could start over again and search for a different SLD with the .com extension.

Can I cancel a domain-name registration?
Any reputable domain-name registration service will let you cancel your registration. On www.hamiltondomains.com you can perform this function from the Manage My Account section of the site. Click on Domain Names, log in, and select from the list the domain you wish to cancel. Next, click Cancel Domains and confirm the cancellation by clicking the Yes, Cancel Domain(s) Now button. Note that canceling a domain-name registration is a permanent action and you cannot undo this action, although you may reregister the same domain later for a new registration fee.

I just paid for a domain name and have designated a host.
Can people access my Web site right away?
No. You generally need to allow 2 to 3 business days after purchase before anyone anywhere in the world will be able to access your site by typing in the name.

What does it mean to forward a domain name?
Suppose you have a free home page from your Internet service provider, but its address is long and complicated, for example, www.yourserviceprovider/ web/users/~yourname. You can use one of the registration sites to register yourname.com (or, if .com is taken, yourname.biz or yourname.ws) and sign up for the (usually free) forwarding service. Then when people type in yourname.com on the address line, they will automatically be redirected to the already existing site. They will, however, see the longer name on the address bar. You can also "forward with

masking," which means that the address the user types in, not the destination address, is the one that stays in the browser's address bar.

How do I find my domain name's expiration date?

All domain name registration services have a "Whois" lookup capability that allows you to access all information pertaining to your account, including the expiration date or dates of all your domain names.

Will my name and contact information be made publicly available?

Information about who is responsible for domain names is publicly available to allow rapid resolution of technical problems, and to permit enforcement of consumer protection, trademark, and other laws. The registrar will make this information available to the public on a Whois site. It is, however, possible to register a domain in the name of a third party, as long as the third party agrees to accept responsibility. Consult your registrar for further details.

How do I find out who owns a domain name?

If you are using hamiltondomains.com to register your name and you select one that is already taken, a link (Already Taken, Click Here for Info) to the Whois function will appear. You will then be able to look up the contact details of that domain's owner.

What can I do if I have misspelled my domain name?

Your domain name cannot be changed after you complete the registration. You will have to register the correctly spelled name and pay the requisite fee.

Step Two: Get a Web Site

Okay, now that you've chosen and registered your domain name, you're going to need a place to use it: your own Web site. Didn't I tell you I'd turn you into a businessperson before you were finished with this book! You're doing great.

I'm going to assume (and pardon me if I'm wrong) that you don't have any hands-on experience with HTML (hypertext markup language—the codes used to mark Web site text so that it has the look the designers want) or Web site design. I'm also going to assume you want a great-looking site, but are underwhelmed at the thought of paying a Web site designer big bucks to create one. Wouldn't it be wonderful if you could easily and quickly design your own Web site and have the ability to change the design, look, and feel of that site as often as you'd like? How about putting files of your own music on there for people to hear? And what if you could do that for under $25 a month? Read on, read on.

Some years ago, one of my fitness and health book publishers suggested I get my own Web site. It would be a place, they said, where anyone, anywhere, could visit and find out more about me and my books, get tips and advice, and ask questions. A great idea, I thought, except for two things: I didn't want to pay thousands of dollars to have it designed and I didn't want to spend a lot of my *own* time learning how to do it.

I did some research and came up with Network Solutions, a company that advertised that I could have my own Web site and be up and running on the Internet in "as little as 10 minutes." I was hooked. In a matter of one evening, I—who had zero experience with Web site design or HTML coding—had designed my own site. It has worked flawlessly ever since. Network Solutions is the company I'm recommending you use, too. I'm sure there are other great companies out there who offer great services, but it seems logical for me to tell you about the one I've used myself. Here's how I did it . . . and how you can, too.

Decide on the Basics: Size and Layout

Network Solutions has quite a few packages to choose from, whether you need a site with only 1 Web page or one with 10 or more. I chose the 10-page option. The thing I liked was that if I ever needed more pages, I could always add them for just a few extra dollars per month.

After choosing my Web site package, I was ready to select one of the many design templates. These templates are grouped in categories and themes (e.g., one category is Sports, and within that category there are 15 different sports themes to choose from). Whatever template you choose essentially becomes the overall visual image people see when they come to your site. Be sure and take lots of time choosing so you'll end up with the one that says, "This is me."

Personalizing Your Site

One of the ways that Network Solutions makes building a Web site easy is by offering different page building blocks for you to choose from. Do you want one page to have all text and no pictures? How about a page that wraps text around a photo? How about two or three photos with text? Or perhaps no text and all photos? The page building blocks offer all these options, and more, and you can mix them in whatever way you want.

At this stage you can also add images and thumbnail pictures along with captions. While you're most likely going to want to use as many of your own photos as possible, you can also choose (without charge) photos and graphics from Network Solution's image and photo library. You can store all your photos on your Web site as well, and change and replace photos from your image library any time you like.

You can also put any of your own designs on any page you want, for example, your band's name in dynamite lettering and your logo. You can put links on your site to other sites anywhere on the Web, such as amazon.com, where they can buy your music. Or one click and they're instantly taken to your Internet radio station!

You can also put music files on your site, whereby viewers can click on the appropriate music link and hear samples of your music. The choices are huge as to what kinds of files, page options, and links you want. You can have your own e-mail address, a feedback and to-contact form, and a guestbook and message board. You can conduct Web polls and add a Web counter that tracks visitor activity. Web counters (which track visitors) are free from Network Solutions, or you can pay one of a number of tracking services out there a minimal fee (e.g., $5.99 or less per month). Plus, you can make unlimited changes (e.g., adding or deleting pictures or pages) and instantly preview how those changes will look before you get your Web site up and running. For an additional fee, you can even put e-commerce on your site: If you set up your own Web store, people can hear samples of your music and then buy your CDs or anything else you're selling.

Go Global

After I had done everything—chosen the design template and colors, set up each page's layout, written the text, added pictures, captions, and links, previewed every page and proofread all text—I was ready to publish my new Web site. All it took was a mouse click. In less than 60 seconds my site was on the Web for the world to see.

Network Solutions also includes one free SubmitWizard search engine submission that automatically submits my site to over 200 of the leading search engines on the Internet. Kind of a nice little bonus.

Step Three: Begin Broadcasting Your Music

Ever dreamed of hearing your music on radio? What about hearing your music on *your* radio station? A few years ago, unless you had millions of dollars, having your own radio station was just that—a dream. Ah, but fast-forward to the twenty-first century. All you need is your home computer, and my friend, you can have your own radio station and begin broadcasting your words and music tonight!

Many record labels and artists already run their own Internet radio stations. It's all about getting the word out, and with the Internet increasing in power and popularity each day, having your own Internet radio station takes you a giant step beyond duplicating promo CDs and flyers that get tossed in the trash—especially if you not only use it for your music, but also give listeners other great information, like artist interviews.

Once you have your own radio station on the Internet—and you can have it in under 10 minutes—you'll be able to broadcast your words and music to a potential audience of more than 500 million people worldwide. In the United States alone, it's estimated that more than 77 million people listen to Internet radio stations. Your station and music can be one of them. If you follow the quick and simple tips in this lesson, you can be on the air for as little as $8 per month.

You might be thinking: What kinds of music are people broadcasting on their stations? How about alternative, ambient, Asian, blues, Christian, classical, classic rock, comedy, country, dance, downtempo, drum 'n' bass, dub, experimental, folk, funk, Goth, government, hard, house, hip-hop, holiday, house indie, rock industrial, international, Irish, jazz, jungle, Latin, metal, new age, oldies, pop, punk, R&B, rap, reality, reggae, religious, rock, soundtracks, swing, talk, techno, trance, UK, garage, Western, world, '50s, '60s, '70s, '80s, '90s. And the list goes on, as new styles constantly evolve.

So how do you do it? You begin by hooking up with a company that specializes in personal Internet broadcasting. There's a big difference between that kind of company and Web sites that simply broadcast other people's music over the Internet. Those are the sites that only allow you to be a listener and not a broadcaster. A site called Live365.com is different.

Billed as "The World's Largest Internet Radio Network," Live365 provides everything necessary to choose the best kind of Internet radio station for your needs. It:

* Helps you upload your tracks (via CD or MP3 format), format your music, and put your music and/or words on your station.
* Places you in a directory so that any of their more than 3 million listeners can tune in to your station.
* Provides you with software so you can send your home broadcast out live directly from your own computer. You can talk into the mic, play tracks on the fly, or relay another broadcast.
* Gives you lots of bandwidth and storage capacity on the Live365 servers and provides a central hub where your station will be based and from which you can play your words and music to a worldwide audience 24 hours a day.

    Live365 offers several different packages, which I'll get to shortly, but if you're new to the world of Internet broadcasting, you need to answer some basic questions about your intended audience and what you want to do.

* How many listeners do you want to reach? (The monthly cost of your station will be tied in to the number of listeners that will be able to tune in to your station at the same time.)

* What kind of broadcasts do you want to do: tracks in a fixed playlist that are available 24/7 even when you're not online, streaming in real time, or rebroadcast of an existing audio stream?
* Do you want to sell advertising or otherwise make money from your station, or do you want to broadcast ad-free?

Personally, I'm into doing things in a top-shelf professional way, but also into doing them (whenever possible) on a budget that saves me money. And I want lots of options. For Internet broadcasting, I want the setup to be fast and easy. I want to broadcast 24 hours a day. I want there to be enough bandwidth (and not have to pay for extra bandwidth) and storage on servers for all of my content (with plenty of room to spare). I don't want to pay for any Internet connections or have to download anything whenever I broadcast.

I want to be the one who is responsible for my station, and I don't want to pay server-licensing fees or even pay to have someone else broadcast my words and music. I don't want to be locked into the same agreement for a fixed period of time. I want to be able to adjust my station—reduce or increase its options, features, and size—whenever I want. And I want to be able to broadcast my words and music either in real time or in an archived loop. What you're about to learn will allow you to do all of those things.

Personalize Your Music and Message

In the music world, not only do you need great songs and a great sound, you also need a great image. You've got to give people something that'll make them want to remember you. One of the things I like about what Live365 does is that they'll build a special "tuner" (or pop-up Player Window) with your own customized look and feel. The Player Window launches directly from your Web site, so visitors never have to leave it in order to listen to your broadcast.

Another feature they offer (for free) is to include your Internet radio station in their directory. This could be a big deal for your music. Live365 tells me their directory is the Internet's largest and they have millions of visitors—from more than 100 countries—who use it each month. Whenever one of those millions of listeners sees your name and chooses it, your Internet station's broadcast will play through the standard Live365 Player Window right there on the spot.

You can also program tracks from Live365's central Music Library. When artists and labels add music to this "record pool," Live365 broadcasters can easily find, preview, and add these tracks directly into their playlists. This is a great way to cross-promote your music with a lot of people.

Know Who's Listening to Your Music

The major labels are known for doing lots of research. Before they sign any new artist or group, they already know what market the new act will attract and how big it will be. It's all about minimizing loss and maximizing exposure and profit—quickly. As a smart Internet broadcaster, you need to have the same kinds of feedback tools at your disposal.

With your station on Live365, you have access to a special customized partner Web page that contains accurate and up-to-date listener data specifically for your broadcast. For example, it tells you:

* How many listeners you had yesterday
* How many listeners you had last month
* How long each person listened

And it provides the information in printable graphs.

In addition, you get valuable feedback from listeners. Through the Live365 interface, listeners can click on a link to purchase a track, get information about a track, add a track to their wish list, and rate a track thumbs-up or thumbs-down. You can also get "live" (e.g., in real time) statistics for artists and labels on these active, real-time responses, as well as the number of overall "plays" and the number of broadcasters who have added your track by choosing it from the Library. Having this information at your fingertips allows you to test tracks with a live audience before spending lots of promotional dollars. It helps you position your music and marketing efforts much more effectively as well.

Another powerful marketing tool you'll have available is a profile of all broadcasters who've included tracks from the Library and all listeners who've heard or actively responded to (e.g., wish-listed) a track. This information—which can be provided on a geographic or demographic basis—gives you insight into audience tastes. It tells you what kinds of music are increasing or decreasing in popularity at any given moment.

You can also get data as to which music genres are most popular among the broadcasters and listeners, and which ones like (or dislike) a track. And you have access to information about the most popular tracks on all stations that play a particular track or artist. This information gives you, the artist, and your label valuable insight into what other kinds of music fans enjoy.

Finally, you can take advantage of having a message board that can launch directly from your own customized Player Window on your station. You'll see message boards on a lot of Web sites and for good reason. You can use them to discuss current issues, to announce events and news, and to receive feedback from your listeners. All of this helps you fine-tune and craft your music and message for your target audience.

Learn How to Promote Your Music

The old line about any kind of publicity being good publicity is so true. With so many artists and songs today, you need to keep your music and message fresh and out there making some noise.

One of the ways to do this with your own Internet radio station is by using targeted e-mail promotions. Live365 features artist and label releases in regular e-mail newsletters that are sent to over 600,000 music fans. These newsletters can be targeted based on genre preferences, demographics, geographic location, or other criteria.

Another promotional vehicle is targeted advertising. Besides having your songs available for anyone to hear in their personal Music Library, you can also use audio and visual ads which can be placed on other Live365 stations by genre or geographic region. A clip of a track of your music can be included to promote the song to broadcasters and listeners. Trading ad space with other Live365 broadcasters is a terrific way to cross-promote each other's music.

Select the Broadcast Package Best Suited to Your Needs

Let's talk about how you're going to send your music out over the airwaves. Live365 gives you four broadcast packages to choose from:

On-Demand Audio. You can offer archived content (programs, speeches, announcements, interviews, and more) to listeners on an "as demanded" basis with On-Demand Audio. Your listeners will be able to tune in to this content from the beginning of each discrete audio track or recording.

Studio365-Live. You can create a live broadcast from your computer in minutes with Studio365-Live. You can broadcast live to the world speeches, musical selections, and anything else you can think of.

Studio365-Basic. You can create maintenance-free broadcasts by storing your content on the Live365 servers with Studio365-Basic. Once you've uploaded your audio content, you no longer need to be online to have your station up and running.

Relay Broadcast. Finally, you can take your current live signal (one you're already broadcasting on the airwaves or on the Internet) and with Relay Broadcast, send that broadcast to more listeners by accessing the world's largest Directory of Internet Radio and using Live365's Relay channel. All you need is Live365's proprietary broadcasting software, a computer, and an Internet connection (ISDN or better recommended). The Relay broadcasting solution is recommended for radio stations or other groups who are already broadcasting.

Create Your Internet Radio Station

Once you choose the broadcast package that fits your budget and needs, all that's left is to create your new Internet radio station. This is where it gets exciting. Go to www.Live365.com and follow their quick and easy steps on how to do it, and you'll see just what I mean.

Questions about Internet Broadcasting

When it comes to something so new as Web broadcasting and having your own Internet radio station, I'm willing to bet you've got a bunch of questions. I asked Steve Chang at Live365 to give me their most frequently asked questions and, of course, their answers.

Can I have a station that plays only songs from one, or a few, of my favorite artists?

Generally, no. With the sole exception of Internet broadcasts that exclusively include recordings in which you own all copyrights (such as recordings featuring your performance or possibly the performance of a band in which you are a member), only Internet broadcasts that are eligible for compulsory licenses may be posted on the Live365.com Web site.

One key rule relates to the number of songs from a particular artist that may be included in an eligible Internet broadcast. In general, in any 3-hour period, you should not intentionally program more than three songs (and not more than two songs in a row) from the same recording (or album); or more than four songs (and not more than three songs in a row) from the same recording artist or anthology/box set. Because of this rule, you cannot legally have a program that plays only music from one artist or a small number of artists.

Is there a way I can link my broadcast to my Web page?

There are a few different ways to launch your station from a Web page. Check out our Launch Examples on Live365.com for examples and instructions.

Can I broadcast music from CDs I have purchased?

Generally, yes. So long as the recordings that you play in your programs are authorized (that is, created originally by the band or record label that owns the copyright), and are not unlawful copies, they may be included in your program without further permission or payment.

This is because Live365.com has taken care of, or is currently in the process of taking care of, all U.S. musical composition performance royalties through its licenses with ASCAP, BMI, and SESAC, and has taken care of U.S. sound recording performance royalties by complying with the terms of recent legislation enacted by Congress.

You should be aware, however, that some songs may be written by writers who are not affiliated with ASCAP, BMI, or SESAC (including, for example, many songs written by local and international songwriters for albums that are not released by a "major" label in the United States).

Such songs are not covered by Live365.com's blanket licenses, and you would need direct permission from the writers (or copyright owners) of such songs before including them in your programs. Generally, the liner notes of your CDs will indicate in small print whether the songwriters are affiliated with ASCAP, BMI, or SESAC.

You may only broadcast sound recordings that are authorized for performance in the United States.

Do DMCA (Digital Millennium Copyright Act) rules apply to me if I live outside the United States?

The rules contained in the DMCA and on Live365.com apply to all users generating Internet broadcasts for transmission via the Live365.com Web site, no matter what country you live in.

However, if you reside outside of the United States, other rules and regulations might also apply to programs that you generate. You should consult a local music organization (such as a performing rights organization) in your country and/or an attorney to determine whether any such rules might apply to you.

Can I broadcast music from MP3 files that I have downloaded?

It depends on whether the MP3 files are legal or unauthorized. Currently, most recordings from major bands available for download on the Internet in MP3 format are not authorized. To the extent that the band's record label (or the band itself, if it controls its copyrights) has not made the recordings available, they probably are unauthorized.

You can usually tell by the type of site from which you downloaded the files. FTP sites, personal Web sites, etc., tend not to be sources of authorized files, while sites operated by the record labels and major Internet retailers tend to offer only authorized files.

As is true with lawful copies of CDs that you own, legitimately acquired MP3 files may be included in your programs. This is generally true whether you obtained such MP3 files for free or for a charge. On the other hand, if the MP3 files are unauthorized, you cannot lawfully include them in your programs, whether you paid for them or not.

Can I transmit certain special programs I've created more than once?

Yes, but subject to certain rules. The DMCA specifies that rebroadcasts of identifiable programs in which recordings are played in a predetermined order (such as published chart countdowns, etc.) and which are preannounced in advance (such as by telling listeners that the program airs at certain times) may be performed at scheduled times. Programs of less than 1 hour may be performed no more than three times in a 2-week period, and programs longer than 1 hour may be performed no more than four times in any 2-week period.

Can I let listeners know in advance what songs will be played in my programs?

Generally, no. Although you may announce a song right before it is about to be played, as well as after it is played, you should not make available, either during your program or in print (or e-mail) form, advance program guides, nor should you use other means to preannounce when particular songs will be played.

This rule applies regardless of whether you list the songs that will be played in the particular order in which they will be played. In other words, it is not permitted to list in advance the songs that are included in your programs in any manner.

Can I include bootleg recordings in my programs?

Generally, no. The only recordings that may be included in Internet broadcasts are ones that are authorized (for example, ones that you purchased from a store). Even if a particular band allows bootleg recordings to be made of its concerts, you should not rely on this fact alone to suggest that you can include such recordings in your programs.

The reason is that, if the band has a recording agreement with a record label, the record label may be able to prevent you from exploiting any recordings you made, despite the band's explicit or implicit authorization of your making a recording in the first place.

If I am based outside the United States, am I subject to any additional requirements to protect against litigation?

The legal issues involving Webcasters outside the United States are evolving and there are at present a number of uncertainties. To some extent, the issue may depend on an analysis of the specific facts involved. You should follow our rules to ensure compliance with respect to your stream as it is transmitted from Live365 servers in the United States.

However, with regard to any transmissions from your own Web site in any country other than the United States or via any other servers besides ours in the United States, then you should look into any requirements by the performing rights organization(s) of that particular country.

It is our understanding that the performing rights organizations in the United States generally have reciprocity agreements with performing rights organizations of many other countries. Therefore, if these agreements are in place with performing rights organizations in the United States, they will make allocation payments to the other country's performing rights organization(s).

Please keep in mind that there are international issues that are still being discussed among the performing rights organizations and among organizations representing record companies in different countries. To the extent that a performing rights organization of a particular country has jurisdiction, then you need to abide by its rules. You should direct these inquiries to the appropriate U.S. performing rights organization or the particular country's performing rights organization for information on how payments are allocated.

We cannot assume responsibility for compliance with any applicable laws or regulations outside the United States, but we are willing to try to assist Webcasters in obtaining information that may be helpful.

What speed is best for encoding my music for my broadcast?
Keep in mind that your broadcast bit rate cannot be higher than the connection speed of your listener. For example, if your listeners have a 56K connection, you will want to encode your music at a lower rate than 56K to allow the music to play without skipping. Here is a chart showing the various connection speeds and corresponding bit rates:

Listener Connection Speed, kpbs	Maximum MP3 Bit Rate Speed, kbps
14.4	8
28.8	16
33.6	24
56.6	32
T1, cable, DSL, ISDN	

Do the licensing guidelines also apply if my station only plays my originally created music and my performance of such music?
Ordinarily, you must abide by the rules as stated in the Digital Millennium Copyright Act. However, if you own the copyrights in both the music and in all sound recordings embodying the performance of such music, you would not need to comply with all the rules that would otherwise be applicable. In addition, you

must still abide by our User's Agreement, Terms of Use, and other guidelines set forth by Live365.com. Please keep in mind that we do require proper documentation from you.

If you are an independent artist and wish to create an Internet radio station featuring your own music, you can do so by forwarding to us written consent from you, as long as you are the sole owner of the copyrights in both the music and in all sound recordings embodying the performance of such music.

If you wish to create an independent artist Internet radio station that features music owned and/or controlled by you, please send us a notice stating that you are in fact the artist being featured and that you own all rights in the music and in all sound recordings embodying the performance of such music (and that no third party, including any record company or other party, owns any such rights) on your Internet radio station. Please provide your DJ name and description of your Internet radio station as well so that we may stamp it as an "independent" station.

If, however, you are featuring someone else's music on your Internet radio station on our site, you must forward to us written consent from the artist and/or artists, and any third parties involved (including record companies) that own any of the copyrights in the music or in any of the sound recordings embodying the performance of such music.

Promoting and Selling Your Music and Web Site

Okay, so you've got a cool-sounding domain name, you've created a great-looking Web site, and you've got a kick-ass radio station ready to broadcast. Way to go! The next step is promoting your music and Web site, and contrary to all the myths you may have heard, you're not going to need a lot of money to do it.

In the history of business, great wealth and opportunity have gone hand in hand with great ideas. Every invention or great business first began as an idea in someone's mind, so you're going to use some creative ingenuity to open doors. What follows are some tips that'll help.

Use Search Engines and Metatags to Direct Traffic to Your Site

You just read about the search engine submission services you can use that'll get you listed on the Internet's biggest search engines. Use them and metatags (i.e., words or phrases to use in your search engine submission description that'll direct people who type in that search word to see your site listed as a search result), lots and lots of metatags, to get your Web site listed and seen by as many people as possible.

Create Tie-ins with Other Sites and Companies

A great way to get your name and music out there in a big way is to be associated with other Web sites and companies you like. And they don't need to be music-related companies. Any company that has customers can be a terrific place to find new ears and eyes.

In exchange for providing music to an individual or a company, ask them to include a link on their site that says "Click here to buy Mymusic." That link will take them to your site where you'll, of course, have plenty of your music available (in many different formats) for them to choose.

Be flexible on the price or deal you're looking for. Start by offering free or reduced-rate music to promote your music and Web site on other sites. As the demand for your music grows, you can always revisit the terms of your agreement.

Associate Yourself with a Powerful Brand

Associating with a powerful brand can open doors for you and your music in a hurry. People go after brand names they're familiar with before they choose lesser-known names. Having you and your music associated with a brand-name company or individual not only gives you instant clout, it also gives you a powerful reference and door-opener to other companies who'll now see you as a major player worthy of playing with the big boys (or girls).

Do Deals with Other Web Sites

There are hundreds of millions of Web sites on the Internet, with one estimate putting the number closer to 3 billion. It's huge, and more new sites are coming online each day. And guess what? Many of them need music content. Bingo! Find the ones you like and do a deal with them to provide musical content for a fee, a trade for promotion and association with them, or a combination of the two.

Not only should you seek out the entertainment providers, companies that specialize in visual content (music and visuals are a powerful pair), but you should consider companies that most people wouldn't associate with a need for music to promote their business—florists, card companies, even auto parts manufacturers.

The Internet is filled with great places to hear MP3s. Make MP3.com the first place to make your music available after you have got your own site up and running.

Sell Your Music on the Internet

First, set up an amazon.com link. It takes only seconds to do. Simply go to ama-zon.com and click on the "become an associate" link and they'll walk you through the setup. As you and millions all over the world know, amazon.com is the place people go for books and music, and having your music for sale on amazon.com will give you presence in front of the eyes of millions. You'll also get a commission on every sale if someone else (e.g., a site you have linked with that directs its customers to Amazon) sells your music. Amazon.com will also buy your CDs from you—the new music business owner of your own record label—directly.

Don't limit yourself to Amazon. Linking with online booksellers or music sellers is easy to do. And the big bonus is, those retailers who may have turned you down in the past when you've wanted them to sell your records in their stores probably won't this time. Why? Because all they have to do is include your name and CD name on their Web site list. There's no warehousing, preorder, or out-of-pocket expenses for them. And you get to be included with all the other major label artists on their site.

Don't forget eBay. Write a great description of you, the artist, and your music, and put your Web address/link in your ad copy that'll direct eBay buyers to your site to hear a free sample of the CD. Include a nice-looking picture of the front and back of the CD cover artwork, include any glowing reviews, price your CD below the cost of others, and get ready to start taking orders!

Sell All Forms of Your Music on Your Site

Give consumers the widest variety of ways to hear your music as possible. Of course, when you're first starting out, funds might be tight and the best you can do might be a CD and MP3 or other music file download for a price. That's fine. Even though CDs are up there at the top as the most preferred way to purchase music, downloads (legal downloads) are skyrocketing in popularity.

The other thing you need to think about is having your sheet music available in electronic form that readers can download and print themselves. All you have to do is create the written version once and put it on your site (or on Sibelius.com, which I told you about in Lesson 8), where it can be downloaded unlimited times by anyone who pays a fee.

Cool Ways to Record, Send, and Receive Music from Anyone, Anywhere, Anytime

You're going to like having your own Internet radio station. Whenever you want, you'll be able to broadcast your music as often and as long as you want. But what if you want to connect and record with other musicians without being in the same room, or even the same city, at the same time? What about if they're in another country half way around the world? In the new music business, your dream has come true. I'm going to tell you about two ways you can musically connect worldwide—one way that uses the Internet and the other approach that uses a dedicated phone line.

The first method is the old tried-and-true way to do it: sending e-mail files to each other that have audio files attached to them. Lots of people do it, so it's got to be working on some level for those folks. While there are quite a few programs that'll help you convert your recorded audio to various Internet audio file formats, a lot of people like to use RealAudio.com. Real Audio helps convert music files to WAV files, which are super easy to transfer. This is a good way to jump into audio file transferring. Another way is by using Advanced Audio Coding (AAC), which is an audio codec which, when compressed at 128 kpbs, delivers audio quality very close to that of uncompressed CD audio.

You might also choose to do it the way the pros do it. When I went to California to interview Bob Clearmountain, he took me on a tour of his amazing studio before we did our interview. Of course he had the best gear you could imagine, but he also had something else: DolbyFax. You might be wondering what the heck a DolbyFax is. It's a device that receives and sends CD-quality audio in real time (with immediate confirmation of audio delivery) by means of standard ISDN phone lines. The basic system allows users to send and receive two discrete 20-kHz bandwidth audio channels in both directions simultaneously, with the option of sending and receiving up to eight audio channels if higher-end versions are used.

Bob told me that by using ISDN (integrated services digital network) lines and the DolbyFax, he's able to receive music from anywhere in the world and mix it right in his studio in California. He's also able to send mixes back to his clients and he never has to leave his home studio. I like the sound of that.

I think you'll find it helpful to understand how an ISDN line and DolbyFax work together. An ISDN is a digital phone line that is able to simultaneously transmit and receive data across the world. It carries voice and data over B Channels (e.g., bearer channels) at between 56 to 64 kilobits (kbs) per second. There can also be a D Channel (e.g., data channel) that handles signals at 16 kbs or 64 kbs. And ISDN uses two kinds of service: primary rate interface (PRI) and basic rate interface (BRI). Primary rate interface is designed for higher-end usage, while BRI offers two channels at 64 kbs and one D Channel at 16 kbs, giving the user 144 kbs.

Many internet service providers and phone companies offer ISDN service. Typically, your home (or studio) needs to be within a certain distance to a phone company's main office in order to get the cheapest rates. For some providers, the further away your location is, the more expensive the service can be, due to the need for repeaters to carry the signal. When using ISDN and ISDN products, both the sender and receiver need to have ISDN routers and ISDN modems.

Because DolbyFax uses ISDN lines as its method of transmitting audio data, it can send and receive much more quickly and efficiently than is possible with DSL, cable, and dial-up services. With DolbyFax (and other, similar products, such as Telos Zephyr, APT Milano, and CCS/Musicam Prima), you can send and receive overdubs, work on scores for TV and movies, record and mix music, and co-create musical ideas with anyone, anywhere, anytime.

Always remember that in the new music business, there are no hard-and-fast rules on how to promote, distribute, and record your music. It's now cheaper than ever for you to get the biggest musical and business bang for the buck. So take advantage of it. Get a domain name, get a Web site, have your own Internet radio station, and begin recording and trading musical ideas with anyone and everyone you can. Do all of this and don't be surprised one year from now, when you look back at what you've done, at just how much your music/business life has changed for the better!

Lessons of Inspiration

Inspiration. We all want it. We all need it. When we *look* for it, it can be very elusive. But often it's just when we are *not* looking anymore—when we've given up—that it finds us. In fact, the possibilities for inspiration are always there, awaiting our discovery. All we need to do is open ourselves and lives to those possibilities. Life is is the greatest of teachers, and, if we are open to learning, will teach us what we need to know at just the right time.

Throughout my life. I've been fortunate to have had many experiences that helped shape who I am. Some of the lessons I learned were taught to me by people I admired. Most were learned from people I didn't know. And many of the lessons have lasted a lifetime. You're about to read a few of those lifetime lessons that I think will put a big smile on your face.

Your life and your talent are gifts of amazing power and potential. With music, you have the power to change people's lives in a big way. You have the power to inspire. Always remember that. Now, let me be the one who inspires you.

Learning from Greatness: The Tommy Tedesco Story

For as long as I can remember, whenever I'd pick up one of the guitar magazines on the stands, one guy's name seemed to always be in it. His monthly column in *Guitar Player* magazine was a reader favorite. He was referred to by studio players and other great guitar players as The King of Studio Musicians. He was a master of many styles. He had the ability to read music like no other studio guitarist. On top of all that, he was one of the most likable human beings you would ever want to meet. His name was Tommy Tedesco. I always wondered what it would be like if I could meet and talk to him.

The first time I came to California was in 1988, and after arriving in Los Angeles, I called the Musician's Union, told them I wanted to contact Tommy Tedesco, and asked if they could give me his number. They did and I called him. The conversation was like one that I might have had with an old friend, and at the end of it, he invited me to visit him the following Thursday.

Thursday couldn't come fast enough. With map in hand, I started out (2 hours early; it was only a 45-minute drive) to meet the man in person and at his house. I couldn't believe it was about to happen.

After getting lost only twice (hey, it was my first time in Los Angeles), I found his home (it was gorgeous) and with 30 minutess to spare, I headed to a nearby 7-11 for some water (dry mouth and nervous, you know) and a pit stop. At 12:55 I pulled up to Tommy's house and walked up and rang the doorbell. I introduced myself to the woman who answered the door, and she told me that Mr. Tedesco would be right down.

I sat down on a massive sofa in the living room, next to a flamenco guitar. I got up when I saw a man with black hair and glasses, wearing an oversized shirt, shorts, and sandals, walk into the room. I was smiling from ear to ear because the man was Tommy Tedesco.

Tommy [holding out his hand with a smile]: Hi Bob. I'm Tommy. Welcome to California and Los Angeles.

Me: Thank you. Thank you. I really appreciate you inviting me to your home and to meet you.

Tommy: So, tell me about you.

Me [not wanting to bore him with all the details]: Well, I was born and raised in St. Louis and I've always wanted to come out to California and Los Angeles. I think I wanted to see what it would be like to be around such great players, learn from them, and be inspired by them. I always wondered what that might do to help me become a better player.

Tommy: Well, there are lots of great players out here.

Me: Yeah, and you're certainly one of the best.

Tommy: That's very kind of you to say and I appreciate that, but I'm just a lucky guy who can play a few different styles, read music okay, and people are nice enough to call me when they think I can help them.

Me [thinking this is a very humble statement from the man whom so many in the business for years have said was the best studio musician in Los Angeles, if not anywhere in the world]: Oh, I think it's more than that, Tommy. You're such a great player and the stories are legend of you being able to read incredibly difficult pieces of music like movie scores, classical and orchestral parts, and the Frank Zappa stuff. . . .

Tommy [laughs]: Good ol' Frank. Yeah, that was fun.

Me: With so many great players out there, can you give me any advice on how I can become a great player too?

Tommy got up from where he was sitting and walked over and picked up the flamenco guitar sitting next to me on the couch. He walked back over to where he had been sitting with the guitar in his hands.

Tommy: What do you see here?

Me: It's a guitar.

Tommy: And do I have three arms and twenty fingers?

Me [laughs]: No, you have two arms and ten fingers.

Tommy: That's right, just like you.

He begins to play a few notes.

Tommy: You see there are lots of people who can play like this. [He rips into some cool-sounding rock riffs.]. There are also lots of people who can play like this. [He effortlessly switches to finger-tapping Van Halen-like leads.] And there are lots of people who can play like this. [He quickly switches to pop and country and Chet Atkins-style fingerpicking.] And there are many people who can play like this. [He starts playing straight-ahead and bebop jazz lines.]

Me: Wow! [By now I'm shaking my head in amazement.]

Tommy: But . . . there are very few who can play like this. [He begins to play lightning-fast finger-picked brilliant flamenco melodies that sound uniquely his own.]

He stopped playing, looked and me, and said, "And that's why my phone always rings."

I was speechless, realizing I had just been taught a very important lesson.

Tommy: You don't need to play everything I just played to be a great player. You don't need to read music to be a great player. You don't need to live in Los Angeles, New York, Nashville, or anywhere else to be a great player. You don't need to copy other people or try to play like anyone else. You've simply got to let what's inside your heart [tapping his chest]—whatever it may be—come out through your fingers, and keep letting the music inside of you come out. When that happens, you will have become a great player.

I have never forgotten Tommy and the lesson he taught me on that fateful Thursday afternoon in his living room. Sadly, he passed away a few years later and much too soon. He was a guy who didn't know me from Adam, yet he invited me into his home and gave of himself to help me. I learned later that throughout his life, he helped many, many people without ever asking for anything in return.

I've carried this lesson and experience around inside of me for many years. And now, looking back, I realize Tommy wasn't talking to me that day; he was talking to you, me, and to all of us. Be true and stay true to your music, he would say. And when you do, you will be walking with Tommy on the road to musical greatness.

On Selling Your Creative Ideas to Noncreative People

I want to tell you a little story about dealing with noncreative people. There's no doubt you're going to come across them on your musical journey (probably you already have), and they can zap the energy and passion right out of you unless you know where they're coming from and how to train them to be receptive to your creative ideas.

The world is full of so-called noncreative people who really are creative, but have closed their creative minds in order that they may fit in with all the other noncreative people they work with. They like things predictable, they tend to be conservative, they don't like taking chances and gambling on new and untested ideas, and they want everything spelled out for them.

You give them an idea and they absolutely love it *until* someone they work with tells them they don't. More often than not, they have little creative or marketing vision and will depend on you to convince them why your ideas are right (even if you're a well-known authority in your field). They want you to tell them—over and over again—why they should believe in and accept what you are telling them.

Don't expect them to see things you may have overlooked or not realized about how your great ideas could be promoted in other ways besides those you give them. Rarely will that happen. Typically, they go with what you tell them and that's it. And for heaven sakes, don't mention anything that gives them a reason to shoot down your ideas.

Too often, I've seen how an artist's passing comment about his or her song or idea that had maybe a hint of negativity about it can be seized on by the noncreative types. They are always looking for any red flag or potential problem (however far from reality), and they'll turn that comment into just the red flag they need to change your idea to something different, use your words against you to give them a better deal or more favorable terms in their favor, or shoot down the idea altogether.

My friends, the music and creative business world we live in is populated by bean-counters who sit inside the four walls of their headquarters and insulate themselves from the people outside. They *say* they want what's fresh and what's new, but what they *do* is seek out the predictable. If so-and-so had a hit song last month with that vibrato-ish funk vibe in the background going on, then they want that on such-and-such's new record too. As the old saying goes, "Imitation is the sincerest form of a lack of imagination."

So what's a creative maverick and visionary like yourself to do? Here are a few tips.

* Come up with lots of ideas, but keep them within a consistent theme.
  The noncreatives love to pick from multiple options, and may not notice that all of the ones you are giving them have a common thread, so whatever one they pick is something you can live with.

* Give them lots of ways to promote your projects. The more ways you give them (read: ways that won't cost them any money), the better. And take all their complaints—that they have little or no budgets for projects, that business is down and they're scaling back right now, that the market has changed, blah, blah, blah—with a grain of salt. They're still in business, so someone, somewhere, is still spending money. If you come up with good ways to promote your ideas (co-op advertising, promo tie-ins with other businesses, etc.), watch how quickly they find a few extra pennies for your project.
* Be ready to give them some real-world education. You'd shake your head at how many people out there have reached positions of power, decision, and influence without having a clue as to what people really want. They make decisions based on what other people, focus groups, trend analysts, and research tell them, and they have the paper to CTA (cover their asses).

So, why then, with all that powerful information, do music and publishing companies lose big dollars year after year? One huge reason is that they've lost touch with the emotional side of things, and it's the emotional that drives people to buy music, dance to music, play music, and love music.

My advice is think like a businessperson when you give them ideas, but always do so with one hand still on the pulse of your heart.

On How to Make Yourself Wanted

We live in a world where people with great talent are often emulated and sought-after—up to a point. If we see them too often or hear them too much, their value decreases, as does our desire for them. Some years ago, before moving to Los Angeles, I had the pleasure of meeting and becoming friends with a gentleman named Reg Park from South Africa.

Park was one of the legends of bodybuilding, having been a Mr. Universe, a star in some of the Hercules movies (the other being Steve Reeves), and friend of Arnold Schwarzenegger. He was wise in the ways of fame, fortune, and human nature and offered me some advice on a decision I was about to make: whether and when I should move to Los Angeles.

In the course of a year, I had traveled many times to Los Angeles to do interviews and write articles for magazine publisher Joe Weider, whose magazines included *Muscle and Fitness, Shape, Flex, Men's Fitness,* and a number of other publications. And each time I was there, Joe would ask what it would take for me to move to Los Angeles and write for his magazines full-time.

I'll admit what with all the phone calls, lunches and dinners, and private meetings at Joe's exclusive home, the attention that the icon of fitness was paying to me was a little overwhelming. While the money he was offering was good, I felt there needed to be a little more guarantee of opportunity before I pulled up stakes and moved from my little town in the Midwest to the big city of Los Angeles.

So I spoke to Reg about it. I told him that I felt the opportunity to learn the magazine publishing business and work for the legendary Joe Weider in Los Angeles could be a once-in-a-lifetime opportunity, but I wanted the timing to be right. Here's what he said first: "One of the reasons you're in demand is because you're reclusive. You have your own business. You live in a little town 1,600 miles away from L.A. You have something they want but can't seem to get. That fact, along with the thought that someone else, some other magazine, could take you, keeps your phone ringing and you on those junkets to Los Angeles."

He wound up with the following advice. "There is no reason for you not to stay right where you are and double your effort to become excellent at the work you do. With each passing month that your writing and articles get better and better, Joe's desire to have you out there working for him will intensify. Be aloof. Be admiring and respectful, but don't be overtaken by awe and by the legend of Joe Weider. And don't become too common—either in the frequency or in the tone of your conversations and appearance. If you do, your value will decrease in their eyes and it's the first step to becoming quickly forgotten."

I took his advice. Soon thereafter, Joe was sending me to many parts around the world on behalf of him and his magazines. A few months later, along with a good salary, he offered me incentives that I just couldn't turn down. I made the move and it turned out to be a positive, life-changing decision. It also taught me an important lesson about music and the people who make it.

Perception is reality. Many times, people treat us the way we train them to treat us. And they can judge our music—not so much based on the reality of how good it is—but on their perceptions of how, who, and where it is made.

You can record music in Los Angeles and it can be great. Yet you can record that same music in London or some exotic locale, and people will think—because of the mystery of where, how, and who recorded the music—that your music is twice as good. Never forget this lesson.

We cherish and value that which we don't have, for we think what we don't have is certainly more desirable than what we do. That's human nature. It's the grass is always greener on the other side story. My advice is to use that to your musical advantage.

Let your music trickle out and start a buzz among people. Be elusive. Be mysterious. Never reveal too much of yourself, your talent, or your craft too quickly. Keep your cards and your music close to your chest. Give out only small bits at a time and keep people hungry to hear more and know more about you. Then wait patiently for the right people and circumstances to appear. When they do, that will be the perfect time to strike.

Shattering the Myth of the Must-Have Music Town: The Studio on Music Row

Many years ago, I worked for an FM radio station that shared the top floor with a recording studio on the famous Music Row in Nashville. Often after work, I'd walk down to the studio and listen to who and what they were recording that day. Each week, studio musicians' cases filled the hall just off the elevator, and it was always a treat to see who was recording.

One evening after work, I was getting ready to catch the elevator down to the parking lot and head home when the studio owner waved his arm in the control room and motioned for me to come in and listen to a record he had just finished recording. He was alone, and the two of us sat down with a couple of cold beers as he rolled tape.

This new artist had a good sound, but I was particularly impressed at the quality of the recording. There was great depth and separation. The sound was full, clean, and very dynamic. I wanted to know more about how he got that sound.

"I really like the sound of this," I commented. "What did you do to get it?"

"Well, we got some new microphones," he said, as he held one up and handed it to me to see. "Then we did a little experimenting and changed some of the sound deflection and absorbing panels in the studio and that made all the difference."

It was his response to what I said next that was about to shatter one of the biggest myths I had believed for years about music.

"Well, listening to what you just played me just goes to show why it's so important to live in a music city and be around all the great studios that can get this kind of sound," I ventured.

He held out his hand as I gave the microphone back to him and he got up and said, "Come with me for a minute."

As we walked into one of the main recording rooms, we stopped and he asked, "Tell me what you see in here."

I looked around for a moment and said, "I see mic stands, direct boxes, headphones, some guitar cables, chairs, sound baffles, and . . ."

He interrupted. "Do you see anything secret in here that you've never seen in any other studio you've ever been in?"

"No," I said. "Not really."

"Of course you don't. What you see in here are four walls, a ceiling, a floor, and equipment that you or anyone, anywhere, can go out tomorrow and buy. Equipment that you can put anywhere you want and get 'that magic sound' you heard in the control room. And you don't need to live in a 'music city' to do it."

I was stunned.

He went on. "A studio is simply four walls with equipment. Anyone who's got got four walls and the same equipment and a little smarts can get the same sound whether they're doing it in Nashville or Whistlestop, North Dakota."

After looking around again and making sure I hadn't missed any secret gear he was hiding, I said, "You know, you're right. Anyone *can* do this anywhere, can't they?"

With a big smile on his face and chuckle he replied. "Yeah, but few believe it and that's one of the reasons why Nashville is 'Music City USA.' And you know what? Next month, like they do every month and have done for years, cars filled with people and their dreams will make the drive down Highway 40 and turn into Music Row so they can get that 'magical sound.'"

I never forgot that night, that man, that studio, and that time in my life. Whoever you are, wherever you are, you can create your music and your dreams anywhere your heart leads you and you don't need to live in a big music city to do it.

On What Inspires Greatness

I'd like to tell you two stories about what I learned from two of the best jazz guitarists to ever play the instrument. It's about how true greatness can't be taught, but is inspired from within.

Early on in my guitar-playing years, I had the good fortune to study with Herb Ellis and Barney Kessel. At the time, I didn't know very much about either of them or jazz, but thought the education and experience would be valuable. It turned out to be valuable in ways I never imagined.

The Herb Ellis experience was a 1-week master class, in which Herb taught a very small group of people about playing jazz guitar. We even got a chance to play one-on-one with him. Of course, being the young, naive guy I was, I wasn't ready to start thinking like a jazz player and it wouldn't be until years later that what I learned could be heard in my playing.

Watching someone of Herb's caliber and ability play was humbling. He used no effects and the only thing between him and his amp was a guitar cord. He wasn't a brilliant finger picker, but he could make his left fingers dance and his right hand and pick race across the strings with pinpoint accuracy and speed.

Watching him play was like watching someone enter into a completely different zone. His eyes were closed and his mouth open as he hummed the notes he was playing. Herb was oblivious to anyone and everything around him. Only when Herb was finished playing would he open his eyes and return to earth.

He also had no idea what he had just played. When people watching him asked him to show us again such-and-such "cool lick," he couldn't. We soon figured out that he never played the same song the same way twice, and we stopped asking him to show us stuff and started watching and listening to what greatness was all about.

While I learned a lot, the biggest lesson I learned didn't have anything specific to do with making music. On the last day of class, Herb told us to get a book called *Psycho Cybernetics,* by Maxwell Maltz. He said the book had really changed his life, and he believed that it would change ours.

I bought the book, and once I started reading it, I couldn't put it down. The author, a famous plastic surgeon in New York City, wrote about his surprising discovery that people who had come in hoping that a changed appearance would lead to a changed life were, for the most part, doomed to disappointment. No matter how successful the procedures had been, the lives of these people were the same as before, as if nothing ever happened.

Dr. Maltz wanted to know why. He discovered that often the beliefs we have about ourselves—our self-images—which we have accepted as truth, are wrong. Yet even though they are wrong, they may guide and direct every action we take or don't take. And many times they lead us in the wrong direction, especially when the self-image is a negative one.

Maltz says that if we can change our self-images—and plastic surgery won't do it—we can change our lives. If we can imagine, then believe in, then truly accept a positive self-image, one that includes our ability to fulfill whatever dreams we have, the job of our brains ("servomechanisms," as Maltz calls them) is to make that self-image a reality. It's really a variation of the old adage, Be careful what you wish for because you're likely to get it. Powerful stuff. It changed my life. It may change yours.

Another person I took a master class with was jazz guitar great Barney Kessel. Barney was not only a legendary player but he, like Ellis, was a great human being who understood life in more than musical terms. Yet it was how he thought as a musician that fascinated me.

During a performance, he had just played a brilliant rendition of a jazz standard tune and when he was asked about why he used a certain chord or phrase for a certain part of the song, he paused and said, "I was imagining myself surrounded by a B major seventh. Everything I played sounded good to my ear and connected to that B major seventh."

That stunned me. Remember, I was still the young wet-behind-the-ears guitar player who wasn't ready for all the heady jazz stuff yet. Still, his approach was inspiring. After that, when I played I would close my eyes and become wrapped up in the music, imagining whatever chord I wanted to play as being all around me. The possibilities were limitless. No longer would I have to keep going back to the same old safe positions, notes, licks, riffs, and runs. I could begin thinking differently, getting results and sounds that would be interesting, different, fresh, fun, and exciting!

Barney Kessel and Herb Ellis became great not because they played the coolest stuff. They were great because they always let what was inside of them be their most important inspiration.

On Getting to Where You Want to Go and Surprising Ways It Can Inspire You

I don't come from a musical family nor did I, when I was 18, have connections to anyone who did. I didn't live in a "music city" (not that that matters today, but some years ago it was a different story) or have any idea which of those magical metropolises would be best for me to move to.

I had to reject New York and Los Angeles because the cost of living in those cities was just too high. Nashville, however, was less than 350 miles from my hometown in St. Louis, it was smaller and cheaper than Los Angeles and New York, and it reminded me a lot of the area where I was raised. And it had lots of music going on, albeit mostly country, but still a good place, I thought, to jump in and get my feet wet musically.

After graduating from college, I moved to Nashville. On my second day in town, I went to the CMA (Country Music Association) office on Music Row to apply for any kind of job they might have. The receptionist was one of the best examples of southern hospitality I had ever met. She asked all kinds of questions about me and where I was from and why I had moved to Nashville. After quizzing me in detail, she informed me that there were no openings at the CMA at the present time, but to stay seated while she made a couple of calls.

As I sat there in the lobby, paging through magazines and watching her talk on the phone, she signaled me over to her desk. She then handed me a name and phone number on a piece of paper and said, "Go see S—— at RCA Records. She knows you're on your way."

The record label's office was just around the corner, so I high-tailed it over there pronto. I was met at the front door by the receptionist, and I told her who I was and who I was supposed to see.

A few minutes later S—— ushered me into her office. She too, was wonderfully kind as she listened to me describe my background and love for music and explain my wanting to work in the music business. She told me that the only entry-level position was a job in the mailroom. I didn't care *what* it was. It was a job working for a major record label and as long it was in the music business, that was all that mattered.

Within a matter of weeks, I was already doing more than delivering mail to everyone at the label (watching how A&R, promotions, the president, and all the other people worked was a priceless education). I was also taking master tapes and lacquers (this was before digital hit big) to the record pressing plants.

Furthermore, I was meeting the record label's recording artists (artists I had heard on radio and watched on TV for years) and making contacts like you wouldn't believe. Even riding the elevator was an adventure. When the doors opened on any given floor, I never knew which major label recording star might be getting in that little elevator car with me.

I also began doing a few demo sessions here and there and getting my feet wet in the studios.

And I was learning some amazing lessons in how to listen to a record as well. One of the friends I made was a quality-control man who vetted the records that were ready for radio release and pressing before they were sent sent out.

It seems like only yesterday that I was sitting in his office watching him check a test pressing. After cranking up the music equipment in his office, he'd sit down at his desk, close his eyes, and listen. "No, the grooves are too wide [or too close] on this," he might say. Or "there's too much distortion in the groove." Or "Have them set the lathe at x and recut." I was listening to exactly what he was listening to, but thinking all the time, "How in the world can he hear that?"

The ears this guy had were incredible, and it was a fantastic learning experience to watch him work his magic on the records that left the Nashville office—and explain just how he did it.

Yet, while the RCA experience was wonderful, perhaps the best decision I made during those early years in Nashville was to go to work for Studio Instrument Rentals (SIR). I met more music people in less than 6 months at SIR than I would have in 6 years on my own. Let me tell you about it.

At that time in Nashville, SIR—like many companies in the bigger music cities— provided cartage (i.e., picking up and delivering music equipment to studios), and also rented music equipment and rehearsal rooms by the hour, day, or week. My duties included picking up, delivering, and setting up studio musician clients' gear for demo and recording sessions in the studios, plus booking rehearsal rooms and dates with clients and setting up sound systems for them. Many of these clients were major label recording artists who would rent the rooms to rehearse either before going into the studio to record a new record or before embarking on a concert tour.

And while the job didn't pay much, I worked every available hour I could—some nights even sleeping at SIR on the sofa in one of the rehearsal rooms—just so I could get a chance to work early and late for anyone and everyone. And it paid off.

One day, the manager at SIR told me that a group of big names had just rented the biggest rehearsal room for the week and he wanted to know if I wanted to mix sound for them while they were there. It was a no-brainer.

The next day, as I was setting up mic, running cables, and checking the system, who walks in but Chet Atkins, The Everly Brothers, Mark Knopfler (who was then lead singer and guitarist of Dire Straits), Emmylou Harris, drumming legend Larrie London, and many others, all of whom were gathered together for the Cinemax Television special starring Chet Atkins and Friends. It was heaven.

One night after everyone had left and I was shutting all the equipment down, I noticed that everyone had closed his or her guitar case except Chet Atkins. Well, being a guitar player, I couldn't let Chet's magical Gibson nylon string just sit there all by itself in the cold air. As I walked over to close the lid on the case, I thought about how beautiful the instrument was and how Chet could coax the sweetest sounds from its mellowed wood as he finger-picked those nylon strings.

I knelt down, reached my hand inside the case, picked up and held the guitar (like a jeweler holding a rare gem), and put my fingers on its frets and strings and began playing. I swear, for those 30 seconds, I sounded like Chet Atkins. And what a shame it was that there was no one in that rehearsal room on that late night in downtown Nashville to hear me.

Ah, but any regrets were quickly forgotten as I gently placed Chet's guitar back in its case and closed the lid. I had touched and played the guitar of one of the greatest musicians who would ever play the instrument. It was an inspiration to me then, and now—many, many years later—the memory still brings a big smile to my face.

The next day, I came back to the rehearsal room hoping that Chet wouldn't find out (he didn't) that my fingers—and not his—had been the last to touch his guitar. Little did I know that something very cool was about to happen.

The Cinemax TV show taping was only one day away and Mark Knopfler wasn't happy with the sounds he was getting from any of the amps he was using. During a break, I went to him and said that I had an amp that I thought he might like and if he wanted, I'd be happy (make that thrilled) to let him use it. He told me to bring it in.

So I rushed home at lunchtime and packed up my Mesa Boogie, brought it back to SIR, and plugged it in. Later, after Mark had listened to a few notes come from it, he looked over at me, smiled, and said, "Thanks, Bob, I'll use it for the show."

The show was taped at Vanderbilt University. On that day, like all the days leading up to it, I was in a dream world, where I was hanging out with musical legends and watching a once-in-a-lifetime event take place. The show, in a word, was a smash.

After the show, as I was packing up my amp, Mark and some of the other stars of the show asked me to come with them to the after-show party at one of Chet's favorite restaurants in Franklin (about 30 minutes south of Nashville). Would there be no end to this musical dream? I sure hoped not. One hour later, there we all were. The restaurant was all ours and the food—catfish, BBQ, sweet tea, and good ol' fashioned southern cooking—was perfect.

So there I was, a young guy from a little town of 15,000 people outside of St. Louis who had just finished working with many of the music legends he grew up listening to, sitting at the same table with those legends: all the musicians I mentioned earlier, plus Michael McDonald, solo artist and former lead singer for the Doobie Brothers, David Pack, producer and lead singer of the group Ambrosia, and many others.

But the famous artists at the table that night weren't the larger-than-life icons that so many people and the press made them out to be. They were people like you and me. People from everyday towns who had humble everyday backgrounds and beginnings. They were born with a gift, a talent, and a desire to play music, to touch people's hearts and lives with that music. And it seemed to me that they would have been just as happy doing it in their local clubs as they were in front of millions.

And once the bright lights had dimmed, the applause had faded away, and the audience had left the building, these legends were who they always had been: ordinary people with extraordinary dreams who let their music come out and take them down the road we call greatness. And for one magical summer night in Nashville, they invited me to become one of them and showed me just how much we all have in common.

Index

A

A&R points, deducted from
    royalties, 24
A&R Recording, 204–205
A/V San, 183
Ableton Live, 145–147
ABSYNTH 2, 155–156
Acoustic Bass (Spectrasonics), 170
Administrative publishing
    agreements, 238
Advertising, radio
    buying airtime, 41–42
    calls to action, 42–44
    to promote music, 44–46
Agents, 91–93
Alliance of Artists and Recording
    Companies, 242
American Society of Composers,
    Authors, and Publishers (ASCAP),
    101, 102, 233, 241
Amplifiers
    Bob Bradshaw on speaker/amp
        combinations, 112–115
    Bob Clearmountain's choices, 199
Amplitube, 151–152
Anderton, Craig, 107
Antares
    Auto-Tune 3, 147–148
    kantos, 149
    Mic Modeler, 147
    Tube, 148–149
Apogee, 194, 198
ASCAP, 101, 102, 233, 241
Atmosphere (Spectrasonics), 171

Attorneys
    ASCAP and BMI as resources, 101
    billable hours, 76–78
    deal parameters, 82–83, 85
    doing without an attorney, 83–84
    finding the right attorney, 78–79,
        101
    Internet resources, 85–87
    negotiating fees, 78–79, 81–82
Audio Home Recording Act of 1992,
    242
Auto-Tune 3, 147–148

B

B4 Organ, 157–158
benedict.com, 87
BMI, 101, 102, 233, 241
Bradshaw, Bob, interview, 106–121
Breakage, deducted from royalties, 24
Broadcasting, Internet
    (*See* Internet radio)
Broadcast Music, Inc., 101, 102,
    233, 241
Broadcast and Production Bundle
    (Waves), 176

C

California labor code, 54
Calls to action
    power of 200 letter and request,
        43–44
    on radio advertising time slots,
        42–43
Case, Steve, 58
Certified Public Accountants, 87–90

Clear Channel, 37, 202

Clearmountain, Bob, interview, 184–202

Cohen, Larry (CPA), 90, 216

Company Corporation, The, 220, 221–224

Compressing music files, 210–211

Computers
audio-computer interface, 124–126
as sound system hub, 123–124

Contracts, artist-label, 48–50
California labor code, 54
major label vs. independent, 71–72

Controlled compositions, 234

copyright.iupui.edu, 86

Copyrights
exploitation of, in music publishing, 241, 242, 243
independent contractors and, 231
registration of, 84
sound recordings, 230–231
term of, 228–229
works for hire and, 231–232

corporate.com, 222

Corporate sponsorship, 59–60

CPAs (*See* Certified Public Accountants)

Cribs, 69

Cubase SX, 142–144

Cycling '74 pluggo 3, 150–151

D

Delaware S corporations, 221–222

Digi 002 Rack, 130

Digi 002, 127–130

Digital audio workstations (DAWs), 126–144
Bob Clearmountain's picks, 199
Digi 002 Rack, 130
Digi 002, 127–130
Bob Ludwig's tips on, 211–212

Mbox, 130–131

MOTU Digital Performer, 131–135

Pro Tools, 127–131

Steinberg Cubase SX, 142–144

Steinberg Nuendo, 138–142

Digital converters, 198

Digital Hollywood Online Entertainment Conference, 48

Digital Millennium Copyright Act, and Internet broadcasting, 261, 262, 263

Digital Performer (MOTU), 131–135

Digital signal processors (DSPs), 197

Discounted product, in calculating royalty percentage, 25–26

Distribution, 32
label-controlled vs. artist-controlled, 32, 55, 56, 58

DolbyFax, 267

Domain names, 249–253

Downloading
music sites, 248
record labels' opposition to, 52–53

DSPs (Digital Signal Processors), 197

DVD Producer, 168–169

Dynamic processing equipment, 197

E

828mkII, 125–126

Electric Base (Spectrasonics), 170

Ellis, Herb, 276

Emagic Logic, 135–138

Equalizers, 197

Exclusivity, in record contracts, 28–29

Expenses, personal record keeping, 90–91

F

Fibredrive, 183

Foreign sales, discounted royalty rate, 25

G

Gigastudio (TASCAM), 174–175
Glazier, Mitch, 50
Glyph Technologies, storage systems, 182
Groove Agent, 173

H

Harry Fox Agency, 241
Home studios vs. large studios, 30

I

IK Multimedia, 151–153
    Amplitube, 151–152
Income taxes
    business expenses, 90–91
    Sample Tank 2, 152–153
    T-RackS, 151
Incorporation
    benefits of, 219–221
    choosing a name, 222
    in Delaware, advantages, 221–222
    IRS regulations, 224–225
    limited liability corporations
        (LLCs), 216–217
    S corporations, 221
    sole proprietorship vs., 216
    state regulations, 225
    tax advantages, 217–219
    The Company Corporation
        (online or telephone incorpora-
        tion), 220, 221–224
Independent contractor, definition, 231
Independent labels, 71–72
Independent promoters, 39–40
Integrated service digital networks
    (ISDN), 267–268
Internet radio, 31–32, 33, 212
    broadcast speed, 263

broadcasting from your own
    station, 249–268
Digital Millennium Copyright Act,
    261, 262, 263
formats, 259
legal issues, 260–263
Live365, 256–260
as marketing tool, 32
personalizing your music, 257
promoting your music, 259, 264
tracking your audience, 258

K

kantos, 149
Kessel, Barney, 276, 277–278
KONTAKT, 158–159

L

law.com, 86
law.cornell.edu, 86
lawinfo.com, 86
legaldocs.com, 86
Legal resources, Internet, 86–87
Library of Congress, 86
Licensing revenue, 233–235
Licensing agreements, 242–245
Limited liability corporations (LLCs),
    216–217
Live365, 256–260
LLCs, 216–217
Love, Courtney, interview, 48–62
Ludwig, Bob, interview, 203–213
Lukather, Steve, interview, 64–74

M

Maltz, Maxwell, 277
Marketing, doing it yourself, 32
Mastering, Bob Ludwig on, 207–209
Masters (Waves), 177
Mbox, 130–131

Mechanical license fees, 234

Metatags, 264

Mic Modeler, 147

Microphones, 199

MIDI

    Emagic Logic and, 135–136

    MOTU's Digital Performer and,
        131–135

    Nuendo and, 141

Mixer points, deducted from royalties,
    24

Mixing

    Bob Clearmountain's mixing
        process, 190–192

    Bob Ludwig on mixing equipment,
        206–207

    mixers, 178

    recording process in, 206–207

    studio equipment list, 197–200

MOTU

    Digital Performer, 131–135

    MachFive, 153–154

MP3 files, Internet broadcasting, 261

MP3.com, 61

Music notation software, 163–165

Music publishing

    basics, 232–233

    revenue sources, 233–235

    self-publishing, 101, 241–245

    writer-publisher agreements,
        236–236

        administrative agreements, 238

        advances, 235

        advantages, 236–238

        copublishing agreements, 239

        negotiating, 239–240

        subpublishing agreements, 237

        terms of, 239–240

N

National Music Publishers Association,
    241–242

Native Instruments, 155–160

    ABSYNTH 2, 155–156

    REAKTOR SESSION, 156–157

    B4 Organ, 157–158

    KONTAKT, 158–159

    TRAKTOR DJ STUDIO, 159–160

New technology, as royalty deduction,
    26

nolo.com, 86

Nuendo, 138–142

O

On-Demand Audio, 259

Outboard gear, 177–178

P

Packaging, as royalty deduction, 26

Performance rights organizations
    (*See* ASCAP, BMI)

Plug-ins, 144–177

    Ableton Live, 145–147

    Antares, 147–149

        Auto-Tune 3, 147–148

        kantos, 149

        Mic Modeler, 147

        Tube, 148–149

    Cycling '74 pluggo 3, 150–151

    IK Multimedia, 151–153

        Amplitube, 151–152

        Sample Tank 2, 152–153

        T-RackS, 151

    MOTU MachFive, 153–154

    Native Instruments, 155–160

        ABSYNTH 2, 155–156

        B4 Organ, 157–158

        KONTAKT, 158–159

Native Instruments (*cont.*)
  REAKTOR SESSION, 156–157
  TRAKTOR DJ STUDIO,
    159–160
Propellerhead, 160–162
  Reason, 160–161
  Rebirth, 161–162
  ReCycle, 162–163
Sibelius, 163–165
  Scorch, 166
  Sibelius 3, 163–165
  G7, 166
Sonic Solutions, 166–169
  DVD Producer, 168–169
  ReelDVD, 167–168
Spectrasonics, 169–172
  Acoustic Bass, 170
  Atmosphere, 171
  Electric Base, 170
  Stylus, 171–172
  Synth Bass, 171
  Trilogy, 169–170
Steinberg, 172–174
  Groove Agent, 173
  Virtual Guitarist, 172–173
  Xphraze, 173–174
TASCAM Gigastudio, 174–175
Waves, 175–177
  Broadcast and Production
    Bundle, 176
  Masters, 177
  Renaissance Maxx, 176–177
  Restoration, 177
Power of 200 letter and request,
  43–44
Pro Tools, 127–131
  mixed down to Sony 3348HR
    and Nuendo, 193
  Studio Network Solutions
    storage systems and, 182

Producer points, deducted from
  royalties, 24
Promotion costs, as royalty deduction,
  26
Promotion, independent, 39–40
Propellerhead, 160–162
  Reason, 160–161
  Rebirth, 161–162
  ReCycle, 162–163
Publishing, music
  (*See* Music publishing)

Q
Quickscribe, 135

R
Radio
  advertising, 36, 38
  buying airtime, 41–42, 44
  calls to action, 42–44
  independent promoters, 39–40
  Internet (*See* Internet radio)
  old school, making it work for you,
    40–46
  record companies and, 35–36
  26-week cycle, 36
REAKTOR SESSION, 156–157
RealAudio.com, 267
Reason (Propellerhead), 160–161
Rebirth (Propellerhead), 161–162
Recording costs, 201
  deducted from royalties, 24
Recording Industry Association of
  America (RIAA), 242
  lobbying efforts, 51
  MP3.com vs., 61
  works for hire and, 50–51
Recording studios, home vs. pro,
  30–31
Recording tools, computer hubs,
  123–124

Record keeping, business expenses, 90–91
ReCycle (Propellerhead), 162–163
ReelDVD, 167–168
Relay broadcasting, 259
Renaissance Maxx (Waves), 176–177
Restoration (Waves), 177
RIAA (*See* Recording Industry Association of America)
Rolling Stones, The, 64–65
Royalties
    deductions, 23–26, 27
    discounted products and, 25–26
    rates, 23, 25, 27

S

Sample Tank 2, 152–153
Sampling, 235
Scorch, 166
Sending and receiving music
    DolbyFax and ISDN, 267–268
    email files, 267
SESAC, 233, 241
Sheet music
    revenue source, 233
    software for transcribing, 163–165
Sibelius, 163–165
    G7, 166
    Scorch, 166
    Sibelius 3, 163–165
Songwriting, Diane Warren on, 100–101
Sonic Solutions, 166–169
    DVD Producer, 168–169
    ReelDVD, 167–168
Sound controllers, 178
Sound Exchange, 242
Sound recording, definition, 230
Sound systems, Bob Bradshaw on, 108–121

Speakers
    Bob Bradshaw on speaker/amp combinations, 112–115
    Bob Clearmountain's choices, 199
Spectrasonics, 169–172
    Acoustic Bass, 170
    Atmosphere, 171
    Electric Base, 170
    Stylus, 171–172
    Synth Bass, 171
    Trilogy, 169–170
Steinberg, 172–174
    Cubase SX, 142–144
    Groove Agent, 173
    Nuendo, 138–142
    Virtual Guitarist, 172–173
    Xphraze, 173–174
Storage systems, 179–183
    A/V San, 183
    Fibredrive, 183
    Glyph Techologies, 182
    Studio Network Solutions, 182–183
Studio equipment
    Bob Clearmountain's choices, 197–200
    old school vs. new school, 30–31
Studio Network Solutions, storage system, 182–183
Studio365-Basic, 259
Studio365-Live, 259
Stylus (Spectrasonics), 171–172
Subpublishing agreements, 237
Synth Bass (Spectrasonics), 171

T

Tape recorders, 198
tapeop.com, 109
TASCAM Gigastudio, 174–175
Tax deductions, business, 217–219

Tedesco, Tommy, 269–271
Tour support, as royalty deduction, 26
T-RackS, 151
TRAKTOR DJ STUDIO, 159–160
Trilogy (Spectrasonics), 169–170
Tube, 148–149

V

Van Halen, Ed, 114–115
Virtual Guitarist, 172–173
VST System Link, 142–143

W

Warren, Diane, interview, 97–104
Waves, 175–177
    Broadcast and Production Bundle,
        176
    Masters, 177
    Renaissance Maxx, 176–177
    Restoration, 177
Webcasting (*See* Internet radio)
Web sites
    artist-controlled distribution, 58
    artist-controlled music sales,
        265–266
    domain name basics, 249–252
    metatags, 264
    Network Solutions, 254–255
    setting up, 249–255
    tie-ins with other companies/sites,
        265
Webcasting software
    Aphex 2020, 195
    Apogee, 194
weblawresources.com, 87
Weider, Joe, 273, 274
Works for hire, 50–51, 231–232

X

Xphraze, 173–174

The Black Family

Essays and Studies

Sixth Edition

ROBERT STAPLES

Wadsworth Publishing Company

I⟨T⟩P® An International Thomson Publishing Company

Belmont, CA • Albany, NY • Boston • Cincinnati • Johannesburg • London • Madrid • Melbourne
Mexico City • New York • Pacific Grove, CA • Scottsdale, AZ • Singapore • Tokyo • Toronto

Sociology Editor: Halee Dinsey
Marketing Manager: Christine Henry
Project Editor: John Walker
Print Buyer: Karen Hunt
Permissions Editor: Susan Walters
Production: Robin Gold, Forbes Mill Press
Cover Design: John Walker
Compositor: Wolf Creek Press / Forbes Mill Press
Printer: Webcom

Printed in Canada
 2 3 4 5 6 7 8 9 10

For more information, contact Wadsworth Publishing Company, 10 Davis Drive, Belmont, CA 94002, or electronically at http://www.wadsworth.com

International Thomson Publishing Europe
Berkshire House
168-173 High Holborn
London, WC1V 7AA, United Kingdom

International Thomson Editores
Seneca, 53
Colonia Polanco
11560 México D.F. México

Nelson ITP, Australia
102 Dodds Street
South Melbourne
Victoria 3205 Australia

International Thomson Publishing Asia
60 Albert Street
#15-01 Albert Complex
Singapore 189969

Nelson Canada
1120 Birchmount Road
Scarborough, Ontario
Canada M1K 5G4

International Thomson Publishing Japan
Hirakawa-cho Kyowa Building, 3F
2-2-1 Hirakawa-cho, Chiyoda-ku
Tokyo 102, Japan

International Thomson Publishing Southern Africa
Building 18, Constantia Square
138 Sixteenth Road, P.O. Box 2459
Halfway House, 1685 South Africa

Library of Congress Cataloging-in-Publication Data

The Black family : essays and studies / [compiled by] Robert Staples.
    — 6th ed.
        p.   cm.
    Includes bibliographical references.
    ISBN 0-534-55296-X
    1. Afro-American families.   I. Staples, Robert.
E185.86.B52553   1998
306.85'089'96073—dc21   98-31016

Contents

Preface   **vii**

PART I ▪ THE CHANGING BLACK FAMILY   **1**

1   The Study of Black Families   **7**

Daniel P. Moynihan: The Tangle of Pathology   7

Robert Staples: Sociocultural Factors in Black Family
Transformation: Toward Redefinition of Family Functions   18

2   Historical Background   **25**

Eugene D. Genovese: The Myth of the Absent Family   25

Rosalyn Terborg-Penn: Women and Slavery in the
African Diaspora   32

Part II ▪ The Dyad   39

3   Dating and Sexual Patterns   45

Gail Wyatt, Hector Myers, Kimlin Ashing-Giwa and
Ramani Durvasula: Sociocultural Factors Affecting Sexual Risk
Taking in Black Men and Women: Results from Two
Empirical Studies   45

Vickie M. Mays and Susan D. Cochran: The Black Women's
Relationship Project: A National Survey of Black Lesbians   59

4   Gender Roles   67

Robert Staples: In a Community of Women:
A Biographical Note   67

Charlotte Perry: Extended Family Support Among Older
Black Females   70

Shanette M. Harris: Black Male Masculinity and Same Sex
Friendships   77

5   Male-Female Relationships   87

Clyde W. Franklin, II and Walter Pillow: Single and Married:
The Black Male's Acceptance of the Prince Charming Ideal   87

Robert C. Evans and Helen L. Evans: Coping: Stressors and
Depression Among Middle Class African American Men   94

6   Marriage and Divorce   103

Howard Wineberg: Separated Black Women: Do They
Reconcile with Their Husbands?   103

Erma Jean Lawson: Black Men After Divorce: How Do
They Cope?   112

7   Black and White Relationships   129

Robert Staples: Interracial Relationships: A Convergence of
Desire and Opportunity   129

Rhett S. Jones: The End of Africanity? The Biracial Assault
on Blackness   137

PART III ▪ THE FAMILY 151

8 The Maternal Role 157

Patricia Hill Collins: The Meaning of Motherhood in
Black Culture 157

Joseph W. Scott: African-American Daughter-Mother
Relations and Teenage Pregnancy: Two Faces of Premarital
Teenage Pregnancy 167

Vidella White and Erma Jean Lawson: Incarcerated Black
Mothers and Their Children 179

9 The Paternal Role 189

Lora Bex Lempert: Other Fathers: An Alternative
Perspective on African American Community Caring 189

William Deryck Allen: To Be, or Not to Be There:
Understanding the Gap Between Adolescent Paternal
Aspirations and Performance 202

10 The Extended Family 223

Sr. Mary Jean Flaherty, Lorna Facteau and Patricia Garver:
Grandmother Functions in Multigenerational Families:
An Exploratory Study of Black Adolescent Mothers and
Their Infants 223

Joseph W. Scott and Albert Black: Deep Structures of African-
American Family Life: Female and Male Kin Networks 232

11 Adolescence and Personality Development 241

Shengming Tang: A Comparison of Trends in Living
Arrangements for White and Black Youth 241

Clyde W. Franklin, II: Sex and Class Differences in the
Socialization Experiences of African American Youth 248

12 Family Violence 259

Robert Staples: Domestic Violence in Black American
Families: The Role of Stress 259

Oliver J. Williams: African American Men Who Batter: Treatment Considerations and Community Response 265

13 Social and Economic Issues 281

Robert Staples: Patterns of Change in the Postindustrial Black Family 281

Center for the Study of Social Policy: World Without Work: Causes and Consequences of Black Male Joblessness 291

14 Health Issues 313

Nanny L. Green: Low Birth Weight and Infant Mortality in the African-American Family: The Impact of Racism and Self-Esteem 313

Erma J. Lawson and La Francis Rodgers-Rose: Social Correlates of Black Women's Health Status 320

PART IV ▪ BLACK FAMILIES AND THE FUTURE 333

15 Alternative Life Styles 339

Joseph W. Scott: From Teenage Parenthood to Polygamy: Case Studies in Black Polygamous Family Formation 339

Susan D. Cochran and Vicki M. Mays: Sociocultural Facets of the Black Gay Male Experience 349

16 Public Policy and Social Problems 357

Grace J. Yoo: Racial Inequality, Welfare Reform and Black Families: The 1996 Personal Responsibility and Work Reconciliation Act 357

Robert Staples: Social Inequality and Black Sexual Pathology: The Essential Relationship 367

Preface

As we approach the millennium, we can no longer defend the Black family as a system characterized by harmonious male-female relationships the majority of its members married, most of its children born in wedlock. Although such a family pattern is increasingly less prevalent among the Euro-American majority in twenty-first century America, it has long been a minority pattern among Black Americans. Hence, it is incumbent on us to understand the reasons why a majority of Black Americans are not conforming to a family pattern its ancestors observed at the start of the twentieth century, a period when they faced massive poverty, violence directed against them, Southern apartheid, and great social and cultural upheaval caused by the large scale migration from the rural South to the urban North.

The articles in this sixth edition of the *Black Family: Essays and Studies,* two-thirds of them new, not only look at the various reasons for this protracted alteration of their family patterns but also describe the alternative forms that have supplanted them. Increasingly, Black Americans are adapting to the new reality that a majority of them will not be imbedded in monogamous, nuclear families over their lifetimes. As true of the previous five editions, we address as many dimensions of the Black family as possible in this new edition. Most of the articles were written in the 1990s and, thus, represent recent information, theories, and statistics.

In this sixth edition, we have reorganized some of the sections and their titles, and expanded greatly the section on parenting, marriage and divorce, and family violence and added new articles on welfare reform, stress and male-female relationships, the movement to redefine the racial labels of Blacks with a recent biracial heritage and sexual risk taking. We continue to strive for a balance between empirical research articles and those based on library research, census articles and those based on library research, census data, or a theoretical orientation. Our goal is to make this new edition undergraduate-student friendly. Many of the research articles are based on qualitative analysis, which retains the human element of empirical research or quantitative research using simple statistical methods and is therefore, readable and comprehensible to undergraduate students.

As true of previous editions, I had the assistance of a number of people. I worked most closely with Robin Gold, who handled production for Wadsworth, and Angela Nava, editorial assistant at Wadsworth, who was very helpful in typing parts of the manuscript and other administrative tasks. Professor E. Lincoln James, the editor of the *Western Journal of Black Studies* was very generous in allowing me to reprint articles from his journal; Robert Kauser continues to go beyond the call of duty in helping to collect permissions to reprint articles. Many of the articles were written expressly for this book, and I am grateful to those authors who contributed them without a lot of advance notice. Professor Talmadge Anderson was very helpful in evaluating articles from the last edition and soliciting additional articles.

Robert Staples

Dedication

Dedicated to the future generation in the Staples–Anthony Family

To

Amber

Alexandria

Brianna

Orrin

Ruby

PART ONE

The Changing Black Family

Many changes have occurred in this country since 1954, covering a wide array of personalities, values, and institutions and bringing about a marked change in the functioning of society as a whole. These changes have been most dramatic within the institution of the family where they have had a most telling effect on our personal lives. We are all, to some degree, affected by increasing sexual permissiveness, changes in sex role expectations, a declining fertility rate, altered attitudes toward childbearing and childrearing, a continuing increase in the divorce rate, and the like.

One would not expect Black families to be immune to the forces modifying our family forms. There is ample evidence that they are not. At the same time, their special status as a racial minority with a singular history continues to give the Black marital and family patterns a unique character. Despite what many allege to be the positive gains of the sixties and seventies, the problems of poverty and racial oppression continue to plague large numbers of Afro-Americans. Black Americans are still spatially segregated from the majority of the more affluent White citizenry, and certain cultural values distinguish their family life in form and content from that of the middle-class, White, Anglo-Saxon model.

Nevertheless, the commonality of the two might be greater than the differences. We lose nothing by admitting this. Moreover, the variations within the Black population might be greater than the differences between the two racial groups. Therefore, it becomes even more important to view the Black family from the widest possible perspective, from its peculiar history to the alternate family life-styles now emerging.

THE CHANGING BLACK FAMILY

It is generally accepted that the precursor of contemporary sociological research and theories on the Black family is the work of the late Black sociologist E. Franklin Frazier. Although Frazier's investigations of the Black family began in the 1920s, his works are still considered the definitive findings on Black family life in the United States (Frazier, 1939). As a sociologist, Frazier was primarily interested in race relations as a social process, and he sought to explain that process through the study of the Black family. Through his training in the University of Chicago's social ecology school under the tutelage of Park, Wirth, Burgess, and others, Frazier came to believe that race relations proceeded through different stages of development to the final stage of assimilation.

Because it is through the family that the culture of a group is transmitted, Frazier chose this group as the object of his sociological study. Using the natural history approach, he explained the present condition of the Black family as the culmination of an evolutionary process, its structure strongly affected by the vestiges of slavery, racism, and economic exploitation. The institution of enslavement and slavery virtually destroyed the cultural moorings of Blacks and prevented any perpetuation of African kinship and family relations. Consequently, the Black family developed various forms according to the different situations it encountered (Frazier, 1939).

Variations in sex and marital practices, according to Frazier, grew out of the social heritage of slavery, and what slavery began—the pattern of racism and economic deprivation—continued to impinge on the family life of Afro-Americans. The variations Frazier spoke of are (1) the matriarchal character of the Black family whereby Black males are marginal, ineffective figures in the family constellation; (2) the instability of marital life resulting from the lack of a legal basis for marriage during the period of slavery, which meant that marriage never acquired the position of a strong institution in Black life and casual sex relations were the prevailing norm; and (3) the dissolution—caused by the process of urbanization—of the stability of family life that had existed among Black peasants in an agrarian society (Frazier, 1939).

Most of Frazier's studies were limited to pre–World War II Black family life. His research method using case studies and documents whose content he analyzed and from which he attempted to deduce a pattern of Black family life. The next large-scale theory of the Black family was developed by Daniel Moynihan (1965); it was based largely on census data and pertained to Black family life as it existed in the sixties. In a sense, Moynihan attempted to confirm statistically Frazier's theory that the Black family was disorganized as a result of slavery, urbanization, and economic deprivation. But he added a new dimension to Frazier's theory: "At the heart of the deterioration of the fabric of Negro society is the deterioration of the Negro family" (Moynihan, 1965: 5). Moynihan attempted to document his major hypothesis by citing statistics on the dissolution of Black marriages, the high rate of Black illegitimate births, the prevalence of female-headed households in the Black community, and how the deterioration of the Black family had led to a shocking increase in welfare dependency (Moynihan, 1965).

This study of the Black family, commonly referred to as the Moynihan Report, generated a largely critical response from members of the Black community. It drew a mixed response from members of the White academic community, some critically supporting most of Moynihan's contentions, others imputing no validity to his assertions (Rainwater and Yancy, 1967; Staples and Mirande, 1980). The reasons for the negative reaction to Moynihan's study are manifest. In effect, he made a generalized indictment of all Black families. And, although he cited the antecedents of slavery and high unemployment as historically important variables, he shifted the burden of Black deprivation onto the Black family rather than the social structure of the United States.

The Moynihan Report assumed a greater importance than other studies on the Black family for several reasons. As an official government publication, it implied a shift in the government's position in dealing with the effects of racism and economic deprivation on the Black community. However, the Moynihan Report did not spell out a plan for action. The conclusion drawn by most people was that whatever his solution, it would focus on strengthening the Black family rather than dealing with the more relevant problems of segregation and discrimination.

HISTORICAL BACKGROUND

The most ground-breaking research on Black families has been conducted by historians. For years the work of Frazier (1939), together with that of Stanley Elkins (1968), had been accepted as the definitive history of Black families and posited as a causal explanation of their contemporary condition. Using traditional historical methods based on plantation records and slave owner testimony, both historians reached the conclusion that slavery destroyed the Black family and decimated Black culture. The first historian to challenge this thesis was Blassingame (1972), whose use of slave narratives indicated that in the slave quarters Black families did exist as functioning institutions and role models for others. Moreover, strong family ties persisted in face of the frequent breakups deriving from the slave trade. To further counteract the Frazier–Elkins thesis, Fogel and Engerman (1974) used elaborate quantitative methods to document that slave owners did not separate a majority of the slave families. Their contention, also controversial, was that capitalistic *efficiency* of the slave system meant it was more practical to keep slave families intact.

Continuing in the vein of revisionist historical research, Genovese (1972) used a mix of slave holders' papers and slave testimony Still, he concluded that Black culture, through compromise and negotiation between slaves and slave owners, did flourish during the era of slavery. Within that cultural vortex, there was a variety of socially approved and sanctioned relationships between slave men and women. The alleged female matriarchy extant during that era was described by Genovese as a closer approximation to a healthy sexual equality than was possible for Whites. Finally, the landmark study by Gutman (1976) put to rest one of the most common and enduring myths about Black families. Using census data for a number of cities between 1880 and 1925, Gutman found that the majority of Blacks of all social classes were lodged in nuclear families. Through the use of plantation birth records and marriage applications, he concluded that the biparental household was the dominant form during slavery. More important than Gutman's compelling evidence that slavery did not destroy the Black family was his contention that their family form in the past era had evolved from family and kinship patterns that had originated under slavery. This contention gives credence to the Africanity model, which assumes African origins for Afro-American family values, traits, and behavior.

Using a classical theory of slave family life, Stanley Elkins made a comparative analysis of the effect of slavery on the bondsman's family life in North and South America. His thesis was that the principal differences between the two regions was the manumission process and the legal basis of marriage between slaves. That is, slaves could become free citizens more easily in South America and those who remained in bondage were permitted to have legal marriage ceremonies. The sanctity of the family was sanctioned in both law and the canons of the Catholic church. The reverse was true, he asserted, in the slave system of the United States. One should view the Elkins research critically because other historians contend that the slave code of which he speaks was not only unenforced but never promulgated in any of the South American countries. In fact, it is claimed, some of the measures encouraging marriage among slaves were designed to bind the slaves to the estates via family ties (Hall, 1970).

However, these historical studies demonstrate that the Black family was a stable unit during slavery and in the immediate postslavery years. The rise in out-of-wedlock births and female-headed households are concomitants of twentieth-century urban ghettos. A doubling of those phenomena is a function of the economic contingencies of industrial America. Unlike the European immigrants before them, U.S. Blacks were disadvantaged by the hard lines of Northern segregation along racial lines. Moreover, families in cities were more vulnerable to disruptions caused by the traumatizing experiences of urbanization, the reduction of family functions, and the loss of extended family supports. To understand the modern Black family, we must look at how its structure is affected by socioeconomic forces.

CONTEMPORARY ISSUES

Understanding the Afro-American family in the twenty-first century means looking at the various segments that make up this group, especially gender, class, and generational membership. Although it was never a monolithic unit, the commonalties peculiar to race allowed empirical generalizations to be made with impunity. Today, a Black, college-educated stockbroker in New York City might have little in common with a teenage mother, high school dropout, in the state of Mississippi. Yet, the stockbroker in ways subtle and overt will still confront the issue of race that condemns that women to a life of poverty in a racially and class, stratified society.

Surprisingly, gender might be the most important variable impacting on Afro-Americans—important because it cuts across class and generational lines. A male child of a Black mother will feel the effects of his mother's disenfranchisement as a human being when being raised by her, the strictures of race, class, and gender eroding his life chances in a society frequently hostile to his aspirations. Having money and a high level of education will diminish the effects of poverty for a Black, female, college graduate. But, there are few ways of circumventing a sex ratio that says there will be at least two Black, female, college graduates competing for the same Black, male, college graduate. And, that is the most optimistic calculation of the odds she faces, which assumes that he will choose a mate within the same race and across gender roles.

Socioeconomic status, if it is in the lower ranks, can define a more dehumanizing existence that only compounds the problems encountered as a consequence of racial and gender membership. It is not a gender specific problem, as some students of the problem suggest. Approximately, two-thirds of all Black male children will grow up in households with incomes below the poverty level. And, according to the Center for the Study of Social Policy (1994), about 43 percent of adult Black males will not be members of the labor force. These lower income groups have lost ground in the last 20 years, as higher income groups gained a greater share of the nations wealth. Obviously the effects of grinding poverty have exacted a serious toll on their family life. Few men in this class have the economic wherewithal to marry and help support a family. And, few women feel they can trust their and their children's futures to men with such dim economic prospects. What we find, instead, are women having children out of wedlock. When living together occurs, it is cohabitation rather than legal marriage.

The males, ineligible for any amount of governmental assistance except for the meager amounts offered by General Assistance, survive by operating in the underground economy or depend on the good will of their families of origin to provide them with food and lodging.

Previous generations of Blacks maintained viable families in the face of unrelenting poverty and racism. The twenty-something generation might have the same aspirations for a loving, devoted spouse and a lifelong marriage. But they will be exposed to a different set of cultural images of marriage and the family. Now, the cultural icons are celebrities who bear their children out of wedlock, and legal marriage is an afterthought. The traditional role models of religious and political leaders are mostly tainted by scandals that are a frequent topic of the broadcast media. Although the rich and powerful violate the moral norms with impunity, a Black teenage mother will witness the destruction of all her dreams, if she has any, once she leaves school prematurely to have an out-of-wedlock child.

Despite these gender, class, and generational variations, Blacks will still intersect around the issues of stress caused by the mundane practice of racism, an imbalanced sex ratio that consigns, theoretically, two million adult Black women to a life of celibacy, and a cultural isolation that finds Blacks alienated from mainstream America and its cultural norms. What does this portend for the Future of Black family life in these United States? Male sexism and White racism were concomitants of a twentieth century that could not withstand the assaults by those it dehumanized. Whatever supplants it will probably be a more equitable social system. Whether the family can survive in a new and different environment remains to be seen.

REFERENCES

Blassingame, J. 1972. *The slave community*. New York: Oxford University Press.

Center for the Study of Social Policy. 1994. *World without work: Causes and Consequences of Black male joblessness*. Washington, D. C.

Elkins, S. 1968. *Slavery: A problem in American institutional and intellectual life*. Chicago: University of Chicago Press.

Fogel, W., and S. Engerman. 1974. *Time on the cross*. Boston: Little, Brown.

Frazier, E. F. 1939. *The Negro family in the United States*. Chicago: University of Chicago Press.

Genovese, E. D. 1972. *Roll, Jordan, roll: The world the slaves made*. New York: Pantheon.

Gutman, H. 1976. *The Black family in slavery and freedom, 1750–1925*. New York: Pantheon.

Hall, G. Midlo. 1970. The myth of benevolent Spanish slave law. *Negro Digest,* 19: 31–39.

Moynihan, Daniel P. 1965. *The Negro family: The case for national action*. Washington, D.C.: U.S. Government Printing Office.

Rainwater, L. ,and W. Yancy. 1967. *The Moynihan Report and the politics of controversy* Cambridge, Mass.: M.I.T. Press.

Staples, R., and A. Mirande. 1980. Racial and cultural variations among American families: A decennial review of the literature on minority families. *Journal of Marriage and the Family* 42: 887–903.

1

The Study of Black Families

The Tangle of Pathology

DANIEL P. MOYNIHAN

In this controversial and much-debated report on the Black family, the author claims that weaknesses in family structure account for many of the problems Afro-Americans encounter in American society. The reason for welfare dependency, out-of-wedlock children, educational failure, crime and delinquency, and so on is the unnatural dominance of women in the family structure. Without tongue in cheek, the author recommends, as remedy, increased involvement of Black men in the military.

■

That the Negro American has survived at all is extraordinary—a lesser people might simply have died out, as indeed others have. That the Negro community has not only survived, but in this political generation has entered national affairs as a moderate, humane, and constructive national force is the highest testament to the healing powers of the democratic ideal and the creative vitality of the Negro people.

But it may not be supposed that the Negro American community has not paid a fearful price for the incredible mistreatment to which it has been subjected over the past three centuries.

In essence, the Negro community has been forced into a matriarchal structure which, because it is so out of line with the rest of the American society, seriously retards the progress of the group as a whole, and imposes a crushing burden on the Negro male and, in consequence, on a great many Negro women as well.

There is, presumably, no special reason why a society in which males are dominant in family relationships is to be preferred to a matriarchal arrangement. However, it is clearly a disadvantage for a minority group to be operating on one principle, while the great majority of the population, and the one with the most advantages to begin with, is operating on another. This is the present situation of the Negro. Ours is a society which presumes male leadership in private and public

Condensed from *The Negro Family: The Case for National Action,* by the Office of Policy Planning and Research, United States Department of Labor (U.S. Government Printing Office, March 1965), pp. 29–44. Tables have been deleted and endnotes renumbered.

affairs. The arrangements of society facilitate such leadership and reward it. A subculture, such as that of the Negro American, in which this is not the pattern, is placed at a distinct disadvantage.

Here an earlier word of caution should be repeated. There is much evidence that a considerable number of Negro families have managed to break out of the tangle of pathology and to establish themselves as stable, effective units, living according to patterns of American society in general. E. Franklin Frazier has suggested that the middle-class Negro American family is, if anything, more patriarchal and protective of its children than the general run of such families.[1] Given equal opportunities, the children of these families will perform as well or better than their White peers. They need no help from anyone, and ask none.

While this phenomenon is not easily measured, one index is that middle-class Negroes have even fewer children than middle-class Whites, indicating a desire to conserve the advances they have made and to insure that their children do as well or better. Negro women who marry early to uneducated laborers have more children than White women in the same situation; Negro women who marry at the common age for the middle class to educated men doing technical or professional work have only four-fifths as many children as their White counterparts.

It might be estimated that as much as half of the Negro community falls into the middle class. However, the remaining half is in desperate and deteriorating circumstances. Moreover, because of housing segregation it is immensely difficult for the stable half to escape from the cultural influences of the unstable one. The children of middle-class Negroes often as not must grow up in, or next to the slums, an experience almost unknown to White middle-class children. They are therefore constantly exposed to the pathology of the disturbed group and constantly in danger of being drawn into it. It is for this reason that the propositions put forth in this study may be thought of as having a more or less general application.

In a word, most Negro youth are in *danger* of being caught up in the tangle of pathology that affects their world, and probably a majority are so entrapped. Many of those who escape do so for one generation only: as things now are, their children may have to run the gauntlet all over again. That is not the least vicious aspect of the world that White America has made for the Negro.

Obviously, not every instance of social pathology afflicting the Negro community can be traced to the weakness of family structure. If, for example, organized crime in the Negro community were not largely controlled by Whites, there would be more capital accumulation among Negroes, and therefore probably more Negro business enterprises. If it were not for the hostility and fear many Whites exhibit towards Negroes, they in turn would be less afflicted by hostility and fear and so on. There is no one Negro community. There is no one Negro problem. There is no one solution. Nonetheless, at the center of the tangle of pathology is the weakness of the family structure. Once or twice removed, it will be found to be the principal source of most of the aberrant, inadequate, or antisocial behavior that did not establish, but now serves to perpetuate the cycle of poverty and deprivation.

It was by destroying the Negro family under slavery that white America broke the will of the Negro People. Although that will has reasserted itself in our time, it is a resurgence doomed to frustration unless the viability of the Negro family is restored.

MATRIARCHY

A fundamental fact of Negro American family life is the often reversed roles of husband and wife.

Robert O. Blood, Jr., and Donald M. Wolfe, in a study of Detroit families, note that "Negro husbands have unusually low power,"[2] and while this is characteristic of all low income families, the pattern pervades the Negro social structure: "the cumulative result of discrimination in jobs

. . . , the segregated housing, and the poor schooling of Negro men."³ In 44 percent of the Negro families studied, the wife was dominant, as against 20 percent of White wives. "Whereas the majority of White families are equalitarian, the largest percentage of Negro families are dominated by the wife."⁴

The matriarchal pattern of so many Negro families reinforces itself over the generations. This process begins with education. Although the gap appears to be closing at the moment, for a long while, Negro females were better educated than Negro males, and this remains true today for the Negro population as a whole.

The difference in educational attainment between non-White men and women in the labor force is even greater; men lag 1.1 years behind women.

The disparity in educational attainment of male and female youth age 16 to 21 who were out of school in February 1963, is striking. Among the non-White males, 66.3 percent were not high school graduates, compared with 55.0 percent of the females. A similar difference existed at the college level, with 4.5 percent of the males having completed 1 to 3 years of college compared with 7.3 percent of the females.

The poorer performance of the male in school exists from the very beginning, and the magnitude of the difference was documented by the 1960 Census in statistics on the number of children who have fallen one or more grades below the typical grade for children of the same age. The boys have more frequently fallen behind at every age level. (White boys also lag behind White girls, but at a differential of 1 to 6 percentage points.)

In 1960, 39 percent of all White persons 25 years of age and over who had completed 4 or more years of college were women. Fifty-three percent of the non-Whites who had attained this level were women.

However, the gap is closing. By October 1963, there were slightly more Negro men in college than women. Among Whites there were almost twice as many men as women enrolled.

There is much evidence that Negro females are better students than their male counterparts.

Daniel Thompson of Dillard University, in a private communication on January 9, 1965, writes

> As low as is the aspirational level among lower class Negro girls, it is considerably higher than among the boys. For example, I have examined the honor rolls in Negro high schools for about 10 years. As a rule, from 75 to 90 percent of all Negro honor students are girls.

In 1 out of 4 Negro families where the husband is present, is an earner, and some one else in the family works, the husband is not the principal earner. The comparable figure for Whites is 18 percent.

More important, it is clear that Negro females have established a strong position for themselves in white collar and professional employment, precisely the areas of the economy which are growing most rapidly, and to which the highest prestige is accorded.

The President's Committee on Equal Employment Opportunity, making a preliminary report on employment in 1964 of over 16,000 companies with nearly 5 million employees, revealed this pattern with dramatic emphasis.

> In this work force, Negro males outnumber Negro females by a ratio of 4 to 1. Yet Negro males represent only 1.2 percent of the males in white collar occupations, while Negro females represent 3.1 percent of the total female white collar work force. Negro males represent 1.1 percent of all male professionals, whereas Negro females represent roughly 6 percent of all female professionals. Again, in technician occupations, Negro males represent 2.1 percent of all male technicians while Negro females represent roughly 10 percent of all female technicians. It would appear therefore that there are proportionally 4 times as many Negro females in significant white collar jobs than Negro males.

Although it is evident that office and clerical jobs account for approximately 50 percent of all Negro female white collar workers, it is significant that 6 out of every 100 Negro females are in professional jobs. This is substantially similar to the rate of all females in such jobs. Approximately 7 out of every 100 Negro females are in technician jobs. This exceeds the proportion of all females in technician jobs—approximately 5 out of every 100.

Negro females in skilled jobs are almost the same as that of all females in such jobs. Nine out of every 100 Negro males are in skilled occupations while 21 out of 100 of all males are in such jobs.[5]

This pattern is to be seen in the Federal government, where special efforts have been made recently to insure equal employment opportunity for Negroes. These efforts have been notably successful in Departments such as Labor, where some 19 percent of employees are now Negro. (A not disproportionate percentage, given the composition of the work force in the areas where the main Department offices are located.) However, it may well be that these efforts have redounded mostly to the benefit of Negro women, and may even have accentuated the comparative disadvantage of Negro men. Seventy percent of the Negro employees of the Department of Labor are women, as contrasted with only 42 percent of the White employees.

Among nonprofessional Labor Department employees—where the most employment opportunities exist for all groups—Negro women outnumber Negro men 4 to 1, and average almost one grade higher in classification.

The testimony to the effects of these patterns in Negro family structure is widespread, and hardly to be doubted. . . .

Duncan M. MacIntyre:

The Negro illegitimacy rate always has been high—about eight times the white rate in 1940 and somewhat higher today even though the white illegitimacy rate also is climbing. The Negro statistics are symptomatic of some old socioeconomic problems, not the least of which are underemployment among Negro men and compensating higher labor force propensity among Negro women. Both operate to enlarge the mother's role, undercutting the status of the male and making many Negro families essentially matriarchal. The Negro man's uncertain employment prospects, matriarchy, and high cost of divorces combine to encourage desertion (the poor man's divorce), increase the number of couples not married, and thereby also increase the Negro illegitimacy rate. In the meantime, higher Negro birth rates are increasing the non-White population, while migration into cities like Detroit, New York, Philadelphia, and Washington, D.C., is making the public assistance rolls in such cities heavily, even predominantly, Negro.[6]

Robin M. Williams, Jr., in a Study of Elmira, New York:

Only 57 percent of Negro adults reported themselves as married—spouse present, as compared with 78 percent of native White American gentiles, 91 percent of Italian-American, and 96 percent of Jewish informants. Of the 93 unmarried Negro youths interviewed, 22 percent did not have their mother living in the home with them, and 42 percent reported that their father was not living in their home. One-third of the youths did not know their father's present occupation, and two-thirds of a sample of 150 Negro adults did not know what the occupation of their father's father had been. Forty percent of the youths said that they had brothers and sisters living in other communities; another 40 percent reported relatives living in their home who were not parents, siblings, or grandparents.[7]

THE FAILURE OF YOUTH

Williams' account of Negro youth growing up with little knowledge of their fathers, less of their fathers' occupations, still less of family occupational traditions, is in sharp contrast to the experience of the White child. The White family, despite many variants, remains a powerful agency not only for transmitting property from one generation to the next, but also for transmitting no less valuable contracts with the world of education and work. In an earlier age, the Carpenters, Wainwrights, Weavers, Mercers, Farmers, Smiths acquired their names as well as their trades from their fathers and grandfathers. Children today still learn the patterns of work from their fathers even though they may no longer go into the same jobs.

White children without fathers at least perceive all about them the pattern of men working.

Negro children without fathers flounder—and fail.

Not always, to be sure. The Negro community produces its share, very possibly more than its share, of young people who have the something extra that carries them over the worst obstacles. But such persons are always a minority. The common run of young people in a group facing serious obstacles to success do not succeed.

A prime index of the disadvantage of Negro youth in the United States is their consistently poor performance on the mental tests that are a standard means of measuring ability and performance in the present generation.

There is absolutely no question of any genetic differential: Intelligence potential is distributed among Negro infants in the same proportion and pattern as among Icelanders or Chinese or any other group. American society, however, impairs the Negro potential. The statement of the HARYOU report that "there is no basic disagreement over the fact that central Harlem students are performing poorly in school"[8] may be taken as true of Negro slum children throughout the United States.

Eighth grade children in central Harlem have a median IQ of 87.7, which means that perhaps a third of the children are scoring at levels perilously near to those of retardation. IQ *declines* in the first decade of life, rising only slightly thereafter.

The effect of broken families on the performance of Negro youth has not been extensively measured, but studies that have been made show an unmistakable influence.

Martin Deutch and Bert Brown, investigating intelligence test differences between Negro and White 1st and 5th graders of different social classes, found that there is a direct relationship between social class and IQ. As the one rises so does the other: but more for Whites than Negroes. This is surely a result of housing segregation, referred to earlier, which makes it difficult for middle-class Negro families to escape the slums.

The authors explain that "it is much more difficult for the Negro to attain identical middle- or upper-middle-class status with Whites, and the social class gradations are less marked for Negroes because Negro life in a caste society is considerably more homogeneous than is life for the majority group."[9]

Therefore, the authors look for background variables other than social class which might explain the difference: "One of the most striking differences between the Negro and White groups is the consistently higher frequency of broken homes and resulting family disorganization in the Negro group."[10]

Further, they found that children from homes where fathers are present have significantly higher scores than children in homes without fathers.

The influence of the father's presence was then tested *within* the social classes and school grades for Negroes alone. They found that "a consistent trend within both grades at the lower SES [social class] level appears, and in no case is there a reversal of this trend: for males, females, and the combined group, the IQ's of children with fathers in the home are always higher than those who have no father in the home."[11]

The authors say that broken homes "may also account for some of the differences between Negro and White intelligence scores."[12]

The scores of fifth graders with fathers absent were lower than the scores of first graders with fathers absent, and while the authors point out that it is cross sectional data and does not reveal the duration of the fathers' absence, "What we might be tapping is the cumulative effect of fatherless years."[13]

This difference in ability to perform has its counterpart in statistics on actual school performance. Non-White boys from families with both parents present are more likely to be going to school than boys with only one parent present, and enrollment rates are even lower when neither parent is present.

When the boys from broken homes are in school, they do not do as well as the boys from whole families. Grade retardation is higher when only one parent is present, and highest when neither parent is present.

The loneliness of the Negro youth in making fundamental decisions about education is shown in a 1959 study of Negro and White dropouts in Connecticut high schools.

Only 29 percent of the Negro male dropouts discussed their decision to drop out of school with their fathers, compared with 65 percent of the White males (38 percent of the Negro males were from broken homes). In fact, 26 percent of the Negro males did not discuss this major decision in their lives with anyone at all, compared with only 8 percent of White males.

A study of Negro apprenticeship by the New York State Commission Against Discrimination in 1960 concluded:

> Negro youth are seldom exposed to influences which can lead to apprenticeship. Negroes are not apt to have relatives, friends, or neighbors in skilled occupations. Nor are they likely to be in secondary schools where they receive encouragement and direction from alternate role models. Within the minority community, skilled Negro "models" after whom the Negro youth might pattern himself are rare, while substitute sources which could provide the direction, encouragement, resources, and information needed to achieve skilled craft standing are nonexistent.[14]

Delinquency and Crime

The combined impact of poverty, failure, and isolation among Negro youth has had the predictable outcome in a disastrous delinquency and crime rate.

In a typical pattern of discrimination, Negro children in all public and private orphanages are a smaller proportion of all children than their proportion of the population although their needs are clearly greater.

On the other hand Negroes represent a third of all youth in training schools for juvenile delinquents.

It is probable that at present, a majority of the crimes against the person, such as rape, murder, and aggravated assault, are committed by Negroes. There is, of course, no absolute evidence; inference can only be made from arrest and prison population statistics. The data that follow unquestionably are biased against Negroes, who are arraigned much more casually than are Whites, but it may be doubted that the bias is great enough to affect the general proportions.

Again on the urban frontier the ratio is worse: 3 out of every 5 arrests for these crimes were of Negroes.

In Chicago in 1963, three-quarters of the persons arrested for such crimes were Negro; in Detroit, the same proportions held.

In 1960, 37 percent of all persons in Federal and State prisons were Negro. In that year, 56 percent of the homicide and 57 percent of the assault offenders committed to State institutions were Negro.

The overwhelming number of offenses committed by Negroes are directed toward other Negroes: the cost of crime to the Negro community is a combination of that to the criminal and to the victim.

Some of the research on the effects of broken homes on delinquent behavior recently surveyed by Thomas F. Pettigrew in *A Profile of the Negro*

American is summarized below, along with several other studies of the question.

Mary Diggs found that three-fourths—twice the expected ratio—of Philadelphia's Negro delinquents who came before the law during 1948 did not live with both their natural parents.[15]

In predicting juvenile crime, Eleanor and Sheldon Glueck also found that a higher proportion of delinquent than nondelinquent boys came from broken homes. They identified five critical factors in the home environment that made a difference in whether boys would become delinquents: discipline of boy by father, supervision of boy by mother, affection of father for boy, affection of mother for boy, and cohesiveness of family.

In 1952, when the New York City Youth Board set out to test the validity of these five factors as predictors of delinquency, a problem quickly emerged. The Glueck sample consisted of White boys of mainly Irish, Italian, Lithuanian, and English descent. However, the Youth Board group was 44 percent Negro and 14 percent Puerto Rican, and the frequency of broken homes within these groups was out of proportion to the total number of delinquents in the population.[16]

> In the majority of these cases, the father was usually never in the home at all, absent for the major proportion of the boy's life, or was present only on occasion.

(The final prediction table was reduced to three factors: supervision of boy by mother, discipline of boy by mother, and family cohesiveness within what family, in fact, existed; it was, nonetheless, 85 percent accurate in predicting delinquents and 96 percent accurate in predicting nondelinquents.)

Researchers who have focused upon the "good" boys in high delinquency neighborhoods noted that they typically come from exceptionally stable, intact families.[17]

Recent psychological research demonstrates the personality effects of being reared in a disorganized home without a father. One study showed that children from fatherless homes seek immediate gratification of their desires far more than children with fathers present.[18] Others revealed that children who hunger for immediate gratification are more prone to delinquency, along with other less social behavior.[19] Two psychologists, Pettigrew says, maintain that inability to delay gratification is a critical factor in immature, criminal, and neurotic behavior.[20]

Finally, Pettigrew discussed the evidence that a stable home is a crucial factor in counteracting the effects of racism upon Negro personality.

> A warm, supportive home can effectively compensate for many of the restrictions the Negro child faces outside of the ghetto; consequently the type of home life a Negro enjoys as a child may be far more crucial for governing the influence of segregation upon his personality than the form the segregation takes—legal or informal, Southern or Northern.[21]

A Yale University study of youth in the lowest socioeconomic class in New Haven in 1950 whose behavior was followed through their 18th year revealed that among the delinquents in the group, 38 percent came from broken homes, compared with 24 percent of nondelinquents.[22]

The President's Task Force on Manpower Conservation in 1963 found that of young men rejected for the draft for failure to pass the mental tests, 42 percent of those with a court record came from broken homes, compared with 30 percent of those without a court record. Half of all the non-White rejectees in the study with a court record came from broken homes.

An examination of the family background of 44,448 delinquency cases in Philadelphia between 1949 and 1954 documents the frequency of broken homes among delinquents. Sixty-two percent of the Negro delinquents and 36 percent of White delinquents were not living with both parents. In 1950, 33 percent of non–White children and 7 percent of White children in Philadelphia were living in homes without both parents. Repeaters were even more likely to be from broken homes than first offenders.[23]

The Armed Forces

The ultimate mark of inadequate preparation for life is the failure rate on the Armed Forces mental test. The Armed Forces Qualification Test is not quite a mental test, nor yet an education test. It is a test of ability to perform at an acceptable level of competence. It roughly measures ability that ought to be found in an average 7th or 8th grade student. A grown young man who cannot pass this test is in trouble.

Fifty-six percent of Negroes fail it.

This is a rate almost four times that of the Whites.

The Army, Navy, Air Force, and Marines conduct by far the largest and most important education and training activities of the Federal Government, as well as provide the largest single source of employment in the nation.

Military service is disruptive in some respects. For those comparatively few who are killed or wounded in combat, or otherwise, the personal sacrifice is inestimable. But on balance service in the Armed Forces over the past quarter-century has worked greatly to the advantage of those involved. The training and experience of military duty itself is unique; the advantages that have generally followed in the form of the G.I. Bill, mortgage guarantees, Federal life insurance, Civil Service preference, veterans' hospitals, and veterans' pensions are singular, to say the least....

In 1963 the Civil Rights Commission commented on the occupational aspect of military service for Negroes. "Negro enlisted men enjoy relatively better opportunities in the Armed Forces than in the civilian economy in every clerical, technical, and skilled field for which the data permit comparison."[24]

There is, however, an even more important issue involved in military service for Negroes. Service in the United States Armed Forces is the *only* experience open to the Negro American in which he is truly treated as an equal: not as a Negro equal to a white, but as one man equal to any other man in a world where the categories "Negro" and "White" do not exist. If this is a statement of the ideal rather than reality, it is an ideal that is close to realization. In food, dress, housing, pay, work—the Negro in the Armed Forces *is* equal and is treated that way.

There is another special quality about military service for Negro men: It is an utterly masculine world. Given the strains of the disorganized and matrifocal family life in which so many Negro youth come of age, the Armed Forces are a dramatic and desperately needed change: a world away from women, a world run by strong men of unquestioned authority, where discipline, if harsh, is nonetheless orderly and predictable, and where rewards, if limited, are granted on the basis of performance.

The theme of a current Army recruiting message states it as clearly as can be: "In the U.S. Army you get to know what it means to feel like a man."

At the recent Civil Rights Commission hearings in Mississippi a witness testified that his Army service was in fact "the only time I ever felt like a man."

Yet a majority of Negro youth (and probably three-quarters of Mississippi Negroes) fail the Selective Service education test and are rejected. Negro participation in the Armed Forces would be less than it is, were it not for a proportionally larger share of voluntary enlistments and reenlistments. (Thus 16.3 percent of Army sergeants are Negro.)

Alienation

The term alienation may by now have been used in too many ways to retain a clear meaning, but it will serve to sum up the equally numerous ways in which large numbers of Negro youth appear to be withdrawing from American society.

One startling way in which this occurs is that the men are just not there when the Census enumerator comes around.

According to Bureau of Census population estimates for 1963, there are only 87 non-White males for every 100 females in the 30-to-34-year age group. The ratio does not exceed 90 to 100 throughout the 25-to-44-year age bracket. In the urban Northeast, there are only 76 males per 100 females 20-to-24-years of age, and males as a percent of females are below 90 percent throughout all ages after 14.

There are not really fewer men than women in the 20-to-40 age bracket. What obviously is involved is an error in counting: the surveyors simply do not find the Negro man. Donald J. Bogue and his associates, who have studied the Federal count of the Negro man, place the error as high as 19.8 percent at age 28; a typical error of around 15 percent is estimated from age 19 through 43.[25] Preliminary research in the Bureau of the Census on the 1960 enumeration has resulted in similar conclusions, although not necessarily the same estimates of the extent of the error. The Negro male *can* be found at age 17 and 18. On the basis of birth records and mortality records, the conclusion must be that he is there at age 19 as well.

When the enumerators do find him, his answers to the standard questions asked in the monthly unemployment survey often result in counting him as "not in the labor force." In other words, Negro male unemployment may in truth be somewhat greater than reported.

The labor force participation rates of non-White men have been falling since the beginning of the century and for the past decade have been lower than the rates for White men. In 1964, the participation rates were 78.0 percent for White men and 75.8 percent for non-White men. Almost one percentage point of this difference was due to a higher proportion of non-White men unable to work because of long-term physical or mental illness; it seems reasonable to assume that the rest of the difference is due to discouragement about finding a job.

If non-White male labor force participation rates were as high as the white rates, there would have been 140,000 more non-White males in the labor force in 1964. If we further assume that the 140,000 would have been unemployed, the unemployment rate for non-White men would have been 11.5 percent instead of the record rate of 9 percent and the ratio between the non-White rate

and the white rate would have jumped from 2:1 to 2.4:1.

Understated or not, the official unemployment rates for Negroes are almost unbelievable.

The unemployment statistics for Negro teenagers—29 percent in January 1964—reflect lack of training and opportunity in the greatest measure, but it may not be doubted that they also reflect a certain failure of nerve.

"Are you looking for a job?" Secretary of Labor Wirtz asked a young man on a Harlem street corner. "Why?" was the reply.

Richard A. Cloward and Robert Ontell have commented on this withdrawal in a discussion of the Mobilization for Youth project on the lower East Side of New York.

> What contemporary slum and minority youth probably lack that similar children in earlier periods possessed is not motivation but some minimal sense of competence.
>
> We are plagued in work with these youth, by what appears to be a low tolerance for frustration. They are not able to absorb setbacks. Minor irritants and rebuffs are magnified out of all proportion to reality. Perhaps they react as they do because they are not equal to the world that confronts them, and they know it. And it is the knowing that is devastating. Had the occupational structure remained intact, or had the education provided to them kept pace with occupational changes, the situation would be a different one. But it is not, and that is what we and they have to contend with.[26]

Narcotic addiction is a characteristic form of withdrawal. In 1963, Negroes made up 54 percent of the addict population of the United States. Although the Federal Bureau of Narcotics reports a decline in the Negro proportion of new addicts, HARYOU reports the addiction rate in central Harlem rose from 22.1 per 10.000 in 1955 to 40.4 in 1961.[27]

There is a larger fact about the alienation of Negro youth than the tangle of pathology described by these statistics. It is a fact particularly difficult to grasp by White persons who have in recent years shown increasing awareness of Negro problems.

The present generation of Negro youth growing up in the urban ghettos has probably less personal contact with the white world than any generation in the history of the Negro American.[28]

Until World War II it could be said that in general the Negro and white worlds lived, if not together, at least side by side. Certainly they did, and do, in the South.

Since World War II, however, the two worlds have drawn physically apart. The symbol of this development was the construction in the 1940's and 1950's of the vast white middle- and lower-middle class suburbs around all of the Nation's cities. Increasingly, the inner cities have been left to Negroes—who now share almost no community life with Whites.

In turn, because of this new housing pattern—most of which has been financially assisted by the Federal government—it is probable that the American school system has become *more,* rather than less segregated in the past two decades.

School integration has not occurred in the South, where a decade after *Brown* v. *Board of Education* only 1 Negro in 9 is attending school with White children.

And in the North, despite strenuous official efforts, neighborhoods and therefore schools are becoming more and more of one class and one color.

In New York City, in the school year 1957–1958 there were 64 schools that were 90 percent or more Negro or Puerto Rican. Six years later there were 134 such schools.

Along with the diminution of white middle-class contacts for a large percentage of Negroes. observers report that the Negro churches have all but lost contact with men in the Northern cities as well. This may be a normal condition of urban life, but it is probably a changed condition for the Negro American and cannot be a socially desirable development.

The only religious movement that appears to have enlisted a considerable number of lower-class Negro males in Northern cities of late is that of the Black Muslims: a movement based on total rejection of white society, even though it emulates white mores.

In a word: the tangle of pathology is tightening.

NOTES

1. E. Franklin Frazier. 1962. *Black bourgeoisie.* New York: Collier.

2. Robert O. Blood, Jr., and Donald M. Wolfe. 1960. *Husbands and wives: The dynamics of married living.* New York: The Free Press, p. 34.

3. Ibid., p. 35.

4. Ibid.

5. Based on preliminary draft of a report by the President's Committee on Equal Employment Opportunity.

6. Duncan M. MacIntyre. 1964. *Public assistance: Too much or too little?* New York: New York State School of Industrial Relations. Cornell University, Bulletin 53–1, December, pp. 73–74.

7. Robin M. Williams, Jr., 1964. *Strangers next door.* Englewood Cliffs, N.J.: Prentice-Hall, p. 240.

8. *Youth in the Ghetto.* New York: Harlem Youth Opportunities Unlimited, p. 195.

9. Martin Deutch and Bert Brown. 1964. Social influences in Negro-White intelligence differences, *Social Issues,* April, p. 27.

10. Ibid., p. 29.

11. Ibid.

12. Ibid., p. 31.

13. Ibid.

14. Negroes in apprenticeship, New York State, *Monthly Labor Review,* September 1960, p. 955.

15. Mary H. Diggs. 1950. Some problems and needs of Negro children as revealed by comparative delinquency and crime statistics, *Journal of Negro Education* 19, pp. 290–297.

16. Maude M. Craig and Thelma J. Glick. 1963. Ten years experience with the Glueck Social Prediction Table, *Journal of Crime and Delinquency,* July, p. 256.

17. F. R. Scarpitti, Ellen Murray, S. Dinitz, and W. C. Reckless. 1960. The "good" boy in a high delinquency area: Four years later, *American Sociological Review,* 25, pp. 555–558.

18. W. Mischel. 1961. Father-absence and delay of gratification: Cross-cultural comparisons, *Journal of Abnormal and Social Psychology,* 63, pp. 116–124.

19. W. Mischel. 1961. Preference for delayed reinforcement and social responsibility. *Journal of Social and Abnormal Psychology,* 62, pp. 1–7; Delay of gratification, need for achievement, and

acquiescence in another culture, *Journal of Abnormal and Social Psychology,* 62, pp. 543–552.

20. O. H. Mowrer and A. D. Ullman. 1945. Time as a determinant in integrative learning, *Psychological Review,* 52, pp. 61–90.

21. Thomas F. Pettigrew. 1964. *Profile of the Negro American.* New York: van Nostrand, p. 22.

22. Erdman Palmore. 1963. Factors associated with school dropouts on juvenile delinquency among lower class children, *Social Security Bulletin,* October, p. 6.

23. Thomas P. Monahan. 1957. Family status and the delinquent child, *Social Forces,* March, p. 254.

24. Ibid., p. 174.

25. Donald J. Bogue, Bhaskar D. Misra, and D. P. Dandekar. 1964. A new estimate of the Negro population and Negro vital rates in the United States, 1930–1960, *Demography,* 1 (1), p. 350.

26. Richard A. Cloward and Robert Ontell. 1965. Our illusions about training, *American Child,* January, p. 7.

27. *Youth in the Ghetto,* New York: Harlem Youth Opportunities Unlimited, p. 144.

28. Nathan Glazer and Daniel Patrick Moynihan. 1965. *Beyond the melting pot.* Cambridge, Mass.: M.I.T. Press.

Sociocultural Factors in Black Family Transformation: Toward a Redefinition of Family Functions

ROBERT STAPLES

In a lecture delivered at Brigham Young University, the author points out that unlike a monolithic unit, the Black family assumes a number of different forms contingent on the primary variables of gender and socioeconomic status. Although the primary causes of dysfunctional Black families are linked to problems of joblessness and poverty, cultural factors, when linked to gender, often fuel "deviant behavior and family structure" among segments of the Afro-American population.

■

For the last 30 years, there have been concerns about the Black American family—where it is going, and what the implications are for other problems in society. Before discussing its current status we need to discuss its history. Although it might not add very much to our understanding of where the Black family is today, we must understand where it has been historically. We know that the Blacks in this country came primarily from the continent of Africa, a continent that at the time, some four or five centuries ago, was highly patriarchal, but, like many patriarchal societies, it was very stable. There was no such thing as divorce and relatively little nonmarital sex, and what existed was institutionalized and controlled by tribes or communities of elders. These patterns and values were brought to the United States. Unfortunately, under slavery the Black family ceased to exist as a legal entity.

A family is, in many ways, a legal entity as well as a social one. The slave had no legal right to a family; the slave family's functions consisted of those that the slave master mandated. There are many claims about what happened to the family of slaves, and those claims are not all consistent with one another. One claim is that the family was destroyed for Black Americans during slavery because the roles of the husband and the father were institutionally obliterated. Others claim that simply for economic reasons, slave owners did not destroy families; for slavery to be an efficient economic system, it was important to keep families intact. Happy workers were thought to be generally more productive workers.

At any rate, recent evidence has indicated that the post-slavery Black family structure was essentially similar to that of White Americans of that period, 1865 to 1925. About 75 percent of all Black families were what one historian calls "simple nuclear families" (Gutman, 1976). Only during the second and third quarters of the twentieth century, during a time of massive immigration and also urbanization, did the Black family begin to disintegrate. Thus after about 1925 the Black family began to face problems brought about by immigration and urbanization. Blacks no longer had the folk culture that had kept them together under the most adverse conditions in the rural South. Hence, we saw several new phenomena: children being raised by mothers, welfare

Reprinted from *American Families: Issues in Race and Ethnicity,* edited by Cardell Jacobson. New York: Garland Publishing Inc. Copyright 1995 by Cardell Jacobson. Reprinted by permission.

dependency, juvenile delinquency, and some educational failures. But such breakdowns have to be viewed in context: Only 10 to 15 percent of all Black families in the period between 1930 and 1950 experienced these problems. In fact, around 1950, the Black and White American families were remarkably similar in their structure, if socioeconomic status differences of the two groups were taken into account.

In 1965 the notorious and much-read Moynihan report (Moynihan, 1965) was published. Officially entitled "The Negro Family: The Case for National Action," the report was written by Daniel Moynihan, who at that time was the Assistant Secretary of Labor, and who later became the senior senator from the State of New York. Moynihan's major thesis was that the root of the problems of the Black community was not economic but rather the deterioration of the Black family. Moynihan was an important government official, so the report seemed to imply a change in direction of government policy toward Blacks and Black American families in the United States. This was 1965, much of the South was still segregated, and Blacks were at the bottom of the caste line according to the Moynihan report. The Black family structure was out of line with the White American family structure. Furthermore, approximately 22 percent of all Black families were headed by women—a "Black matriarchy," in Moynihan's words. These families were dominated by women simply because there was no one to challenge them for power and control. The men obviously were not part of these families, but Moynihan claimed that even when men were present, they were weak and spineless; the women basically ruled the roost and, as a result produced ineffective, effeminate, and, by implication, homosexual males. Moynihan based many of his conclusions on rather flawed research evidence supplied to him by two sociologists (Blood and Wolf, 1960).

In addition, Moynihan noted that 23.6 percent of all births to Black women were out of wedlock—approximately one out of four. As a result, he said that this had led to welfare dependency and educational failures, and again to spineless men. In fact, many people cannot believe, or simply do not know, what Moynihan's solution to the "problem" was. Moynihan recommended that Black men go someplace where men could be men. At that time, he believed that place to be the United States military. Of course, the Black man also had a fairly high chance of being killed if he joined the army at that time because many men in the military were serving in Vietnam. Some claim Moynihan has subsequently been vindicated; the figures he cited in 1965 have grown increasingly worse, so that by 1992, according to the latest figures I have, 60 percent of Black births were out of wedlock. If this has been the basic reason for lack of black achievement, the problem has gotten worse. But these same figures are now also higher for White families: 22 percent out-of-wedlock births for White women, and approximately 26 percent of White women heading families with children. What are we then to say about the White American family in 1992? Sociologists have debated the question for years: "Is the family the engine that drives the car, or is it the car that is being driven by the engine?" In other words, does the family determine the economic status of individuals, or does the economy determine the structure of a family?

Let us now examine what is happening in Black families in the 1990s. First, let us understand the variations within Black subgroups in the United States; the Black family in the United States is not a monolithic unit. Approximately 35 to 40 percent of Black families would be considered middle class, depending on what definition is used. Most successful Black Americans are not just those who are highly educated; gender plays a factor. Success is also not just socioeconomic status; it actually turns out to be marital status. If you are a Black married couple in the United States, as Martin Luther King Jr. might have said, "You have reached the promised land." We actually find that Black married couples in the northeastern part of the United States have a median income of approximately $43,000 a year, about parity with White married couples in that same geographic area of the country. Relatively few of the children of Black married couples will be poor. In comparison to single-parent households, in which 65 percent of the children are poor, only 18 percent of the children in married couple households are poor, again a figure comparable to that for White American families. What Blacks essentially need to achieve equality is to be married. Obviously, one result of being married is that, particularly for Black families, they have two incomes. The problem with Black Americans, of course, is that one consequence of the travail of the 30 years since the Moynihan report was published is that approximately 40 percent of Black adults over the age of 16 are married. This low figure represents one of the steepest declines, certainly in the western industrialized world, for a particular racial group. Only one-third of Black women over the age of 16 are currently married and living with a spouse. Thus, the fairly positive economic state for Blacks, in terms of marital status, applies to only about 40 percent of the Black American population. Yet despite these positive results, the poverty rate has increased by 3 percent among Black married couples in the last two to three years.

Another key indicator of variations within the Black community is gender. Approximately 85 percent or 90 percent of college-educated Black males with an income of more than $25,000 a year are married and live with their spouse. Again, the unfortunate part is that Black males are currently only about one-third of all the Blacks enrolled in college, and they represent even a smaller percentage of those who will graduate from college. But reasonably well-educated Black males have no shortage of eligible and desirable mates, and they will have a fairly stable marital life.

Black women, who are two-thirds of the Black college graduates, on the other hand, find themselves in a much different situation. Maybe half, or perhaps only 25 percent of them, will find comparably educated Black men who are available for marriage. Several years ago, I was struck by a 1978 figure, and I don't think it has changed. I was looking at educational levels and marital status of college graduates. I happened to look at the column for Black women between the ages of 35 and 54, who had five or more years of college who had not been formerly married. The census bureau listed about 15,000 Blacks in that category. One might assume that those Black women would also like to marry a Black male with similar characteristics. I looked at the column for Black males that had the same characteristics. The census bureau did not list any. In other words, the ratio of Black women to Black men, who had five or more years of college, who had been formerly married, and who were between the ages of 35–54, was 100:0.I knew that technically this was an error, because I was in that category. The Census Bureau told me that because of statistical variance, it had calculated that the number was less than 500. That meant that at best, according to Census Bureau statistics, there were about 15,000 Black women in that particular category and 499 Black males— a dismal marriage pool for those who want to marry within the race. And, of course, approximately 97 percent of all Black American women do marry within their race. Thus, gender is an important variable, for it (1) determines your chances of finding a sufficient number of people in the marriage pool, and (2) if you get married, as these 15,000 women have done, and get divorced, it determines in large part your chances of getting remarried. And if you want to have a marriage of socioeconomic equals, you are looking at very low prospects for Black American women who have graduated from college.

Another factor, of course, is socioeconomic status in general. What we find is that middle-class Black families also have problems. We don't really hear about problems of Black middle-class families because much of the concern over Black American families is distorted in the media. There are these problems, but they are not problems of an economic nature, and therefore the government is not concerned. One problem is the downward mobility for many Black middle-class families in the sense that they are simply not able to transmit their class status to their children in the way that many White families do. Black women must also deal with the problem of a declining marriage pool, which forces women, in many cases, to marry down. These marriages have the highest divorce rate—at least they did in the past—of almost all marriages. So, the divorce rate for Black women in middle-class marriages is fairly high and remarriage rate is very low, simply because of the low numbers and the sex ratios in the marriage pool. We also know that the marriage pool is reduced even further by other kinds of behavior or statuses, such as high rates of interracial marriages by the middle-class Blacks. Even the highest rate of homosexuality also appears to be in that group, although we are not really sure because data are so unreliable on homosexuality.

So the problem of the middle class is in many ways a problem of gender. Gender brings about other kinds of behavior less closely associated with the middle class. For instance, *Newsweek* published figures showing that even among Black women who earned more than $75,000 a year, approximately one out of five had a child out of wedlock, one of the most famous examples being a TV news anchor in Boston. Again, this is a function of gender, although it is also a function of socioeconomic status, because the inability of many Black men to rise up to the level of Black women creates this low number in the marriage pool.

These are, in a nutshell, some of the key factors, but what about the explanations? As has been already mentioned, there is a demographic relationship and imbalance in sex ratios. Approximately 46 percent of Black men, for a number of reasons, are not in the civilian labor force. Between the ages of 20 and 30, almost 25 percent are in jail, on probation, or on parole. The mortality rate in that same age range is about five times higher for Black men than for Black women. The largest cause of death is homicide, the second largest is accidents, the third largest is suicide, and the fourth largest—a cause that just basically came into existence in the 1980s—is

AIDS. As of 1992, 46 percent of those who died from AIDS were either Black or Latino males. It is little wonder that for Black women, the out-of-wedlock birthrate is about 70 percent, simply because there are no men who are able to meet the basic requisites of being employed, drug-free, and able to carry out the normative functions of husbands and fathers.

This situation does not exist to the same extent in the white community. Black males are eight times more likely to be in prison than White males, about eight times more likely to die from homicide than White males, about eight times more likely to be out of the labor force. And even those who are in the military are often not in places where they can carry on functional marriages, because they are often stationed in places like Somalia, the Philippines, Spain, and elsewhere abroad.

We must look closely at these social causes that bring about such demographic relationships. We also must consider, and this we do not often do, the social and cultural factors. Seventy-five percent of births being out of wedlock is not all socioeconomic or even demographic. High rates of out-of-wedlock births are also beginning to appear, as I have already pointed out, among middle-class Whites. What we also need to understand is that the increase among Whites has been considerably greater than among Blacks. In fact, if Blacks had increased their rates of divorces, out-of-wedlock children, and single-parent households at the same rate as Whites, they would now be beyond 100 percent. That is, there would be no Black married couples in the United States. Because Blacks were at a higher level in the beginning, their percentage is now larger, but the rate of increase is smaller.

Some of these factors are social and cultural, and it is not always popular to talk about them. Among these factors is the change in sex roles. Just as a dictatorship is more stable than a democracy, when the subordinate person has no viable option, so we find a statistical norm of family stability under the unchallenged system of patriarchy. Gender equality is a fairer system, but in the transitional stage may produce some family instability. Thus, at this point of transition when we are striving for gender equity, families are under stress. The tensions, disagreements, and dissonance that occur at a time when we are trying for this noble goal are having a very disruptive effect on the family. This is, of course, by no means an endorsement of patriarchy; it simply points out what should be a fairly clear-cut fact: It is easier to have order in a dictatorship than in a democracy.

The media and the role models available to us through the media have essentially made nonmarital sex, and even antimarriage attitudes, normative in this country. I can hardly think of a well-known celebrity in a conventional marriage who is living the normative lifestyle of husbands and wives as we have traditionally defined it. Most of them, and certainly the more visible ones, often have children out of wedlock, are cohabitating, and are certainly in agreement with permissive attitudes towards sex and even drugs. This eventually has an impact on the most impressionable sector of the Black population, the youth, as well as on the White population. It is among that population where we have the largest number of out-of-wedlock births and the most sexually active population. As long as society, which really has no choice in a democracy, allows this sort of media impact of role models, who are entertainers and other prominent people, including those in the highest levels of government, the message is that this is desirable behavior.

There are a combination of factors for Black Americans. The most imminent and decisive factor still tends to be the economic one, but it is also cultural, which means that it is beginning to have an impact on the middle class as well as the lower class.

What is the "solution"? I am not sure that we know. We assume that a two-parent household is preferable to a single-parent household, and I would add that a two-parent household in which husbands and wives are in a loving and caring relationship might be more preferable than a single-parent household in which the

woman has to struggle with sorts of roles; in that case, a two-parent household is preferable. The significant thing about this whole debate about two-parent versus one-parent households has to do with the subtle problems that ostensibly come from the one-parent household: educational failures, crime, delinquency, welfare dependency, and so forth. We have never really been able to sort this out, simply because most single-parent households (and this is particularly true of Black single-parent households) actually have about 40 percent of the income available to them that Black married couple households have. Thus we are looking at two groups with very different resources, and when we talk about crime, when we talk about educational failures and welfare dependency caused by female heads of households, we also know that those are the poorest households. And until we have carefully constructed studies that can show that, with socioeconomic status controlled, we are still going to have these problems, we cannot really direct all the blame or responsibility to the one- or two-parent structure of such households.

Moreover, remember that when we talk about certain factors like crime, it is one of the easiest things in the world to say that crime in this country is primarily a function of its definition and its enforcement. Certainly, like everyone else, I would prefer to have the criminal that comes into the bank and robs it and kidnaps all the customers put behind bars. He is, in many ways, a much greater threat to my safety and well-being than the white-collar criminal who manages to steal millions through the use of a computer. On the other hand, the person who robs the bank generally gets only $1,000 to $2,000. The white-collar criminal who generally has access to the computer through what we call "human capital," "credentials,"—a degree, job experience, good recommendations—steals a lot more. They both commit crimes, but essentially we punish the crimes of the poor, we enforce the law against the poor, and the poor are less likely to have a defense because they are less likely to be able to afford a good lawyer who can get them off. We really do not want to talk about crime as coming from these one-parent families because, obviously, the white-collar criminal comes from a more privileged family that is likely to be a two-parent family. We must consider which is the worse crime. Certainly in magnitude, the white-collar criminal gets away with more.

Educational problems are widespread in society. They are no longer unique to the lower class. They exist in the suburbs; that is why we have initiatives to establish vouchers so that everybody can go to private schools, except for the most intransigent students, who will be left in the public schools, along with their teachers, who I would suggest should arm themselves and not worry about teaching.

So, we are at this point where we have to consider all American families in the overall context of American society, and the family's function in society. Certainly many of its traditional functions are no longer carried out in most of the United States. Statistically, probably only 18 percent of Americans belong to what we would consider the traditional American family, that is, a two-parent family in which the wife stays at home, and the parents have approximately 1.8 children. That family is a small minority nowadays. We will have to go beyond these traditional models and figure out a niche, a role, a function, for families in American society. The Black American family, in a sense, is in the vanguard of these changes. We will not know whether these changes are positive or negative until the economic basis of these family structures has been reduced or eliminated.

REFERENCES

Blood, Robert, and Donald Wolf. 1960. *Husbands and wives: The dynamics of married living.* New York: Free Press.

Gutman, Herbert. 1976. *The Black family in slavery and freedom, 1750–1925.* New York: Pantheon.

Moynihan, Daniel Patrick. 1965. *The Negro family: The case for national action.* Washington, DC: Office of Policy Planning and Research. U.S. Department of Labor.

Newsweek, 1993. Endangered family. August 30, pp. 17–29.

2

Historical Background

The Myth of the Absent Family

EUGENE D. GENOVESE

This article examines some common myths about the Black family during the period of slavery. Genovese finds that despite considerable constraints on their ability to carry out normative family roles and functions, the bondsmen created impressive norms of family life and entered the post-emancipation era with a strong respect for the family and a comparatively stable family base.

■

The recent controversy over the ill-fated Moynihan Report has brought the question of the Black family in general and the slave family in particular into full review. Largely following the pioneering work of E. Franklin Frazier, the report summarized the conventional wisdom according to which slavery had emasculated Black men, created a matriarchy, and prevented the emergence of a strong sense of family.[1] Historians and sociologists, Black and white, have been led astray in two ways. First, they have read the story of the twentieth-century Black ghettos backward in time and have assumed a historical continuity with slavery days. Second, they have looked too closely at slave law and at the externals of family life and not closely enough at the actual temper of the quarters.

During the twentieth century Blacks went north in great waves and faced enormous hardship. The women often could find work as domestics; the men found themselves shut out of employment not so much by their lack of skills as by fierce racial discrimination. Some disorientation of the Black family apparently followed; evaluation of its extent and social content must be left to others who can get beyond simple statistical reports to an examination of the quality of life.[2] But those inclined to read the presumed present record back into the past have always had a special problem, for by any standard of judgment the southern rural Black family, which remained closer to the antebellum experience,

From *Roll, Jordan, Roll: The World the Slaves Made,* by Eugene D. Genovese. Copyright 1972, 1974 by Eugene D. Genovese. Reprinted by permission of Pantheon Books, a Division of Random House.

always appeared to be much stronger than the northern urban family.[3]

The evidence from the war years and Reconstruction, now emerging in more systematic studies than were previously available, long ago should have given us pause.[4] Every student of the Union occupation and early Reconstruction has known of the rush of the freedmen to legalize their marriages; of the widespread desertion of the plantations by whole families; of the demands by men and women for a division of labor that would send the women out of the fields and into the homes; of the militancy of parents seeking to keep their children from apprenticeship to Whites even when it would have been to their economic advantage; and especially of the heart-rending effort of thousands of freedmen to find long-lost loved ones all over the South. These events were prefigured in antebellum times. Almost every study of runaway slaves uncovers the importance of the family motive: thousands of slaves ran away to find children, parents, wives, or husbands from whom they had been separated by sale. Next to resentment over punishment, the attempt to find relatives was the most prevalent cause of flight.[5]

These data demand a reassessment of slave family life as having had much greater power than generally believed. But a word of warning: the pressures on the family, as E. Franklin Frazier, W. E. B. Du Bois, Kenneth M. Stampp, Stanley M. Elkins, and other scholars have pointed out, were extraordinary and took a terrible toll. My claims must be read within limits—as a record of the countervailing forces even within the slavocracy but especially within the slave community. I suggest only that the slaves created impressive norms of family life, including as much of a nuclear family norm as conditions permitted, and that they entered the postwar social system with a remarkably stable base. Many families became indifferent or demoralized, but those with a strong desire for family stability were able to set norms for life in freedom that could serve their own interests and function reasonably well within the wider social system of White-dominated America.

The masters understood the strength of the marital and family ties among their slaves well enough to see in them a powerful means of social control. As a Dutch slaveholder wrote from Louisiana in the 1750s: "It is necessary that the Negroes have wives, and you ought to know that nothing attaches them so much to a plantation as children."[6] No threat carried such force as a threat to sell the children, except the threat to separate husband and wife. The consequences for the children loomed large in the actions of their parents. When—to take an extreme example—a group of slaves planned a mass suicide, concern for their children provided the ground for sober second thoughts.[7]

Evidence of the slaveholders' awareness of the importance of family to the slaves may be found in almost any well-kept set of plantation records. Masters and overseers normally listed their slaves by households and shaped disciplinary procedures to take full account of family relationships. The sale of a recalcitrant slave might be delayed or avoided because it would cause resentment among his family of normally good workers. Conversely, a slave might be sold as the only way to break his influence over valuable relatives.[8] Could Whites possibly have missed the content of their slaves' marital relationships when faced with such incidents as the one reported by James W. Melvin, an overseer, to his employer, Audley Clark Britton?

> [Old Bill] breathed his last on Saturday the 31st, Jan. about 8-1/2 o'clock in the morning. He appeared prepared for Death and said he was going to heaven and wanted his wife to meet him there. When he took sick he told all it would be his last sickness—I was very sorry to lose him.[9]

The pretensions of racist propagandists that slaves did not value the marriage relation fell apart in the courts, which in a variety of ways wrestled with the problems caused by the lack of legal sanction for slave marriages. However much they insisted on treating the slaves' marriages as mere concubinage, they rarely if ever denied the moral content of the relationship or the common devotion of the parties to each other. Thus, Georgia and Texas illogically and humanely would not permit slave wives to testify against their husbands while continuing to insist that their relationship had no standing at law. The high courts of South Carolina and other states took a more consistent stand on the question of testimony but repeatedly acknowledged the painful problems caused by the lack of legal sanction for relationships everyone knew to be meaningful and worthy of respect.[10]

Many slaveholders went to impressive lengths to keep families together even at the price of considerable pecuniary loss, although, as Kenneth Stampp forcefully insists, the great majority of slaveholders chose business over sentiment and broke up families when under financial pressure. But the choice did not rest easy on their conscience. The kernel of truth in the notion that the slaveholders felt guilty about owning human beings resides largely in this issue. They did feel guilty about their inability to live up to their own paternalistic justification for slavery in the face of market pressure.[11]

The more paternalistic masters betrayed evidence of considerable emotional strain. In 1858, William Massie of Virginia, forced to decrease his debts, chose to sell a beloved and newly improved homestead rather than his slaves. "To know," he explained, "that my little family, White and *Black,* [is] to be fixed permanently together would be as near that thing happiness as I ever expect to get. . . . Elizabeth has raised and taught most of them, and having no children, like every other woman under like circumstances, has tender feelings toward them."[12] An impressive number of slaveholders took losses they could ill afford in an effort to keep families together.[13] For the great families, from colonial times to the fall of the regime, the maintenance of family units was a matter of honor.[14] Foreign travelers not easily taken in by appearances testified to the lengths to which slaveholders went at auctions to compel the callous among them to keep family units together.[15] Finally, many ex-slaves testified about

masters who steadfastly refused to separate families; who, if they could not avoid separations, sold the children within visiting distance of their parents; and who took losses to buy wives or husbands in order to prevent permanent separations.[16] Stampp's insistence that such evidence revealed the exception rather than the rule is probably true, although I think that exceptions occurred more frequently than he seems to allow for. But it does demonstrate how well the Whites understood the strength of the slaves' family ties and the devastating consequences of their own brutal disregard of the sensibilities of those they were selling.

Masters could not afford to be wholly indifferent to slave sensibilities. "Who buys me must buy my son too," a slave defiantly shouted from an auction block. "Better to buy in Virginia than Louisiana," wrote J. W. Metcalfe to St. John R. Liddell, "for we stand a better chance of buying whole families, whose attachments will make them better and less troublesome workers." Enough slaves risked severe punishment in demanding that their families be kept intact to make masters thoughtful of their own self-interest.[17] So far as circumstances permitted, the slaves tried to stay close to brothers and sisters, aunts and uncles.[18] A woman with a husband who struck her too freely might turn to her brother for protection. A widowed or abandoned aunt could expect to live in a cabin with an affectionate niece and her husband. An old slave without spouse or children could expect attention and comfort from nieces, nephews, and cousins when facing illness and death.[19] Brothers looked after their sisters or at least tried to. An overseer killed a slave girl in Kentucky and paid with his own life at the hands of her brother, who then made a successful escape. In Virginia terrible whippings could not prevent a young man from sneaking off to visit a cherished sister on another plantation.[20]

The more humane masters took full account of their slaves' affection for and sense of responsibility toward relatives. Charles West wrote to the Reverend John Jones of Georgia to ask if a certain Clarissa was alive and about, for her sister, Hannah, in Alabama wanted to visit her during the summer. Dr. Bradford, a slaveholder in Florida, hired out three sisters at a lower price than he could have gotten because he would not separate them even for a year.[21] Few slaveholders took such pains to respect the strong ties of brothers and sisters, but fewer still could claim as excuse that they did not have evidence of the slaves' feelings. Three-quarters of a century after slavery, Anne Harris of Virginia, at age ninety-two, told her interviewer that no White person had ever set foot in her house.

> Don't 'low it. Dey sole my sister Kate. I saw it wid dese here eyes. Sole her in 1860, and I ain't seed nor heard of her since. Folks say White folks is all right dese days. Maybe dey is, maybe dey isn't. But I can't stand to see 'em. Not on my place.[22]

In the late antebellum period several states moved to forbid the sale of children away from their mother, but only Louisiana's law appears to have been effective. At that, Governor Hammond of South Carolina had the audacity to argue that the slaveholders deserved credit for efforts to hold slave families together and that the slaves themselves cared little.[23]

Masters not only saw the bonds between husbands and wives, parents and children, they saw the bonds between nieces and nephews and aunts and uncles and especially between brothers and sisters. Nowhere did the slaveholders' willful blindness, not to say hypocrisy, concerning the strength of their slaves' family ties appear so baldly as in their reaction to separations attendant upon sales. They told themselves and anyone who would listen that husbands and wives, despite momentary distress, did not mind separations and would quickly adjust to new mates. Not content with this fabrication, some slaveholders went so far as to assert that separation of mothers from children caused only minimal hardship. Most slaveholders knew this claim to be nonsense, but they nevertheless argued that

the separation of fathers from their children was of little consequence.

From time to time a slave did prefer to stay with a good master or mistress rather than follow a spouse who was being sold away. In these cases and in many others in which slaves displayed indifference, the marriage had probably already been weakened, and sale provided the most convenient and painless form of divorce. Such incidents reveal nothing about the depth of grief aroused by the sale of cherished wives and husbands. The slaveholders knew that many slave marriages rested on solid foundations of affection. Slaves on all except the most entrenched and stable plantations lived in constant fear of such separations and steeled themselves against them. When the blow came, the slaves often took it with outward calm. A discernible decline in a master's fortune or growing trouble with the overseer or master might have given warning of what was coming. If the slaves suffered quietly and cried alone, their masters had an excuse to declare them indifferent.

No such excuses, frail as they were, could explain the slaveholders' frequent assertions that mothers and children adjusted easily to separations. The slaveholders saw the depth of the anguish constantly, and only the most crass tried to deny it. John A. Quitman said that he had witnessed the separation of a family only once. It was enough: "I never saw such profound grief as the poor creatures manifested." Mary Boykin Chesnut remarked to a visiting Englishwoman as they passed a slave auction, "If you can stand that, no other Southern thing need choke you."[24]

John S. Wise's testimony may stand for many others. An apologist who put the best face he could on the old regime, he described an auction in which a crippled man of limited use was in danger of being separated from his wife and children. Israel, the man, spoke up in his own behalf:

> "Yes, sir, I kin do as much ez ennybody; and marsters, ef you'll only buy me and de chillum with Martha Ann, Gord knows I'll

wuk myself to deth for you." The poor little darkeys, Cephas and Melinda, sat there frightened and silent, their white eyes dancing like monkey-eyes, and gleaming in the shadows. As her husband's voice broke on her ear, Martha Ann, who bad been looking sadly out of the window in a pose of quiet dignity turned her face with an expression of exquisite love and gratitude towards Israel. She gazed for a moment at her husband and at her children, and then looked away once more, her eyes brimming with tears.[25]

Wise's story—of course—ended happily when a slaveholder accepted a loss he could not easily afford in order to buy the family as a unit. But Wise, a man of the world, had to know, as Brecht later reminded us, "In real life, the ending is not so fine/Victoria's Messenger does not come riding often."

John Randolph of Roanoke, a slaveholder himself, who had known Patrick Henry, Henry Clay, and all the great political orators of the day and who himself ranked at the top, was asked whom he thought to have pride of place. "The greatest orator I ever heard," he replied, "was a woman. She was a slave and a mother and her rostrum was an auction block."[26]

All except the most dehumanized slaveholders knew of the attachments that the slaves had to their more extended families, to their friends, and to most of those who made up their little communities and called each other "brother" and "sister." Kate Stone wrote in 1862: "Separating the old family Negroes who have lived and worked together for so many years is a great grief to them and a distress to us."[27] Those who pretended that the separations came easy never explained why so many ruses had to be used to keep men and women occupied while one or another of their children was being whisked off. Robert Applegarth, an Englishman, described a common scene in which slaves suffered threats and punishments at auctions in response to their wailing and pleading to be kept together.[28] So

well did the slaveholders understand the strength of these family ties that the more humane among them found it useful to argue against separations on the grounds of economic expediency by pointing out that the slaves worked much better when kept together.[29]

The extent of separation of wives from husbands and children from parents will probably remain in dispute. The impressive econometric work by Robert Fogel and Stanley Engerman suggests that separations occurred less frequently than has generally been believed, but the data do not permit precise measurement.[30] The nostalgic son of an antebellum planter did not fear contradiction when he recalled long after emancipation: "Were families separated by sale, etc.? Yes, quite often."[31] The potential for forced separation—whatever the ultimate measure of its realization—struck fear into the quarters, especially in the slave-exporting states of the Upper South. If the rich and powerful Pierce Butler of the Sea Islands had to sell hundreds of slaves to cover debts in the 1850s, was anyone safe? Even planters willing to take financial losses to keep families intact could not always control events. Once slaves passed out of the hands of their old masters, their fate depended upon the willingness of professional traders to honor commitments to keep families together or upon the attitude of new masters. And many masters did not respect their slaves' family feelings and did not hesitate to sell them as individuals.

Frederick Douglass referred to "that painful uncertainty which in one form or another was ever obtruding itself in the pathway of the slave."[32] Perhaps no single hardship or danger, not even the ever-present whip, struck such terror into the slaves and accounted for so much of that "fatalism" often attributed to them. If the spirit of many did crack and if many did become numb, nothing weighs so heavily among the reasons as the constant fear of losing loved ones. In the weakest slaves it instilled reckless irresponsibility and a fear of risking attachments—of feeling anything—and in the strongest, a heroic stoicism in the face of unbearable pain. A majority of the slaves probably suffered from some effects of these fears, but their vibrant love of life and of each other checked the slide into despair.

But the pain remained, and the slaveholders knew as much. Is it possible that no slaveholder noticed the grief of the woman who told Fredrika Bremer that she had had six children, three of whom had died and three of whom had been sold: "When they took from me the last little girl, oh, I believed I never should have got over it! It almost broke my heart!"[33] Could any White southerner pretend not to know from direct observation the meaning of Sojourner Truth's statement: "I have borne thirteen chillun and seen 'em mos' all sold off into slavery, and when I cried out with a mother's grief, none but Jesus heard. . . ."[34] Whatever the Whites admitted to others or even themselves, they knew what they wrought. And the slaves knew that they knew. A Black woman, speaking to Lucy Chase, recalled her first husband's being sold away from her: "White folks got a heap to answer for the way they've done to colored folks! So much they won't never pray it away!"[35]

NOTES

1. Lee Rainwater and William L. Yancey, *The Moynihan Report and the Politics of Controversy* (Cambridge, Mass. 1967), which includes the text of the report; Frazier. *Negro in the United States* and *Negro Family*; Elkins, *Slavery*.

2. For a brief general critique of prevailing notions of family disorganization see Charles V. Willie, "The Black Family in America," Dissent. Feb., 1971, pp. 80—83. The specialized literature is growing rapidly. For one of the most careful and responsible of the older studies see Drake and Cayton, *Black Metropolis*, II, 582–583.

3. See, e.g., Myrdal, *American Dilemma*, p. 935; Jessie Bernard, *Marriage and Family among Negroes* (Englewood Cliffs, N.J., 1966), p. 21; Powdermaker, *After Freedom*, p. 143.

4. See esp. Peter Kolchin, *First Freedom: The Responses of Alabama's Blacks to Emancipation and Reconstruction* (Westport, Conn., 1972), Ch. 3.; Herbert G. Gutman, "Le Phénomène invisible: La Composition de la famille et du foyer flairs après la Guerre de Sécession," *Annales: Économies, Sociétés, Civilisations,* XXVII (July–Oct., 1972), 1197–1218. Of special interest in these studies are the data from marriage certificates in the Union archives,

which show an impressive number of cases in which slaves had lived together for ten years and longer, sometimes much longer.

5. Mullin, *Flight and Rebellion,* p. 109; Sydnor, *Slavery in Mississippi,* p. 103; Bancroft, *Slave Trading,* p. 206.

6. Quoted in M. Le Page Du Pratz, *History of Louisiana or of the Western Parts of Virginia and Carolina* (London, 1924), p. 365.

7. WPA, *Negro in Virginia,* p. 74; Fisk University, *Unwritten History of Slavery,* p. 136.

8. See, for example, Agnew Diary, Aug. 19, 1862 (II, 124a–124b); Sitterson, *Sugar Country,* pp. 103–104; the correspondence of Charles C. Jones, Jr., and C. C. Jones, Oct., 1856, in Myers, ed., *Children of Pride.*

9. James W. Melvin to A. C. Britton, Feb. 11, 1863, in the Britton Papers.

10. Catterall, ed., *Judicial Cases,* I, passim; III, 89–90, 160; V. 182; also C. P. Patterson, *Negro in Tennessee,* pp. 57, 154.

11. Kenneth Stampp, having studied the wills of a large number of slaveholders, concludes that the financial return to the heirs constitutes the overriding consideration; see *Peculiar Institution,* p. 204. But see also J. B. Sellers, *Slavery in Alabama,* p. 168, for a somewhat different reading.

12. Quoted in Phillips, *Life and Labor,* p. 243.

13. For same evidence of masters who went to great lengths to keep the families of even recalcitrant slaves together, or who took financial losses to avoid separations, see the Witherspoon-McDowall Correspondence for 1852; Richard Whitaker to A. H. Boykin, Nov. 17, 1843, in the Boykin Papers; J. B. Hawkins to Charles Alston, Nov. 28, 1847, in the Aiston Papers; William Otey to Octavia A. Otey, Nov. 20, 1855, in the Wyche-Otey Papers; Ernest Haywood Correspondence, 1856–1857; Lewis Stirling to his son, Jan. 10, 1843; Henry A. Taylor to B. O. Taylor, Jan. 5, 1835; Correspondence of Joseph Bryan of Savannah, Ga., a slave trader, in the Slave Papers, Library of Congress; Gavin Diary, July 2, 1857; George W. Clement to Capt. John P. Wright, Oct. 28, 1849, in the Pocket Plantation Record. For evidence and analyses in secondary works see especially R. H. Taylor, *Slaveholding in North Carolina,* p. 85; Phillips, *Life and Labor,* pp. 274–275; McColley, *Slavery and Jeffersonian Virginia,* pp. 66–68.

14. See, for example, Morton, *Robert Carter of Nomini Hall,* p. 111; Joseph Clay to Edward Telfair, Dec. 6, 1785, in the Telfair Papers; Heyward, *Seed from Madagascar,* p. 88; W. T. Jordan, *Hugh Davis,* passim; Myers, ed., *Children of Pride,* passim; John Lynch to Ralph Smith, Oct. 13, 1826, in *Pocket Plantation Record;* J. B. Grimball Diary, June 20, 1835, Jan. 11, 1860, July 17, 1863; C. C. Mercer to John and William Mercer, July 28, 1860; wills dated Dec. 12, 1849, July 9, 1857, Feb. 2, 1862, in the Lawton Papers; A.G.G. to Thomas W. Harriss, Oct. 28, 1848, in the Harriss Papers; Gavin Diary, Sept. 9, 1856; William McKean to James Dunlop, April 4, 1812, in the McKean Letterbook; Eaton, *Henry Clay,* pp. 120–121; John Kirkland to his son, Sept. 15, 1858, in the Wyche-Otey Papers.

15. See, for example, Lyell, *Second Visit,* I, 209–210; Stirling, *Letters from the Slave States,* p. 260.

16. Fisk University, *Unwritten History of Slavery*, pp. 1, 33; Rawick, ed., S. C. Narr., 11(1), 206; III (3), 2; Texas Narr., IV (2), 110; Indiana Narr., VI (2), 10; George Teamah Journal, Pts. 1–2, p. 31, in the Woodson Papers.

17. Schoepf, *Travels in the Confederation*, II, 148; Metcalfe to Liddell, June 24, 1848, in the Liddell Papers. Also Charles M. Manigault to Louis Manigault, Jan. 8, 1857; John W. Pittman invoice and note, in the Slave Papers, Library of Congress.

18. In general see Rawick, *Sundown to Sunup*, p. 90.

19. For illustrations of each of these cases see Fisk University, *Unwritten History of Slavery*, pp. 140, 143; Phillips, *Life and Labor*, p. 270; Henry [the Driver] to William S. Pettigrew, July 1, 1857, in the Pettigrew Papers; Eliza G. Roberts to Mrs. C. C. Jones, May 20, 1861, and Mary Jones to Mary S. Mallard, Nov. 7, 1865, in Myers, ed., *Children of Pride.*

20. Rawick, ed., Kansas Narr., XVI, 71; Ohio Narr., XVI, 12.

21. West to John Jones, July 23, 1855, in the John Jones Papers; Chatham, "Plantation Slavery in Middle Florida," unpublished M.A. thesis, University of North Carolina, 1938, p. 80. See also Father Henson's *Story of His Own Life*, pp. 147–148, 157; Fisk University, *Unwritten History of Slavery*, p. 78.

22. WPA, *Negro in Virginia*, p. 34.

23. DBR, VIII (Feb., 1850), 122. For a discussion of the state laws designed to protect families from separation see Bancroft, *Slave Trading*, pp. 197–199.

24. Quitman as quoted in Bancroft, *Slave Trading*, p. 308; Chesnut, *Diary from Dixie*, p. 18.

25. Wise, *End of an Era*, p. 84; also pp. 85–86.

26. As quoted by R. E. Park in his introduction to Doyle, *Etiquette of Race Relations*, p. xxvii.

27. Kate Stone, *Brokenburn*, p. 84. Or see the remarks of the court in *Nowell v. O'Hara* (S.C.), 1833, in Catterall, ed., *Judicial Cases*, II, 352.

28. See Applegarth's statement in the Slave Papers, Library of Congress.

29. See, e.g., Judge DeSaussure of South Carolina in *Gayle v. Cunningham*, 1846, in Catterall, ed., *Judicial Cases*, II, 314; or Judge Slidell of Louisiana in *Bertrand v. Arcueil*, Ibid., III, 599–600.

30. Fogel and Engerman, *Time on the Cross*, pp. 126–144. See also the suggestive article by William Calderhead, "How Extensive Was the Border State Slave Trade: A New Look," *CWH*, XVIII (March, 1972), 42–55.

31. J. A. McKinstry to H. C. Nixon, Feb. 11, 1913, in Correspondence: Slavery, Tennessee State Library and Archives. In general, see Bancroft, *Slave Trading*, especially Chs. 2 and 10.

32. *Life and Times of Frederick Douglass*, p. 96.

33. Bremer, *Homes of the New World*, II, 93.

34. Quoted in Du Bois, *Gift of Black Folk*, p. 143.

35. Swint, ed., *Dear Ones at Home*, p. 124.

Women and Slavery in the African Diaspora: A Cross-Cultural Approach to Historical Analysis

ROSALYN TERBORG-PENN

In this comparative review of the study of women and slavery in the African diaspora, the author begins with an assessment of the demographic impact of slavery upon African females. She raises several questions about the relationship of enslaved women to men of the master-class. Among the other factors considered are the role of free women in the master-class, the extent to which female slaves assimilated into the society of the master-class, and how they fitted into the kinship structure of the society.

■

AFRICAN DIASPORA WOMEN'S HISTORY

The subject is Black women and slavery, a topic of growing interest among scholars, but one which is rarely studied cross-culturally by historians. As a result, theoretical models for examining the historical impact of enslaving women of African descent are in the pioneering stages. A cross-cultural analysis of slavery and Black women belongs in the realm of African Diaspora Studies, an interdisciplinary area of scholarship. Whether to use interdisciplinary approaches to historical analysis or not is a debate that re-emerges periodically among historians. A theory for African Diaspora Women's History which includes the use of interdisciplinary methods will stimulate this debate even further. Nonetheless, such an approach seems quite viable, and anthropologist Filomina Chioma Steady's concept, which she calls African feminism, lends itself to an historically based theoretical framework.[1]

In essence, the theory is used to approach the study of Black women's lives through an analysis of their own networks and to view Black women's plight and goals to overcome their problems cross-culturally. Beginning with an examination of the values which foster the customs of free women in traditional African societies, historians can plot how these traits have changed, yet the values remained somewhat the same, as women of African descent were forcibly transported throughout Africa, Europe and the Western hemisphere. Perhaps the two most dominant values in African feminist theory, traceable through a time perspective, are developing survival strategies and encouraging self-reliance through female networks. Historically, this combination has not been present among females in the Western world, but can be traced among women of African descent in New World societies as well as in Africa.[2]

The dispersal of Africans through the slave trade is the process by which the African diaspora phenomenon was created. Before we look at the role of African women in this process, it is important to define the term "African diaspora." Traditionally, scholars refer to Africans sent away from

From *SAGE: A Scholarly Journal on Black Women*, 3 (Fall 1986): 11–15. © 1986 by the SAGE Women's Education Press, Inc. Reprinted by permission.

the continent as those who become part of the diaspora. At times these people of African descent are called "Africans abroad."[3] It seems that to limit the diaspora to areas outside of the continent of Africa is valid for the study of African men, but not for African women, because during the height of the transatlantic slave trade—from the seventeenth century into the first decade of the nineteenth century—the majority of African women enslaved were sent throughout the continent of Africa. African women were removed from their local areas and taken to other regions or to nearby areas in Africa, but usually to places outside of their kinship network, often to societies foreign to them in language, customs and environment. As a result, the majority of men enslaved during this period were dispersed throughout the Western hemisphere or New World societies, while the majority of women enslaved were dispersed throughout Africa. Consequently, the disruption and alienation that most men experienced with enslavement throughout the diaspora, women experienced on the continent of Africa.

The enslavement of African women has been a topic of limited interest to scholars of the past, be they Africanists, Americanists or Caribbeanists. Only in the 1980s has the trend to analyze enslaved women of African descent developed to the point where anthologies and monographs written in English have been published. Scholars in African history have taken the lead, notably Claire Robertson and Martin A. Klein.[4] Scholars in Afro-American history have followed, notably Deborah Gray White.[5] However, those in Latin-American and the Caribbean histories fall behind. Nonetheless, there are limited data that can be used to look at Latin America and the Caribbean to determine why African Diaspora women's history has developed more slowly than that of other regions. In addition, we can begin to make some assumptions about women enslaved in the southern regions of the Western hemisphere.

Before beginning this introduction to a cross-cultural view of enslaved Black women, it is important to look at the term "Black," because not all women of African descent identify equally with this term. In the United States, for example, by law, people with any "measurable" degree of African ancestry are considered to be Black. As a result, since slavery, women of African descent, regardless of skin color, have been perceived as and often have perceived themselves as "colored," or as "Negro," or as "Black." In this sense, "Black" becomes a manifestation of a cultural milieu, more than a color. On the other hand, in many Caribbean and South American societies, women of African descent vary in colors that determine legal status as well as cultural association. Hence, a mulatto woman in the British-speaking West Indies, for example, does not identify as Black, whereas the same woman born in the United States may choose to or is forced by the society to do so. Differences in legal and cultural identification by race cause barriers to reconstructing the past, especially for researchers studying countries such as Argentina and Brazil, where Black as a racial category has not been enumerated in the population census for several generations.

The key to historical reconstruction of slavery or any other institution must then rest first upon how women perceive themselves and second on how they are perceived by the society in which they live. In the cross-cultural historical reconstruction of enslaved Black women's lives, color and cultural perception should be taken into consideration and questions relating to these factors raised for each society under study. Likewise, questions about the master-class and the female slaves' relationship to it must be considered: What was the numerical relationship between slaves and masters in a given society? What was the role of free women in the master-class? What determined kinship and how did slaves fit into the kinship structure of the society? To what extent did female slaves assimilate into the society of the master-class? To what extent did female slaves resist their status as slaves? Finally, time must be considered in any comparative study. Comparing colonial slavery in the British Caribbean with early nineteenth-century slavery in the United States and with late nineteenth-century slavery in West Africa may result in misleading conclusions, if time periods and changes in the various institutions of slavery are not taken into consideration.

ENSLAVING WOMEN OF AFRICAN DESCENT

To begin this comparative review of the study of women and slavery in the African diaspora, let us look at the demographic impact of slavery upon African females. Women of African descent had been transported for sale from the mid-seventh century through the early twentieth century. The slave trade began as the Trans-Saharan trade on the African continent in about 650. It was supplemented by trade routes to the Red Sea and to East Africa by 800, creating a trade which shipped Africans away from the continent. With the colonization of the Western hemisphere by Europeans in the sixteenth century, the Atlantic slave trade became dominant, pulling Africans from Central and West Africa to the west African coast. The Atlantic trade peaked in the mid-eighteenth century, declining by the early nineteenth century and ending in the late 1800s.[6] By the turn of the twentieth century, vestiges of the trade remained on the African continent, where the largest number of slaves traded remained, and where the largest number of slaves traded throughout the history of slaving had been women. There is evidence that African women were still exchanged as pawns as late as the 1930s. Surprising as it may seem, the demographics of the slave trade in African women reveal a continuous demand for nearly 1300 years, mainly among Africans themselves, who paid more for adult female slaves than for adult male slaves.[7]

Recent studies about the role of women in the African slave trade astonish Americanists who have assumed that since the majority of slaves brought to New World societies were male, fewer African women were enslaved. Refocusing research about slavery toward women paints a new picture about the dynamics of slavery and the role of African women in the diaspora. Subsequent studies of slavery and women in the Western hemisphere should surely revise preconceived notions about African women transplanted into the New World.

Africanists have speculated about why more men than women were slated for the Atlantic slave trade, concluding that women were more valuable as slaves in African societies for both their productive and their reproductive functions. In most traditional African societies, women produced most of the food consumed by the community. Food producers included free and enslaved women, whose labor freed men to participate in war, long-distance trade, hunting and fishing. In addition, slave women were often used as rewards to free and enslaved males who sought wives to reproduce and to care for children, expanding the lineage of masters. Because slaves were considered to be kinless people, they remained loyal to their master's lineage. Masters who married slave women did not fear accountability to their slave wives' kin as they would if they had married free women. Slave women had no kin to protect them from spousal abuse and no kin to demand a bride-price. In addition, it was believed that women could be more easily assimilated into the society of the master-class. Furthermore, in many African societies, free women also benefited from enslaving women because slaves could increase food production and create a greater surplus, profits from which free wives often kept for themselves. In the case of secluded Muslim women, female slaves traded goods in public markets on behalf of their secluded mistresses. All of these factors made the demand for African women on the continent of Africa greater than the demand for men throughout most of the slave trading period.[8]

The high demand for enslaved women resulted in a lower price for enslaved men, many of whom would have been executed after being captured in wars if there had not been an outlet for their sale to European traders in the Atlantic slave trade. At first Europeans acquired more male slaves because they believed a strong, young male would work harder than a female. Ironically, when women were enslaved on plantations in both North America and in the Caribbean, the gender division of labor common throughout Africa broke down. New World masters worked many female slaves in the fields alongside of males and worked the females as hard as they worked male slaves.[9]

Here we see differences in work patterns among African women enslaved on the continent and those enslaved in the Western hemisphere. Gender determined work assignments in African societies, but less so in New World societies. Nonetheless, preconceived Western notions about women's work prevented European slave masters from seeking women during the first 200 years of the Atlantic trade. One common factor shared among enslaved women in African as well as in New World societies was work associated with childrearing and domestic duties. Slave women's daily chores included work for the master as well as domestic activities for the family unit wherein the woman functioned. Male slaves who lived in family units did not have this universal double work load forced upon women.

Reproducing the slave population is another topic that can be viewed comparatively. In the Caribbean, masters' attempts to reproduce the slave population did not become universal until the last century of the slave trade, as European abolitionists successfully limited access to a continuous, inexpensive stream of fresh slaves to replace those who died, usually within seven years. In North America, the slave trade developed about 100 years later, yet the preference for males remained until the early seventeenth century. Then American masters sought men and women and encouraged slaves to reproduce themselves in family units.[10]

Reproduction as a function of enslaved women remains a controversy, especially among African-Americanists, when it comes to the issue of enslaved women resisting reproductive functions imposed upon them by masters. Some scholars of African-American history, who look to the prestigious role of the African woman as mother, argue that deliberate attempts to limit reproduction or to abort fetuses by enslaved women appear contrary to African values. Nonetheless, the literature about

Africa and the United States indicates evidence of abortive practices among slave women.[11]

Although African-Americanists debate about whether abortion was atypical of women enslaved in the United States because African women brought their beliefs about the value of children and motherhood with them, we can now presume that there were two statuses for traditional African women during the height of the African slave trade—free and non-free women who were slaves or pawns. The evidence has yet to reveal how many of the women who were brought to the Western hemisphere were captured as free women or were previously slaves before being shipped to the Americas. Values about motherhood would have been influenced by previous status.

Enslaved women in both Africa and in the Americas had no control over their offspring. In Zaire and in the western Sudan, the birthrate among slave women was considerably lower than the birthrate among free women.[12] In the plantation South of the United States, however, slave women bore more children than free white women. Nonetheless, slaves appeared to have limited conception to a later time than hoped for by their masters. Black women were often able to restrict pregnancy for several years after reaching puberty, despite masters' attempts to have them breed earlier as their life cycle enabled them.[13]

Several issues still remain: Did overwork, disease and poor diet—conditions prevalent among enslaved women universally—lead to miscarriages and spontaneous abortions, or did some slaves practice abortion by use of herbs and roots? Similarly, did victimization leave women little control over their bodies, or did some enslaved women make rebellious choices about bringing children into the master's world, a world which the women could not otherwise control?

COMPARATIVE HISTORICAL RECONSTRUCTION

Earlier in this discussion we looked at several questions about enslaved women and about their relationship to the master-class. Answers to these questions are essential for establishing a framework for the historical reconstructive process cross-culturally. The published data about female slavery in Africa, in the United States, and in Latin America/the Caribbean can give us only partial answers to these reconstruction processes. Nonetheless, these factors can provide clues to the direction future research about Black women and slavery should take.

Perceptions about race and color have been established as factors to consider in reconstructing women's attitudes and responses to slavery. The numerical relationship between Black slaves and white masters often influenced these perceptions. Data about these numerical relationships are available for New World societies, where, unlike Africa, racial differences were significant, thus influencing self-perception as well as culture. In the Caribbean, during most of the Atlantic slave trade period, Africans and their descendants outnumbered white masters. A population survey of the British West Indies in 1791 reveals that in ten of the twelve British-held islands, Blacks outnumbered whites by almost ninety percent. In Jamaica, for example, the white population estimate was 30,000, while Blacks numbered about 250,000. Of the Blacks, 10,000 were believed to be free, leaving a slave population of about 240,000. During this period, masters and the colonial government encouraged the slave women to reproduce; therefore imports of African women increased. Although at this point it is difficult to estimate the numbers of female slaves in Jamaica, it is clear that Blacks were in the majority and that most of them lived on plantations where their interaction with whites was minimal. As a result, the impact of the master-class culture was less significant than it would be for women enslaved in Bermuda, where whites comprised fifty-two percent of the population.[14]

In turning to another English-speaking slave society of the time, the United States represented what Graham Irwin calls the "white settler society of the temperate zones."[15] In societies such as

this, whites outnumbered Africans significantly and European culture was re-created with modifications. Most of North America and the Spanish-speaking slave societies of Argentina and Chile fell into this category. In these areas, the white population overwhelmed the Black; hence, the impact of the master-class culture was significant. Even in areas like the plantation South in the United States during the antebellum period, where Blacks comprised somewhat more than fifty percent of the population, Euro-American culture could not be ignored by slaves. In comparing the culture and self-perception of enslaved Black women in New World societies, the impact of the master-class culture must be considered, for mainstream standards of beauty, family organization, and women's worth often clashed with African standards. Influence variables include not only the percentage of whites and Blacks, but the degree to which the master-class attempted to assimilate slaves into the mainstream. In the United States, as in most English-speaking societies, the effort was discouraged, whereas in Spanish-speaking countries such as Argentina and Chile, assimilation was ultimately encouraged. The assimilation of Blacks makes it difficult to reconstruct the culture of female slaves, because retaining elements of the African past was not rewarded by the mainstream society.

Other related factors for comparative consideration are the role of free women in the master-class, the extent to which female slaves assimilated into the society of the master-class, and how female slaves fit into the kinship structure of the society. For these comparisons we can look first to Africa, where free African women often owned and usually supervised the work, the rewards and the punishment of slave women. The available studies, however, dwell more upon the ways in which mistresses victimized their slaves rather than upon the socialization and assimilation process of slave women by free women.[16] Since female slaves were valued for their ability to become more assimilated into their master's society than male slaves, the process must have been initiated with the free women who supervised the slave women. In addition, as wives and concubines, slaves were part of the master's compound, as were his free wives. Networking for survival was essential to these food producers and child-rearers, who may have established fictive kinship relationships. Even if the free wives did not establish support systems with enslaved women, female slaves probably did. Just because a slave woman was considered kinless in the eyes of the master's lineage does not mean that she did not relate to other female slaves, especially those enslaved at the same time as she was, thus experiencing the same initiation into the community of the master.[17]

For the United States, free women of the master-class may have worked closely with slave women if the master owned a small farm and one or two slaves, who contributed to the upkeep of the household, including family and surplus food production. However, if the mistress was the wife of a plantation owner, she did no manual labor, but probably supervised household slaves. Nonetheless, white slaveholding masters held the final word about the treatment of slaves. Assimilation and socialization on plantations were left to the individuals in the slave community, not to the mistresses, who rarely had contact with field slaves who worked in agricultural production.

On many plantations young female slaves entering puberty often worked in squads of slave women in the fields. The squads were called "trash gangs," and were comprised also of pregnant women and older women who could not do the intensive labor other female slaves and male slaves performed. In the "trash gangs" younger slave women learned from the elders about work, plantation survival, male-female relations, motherhood and networking.[18] Kinship included blood relations and fictive kin—all providing the extended kinship relationships, the concept of which originated for African-Americans in Africa, but practices were adapted and transformed by the realities of New World slavery. The studies about plantation slavery in the United States, however, deal with the antebellum period or the first half of the nineteenth century, when the sex ratio among the slaves was nearly equal. Here the use of a time perspective is important to determine what types of kinship and assimilation practices occurred during the eighteenth century and earlier.

The emphasis upon lineage among Africans, who distinguished slaves as kinless people, appears totally different from family structure in New World societies. Yet slaves throughout the diaspora, whether in alien environments on the African continent or in the Western hemisphere, constructed survival mechanisms, including modified kinship structures, which retained values and elements of African family life.[19]

The final factor is female resistance to slavery or slave status. Both on the African continent and in New World societies there is evidence of both covert and overt female resistance. Abortion and the refusal to conceive children are covert forms previously discussed. Overt resistance took the form of running away or open revolt. African women enslaved on the continent escaped and protested slave status to higher authorities. On slave ships crossing the Atlantic from Africa, African women were known to assist in slave revolts. In the Caribbean, slave women participated in Maroon communities of runaways, where resistance to re-enslavement was an ever-present threat. In the United States slave women participated in the Underground Railroad and in open rebellion. Women such as these were revered for their wisdom, leadership and courage. The memory of their deeds has been passed down by women during slavery and in the post-slavery eras. Studies about female slave resistance and protest against slave status provide views of women's choices about the acceptance or the rejection of victimization.[20]

FUTURE RESEARCH

Much has to be done to prepare the theoretical framework, to select the factors for historical reconstruction, but most importantly, to collect the data needed for the various diaspora societies to be studied. For some areas, much of the groundwork has been established, but for others, especially key countries like Brazil, very little scholarly work about female slaves has been published by historians in either Portuguese or English.

Scholars have choices about using a female perspective or not. Hopefully, those who consider African diaspora women's history will choose a female perspective. Writing about women does not guarantee a feminist interpretation, especially in this case if the focus avoids the interaction among slave women themselves, or the survival mechanisms female slaves adopted and implemented. For the United States and Africa, the use of slave testimony by women, though infrequent, is producing data banks that can be used for cross-cultural analysis.[21] Sources of this kind are not readily available for Latin America/the Caribbean, but should be sought out.[22] Finally, challenges that re-define or reverse previous interpretations about women in African, Latin America/Caribbean, and African-American histories are important when the research has been carefully and thoroughly conducted and evaluated.

NOTES

1. Filomina Chioma Steady, ed. 1981. *The Black woman cross-culturally*. Cambridge: Schenkman.

2. Steady, Introduction and Overview, pp. 1–41.

3. Joseph E. Harris, ed. 1982. *Global dimensions of the African diaspora*. Washington: Howard University Press, pp. 3–5.

4. Claire Robertson and Martin A. Klein, eds. 1983. *Women and slavery in Africa*. Madison: University of Wisconsin Press.

5. Deborah Gray White. 1985. *A'rn't I a woman? Female slaves in the plantation South*. New York: Norton.

6. Paul E. Lovejoy. 1983. *Transformations in slavery: A history of slavery in Africa*. Cambridge: Cambridge University Press, pp. 25–27.

7. Herbert S. Klein. 1983. African women in the Atlantic Slave Trade. In Claire Robertson and Martin A. Klein, eds., *Women and Slavery in Africa*, pp. 29–39.

8. Klein, pp. 34–37; John Thornton. 1983. Sexual demography: The impact of the slave trade on family structure, pp. 45–46; Martin A. Klein, Women in slavery in the Western

Sudan, pp. 68–77. Both in Claire Robertson and Martin A. Klein, eds., *Women and Slavery in Africa*.

9. Claire C. Robertson and Martin A. Klein. Women's Importance in African Slave Systems, in *Women and Slavery in Africa*, p. 10.

10. White, pp. 67–69.

11. Herbert G. Gutman. 1976. *The Black family in slavery and freedom, 1750–1925*. New York: Pantheon, p. 60, fn l; Darlene Clark Hine and Kate Wittenstein, Female slave resistance: The economics of sex, in Filomina Chioma Steady, ed., *The Black woman cross-culturally*, pp. 292–95; Robert Harms, Sustaining the system: Trading towns along the Middle Zaire, in Claire Robertson and Martin A. Klein, eds., *Women and Slavery in Africa*, pp. 105–7; White, pp. 85–88.

12. Klein, Women in slavery in the Western Sudan, p. 73; Harms, p. 105.

13. White, pp. 97–99.

14. Population of the British West Indies, 1791, in Graham W. Irwin, ed., 1971. *Africans abroad: A documentary history of the Black Diaspora in Asia, Latin America, and the Caribbean during the Age of Slavery*. New York: Columbia University Press, pp. 202–203.

15. The Experience of Slavery in *Africans abroad*, p. 185.

16. Klein, pp. 84–86; Harms, pp. 100–102.

17. Marcia Wright, Bwanikwa: Consciousness and protest among slave women in Central Africa, 1886–1911. In Claire Robertson and Martin A. Klein, eds., *Women and Slavery in Africa*, pp. 255–58.

18. White, p. 95.

19. Niara Sudarkasa. 1981. Interpreting the African heritage in Afro-American family organization. In Harriette Pipes McAdoo, ed., *Black Families*. Beverly Hills: Sage, pp. 44–48.

20. Wright, pp. 250–66; White, pp. 62–64; Kenneth Bilby and Filomina Chioma Steady, Black women and survival: A Maroon case, in Filomina Chioma Steady, ed., *The Black woman cross-culturally*, pp. 451–65; Rosalyn Terborg-Penn. 1986. Black women in resistance: A cross-cultural perspective, in Gary V. Okihiro, ed., *In resistance: Studies in African. Caribbean, and Afro-American History*. Amherst: University of Massachusetts Press, pp. 250–55.

21. Edward A. Alpers, The story of Swema: Female vulnerability in nineteenth century East Africa. In Claire Robertson and Martin A. Klein, eds., *Women and Slavery in Africa*, pp. 185–200; Sojourner Truth. 1970. *Narrative of Sojourner Truth: A bondwoman of olden time* (Chicago: Johnson; Elizabeth Keckley. 1968. *Behind the scenes: Thirty years a slave and four years in the White House*. New York: Arno Press and the New York Times; Linda Brent. 1973. *Incidents in the life of a slave girl*. New York: Harcourt Brace Jovanovich.

22. For a study published outside the United States, see (political economist) Rhoda Reddock, 1985. Women and slavery in the Caribbean: A feminist perspective, *Latin American Perspective,* 12 (Winter).

PART TWO

The Dyad

DATING AND SEXUAL PATTERNS

Each unit of the family begins as a dyad, usually two members of the opposite sex who occupy a range of roles based on the stage of their relationship. Historically, the first stage in the process of forming a family has been dating and courtship. Changes in attitudes toward the family have brought about variations in the practice of these behaviors. Among the most marked changes in the dating and courtship system are the differing characteristics of its participants, the changing purpose of dating, and variations in its form. Dating, for instance, now involves not only the very young; the increasing numbers of individuals who remain unmarried until fairly advanced ages means that a dating partner could as easily be 38 as 18. Spiraling divorce and low remarriage rates create another large pool of dating partners. Dating has also become time contained, often existing only for the moment for sexual or recreational purposes and is no longer automatically presumed to be a prelude to courtship or marriage. Even the concept of dating has been modified as men and women get together without making formal arrangements for an evening out in a public setting.

Much of this description is relevant to the White middle class, which has developed a new ideology about the nature and content of the dating system. There are limitations to the generalizations we can make about Black dating because there is less literature on the subject. The practice of Black dating varies by region, epoch, and social class. In the past, when Blacks formed a small, cohesive community in the rural and urban South, what might be called dating behavior centered on the neighborhood, church, and school. In general it was a casual process where men and women met, formed emotional attachments, and later married. Most of the participants were members of larger social units whose members or reputation were generally known to the community. As Blacks moved into urban areas outside of the South, the anonymity of individuals in these settings modified dating patterns. The school and house party became centers for fraternizing between the sexes, particularly among the lower class. In the middle-class group, dating habits took on the characteristics of mainstream culture as they included more activities like movies, dances, or bowling.

Black sexuality is another area of Black family life neglected in the literature. This is particularly difficult to understand in light of the special role accorded to Blacks—that of a peculiarly desirable or essentially different sexual object. Yet, although we have witnessed a full-blown sexual revolution, at least in the media, a reliable study of Black sexuality is hard to find. Blacks rarely are included in the many studies on White sexual attitudes and behavior. The paucity of past research on Black sexuality makes it difficult to assess what, if any, changes have occurred as a result of the fundamental transformation of sexual attitudes and practices occurring among the general population.

We do know that historically Black sexuality differed from its white counterpart in a number of ways. This difference began with the African and European conceptions of the nature of human sexuality. While Europeans traditionally have viewed sex as inherently sinful, Africans have viewed it as a natural function that should be enjoyed. These contrasting views may suggest a dichotomy of permissiveness versus puritanism. However, within the African continent a wide range of sexual codes and practices coexisted, differing from the European sexual traditions in the secular basis for the code as well as in the belief that sex is a natural function for humans.

Slavery exercised another influence on Afro-American sexuality. Women in bondage, unlike their White counterparts, had no way to protect their sexual purity. This fact has led to the assumption that because Black women could not be accorded any respect for, or defense of, their sexual integrity, it failed to have any strong value for them. Although such an assumption might be logical, it ignores the existence of moral codes related to sex in the Black community that, although different from mainstream norms, do regulate sexual activity for both men and women.

GENDER ROLES

In recent years, the issue of sex roles and their definition has received much attention. The debate has centered on the issue of female subordination and male dominance and privilege, but Blacks have considerably different problems with their sex role identities. They must first overcome certain disabilities based on racial membership, not gender affiliation. However, this does not mean that sex role identities within the Black community do not carry with them advantages and disadvantages. In many ways they do, but instead of fighting over the question of who is the poorest of the poor, Blacks must contend with the plaguing problems of an unemployment rate that is as high as 45 percent among Black men. Correlates of that central problem are the declining life expectancy rate of Black men and rises in drug abuse, suicide, crime, and educational failures. These facts do not warrant much support for a movement to equalize the condition of men and women in the Black community.

Along with the economic conditions that impinge on their role performance, Black men are saddled with a number of stereotypes that label them as irresponsible, criminalistic, hypersexual, and lacking in masculine traits. Some of these stereotypes become self-fulfilling prophecies because the structure of the dominant society prevents many Black men from achieving the goals of manhood. At the same time, the notion of the castrated Black male is largely a myth. While mainstream culture has deprived many Black men of the economic wherewithal for normal masculine functions, most of them function in such a way as to gain the respect of their mates, children, and communities.

Along with all the dynamic changes occurring in U.S. society are slow but perceptible alterations in the role of Black women. The implications of these changes are profound given that women are central figures in the family life of Black people. Historically, the Black woman has been a bulwark of strength in the Black community. From the time of slavery onward, she has resisted the destructive forces she has encountered in American society. During the period of slavery she fought and survived the attacks on her dignity by the slave system, relinquished the passive role ascribed to members of her gender to ensure the survival of he people, and tolerated the culturally induced irresponsibility of her man in recognition of this country's relentless attempts to castrate him.

Too often the only result of her sacrifices and suffering has been the invidious and inaccurate labeling of her as a matriarch, a figure deserving respect but not love. The objective reality of the Black woman in America is that she occupies the lower rung of the socioeconomic ladder of all sex-race groups and has the least prestige. The double burden of gender and race has put her in the category of a super-oppressed entity. Considering the opprobrium to which she is sub-jected, one would expect her to be well represented in the woman's liberation movement. Yet that movement remains primarily White and middle class. This is due in part to the class-bound character of the women's movement, which is middle class while most Black women are poor or working class. Their low pro-file in that movement also stems from the fact that many of the objectives of White feminists relate to psychological and cultural factors such as language and sexist behavior, while the Black woman's concerns are economic.

There is a common ground on which Blacks and women can and do meet: on issues like equal pay for equal work, child-care facilities, and female parity in the work force. Instead of joining the predominantly White and middle-class women's movement, many Black women have formed their own organizations such as the Welfare Rights Organization, Black Women Organized for Action, and the Black Feminist Alliance. There is little question that there is a heightened awareness among Black women of the problems they face based on their sex roles alone. Whether the struggle of Black women for equal rights will come in con-flict with the movement for Black liberation remains to be seen. It is fairly clear that Black women have to be freed from the disabilities of both race and sex.

MALE/FEMALE RELATIONSHIPS

Relationships between Black men and Black women have had a peculiar evolu-tion. Unlike the White family, which was a patriarchy and was sustained by the economic dependence of women, the Black dyad in North America has been characterized by more equalitarian roles and economic parity. The system of slav-ery did not permit the Black male to assume the superordinate role in the family condition because the female was not economically dependent on him. Hence relationships between the sexes were based on sociopsychological factors rather than on economic compulsion to marry and remain married. This fact, in part, explains the unique trajectory of Black male-female relationships.

Finding and keeping a mate is complicated by a number of sociopsychologi-cal factors as well as structural restraints. Social structure and individual attitudes interface to make male-female relationships ephemeral rather than permanent. The imbalance in the sex ratio will continue to deny large numbers of profes-sional Black women a comparable mate, and there are only a limited number of ways to deal with that irreversible fact of life. At the same time there exists a pool of professional Black males who are available to this group of women, and the tension between them builds barriers to communicating and mating. This is a complex problem, and there is no easy solution.

Although there are some Black men who are threatened by the successful Black woman, further investigation reveals other underlying forces. Men are torn between the need for security and the desire for freedom, between the quest for a special person to call their own and the temptation of sexual variety. They see marriage as a way of establishing roots but are seduced by the enticement of all the attractive, possibly "better," women in their midst. Given the advantage they have as males in a sexist society, and a high prestige (which is in short supply in the Black community), Black males have little incentive to undertake the actions needed to meet the needs of women. Consequently, women who feel that their emotional needs are not being met begin to recoil and to adopt their own agenda based on a concept of self-interest.

Some recognition must be made of the changing relations between men and women. The old exchange of feminine sexual appeal for male financial support is declining. Women increasingly are able to define their own status and to be economically independent. What they seek now is the satisfaction of emotional needs, not an economic cushion. While men must confront this new reality, women must realize that emotional needs can be taken care of by men in all social classes. Although similar education and income can mean greater compatibility in values and interests, they are no guarantee of this compatibility nor of personal happiness. Common needs, interests, and values are more a function of gender than of class.

We should not be deluded by the ostensible reluctance of many Black singles to enter the conjugal state. People who have not been able to develop a lasting permanent relationship with a member of the opposite sex must make the best of whatever circumstances they have at the moment. The industrial and urban revolution has made singlehood more viable as a way of life, but it has also made the need for belonging more imperative. The tensions of work and the impersonality of the city have created a need to escape depersonalization by retreating into an intimate sanctum. This is especially imperative for Blacks in the middle class who have their personhood tested daily by a racist society and who often must work and live in isolation. In modem society individuals are required to depend on each other for permanence and stability. That function was previously served by a large familial and social network.

The fear that even marriage no longer provides permanence and stability causes people to enter and exit relationships quickly. The fear of failure comes from failure. Until Black singles develop the tenacity to work at relationships as they did at schooling and jobs, we will continue to see this vicious cycle repeated again and again. Marriage and the family continue to be the most important buffer for Blacks against racism and depersonalization. When we look at the strongest predictors of happiness in the United States, they are inevitably social factors such as marriage, family, friends, and children. Across the board, married people tend to be happier than unmarrieds. The best confirmation of this fact is that most people who divorce eventually remarry. Before people can find happiness in a marriage, they have to form a strong basis for marriage. That task continues to perplex Black singles.

We are all aware that marriages are very fragile nowadays. Fewer people are getting married and the divorce rate in the United States is at an all-time high. It is estimated that the majority of marriages no longer will last a lifetime. Many forces are responsible for this changing pattern, including changing attitudes and laws on divorce, changing and conflicting definitions of sex roles and their functions in the family, economic problems, and personality conflicts. The increase in divorce cuts across racial and class lines, but divorce is still more pronounced among Blacks. Only one out of every three Black couples will remain married longer than ten years.

It is not easy to pinpoint unique causes of Black marital dissolution because they are similar to those for their White counterparts. In some cases, the severity of the problems they face are the difference. Economic problems are a major factor in marital conflicts, and there are three times as many Blacks with incomes below the poverty level as Whites. The tensions Blacks experience in coping with the pervasive incidents of racism often have their ramifications in the marital arena. A peculiar problem Blacks face is the imbalanced sex ratio, which places many women in competition for the available males. Too often the males they compete for are not available, and this places serious pressure on many Black marriages.

At the same time, many Blacks are involved in functional marriages. Many adult Blacks are married and have positive and loving relationships with their spouses. Unfortunately, practically no research exists on marital adjustment and satisfaction among Blacks. What little research we have does indicate that Black wives are generally less satisfied with their marriages than are White wives. But the source of their dissatisfaction is often associated with the problems of poverty and racism.

BLACK-WHITE RELATIONSHIPS

Interracial dating and marriage continue to captivate the interest of Americans of all races. Among groups other than Blacks and Whites, it is no longer a novelty. In some California counties, a majority of Asian women are in outmarriages. Only among Black Americans is the percentage of outmarriages lower than five percent. The reasons why are varied, but include the greater amount of spatial segregation in the Black community. Studies have also consistently shown that Black Americans are the least socially acceptable of the major racial groups in the United States, indicating that White, even Asian, resistance, to Blacks is greater than to other non-White groups. Given the current racial divide, it is realistic to expect interracial marriages to be low in the Afro-American community. Increases might be incremental and might be significant in outmarriages to other people of color in the twenty-first century.

3

Dating and Sexual Patterns

Sociocultural Factors Affecting Sexual Risk-Taking in African American Men and Women: Results from Two Empirical Studies

GAIL E. WYATT, HECTOR F. MYERS, KIMLIN ASHING-GIWA, & RAMANI DURVASULA

INTRODUCTION

In the past decade, we have witnessed a marked increase in the attention given to the sexual attitudes, knowledge, beliefs and behaviors of African Americans. This attention is due, in large part, to the growing recognition of the shift in the populations of greatest risk for HIV-1 infection and AIDS from gay White males to African American and Latino men, women and children (CDC, 1997). Current evidence indicates that between the ages of 25 to 44, Black women and men constitute the group at greatest risk for HIV infection, and are one of the groups at disproportionate risk for other STDs (CDC, 1997). Of particular concern are young adults and adolescents who continue to engage in high risk behaviors, despite growing recognition in the Black community that HIV is no longer a disease of gay White males (d'Ardenne, 1996). Women between the ages of 49 and 50 are also at risk because they may be divorced or widowed and do not fully understand how to prevent diseases from being transmitted (CDC, 1 997). Thus, this increased attention on Black sexual attitudes and behavior is an attempt to understand the shift in the pattern of infection risk in the population, as well as to inform the design of appropriate prevention programs.

Despite the increased attention, however, the empirical literature on African American sexuality continues to be limited, and suffers from many conceptual and methodological limitations. For example, many studies are largely

Affiliations: Wyatt and Durvasula, Department of Psychiatry, University of California, Los Angeles; Myers, Department of Psychology, University of California, Los Angeles; Ashing-Giwa, California School of Professional Psychology, Los Angeles. Preparation of this chapter was supported in part by Grants No. R0l MH 48269 and R0l MH 00269–16 to the first author from the National Institute of Mental Health, and by Grant No. DA06597 from the National Institute on Drug Abuse (NIDA) to the second author. From a previously unpublished paper, 1998. Reprinted by permission.

comparative in nature (i.e., focus on describing Black-White differences in sexual behaviors), and as such emphasize similarities and differences in discrete behaviors between the groups, but fail to investigate the diversity of experiences and behaviors within groups. Also, while it is useful to identify group differences in the risk behaviors of interest, it is even more important to understand the sociocultural contexts that contribute to these differences, especially for the ultimate goal of behavior change.

In addition, because the primary concern is often to understand pathways of HIV infection, many studies on Black sexual behaviors compare "high risk" groups within the community (e.g., street IDUs, gays and bisexuals who frequent gay bars, men and women who attend STD clinics, persons in drug and alcohol treatment programs, college students, inner-city teens, etc.), but few include large, diverse community samples who differ in HIV risk. While targeting high risk groups is both necessary and cost-effective in light of the AIDS epidemic, the sexual attitudes, beliefs and behaviors of these high risk groups cannot be interpreted as "representative" of African American adults.

Perhaps the most important conceptual limitation in the extant literature on African American sexuality, however, is the relative dearth of studies that place these behaviors in their appropriate sociocultural and psychosocial contexts. For example, while it is important to be able to document risk behaviors, it is even more important to understand what factors contribute to their occurrence, what factors maintain them, and what points of leverage might be used to change them (Wyatt, 1994; Jemmott, et al., 1995). Of particular relevance here are those factors that shape sexual decision-making within the context of relationships or the absence thereof (Wyatt and Riederle, 1994).

Finally, there are a host of methodological issues that arise when assessing sexual behaviors across ethnocultural groups. For example, cultural rules governing the disclosure of a variety of sexual attitudes and beliefs and the language

of sexuality varies across groups (Bowser, 1994; Mays, et al., 1992; Mays and Cochran, 1990). Thus, the language, type of questions asked, and the training of interviewers who are administering structured interviews of sexual behaviors to African Americans and other ethnic minorities can influence the validity of the findings obtained (Mays and Jackson, 1991; Wyatt, 1991).

The next generation of studies of Black sexuality will need to address these issues if we are to advance the quality and utility of the empirical evidence available to us.

In the present chapter, we will offer a conceptual framework for thinking about African American male and female sexuality that considers cultural, socioeconomic and structural factors that shape sexual socialization, then we report the results of two studies of sexual risk behaviors in African American men and women—The Los Angeles Women's Project (LAWP) and the African American Health Project (AAHP). Implications of the findings from these situations and directions for future research that will be needed to advance the field will be discussed.

THE SOCIOCULTURAL CONTEXT OF AFRICAN AMERICAN FEMALE SEXUALITY

There are three major factors that influence African American women's sexuality and the behaviors they willingly engage in: Sexual socialization; economic dependence and structural influences on partner availability; and cultural beliefs about sex and relationships.

Sexual Socialization of African American Women

How women were taught to view their sexuality and how they are to behave sexually are important aspects often overlooked in sex research. Sexual socialization influences how individuals think and feel about sex (Wyatt and Ashing-

Giwa, 1994; Yarber and Greer, 1986). One of the primary tasks for adult women, regardless of serostatus, is procreation (White, 1984; Wyatt, 1994). The status of motherhood and fatherhood are almost synonymous with those of womanhood and manhood (White, 1984). Sexual socialization can influence women's comfort in discussing sex with others including partners, deference to their partners' initiation of sex and reasons for engaging or not engaging in a variety of sexual behaviors, as well (Wyatt, 1997). Women's gender and sexual roles are taught in childhood, reinforced during adolescence, and sometimes realized optimally through marriage or a committed relationship in adulthood (Norris and Ford, 1991).

Research indicates that African American women's sexual socialization emphasizes no sexual knowledge, no sexual contact before marriage and a preference for vaginal-penile sex as a primary source of gratification (Tucker and Taylor, 1989; Wyatt, 1982, 1997). A woman's sexuality is often defined through her relationship with her partner and she is expected to be sexual only in the context of that relationship (Norris and Ford, 1991). More importantly, sexual socialization dictates that African American women should comply with their partners' sexual needs and value their partners' pleasure over their own (Holland, Ramazonoglu, Sharpe, and Thompson, 1992; Wyatt, 1997). Relinquishing sexual control and fostering sexual submissiveness are primary components of women's sexual socialization which are also culturally sanctioned. (Amaro, 1995; Wyatt, 1997). Thus, women's sexual socialization has resulted in a lack of emphasis on women taking responsibility for their own bodies in order to avoid negative outcomes such as unintended pregnancies and STDs including HIV (Wyatt, 1991, 1997).

Socio-Structural and Economic Factors

Among African Americans, single women have lower personal incomes than married women even when their educational backgrounds are the same (Tucker, 1989). Several studies report that socioeconomic conditions affect sexual-risk-taking and the perceived ability to change behavior (Gasch, Poulson, Fullilove, and Fullilove, 1991; McCoy and Inciardi, 1993). According to 1993 Census data, Black families supported by mothers with children had a median income of $10,380—which is below the poverty level. Further, since 1970, the proportion of children living with one parent (usually the mother) increased from 32 percent to 58 percent (Bennett, 1994). These figures indicate that women and children's economic dependence decrease the likelihood that women may make sex-related decisions that are independent of their partners' approval, especially if the partner makes financial contributions to the family. Cultural standards and economic necessity dictate that women seek relationships with partners who can provide some financial support. Therefore, African American women may be highly motivated to seek a partner, and those who are economically disenfranchised may be more vulnerable to enter into risky relationships in the process (Jemmott, Catan, Nyamathi, and Anastasia, 1995; Ulin, 1992).

Relationship status is also related to other distinctive feature of African American life, i.e., African American women marry later and are less likely to ever marry than women in any other major ethnic group in the United States (Tucker and Mitchell-Kernan, 1995). The decline in the number of eligible Black men has severely limited the pool of potential partners who share cultural values around marriage and family. Further, the divorce rate of African Americans is triple that of the general population, and they are less likely to remarry after divorce. These trends are due, in large part, to the declining availability of African American men for marriage as a consequence of higher male mortality and the decreased economic viability of poorly educated Black men (Tucker and Mitchell-Kernan, 1995). African American women are therefore likely to spend substantial portions of their adult lives outside of marriage.

Sociocultural Factors

The concept of interconnectedness in African American culture is based on the notion that individuals are linked together so that perceptions of individual identity and purpose are defined through the group (Baldwin, 1984; Greene, 1994, Nobles, 1986). Akbar (1979) described this attribute in the phrase "I am because we are." This concept of interconnectedness is comparable to self-in-relation theory posited in psychology. The basic tenant of the "self-in-relation" theory is that a woman's identity or self-definition is created by and exists through her relationships (Miller, 1991; Surrey, 1991).

While individuals are often dependent on family support for their acceptance and affirmation, for many women, the expression of interconnectedness is most meaningful within an intimate relationship that includes intense emotional ties and loyalty to one's partner. Traditional cultural and religious beliefs do not reinforce planning for sex or contraceptive use, because to plan sex represents a conscious decision to violate standards of acceptable behavior. Selection and use of contraceptives can vary with ethnicity, age, marital status, income, plans for children, past experience with contraceptives, or partner support or resistance to contraceptive use (Wyatt, 1997).

An interesting contrast of contraceptive patterns is highlighted by ethnic group comparisons. For example, African American women were twice as likely not to use any form of contraception currently compared to White women (Wyatt and Riederle, 1994), and two times more likely not to have ever used any contraceptive. Additionally, among those African American women using a contraceptive, the birth control pill was most commonly reported.

Finally, another important aspect of sexuality about which we know little is the degree to which women are socialized to touch their bodies. While body touching may be an important antecedent to contraceptive patterns and condom use, it is not culturally condoned nor endorsed by most religious groups (Wyatt, 1997). However, life long patterns of infrequent body touching may interfere with safer sex intervention programs that require touching of oneself or one's partner (Wyatt and Riederle, 1994). Wyatt (1991) found that African American women tend to engage less in body touching and masturbation than their White peers, and generally are more conservative in terms of sexual behavior.

These three factors increase women's sexual risk-taking and need to be incorporated into studies of African American women's sexuality.

THE SOCIOCULTURAL CONTEXT OF AFRICAN AMERICAN MALE SEXUALITY

There is growing interest in and attention to the sexual attitudes, beliefs and behaviors of African American men, especially in response to their recognized disproportionate prevalence of sexually transmitted diseases (d'Ardenne, 1996) and risk for HIV infection (CDC, 1997). Most of the studies to date have focused their attention on ethnic differences in sexual behaviors (Samuels, 1997; Johnson, et al., 1994; Catania, et al., 1992), on the sexual behaviors of gays and bisexuals (Peterson, et al., 1995; Stokes, Venable, and McKirnan, 1996; McKirnan, et al., 1995; Doll, et al., 1992), on the risk behaviors of inner-city IDUs (Friedman, et al., 1993; Kim, et al., 1993), and on the attitudes, beliefs and sexual behaviors of Black teens and college students (Gilmore, DeLamater, and Wagstaff, 1996; Johnson., Douglas, and Nelson, 1992; Jemmott and Jemmott, 1990, 1992).

While there is substantial justification for attending to sexual risk behaviors in African American men in the context of HIV/AIDS risk, there is growing recognition of the need to understand the broader psychosocial context of African American male sexuality. Both conceptual and methodological limitations in the studies to date have hampered these efforts. For example, most studies have indicated that despite being one of the groups at highest risk for HIV infection, high risk sexual practices continue to be prevalent in this population, especially among young gays and bisexuals, and among injection drug users. Risk reduction education efforts have yielded some beneficial results, at least in improving knowledge about HIV risk especially among the more educated, but these efforts have yielded limited results among the less educated and those at greatest risk. Efforts to explain these results have been hampered by the limited conceptual perspectives we have taken in addressing these questions, and the failure to appreciate both the variety of sexual attitudes and beliefs of Black men, the cultural rules governing disclosure of sexual behaviors and the language of sexuality used (Bowser, 1994; Mays, et al., 1992; Mays and Cochran, 1990). For example, Bowser (1994) noted that Black men's sexuality is quite varied, and its expression is conditioned over the life course and by the Black men's socioeconomic status and participation in mainstream economy. A central implication of these findings is that the picture of Black male sexuality that we obtain is likely influenced by the generation and social class of the sample of men studied. Unfortunately, and as a predictable consequence of our focus on sexual risk behaviors in the context of HIV/AIDS, much less information is available about "normative" sexual beliefs, attitudes and behaviors of Black men, especially as a function of the relationships in which these behaviors occur.

The study of Black male sexuality is further complicated by the limited attention we have given to methodological issues involved in sex research with this population. For example, African American men are often unwilling to identify as gay or bisexual even when they acknowledge having sex with men. Whether or not they identify as gay or bisexual appears to be influenced by the reasons for these sexual contacts (e.g., pleasure vs. in exchange for money, drugs, or other goods), the context in which these behaviors occur (e.g., while incarcerated vs. in bars, clubs or other areas frequented by male prostitutes), and the role played during the sex act (e.g., being the receptive vs. the insertive partner). Therefore,

there are likely to be discrepancies between what an African American man does and how he identifies his sexual orientation.

Sexual behaviors are also influenced by the nature of the relationship in which these behaviors occur. Therefore, factors such as whether men are in a casual or committed relationship, their relationship history, the history of the current relationship, and the degree of satisfaction with the relationship are also likely to influence what sexual behaviors are reported. For example, there is substantial evidence indicating greater sexual experimentation and more risky sexual behaviors in men who are single and unattached, low SES and non-religious. These men are more likely to have multiple sexual partners, to have sex with strangers, to experiment more sexually, and to have sex under the influence or alcohol and/or drugs than those in committed relationships (Myers, 1997). Recent evidence suggest some Black-White differences in these behaviors, with Black men somewhat more likely to report beginning sexual activities are at earlier age, participating in high risk sexual activity more frequently and with more sexual partners than White men (Samuels, 1997; Graves and Hines, 1997; Peterson, et al., 1993).

A growing number of studies have also begun investigating ethnic differences in attitudes and behaviors among gay and bisexual men. These studies indicate that African American men who had sex with men were more likely that their White counterparts to perceive their neighbors as more critical and less accepting of homosexual behavior, to identify as bisexual rather than homosexual, to have had fewer male sexual partners, to report more insertive anal sex, and to have exchanged sex for money or drugs. On the other hand, they were less likely to report receptive oral sex with men, to report their homosexual behavior to any female sexual partners, and to be less involved in the gay community (Stokes et al., 1996; McKirnan. et al., 1995; Doll, et al., 1992).

These issues point to the need for more systematic research on the sexual attitudes, beliefs and behaviors of African American women and men.

AFRICAN AMERICAN WOMEN'S SEXUAL DECISION MAKING: RESULTS FROM THE LA WOMEN PROJECT

Sample Selection

Stratified probability sampling was used to recruit comparable samples of African American, Latina, and White American women, 18 to 50 years of age in Los Angeles County, as part of a larger study of women's sexual decision-making in 1992–1993. The sample was obtained through random digit telephone dialing procedures in Los Angeles County conducted by the Institute of Social Science Research at the University of California, Los Angeles. The study sample included 305 African American women. To be eligible to participate, they had to identify themselves ethnically as an African-American/Black and have lived in the United States for at least the first six years of their lives to ensure that they were socialized about sexuality in America. Of the 305 African American women, those who had not been sexually active within the year prior to the interview (n = 37) were all included for the study. Thus, a total of 305 African American women, 217 of whom were single and 88 of them married or cohabitating and all of them reportedly HIV-negative, were included in this study. For additional information about the sample and sampling procedures, please see Wyatt, et al., (1998).

Procedure

Each participant was interviewed face-to-face by a trained female interviewer of the same ethnicity at the participant's location of choice (her home, UCLA, or another location). The interviews ranged in length from three to eight hours and were tape-recorded to ensure the accuracy of the interviewer's transcription of responses during data collection. Respondents were paid $32 for their time and given referral information for mental health services upon request (fewer than 5 percent of the sample requested this information).

Instrumentation

The Los Angeles Structured Interview (LASI) consists of 913 open- and closed-ended items designed to obtain both retrospective and current data about women's sexual socialization, sexual and physical abuse, sexual attitudes, practices, and risk-taking, as well as contraception and reproduction. For additional information on the measure, see Wyatt (1998). Reliability was established for various portions of the LASI. Interrater reliability (using the kappa coefficient), established on a weekly basis among 30 interviewers, averaged .95.

Description of the Sample

African American women had had a mean age of 34 years and were moderately well educated (13 years). Over one in four were married (29 percent), 50 percent were employed full time and 18 percent were unemployed. Of those who worked, 47 percent were in technical/administrative positions. Six percent had been homeless.

Age of First Intercourse

African American women reported age 17 as the mean age of intercourse and 38 percent used some form of birth control the first time they had sex. The mean age of first use of birth control, however, was age 18 for the sample. The average age of their first partner was 20 (SD 4.47).

Health, Pregnancy, and STD History

African American women reported going to the doctor between 6 months to 1 year, primarily for a pap smear. Women had an average of 3.4 pregnancies, of which 2.2 were unintended. Yeast infections (71 percent), Trichomoniasis (24 percent), Gonorrhea (11 percent) and pelvic inflammatory disease (8 percent) were the most common sexually transmitted diseases reported by these women.

The Importance of Relationships

We found that 94 percent of the women in their current sample indicated that being in a long-term relationship was important. Additionally, importance of being in a relationship did not vary by marital status, age, income or education $(F (4,174) = 2.04, p = 0.09)$. Further, 86 percent stated that it was very important for both the woman and the man to be faithful to each other.

Women's Risky Sexual Behavior

Regarding the number of sexual partners in the past year, 12 percent stated that they had no sexual partner, 69 percent stated that they had one partner, and 19 percent indicated that they had more than one partner. These women reported poor and inconsistent condom use: 42 percent indicated that they never use condoms with partners, 35 percent stated that they rarely use condoms and 23 percent stated that they almost always use condoms. When asked about condom use at last sexual intercourse, 23 percent stated that they did and 77 percent reported that they did not use a condom the last time they had sex. However, 53 percent reported that they had been tested for HIV in the past 12 months.

Little additional sexual risk-taking was reported by these women: 2 percent reported injecting drugs, having sex with a prostitute, and engaging in prostitution, 6 percent stated that they currently have sex with more than one partner, and 9 percent reported that they have exchanged sex for money. Regarding drug use while having sex, about 15 percent reported some alcohol use before sex, 8 percent reported marijuana use and 2 percent reported cocaine use in conjunction with sex. Of the women who reported using drugs before sex, 25 percent indicated that both she and her partner decided and 14 percent reported that it was her decision to use the drugs.

A sexually risk taking composite score was generated from the following items: number of sexual partners in the past year, having sex outside the primary relationship, engaging in prostitution, engaging in sex for money, having sex with a prostitute or gigolo, using drugs before sexual activity and injecting drugs. Neither age, marital status, nor income predicted sexual risk-taking $(F (4,174) = 0.78, p < 0.5414)$; however, more educated women were somewhat more likely to report engaging in risky sexual behaviors.

Sexual Practices of Women's Partners

With regards to risky sexual partners, none of the women reported having sex with a man who was HIV positive, only one woman reported having sex with an injecting drug user, only 1 percent reported having sex with a man who had had a blood transfusion, or who had sex with other men, or who engaged in partner swapping. However, 41 percent stated that their partner had been tested for HIV in the past 12 months.

A risky sexual partner composite score was generated from the following items: number of sexual partners in the past year, having a blood transfusion, engaging in sex with other men, ever having been incarcerated, engaging in partner swapping, using injection drugs and testing HIV positive. Marital status, age and income only slightly predicted risky sexual partners, however better educated women were significantly more likely to be associated with having risky sexual partners $(F (4,174) = 2.89, p = 0.02)$.

Women's Self-Pleasuring

The results indicated that 46 percent of the African American women reported that they had masturbated, with more educated women being almost twice as likely to have masturbated than less educated women $(SE = 0.018, OR = 1.943)$. However, only about 10 percent stated that they masturbated with some frequency. The low frequency of self-pleasuring sexual activities in African American women was similar across age, income, and relationship status $(F (4,24) = 0.76, p = 0.517)$.

Sexual Initiation

Women indicated that their male partner's regularly and consistently initiated sex about 80 percent of the time. Neither marital status, income nor education had an impact on sexual initiation ($F(4,167) = 1.45$, $p < 0.2198$); but older women were significantly more likely to report that their partners initiated sexual activity ($p < .03$). Additionally, only 25 percent of African American women regularly initiated sex with their partners. Neither marital status, income nor education had an impact on sexual initiation ($F(4,167) = 0.55$, $p = 0.70$). However, younger women were somewhat, although not significantly, more likely than older women to initiate sex with their partners ($p < 0.08$).

SEXUAL BEHAVIORS OF AFRICAN AMERICAN MEN: RESULTS FROM THE AFRICAN AMERICAN HEALTH PROJECT

The African American Health Project (AAHP)

Our group recently completed a large, federally-funded, collaborative study of African American men impacted by HIV/AIDS. This study, the African American Health Project (AAHP) was designed to investigate the neurobehavioral and psychosocial sequelae of HIV/AIDS in a community-resident sample of African American men (Myers, et al., 1997). Specifically, a sample of 502 African American men ages 18–50 who differed by serostatus (HIV+, HIV-), sexual orientation (heterosexual, gay, bisexual), and substance use history were recruited from the greater Los Angeles Metropolitan Area. A comprehensive assessment battery of neuropsychological tests, psychiatric interview, neurological examination, behavioral lifestyle and psychosocial measures was administered by an experienced, primarily African American team of interviewers and examiners.

The sample was relatively young (mean age = 34.5 years) and moderately well educated (mean education = 13.5 years), but with a modest income relative to their education (mean income = $17,764/annum). They were also underemployed (25.3 percent employed full-time or part-time), and living alone (23 percent married or cohabiting). Most of the sample was HIV-negative (63 percent) and 51 percent described themselves as exclusively heterosexual (51 percent), 25 percent identified as gay and 24 percent as bisexual. Slightly more than half of the sample (56 percent) reported using illicit drugs in the past year, especially cannabis (41 percent) and cocaine (36 percent), but very few reported injection drug use (3 percent). Finally, a larger than expected percentage (56 percent) reported a history of STDs.

Of specific relevance to this report are the data collected on sexual lifestyle, which affords us the opportunity to compare the pattern of reported high risk sexual behaviors of African American heterosexual, homosexual and bisexual men. In order to provide a context for these sexual practices, comparisons are reported between those in committed relationships ("attached") versus those who are single and "unattached." In general, homosexuals and bisexuals were significantly more likely to be unattached than the heterosexuals (66 percent and 70 percent vs. 51 percent; $X^2 (2) = 15.5$, $p < .0005$). Analyses testing for demographic differences as a function of sexual orientation and relationship status indicated that the groups did not differ on age, but differed on education ($F (2) = 4.00$, $p < .02$), and income ($F (1) = 13.05$, $p < .0005$). Homosexuals and bisexuals reported having more education than heterosexuals (13.9 years and 13.7 years vs. 13.3 years respectively). Heterosexuals and bisexuals who were in committed relationships had more education than their unattached counterparts, while unattached homosexuals had higher education than their attached counterparts ($F (2) = 4.44$, $p < .01$). Also, and consistent with expectations, unattached men reported lower annual household incomes than those in relationships ($14,479/annum vs. $21,831/annum). Finally, more heterosexuals were employed, at least part-time (35 percent) than homosexuals (30.2 percent) and bisexuals (27.8 percent). This latter difference is partly attributable to the disproportionate representation of the homosexuals and bisexuals among the HIV-infected or with AIDS.

In our review of sexual practices, specific attention is given to those sexual behaviors that place men at increased risk of infection and transmission of HIV-1 and other STDs. Two specific hypotheses are addressed: 1) we expected that men who are in committed relationships would be less likely to engage in high risk sexual behaviors, and 2) that bisexuals, many of whom conceal their sexual orientation and same-sex activities from their partners, would be more likely to engage in more high risk behaviors than their heterosexual and gay counterparts regardless of their relationship status.

Age at First Sexual Experience

Previous studies have reported that African American men typically initiate sexual experiences earlier than White men (Kim et al., 1993). In this sample, the average age of first coitus was 14 years, with significant differences in age of first coitus as a function of sexual orientation and relationship status (F (2) = 3.2, $p < .04$). Gays and bisexuals who were currently in committed relationships reported earlier age of first sexual experience than heterosexuals in committed relationships, while currently unattached heterosexuals reported first coitus at a younger age than unattached gays and bisexuals.

Although not significant, more bisexuals who were currently in committed relationships (63 percent) reported first coitus prior to age 15 than their gay and heterosexual counterparts (47 percent and 46 percent).

Number of Sexual Partners

Research on ethnic differences in number of sexual partners is mixed, while there is greater consistency in the evidence of multiple partnerships

among gays and bisexuals. The men in the current sample reported an average of 7.8 partners in the past year, with gays reporting significantly more partners on average (13.20) than bisexuals (7.38) and heterosexuals (5.24) (F (2,5) = 3.27, p<.04). In addition, those in committed relationships reported significantly fewer partners than those who were unattached (10.2 vs. 4.6) (F (1,5) = 4.34, p<.04). However, the one exception to this rule was among the bisexuals, with the attached bisexuals reporting significantly more partners in the past year than their unattached counterparts (11.3 vs. 5.50) (F (2,5) = 6.02, p<.003).

These findings are confirmed when we look at the percentage of each group who reported having multiple sexual partners, with a larger percentage of gays and bisexuals reporting multiple partners than heterosexuals (62.7 percent and 70.9 percent vs. 58.7 percent), and fewer of those in committed relationships reporting multiple partners than those who were unattached. It is especially noteworthy that while the discrepancy in the percentages of the multiply partnered were striking among heterosexuals and homosexuals, the difference in multiple partnering among the bisexuals was small. Regardless of their relationship status, the majority of bisexuals reported having multiple sexual partners in the past year.

Exchanging Sex for Drugs or Money

A major contributor to risk for sexual transmission of HIV/AIDS is the bartering (i.e., giving or receiving) of drugs or money for sex. Despite growing concerns about HIV/AIDS in the African American community, almost a third of the sample (32.3 percent) reported having had sex for money or drugs. Overall, a larger percentage of bisexuals had sex for money or drugs (79.9 percent) than homosexuals (53.1 percent) and heterosexuals (58.7 percent). Also, as expected and regardless of sexual orientation, a smaller percentage of those in committed relationships reported exchanging sex for money or drugs than those who were unattached (20.3 percent vs. 41.5 percent).

Having Sex While Under the Influence of Alcohol and Drugs

It is generally accepted that having sex under the influence of alcohol and/or recreational drugs confers risk for HIV infection because it impairs judgment, is often associated with engaging in riskier sexual behaviors, and is more likely to occur when having sex with strangers or new sexual partners (Leigh and Stall, 1993; Caetano and Hines, 1995). Overall, a slightly higher percentage of those who were unattached reported having sex always or sometimes under the influence of alcohol and/or drugs than those in committed relationships (33.9 percent vs. 31.6 percent). This was true for homosexuals and bisexuals but not for heterosexuals, where slightly more of those who were attached reported having sex under the influence than their unattached counterparts. This is a somewhat counterintuitive finding, and may reflect the fact that more of the heterosexuals were heavy alcohol and drug users than the homosexuals or that more of the attached heterosexuals had incorporated the use of alcohol and/or drugs into their regular sexual activities with their partner. This finding is intriguing, especially in light of later findings regarding condom use in those in committed relationships and requires further investigation.

Having Sex in Jail

The risk of same sex experiences, both voluntary and coerced is significantly high when incarcerated, and many heterosexuals report having their first same sex experiences in jail. In addition, most of these experiences are unprotected, therefore, they constitute a significant source of transmission of HIV and other STDs. For African American men, this is of particular concern since a disproportionately large percentage of African American men have a history of incarceration. In the present sample, 28 percent of the men reported having been incarcerated, and of those, only a relatively small percentage (17 percent) admitted having had sex in jail. A significantly larger percentage of bisexuals and homosexuals reported having sex in jail than the heterosexuals (17.9 percent and 15.4 percent vs. 1.6 percent), and unattached males regardless of their sexual orientation reported sexual experiences in jail compared to those in committed relationships (21.4 percent vs. 7.2 percent). Because there is likely to be considerable embarrassment in admitting to having sex under these circumstances, especially for the heterosexual men, these figures are likely to be underestimates of the true prevalence of these experiences, and therefore, they should be treated with caution.

Having Sex with Strangers

Another major risk factor for HIV and other STD infections is having sex with strangers. The evidence here is mixed since the available evidence is equivocal with respect to whether condoms of more or less likely to be used when having sex with strangers (Peterson, et al., 1993; Choi, et al., 1994). In any event, participants in the AAHP were queried about having had sex with one or more strangers in the past year, and 15 percent of the sample admitted to doing so. Not surprising, and regardless of sexual orientation, a larger percentage of unattached men reported having sex with strangers than those in committed relationships (21.1 percent vs. 6.4 percent). There were only slight differences in the percentage of those who were unattached who had these experiences, but among those who were in committed relationships, a significantly larger percentage of bisexuals had these experiences than their gay and heterosexual counterparts (17.1 percent vs. 4.7 percent and 4 percent respectively).

Infrequent Use of Condoms

Finally, it is generally accepted that except for abstinence or maintaining a monogamous sexual relationship with an uninfected partner, the only reasonable protection against infection is the consistent and proper use of barrier protection (i.e., condoms). All participants were queried about their use of condoms, and the percentage of those who reported rarely or never using condoms were compared as a function of sexual orientation and relationship status. Previous evidence indicates that persons in ongoing relationships are less likely to use condoms with their primary or regular partner (Messiah and Pelletier, 1996). This is confirmed among the heterosexuals and homosexuals, but not among the bisexuals, where slightly fewer of those in committed relationships reported rarely or never using condoms. This suggests, that while the bisexual men appear to be the group that is the greatest threat to HIV transmission to the African American heterosexual community, more of them engage in protective behavior in their primary relationships, but not in their other sexual relationships.

Cautionary Note

Caution must be exercised in interpreting the findings from the men's study, especially in terms of inferring their generalization to the broader community. The specific objectives of the AAHP required the inclusion of sufficient numbers of African American men who were substance abusers, as well as those who were HIV+ and with full-blown AIDS. As a result, our findings may be more representative of these subgroups of Black men than of the general population of Black men. Nevertheless, these results underscore the need for more basic, normative research on the sexual attitudes, beliefs and behaviors of African American men. Of specific value are studies that take a more comprehensive approach to Black male sexuality using larger study samples that are more representative of men from all walks of life.

DISCUSSION

This chapter describes some of the sexual experiences of Los Angeles community samples of African American women and men ages 18 to 50 that may increase their sexual risks for unintended pregnancies, STDs and HIV. The research grows out a lack of information available that includes some of the cultural factors influencing sexual practices. Heretofore, research on African American sexuality has concentrated on describing primarily high risk behaviors without incorporating background factors, cultural, economic, or structural aspects of relationships that influence these practices. Examining sexual behaviors without a context can result in misattributing risky behaviors to promiscuity, or immorality. These assumptions have, in part, contributed to the lack of attention paid to research describing a variety of sexual experiences some that are risky and others that reflect health promotion among African Americans. The sentiment among far too many researchers, clinicians and public policy makers is that "we know all we need to about Black sexuality." Unfortunately, what is known is based on biased samples who often lack an adequate understanding on how to maintain sexual health. When these individuals do not change their behavior as a result of involvement in prevention or intervention programs, it is often concluded that African Americans are resistant to change. However, another interpretation of resistance to change may be that these programs target behaviors and seldom address the context or circumstances in which they occur, or they recommend behavioral alternatives that are outside of culturally accepted standards for sex.

These findings, however, offer a different perspective. Data from the African American women suggest that most of the sexual practices reported here were not associated with women's demographic characteristics or financial resources. The dynamics of relationships and their perceived importance may influence women's sexual risk-taking, especially if they are economically dependent on a partner. If African Americans value being with a partner, it is possible that the end goal of being interconnected is perceived as justification for some behaviors in order to attain a lasting relationship. Unfortunately, this may include un-protected sex and unwanted outcomes, a high price to pay.

The findings for African American women correspond to dimensions of the Sexual Health and Risk-Taking Model (Wyatt and Ashing-Giwa, 1995). SHM is designed to assess sexual health and risk-taking dimensions for women. Specifically, women's sexual socialization, atti-tudes about interconnectedness, body touching, sexual ownership, taking responsibility for sexual health, sexual judgment (sexual decision mak-ing) and women's sexual practices can increase their risks for unwanted sexual outcomes. The SHM is based on a sociocultural framework that includes concepts from social-learning theory (Bandura, 1986) (sexual socialization, body touching and sexual practices), cognitive theo-ries (Ajzen and Fishbein, 1980) (sexual owner-ship and sexual judgment), and an affective component (Akbar, 1979) (interconnectedness), across the life span. This model helps us to un-derstand the context of sexual health for women that extends beyond HIV prevention to incor-porate all of the risks that women face—preg-nancy, STDs, and HIV. All of these dimensions need to be assessed in order to develop appropri-ate prevention and intervention programs.

The men's data, on the other hand, demon-strates that sexual behaviors can range from tra-ditional to very risky, and the circumstances of risk-taking are often due to environmental fac-tors such as incarceration, to limited financial re-sources, or drug use.

Given the silence between African American partner's about past or current risk-taking expe-riences, it is highly probable that women may be unaware of the risks that they face in attempting to conform to cultural beliefs that are reinforced by past socialization and values about partner seeking and men are not disclosing their risks to give them a choice. This is especially likely in couples where the male is a "closeted" bisexual.

These findings highlight the need for commu-nity based prevention programs and couples coun-seling to help individuals or those in relationships

to make the necessary changes in risky practices. However, this information also suggests that the circumstances in which risk-taking occurs often influences the degree of risks that women and men take. Far too many, however, may be will-ingly sacrificing their lives in the service of main-taining a relationship to express their sexuality. There is no one worth dying for and sexual health demands that individual and relationship needs be reconciled with the realities of being sexually ac-tive in the twenty-first century.

BIBLIOGRAPHY

Akbar, N. (1979). African roots of personality. In W. Smith, K. Burlew, M. Mosely, and W. Whitney (eds.), *Reflections on Black psychology* (pp. 79–87). Washington, D.C.: University Press of America.

Amaro, H., (1995). Love, sex and power: Considering women's realities in HIV prevention. *American Psychologists,* 50(6), 437–447.

Baldwin, J. (1984). African self-consciousness and the mental health of African American. *Journal of Black Studies, 15,* 177–194.

Bennett, C. (1994). The Black population in the United States: March 1994 and 1993. U.S. Dept. of Commerce, Bureau of the Census, Washington, D.C.

Bowser, B. J. (1994). African-American male sexuality through the early life course. In A. S. Rossi (ed.). *Sexuality across the life course.* The John D. and Catherine T. MacArthur Foundation Series on Mental Health and Development: Studies on Success-ful Midlife Development. Chicago: University of Chicago Press, pp. 127–150.

Catania, J. A., T. J. Coates, S. Kegeles, M. T. Fullilove, M. T., (1992). Condom use in multi-ethnic neighborhoods of San Francisco: The population-based AMEN (AIDS in Multi-Ethnic Neighborhoods) study. *American Journal of Public Health,* 82(2), 284–287.

Center for Disease Control (1997). Update: Trends in AIDS incidence, deaths, and prevalence - United States, 1996. *Mor-bidity and Mortality Weekly Report* 46(8), 165–173.

d'Ardenne, P. (1996). Sexual health for men in culturally diverse communities—some psychological considerations. *Sexual & Marital Therapy,* 11(3), 289–296.

Doll, L. S., L. R. Petersen, C. R. White, E. S. Johnson (1992). Homosexually and non-homosexually identified men who have sex with men: A behavioral comparison. *Journal of Sex Research,* 29(1), 1–14.

Friedman, S. R., P. A. Young, F. R. Snyder, V. Shorty (1993). Racial differences in sexual behaviors related to AIDS in a nineteen-city sample of street-recruited drug injectors. *AIDS Education & Prevention,* 5(3), 196–211.

Gasch, H., D. Poulson, R. Fullilove, and M. Fullilove. (1991). Shaping AIDS education and prevention programs for African Americans amidst community decline. *Journal of Negro Education, 60*, 85–96.

Gilmore, S., J. DeLamater, and D. Wagstaff. (1996). Sexual decision making by inner-city Black adolescent males: A focus group study. *Journal of Sex Research, 33*(4), 364–371.

Graves, K. L., and A. M. Hines, A.M. (1997). Ethnic differences in the association between alcohol and risky sexual behavior with a new partner: An event-based analysis. *AIDS Education & Prevention, 9*(3), 219–237.

Greene, B. (1994). African American women. In L. Comas-Diaz and B. Greene (Eds.), *Women of color: Integrating ethnic and gender identities in psychotherapy* (pp. 10–30). New York: Guilford.

Holland, J., C. Ramazonoglu, S. Sharpe, and R. Thompson. (1992). Pleasure, pressure and power: Some contradictions of gendered sexuality. *Sociological Review, 40*, 645–674.

Jemmott, L., V. Catan, A. Nyamathi, and J. Anastasia. (1995). African American women and HIV risk-reduction issues. In A. O'Leary and L. Jemmott (eds.), *Women at risk: Issues in the primary prevention of AIDS.* (pp. 131–157). New York: Plenum.

Jemmott, L. S., and J. B. Jemmott. (1990). Sexual knowledge, attitudes, and risky sexual behavior among inner-city Black male adolescents. *Journal of Adolescent Research, 5*(3), 346–369.

Jemmott, L. S., and J. B. Jemmott. (1992). Family structure, parental strictness, and sexual behavior among inner-city Black male adolescents. *Journal of Adolescent Research, 7*(2), 192–207.

Johnson, E. H., L. A. Jackson, Y. Hinkle, D. Gilbert, (1994). What is the significance of Black-White differences in risky sexual behavior? *Journal of the National Medical Association,* 86(10), 745–759.

Johnson, R. L., W. Douglas, and A. Nelson. (1992). Sexual behaviors of African-American male college students and the risk of HIV infection. *Journal of the National Medical Association,* 84(10), 864–868.

Kim, M. Y., M. Marmor, N. Dubin, H. Wolfe. (1993). HIV risk-related sexual behaviors among heterosexuals in New York City: Associations with race, sex, and intravenous drug use. *AIDS, 7*(3), 409–414.

Mays, V. M, and S. D. Cochran. (1990). Methodological issues in the assessment and prediction of AIDS risk-related sexual behaviors among Black Americans. In V. R. Voeller, J. M. Reinisch, and M. S. Gottlieb (eds.). *AIDS and sex: An integrated biomedical and biobehavioral approach: Vol. 4 Kinsey Institute Series,* pp. 97–120. New York: Oxford University Press.

Mays, V. M., S. D. Cochran, G. Bellinger, R. G. Smith, (1992). The language of Black gay men's sexual behavior: Implications for AIDS risk reduction. *Journal of Sex Research, 29*(3), 425–434.

Mays, V. M., and J. S. Jackson. (1991). AIDS survey methodology with Black Americans. *Social Science & Medicine, 33*(1), 47–54.

McCoy, H., and J. Inciardi. (1993). Women and AIDS: Social determinants of sex-related activities. *Women and Health, 20*, 69–86.

McKirnan, D. J., J. P. Stokes, L. Doll, R. G. Burzette. (1995). Bisexually active men: Social characteristics and sexual behavior. *Journal of Sex Research, 32*(1), 65–76.

Miller, J. (1991). The "self-in-relation." A theory of women's development. In J. D. Jordan, A. G. Kaplan, J. B. Miller, I. P. Stiver, and J. L. Surrey (eds.), *Women's growth in connection* (pp. 202–220). New York: Guilford.

Myers, H. F., P. Satz, B. E. Miller, E. G. Bing (1997). The African American health project (AAHP): Study overview and select findings on high risk behaviors and psychiatric disorders in African American men. *Ethnicity & Health, 2*(3), 183–196.

Nobles, W. (1986). *African Psychology: Towards its reclamation, reascension and revitalization.* Oakland, Calif.: Institute for the Advanced Study of Black Family Life and Culture.

Norris, A., and K. Ford. (1991). AIDS risk behaviors of minority youth living in Detroit. *American Journal of Preventive Medicine, 7*, 416–421.

Peterson, J. L., T. J. Coates, J. A. Catania, B. Hilliard (1995). Help-seeking for AIDS high-risk sexual behavior among gay and bisexual African American men. *AIDS Education & Prevention, 7*(1), 1–9.

Peterson, J., J. Catania, M. Dolcini, and B. Faigeles. (1993) Multiple sexual partners among Blacks in high-risk cities. *Family Planning Perspectives, 25*, 263–267.

Samuels, H. P. (1997). The relationships among selected demographics and conventional and unconventional sexual behaviors among Black and White heterosexual men. *Journal of Sex Research, 34*(1), 85–92.

Stokes, J. P., P. A. Venable, and D. J. McKirnan. (1996). Ethnic differences in sexual behavior, condom use and psychosocial variables among Black and White men who have sex with men. *Journal of Sex Research, 33*(4), 373–381.

Surrey, J. (1991). Relationship and empowerment. In J. D. Jordan, A. G. Kaplan, J. B. Miller, I. P. Stiver, and J. L. Surrey (eds.) *Women's growth in connection* (pp. 162–180). New York: Guilford.

Tucker, M. B., and C. Kernan. (1995). *The decline in marriage among African Americans.* New York: Russell Sage Foundation.

Tucker, M. B., and R. J. Taylor. (1989). Demographic correlates of relationship status among Black Americans. *Journal of Marriage and the Family, 51*, 655–665.

Tucker, S. (1989). Adolescent patterns of communication about sexually related topics. *Adolescence, 24*, 269–273.

Ulin, P. (1992). African women and AIDS: Negotiating behavior change. *Social Science Medicine, 34*, 63–73.

White, J. (1984). *The psychology of Blacks.* Englewood Cliffs, N.J.: Prentice-Hall.

Wyatt, G. (1994). The sociocultural relevance of sex research: Challenges for the 1990s and beyond. *American Psychologist, 49*, 748–754.

Wyatt, G. E. (1991). Ethnic and cultural differences in women's sexual behavior. In S. Blumenthal, A. Eichler, G. Weissman. *Women and AIDS: Promoting healthy behavior* (pp. 174–182). DHHS Publication. Washington D.C.

Wyatt, G. (1982). Sexual experience of African American women. In M. Kirkpatrick (ed.) *Women's sexual experiences: Explorations of the dark continent.* New York: Plenum.

Wyatt, G. E., and K. Ashing-Giwa. (1995). *The sexual health and risk-taking model.* Work in progress.

Wyatt, G. E., and K. T. Ashing-Giwa. (1994). Factors affecting African American women's sexual health and HIV related risk: A focus group discussion. Unpublished.

Wyatt, G., and M. Riederle (1 994). Reconceptualizing issues that affect women's sexual decision-making and sexual functioning. *Psychology of Women Quarterly, 18,* 611–625.

Wyatt, G. E. (1 997). *Stolen Women: Reclaiming our sexuality, taking back our lives.* New York: John Wiley & Sons.

Yarber, W., and J. Greer (1986). The relationship between the sexual attitudes of parents and their college daughters' or sons' sexual attitudes and sexual behavior. *Journal of School Health,* 56, 68–72.

The Black Women's Relationships Project: A National Survey of Black Lesbians

VICKIE M. MAYS & SUSAN D. COCHRAN

This article is a study of sexual orientation as a salient social status characteristic shaping the experiences of a subgroup of Black women. The authors' sample included 530 self identified Black lesbians and 66 bisexual women. Primarily a descriptive study, this article looks at how sociocultural factors influence the development, maintenance, and dissolution of lover, friend, and community relationships of Black lesbians.

■

Black lesbians are relatively invisible in our society. Despite popular stereotypes, we actually know very little about their lives. Research on lesbians (see Peplau & Amaro, 1982 for review) has generally focused solely on Anglos. In a recent search of psychological research on lesbians using *Dialogues* and *Psych Info* databases, we found that only two of over 300 references contained "Black women" in the title or abstract. Turning to the social science literature on Black women also provides little assistance. Most written information on Black lesbians is found (even here only rarely) in popular magazines, gay publications or in the form of published poetry, short stories or autobiographies.

Why is there so little psychological research on Black lesbians? There are probably several reasons. First, social scientists have, for the most part, neglected sexual orientation as a variable of interest in psychological research in general. Psychology, while well developed in race relations

research, particularly with Black Americans, has not yet incorporated sexual orientation as a variable of interest to any great extent. Yet, like gender or ethnicity, sexual orientation represents a social status characteristic that may have important implications. Potentially, it can structure an individuals' experiences of being in the world and expectations for social interactions (for a review see Webster and Driskoll, 1985).

A second possible reason for the dearth of Black lesbian-related research is that much current research on the lives of lesbians arose out of feminist academic roots, which have been predominantly Anglo in focus. To address the topic of Black lesbians adequately, one must meld both the issues of race and sexual orientation.

CONCEPTUAL ISSUES

Psychological research from the areas of stereotyping, status expectations, the contact hypothesis or social cognition can give us some potential insight into what happens when a person has one salient status or characteristic, such as ethnicity, social class or gender. Only in recent years have researchers begun utilizing clearly formulated ideas about the conditional relationship between two or more status's (e.g., gender and ethnicity) in behavior. The thrust of much of this research has been to approach these

From *A Sourcebook of Gay/Lesbian Health Care* (M. Shernoff and W. A. Scott, eds.) Washington, D.C.: National Gay and Lesbian Health Foundation, 2nd ed., 1988, pp. 54–62. Copyright 1988 by the National Gay and Lesbian Health Foundation. Reprinted by permission. An earlier version of this chapter was presented at the annual meeting of the American Psychological Association, Washington, D.C., August 25, 1986. The authors wish to acknowledge L. Anne Peplau's work on this project as well as her comments on an earlier version of this manuscript.

status's from the perspective of an additive model rather than examining the simultaneous contribution of these status's as interactive, interdependent or interrelated (Kessler and Neighbors, 1986). In the latter perspective, the goal is to investigate the complex web of hierarchical social arrangements generating different experiences (Zinn, Cannon, and Dill, 1984), modified by combinations and salience of the status characteristics.

It is from this conceptual framework that the Black Lesbian's Relationship Project was begun. The survey is the first of four related studies that are now in progress. These include investigations of relationship issues among Black heterosexual women; Black heterosexual men, with a particular emphasis on their relationships with Black women; Black gay and bisexual men, with an emphasis on how AIDS has impacted upon their relationships; and the intimate relationships of Black lesbians. This chapter will focus on the Black lesbians we have surveyed.

Our Black lesbian research adds the dimension of sexual orientation as a salient social status characteristic shaping the experiences of a subgroup of Black women. Like gender and ethnicity, sexual orientation can be a status characteristic when it is an obvious or known factor about the person. Yet, it also differs from gender and ethnicity in that it can be, at times, a hidden characteristic. While we expect direct relationships between the various social statuses and women's life experiences (e.g., a direct relationship between race discrimination and mental health factors such as depression or drug problems), we are particularly interested in exploring the interactions among our status characteristics. For example, we believe that social support structures, so necessary to protect one from the psychological effects of discrimination, will be influenced by one's sexual orientation, and may differ depending upon the salience of the latter characteristic. Elsewhere it has been shown that we are most likely to receive help from similar others (Thoits, 1986).

METHODOLOGICAL CONCERNS

Early research of homosexuality and lesbianism tends to formulate questions collect data, and interpret results in ways reflecting ethnocentric, male, heterosexist or class biases (Morin, 1977; Suppe, 1981). Obviously, we hoped to avoid making similar mistakes. Since social scientists have never had access to scientifically valid or nationally representative data on the lives of Black lesbians, we were especially concerned about capturing the diversity present in this group of women. Our aim was to gather data on Black lesbian relationships that would be both scientifically valid and sensitive to ethnic and cultural contexts. In structuring our research, we focused on developing both instruments and recruitment methods that would accomplish our goals.

INSTRUMENT DEVELOPMENT

There are several special issues of concern in devising an appropriate survey instrument for Black lesbians. First, research on Black Americans has been hampered by the inapplicability of standard measures and procedures of survey data collection (Jackson, Gurin, and Hatchett, 1979). The National Survey of Black Americans clearly demonstrated the need for specialized procedures across all aspects of research design, data collection and analysis. For example, in asking about health problems, it was important to use the term, "high blood pressure," rather than hypertension a term unfamiliar to many participants.

Second, survey research methods developed for use with Black Americans assumes a heterosexual orientation of respondents while research instruments developed for use with lesbians targets primarily Anglo populations. Neither captures the unique concerns of Black lesbians. For example, previous research has documented that the family of origin plays a central role in the lives of Black women (Brown and Gary, 1985; Vaux, 1985).

Black lesbians, in contrast to White lesbians, may be more likely to remain a part of the heterosexual community, maintaining relationships outside of the lesbian population. This may happen for several reasons. First, Black community values emphasize ethnic commitment and participation by all members of the community. Second, the relatively smaller population of Black lesbians (a minority within a minority) puts more pressure on these women to maintain their contacts with a Black heterosexual community in order to satisfy some of their ethnically-related social support needs. Third, Black lesbians may contribute much needed financial and informational resources to their families of origin. This assistance may be critical for the maintenance of a reasonable standard of living. In contrast, for White lesbians, there may be a sufficiently large lesbian population (a similar minority, but drawn from a larger population) from which to derive most ethnic/cultural, social and emotional needs. Also, distance from family of origin may be more achievable for a greater percentage of White lesbians due to greater financial resources within the family system. Thus, Black lesbians may find that the need to juggle family of origin demands and their lives as lesbians is somewhat more complicated.

It was our goal to collect data that would allow for an exploration of how these sociocultural factors influence the development, maintenance and dissolution of lover, friend and community relationships of Black lesbians. Most investigations of relationships have centered mainly on interpersonal or intrapersonal aspects. While this focus is important, our research team felt that other factors (such as availability of Black lovers, perceptions of discrimination within the primarily Anglo lesbian community or perceived class discrimination within the Black lesbian community) may be additional mediating factors in explaining relationship choices as well as overall psychological well-being.

Generally there is insufficient questioning in survey research whether or not underlying assumptions or universal applications of concepts, measures or procedures are appropriate (Schumann, 1966; Warwick and Lininger, 1975; Jackson et al., 1979). It was our strong belief that development of an effective questionnaire necessitated initial field work to establish even the types of questions that we needed to ask of our participants.

Development of the questionnaire incorporated a variety of methodological techniques. These included the use of focus groups, employment of a modified back translation procedure (Jackson et al., 1979; Warwick and Osherson, 1973) and random probes (Schumann, 1966; Jackson et al., 1979).

COLLECTION OF QUALITATIVE DATA

We began our research in 1984 by listening carefully to the experiences of Black lesbians. A pilot study, using extensive individual interviews with Black lesbians, gathered information on women's perceptions of how discrimination influenced their interpersonal relationships and participation in various community activities (Mays, 1988). Responses to open-ended questions were tape-recorded and later transcribed. These transcriptions served as one basis for development of the first pre-test instrument.

Next, we conducted two focus groups, one with single and one with coupled Black lesbians, to help identify relevant issues in relationship values, social support, community participation and sources of discrimination. The focus groups were conducted in a relaxed atmosphere designed to encourage participants to talk openly about past and present relationship experiences. These focus groups supplied detailed information assisting us in decisions about appropriate language and meaningful concepts to be included in the questionnaire.

FINALIZING THE QUESTIONNAIRE

A pool of questions was then written, aided by previous research on Anglo lesbians (Aura, 1985; Peplau, Cochran, Rook and Padesky, 1978), Anglo gay men (Peplau and Cochran, 1981), Anglo heterosexual college students (Cochran and Peplau, 1986) and heterosexual Black men and women (Jackson et al., 1979). Many questions needed to be "translated" into culturally-relevant phrasing determined from the interview and focus group sessions. As an example, we found that the word, "lover" rather than the previously used terminology, "romantic/sexual partner" (Cochran and Peplau, 1986; Peplau and Cochran, 1981; Peplau et al., 1978), was important when referring to a woman's sexual significant other. Unlike Anglo lesbians, Black lesbians often use "partner" to refer to a good friend one travels about with to various activities (social, family visits, business).

From this process, we developed a 28-page questionnaire. The questionnaire covered a wide range of topics including questions about participants' friendships and love relationships, perceptions of support and discrimination, openness about being lesbian and problems experienced. Included also was the Center for Epidemiological Studies Depression Scale, a standard measure of depressed mood with norms for the Black population (Radloff, 1977).

After the initial questionnaire was developed, it was piloted with a small sample of Black lesbians. Attempts were made to have this pretest group as heterogeneous as possible. Women varied in relationship status (single versus coupled), age (ranging from 18 to 52), class background and whether or not they had children. After the women completed the questionnaire, they were then interviewed extensively regarding the meaningfulness of the concepts and the completeness of the items. This was done to assure ourselves that the instrument was clear and functioned as intended. We used a variant of the random probe technique to determine the shared meaning of items. This use of the random probe parallels the procedures of the National Survey of Black Americans (Jackson et al., 1979). It ensures the validity of questions. The questionnaire was then modified to arrive at our final version.

COLLECTION OF SURVEY DATA

Sampling

Sampling our subjects also provided its own set of special concerns. Random probability sampling of a gay or lesbian population is impossible (Gatozzi, 1986; Morin, 1977) although the larger and more diverse the sample, the more likely results will be externally valid. Recruiting a diverse, large sample of Black lesbians from across the country was not an easy task. The Black lesbian community is small, isolated and relatively invisible. However, we developed a variety of techniques that proved successful in finding Black lesbians.

Participants were recruited using a variant of the "snowball" technique. We started with large mailings to potential participants. Several organizations and social and political groups, including the National Coalition of Black Lesbians and Gays, mailed the questionnaire to their lesbian members. Participants who returned the questionnaire to us were also given the opportunity to separately return a postcard requesting additional questionnaires for friends. These were then mailed to the participant who personally recruited additional participants.

Distribution of the questionnaire also involved less focused tactics. The questionnaire was handed out by volunteers at several major lesbian events throughout the United States. In addition, press releases were periodically mailed to lesbian and gay newspapers, such as the *Gay Community News* in Boston, *Off Our Backs,* or the *Washington Blade,* all of which have a sizable Black lesbian readership, inviting participation. Flyers and questionnaires were sent to lesbian and gay bookstores and bars around the country where

Black gay men and lesbians might frequent. And finally; announcements of the study were distributed to gay and lesbian radio programs throughout the country.

Approximately every three months during the field phase of this project, the demographic characteristics of respondents were tabulated. Those aspects of the community or geographic region that appeared underrepresented were then targeted for more concentrated recruitment efforts. For example, based on the U.S. Census statistics on the number of Black women in the Midwest, we decided that our response rate for the major midwest urban areas did not reflect expected percentages. To correct this, the field phase of our study was extended. We remained in the field for approximately 18 months distributing approximately 2,100 questionnaires. Our final sample consists of responses from 530 self-identified Black lesbians and 66 bisexual women.

Inclusionary and Exclusionary Criteria

Even after receiving the 612 completed questionnaires from potential study participants, decisions had to be made about whom to include and whom to exclude. At first, it may seem that the inclusion criteria for this study would be relatively easy. Yet, the measurement of ethnicity and sexual orientation is not always simple. We decided to include in the sample any woman who was Black American, including two women from the Caribbean. Additionally, the participant also had to self-identify herself as a lesbian or bisexual woman and report at least one prior sexual experience with a woman. Thus, a few women who had not had a same-sex sexual experience were dropped from our sample. Notice that our definition of lesbian or bisexual status refers only to those individuals who are currently or have been sexually active with women. Obviously, it is possible to consider oneself a lesbian without ever having had a lesbian sexual experience. However, for the purposes of our study, we felt that sexual experience was an important criterion; a lack of

sexual experience might also indicate a relative inexperience with the lesbian lifestyle.

Characteristics of the Sample

Turning now to a description of the sample, the focus will be on our lesbian respondents. Demographic characteristics of the 530 women are given in Table 1. The women ranged in age from 18 to 59 (mean age = 33.3 years). Most of the women were somewhat religious, although this varied considerably They were also, by and large, fairly well educated. Nearly half reported having completed a college education or more. Most of the women held jobs, with approximately 84 percent employed at least half-time. Their median yearly income (1985—1986) was $17,500. On the average, respondents categorized themselves as coming from the middle class. Approximately a third of the sample had children. While one-third of the women lived alone, another third lived with their partner or lover. Two-thirds of our sample were currently in a serious/committed relationship. Almost half of our sample came from the Western United States, primarily California; another 21.3 percent were drawn from the East Coast/Northeast, 14.3 percent from the Midwest and 14.3 percent from the South.

Clearly from our demographics, we have for the most part BLUPPIES (Black Lesbian Upwardly Mobile People); a group of Black lesbians who are relatively well educated, have reasonable incomes and consider themselves as coming from class backgrounds considered middle class in the Black community. While our sample is perhaps not representative of the Black lesbian community as a whole, it does present us with an opportunity to examine in detail a particular segment of that community. One useful aspect of the sample is that these are women who, on the average, are in their thirties and have been lesbians for quite some time. Thus, their views and adjustments to life probably reflect those of women with a relatively committed lesbian lifestyle. On the negative side, we have too few respondents with lower incomes and less education. This

TABLE 1 Demographic Characteristics of the Black Lesbian Sample

Mean Age	33.3 years (range = 18 to 59)
Religious Background (in percentages)	33.3% Baptist
	16.8% Protestant
	16.3% Catholic
	33.6% Other
Mean level of religiosity (5-point scale where 3 = somewhat religious	3.9
Socioeconomic background	3.0 (reflecting middle class)
Mean years of schooling	15.4 (consistent with junior year in college)
Women possessing four-year college degree or more	46.0% (in percentage)
Annual income (1985-1986)	
Less than $5,000	8.3%
$5,000 to $10,999	17.5%
$11,000 to $19,999	34.5%
$20,000 or more	39.7%
Median yearly income	$17,500
Women employed at least 20 hrs/week (in percentage)	83.6%
Geographic location of respondent (in percentages):	
West/Northwest/Southwest	49.7%
Northeast/East	21.2%
Midwest	14.3%
South/Southeast	14.3%
Women who have given birth to at least one child	33.1%
Women who:	
live alone	32.1%
live with relationship partner	35.1%
live with others	32.8%
Women who are currently in a committed relationship	65.7%

Note: N = 530

could have resulted from several factors, including demand characteristics of the study instrument, such as reading level or sampling bias. Nonetheless, we do have a small group of this segment of the Black lesbian community which will allow us to make some comparisons on the basis of income, education or class.

Looking at Table 2, we get a picture of the relationship experiences of the sample. The mean age at which they reported first being attracted to a women was 15.8 years (median = 14.0 years). Their first lesbian sexual experience occurred at approximately 19 years of age. Almost all of the participants had had a sexual relationship with a Black woman, approximately two–thirds with an Anglo woman and 39 percent with other women

of color. In general, particularly with the number of West Coast women completing our sample, we were surprised by the relatively low percentage of sexual and committed relationships with other women of color. The median number of sexual partners was nine, which is similar to research on other lesbian samples (Bell and Weinberg, 1978; Peplau et al, 1978).

While the means and medians give you some insight into our sample, they do not really capture the richness of our data set. On each of the variables we have discussed, we have a wide range of responses. There are unique possibilities that derive from the fact that our data are based on a large national sample of Black lesbians. In contrast, the largest previous sample of Black lesbians

TABLE 2 Participants' Reports of Lesbian Sexual and Relationship Experiences

Mean age of first attraction to women	15.8 years (range = 4 to 52 years)
Mean age of first sexual experience	19.5 years
Median number of sexual partners	9.0
Women reporting at least one sexual relationship with:	
a Black woman	93%
an Anglo woman	65%
other women of color	39%
Median number of lifestyle/serious/committed lesbian relationships	3.0
Women reporting at least one committed relationship with:	
a Black woman	83%
an Anglo woman	40%
other woman of color	17%
Median length of longest relationship	42.0 months (range = 1 month to 20 years)

Note: N = 530

consisted of 64 young women recruited from the San Francisco area (Bell and Weinberg, 1978). To date, knowledge of the Black lesbian community has been limited by our lack of information. Therefore, some of our most straightforward analyses will involve the simple documentation of relationships and the heterogeneity of Black lesbians themselves in relation to such characteristics as age, economic status, social support networks, friendship patterns, problems and levels of psychological distress and openness of sexual orientation (Cochran and Mays, in press). For example, two manuscripts that are currently in preparation examine the mental health aspects of depressive symptomatology (Cochran and Mays, 1987) and drinking/drug use (Mays and Cochran, 1987) in this sample. Our focus in these manuscripts has been less on the documentation of pathology than the identification of subgroups of Black lesbians that are at higher risk for depression and substance abuse. We know that our sample, as a whole, has levels of depressive symptomatology no different than the population of Black women (as measured by the CES-D) (Cochran and Mays, 1987). However, some of our participants evidence considerable levels of depression. Prelimi-

nary analyses suggest that Black lesbians who are isolated from other Black lesbians and participate more extensively in the Anglo lesbian community are more likely to suffer from depression. In contrast, women who are more integrated into the Black lesbian community (in terms of sources of support, ethnicity of sexual partners and lovers) than the average woman in our sample are more likely to have drug and alcohol problems. In future analyses, we will be able to use our large sample to explore factors that put particular segments of the Black lesbian community at risk for emotional problems. Our data can help to identify strategies for intervening with these at risk women as well as assisting therapists and other helpers by better identifying the role of structural factors (i.e., discriminations) versus intrapersonal dynamics in the development and maintenance of emotional problems. The need to document this heterogeneity is particularly important to aid in eradicating the negative stereotypes that exist about Black lesbians.

Other analyses will tackle more complex issues. Two major themes in our dataset are social support and discrimination—concepts of particular importance for Black Americans. Much of the research on Black Americans has discussed the importance of the Black family and social networks to the psychological well-being and survival of this group. Our data allow us to investigate the relationship between social support and sexual orientation. This can take many forms from the particular stresses of an interracial relationship (where the interracial pairing may make the lesbian status more salient to others) (Mays and Cochran, 1986) to the relative importance of ethnicity versus sexual orientation in defining social support structures (Cochran and Mays, 1987).

A final area of interest is in the factors that predict achieving and maintaining a satisfying close relationship. As with Anglo lesbians (Peplau, Padesky, and Hamilton, 1982), the Black lesbians in our sample reported their relationships as generally satisfying and close (Peplau, Cochran and Mays, 1986). Further work in the area will seek to determine which factors are important in generating a positive relationship.

We are hopeful that this study will aid in bringing the lives of Black lesbians out of the research closet they have inhabited for so many years.

REFERENCES

Aura, J. 1985. Women's social support: A comparison of lesbians and heterosexuals, doctoral dissertation. University of California, Los Angeles.

Bell, A.. and M. Weinberg 1978. *Homosexualities: A Study of Diversity in Men and Women.* New York: Simon and Schuster.

Brown, D. R. and L. E. Gary 1985. Social support network differentials among married and nonmarried Black females. *Psychology of Women Quarterly*, 9, pp. 229–241.

Cochran, S. D.. and L. A. Peplau 1985. Value orientations in heterosexual relationships, *Psychology of Women Quarterly*, 9, pp. 477–488.

Gatozzi, A. 1986. *Psychological and social aspects of the Acquired Immune Deficiency Syndrome: Early findings of research supported by the National Institute of Mental Health.* Unpublished working paper. Office of Scientific Information, National Institute of Mental Health.

Jackson, J. S., Gurin, G., and Hatchett, S. 1979. A study of Black American life and mental health. Proposal submitted to the National Institute of Mental Health.

Kessler, R. C., and H. W. Neighbors 1986. A new perspective on the relationships among race, social class, and psychological distress, *Journal of Health and Social Behavior*, 27, pp. 107–115.

Mays, V. M. 1985. Black Women working together: Diversity in same sex relationships, *Women's Studies International Forum*, 8, pp. 67–71.

Mays, V. M., and S. D. Cochran 1986. *Relationship experiences and the perception of discrimination.* Paper presented at the meetings of the American Psychological Association, Washington, D.C., August.

Morin, S. E. 1977. Heterosexual bias in psychological research on lesbianism and male homosexuality. *American Psychologist*, 32, pp. 629–637

Peplau, L. A., and S. D. Cochran 1981. Value orientations in the intimate relationships of gay men, *Journal of Homosexuality*, 6, pp. 1–19.

Peplau, L. A., S. D. Cochran, and V. M. Mays 1986. *Satisfaction in the intimate relationships of Black lesbians.* Paper presented at the annual meeting of the American Psychological Association, Washington, D.C., August.

Peplau, L. A., Cochran, S., Rook, I. C., and Padesky, C. 1978. Loving women: Attachment and autonomy in lesbian relationships, *Journal of Social Issues*, 34, pp. 7–27

Peplau, L. A., C. Padesky, and M. Hamilton 1982. Satisfaction in lesbian relationships, *Journal of Homosexuality*, 8, pp. 23–35.

Radloff, L. S. 1977. The CES-D Scale: A self report depression scale for research in the general population. *Journal of Applied Psychological Measurement*, 1, pp. 385–401.

Schumann, H. 1966. The random probe: A technique for evaluating the validity of closed questions, *American Sociological Review*, 32(2), pp. 218–222.

Suppe, F. 1981. The Bell and Weinberg Study: Future priorities for research on homosexuality, *Journal of Homosexuality*, 6, pp. 69–97

Thoits, P. A. 1986. Social support as coping assistance, *Journal of Consulting and Clinical Psychology*, 54, pp. 416–423.

Vaux, A. 1985. Variations in social support associated with gender, ethnicity and age, *Journal of Social Issues*, 41, pp. 89–110.

Warwick D. P., and C. A. Lininger 1975. *The sample survey.* New York: McGraw Hill.

Warwick D. P., and D. Osherson 1973. *Comparative research methods.* Englewood Cliffs, N.J.: Prentice-Hall.

Webster, M., and J. E. Driskoll 1985. Status Generalization, In J. Berger and M. Zeditch (eds.) *Status Rewards; and Influence.* San Francisco: Jossey-Bass, 1985.

Zinn, M. B., L. W. Cannon, and B. T. Dill 1984. *The costs of exclusionary practices in women's studies.* Unpublished manuscript.

4

Gender Roles

In a Community of Women: A Biographical Note

ROBERT STAPLES

Writing about my relationship with female kin is a particularly liberating experience for me. Anyone who is familiar with the recent feminist attacks on me would naturally assume these experiences to be negative. Such an assumption belies my real history with, and attitudes toward, Black women in general and my female kin in particular. The first of my books to contain a dedication was devoted to my two grandmothers, who had died a year before its publication (*The Black Family: Essays and Studies,* 1971). My third book was on Black women (*The Black Woman in America: Sex, Marriage and the Family,* 1973) and was used in classes taught by Johnetta Cole, Patricia Bell-Scott, and Angela Davis. One of my first articles, "The Myth of the Black Matriarchy" (1970), was widely praised and used by Black feminists in their classes and writings. And I did not, in later years, become a neo-sexist but rather was victimized by changing norms relating to Black women's liberation.

My special history with Black female kin has shaped my ideology on the woman question. First, I should note that male kin played an instrumental role in my achievements, but their influence was felt more in my young adulthood than in other phases of my life. And I will not discuss my mother, for whom I have such a special love that all other relationships pale in comparison. Growing up as a child of the 1950s, in a segregated South, I was quite small and shy. The male kin often ignored me or felt I was too withdrawn to attempt communication or interaction with. That did not seem to bother my female kin, who would make the effort to determine how I felt. Moreover, I always perceived the male kin as disciplinarians and stood in awe of them, never knowing when they would punish me for some violation of Black or Southern norms.

Sociological and anthropological research have shown that, despite a bilateral descent system, Americans often behave in a unilateral descent manner. That is, one side of the family is often more important than the other. As a rule, children often interact more and are closer to the maternal side of their family than the paternal. Daughters remain a concern of their family of origin, and their children are often the favored grandchildren. Although the maternal side was not that much more important than my paternal relatives, certain differences were dictated by geography. When I was growing up in Roanoke, Virginia, only my mother had close relatives who lived in the same city. Her mother and step-father and one brother's family all lived in Roanoke. All my father's family lived in other parts of Virginia. Behavioral differences created an even stronger affinity for the maternal side. My mother's family was more expressive—big huggers and kissers. The paternal relatives were more reserved, albeit just as loving in their stoic demeanor.

As a young boy, my greatest love was for my two grandmothers. Typical of grandparents, they could play a pure nurturing function because my two parents were my disciplinarians. My biological grandfathers both died before my birth and my step grandfathers, whom I never knew well, also passed away when I was very young. Momma Daisy, as my maternal grandmother was called, was who I spent most of my time with. She was a petite woman, with only one fourth Black ancestry and the phenotype of an average White woman; I rarely had to share her time or affection as I did with my mother. As the oldest of five children, I had first claim on Momma Daisy's attention for much of my childhood.

Speaking of Momma Daisy, I find it difficult to condense my memories of her to a few pages. What I remember most are the mundane events. I began elementary school only a block from her house. Every lunch hour I would trek to her little white house, with the picket fence, and she would greet me at the door with a big kiss. Later, she would give me a bowl of Jello and some vanilla wafers. We would sit on her porch, during the warmer days, and just look out and talk with her neighbors. Because she lived on Sixth Avenue all of my childhood, and my parents moved us about ten different times, Momma Daisy's neighborhood became the more familiar source of friendships than any other I ever lived in. Next door to Mamma Daisy lived my godmother, "Big Sis," Mr. Johnny, and my godsister Cloteal. When I graduated from high school, most of the people who gave me gifts were women in Momma

Daisy's neighborhood. Besides my daily visits to her house on school days, I generally went to the movie theater on Saturday mornings and had to pass near her house. On that day, when I didn't have my school lunch, I was treated to her special dish of macaroni and cheese.

It is impossible to describe the angelic nature of Mamma Daisy. Suffice it to say that she was the Mother Theresa of Roanoke. Blessed with an indescribable beauty, she married well and never worked outside the home. Much of her time was spent helping my mother, who had her hands full with five young children. But Momma Daisy also devoted time, attention, and money to helping the needy, the ill, and the elderly. Many times she took me to a neighbor's house, where she would help with the housework because the neighbor was ill. And she was always giving money to people who were down on their luck. Although such neighborly assistance was not uncommon in the 1950s South, her generosity spread to a very large number of people.

Momma Daisy often preached the virtue of family togetherness. And she was the anchor of our small family. Two of her children lived in Roanoke, and two of them lived in New York. Each summer, without fail, the entire clan gathered in Roanoke at some time during the summer to pay homage to her. All her children took seriously her exhortation to remain together as a family. When her youngest son, James, moved from New York City to Los Angeles in the 1950s, he managed, through his family's generosity and sacrifice, to move us all (except the New York sister) to the state of California. For fifteen years afterwards, Mama Daisy stayed in Roanoke with her lifelong friends, and Uncle James brought her out to California during the winter. On her return from California in April 1968, I was in Roanoke for a brief visit and saw a very weak and frail Momma Daisy. I wrote my New York aunt to say that I was worried about the state of her health. Despite her desire to remain in Roanoke, Aunt Cora took Momma Daisy to live with her in New York. Some months later Momma Daisy was moved to Los Angeles, where she lived with her children until her death, from emphysema on

January 31, 1970, at the age of seventy-eight. As she often wanted, the family is still together. Each year, on Memorial day, flowers are placed on her grave in North Hollywood, California, as our way of saying, "We miss you so very much, and thank you for the model of human decency you gave us."

Although Momma Daisy was a very positive influence in my life, there were others. One of the strong ones was Grandma Ella, my father's mother. Unlike with the maternal side, I had a very special status in my father's family. After six granddaughters, I was Grandma Ella's first grandson. As a result, I was lavished with much attention and affection from her, the unmarried daughter who lived with her, and all my older female cousins. Again I was surrounded, embraced, and nurtured by a community of women. Because of my unique status, I was the only grandchild to spend each summer at Grandma Ella's house in the small town of Stuart, Virginia (population 2,800). My father and his family were a typical upwardly mobile Black family, Grandma could not read or write, and my father only completed the 8th grade. All my female cousins graduated from college, despite the restrictions imposed on them by small town Southern society.

Although limited in education, my paternal family members were property owners and merchants. At one time, Grandma had a 10-acre farm with horses, cows, pigs, and chickens. She owned the only Black business, other than the mortuary, in Stuart. On this 10-acre estate, she rented out her smaller houses, sold sodas and confectioneries, and ran a dance hall. Her house also served as an informal community center where Black folks from miles around gathered to visit, listen to music, and court each other. Each summer I helped sell the snacks, collect tickets in the dance hall, kill the chickens, and slaughter the pigs. It was my only experience with rural America, and it certainly shaped my adult identity.

Again I was enmeshed in a network of female kin. Because I tended to be around women most of the time, it socialized me into norms of compassion, tenderness, sensitivity, and emotional warmth. The lesson of my involvement with female kin was the importance of unconditional love. Although I had achieved nothing as a child, I was valued for my mere humanity. These women all loved me for myself, not for what I was to become. And that love would have been there whether I had gone to get a Ph.D. and write books or if I had gone to jail and become a career criminal. The male kin were more likely to demand achievement of me and to be less expressive with their emotions, a male model that I, to a certain degree, emulate.

Not that my female kin failed to encourage my educational and occupational aspirations. When my Uncle James encouraged me to go to college and live with them in California, all the people, with the exception of my father, who gave me money for my expenses were women. Many of them were household employees who earned less than $5 a day. A gift of $25 from one of them represented a week's wages. Even my aunts related by marriage looked out for my welfare in a way that the male kin did not understand. Although my uncles, in particular, were very supportive of me in young adulthood, I faced harsh sanctions if I did not work and study hard. If I were to remain in good standing in the family, they required that I avoid the temptations of substance abuse, sexual promiscuity, and indolence. Continual and unconditional love? It can make a difference.

In many ways, I remain involved in a community of women. As a child I was closest to my cousin Carolyn and have more communication as an adult with my paternal cousin Gwen and maternal cousin Barbara than others. The male elders in my family have often gone to early graves. My Aunt Cora is the only kin of her generation to maintain an ongoing correspondence with me and has always represented a source of support. In the most objective sense, there might not be biologically rooted ways of behaving by gender. We are all the products of our socialization. I was fortunate to be enmeshed in a community of women who cared about me and made me care about them. They made me want to achieve success to justify their faith in me. For me, there was no need for my male kin's conditional love. I wanted so much to vindicate their belief in me.

Extended Family Support Among Older Black Females

CHARLOTTE PERRY

This paper is a review of selected demographic data and empirical research. It discusses current family and social issues affecting the lives of older females in the Black American community. Its purpose is to present an overview of the literature about elderly Black females, their extended family relationships, and social support systems. The author finds that older Black women tend to interact frequently with family members and are simultaneously involved in the roles of parent, grandparent, and great-grandparent. The challenge of the 1990s will be to develop new perspectives on family support within the Afro-American family.

■

INTRODUCTION

Society in general, and policymakers in particular, view the family as the core support system for the older adult. It is estimated that adult children provide nearly 80 percent of all long-term social support the older adult receives (Cohen and Syme, 1985; Horowitz, 1985). However, social policy is leaning toward a philosophy of increased familial responsibility for the older adult. The lack of formal supports to assist families will have an adverse impact on the African-American family. This paper is a review of selected demographic data and empirical research that discusses current family and social issues affecting the lives of older females in the African-American community

African-American females tend to outlive men and dominate the elderly Black population. Population projections indicate that women will continue to outlive men, and the longer life expectancy for women has important implications for older Black women and their families. For the most part, older African-American females, during their younger years, were concentrated in low-paying female-dominated jobs, a work history that negatively affects retirement income. Their Social Security benefits are minimal and retirement pensions are practically nonexistent. Therefore, this group of women must rely on their families or public programs for assistance. On the contrary, a smaller group of Black females aged 65 and over have adequate retirement incomes and rely on families for expressive or emotional support (Claude, 1986; Ladner, 1986).

Considering the majority however, national data indicate that civilian noninstitutionalized elderly do have greater dependency needs with advancing age (National Center for Health Statistics, 1986). An analysis of these data revealed that older Black females, when compared to older Black males, had limitations in doing heavy housework and handling money (Jackson and Perry, 1989). The findings from this study suggest the levels of support older Black females need from family and friends.

The importance of family functioning to older Black females has been emphasized in the ethnographic literature (Aschenbrenner, 1975; Shimkin, Shimkin, and Frate, 1978; Stack, 1974). The reciprocal nature of support from older adult females has also been crucial to the family life of the younger generation (Martin and Martin, 1978; Stack, 1974). Allen (1979) reported that

A previously unpublished paper, 1993. Printed by permission of the author.

the Black extended family structure was most commonly found within the lower socioeconomic groups, and this family structure served a survival function. On the contrary, Jackson (1981) claimed that relics of this structural pattern are found across all socioeconomic groups, suggesting that a structural connectedness of the family is culturally pervasive.

The family member who traditionally provides support to parents is the adult daughter. Population trends within the African-American community indicate that the ability of the adult daughter to provide support is gradually diminishing. This diminished ability can be attributed to the changes in family structures among the younger generations, changes that affect women primarily (Ladner, 1986; Staples, 1986; Wilkinson, 1978; Worobey and Angel, 1990a). For example, in comparison to Whites, there is a disproportionate number of black middle-aged females functioning as heads of households. The high divorce rate among blacks and the high mortality rate among young and middle-aged black men have been partly responsible for this phenomenon during the past two decades. Unemployment and underemployment of the black male have also contributed to the increase in female-headed households (Claude, 1986; Ladner, 1986; Wilkinson, 1978). A large number of black women in two-parent families are also members of the labor force. These changing family structures within the middle generation have not only reduced available resources to this group, but also reduced their ability to provide support to older women. Despite this observation, White-Means and Thornton (1990) found that, among four ethnic groups, African-American families were providing more caregiving hours to the elderly when compared to German, Irish, and English families. The investigators also found that, if the elderly people had limitations in performing instrumental activities of daily living (such as traveling, housework, and meal preparation), more assistance was provided by the African-American families than by the other groups. Most often the daughters provided the

assistance, without reducing their hours in the labor market. If the elderly people had limitations in performing physical activities of daily living (such as eating, dressing, and bathing), the African-American families again provided more assistance than the others, but at the cost of a reduction of hours in the labor market. Worobey and Angel (1990b) found that African-American elderly who experienced functional declines were more likely to remain at home alone than were Euro-American elderly. African-American elderly are, in general, highly impoverished and dependent and require strong support networks. Given the demographic trends of African-American families and the status of older Black females and their families, it is not understood whether adequate support networks exist to assist community living of this highly vulnerable group.

The research of Taylor (1986) suggested that the support needs of older Black adults are not being met. Taylor's study, which used data from the National Survey of Black Americans (NSBA), refuted earlier works regarding levels of support received from extended family members. Although most respondents in Taylor's study reported frequent interactions with family members, residential proximity, and family closeness, the picture was not so bright for those over 65. When comparisons were made for support provided to younger and older respondents, those age 65 and older received the least support. The negative relationship found between age and receipt of support in the NSBA research refuted the earlier works of Martin and Martin (1978) and Wylie (1971), who reported that Black elderly persons were highly respected and received high levels of support among extended family members. Taylor's study also compared the support received by elderly persons with adult children to that received by elderly persons without children. Those with children were more likely to receive support.

In general, the presence of an adult child tends to reduce the negative effects of age, and elderly Black adults with children tend to have larger networks composed of immediate family members. Taylor (1986) reported that assistance from extended family is usually more available to older Black adults with at least one adult child than to those without adult children. Other research with older Black adults found that social support was a function of marital status (Chatters, Taylor, and Jackson, 1986). These data suggested that never-married persons received the most support and that widowed persons received the least support. Widowed Black elderly, compared to married Black elderly, were reported to have smaller informal support networks of adult children, siblings, and friends (Chatters, Taylor, and Jackson, 1986).

The "hierarchical compensatory model" (Cantor, 1979a: 453) is a useful approach for explaining the social support available to older Black females. This model suggests that older Black adults receive support from distant kin, and non-kin when close kin are not available. Gibson and Jackson (1987) also found that distant relatives and non-kin were important to a group of elderly Blacks who had few immediate kin. As a result, the number of persons available to the older adult was unaffected by the absence of close kin.

The needs associated with being elderly and having limited income and education have not conclusively predicted support relationships. Taylor (1986) explored the influence of socioeconomic status on the social support relationships of older Black adults. Taylor found that socioeconomic status among older Black adults was not consistently related to the receipt of support. Income was positively related, but education was negatively related to the frequency of support received. These findings suggest that elderly Black adults with limited income and education tend to have smaller support networks of family members than those with more income and education. In contrast, elderly persons in higher socioeconomic groups tend to broaden their networks by including friends (Ferraro, Mutran, and Barresi, 1984; Lee, 1985).

Role changes are inevitable as one experiences aging. The older Black female tends to become more involved with her kin. For instance, the spousal role is relinquished in widowhood, but the grandparent role may be acquired or take on a different meaning. Moreover, older Black females may occupy and function simultaneously in a variety of vertical roles such as parent, grandparent, and great-grandparent. A family in which one or more members play vertical roles has been referred to as a verticalized intergenerational family (Burton and Dilworth-Anderson, 1991).

MULTIGENERATIONAL HOUSEHOLDS

Elderly Blacks, like the elderly in general, prefer to live alone. Widowhood, poor health, and limited income are factors that often require them to live in an extended family, however (Hess and Markson, 1980; Jackson and Ensley, 1990–1991; Worobey and Angel, 1990b).

Older Black females, widows in particular, are noted for taking into their homes grandchildren, nieces, nephews, other relatives, fictive kin, and non-kin to combine the resources of the extended family and provide child care (Hill and Shackelford, 1975). Previous works (Herskovits, 1958; Shimkin, Louie, and Frate, 1975) have traced this practice to the culture of the tribes of West Africa. Some researchers (Ladner, 1986; Mitchell and Register, 1984) have suggested that this phenomenon is common in African-American families across all socioeconomic groups. Furthermore, Allen (1979) and Wilson (1986), in particular, have stressed the importance of researchers adopting a cultural variant perspective in an extended family model to examine the uniqueness of the African-American family.

RESIDENTIAL PROXIMITY AND FAMILY CONTACT

Frequency of contact is associated with residential proximity of family members among the general population of older adults (Antonucci and Akiyama, 1987; Kahn, Wethington, and Ingersoll-Dayton, 1987). Results from the NSBA study also supports this finding (Taylor, 1986). Increased geographical distance between the older person and relatives tends to reduce the frequency of contact. Jackson (1971) reported that a curvilinear relationship exists between proximity of kin and satisfaction. Elderly mothers were dissatisfied with too little contact when adult children lived far away and dissatisfied with too much contact when an adult child shared the residence.

SOCIAL SUPPORT FROM FAMILY, FRIENDS, AND NON-KIN

Frequency of contact is also an important predictor of the receipt of support for older Black adults. Elderly Blacks tend to have face-to-face interactions with adult children or extended family members as often as once a week (Taylor, 1986). Lopata's work (1973, 1979) with widows confirmed the importance of adult children in the support network. Older widowed Black females who reported contact with adult children indicated that contact was frequent. In another study (Scott and Kivett, 1980) older widowed Black women reported that, in general, they had as much contact as they wanted with a personal confidante.

Exchanges of services are common within the African-American family, and elderly females tend to play a major role. The older adult is often responsible for maintaining the kinship network of the extended family, planning family celebrations, and providing child care (Taylor, 1986). These services are considered a part of the service exchange system. Adult children participate in this exchange by providing extra income to the total household if the family resides in a multigenerational living arrangement. Adult children also provide instrumental and other tangible supports to elderly parents who maintain independent living arrangements. Additionally,

the adult child provides care to the elderly parent as the parent's health declines.

The pattern of younger Black females providing assistance to older Black females is consistent with the literature in general. Studies have reported that elderly Blacks receive family support for personal care and assistance with household tasks (Cantor, 1979a; McAdoo, 1978; Taylor, 1986). Daughters, daughters-in-law, and sisters were usually reported as providers. They provided instrumental and emotional support, care when ill, meal preparation, and reassurance. Sons and grandchildren provided money, transportation, shopping services, and home repairs.

Friends are also important providers of support to older Black adult females. Engaging in fictive-kin relationships is common to African-American culture, where close friends are regarded as kin. This is probably more true for childless and spouseless elderly Black females than for married persons (Aschenbrenner, 1973; Wolf et al., 1983). Fictive kin take on the rights and obligations associated with kin status and actively provide support. Gibson and Jackson (1987) found that geographical differences occur in the perception of fictive kin. When fictive-kin relationships were compared for the four United States geographical regions, the relationships were more prevalent among Southern older Black adults who did not consider themselves affectively close to their families. Recently, Johnson and Barer (1990) looked for fictive-kin relationships among an inner-city elderly Black female sample in California. They found that some women had created fictive-kin relationships with friends and with choreworkers. I (Perry, 1991) found that older African-American widows who lived in an urban area of North Carolina reported receiving expressive support (affection, for example), but seldom reported receiving instrumental support (such as help with daily tasks) from fictive kin.

Other studies (Cantor, 1979b; Chatters and Taylor, 1986; Taylor and Jackson, 1986) have suggested how family and friends are selected by older adults to provide informal support. Chatters and associates (1986) explored the informal support provided among a sample of 581 Black adults who had an impairment. The major purpose of the study was to determine which category of helper would most often be selected by the respondent. The findings suggest that a consistent pattern of helper choices was made irrespective of the elderly person's health status. For example, the respondent in poor health continued to select the same helpers, although those persons were not the most capable of providing the necessary supports. Spouses, if available, were chosen as first preference. This held true even though help from others was available. Adult children were selected over siblings and friends. Unmarried older adults tended to select siblings, friends, and neighbors, in that order. The investigators concluded that poor health status did not change helper selection. The conclusion suggests that in helper selection, pre-existing relationships, such as marital and parental status, are more important than the older adults support needs.

Barresi and Menton (1990) reviewed informal support for elderly African-Americans. They concluded that frequency of contact and number of support members are influenced by residential proximity of family members, family affection, presence of children in the home, being female, living in Southern regions, age, martial status, health status, and respect for youth and older persons.

SUMMARY

The purpose of this paper was to present an overview of the literature about elderly Black females, their extended family relationships, and social support systems. The research indicates that an increased life span, among the elderly in general, has made it necessary for gerontologists to discuss older adults in the context of young-old, middle-old, and old-old. According to the available literature about the extended family relationships of older Black females, family members tend to interact frequently and have close affective bonds. Pooling limited resources in multigenerational households has been a common practice among Black families. Older African-American women, in general, tend to interact frequently and affectively with family members and are simultaneously involved in the roles of parent, grandparent, and great-grandparent. This family structure is considered a cultural variation not generally seen in Euro-American family structures. African-American widows tend to take grandchildren, nieces, and nephews into their homes. Reciprocity among kin, fictive kin, and non-kin is a common family theme. Services for child care, household tasks, transportation, and care when ill are often exchanged.

Social support is provided by substituting the next social support member in the hierarchy. Older Black mothers, in particular, expect adult children to provide for their needs, as necessary. Support expectations regarding daughters and sons are usually gender-typed. Research studies have also indicated that an inverse relationship exists between age and receipt of support. As a person gets older, less support is received. Childless widows increase the number of support providers by including friends and neighbors. The literature has also shown that, with limited resources, older Black females frequently give more support than they receive.

Social scientists are beginning to question whether family support for older African-Americans is diminishing as a result of changing family structures. The challenge for the 1990s will be to develop studies to address this question and to develop new perspectives on family support within the African-American family.

REFERENCES

Allen, W. R. 1979. Class, culture and family organization: The effects of class and race on family structure in urban America. *Journal of Comparative Family Studies,* 10: 301–313.

Antonucci, T. C., and H. Akiyama. 1987. Social networks in adult life and a preliminary examination of the Convoy model. *Journal of Gerontology,* 42(5): 519–527.

Aschenbrenner, J. 1973. Extended families among Black Americans. *Journal of Comparative Family Studies,* 4: 257–268.

Aschenbrenner, J. 1975. *Lifelines: Black families in Chicago.* New York: Holt, Rinehart & Winston.

Barresi, C. M., and G. Menton. 1990. Diversity in Black family caregiving. In *Black Aged. Understanding Diversity and Service Needs,* Z. Hare, E. McKinney, and M. Williams, editors. Newbury Park, CA: Sage.

Burton, L. M., and P. Dilworth-Anderson. 1991. The intergenerational family roles of aged Black Americans. *Marriage and Family Review,* 16(3–4): 311–330.

Cantor, M. H. 1979a. Neighbors and friends: An overlooked resource. *Research on Aging,* 1(4): 434–463.

Cantor, M. H. 1979b. The informal support system of New York's inner city elderly: Is ethnicity a factor? In *Ethnicity and aging: Theory, research, and policy,* D. E Gelfand and A J. Kutzik, eds. New York: Springer.

Chatters, L. M., R. T. Taylor, and J. S. Jackson. 1985. Size and composition of the informal helper networks of the elderly Black, *Journal of Gerontology,* 40: 605–614.

Chatters, L. M., R. T. Taylor, and J. S. Jackson. 1986. Aged Blacks' Choices for an informal helper network, *Journal of Gerontology,* 41(1): 94–100.

Claude, J. 1986. Poverty patterns for Black men and women, *Black Scholar,* 17(5): 30–33.

Cohen, S., and S. L Syme 1985. *Social Support and Health.* New York: Academic.

Ferraro, K. F., E. Mutran, and C. M. Barresi. 1984. Widowhood, health, and friendship support in later life, *Journal of Health and Social Behavior,* 25: 245–259.

Gibson, R. C., and J. S. Jackson. 1987. The Health, physical functioning, and informal supports of the Black elderly, *Milbank Quarterly,* 65(2): 421–454.

Herskovits, M. 1958. *The myth of the Negro past.* Boston: Beacon.

Hess, B. B., and E. W. Markson. 1980. *Aging and old age.* New York: Macmillan.

Hill, R. B., and L. Shackelford. 1975. The Black extended family revisited. *Urban League Review,* 1: 18–24.

Horowitz, A. 1985. Family caregiving to the frail elderly. In *Annual Review of Gerontology and Geriatrics,* Volume 5, C. Eisdorfer, ed. New York: Springer.

Jackson, J. J. 1971. Sex and social class variations in Negro older parent–adult child relationships. *Aging and Human Development,* 2: 96–107.

Jackson, J. J. 1981. Urban Black Americans. In *Ethnicity and Medical Care,* A. Harwood, ed., pp. 37–129. Cambridge, Mass.: Harvard University Press.

Jackson, J. J., and D. E. Ensley. 1990–1991. Ethnogerontology's status and complementary and conflicting social and cultural concerns for American minority elders, *Journal of Minority Aging,* 12(2): 41–78.

Jackson, J. J., and C. M. Perry. 1989. Physical health conditions of middle-aged and aged Blacks. In *Aging and Health,* K. S. Markides, ed., pp. 111–176. Beverly Hills, Calif.: Sage.

Johnson, C. L., and B. M. Barer. 1990. Families and networks among older inner-city Blacks. *Gerontologist,* 30(6): 726–740.

Kahn, R. L., E. Wethington, and B. Ingersoll-Dayton. 1987. Social support and social networks: Determinant, effects and interactions. In *Life-Span Perspectives and Social Psychology,* R. P. Abeles, ed., pp. 139–165. New York: Lawrence Erlbaum.

Ladner, J. 1986. Black women face the 21st century: Major issues and problems. *Black Scholar,* 17(5): 10–18.

Lee, G. R. 1985. Kinship and social support: The case of the United States. *Aging and Society,* 5(3): 19–38.

Lopata, H. Z. 1973. *Widowhood in an American City.* Cambridge, Mass.: Schenkman.

Lopata, H. Z. 1979. *Women as widows.* New York: Elsevier.

Martin, E., and J. Marlin. 1978. *The Black extended family.* Chicago: University of Chicago Press.

McAdoo, H. P. 1978. Factors related to stability in upwardly mobile Black families. *Journal of Marriage and the Family,* 40(11): 762–778.

Mitchell, J., and J. C. Register. 1984. An exploration of family interaction with the elderly by race, socioeconomic status, and residence. *Gerontologist* 24: 48–54.

National Center for Health Statistics 1986. Current estimates from the National Health Interview Survey United States, 1984. *Vital and Health Statistics* Series 10, No. 156. (DHHS Publication No. (PHS) 86–1584.) Washington, D.C.: U.S. Government Printing Office.

Perry, C. M. 1991. *The relationship of social support networks and support network function to the health status of older widowed Black females.* Unpublished doctoral dissertation, University of North Carolina at Greensboro.

Scott, J. P., and V. R. Kivett. 1980. The widowed, Black older adult in the rural South: Implication for policy. *Family Relations,* 29(1): 83–90.

Shimkin D., G. J. Louie, and D. A. Frate. 1975. *The Black extended family: A basic rural institution and mechanism of urban adaptation.* Urbana: University of Illinois.

Shimkin, D., E. E. Shimkin, and D. Frate. 1978. *The extended family in Black sciences.* Chicago: Aldine.

Stack, C. 1974. *All our kin.* New York: Harper & Row.

Staples, R. 1986. Change and adaptation in the Black family. In *The Black family: Essays and studies,* R. Staples, editor, pp. 251–254. Belmont, Calif.: Wadsworth.

Taylor, R. J. 1986. Receipt of support from family among Black Americans: Demographic and familial differences. *Journal of Marriage and the Family,* 48(2): 67–77.

Taylor, R. J., and L. M. Chatters. 1986. Church-based informal support networks of elderly Blacks. *Gerontologist,* 26: 637–642.

White-Means, S. I., and M. C. Thornton. 1990. Labor market choices and home health care programs among employed ethnic caregivers. *Gerontologist,* 30(6): 769–775.

Wilkinson, D. Y. 1978. The Black family past and present: A review essay. *Journal of Marriage and the Family,* 40: 829–835.

Wilson, M. N. 1986. The Black extended family: an analytical consideration. *Journal of Developmental Psychology,* 22(2): 246–258.

Wolf, J. H., N. Breshu, H. Ford, H. Ziegler, and A. Ward. 1983. Distance and contacts: Interactions of Black urban elderly and family and friends. *Journal of Gerontology,* 38: 465–471.

Worobey, J. L., and R. J. Angel. l990a. Poverty and health: Older minority women and the rise of the female-headed household. *Journal of Health and Social Behavior,* 31(12): 370–383.

Worobey, J. L., and R. J. Angel. 1990b. Functional capacity and living arrangements of unmarried persons. *Journal of Gerontology,* 45(3): S95–101.

Wylie, F M. 1971. Attitudes toward aging and the aged among Black Americans: Some historical perspectives. *Aging and Human Development,* 2: 66–70.

Black Male Masculinity
and Same Sex Friendships

SHANETTE M. HARRIS

This paper explores how alternative masculine behaviors are expressed within same-sex peer groups and friendships. The author argues that Black males have developed an alternative style of masculinity to cope with social and interpersonal pressures. In many cases, this coping style is dysfunctional, associated with specific negative consequences, and destructive for the participants. She concludes that Black male masculinity can present a threat to the Afro-American community.

■

The subject of same-sex friendships originates from research studies that have identified gender differences in friendship patterns and networks throughout the lifecycle (Dickens and Perlman, 1981; Kon, 1981; Rubin, 1980). Findings of consistent gender differences in friendship patterns is assumed to reflect stereotypical gender-role behaviors that differentiate between masculinity and femininity. However, theorists have recently proposed that masculinity may be expressed differently for African American and Euro-American males (Oliver, 1989; Staples, 1982). The recognition that African American male masculinity may differ from Euro-American masculinity suggests that African American friendship patterns may also differ in a manner consistent with a culturally distinct standard of masculinity.

In particular, male same-sex friendships referred to as "gangs" have been recently identified as a major social problem in urban areas. The presence of youth gangs in American urban areas, however, is not a recent occurrence. Urban youth gangs first appeared in America during Colonial times (Fox, 1985). Unfortunately, since the late 1960s, few studies have been conducted regarding this particular friendship pattern (Fox, 1985). The preponderance of research on same-sex friendships has focused on relationships formed between middle-class, Euro-American adolescents and young adults. An absence of research on African American male friendships makes it difficult to answer important questions regarding the relationship between friendship dynamics and expressions of masculinity adopted by African American males.

The purpose of this article is to examine how alternative masculine behaviors are expressed within same-sex peer groups and friendships. The writer proposes that African American males have adopted an alternative style of masculinity to cope with social and interpersonal pressures that is similar to but fundamentally different from traditional masculinity. This coping style mitigates against various structural stressors, although in many instances is dysfunctional and associated with specific negative consequences (for example, violent gang behavior).

AFRICAN AMERICAN MALES AND EURO-AMERICAN MASCULINITY

Masculinity has traditionally been associated with qualities assumed to be necessary for the adaptive functioning of all American males (Bem,

From *The Western Journal of Black Studies,* Volume 16, No. 2. 1992: 74–81. Copyright © 1992 by Washington State University Press. Reprinted by permission.

1981; Spence and Helmreich, 1978). Psychologists have described the masculine role as representing socially desirable behaviors for males such as independence, assertiveness, competitiveness, and high achievement needs and motivation. Doyle (1989) summarized much of the literature on masculinity and proposed that five themes encompass the male role: (1) antifemininity (2) success, (3) aggression, (4) sexuality, (5) self-reliance. Brannon (1976) postulated four dimensions of the masculine role: a) "No Sissy Stuff" (rejection of feminine aspects of the self); (b) "The Big Wheel" (status and power); (c) "Give Em Hell" (aggression and toughness); and (d) "The Sturdy Oak" (emotional strength and invulnerability). The most notable of the four, according to Brannon (1976), is "No Sissy Stuff," referring to the rejection and avoidance of femininity.

Teachings of Christianity have also been influential in delineating behaviors and characteristics affiliated with the masculine construct. For example, the connection between dominance, power, and masculinity stems from teachings that men are primarily responsible for the economic and moral well-being of the family (Pleck, 1987). The prominence of the church has declined, and economic changes require that a significant number of women work to assist with household finances. However, the view that males are primarily responsible for fulfilling roles of family protector and provider continue to be associated with desirable masculine behaviors (Pleck, 1987).

The social power and privilege extended to masculine role qualities contribute to both male and female views of masculinity as a beneficial commodity. The value of masculinity has also been discussed within the gender-role literature (Whitley, 1983). However, research findings from women's studies linking negative outcomes with rigid adherence to gender-role behavior have influenced the types of questions asked about masculinity Studies conducted to explore possible negative outcomes of adherence to masculinity indicate that masculine gender-role behavior is correlated with physical, psychological emotional, and interpersonal difficulties (Pleck, 1981).

For example, men predominate in alcoholism, antisocial behaviors, and sexual deviance (Gove, 1979). Similarly death rates from accidents, homicide, and suicide indicate that males incur significant health risks as a result of a gender role which prescribes that men should behave in aggressive and adventurous ways. In addition, men have been taught not to experience and report feelings and symptoms that could be perceived as signs of weakness. The inability to admit vulnerabilities is associated with the repression of emotions leading to stress-related disorders (such as heart attack, gastrointestinal disturbances) and interpersonal difficulties (Pleck, 1981). Internalized pressures to adhere to masculine norms and social pressures to serve as family provider and protector combine with potentially life-threatening behaviors (such as smoking, drinking alcohol) to decrease the life expectancy of males (Johnson, 1977). These behaviors and outcomes, however, have been linked almost exclusively to masculinity expressed by Euro-American middle-class males. The gender-role and men's studies literature have neglected the contributions of history social class, and racial differences among males that may influence masculine behaviors and outcomes. In particular, African American males have not been proportionately represented in studies of masculinity

Historically as regards masculinity, African American men have been placed in a double bind. Slavery, in particular, can be viewed as a period of African American male de-masculinization. Physical and psychological forms of coercion were used to discourage African American male slaves from expressing conventional forms of masculinity. Assertiveness, for example, was discouraged, and punishment was delivered for behaving in ways that conflicted with slaveowners' policies. The role of provider was also undermined because the slave-owner assumed primary responsibility for the distribution of material goods within slave households. In addition, unlike Euro-American males, African American male slaves were prevented from protecting their wives and children from external harm. At the discretion of slave-owners and overseers, families were separated and the wives of male slaves forced to submit to their owner's or overseers wishes. Thus the institution of slavery limited the actual and perceived independence, self-confidence, aggression, power, and even sexual behavior of African American men and introduced a style of manhood which they were prevented from displaying but eventually aspired to emulate. Ironically, after slavery was abolished, African American men were confronted with expectations from Euro-Americans and the African American community to behave, feel, and think according to traditional masculine norms. Conflicting values and expectations regarding masculinity engendered a conflict within African American males that continues today.

Despite a history of discouragement, research indicates that African American males have internalized and accepted norms and standards of Euro-American masculinity. For example, Cazenave (1987) investigated the significance of the provider role and found that African American males were more likely than African American females and Euro-Americans to agree or strongly agree that the role of economic provider was important. Although other research supports this finding (Staples, 1982), African American males encounter barriers in expressing behaviors consistent with these values.

Inequities are also reflected in earning potential and employment. African American males between 20 and 22 years of age have experienced a greater decline in annual earnings than Euro-American and Hispanic Americans in the same age group, an approximate loss of 28 percent between 1973 and 1987 (Sum and Fogg, 1990). The number of African American males with no earnings has also increased in the last 14 years. Sum and Fogg (1990) attribute these differences to both structural and cultural factors including: changes in the composition of jobs, low earnings opportunities available in industrial jobs, deficiencies in training and education required to acquire such positions and the lack of a vocational orientation during early years of development.

Restricted access to educational and employment opportunities representative of conventional masculine status obstruct the expression of behaviors consistent with Euro-American standards (Sum and Fogg, 1990; Wilson and Melendez, 1986). In part because of denied access to achieving aspects of traditional masculinity, many African American men reduce conflict by employing alternative ways of proving their manliness.

BLACK MALE MASCULINITY: AN ADAPTIVE COPING STRATEGY

African American males have developed distinct mannerisms and behaviors which serve to maintain positive feelings toward the self. The literature refers to these mannerisms and behaviors as "the expressive lifestyle" (Kochman, 1981; Majors, 1989; Oliver, 1989). This expressive pattern is a manifestation of behaviors that include physical postures, content and flow of speech, gestures, clothing style, styles of walking, types of dance, handshakes, and demeanor. This alternative masculinity is also concerned with roles, values, and self-presentation.

These behaviors are dynamic and evolve in relation to immediate environmental and structural stressors that emanate from sociopolitical factors at different points in history. During slavery, some behaviors specific to African American males included the oration of humorous stories, an emphasis on "shucking and jiving" and "dummying up." However, political and community changes during the civil rights era resulted in modifications of earlier behavioral and interactional styles. In the 1960s, hairstyles (such as the afro), handshakes (such as agreement skin, complimentary skin, Black power handshake), physical stances (player stance, pimp stance, peeping), and within-group forms of verbal communication (such as using the terms *brother* and *sister*) became representative of the new sociopolitical spirit (Cooke, 1980). More recently, new forms of handshakes (high and low five), dances (breakdance, cabbage patch), and hairstyles (relaxed hair, fade cuts) have emerged as forms of self-expression.

Black male masculine behaviors and expressions are influenced by the attempts of some African American males to disguise painful emotions such as shame and sadness induced by frustrations encountered within mainstream society. Consistent with the dimensions of traditional masculinity, failure to adhere to masculine norms by publicly expressing emotions (other than anger) is indicative of personal weakness and failure. However, the norms and standards characteristic of Black male masculinity are more restrictive than those of conventional masculinity because African American males have many more painful emotions to conceal from others. Characteristics, such as aloof expressions, detached behaviors, fearlessness, and expressionlessness are some of the noticeable defenses employed to minimize strong emotions.

The behaviors adopted by African American males, however, are not perceived by similar others as defenses against pain and sadness, but representative of power, strength, courage, and pride. This repertoire of behavioral expressions is an adaptive style that has evolved as a strategy for coping with frustration and alienation. This style exudes energy and activity rather than depression and defeat. In many ways, this type of masculinity provides another route by which African American males can obtain the rites and privileges of manhood. Black male masculinity, then, is a construct that describes and organizes the ways in which personal style is employed as a coping strategy by many low-income African American males. These mannerisms and gestures enhance self-esteem and insulate African American males from the harsh experiences of minority status. These behaviors also elicit respect and allow African American males to function as "men" within an environment often perceived as hostile and threatening.

The internal and external responses of Black male masculinity assist with the reduction of stress. According to Taylor (1981), both "achievement-related" pressures (pressures to complete tasks of upward mobility, for example) and "security-related" stressors are experienced more frequently by African American males than their Euro-American counterparts. Unlike low-income Euro-American males, racial membership and a greater likelihood of low socioeconomic status make it likely that African American males rarely have access to information and resources required to manipulate stressful conditions in their favor.

Given the greater likelihood of security-related stressors and minimal external resources to cope with stressors, African American males adapt by using resources most available (such as their own personal style). The degree to which African American males employ alternative masculine behaviors, however, is dependent upon individual variation in access to conventional symbols of manhood (for example, high school diploma, college education). That is, African American males who complete college and obtain satisfactory employment are less likely to display behaviors associated with Black male masculinity as compared to those who are less able to express masculinity in a traditional manner. However, because of existing inequities that stem from racial membership, some percentage of middle-class African American males resort intermittently to alternative masculine behaviors as well.

Thus, Black male masculinity can be conceptualized as a set of related thoughts, feelings, and behaviors that are based on long-standing African American traditions. These behaviors (such as behavior to manage overt feelings) indirectly promote African American male empowerment and survival and are enacted to reduce feelings of anger and mistrust experienced because of historical and ongoing racial oppression. To this extent, African American males—regardless of economic standing, educational level, marital status, or appearance—can achieve power and status. Status derived from this masculinity, however, is not based on the decisions of mainstream society nor evaluated according to Euro-American standards, but determined by the individual. These behaviors, beliefs, and feelings have been transmitted intergenerationally for many years and continue to serve as determinants of adulthood for African American male youth.

Same-Sex Peer Relationships and the Expressive Style

Peer relationships are one of several primary socialization agents in which African American males learn and exhibit Black male masculinity. Although few empirical studies have been conducted with this subpopulation, some of the findings from studies conducted with Euro-American male participants appear to be applicable to African American same-sex relationships.

Young males, unlike females, form extensive ties with large groups of similar others as opposed to intimate relations with two or three friends (Farrell, 1986). These friendships are generally less concerned with closeness and focus upon shared activities, rather than affection and sharing of feelings. Gender differences in friendships are even more pronounced for the same-sex friendships of low-income male youth because peer alliances become of importance early on in their development. For example, the conformity of middle-class youth to peer group norms increases during middle childhood and peaks during late elementary school years, whereas low-income youth align with peers at earlier ages and show greater dependence on their peers for support and approval (Silverstein and Krate, 1975).

Family dynamics and characteristics contribute to the earlier peer conformity of low-income youth. Children with several siblings and parents who express little affection but use restrictive and punitive forms of discipline are likely to form early peer group affiliations (Silverstein and Krate, 1975). Father-absent homes in which no other male models are present have also been associated with young males' greater reliance on peers than adults and family members (Wilkinson, 1974). Unfortunately, these findings apply to many African American male youth because almost half of all African American children under 18 years of age are of low-income socioeconomic status (Edelman, 1989).

The early separation of low-income male youth from parents increases their reliance upon peers for support and self-esteem. This need for approval and support increases the importance of the punishments and rewards delivered by peer members and minimizes the influence of family values and standards. However, the support offered by male peers consists of activities and companionship as compared to the conversation and intimate self-disclosure preferred by females. Competitive and combative activities also have a significant role in the development and maintenance of male same-sex friendships. Such interactions serve to enhance well-being and validate members' masculinity.

The competitive nature of male same-sex friendships is partly responsible for members' adherence to group norms that devalue affection and closeness (Lewis, 1978). Males are expected to surpass peers in various skills and abilities. Skills in physical, verbal, and emotional areas are especially encouraged as demonstrations of manliness. As early as the third grade, success in fighting, athletics and risk-taking are perceived as "manly" (Kunjufu, 1986). The ability to outwit peers and authority figures by "sounding" or "playing the dozens" (usually involving verbal insults and abusive comments) and the ability to accept such taunts are aspects of masculinity. Learning to accept verbal insults teaches low-income youth to suppress emotions and conceal painful responses from themselves and observers. "Rapping" is also a verbal prerequisite for status among African American male peers. This behavior usually begins during adolescence when masculinity is evaluated according to the number of sexual favors obtained from females, although references to sexual behavior frequently occur much earlier (Silverstein and Krate, 1975).

Peer norms exert a significant degree of control over members' behaviors and, depending upon feelings of loyalty to group norms, can either decrease or increase feelings of self-esteem. African American males most capable of expressing "Black male masculinity" are perceived as attractive by peers, females, and other youth. Males skilled in alternative behaviors acquire group status and recognition as decision makers and leaders. Specifically, males who show competence in rapping, playing the dozens, fighting, participating in sports, and reporting actual or contrived sexual conquests are conferred with different privileges than members less competent in these areas. Similarly, those who are less capable of expressing alternative masculine behaviors are likely to be ridiculed and rejected by peers. Such treatment has been associated with negative feelings about the self, social isolation, and poor interpersonal relations.

Related to the failure to adhere to peer norms are the consequences of peer disapproval involving the fear of being perceived as feminine. This fear is pervasive among African American male same-sex relationships and serves as a primary method for enforcing peer norms and values. The disdain for feminine aspects of the self, however, is not limited to Black male masculinity but a dimension of conventional masculinity as well (Doyle, 1989). Yet the consequences for failing to express masculinity among male peer groups appear to be more negative. Use of derogatory and sexist labels such as *faggot, queer, wimp,* and *girl* to refer to a male who does not follow peer group standards can often erupt into physical violence and have deleterious effects on the self-image.

Stimuli that cue antifeminine insults also appear to differ for African American and Euro-American males. Euro-American males who perform well academically and cooperate with teachers and adults tend to be regarded by peers as sociable and "nice young men." At the worst, they are not harassed and disrespected for these behaviors and, in some instances, are rewarded. However, these standards do not usually apply to low-income African American male youth. In fact, African American males who achieve academic success and rarely encounter conflict with authority figures are often perceived as sissified and lacking in manliness. The tendency to prefer academics to activities of the peer group equate to an absence of manhood; the lack of manhood is most always perceived as feminine. The male peer group then, operates under the assumption that a display of feminine aspects of

the self is evidence of weakness. African American male peers further assume that cooperation and compliance with standards of mainstream social institutions is inconsistent with being male. To this extent, academic success and respect for authority come to be synonymous with femininity. As a result, many African American male youth forego excellence in education to avoid ridicule and rejection which stems from their own homophobia and that of their same-sex peers.

African American Males and Gang Behavior

Urban African American friendships in the form of gangs have evoked considerable controversy within both the African American community and Euro-American culture. Most of the negative reactions to urban youth gangs can be attributed to the association between the terms *gang, violence,* and *drugs* (Fagan, 1989; Yablosky, 1963).

Although the relationship between drug behavior and violence among gangs is basically clear, diversity exists among these same-sex friendships just as among adolescent peer groups. In many ways, urban gangs are similar to adolescent peer populations discussed earlier. African American youth gangs reflect the exaggerated masculine behaviors found among other low-income African American male same-sex friendship groups. Many behaviors engaged in by male adolescents—behaviors such as conflict with authority figures, truancy, and disobedience-are overt symbols of group affiliation. Loyalty to the peer group above and beyond that felt for adults and family members are also displayed by gang members. Such an orientation enables low-income African American males to survive amidst realities of poverty to which they have been accustomed.

African American males join gangs to meet intrapersonal and interpersonal needs that are not met in more socially acceptable ways. The absence of recreational and social outlets in low-income communities and economic and educational deficits of low-income families contribute to gang membership as a viable alternative for meeting the developmental needs of male youth. The tendency for low-income males to form early superficial bonds with several friends based upon shared ritualized activities, competitiveness and combativeness (as opposed to relationships that promote verbal communication, affection, and acceptance) increases the attractiveness of gang membership. The interdependence of gang members also reduces feelings of isolation and alienation experienced when confronting oppressive structural conditions. The fact that African American male youth and youth in general attach great importance to the status of adulthood also adds to the lure of such friendships. However, this sought-after adult status is emblematic rather than a quest for actual adult responsibilities.

Gang membership and associated activities provide African American male youth with opportunities to acquire trappings of manhood by offering social status, economic opportunity and social support. Similar to mainstream social organizations gangs are composed of social structures within which young males are able to advance in a hierarchical manner. However, the skills and characteristics required to progress within conventional organizations differ significantly from those necessary for success within the gang hierarchy. In contrast to the years of education, styles of interacting and perceived "feminine" ways of acquiring conventional symbols, gang membership and upward mobility are oftentimes dependent upon an individual's desire to "succeed" and the ability to manipulate one's own feelings and behaviors. Thus, the illegal activities of some gangs are more compelling to this male subpopulation. In addition, it is likely that for male youth who have been reared in low-income dwellings, gang members have served as childhood role models and primary adult reference groups. For example, like any business, drug involvement provides gang members with income, advancement potential, and social status (Moore, 1978). Youth who feel unable to attain

the outward signs of manhood in conventional ways may view gang organizations as an employment opportunity in which they are more likely to succeed as compared to traditional vocations.

Violence is also a part of the gang process and, in many instances, is not far removed from the family and peer interactions experienced by many male youth. Like homophobia in other adolescent peer groups, violence is used as a method of controlling the behavior of individual gang members. Violent acts toward other gangs may also be used to protect the gang as a social unit from external threats.

Black male masculine behaviors are assets among gang members. These behaviors often determine the role and position of members within the gang hierarchy Certain masculine behaviors such as toughness and fighting are especially valuable to gang members' drug trafficking and violent operations. The use of emotional detachment and indications of fearlessness that appear as toughness to observers, facilitate dangerous interpersonal transactions with life-threatening consequences. The ability to obscure fear and panic commands respect from members of one's own gang and opposing gangs. Images of toughness also increase group solidarity by reflecting the importance of this particular norm to each gang member. The facade of toughness also reduces any feelings of guilt or remorse that individual members might experience after engaging in socially inappropriate acts.

Demonstrations of toughness protect the longevity of gangs by removing members who are unable or unwilling to show this type of masculinity. Similar to other male peer groups, those who do not adhere to gang norms and values are verbally and physically harassed and eventually rejected. However, the pressure to conform and the absence of other types of support influences gang members to behave according to prescribed standards. As with other peer groups, the need to conform leads males to engage in behaviors they inwardly may disapprove of in order to maintain an aura of "manliness." Fighting, drinking, drug use, and other maladaptive behaviors are intertwined with the "tough-guy" image and produce group cohesion, prevent encroachment by other gangs, assist with the maintenance of behavioral norms, and determine the pace at which members will assume primary positions among the "organizational hierarchy." The reemergence of gangs in low-income areas appears to suggest that families, churches, communities, and society in general have failed to satisfy the developmental needs that gang membership seems able to meet for some minority male youth. For many low-income African American youth, gangs fulfill normal male adolescent strivings to become men under oppressive conditions.

Expressions and mannerisms associated with masculinity are regarded highly by both African American male peer groups and friendships referred to as gangs. However, masculine behaviors associated with positive self-esteem for this population conflict with the norms and standards of masculinity promoted by mainstream America. As a result, these behaviors are associated with negative consequences for participants. Limited emotional expressions, low self-disclosure, indirect expressions of anger, sexism, homophobia, and roughness generalize to situations in which behavior and performance are evaluated according to more conventional standards. This type of personal style produces several problems for African American males, including: restricting their abilities to relate emotionally and behaviorally within intimate relationships, reducing employment opportunities, decreasing the favorability of college attendance and progression, and increasing the attractiveness of activities that can lead to incarceration. Opportunities for interpersonal learning experiences are also minimized because of similarities that exist among peer group and gang members. Thus, behaviors characteristic of alternative Black male masculinity within same-sex peer groups appear to have some positive consequences (such as group cohesion, self-confidence, and peer status) but are also associated with many maladaptive patterns of relating.

SUMMARY AND CONCLUSION

This article has discussed the way in which African American male masculinity, referred to as Black male masculinity, is *learned* and *expressed* within male same-sex peer relationships. This form of masculinity protects the self from pain and frustration associated with perceived and actual oppression and stigmatization. As a minority group member, these behaviors provide for affiliation and achievement needs not met by other social institutions, increase feelings of power and mastery, and inspire feelings of optimism and superiority. This lifestyle also serves as a channel for the release of anger and resentment towards the existing social structure. Unfortunately, the exaggeration of these behaviors and mannerisms within same-sex friendships self-defined as "gangs" are associated with maladaptive and dysfunctional patterns that are destructive for the participants, the African American community, and society in general. As a result, this alternative to conventional manhood has an opposite and equal negative effect, leading to a greater number of closed doors to opportunities (imprisonment, suicide, homicide, and poor health problems, for example) than existed on the traditional route to masculinity.

In addition, just as traditional Euro-American masculinity is associated with power and social benefits at the expense of Euro-American females, so too does Black male masculinity present an equal, if not greater, threat to the African American community. Attempts to define masculinity and manhood at the expense of African American females is unlikely and inevitably associated with an even greater loss to male self-esteem. Thus, the relationship between African American male same-sex friendships and masculinity must be redefined to exclude themes of domination and superiority in conjunction with other dysfunctional behaviors. In this instance, African American males can learn much from the illustrations provided by the self-defeating patterns of Euro-American male masculinity.

REFERENCES

Bern, S. L. 1981. Gender schema theory: A cognitive account of sex typing. *Psychological Review,* 88: 354–364.

Brannon, R. 1976. The male sex role: Our culture's blueprint of manhood, and what's it's done for us lately. In *The forty-nine percent majority,* D. David and R. Brannon, eds. Reading, Mass.: Addison-Wesley.

Cazenave, N. A. 1987. Men's work and family roles and characteristics. In *Changing men: New directions in research on men and masculinity,* M. S. Kimmel, ed. Newbury Park, Calif.: Sage.

Cooke, B. 1980. Nonverbal communication among Afro-Americans: An initial classification. In *Black Psychology* (2nd ed.), R. L. Jones, ed. New York: Harper & Row.

Dickens, W J., and D. Perlman. 1981. Friendship over the life cycle. In *Developing personal relationships,* S. Duck and R. Gilmour, ed. London: Academic.

Doyle, J. A. 1989. *The male experience* (2nd ed.). Dubuque, Ia.: W. C. Brown.

Edelman, M. 1989. Black Children in America. In *The state of Black America, 1989,* J. Dewart, ed., pp. 63–76. New York: National Urban League.

Fagan, J. 1989. The social organization of drug use and drug dealing among urban gangs. *Criminology,* 27: 633–667

Farrell, M. P. 1986. Friendship between men. *Marriage and Family Review,* 9:163–197.

Fox I. 1985. Mission impossible? Social work practice with Black urban youth gangs. *Social Work,* January–February: 25–31.

Gove, W. R. 1979. Sex differences in the epidemiology of mental disorder: Evidence and explanations. In *Gender and disordered behavior: Sex differences in psychopathology,* E. S. Gomberg and V. Franks, eds., pp. 23–68. New York: Brunner/Mazel.

Johnson, A. 1977. Recent trends in sex mortality differentials in the United States. *Journal of Human Stress,* 3: 22–32.

Kochman, T. 1981. *Black and White styles in conflict.* Chicago: University of Chicago Press.

Kon, I. S. 1981. Adolescent friendship: Some unanswered questions for future research. In *Developing personal relationships,* S. Duck and R. Gilmour, eds. London: Academic.

Kunjufu, J. 1986. *Countering the conspiracy to destroy Black boys,* Volume II. Chicago: African American Images.

Lewis, R. A. 1978. Emotional intimacy among young men. *Journal of Social Issues,* 34: 108–121.

Majors, R. 1989. Coolpose: The proud signature of Black survival. In *Men's lives: Readings in the sociology of men and masculinity,* M. Messner and M. Kimmel, eds., pp. 83–87. New York: Macmillan.

Moore, J. W. 1978. *Homeboys.* Philadelphia: Temple University Press.

Oliver, W. 1989. Sexual conquest patterns of Black-on-Black violence: A structural-cultural perspective. *Violence and Victims,* 4:257–273.

Pleck, J. H. 1981. *The myth of masculinity.* Cambridge, Mass.: MIT. Press.

Pleck, J. H. 1987. American fathering in historical perspective. In *Changing men: New directions in research on men and masculinity,* M. S. Kimmel, ed. Newbury Park, Calif.: Sage.

Rubin, Z. 1980. *Children's friendships.* Cambridge, Mass.: Harvard University Press.

Silverstein, B., and R. Krate. 1975. *Children of the dark ghetto: A developmental psychology.* New York: Praeger.

Staples, R. 1982. *Black masculinity: The Black males' role in American Society.* San Francisco: Black Scholar.

Spence, I. T., and R. L. Helmreich. 1978. *Masculinity and femininity: Their psychological dimensions, correlates, and antecedents.* Austin: University of Texas Press.

Sum, A., and N. Fogg. 1990. The changing economic fortunes of young Black men in America. *Black Scholar,* January–February–March: 47–55.

Taylor, R. 1981. Psychological modes of adaptation. In *Black men,* L. E. Gary, ed. Newbury Park, Calif.: Sage.

Whitley, B. E. 1983. Sex role orientation and self-esteem: A critical meta-analytic review, *Journal of Personality and Social Psychology,* 44: 765–788.

Wilkinson, K. 1974. The broken family and juvenile delinquency: Scientific explanation or ideology. *Social Problems,* 21: 726–739.

Wilson, R., and S. Melendez. 1986. *Fifth annual status report on minorities in higher education.* Washington, D. C.: American Council on Education, Office of Minority Concerns.

Yablosky, L. 1963. *The violent gang.* New York: Macmillan.

5

❀

Male-Female Relationships

Single and Married: The Black Male's Acceptance of the Prince Charming Ideal

CLYDE W. FRANKLIN II & WALTER PILLOW

The Prince Charming ideal is the other half of the Cinderella complex, which encourages women to repress full use of their minds and creativity and to become dependent upon others. The Prince Charming ideal holds that becoming a mature man means assuming a protective, condescending, patriarchal role toward one's female mate and toward women in general. The authors differentiate between internalization of the Prince Charming ideal and acting in accordance with it. They develop a model of these differences and discuss the implications for male-female relationships.

■

Jeanne Noble's *Beautiful Also Are the Souls of My Black Sisters* and Colette Dowling's *The Cinderella Complex* serve as points of departure in this paper, which is devoted to an exploration of the Black male role and its effect on Black male-female social interaction (Dowling, 1981; Noble, 1978). The above books are provocative in that their theses propose two distinct, though related, empirical statements about male-female relationships in the United States. Of the two, Noble's book admittedly is more specific and more critical of Black men. She suggests that Black males have destructive, sexist attitudes. Dowling's work, which is oriented more toward sex role relationships in the United States generally, characterizes women as being engulfed in a destructive and debilitating fear of independence which is posited as the main reason for female subjugation in our society.

Noble's thesis implicitly blames Black men for negative social interaction between themselves and Black females. Dowling's thesis implies that a complex set of factors may be responsible for the state of Black male-female relationships. It is within the context of the latter thesis that we explore the role of the Black male and its effects on intersex social interaction.

From *Black Caucus* 13 (Spring 1982): 3–7. © 1982 by the National Association of Black Social Workers. Reprinted by permission.

Two important assumptions underlie our efforts. The first is that, despite Dowling's contention, which is based on Homer's studies indicating that Black females appear to be less fearful of independence than are White females *and* Black males, another observation might be more accurate. This is due to the fact that Homer's studies, which were conducted at the University of Michigan during the middle of the late 1960's, might be outdated. We suggest instead that present day Black women only *appear* to be more independent than are White women and Black men due to their historically imposed independent subsistence relative to the former. In actuality, Black females internalize values regarding not only their roles in society, but also those of Black males that are similar to the ones internalized by their White counterparts. The result is that Black females are just as emotionally dependent upon Black men as White women are on White men.

A second assumption is that Black men presently are socialized into the Prince Charming ideal *to the same extent* as are White males with one exception—they do not receive either the means or the societal support by which to approximate the ideal as do their White counterparts. Moreover, Black males oftentimes accede to the idea that Black females are independent, assertive, and so forth. Wallace's observations are instructive here:

> Black men and women were separated, given conflicting roles, and the creation of various myths assured our nation would be disunified. One of the most harmful myths was... the idea of the Black matriarchy. The Black woman's role was defined in such an intentional manner as to emasculate our men and give them limited responsibility (Wallace, 1979:122)

Because Black females actually *are* dependent upon Black males and many Black males' role responses are not congruent with Black female dependence, Black male–Black female social interaction suffers. The purpose of this paper,

therefore, is *to explore factors within the Black male role which militate against fulfilling dependency needs in Black females.* These factors, we submit, are entrenched in *Black male responses to the "Prince Charming" ideal*—the role model for males to use in their relationships with females in the United States. This ideal, Black male responses to the ideal, and the implications of those responses to Black male–Black female relationships are the subject of this article.

THE PRINCE CHARMING IDEAL

In the fairy tale, not only was there a Cinderella, but there was also a Prince Charming. Dowling's book concentrated on Cinderella; we focus our attention on Prince Charming—at least the "Prince Charming" ideal which is just as pervasive in the fantasies of Black men and Black women as it is in the fantasies of their White counterparts. Dowling defines the "Cinderella complex" as "a network of largely repressed attitudes toward the full use of their minds and creativity.... That psychological dependency—the deep wish to be taken care of by others—is the chief force holding women down today" (Dowling, 1981:31).

While Dowling's thesis certainly is thought-provoking, we contend that more than the Cinderella complex holds women down today. More specifically, the Prince Charming ideal also contributes to the subordination of women in society. In fact, the authors contend that the Prince Charming ideal negatively affects the Black male in the performance of his role as he interacts with the Black female. The Prince Charming ideal may be defined as the *philosophical belief that being a responsible, mature male means the assumption of a protective, condescending providing and generally patriarchal role regarding one's female mate and women in general.* Implicit in this definition is a denial of the ability of women to fend for themselves as well as all of the psychological implications of the philosophical stance. Goldberg describes the syndrome in detail in his book, although he does not refer to the "Prince Charming" labels (Goldberg, 1976). Instead, he refers to so-called masculine traits such as competition, internalization of the Protestant work ethic, domination, emphasis on independence, intellect, activity, and the like.

It is interesting to note that, prior to the Black male-led civil rights movement of the late '60s and early '70s, relatively few Black Prince Charmings existed in the Black subculture in America because few Black Cinderellas existed. We contend that this social movement had the latent function of producing Black Cinderellas and Black Charmings without a fairyland. Let us explore this contention further.

Antecedent to the modern day civil rights movement, Black women generally were taught to be much more assertive, competitive, and active than were Black men. Black parents, fearing for the safety of their male offspring, generally taught them to assume the deferential mask.... to be submissive. In 1968, Grier and Cobbs wrote at length about how Black parents tended to curb aggression, competitiveness, and domination in their male offspring for fear that it was too dangerous for them to exhibit such traits in the United States (Grier and Cobbs, 1968:62). Because Black females were not perceived by White American society to be as threatening as were Black males, Black females generally were allowed greater access to the meager opportunities for social mobility available to Blacks. This resulted in widespread perceptions of the Black females as the more dominant, aggressive, and authoritarian figure in the Black race substructure. This perception was held not only by the larger American society, but also by many Black men at the outset, and during the course, of the Black movement. These "new" Black males who were leaders and supporters of the movement, viewed the Black male as a sexual victim of matriarchal tyranny (Porter, 1979). As a result, Black females were exhorted to assume supportive rather than leadership roles in the movement, to get behind Black men, to become less aggressive and domineering, and to become more submissive in social interaction with Black men. Succinctly stated, many Black men felt that for the

first time in American history they were ready to become Black Prince Charmings. Of Black female response to the Black male and Black female sex-role modification, Wallace states, "When she stood by silently as he (the Black male) became a man, she assumed that he would finally glorify and dignify Black womanhood just as the White man had done for White women" (Wallace, 1979:14). Wallace could have stated that Black females transformed themselves from self-reliant, independent, confident, and mature adults into Black Cinderellas waiting for their Black Prince Charmings. The length of the waiting period is what has troubled growing numbers of Black females and is the topic of our next section.

BLACK MALE RESPONSES TO THE PRINCE CHARMING IDEAL

Once Black males and Black females accepted the Prince Charming ideal for Black males, Black male role expectations changed appreciably. The responses to these changes are the focus of our attention in this section. In a sense, it is possible to say that Black males respond to the Prince Charming ideal on two levels: an *internalization level* and an *action level*. Let us consider the nature of these responses.

Black Male Responses on an Internalization Level

Black males learn the Prince Charming ideal (that is, the "appropriate" male role), both formally and informally. Sources for this instruction are both external and internal to the Black race subculture. Instruction on the appropriate role models for men in our society may result when Black men are exposed to formal socialization from educational institutions, religious institutions, the mass media, and other basic societal institutions. While such instruction historically has occurred, it was not until the civil rights movement that increasing numbers of Black males *adopted,* and numerous Black females submissively *accepted,* the

Prince Charming ideal. As a result, the Black subculture as a whole began to accept this role model. This acceptance paved the way for subcultural support of the internalization of the Prince Charming ideal by young Black males who were being instructed in appropriate male sex roles. Moreover, it is suggested that many older Black males similarly became resocialized with respect to the appropriate male sex roles which Black men should internalize.

As a result of this change in Black male sex role socialization, we submit that a majority of Black males have internalized the Prince Charming ideal. This position places us diametrically opposite popular beliefs which posit that one reason for disharmony among increasing numbers of Black males and Black females is a failure of Black males to internalize a male sex role which emphasizes the assumption of responsibility, self-reliance, assertiveness, competitiveness, independence, and the like. Indeed, the myth of Black males' noninternalization of the normative male sex role probably persists because of the failure of many persons to distinguish between the two levels of Black male responses to the role ideal—that is, internalization and action. Internalizing the ideal does not automatically result in behavior congruent with the ideal, as will be shown below. Given the inordinate number of societal constraints Black males experience when they attempt to exhibit behavior congruent with their internalized values, it is not surprising that, on the whole, Black male actions are viewed as being divergent from the Prince Charming ideal. Such perceptions seemingly support the notion that a majority of Black males reject the ideal and, therefore, do not act in accordance with the ideal. The authors contend that this is not the case and, instead, offer an alternative explanation of Black male action on the ideal.

Black Male Response on an Action Level

For Black males, unlike counterparts in our society, there is not a linear relationship between internalization of the Prince Charming ideal and action congruent with the ideal. On the contrary, for Black males, numerous societal factors militate against their actualization of the Prince Charming ideal. Such factors are well known, and have been explored extensively. The important point to note is that a failure to act upon the ideal may not reflect a rejection of the ideal. Acting upon the ideal is some function of class status for Black males just as it is for White males. However, for Black males, unlike White males, it is also some function of actual and perceived opportunities for obtaining the means by which to act upon the ideal. This means that Black males continue to be inhibited in their efforts to act upon the Prince Charming ideal. The existence of this inhibition illuminates the need for social science scholars and practitioners to conduct research and respond to clients on the basis of a model of the Black male role as one that involves not only internalizing and acting upon the ideal, but also a failure to do so. The accompanying table shows the proposed model.

At a simple action response level, Black males either act or fail to act in accordance with the Prince Charming ideal. Because two levels of Black male responses are suggested, Black male responses always involve at least two variables *and* one of two subtypes of each variable. Thus, the Black male response to the Prince Charming ideal at the most simple level assumes one of four possible forms. First, some Black males (category one) internalize the ideal and exhibit behavior congruent with the ideal. Black males most likely to be characterized in this manner typically are middle class, although they can be found throughout the Black social stratification. When such males come from the lower socioeconomic classes, they have usually acquired the necessary means for actualizing the ideal. Entertainers and sports figures who, after years of poverty, suddenly acquire great wealth are highly visible examples of lower class Black males who become socially mobile and, therefore, are able to actualize the internalized Prince Charming ideal. Other less visible Black males in this category include those who become socially mobile through education, hard work, and rare opportunities.

Category two calls attention to those Black males who, for a variety of reasons related to their socialization experience (both formal and informal), *do not* internalize the Prince Charming ideal, but rather act in a ritualistic manner regarding the ideal. These males, then, act in accordance with the ideal and may superficially resemble those Black males in category one. The characteristic that distinguishes the Black male category two from all of the others is a tendency to actualize his resentment of the roles he performs. In addition, when the opportunity presents itself, such Black males are extremely likely to discard the "performing" role. We contend that some unknown proportion of Black males who reject parental and spousal obligations fall into this category. However, not all Black men who initially act on the ideal but who do not subsequently continue to do so should be characterized as having failed to internalize the Prince Charming ideal, as we show later.

A third response category in which we feel a large number of poor Black males can be placed is category three. Black males in this category *do* internalize the Prince Charming ideal, but the behaviors which they exhibit are not congruent with the internalized values. Many of these Black males, we feel, come from the lower Black social stratum, while the remainder have experienced *downward social mobility*. The distinguishing feature of the males in this category is the high probability that they will engage in self-destructive behavior as well as anti-social behavior, that is, physically abusive behavior toward their mates. Such behavior, when viewed by the uninformed, is likely to be perceived as a failure to internalize the ideal. To the contrary, we believe that such behavior reflects feelings of poor self-esteem due to the lack of means by which to actualize the internalized and societally supported Prince Charming ideal. Additionally, such feelings and the resulting anti-social behavior may be increased when the Black female in such a relationship also holds expectations for the Black male that are congruent with the ideal.

The fourth Black male response category describes the Black male who does not internalize

Black Male Responses to the Prince Charming Ideal

		Black Male Internalization Response Related to the Prince Charming Ideal	
		Internalize	Failure to Internalize
Black male action responses related to the Prince Charming ideal	Act in accordance with the ideal	1	2
	Fail to act in accordance with the ideal	3	4

the ideal and who fails to act in accordance with the ideal. These Black males can include two types: (1) those who appear to be estranged from Black females (and females in general), often by exhibiting boorish behavior and an apparent lack of respect for women; and (2) those Black males who in the vernacular seemingly "have it all together," but who refuse to allow Black females to become emotionally dependent upon them or to act in a protective, condescending, and generally patriarchal manner toward Black females. Because of the influence and pervasiveness of the Prince Charming ideal, however, we believe that Black males falling into this category are relatively few in number in comparison to those in the other three categories.

THE IMPLICATIONS OF BLACK MALE RESPONSES FOR BLACK MALE–BLACK FEMALE RELATIONS

By now, the implications of Black male responses to the Prince Charming ideal for social interaction between Black males and Black females are probably apparent. Black males who interact with Black females from the vantage point of category one (internalization of the ideal and action in accordance with the ideal) usually do so with a minimum of difficulty. Both the male and the female generally experience a positive interaction. This is to be expected, since both individuals have similar expectations about the roles of Black males and Black females involved in social interaction. Moreover, hidden resentment is less likely to characterize the male involved in the interaction. In this case, Black Prince Charming is meeting his own expectations as well as the expectations of the Black Cinderella.

But, what happens to Black male–Black female relationships when Prince Charming does *not* internalize the Prince Charming ideal (category two)? Such relationships can superficially appear to be positive for years. This is true because the Black male's visible behavior under these circumstances may be no different from that of the true Black Prince Charming. However, the possible exception is that the Black male in category two strictly fulfills the overt behavioral requirements of his role and *demands* that Black Cinderella fulfill the requirements of her role. In such instances, the Black male is likely to be hypercritical of the Black female—making extreme demands on her and placing her in impossible situations (Goldberg, 1976). Her inability to meet these demands or to extricate herself from such situations provides the needed excuse for him not to *fulfill* his own and her expectations of his role. When this occurs, the Black male is inclined to leave the relationship. If he remains in the relationship, the situation usually becomes intolerable for the Black female and she is forced to flee the relationship. When both remain, the relationship becomes an overtly conflict-ridden one with both parties feeling that the expectations for the other are not being met.

Black male–Black female relationships are most visibly conflict-ridden when Black males fall into category three….(when they have internalized the Prince Charming ideal, but do not have the means by which to act on the ideal). Black males in these situations suffer from poor

self-esteem *and* a loss of respect from Black females. These men are much more likely than are those in any other category to be physically abusive toward the Black female, who is perceived as demanding, nagging, domineering, and aggressive. On another level, however, such males feel that they are not adequately fulfilling their self-internalized roles. The Black female who also has accepted the definition of the Black male's role as that of "Prince Charming" and who exhibits behavior congruent with this acceptance is viewed by this Black male as a constant reminder of his failure to live up to his own ideals. Hostilities which Black males in this category direct toward these women may be construed as efforts to eradicate the "reminder."

Category four characterizes Black males who neither internalize nor act upon the Prince Charming ideal. The implications of this Black male response for Black male–Black female relationships take two diverse directions. One direction leads to unstable relationships between Black males in this category and Black females. The other direction, given modifications in the expectations for Black males held by many Black females, can lead to stable and positive relationships between these Black males and Black females.

With respect to the first direction, Black males who have neither internalized nor acted upon the ideal include those who visibly shirk all responsibility and act contrary to the male role ideal. Such men indicate verbally and by their actions that they have no intention of participating in a stable relationship with any Black female. Obviously, a proliferation of Black males who perform their roles in this manner foretells doom for Black male–Black female relationships.

Yet, there is a small and growing cadre of Black males who epitomize category four, but who believe that Black females should renounce many elements of the Cinderella complex and, therefore, modify their expectations of the role of Black men in Black male–Black female relationships. Such men *are* responsible and behave responsibly toward Black females, respecting Black females as mature adults. When these males form relationships with Black females who have modified their conceptions of the Black male's role in Black male–Black female relationships, stable relationships between the two may be obtained. Men and women who begin their relationship in this manner can be characterized in sex-role parlance as having an androgynous sex-role orientation. Moreover, we suggest that such relationships can be fulfilling to both parties. Given the fact that support exists in our society for less dependent, more assertive women and for less aggressive, less domineering men, those possessing an androgynous sex-role orientation may increase the probability that the relationships they form are both positive and powerful.

CONCLUSION

A latent but persistent theme in our analysis of Black male responses to the Black male's role in Black male–Black female relationships has been that Black men may respond in several ways. In addition, we indicated that there may not be a linear relationship between internalization of the traditional male role and the exhibition of behavior which is congruent with that role. Societal constraints on acting upon the Prince Charming ideal, noninternalization of the ideal, and an inability to act upon the ideal, among the factors, may all be responsible for Black male behavior which appears to be contrary to the Prince Charming ideal.

An additional feature of our analysis is that both the Prince Charming ideal and the Cinderella complex lock persons into social roles, which may be difficult to fulfill in a modern society. The Black male role may be the most difficult of all to fulfill, given the complexities of, and the contradictions inherent in, his role in a

society which is often diametrically opposed to his interests.

Given the above statements, social scientists (both theoreticians and practitioners) should begin to view Black male responses in terms of the multiplicity of possible meanings of the responses. Traditionally, Black male responses deemed to be inappropriate in Black male–Black female relationships have been defined as meaning noninternalization of what we call the "Prince Charming ideal." As we have seen, this perception may or may not be accurate. Moreover, when disruptive responses are defined in this way, measures designed to alter the responses may be inadequate. Certainly, the model presented in this paper to represent possible meanings underlying Black male responses is simplistic. Some Black males, for example, may partially internalize the ideal, act upon the ideal only part of the time, and so forth. Yet, we believe that approaching a particular case from the framework presented—with whatever modifications may be required by that case—may improve the rate of problem resolution between Black males and Black females. This undoubtedly will contribute to the unification of Black men and Black women in America.

REFERENCES

Dowling, Colette. 1981. *The cinderella complex*. New York: Summit.

Goldberg, Herb. 1976. *The hazards of being male*. New York: New American Library.

Grier, William H., and Price M. Cobbs. 1968. *Black rage*. New York: Basic Books.

Noble, Jeanne. 1978. *Beautiful also are the souls of my Black sisters*. Englewood Cliffs, N.J.: Prentice-Hall.

Porter, John R. 1979. *Dating habits of young Black Americans*. Dubuque, Ia.: Kendall/Hunt.

Wallace, Michelle. 1979. *Black macho and the myth of the superwoman*. New York: Dial.

Coping: Stressors and Depression among Middle Class African American Men

ROBERT C. EVANS & HELEN L. EVANS

The authors designed a study to test the association be-tween stressors, depression, and styles of coping among middle-class Black men. Using a purposive sample of young to late middle-age Black professional men and graduate students preparing for professional employ-ment, the authors sent out a questionnaire to measure this association. They found that most of the men were not depressed. Among the men who were depressed, a relationship with a "significant other" was the primary source of their stress in the last 12 months. There was little relationship between depression and stressors. The men who experienced problems in their relationships were more likely to use confrontive, accepting responsi-bility and escape avoidance coping strategies.

■

INTRODUCTION

African-American men have become a critical group to understand in order to provide appro-priate social and psychological services to the African American community. The 1990 census data profiles African-American men (A.A. men) as being challenged to cope with a number of personal and societal factors that profoundly im-pact their emotional state. A.A. men were more than twice as likely as White men to be divorced in 1989. Forty-one percent of A.A. men 16 years old and over were not in the labor force in 1989. Twelve percent of A.A. men versus 4.5 percent of White men in the labor force were unem-ployed in 1989. The average life expectancy of A.A. men in 1989 was, on the average, seven years shorter than that of White men. Suicide for

A.A. men had increased from 8/100,000 in 1970 to 12/100,000 in 1988. While White men com-mit suicide at higher rates after age 65, A.A. men from 25 to 34 years of age committed suicide at a rate more frequent than other A.A. men grouped by age. One hundred and thirty-seven A.A. men per one hundred thousand experienced death from accidents or violence in 1988, as compared to 83/100,000 for White men. Fifty-eight per one hundred thousand A.A. men were murdered in 1988, as compared to 8/ 100,000 White men. AA. men in 1988 accounted for 47 percent of all persons incarcerated in state prisons and 41 per-cent of the inmates in city, county, and local jails. The latter and former are significant data, given that A.A. men make up only 5 percent of the U.S. population (Bureau of the Census, 1991).

The above statistics present a limited but sig-nificant picture of the kind of stressors which might create a high risk for depression among A.A. men. These kinds of stressors influence how A.A. men experience and cope with their envi-ronment (Jones, 1984; Crawley and Freeman, 1992). Some A.A. men might blame themselves for not being able to resolve personal problems which then might cause self-doubt (Steele, 1990). Alternatively, Crawley and Freeman (1992) using an ethnographic survey, found that both young and older A.A. men might manage stressful life events by talking things over with other men. Other researchers have found that some A.A. men experience depression as a result of environ-mental stressors (Jones, 1984; Gary, 1985).

The economic, legal, social and mental health concerns of A.A. men should be understood and addressed at the societal, community and personal levels. This article provides empirical data about how A.A. men cope with relationships, jobs and other life stressors. Given the environmental and social stressors that A.A. men might encounter, many are likely to experience depression. How they cope with stress and depression will greatly influence the quality of their lives.

REVIEW OF LITERATURE

Jones (1984), in a survey of psychiatrists who had treated African-American men, found that the most reported initial problem and diagnosis was depression. The primary issues associated with being depressed were family issues, employment issues, environmental factors and racism. Gary (1985), in a study of 142 males, reports that employment status and conflict between a male and his female partner were the best correlates of depressive symptoms. Family income and conflict between the men and their partners accounted for 20 percent of the sample's variance in severity of depressive symptoms.

Jones (1984) found that racial discrimination was a significant conflict area for men. Low self-esteem was also a factor for a majority of the study's subjects. The most frequent means of coping was denial. Cazenave (1983), in a study of 155 A.A. men, reported that one of the critical areas of conflict for the males and their female partners was communication. The stress of poor communication was associated with withdrawal and blaming one's partner as ways of coping. This pattern is similar to behaviors described in Lazarus' escape avoidance coping subscale (Lazarus, 1984) in which not believing the stressful event happened, avoiding being with people and thinking of unreal things might be ways of coping with stress.

Lazarus' model suggests that coping refers to both how a person thinks and behaves towards environmental stress. A person under stress might attempt to solve the cause of stress or absorb the emotional stress of the situation. In a study of middle age Whites using Lazarus' (1984) coping scale, Coyne et al. (1981) found that depressed persons had a greater use of the appraisals (continually reevaluated judgments about environmental demands and constraints) of "need more information," wishful thinking," and "seeking of emotional support," and not-depressed persons had greater use of "must accept." As Coyne noted, depressed and not-depressed persons did not differ in "self-blame" or "problem focused" coping responses. Depressed persons coped differently at work and in family situations than those not depressed. At work depressed persons sought emotional support and in the family they relied very heavily on wishful thinking and self-blaming. The notion of "wishful thinking" is similar to Lazarus' escape avoidance concept and seeking emotional support seems to parallel Lazarus' "seeking social support" (Lazarus, 1984). Heppner et al. (1983) observed that effective coping was associated with positive self concept, problem focused coping and lower self blame. The current researchers believe, based on clinical practice, that the coping patterns of A.A. men are influenced by racial identity, the ability to influence one's immediate environment and the quality of one's relationship with a spouse or partner.

The studies by Jones (1984), Gary (1985), and Cazenave (1983), on African American men and coping each suggest that relational conflict with a female partner is associated with depressive behaviors. Based on the previously mentioned studies, African American men who exhibited depressive behaviors of denial, withdrawal, poor communication were more likely to be related to having had conflict with a female partner. It is not clear which factor occurs first, according to the studies. Using Lazarus' scale in the current study will permit the subjects to identify the initial source of their stress and their resulting method of coping. Lazarus' scale encourages the subject to consider the sequence of events (i.e., stressor leading to a coping strategy). Jones, Gary and Cazenave each suggest that the subjects in their studies used avoidance behaviors when confronting relational stressors. Thus, the present research addressed the following question. What is the association between stressors, depression and styles of coping among middle-class African American men? The following relationships were tested:

1. Men who report stress related to conflict with a significant female partner are more likely to report experiencing depression.
2. Escape-avoidance coping as defined by Lazarus will be used more by men who report stress related to conflict with a significant female partner.
3. There will be a positive association between depression and using escape-avoidance coping.

Knowing some of the critical stressors and coping patterns in the personal lives of A.A. men will help researchers and clinical psychotherapists to understand this group and to develop appropriate services. The current research is based on self report survey data. This method was chosen to ensure anonymity and thus to increase the return rate.

Methodology

A purposive sample of middle class African American men was used, drawn in a large Midwestern city. The mailing addresses of potential participants were obtained from men's groups at churches, the local graduate chapter of a fraternity, graduate schools of social work, and African American professional associations (i.e., lawyers, social workers, psychologists). Two-hundred questionnaires were mailed, and by the end of follow-up procedures, 108 (54 percent response rate) were returned completed. The respondents ranged from 18 to 82 years of age. More than half (54 percent) of the respondents were employed professionals, 40 percent were graduate students and 6 percent were retired.

The questionnaire included the Beck Depression Inventory, Lazarus' Ways of Coping Scale, and background information. The scales are standardized with reported reliability and validity data

(Beck, 1975; 1979; Lazarus, 1984). The Beck Depression Inventory consists of 21 items with four response choices each of which estimate depression on cognitive, behavioral and emotional dimensions. The scale is scored summatively. A score of 17 is clinically significant (Burns, 1980). An example of a scale item is:

0. I do not feel sad
1. I feel sad
2. I am sad all the time and I cannot snap out of it
3. I am so sad or unhappy that I can't stand it

The Ways of Coping Scale ask respondents to identify a significant stressor which occurred in the last 12 months and includes a 67 item scale which estimates the use of 8 coping strategies (confrontive, distancing, self-controlling, seeking social support, accepting responsibility, escape-avoidance, planful problem-solving and positive reappraisal) (Folkman et al., 1986). The scale has response values and anchors which range from 0 "not used" to 3 "used a great deal?" For purposes of the current research the scale was scored summatively.

Confrontive coping (6 items) indicates using direct aggressive strategies to cope with stress. Examples of scale items include "Stood my ground and fought for what I wanted" and "I expressed anger to the person(s) who caused the problem." *Distancing* (6 items) as a coping strategy is similar to using denial. Examples of scale items include "Went on as if nothing had happened" and "Tried to forget the whole thing." *Self controlling* coping (7 items) involves not allowing true feelings or thoughts to be known. Examples of scale items are, "I tried to keep my feelings to myself" and "Kept others from knowing how bad things were?" *Seeking Social Support* (6 items) as a coping strategy involves discussing one's stressful situation with others and getting advice. Scale items include "Talked to someone who could do something concrete about the problem" and "Talked to someone about how I was feeling." *Accepting Responsibility* (4 items) as a way to cope indicates that the individual assumed the blame for their stressful situation. Example scale items are "Criticized or lectured myself" and "Realized I brought the problem on myself" *Escape-Avoidance* coping (8 items) involves wishfully thinking the stressor would disappear. Sample items of this scale are "Hoped a miracle would happen" and "Wished that the situation would go away or somehow be over." *Planful Problem Solving* (6 items) as a way to cope indicates using assertive behaviors. Examples of scale items are "I made a plan of action and followed it" and "I knew what had to be done, so I doubled my efforts to make things work." Lastly, *Positive Reappraisal* (7 items) as a coping style suggest that the individual changed their way of thinking about the stressful situation. Individuals would be more likely to reaffirm their goodness or adopt a positive future outlook. Examples of scale items are "Changed or grew as a person in a good way" and "I came out of the experience better than when I went in."

Background information was gathered about age, occupation, education and marital status. These items appeared at the end of the questionnaire.

The study data was analyzed using one-way analysis of variance and the 't' test. Results were consistent with hypotheses; however, as the sample was purposive and not large enough to be considered representative of men in the population, the findings cannot be generalized beyond the sample. Despite this limitation, the study is important because it has investigated a segment of the population that is usually not studied or written about in journal articles.

RESULTS

Reliability and Validity of the Measures

Cronbach's test of reliability was computed for each measure as there were no reports of the scales being used primarily with A.A. men (see Table 1). The Beck Depression Scale (21 items)

TABLE 1 Reliability of Scales

Reliability	Alpha
Depression (21 items)	.87
Hopelessness (20 items)	.67
Ways of Coping	
full scale-67 items	.96
subscale	
1. Confrontive coping	.76
2. Distancing	.72
3. Self controlling	.70
4. Seeking social support	.77
5. Accepting responsibility	.71
6. Escape avoidance	.83
7. Planful problem solving	.85
8. Positive reappraisal	.83

achieved an alpha rating of .87. Thus, there was very high inter–item correlation. The Ways of Coping Scale (67 items) obtained a full scale alpha rating of .96. The Ways of Coping Scale's subscales achieved alpha levels which ranged from .70 to .85. To investigate the construct validity of depression, Beck (1975) suggests that the hopelessness scale would positively correlate with depression. The strong positive correlation found here between depression and hopelessness was in the expected direction ($r = .56$, $p = .01$). (Note: The hopelessness scale achieved an alpha of .67.)

Frequency Description of the Sample

The mean age of the respondents was 36 (see Table 2), the median age was 36, and the range was from 18 to 82 years. Within the sample, 7 (6 percent) respondents were retired professionals, 43 (40 percent) were graduate social work or psychology students and 58 (54 percent) were employed professionals. The mean score of depression was 5, the median was 3, and the range was 0 to 32. According to Burns (1980), the clinically significant depression scores are 17 and

TABLE 2 Stress, Depression, and Coping within a Sample of African-American Males

	Age N = 108	
Mean	36	
Median	36	
Range	18-82	
	Occupation N = 108	
Categories	**N**	**%**
Retired professional	7	6
Student	43	40
Professional	58	54
	Depression N = 108	
Mean	5	
Median	3	
Range	0-32	

above, and mood disturbance is indicated by scores between 10 to 16. There were 8 persons who self reported clinical depression.

A brief description of how the men responded on the 8 Lazarus subscales provides an overview of the general coping patterns used. *Confrontative Coping* (6 items) scores exhibited a range of 0 to 17, mean of 5.97 and a standard deviation of 3.8. More than 50 percent of the men reported using aggressive coping strategies to deal with stress. *Distancing Coping* (6 items) achieved a range of 0 to 17, a mean of 5.96, and a standard deviation of 3.8. More than 50 percent of the men reported using some form of denial to cope with stressful circumstances. *Self Controlling* (7 items) scores demonstrated a range of 0 to 19, a mean of 9.50, and a standard deviation 4.47. More than 50 percent of the men reported regular use of self-control by not showing their true feelings as a way of coping. *Seeking Social Support* (6 items) scores achieved a range of 0 to 18, a mean of 8.38 and a standard deviation of 4.49. About 50 percent of the men

reported that they talk to other people and ask for their advice as a way to cope with stress. *Accepting Responsibility* (4 items) exhibited a range of 0 to 12, a mean of 4.68, and a standard deviation of 3.21. More than 50 percent of the men reported often using self-blame as a method of coping. *Escape Avoidance* (8 items) scores demonstrated a range of 0 to 24, a mean 6.20, and a standard deviation of 5.26. Slightly less than 50 percent of the men reported using this method which involves wishful thinking on a somewhat regular basis. *Planful Problem Solving* (6 items) achieved a range of 0 to 18, a mean of 10.01, and a standard deviation of 5.12. About 50 percent of the men reported regular use of thoughtful assertive ways of coping. Lastly, *Positive Reappraisal* (7 items) scores exhibited a range of 0 to 21, a mean of 11.19 and a standard deviation of 5.65; slightly more than 33 percent of the men reported regular use of changing their way of thinking about the stressful situation as a way to cope. Thus, in general, it appears that many of the men were likely to use most of the coping strategies above.

Stressors

Table 3 indicates that 79 men (73 percent) reported having experienced a stressor in the last twelve months. Twenty-nine men (27 percent) reported not experiencing a stressful situation. Of those men reporting stressors, fifteen (19 percent) reported job stressors (i.e., production, evaluations, pay reductions). One man (1 percent) reported race relation stress. This situation was job related and was added to job related stress. Thirty-six men (46 percent) reported relational stress in the last 12 months. Twenty-seven men (34 percent) reported having health, financial and other stressors in the past 12 months.

Stressors and Depression

The first hypothesis, that "men who report stress related to conflict with a significant female partner are more likely to report experiencing

TABLE 3 Stressors Reported on the Ways of Coping Scale
N = 108

	N	%
No stressor in last 12 months	29	27
Stressor reported for last 12 months	79	73

Types of Stressors Reported
N = 79

	N	%
Job related	15	19
Race relation	1	1
Relationship	36	46
Health, finance, etc.	27	34

depression," was not confirmed. Depression did not vary significantly across the various stressors reported by the men in the current sample (F = 1.62; p = 19). This result might be somewhat a reflection of the middle class status of the men and the fact that many were in stable (married) relationships (N = 49, 45 percent).

Ways of Coping

Ways of coping cross-classified by stressors are exhibited in Table 4. Confrontive, accepting responsibility, and escape avoidance coping strategies varied significantly across the stressors. Men who reported job or relationship stressors were more likely to use confrontive coping whereas men who reported no stressor or other stressors reported using it least. Also men who reported a relationship stressor reported using accepting responsibility more often than men who reported job, other and no stressors. The latter might indicate the importance those men placed on maintaining a positive relationship with their partners. Men who reported a relationship stressor also estimated themselves as using escape-avoidance coping more often than men who reported having job, other or no stressors. The latter and former findings suggest that men who reported a relationship stressor were more likely

to use different coping strategies to deal with conflict with their wives or girlfriends. The differential use of coping strategies might result from contextual issues relating to the stressor or varied personality characteristics of the men. The remaining ways of coping did not vary significantly across the stressors.

Tukey's range test on confrontive and accepting responsibility as ways of coping revealed that the men who reported experiencing a relationship stressor significantly differed from men who reported "other" stressors (health problems, automobile accidents, financial, etc.) (range = 3.69, p = .05). The Tukey range test on escape-avoidance coping indicated that men who experienced a relationship stressor differed significantly from men who reported not experiencing a stressor (range = 3.69, p = .05). No other comparisons were significant. These comparisons suggest that experiencing different kinds of relationship stressors might have a significant influence on the kind of coping strategy men might use. The latter finding confirms the *second hypothesis* that escape-avoidance coping will be used more by men who report stress related to conflict with a significant female partner.

Depression

The ways of coping strategies classified by level of depression are presented in Table 5. Self controlling, accepting responsibility and escape-avoidance responses achieved significant inverse relationships across the levels of depression. The group characterized as having "some depression" achieved the highest means on each significant coping strategy. This indicates that the more depressed the men were the more likely they were to use self-controlling, accepting responsibility and escape avoidance to cope.

Hypothesis 3 that there would be a positive association between depression and using escape-avoidance coping was confirmed (T = 2.70 df 24, p = .01). Depressive men were more likely to cope by escape and avoidance of stressful situations.

TABLE 4 Ways of Coping by Stressors

Ways of coping	Means of Stressors					
	Job (N = 16)	Relationship (N = 36)	Other Stressor (N = 27)	No Stressor (N = 29)	"F" (df3, 104)	P
Confrontive	8.31	8.42	5.56	6.90	2.72	.05*
Distancing	5.75	7.00	4.74	5.93	1.88	.14
Self-controlling	9.38	10.5	8.44	9.24	1.78	.32
Seeking social support	10.25	8.64	8.74	6.69	2.50	.06
Accepting responsibility	3.81	6.08	3.85	4.17	3.8	.01*
Escape-avoidance	6.56	8.00	6.04	3.93	3.47	.02*
Planful problem-solving	12.87	9.72	9.19	9.55	2.08	.11
Positive reappraisal	12.94	11.53	10.44	10.52	.84	.47

*significant at .05 or lower

TABLE 5 Ways of Coping by Level of Depression

Ways of Coping	No Depression Score 0-9 (N = 90)		Some Depression Score 10-32 (N = 18)		"T"	df	P
	Mean	SD	Mean	SD			
Confrontive	7.11	4.38	8.11	4.27	−.90	25	.38
Distancing	5.67	3.70	7.44	4.08	−1.71	23	.10
Self-controlling	9.11	4.48	11.39	4.03	−2.15	26	.04**
Seeking social support	8.11	4.17	9.72	5.77	−1.40*	106	.17
Accepting responsibility	4.24	3.03	6.83	3.28	−3.10	23	.005**
Escape-avoidance	5.60	5.08	9.22	5.21	−2.70	24	.01**
Planful problem solving	10.20	5.32	9.05	3.93	1.06	31	.29
Positive reappraisal	10.91	5.78	12.61	4.85	−1.31	28	.20

*Based on pooled variance

**Significant at .05 or lower

DISCUSSION

The sample consisted of young to late middle-age African American men who were engaged in professional employment or were graduate students preparing for professional employment. Most of the men were not depressed. However, 18 of the 108 scored in the depressive range (mood disturbance 10, depressed 8).

The current finding regarding the significance of relationship stress supports Gary's (1985) findings that A.A. men are likely to report that a relationship with a significant other had been their primary source of stress in the last 12 months. Job related stressors and various other stressors (financial, health, accidents, death of relative, fear of failure) followed relationship stressors in order of frequency.

There was little association between depression and stressors. Gary (1985) found that 20 percent of the sample variance on depression was accounted for by conflict between the men and their partners. The current research does not support that finding, and this might reflect that most of the men in the current study were not depressed and 45 percent of them were married. It is likely that the reasons for being depressed might be accounted for by a complex combination of stressors and not a single one. Lazarus (1984) suggests that a better estimate of stress might be daily hassles as they seem to predict depression better.

Men who experienced relational stressors were more likely to use confrontive, accepting responsibility and escape avoidance coping strategies. The significant difference between use of confrontive and accepting responsibility was accounted for by men who experienced relational problems with their female partners and men who experienced "other" stressors. It is likely that men who experienced "other" stressors used less confrontive and accepting responsibility coping because their stressors might have been perceived as beyond their control. By contrast, men who had relationship problems might have been more likely to see their problems as internal to themselves which required accepting responsibility for what had gone wrong and confronting the situation in an attempt to problem solve. Additionally, escape avoidance coping was used significantly more by men who experienced a relationship stressor. There was a significant difference between men who had experienced a relationship stressor and men who reported not having any stressors in the last 12 months. Cazenave (1983) found that conflict between men and their partners might be related to the men's perception of their partner's professional success. The latter is an area that needs further research.

Somewhat depressed A.A. men are likely to cope in some ways similar to the general population. This is suggested by the inverse relationship between the not depression and some depression groups on self controlling, accepting responsibility and escape avoidance Coyne (1981) and Heppner (1983) found that depressed persons were more likely to use self blaming and withdrawal from stressful situations as ways to cope. The current research shows that somewhat depressed A.A. men used these strategies more than men who were not depressed.

FUTURE RESEARCH

In future research, to provide more depth to the mental health knowledge regarding African American men, it would be important to investigate, in addition to affect and coping, their overall self concept and personal regulatory system (i.e., goals, standards and beliefs). Additionally, as Lazarus (1984) pointed out, it might be better to evaluate daily hassles as opposed to stressors, as the former has been found to predict depression better than stressors. The evaluation of anger and the management of it might also add some important information about these men. Another area which needs some close investigation is the quality of economic levels. significant intimate male-female relationships as they relate to coping and depression. It appears that these interpersonal relationships have critical influence on the behavior and affect of the men. Future research also needs to include men from more varied socioeconomic levels.

REFERENCES

Beck, A. et al. 1975. The hopeless scale. *Journal of Consulting and Clinical Psychology,* 42: 861–865.

Beck, A. et al. 1979. *A Cognitive Therapy of Depression.* New York: Guilford.

Burns, D. 1980. *Feeling Good.* New York: Signet.

Cazenave, N. July, 1983. Black male-black female relationships: The perceptions of 155 middle class black males. *Family Relations,* 34: 341–350.

Cheek, D. 1976. *Assertive Black. . . puzzled White.* San Luis Obispo, Calif.: Impact.

Corcoran, K. and Fischer, J. 1987. *Measures for clinical practice.* New York: Free Press.

Crawley, B., and Freeman, F. M. 1992. Themes in the life views of older and younger African American males. *Journal of African American Male Studies,* 1(1): 15–29.

Coyne, J. C., Aldwin, C., and Lazarus, R. S. 1981. Depression and coping in stressful episodes. *Journal of Abnormal Psychology,* 90: 439–447.

Davis, R. September, 1980. Suicide among young black . . . *Phylon,* 41(3): 223–229.

Franklin, C., II. December, 1984. Black males-black female conflict. *Journal of Black Studies,* 15(2): 139–154.

Folkman, S., Lazarus, R., Dunkel-Shetter, C., DeLongis, A., and Gruen, R. 1986. The dynamics of a stressful encounter: Cognitive appraisal, coping, and encounter outcomes. *Journal of Personality and Social Psychology,* 50: 992–1003.

Gary, L. (October) 1985. Correlates of depressive symptoms among a select population of black males. *American Journal of Public Health,* 75(10): 1220–1222.

Gite, L. November 1986. Black males and suicide. *Essence,* 17(7): 64–66, 134.

Helms, J. E., and Parham, T. A. 1985. *The Racial Identity Attitude Scale.* University of California, Irvine.

Hendrix, B. 1980. The effects of locus of control on the self esteem of black and white youth. *The Journal of Social Psychology,* 112: 301–302.

Heppner, P. P., Reeder, B. L, and Larson, L. M. 1983. Cognitive variables associated with personal problem-solving appraisal: Implications for counseling. *Journal of Counseling Psychology,* 30(4): 537–545.

Jones, B., and Gay, B. 1984. Similarities and differences in black males and women in psychotherapy. *Journal of the National Medical Association,* 76(1): 21–27.

Jones, B., and Gay, B. (January 1983. Black males and psychotherapy. *American Journal of Psychotherapy,* 37(1): 77–85.

Jones, B., and Gay, B. (September 1982. Survey of psychotherapy with black males. *American Psychiatric Association,* 139: 1174–1177

Kanner, H. D. et al. 1981. Comparison of two models of stress management: Daily hassles and uplifts vs. major events. *Journal of Behavior Medicine,* 4(10).

Kochman, T. 1981. *Black and White styles in conflict.* Chicago: University of Chicago Press.

L'Abate, L, and Milan, M. 1985. *Handbook of social skills training and research.* New York: John Wiley.

Lazarus, R. S. et al. 1984. *Stress Appraisal and Coping.* New York. Springer.

McMullin, R., and Giles, T. 1981. *Cognitive behavior therapy.* New York: Grune & Stratton.

Norment, L. (August) 1985. 21st century forecast: Male/female relationships. *Ebony,* 40: 76–79.

Steele, S. 1990. *The content of our character.* New York: Harper Perennial.

U.S. Bureau of the Census. 1991. *Statistical Abstracts of the United States: 1991* (11th ed). Washington, D.C.

6

❦

Marriage and Divorce

Separated Black Women: Do They Reconcile with Their Husbands?

HOWARD WINEBERG

This study, using 1987–1988 National Survey of Families and Households data, examined the prevalence and characteristics of ever-separated Black women who attempt a marital reconciliation in their first marriage. Marital reconciliations are quite common, as 45 percent of the separated women attempt a reconciliation. Women with children and those who are in marriages in which either spouse changed religion after marrying have a significantly increased likelihood of attempting a reconciliation. These findings provide some support for the thesis that those who have the most invested in the marriage or the greatest reliance on the relationship are the most likely to attempt a reconciliation. The implications of these findings are discussed.

■

INTRODUCTION

Marital dissolution continues to occur at a high rate in the United States with approximately half of the recent first marriages expected to end in divorce (Martin & Bumpass, 1989; Norton & Moorman, 1987). Researchers routinely consider the marriage ended at the date of separation rather than at the date of divorce (Martin & Bumpass, 1989; McCarthy, 1978). Marriage as a social union can be thought of as having ended when a couple permanently stops living together, even though the legal union continues until a divorce is obtained. Researchers have found that there are systematic variations in populations with regard to both the extent to which all separations are followed by legal divorces and the duration between separation and divorce. In particular, the duration between separation and divorce is much longer for Blacks than Whites (McCarthy, 1978)

From the *Western Journal of Black Studies,* Vol. 20, No. 1, 1996: 21–27. Copyright 1996 by the Board of Regents, Washington State University, Pullman, WA 99164. Reprinted by permission.

and Blacks are much more likely than Whites to rely on separation as a way of functionally ending a marriage (Morgan, 1988).

Although the pattern of divorce among various subgroups of American society has been well documented, little is known about the paths taken by separated women. Separation does not always denote the end of the marriage since some separated women reconcile with their husbands. In this study, we examine the characteristics of Black women who separate and then reconcile with their husbands.

LITERATURE REVIEW

Several researchers have examined reconciliations following separations. Bloom, et al. (1977) conducted a survey of households in Boulder, Colorado in 1975–76 to gather information on the prevalence and duration of marital separation. They found that 12 percent of ever-separated women had reconciled and were currently living with their spouses, and these women were younger and had shorter separations than persons who divorced.

Morgan (1988) used data from the National Longitudinal Surveys Cohort of Mature Women, 1967–1982, to examine the characteristics of separated women who divorce, reconcile, and remain in long-term separations; these women were between the ages of 30 and 44 when the panel study began. She found that non-Whites had a reduced probability of moving from separation to divorce; rather, they were significantly more likely to remain in long-term separations. Completing education beyond high school substantially reduced the probability of reconciling. The primary drawback of this study was that it provided no information on women under age 30.

In a more recent study, Wineberg and McCarthy (1993) used National Survey of Families and Households data to document the prevalence of separation and reconciliation among ever-married American women. They found that among currently married women about

9 percent of Whites and 14 percent of Blacks (or about 5,000,000 currently married couples in the United States) had experienced a separation and reconciliation in their marriage. Among women whose first marriage had ended, about 30 percent reported that, at some stage in the process of dissolving the marriage, they separated and reconciled before divorcing.

Lawson and Thompson (1994), in a review of the causes of divorce among Blacks briefly discussed separation. They noted that Blacks were substantially more likely to be currently separated than Whites. Additionally, the length of separations among Blacks suggested the possibility of Blacks moving between separation and reconciliation. They concluded that substantial research is needed on marital dissolution among Blacks.

OBJECTIVE

The purpose of this study was to help further our knowledge of the resolutions of separation by examining the patterns of marital reconciliation among separated Black women. In particular, we tried to document any significant differences in the characteristics of those moving from separation to reconciliation as compared to those who either remained in long-term separations or who moved directly from separation to divorce. The results of this study should provide some baseline data about the paths taken by separated Black women, thus improving our understanding of marital processes among Blacks. The relative scarcity of marital dissolution research for Blacks (Lawson and Thompson, 1994) and the fact that marriage is viewed differently by Blacks and Whites makes it appropriate for this study to focus exclusively on reconciliations among Blacks.

In discussing the characteristics of those moving from separation to reconciliation, we hypothesized that those who had the most invested in the marriage or the greatest reliance on the marital relationship may be the most likely to have a reconciliation. For example, it may be easier for someone who had been married a short time and has shared few marital experiences to end a marriage than someone who had been married for many years before separating. The psychological, emotional, and financial investment of long-time married couples may make it difficult for them to end the marriage and thus they may reconcile in the hopes of saving their marriages. Commitment to marriage may be expected to be related to an increased probability of moving from separation to reconciliation.

To the extent that changing religion in connection with their marriage is a proxy for marital commitment (investment), it may be expected that women who are in a marriage in which one of the spouses has changed religion maybe more likely to move from separation to reconciliation than to consider the marriage ended when they become separated. Additionally, women with children may need the financial and psychological security associated with marriage and thus they may attempt a reconciliation despite dissatisfaction with their marriage. Our analyses will try to shed some light on whether or not there is any evidence to support the hypothesis that marital investment, or reliance on the marital relationship, is associated with having a reconciliation.

DATA AND METHODS

The data source for this study was the National Survey of Families and Households (NSFH), which is a probability sample of the non–institutionalized United States population aged 19 and older. Interviews were carried out in 1987 and 1988, with primary respondents randomly selected from households. The NSFH collects information on many aspects of family life; the detailed marital history questions provide the basic focus of this study. In particular, ever-married respondents were asked questions about separations and reconciliations in their current (and first) marriage. (For a detailed description of the NSFH, see Sweet, et al, 1988).

The study population consisted of 320 non-Hispanic Black women who had been married once or twice, whose first marriage occurred between 1960 and 1988, and who had experienced a marital separation in their first marriage. To maximize recall accuracy, our analyses excluded women whose first marriage had occurred before 1960. We also excluded women who had been married more than two times because of possible recall accuracy concerning events in their first marriage. This exclusion should have little effect on the results since only 3 percent of the women who first married after 1960 had had more than two marriages.

The event of interest in this study was whether or not a woman who experienced a separation in her first marriage was likely to reconcile with her husband. We were not concerned with the successfulness of the reconciliation; for information on this issue, see Wineberg, 1996. We did not perform a separate analysis for reconciliations by men because marital data (as well as other data) reported by men are considered less reliable and precise than marital data reported by women (Cherlin, Griffith, and McCarthy, 1983; Sweet, 1990). The NSFH has virtually no information on the woman's second husband for women whose second marriages have ended. Consequently, our analysis focused on reconciliations occurring in first marriages only.

The NSFH collected information on separation, reconciliation, and divorce, making it an ideal data source for this study. Like other data sets, however, the NSFH does have limitations. Because both the husband and wife are involved in marital decisions, ideally, information on both spouses should be included in the analysis. However, we have no data indicating how the separated spouses collectively decide whether or not to attempt a reconciliation. Thus, in this study, the focus is on the resolution of separation from a woman's perspective. Some data that may impact whether a separated woman attempts a reconciliation (e.g., the income the woman earned while she was separated) were not collected in the NSFH. Despite the data limitations, this study should further our knowledge of which groups of separated Black women are likely to reconcile.

ANALYSIS

Initially, we calculated the proportion of ever-separated women who attempt a reconciliation. We then used a multivariate analysis to estimate the relationship between the sociodemographic variables and reconciling, with other variables held constant. The multivariate analysis used in the study is a discrete history analysis (discrete-time logit model) using logistic regression to estimate the parameters of the event history model.

In the multivariate analysis, the dependent variable was whether or not a separated woman reconciled with her husband. Women were followed from the date of their first separation until they reconciled, divorced, or were interviewed. The duration between the first separation and the reconciliation, divorce, or interview (whichever came first) was partitioned into discrete intervals.[1] If the woman reconciled during the interval the dependent variable was coded 1, or 0 otherwise. Each interval included only women who were in their first separation at the beginning of the interval. That is, if a woman reconciled, divorced, or was interviewed in a particular interval, she was included in that interval but excluded from subsequent intervals. For example, a woman who reconciled in the fifth interval would yield 5 intervals to the analysis whereas a woman who divorced in the second interval would yield 2 intervals to the analysis. All intervals were pooled into one sample for the purpose of analysis, which was accomplished using logistic regression. Although the sample contained only 320 women, because of data pooling the results in the multivariate analysis were based on 1052 observations.

RESULTS

In Table 1 the percentages are based on weighted numbers in order to correct for differential selection and response probabilities.

Table 1 shows that about 45 percent of Black women who experienced a separation in their first marriage had a reconciliation. It is probable that the proportion of separated women who reconcile could have been slightly higher than 45 percent since some of the currently separated women might have reconciled with their husbands after the date of interview. That about 85 percent of the separated women reconciling did so within six months after separating (results not shown) suggests that our results ever so slightly underestimated the proportion of separated Black women who move from separation to reconciliation.

It is clear from Table 1 that there were differences in the percentage reconciling among subgroups of Black women. In particular, the duration between marriage and first separation has a strong negative relationship with attempting a reconciliation. Approximately 55 percent of the women who separated within two years after marrying had a reconciliation; the proportion declined to 44 percent for women separating in the third to fifth year of marriage. Among women separating in the sixth to tenth year of marriage, 38 percent reconciled, and only 18 percent of women married 10 years before separating had a reconciliation.

Among women separating before age 23, about 54 percent had a reconciliation. The proportion reconciling declined to about 45 percent for those separating between the ages of 23 and 27. For those separating after age 28, the percentage having a reconciliation is only 28 percent. A similar pattern was found for age at marriage. Slightly more than one-half of the women who married before age 19 had a reconciliation, whereas only about 31 percent of those who first married after age 25 had a reconciliation.

Considering the age difference between the spouses, the lowest proportion of reconciliations occurred among women who married a husband of the same age (39 percent). Reconciliations were most common among women who married a younger man (50 percent). Women with one or two children at separation were substantially more likely to reconcile than childless women (46 percent to 34 percent).

TABLE 1 Percentage (Weighted) of Afro-American Women Attempting a Reconciliation among those Experiencing a Separation in their First Marriage

Variable	Percentage	Variable	Percentage
Total	44.9	Premarital Fertility	
		yes	49.1
Age at first separation		no	44.3
<20	54.0	Frequency of religious attendance	
20–22	53.6	<1 a week	44.5
23–27	45.1	1+ a week	46.3
28+	28.0	Cohabit with spouse before first marriage	
Parity at first separation		yes	53.1
0	34.1	no	42.3
1–2	45.5	Spouse previously married	
3+	37.2	yes	36.8
Duration between marriage and first separation		no	43.7
< 24 months	55.2	Age difference between spouses at marriage	
24–59 months	43.5	man 5+ years older	42.8
60–119 months	38.0	man 1–4 years older	42.7
120+ months	17.5	same age	38.8
Age at first marriage		woman 1+ years older	50.0
<19	53.9	Same religion as spouse	
19–20	44.2	yes	42.3
21–24	46.1	no	44.0
25+	30.6	Either spouse change religion after marriage	
Education		yes	53.7
<12	52.4	no	41.9
12	47.1	Total Number of Cases (unweighted)	320
13–15	34.2		
16+	49.4		

Among the three variables that measured some aspect of religion, only religious conversion was related to reconciling. In 54 percent of the marriages in which one or both of the spouses changed religion after marrying, a reconciliation was attempted. Reconciliations occurred in 42 percent of the marriages in which there was no change in religion associated with becoming married.

Women who cohabited with their spouse before marrying were more likely to have a reconciliation than women who did not cohabit with their spouse before marrying (53 percent to 42 percent). Reconciliations were slightly less likely to occur for women whose husbands were previously married than for women whose husbands were not previously married (37 percent to 44 percent). Education and premarital fertility did not appear to be related to whether or not a separated woman reconciled with her husband.

Table 2 presents the logit model for separated women having a reconciliation in their first marriage.[2] For ease in interpretation, the coefficients have been transformed to show the relative odds of women reconciling. Relative odds greater than 1.0 indicate an increased probability of having a reconciliation whereas relative odds less than 1.0 indicate a reduced probability of reconciling, other variables held constant.

Women with children at first separation had a significantly increased probability of having a reconciliation. In particular, women who have one or two children when they separate were about 2.4 times more likely to reconcile, and women with at least three children at separation

TABLE 2 Logistic Regression of Afro-American Women Attempting a Reconciliation Among Those Experiencing a Separation in Their First Marriage

Variable	Relative Odds
Age at first separation	
<20	1.12
20–22	1.00
23–27	0.91
28+	0.62
Parity at first separation	
0	1.00
1–2	2.43*
3+	2.84*
Duration between marriage and first separation	
<24 months	3.22**
24–59 months	1.00
60–119 months	1.05
120+ months	0.50
Education	
<12	1.68
12	1.00
13–15	0.83
16+	2.09
Age difference between spouses at marriage	
man 5+ years older	1.11
man 1–4 years older	0.74
same age	1.00
woman 1+ years older	0.85
Premarital fertility	0.55*
Frequency of religious attendance	1.17
Cohabit with spouse before first marriage	1.63
Spouse previously married	0.69
Same religion as spouse	0.93
Either spouse change religion after marriage	3.09**
N	1052

*p<.05. **p<.01

are about 2.8 times more likely to have a reconciliation than childless women.

Premarital fertility was associated with a significantly decreased likelihood of moving from separation to reconciliation. Women giving birth before marriage were about one-half as likely to have a reconciliation than women not giving birth before marriage.

Considering the three variables that measure some aspect of religion, only religious conversion is significantly related to having a reconciliation. Women who are in a marriage in which one of the spouses changed religion in connection with the marriage were about 3 times more likely to have a reconciliation than women who were in marriages in which no religious conversion occurs.

The duration between marriage and first separation had a negative, albeit not monotonic, relationship with having a reconciliation. Women separating within two years after marrying were significantly more likely to reconcile than women separating three to five years after marrying. It may be that women separating early in their marriage were still naive about marriage and they may believe that they can save their marriage if they worked a little harder at it; thus, they had a reconciliation. Women married more than 10 years before separating have a lower, albeit not significant, probability of having a reconciliation than those married three to five years before separating.

The remaining sociodemographic variables (premarital cohabitation, number of times the husband has been married, age at first separation, education, and age similarity of the spouses) are not significantly related to having a reconciliation.

CONCLUSION

This study using 1987–88 NSFH data, provided some insight as to the prevalence and characteristics of ever-separated Black women who had a marital reconciliation in their first marriage. Reconciliations are quite common as about 45 percent of the separated women reconciled with their husbands. Clearly, divorce was not necessarily imminent after separation and it may be premature to consider a marriage ended when a Black woman separated from her husband. The high proportion of separated women who reconciled was consistent with the thesis espoused by Furstenberg and Cherlin (1991) that many couples begin the process of separation undecided about its outcome. It also suggests that the decision to separate should not be equated with the decision to end the marriage.

Approximately one-half of the reconciliations occurred within one month after separation suggesting that some separations may have been the result of impulse or may have been used as a way to dissipate anger or create psychological space (Kitson, 1985). That many of the separations were short-lived may be beneficial to children in that there was a disruption in their living arrangements for only a short time. However, a very short separation may not provide the couple with sufficient time to work on the problems that caused the separation.

Differentials in the probability of having a reconciliation were found among subgroups of Black women. In particular, women giving birth before marriage had a significantly decreased likelihood of moving from separation to reconciliation. It is possible that the marital discord associated with the rearing of stepchildren may act to discourage the separated couple from reconciling. That is, in those households in which the husband was a stepfather, school-aged stepchildren may play one parent off against their stepparent, and they may resent a new stepfather being part of the picture for fear their natural father may be pushed out of the picture.

Additionally, stepchildren may provide ties to a relationship outside the marriage which may cause marital tension. Although in some instances women giving birth before marriage may have subsequently married the child's father, the father's parental responsibilities were probably more time consuming and stressful when he lived with his children on a full-time basis than when he cared for his children on a part-time basis. That premarital fertility is significantly associated with moving from separation to reconciliation may have a substantial impact on the overall number of reconciliations occurring among Black women since about two-thirds of all Black children are born to unmarried women (Ventura et al., 1994).

Our findings show moderate support for the hypothesis that greater marital investment is associated with a greater likelihood of a separated woman reconciling. In particular, that women having children at separation and religious conversion are associated with an increased probability of reconciling suggest that greater marital investment is related to moving from separation to reconciliation. However, results show that women married 5–10 years before separating were similarly likely to reconcile and women married more than 10 years before separating were less likely, albeit not significantly, to reconcile than women married 3–5 years before separating. This finding does not support the thesis that greater marital investment is related to an increased probability of moving from separation to reconciliation.

Separated women with children are probably in greater need of the financial and psychological security associated with marriage than childless women and thus they may be more likely to reconcile. It may be quite difficult for women with children to sever their marital bonds since substantial lifestyle changes often accompany separation and divorce (e.g., loss of social networks and change in residence). Conversely, it is probably easier for childless women to move directly from separation to divorce since they have no childrearing responsibilities to consider when deciding how to resolve their separation.

That one of the spouses changes religion in connection with the marriage suggests a strong commitment to the marriage in that a high priority may have been placed on religious compatibility during the search (courtship) process (Lehrer and Chiswick, 1993). Additionally, the process of religious conversion can be quite arduous for some religions suggesting greater marital investment among couples in which one of the spouses changed religion in connection with the marriage.

Our results suggest that some correlates may operate at several stages in the marital dissolution process and other correlates may operate at only one stage in the marital dissolution process. For example, several sociodemographic variables (e.g., premarital fertility, childlessness, and no religious conversion) were related to an increased probability of separation and a decreased probability of a reconciliation. It thus appears that the impact that these sociodemographic variables may have on the decision to separate is carried over to the decision of how to resolve the separation.

Several variables (e.g., education, frequency of religious attendance, and religious homogamy of the spouses) appear to be related to separation but have little impact on whether or not there is a reconciliation. Other variables (e.g., marital duration) appear to be associated with separation in a different manner. For example, women married a short time at separation are the most likely to reconcile; yet, the yearly risk of becoming separated is quite high in the early years of marriage. Researchers may wish to explore further the interrelationship between sociodemographic correlates and the various stages of the marital dissolution process.

That about 60 percent of recently married Black women may be expected to separate from their first husband (Martin and Bumpass, 1989), suggests that each year a substantial number of separated women may reconcile with their husbands. Consequently, in addition to programs for divorce counseling, it may be prudent to develop programs to help couples and their children to make a smoother transition from separation to reconciliation. Included in these programs should be guidance on how a separated couple may work together to overcome marital problems and help increase the likelihood of a successful reconciliation. Additionally, it may be time to reassess society's emphasis on couples and marriages, especially its desire for married couples to remain married despite marital dissatisfaction.

This study focused on the paths taken by separated Black women, thus increasing our understanding of the process of marital dissolution among Blacks. The effects that trial separations and failed reconciliations have on family members may have implications on the consequences of separation and divorce and thus are interesting topics for future research that may add to our overall understanding of marital processes.

NOTES

1. The first month of separation is divided into three intervals: the first week, the second week, and the remainder of the month. Separation durations are divided into monthly intervals in the second through sixth months. Separation durations lasting seven or more months are combined into one interval.

2. Age at first marriage is not included in the logit model since knowing age at first separation and duration between marriage and first separation gives one the age at first marriage.

REFERENCES

Bloom, B. L, Hodges, W. F., Caldwell, R. A., Systra, L., and Cedrone, A. R. 1977. Marital separation: A community survey. *Journal of Divorce, 1,* 7–19.

Cherlin, A., Griffith, J. and McCarthy, J. 1983. A note on maritally disrupted men's reports of child support in the 1980 current population survey. *Demography, 20,* 385–390.

Furstenberg, F. F., Jr., and Cherlin, A. J. 1991. *Divided families: What happens to children when parents part.* Harvard University Press, Cambridge, Mass..

Kitson, G. C. 1985. Marital discord and marital separation: A county survey. *Journal of Marriage and the Family, 47,* 693–700.

Lawson, E., and Thompson, A. 1994. Historical and social correlates of African American divorce: Review of the literature and implications for research? *Western Journal of Black Studies, 18,* 91–103.

Lehrer, E. V., and Chiswick, C. V. 1993. Religion as a determinant of marital stability. *Demography, 30,* 385–404.

Martin, T. C., and Bumpass, L. L. 1989. Recent trends in marital dissolution. *Demography, 26,* 37–51.

McCarthy, J. 1978. A comparison of the probability of the dissolution of first and second marriages. *Demography, 19,* 345–359.

Morgan, L. A. 1988. Outcomes of marital separation: A longitudinal test of predictors. *Journal of Marriage and the Family, 50,* 493–498.

Norton, A. J., and Moorman, J. E. 1987. Current trends in marriage and divorce among American women. *Journal of Marriage and the Family, 49,* 3–14.

Sweet, J. A. 1990. Differential in precision of reporting of dates of marital events in the national survey of families and households. (NSFH Working Paper No. 20). Madison: University of Wisconsin, Center for Demography and Ecology.

Sweet, J. A., Bumpass, L. L., and Call, V. 1988. The design and content of the national survey of families and households. (NSFH Working Paper No. 1). Madison: University of Wisconsin, Center for Demography and Ecology.

Ventura, S. J., Martin, J. A., Taffel, S. M., Mathews, T. J., and Clarke, S. C. 1994. Advance report of final natality statistics, 1992. *Monthly Vital Statistics Report,* Vol. 43, No. 5, Suppl. Public Health Service, Hyattsville, Md.

Wineberg, H. 1996. The prevalence and characteristics of Blacks having a successful marital reconciliation. Forthcoming in: *Journal of Divorce and Remarriage.*

Wineberg, H. and McCarthy, J. 1993. Separation and reconciliation in American marriages. *Journal of Divorce and Remarriage, 20,* 21–42.

Black Men After Divorce:
How Do They Cope?

ERMA JEAN LAWSON

Previous research has reported that postdivorce adjust-ment is non-problematic for Black men. However, the reasons for Black men's positive postdivorce adjustment remain unspecified. This study, using in-depth inter-views from 50 divorced working and middle class Black men, examines strategies they used to cope with di-vorce. The findings suggest that: (a) family and friends' support, (b) social and religious participation, (c) a cog-nitive style of optimism based on the historical experi-ences of Blacks in America, (d) initial maintenance of postmarital relationships, and (d) heterosexual rela-tionships assisted Black men to cope with divorce. The findings suggest that previous divorce literature has ig-nored Black families, friends, community groups, and religious institutions as resources for coping with di-vorce. It is argued that the dynamics of race, culture, and class have forged varied definitions of Black social support in a crisis, which are obscured by politicized images of the vanishing Black family and the deterio-rating Black community. Consequently, the adjustment of Black men to divorce is more complicated than re-searchers had presumed.

■

INTRODUCTION

During the past decade, enormous changes have occurred in Black families. These transitions have included the growth of marital dissolution by di-vorce and separation. Two thirds of all Black mar-riages end in divorce and two of three Black children will experience the dissolution of their parents' marriage by age 16 (U.S. Bureau of the Census, 1995). The separation rate is also higher for Blacks. Approximately, 16 percent of Black women between the ages of 18 and 44 are sepa-rated, compared to 4 percent of comparable White women (U.S. Bureau of the Census, 1995). Racial differences in divorce and separation rates persist independently of education and parental marital stability (Cherlin, 1992; Davis, 1993; Dickson, 1993; Weingarten, 1985; Willie, 1991).

Divorce demands tremendous psychological, social, and economic adjustments, which includes severance of complex marital bonds, negotiation of custody arrangements, and adjustment to a single lifestyle (Amato and Keith, 1991; Ardnell, 1995; Demo and Ganong, 1994; Kitson and Holmes, 1992; Reissman, 1990; Vaughan, 1986; Wymard, 1994). However, there is an absence of studies that have examined Black men's adjustment to divorce. This lack of research is surprising since studies have reported that Black men experience little postdi-vorce distress, suggesting that they regard marriage as less important compared to their White counter-parts (Kitson and Holmes, 1992; Thoits, 1986).

This article explores the strategies working/middle class divorced Black men used to reestab-lish their lives. It considers reliance on family and friends, religious and community participation, postmarital relationships, and the establishment of heterosexual relationships as approaches to ad-just to divorce. An examination of divorced Black men's coping strategies is a particularly salient issue given the high rate of marital disso-lution among Blacks and the paucity of research on Black divorced men (Fine, McKenry and

---

Previously unpublished paper ,1998. Reprinted by permission of the author.

Chung, 1992; McKenry and Price, 1991; Taylor, Chatters, Tucker, and Lewis, 1990).

MODERATORS OF POSTDIVORCE ADJUSTMENT

Family and Friends' Support

Social support has been correlated with positive postdivorce adjustment (Ambert, 1989; Kitson and Morgan, 1990; Milardo, 1987; Reissman, 1990). Divorced women, however, are more likely to find satisfaction in their friendships and to seek social support compared to divorced men (Albrecht, Bahr, and Goodman, 1983; Amato and Booth, 1991). On the other hand, White divorced men are more socially isolated than White divorced women, indicating that they adjust poorer to divorce due to lack of supportive friendships (Albrecht, 1980; White and Bloom, 1980; Reissman, 1990; Vaughan, 1986).

The availability of social support may be particularly problematic during divorce (Kitson and Holmes, 1992; Spanier and Castro, 1979; Spanier and Thompson, 1983). First, friendships are often changed during the disruption of a marriage. Second, the divorced may find that most friends engage in couple-oriented activities. Third, patterns of family and friends interactions might be strained because they disapproved of the divorce (Kitson and Holmes, 1992). Fourth, friends may feel threatened since the marital dissolution of a close friend may cause an examination of their marriages (Albrecht, 1980; Gray, 1978). Other friends may remain aloof because they feel awkward and ambiguous about the situation (Amato and Booth, 1991; Arendell, 1995; Spanier and Thompson, 1984). Friends may also take sides out of loyalty to one of the other divorcing spouse, and reject the other (Masheter, 1990; Milardo, 1987; Weiss, 1975).

Social Participation

Social participation correlates with lower distress and facilitates postdivorce adjustment (Ambert,

1988; Kitson and Morgan, 1990). Studies have shown that among divorce males, social participation increases (Hetherington et al., 1976; Reissman, 1990; Weiss, 1976). While they become more involved with clubs and organizations, females increase contact with family members (McKenry and Price, 1991; Wallerstein and Blakeslee, 1990). Because men usually have to make an effort to form relationships, they use athletic clubs, or hobby groups to adjust to divorce. In fact, men often experience a sense of public glory in athletics, which helps them to distance themselves from the emotional pain of divorce (Reissman, 1990).

Social participation in self-help groups have been reported to minimize the distress of divorce. Such groups have targeted single mothers (Leslie and Grady, 1988), single fathers (Tedder, Scherman, and Scheridan, 1984), or older divorced women (Langelier and Druckert, 1980). Support groups for divorced men are effective when they focus on affective responses to facilitate self-development, indicating that divorce stimulates men to examine an intimate aspect of themselves (Reissman, 1990; Wallerstein and Kelly, 1980; Weiss, 1975; White and Bloom, 1991; Wymard, 1994).

Forming New Relationships

There is evidence that establishment of a satisfying intimate relationship facilitates transition to a new lifestyle (Berman, 1988; Hetherington, 1989; Reissman, 1990; Wallerstein and Kelly, 1980). First, new heterosexual relationships familiarize the divorced to customs and values of singlehood, which lowers postdivorce distress. Second, forming intimate relationships results in needed self-appraisal (Thomas, 1982; Wymard, 1994). Although dating a variety of people is as effective as forming a very close relationship, dating decreases postdivorce stress for males but not for females (Diedrick, 1991; McKenry and Price, 1991; Reissman, 1990). Moreover, since sexual performance is a crucial area for the enactment of masculinity, a large number of men have reported sexual freedom as a major benefit of divorce (Kimmel, 1987; Spanier and Thompson, 1984; Pleck, 1982)

Black men may be disadvantaged in the dating process compared to White men (Chapman, 1988; Franklin, 1980). First, they usually have less financial resources to spend on dates (Hill, 1993; Hunter and Davis, 1992). Second, they may be constrained by work schedules since a large number work various shifts and part-time jobs (Lawson and Thompson, 1996). Third, fears of rejection also may prohibit some Black men from dating (Aldridge, 1989; Braithwaite, 1981; Staples, 1982).

Postmarital Relationships

Studies have shown that postmarital relationships can influence postdivorce adjustment (Amato and Booth, 1991; Goldsmith, 1981; Reissman, 1990). For example, Weiss (1975) reported that divorce results in loss of attachment, and thus separation distress. Divorced individuals, therefore, search for the familiar attachment of a former spouse. Further, attachment to former spouses persists even though other heterosexual relationships may develop. As a result, the inaccessibility of former spouses leads to separation distress as well as continued ambivalent postmarital relationships (Weiss, 1975).

Attachment also has been correlated with postdivorce adjustment (Kitson and Holmes, 1992). For example, Kitson (1982), developed a scale for postdivorce attachment. The scale consisted of four items: (1) wondering what the ex-spouse is doing, (2) spending a large majority of time thinking about the ex-spouse, (3) disbelief of a divorce, and (4) feeling that the person will not adjust to the divorce. Those attached demonstrated postdivorce adjustment difficulties, including problems in living alone and forming new relationships (Kitson, 1982). Additionally, Berman (1988) reported that the marital quality and post-marital relationships predict postdivorce attachment. It is unknown, however, whether these findings can be generalized to Black men. This study focuses on the following questions:

(a) What strategies do Black men use to cope with divorce? (b) What social-environmental supports are available to divorcing Black men to facilitate transition to a new lifestyle?

Methods

Fifty divorced Black men who had been divorced for no more than three years, the period most salient in making sense of their past marriages, were interviewed (Reissman, 1990). The men were located through referrals from individuals contacted through Black organizations such as the Urban League, Black churches, and the National Association for the Advancement of Colored People. Recruitment was restricted to: (a) men who were currently divorced and had not remarried; (b) men who were currently in the labor force; (c) men who had experienced only one divorce; and (d) men who had been married at least two years. The men were apprised of the study through phone calls, and appointments were made for interviews. Not one man contacted refused to be interviewed. The purpose of selecting men in the labor force was to eliminate the psychological distress associated with unemployment.

The research was described as a study of Black divorced men. All respondents who were asked agreed to participate, stating, "It is time that the voices of Black divorced men are heard." The men interviewed referred other Black divorced men.

Interviews

The data were collected through face-to-face interviews and were conducted in the respondents' home or place of employment. The interviews were tape-recorded and transcribed. The tapes were transcribed verbatim, with the average length of each transcript ranging between 30 and 40 single-spaced pages.

The respondents were asked to be informal and spontaneous in telling a story that included: "the quality of marital life preceding the separation and postdivorce; experiences during divorce and postdivorce; and support and coping strategies postdivorce." A list of probes were addressed to respondents if they failed to discuss a topic of interest.

The coding process involved several steps. First, the data were coded for the respondents' assumptions, meanings, feelings, actions, and beliefs. Second, analytical categories were developed and refined (Strauss, 1986). Third, observations were noted and coded when respondents cried (e.g., tears) or laughed during the interview.

Participant Observation

Participant observation of the respondents social world was conducted for two years. Participant observation methodology is defined as observation of behavior within natural settings (Bogden, 1972; Denzen, 1970). The men provided a list of their social activities and places they frequently visited. I visited those places, including church activities, Black lodges, fraternity meetings, community meetings, and social events.

RESULTS

The Sample Characteristics

Approximately 34 percent of the sample were between 40 and 44 years of age; 80 percent had 1–2 years of college education, 45 percent reported an annual income between $30,000 and $50,000; 30 percent were raised by two parents; and 32 percent of the respondents married women who had children prior to the marriage. A large percentage were parents (100 percent); had been married between 10 and 15 years (42 percent) and had been divorced between 1 and 3 years (56 percent). With the exception of one man, all mothers gained custody of the children; 32 percent of the men had a child born before marriage. Table 1 shows that the sample consisted of middle-aged, working/middle class Black men who were recently divorced for the first time, and were parents.

TABLE 1 Demographic Characteristics of the Sample (N = 50)

	Percent
Age	
20-34	18.0
35-39	20.0
40-45	34.0
46-50	18.0
Over 50	10.0
Education	
0–12 years	15.0
1–2 years of college	70.0
4 or more years of college	15.0
Income	
$20,000–$29,999	20.0
$30,000–$39,999	20.0
$40,000–$49,999	45.0
$50,000 or more	15.0
Length of Divorce	
1–3 years	56.0
4–9 years	42.0
10 years or more	2.0
Length of Marriage	
1–5 years	6.0
6–9 years	24.0
10–15 years	42.0
16-20 years	28.0
Biological Children	
1–2 children	82.0
3 or more children	18.0
Family of Origin	
Two–parent family	20.0
Mother only	50.0
Extended family only	30.0
Married Women with Children	
Wife had no children	66.0
Wife had 1–2 children	32.0
Wife had 3 or more children	2.0
Children Before Marriage	
0 children	68.0
1–2 children	32.0

Social Support and Divorce

In contrast with previous research examining White males (i.e., Albrecht, 1980; White and Bloom, 1981), the respondents requested and relied on the support of friends and family members to cope with the psychological stress of divorce. Because of perceived racist attitudes and behaviors in traditional counseling services, they were reluctant to seek professional advice. Additionally, they believed that counseling practices often failed to incorporate an understanding of Black men in America and counselors often lacked sensitivity to the Black experience. As a result, the respondents formed their own support group. Lennie said: "I hand-picked my support group from friends who had been in a similar situation. These friends were open-minded and saw both sides of the situation. We met every week." Elaborating on the specific actions of his friends Curtis also said:

> I talked to my friends about the situation and that helped me to cope. They helped me to ponder the question whether I was addicted to a cycle of turmoil. We talked about my deep-seated anxieties of no matter how close I was to establishing a successful life, I would eventually find a way to blow it. We also talked about the experiences of being a Black man in America. We have the same feelings of being restricted by forces beyond our control and having fears of never knowing what we could really be and do within a system that is not plagued by racism. Divorce compounds the stress of coping with racial stereotypes and my friends understood that.

A large majority of men (70 percent) viewed male friends as supportive. Unlike predominately White samples (i.e., Albrecht, 1980; Spanier and Castro, 1979; Weiss, 1975*)*, respondents did not isolate themselves from friends, feeling that they no longer fit in. Moreover, friends *did not view* the respondents as a threat to their own marriage, a sexual competitor, or a reminder of possible marital failure. Although friends were married, they involved the respondents in card parties, cook-outs, concerts, and vacations.

Of interest, the respondents reported that their mothers provided emotional and tangible support. Allen recalled, "My mother helped me by providing emotional support, and she took care of kids until I returned from work." Gerald emphasized the financial support he received

from his mother: "My mother got me a lawyer, the best lawyer in town, and paid for the divorce." Anton also underscored the moral support received from his mother:

> My mother gave me so much emotional support that helped me to cope with the divorce. She understood that I was losing a wife and that it would be painful. That helped a lot. One day mom asked, "Have you tried praying?" From then on, Mom and I often read the Bible together and prayed. Mom provided so much positive support and it was a relief to know she was there for me.

Ivan's mother gave him a car; Mat lived with his mother and viewed it as practical, convenient, and temporary. Mothers exercised authority coupled with love, in ways few studies have reported with White samples. In fact, since mothers usually agreed with their sons about the characteristics of former spouses, some men reported that their mothers were actually happy the marriage had ended. Frank recalled the remarks of his mother. He said,

> My mother said, "I've talked to God about this, and told God I can't put up with this anymore. Your wife is destroying you. Can't you see that? I'm glad you are away from her. We will go to court and file the papers." My mother and I did just that. She was relieved that I was out of the marriage.

Participant observation revealed that mothers and sisters volunteered to take children to parks, sport activities, and church. Black family members, especially female members, also provided child care, mutual aide, advice, therapeutic comfort, and tangible support.

Approximately 40 percent of the men mentioned support of opposite-sex friends with whom they shared confidences and described them as stable and valuable. These friends provided an atmosphere whereby the men could receive a "woman's view of the situation." The following is Barry's description of such a relationship:

I have had this woman friend for about twenty years. Sometimes we get together and I just talk to her. There is no romantic interest; she is somebody nice to talk to. Since she is a woman, I get her point of view. I like her company better than the men I know 'cause she understood and responded sympathetically than most of my male friends.

Men appreciated a woman's emotional side and problem-solving skills. They talked about a woman's friendship as providing nurturance, pampering, and intimacy which was unavailable in their relations with men. These women served as confidantes which allowed men to explore private aspects of their lives and often taught men to express broader range of feelings. As Ben reported, "With Beth, my female friend, I became less defensive and expressed a range of feelings as they surfaced during the divorce." Opposite-sex friends also provided housing, financial support, and assisted with child care. Previous research has shown that female friends provide distinctive types of support to men postdivorce (Gerstel, 1988; Spanier and Thompson, 1984).

Religious Support

Approximately 36 percent of respondents reported that increased involvement in church activities and a religious community moderated postdivorce distress. Arthur explained: "I pulled myself together and started going to church. The church community helped me to deal with the pain by helping me to forgive my ex-wife." Bert recalled help received from his pastor. He said: "My pastor was understanding and forgiving. I felt a tremendous relief telling him about my past. He didn't moralize. I didn't need that. He did not preach to me. He just listened and I needed that." Barry also explained the role of the church in facilitating adjustment postdivorce. He said:

I wanted to kill Jennifer, and the church pastor showed me if you have God in your life you can conquer anything. We had

weekly talks about the pain and hurt I felt. He does not know it, but he may have saved Jennifer's life. I had to acknowledge my hurt through a church community or I would have destroyed myself, or killed Jennifer.

Other men reported that church pastors, members, and activities as well as prayer provided emotional support. A religious social network also provided advice, instrumental support, and referrals to other sources of aid.

Participation observations of church services added another dimension to the study. While interviews enabled assessment of patterns of experiences, direct observation of church members allowed examination of the supportive role religion played in mitigating postdivorce distress. For instance, ministers emphasized a need to love—to love one's neighbors, one's friends, and even one's enemies. Fervent prayers were offered on behalf of the respondents. For example, a church member opened the service by reading a chapter from the Bible; this was followed by a congregational hymn. The church member then prayed. She began each sentence with, "O Holy Father," and asked Him to bless the respondent during his trials and tribulations. "We ask you, Holy Father, to look on him and to give him strength during these difficult days." The prayer was very personal, therefore, the respondent could regard himself superior because he followed Christ's precepts better than that of his former spouse.

Several men reported "getting religion" after the divorce and even "shouted" in church. They indicated that the Lord had changed their lives. Before the divorce, their lives were "heavy with sin" and they prayed to God for forgiveness. Because their sins had been forgiven, they felt "light as a feather." This feeling propelled them to make behavioral and attitudinal changes, such as abstaining from smoking, drinking, and examining priorities.

The men's church activities also included participation in church conventions, weekly revival meetings, discussion groups, and social events, such as boat cruises, Broadway plays, and trips to health spas. The men also participated in church cookouts and planned events to pay off church debts, to help needy church members, and to beautify the church. For example, Stanley and Sam organized a bake sale to help the church purchase a new furnace. Lennie organized events during Black History Month, which included a father-son night and several speakers from the local university.

Increased Social Participation

Approximately, 80 percent of the respondents coped with the divorce by increasing their time commitment to work and engaging in self-improvement activities. For example, Jim, Curtis, Leon, Kenneth, Willy, and Henry worked overtime; Todd, John, Jim, and Bernie worked part-time jobs; Dwayne, Bronson, Stanley, and Barry worked evening full-time jobs. Vincent enrolled in a weigh-lifting course; Eric and Graham learned to play golf; James coached a basketball team, Allen biked cross-country, and Clyde became a Big Brother. Henry detailed the benefits of work to cope with divorce, he explained,

> I used my job as a tool to cope with the divorce. I kept my mind busy and over a period of time the pain wore off. I would tell any divorcing man to make sure he gets involved with work because if he does not, he might end up shooting himself or killing someone else. I also fished, hunted, and spent a lot of time on my boat.

Similarly, men in Hetherington's (1979) study reported spending more time at work. However, unlike samples of Whites (Albrecht 1980; Weiss, 1975) not one man, in this study, reported their work suffered as a result of the divorce. Work aided in postdivorce adjustment because it provided supportive social relationships. For instance, Kenneth said:

> The men at the police department were so supportive. They really understood what I was going through. They recommended a

good lawyer and made suggestions about how to deal with the hurt and pain, like introducing me to single women.

The respondents also increased their involvement in social activities including Black fraternity events and political functions. Participant observation revealed that Lawrence, Graham, and Barry joined community committees that opposed school busing. John, Maurice, and Bert formed a group to repair parks in Black neighborhoods. Ernell, who formed the group, detailed his involvement. He said:

> I wrote a letter to the Park and Recreations board when I saw Black kids playing in a park with broken swings and dangerous equipment. The city council asked me to attend a board meeting. The city had constructed a golf course that costs about four million dollars in a White neighborhood and neglected to repair parks in Black neighborhoods. I spoke in front of the city's park and recreation commission and even met with the mayor about the need for better recreational facilities in Black neighborhoods.

Truman reported that he belonged to the Elks club and was chair of a committee to increase scholarships for Black youth and attributed these activities to the moderation of emotional pain following the divorce. He said, "I organized a fund-raising drive for scholarships to give to Black youths who want to go to college. I raised over $50,000 and received a plaque of appreciation, and had my picture in the paper. This helped me adjust to living alone and the pain of the divorce."

Participation in Black community activities reinforced the postdivorce identities of the respondents as respectable which increased their self-worth and provided an antidote to a sense of failure. Other activities that moderated postdivorce distress, included attending movies, traveling, visiting museums, collecting Black art, and enrolling in college courses. According to the respondents, these activities were previously constrained by family obligations and represented a form of self-expression which facilitated transition to a new lifestyle.

Cognitive Style

The optimism of Blacks has been documented extensively by a number of scholars (Hill, 1993a; Hill, 1971; Billingsley, 1992; Staples, 1985). This cognitive style has been characterized as an unfaltering faith and a strong religious orientation. Historically, Blacks have believed in and practiced the paradox of faith—the certainty of the uncertainty. According to Hill (1993b), this cognitive characteristic of Blacks represents a survival strategy used to cope with social and economic marginality. Blacks would not have survived, if a sense of optimism had not existed. This outlook involves the belief that when life has devastated Blacks, they will triumph. For example, Leon discussed optimism in the context of the historical experiences of Blacks in America. He said,

My ancestors suffered and believed that they would over come oppression one day. My forefathers and foremothers kept on going, even though they were slaves. Knowledge of their strength has given me determination and inspiration to keep on going, despite obstacles I face in trying to re-establish my life.

Truman also said,

I strongly believe that life has a way of working out 'cause as a Black man, I've had to believe that or I would have killed myself long time ago. That was the theme of slaves, and they were eventually freed.

The men's sense of optimism represents a resilience to adapt to divorce. Although some respondents experienced much pain and had been economically bankrupted, they expressed a strong unfaltering faith that their situation would improve. According to the respondents, spirituality also referred to reliance on inner strength

during a crisis and provided positive meaning to stressful life events. Indeed, the spiritual beliefs and the history of coping with oppression underscores the strength of Blacks (Hill, 1993b; Nobles, 1974; Randolph, 1995).

Grier and Cobb (1969) reported that the survival skills of Blacks have been passed from generation to generation and continue as contemporary coping strategies. For example, optimism has helped Blacks to cope with an American ethos which include the assumption that Blacks are inferior and are born for physical labor (Grier and Cobb, 1969). In the struggle to survive, Blacks, however, have developed a style of life which has influenced music and a broad canvas of creativity. As Bronson said:

Take a look at Blacks, who as slaves, took the leftover trash intestines that White folks gave them from the hog and turned it into a delicacy, chitterlings. Blacks took the painful experiences of slavery and created the blues and jazz that the White world loves.

This finding suggests that the strategies which enabled men to cope with social marginality and discrediting were activated to cope with postdivorce psychological distress.

Postmarital relationships

Approximately 80 percent of men reported attachment to former spouses during the first year postdivorce which facilitated adaptation to divorce. However, attachment feelings and behaviors decreased over time. For example, divorced for five years, Anton did not understand why Thelma filed for a divorce. He said:

Initially, I called about everything—to see if the car insurance had been paid, to see if the grass had been cut, or if the garbage had been taken out. After a year, I stopped calling and waited for Thelma to get in touch with me, in other words, the relationship just faded. But, our initial relationship helped me to adjust to living alone. Thelma even spent the night over my house a couple of times and helped me furnish my apartment.

Of interest, the respondents' reported that former spouses were more likely to display attachment behaviors three and two years postdivorce. Curtis, who had been divorced for three years, said,

> As recently as yesterday, Julie wanted me back, but I know it will not work. She will put me on a roller coaster again, and I can't go through that again. I keep Julie at a distance. When I am friendly to her, she wants to know where the relationship is leading. I could not just have caring feelings for her. It had to be, O.K., where are we going with this?

Respondents also indicated that although the legal bond of their marriages was broken, former spouses remained devoted and connected to their families through frequent visits and by weekly telephone calls. Clyde explained his ex-wife's behavior:

> Betty told me that no matter what happens to our relationship, she would always remain close to my family. She visits my mother and talks to my sister frequently. She sends Easter and Christmas cards. In fact, Betty had Thanksgiving dinner with my family. Even though we have been divorced for five years. Betty refuses to let go.

In contrast to previous research of White samples (i.e., Albrecht, 1990; Albrecht et al., 1983; Kitson, Babri and Roach, 1985; Kitson and Holmes, 1992; Spanier and Thompson, 1984; Reissman, 1990; Weiss, 1975), ex-wives professed love for, and desired to interact with the respondents even though they both may have developed other heterosexual relationships. This finding suggests that gender may be an important variable in the postdivorce attachment process of Blacks.

One explanation for Black women's postdivorce attachment is their attachment to Black family relationships, rather than to ex-husbands, as found in mostly White samples. In other words, the survival of postdivorce in-law relationships may be extremely important for Black women because of the value they place on the sense of belonging that a family fosters. Further, Black women's attachment to ex-husbands can be explained by the imbalanced sex ratio. The result is a marked shortage of potential marriage partners for Black women. Consequently, an ex-husband may be viewed as particularly attractive for Black women, given their available options.

Overall, Black divorced couples offered each other company and solace within an environment perceived as hostile. For example, former spouses called the respondents to receive assistance with insensitive teachers and advice about coping with racist employers, absentee landlords, and incompetent, exploitative automobile mechanics. They also informed each other of a family member's death or illness. Couples who had friendly postmarital relationships lived apart, but entered into a platonic friendship. In many instances, those relationships will remain until death. As Kenneth explained: "Mary will be in my life until I die. We will even talk about our grand-children and great grandchildren, but there is no chance of us getting back together." Kenneth's comments suggest that divorce often does not end former spouses relationships, it merely changes it. Continued positive interactions with former spouses assisted the transition to divorce by "having someone to talk things over with." Ironically, in the absence of marriage, often men discovered the value of relationships and self-disclosure, which explains why some respondents reported, "My ex-wife is my best friend now; when we were married we were enemies."

Heterosexual Relationships

According to the men, forming new heterosexual relationships facilitated postdivorce adjustment. A majority of the respondents did not engage in "frenzied dating activity" because it was expensive, which required energy and time to arrange. Approximately 70 percent (N = 35) of the respondents became involved in a close relationship one year postdivorce, which often resulted in cohabitation. Although the men recognized that cohabitation was a major commitment, it seemed to happen casually. Brent said, "It took me 'bout one year to even want to talk to another woman again. I went back to church and met this wonderful lady who loved me as me, and we started living together. A lot of my friends are living together and they seem happy." Brent also asserted that the living arrangement was a prelude to marriage to "see if we could get along," and merged into a collective identity with his mate. Additionally, cohabitation was preferred over dating since men viewed forming new relationships as emotionally draining. In fact, some relationships were formed with women whom respondents had known prior to the marriage.

Indeed, not *one* respondent expressed positive views about living single, but only one man was engaged to be married. The desire for a stable family life appeared to underlie the reason men yearned for an intense emotional relationship. "I enjoy the family fife, that is, having one special person in my life, rather than dating a number of women" was a recurrent comment. Some men also became involved with women who had children because it provided them with a sense of belonging and served as a substitute for their own children. Gerald explained,

> I live with my girlfriend and her daughter. Since I can't raise my own daughters, I can protect and provide security for my girlfriend's daughter. I always wanted to raise a daughter, so my girlfriend and her two-year-old daughter live with me.

Participant observation revealed that social events reinforced the belief that marriage and romance were necessary prerequisites for personal fulfillment. For example, songs in the tradition of "soul music" such as the Temptations' "My Girl," and the melodies of Luther Vandross often played during social events, suggested that relationships were extremely significant.

Black fraternity parties, family reunions, and church socials also emphasized the importance of conjugal relationships. For instance, men and women were usually introduced as the wife or husband of someone, and individuals who were single often sat together while those who were married formed their own social group. There was a high social status attached to being coupled. Compliments were paid to couples who had been together for years and who were celebrating a twenty-fifth wedding anniversary. In fact, in the respondents' social circle, wedding anniversaries were celebrated events, costing between $3,000 and $5,000 with professional caters and live bands. Consequently, the men organized their postmarital lives with an intimate friend who they could talk to, who they could go places with, and who was committed to monogamy. These women, however, represented little risk of a permanent connection. After a few months, some respondents desired to diversify their social world and began forming a relationship with another woman. Thus, winning a new relationship often became a central concern for a number of men.

Barriers to Intimacy

Because intimate relationships often were viewed as threatening, some men had difficulty with commitment. For example, Sam felt apprehensive about making a long-term emotional commitment for fear of being hurt or rejected. He said: "I told my girlfriend that I am holding my emotions back 'cause I didn't want to go through more hurt and pain" Similarly, Larry also restrained emotions in his current relationship. He said,

> I'm hard on women because of my marriage. I don't want to love anymore. As long as I don't put myself completely out there, my relationships go fine. Every time a woman thinks a man loves her, some thing goes off in her head. So, I have a hard time trusting women. I am clear that nothing lasts forever. I thought I would be married to Pat until death. Today, I am clear that there is no guarantee that a marriage will last.

Anton also expanded on his inability to trust a relationship and being unable to reciprocate a partner's feelings of love. He said,

> Even though I am involved in a close relationship, I always say, Is she telling me the truth? Does she really care for me the way she says? Does she really understand what I need in a relationship? If I marry her, will the marriage end the way my first marriage ended? I ask myself these questions constantly. I have a hard time believing women after the divorce.

Although some men were involved in an intimate relationship, they were hesitant to totally entrust their well-being to a woman. They wondered if their future marriages would remain vital and warm, and if their love would continue to excite another woman forever. They also wondered if they would sleep every night with a spouse and reach for her with the same desire and eagerness. Although they hoped a marriage would endure forever, they wondered if that belief was a fantasy. Consequently, in some instances, a new relationship was imagined than real since a new partner may have lived in another state, or was emotionally distant.

Some men had difficulty establishing an intimate relationship because they feared losing their newly acquired sense of autonomy. The divorce allowed them to establish a routine without constraints. According to Ivan, the divorce allowed him to live alone for the first time in his life and liberated him from the demands of adjusting to a woman's plans. Other men also discovered that they were free to do what gave them pleasure and relished in being able to come and go as they pleased, and some even described divorce as "being released from prison."

Similarly, Reissman (1990) found a large number of divorced White men described a sense of freedom following the termination of their marriages. Thus, respondents in this study, had a series of superficial relationships with little emotional involvement and avoided using the term love to maintain a comfortable emotional distance. For example, Tony said, "I tell women, I don't want anything serious, don't bring up the sex issue, don't get too close to me. Let's be two friends. We can go out and have a good time, but please don't want to go home with me." These relationships facilitated the respondents' adjustment to divorce because they permitted men to distance themselves from emotional intimacy and to construct a transformed identity.

The presence of minor children also served as a major barrier to relationship development. For example, a number of men said that their energy and attention were concentrated solely on their children. Eric said:

> Right now I am pretty happy 'cause all of my energy and attention is solely devoted to my sons. They are only ages five, nine, and ten and they need me now more than ever. I spend a lot of time taking them to parks, fishing, and just hanging out. I do things that will last in their memories.

Because Eric devoted a large amount of time to his sons, he had insufficient time, energy, or money to become involved with a woman. In agreement, Edsel said that his life was harried by taking his kids to basketball games, football practice, and community events and he did not have time for an intimate relationship. Other men reported that children gave their lives structure and purpose, which bonded them to family members and to the community. Children, therefore, often provided a substitute for an intimate relationship and facilitated adjustment to divorce.

Additionally, children often felt threatened and reacted negatively to the respondents' dates, thus men concealed new partners from children. As a result, often new heterosexual relationships were characterized by no obligation other than being accessible when convenient. Consequently, men gained reassurance of their self-worth from a partner's sexual consent and interpreted it as acceptance of a transformed identity. Some respondents, therefore, struggled to conquer anxieties resulting from their social identity reduced to a physical entity while simultaneously viewing sexual freedom as a positive outcome of divorce which decreased postdivorce distress.

Overall, most men proceeded with relationships pragmatically and slowly. As a result, coupling was viewed as preferable to no relationship, but seldom evolved into marriage. Temporary serial heterosexual monogamous relationships were appealing because they involved few constraints. Paradoxically, these relationships often prohibited remarriage and were viewed as a legitimate alternative to marriage. This finding indicates that men continue to negotiate and re-negotiate intimate relationships as they coped with divorce, suggesting that Black men's adjustment to divorce may be more complicated than previous researchers had presumed.

DISCUSSION

The analysis suggests that previous postdivorce adjustment research has ignored the complexities of divorce as a cultural construct for family, friends, religious, and community support mobilization. The findings showed that the availability of coping strategies were extensive, including reliance on family and friends, (b) involvement in church-related activities, (c) increased social participation, (d) reliance on an optimistic cognitive style, (e) postmarital relationships and (f) heterosexual relationships.

Family and Friends Support
Most striking was the instrumental, emotional, and often economic support received from the respondents' mothers. A possible reason for this finding is that mothers have assumed a variety of roles in Black families which created an enduring bond postdivorce. Indeed, Black mothers have been shown to be extensively involved in kin-help exchange networks as well as receive help from sons (Burton and Dilworth-Anderson, 1991; Kivett, 1993).

Moreover, the key role men played in the provision of resources to mothers pre-divorce facilitated support postdivorce. Although some men experienced employment instability, they provided human resources within their support system. For example, a large number of men provided tangible support to mothers including repairing household appliances, mowing lawns, cars, and painting houses as well as often providing economic resources. Further, because of their relatively higher status as males in the traditional social structure of many Black families, a crisis such as divorce intensified interactions with mothers.

Clear evidence of the mother's central role is provided by warm mother-son interpersonal relationships. Indeed, similar findings have been interpreted in past studies as evidence of a "Black matriarchy." Nevertheless, it is important for future research to investigate the central role mothers play in the lives of adult sons while acknowledging that these patterns are derived from the unique cultural histories of Black families. Moreover, it is unknown from the data, whether a mother's perception of a particular son or her disapproval of the marriage might affect his adjustment postdivorce. This possibility is worthy of future research attention.

Church Support
The findings indicate that church-related activities, pastoral support, and supportive church members were critical coping mechanisms for men. Historically, religious institutions have been important sources of support for Blacks. For example, Blacks share a religious tradition dating to Africa—where the sacred and secular are inseparable. Thus, Black men who are not involved in religious institution and their adjustment postdivorce warrants further investigation.

Optimistic Cognitive Style
Of interest, the respondents used a coping style grounded in the social historical experiences of Blacks to adjust to divorce. This style led to a reinvestment of mental energy and freedom from debilitating psychological states. This finding coincides with Sudarkasa's (1988) suggestion that it is important to remind Black and White communities the roles Blacks played in surviving and

achieving in America. Future research might determine what differentiates divorced Black men who use an optimistic cognitive coping style and those who do not, and if there are differences in postdivorce adjustment between groups.

Postmarital Relationships

Relationships with former spouses assisted Black men to cope with the loss of their marriages. They often confronted the dissolution of their marriages by maintaining involvement with ex-spouses particularly when children were present. In contrast with previous studies, former spouses behaved in ways to increase attachment. These data suggest that Black postmarital relationships continue which satisfied adult attachment needs, perhaps due to shared parenting and social networks.

Generally, divorce is thought of as a bitter battle between two adversaries. Frequently this is the case. However, in the interviews here, postmarital relations provided continuity and assisted men in the grieving process, which had important consequences for their mental health and well-being. Because both husband and wife are involved in postmarital relationships, ideally information on both spouses should be included in the analysis. Therefore, future research should explore former spouses as central to the postdivorce adjustment process. Additionally, more studies need to investigate both partners adjustment to divorce, and include children in the analysis.

Heterosexual Relationships

Heterosexual relationships assisted in postdivorce adjustment. However, most postdivorce relationships were characterized by ambivalence and often involved cohabitation. This trial marriage eliminated the fears of a major financial commitment and dealing with custody and child-support issues. Most of these relationships occurred with little conscious planning or decision and began as a convenience such as saving travel time between residence. Although some postdivorce relationships were casual sexual encounters, men gained

reassurance of worth from a partner's sexual consent. Thus, the study of new intimate relationships postdivorce can assist in understanding how Black relationships develop. Future research topics, such as mate selection, remarriage stability, and relations with former in-laws may increase our overall understanding of Black men's postdivorce adjustment.

Implications for Family Practitioners

The results suggest that programs for divorce counseling coordinated with Black churches and university-based counseling programs could be a collaborative effort to address the needs of divorced Black men. This strategy would identify lay helpers, in particular Black mothers, who are customarily relied upon for informal assistance and involve them in postdivorce training. Indeed, programs and policies should strengthen natural support systems of the families (Kivett, 1992). Clearly, more information is needed about which kinds of counseling programs are most effective for Black men and under what conditions. There also is a critical need for services geared toward strengthening Black marriages and to assist spouses to acquire skills that facilitate marital stability (Dilworth-Anderson and McAdoo, 1988; Ho, 1987; Thomas, 1990).

Findings from the study also suggest that counselors should view some Black postmarital relationships as changing, rather than ending with divorce ex-spouses may remain as a source of support. Moreover, counselors have an obligation to increase their understanding of the historical discrediting of Blacks, which have had a profound effect on the Black male's psychology and his relationship with Black women (Wilkinson, 1978). Thus family practitioners should demonstrate an understanding of the diverse Black male divorced population, show an awareness of societal actions that malign Blacks, and acknowledge strategies Blacks employ to manage racial stereotypes. Thus counselors for divorced Black men must address the context in which Blacks live and incorporate such perspective in their treatment efforts (Lawson and Thompson, 1995).

The limitation of this study should be noted. First, qualitative methods and cross-sectional data identified coping strategies of divorced Black men. Longitudinal data and random samples are needed to address the causal order of coping responses and long-term outcomes in Black divorced male population. Second, the sample size of this study was small and findings can be generalized only to Black working class/middle-class divorced men. However, the sample was large enough to understand how Black men cope with divorce. However, the sample was large enough to understand how Black men cope with divorce.

REFERENCES

Albrecht, S. L. 1980. Reactions and adjustments to divorce: Differences in the experiences of males and females. *Family Relations, 29,* 59–60.

Albrecht, S. L., Bahr, H. and Goodman, K. 1983. *Divorce and remarriage: Problems, adaptations, and adjustments.* Westport, Conn.: Greenwood.

Aldridge, D. P. 1989. (ed.). *Black male-female relationships.* Dubuque, Ia.: Kendall/Hunt.

Amato, P. R. 1988. Parental divorce and attitudes toward marriage and family life. *Journal of Marriage and the Family, 50,* 453–461.

Amato, P. R., and Booth, A. 1991. The consequences of divorce for attitudes toward divorce and gender roles. *Journal of Family Issues, 12,* 306–322.

Amato, P. R., and Keith, B. 1991. Parental divorce and adult well-being. A meta-analysis. *Journal of Marriage and the Family, 53,* 43–58.

Ambert, A. M. 1989. *Ex-spouses and new spouses: A study of relationships.* Greenwich, CT: JAI .

Arendell, T. 1995. *Fathers & divorce.* Thousand Oaks, Calif.: Sage.

Billingsley, A. 1992. *Climbing Jacob's Ladder: The enduring legacy of African-American families.* New York: Simon & Schuster.

Berman, W. H. 1988. The role of attachment in the post-divorce experience. *Journal of Personality and Social Psychology, 54,* 496–503.

Braithwaite, R. 1981. Interpersonal relations between Black males and Black females. In L. E. Gary (ed.), *Black men* (pp. 269–276). Beverly Hills, Calif.: Sage.

Bogden, R. 1972. *Participant observation in organizational settings.* Syracuse, N.Y.: Syracuse University Press.

Burton, L. M., and Dilworth-Anderson, P. 1991. The intergenerational family roles of aged Black Americans. In S. K. Pfieffer and M. B. Sussman (eds.), *Marriage and family review* (pp. 311–330). New York: Haworth.

Chapman, A. 1988. Male-female relationships. In H. P. McAdoo (Ed.), *Black families* (2nd ed., pp. 190–200). Newbury Park, Calif.: Sage.

Cherlin, A. J. 1992. *Marriage, divorce, remarriage.* (Rev. ed.). Cambridge, Mass.: Harvard University Press.

Davis, R. A. 1993. *The Black family in a changing Black community.* New York: Garland.

Demo, D. H., and Ganong, L. H. 1994. Divorce. In S. Price and P. McKenry (Ed.), *Families and change: Coping with stressful events* (pp. 197–218). Thousand Oaks, Calif.: Sage.

Denzen, N. K. 1970. *The research act: A theoretical introduction to sociological methods.* Chicago: Aldine.

Dickson, L. 1993. The future of marriage and family in Black America. *Journal of Black Studies, 23,* 472–491.

Diedrick, P. 1991. Gender differences in divorce adjustment. *Journal of Divorce and Remarriage, 14,* 33–35.

Dilworth-Anderson, P., and McAdoo, H. P. 1988. The study of ethnic minority families: Implications for practitioners and policy makers. *Family Relations, 37,* 265–267.

Fine, M. A., McKenry, P. C., Chung, H. 1992. Post-divorce adjustment of Black and White single parents. *Journal of Divorce and Remarriage, 17,* 121–134.

Franklin, C. W. 1980. White racism as a cause of Black male-female conflict: A critique. *Western Journal of Black Studies, 4,* 42–49.

Goldsmith, J. 1981. The relationships between former spouses: Descriptive findings. *Journal of Divorce, 4,* 1–19.

Gray, G. M. 1978. The nature of the psychological impact of divorce upon the individual. *Journal of Divorce, 1,* 289–301.

Grier, W., and Cobb, P. M. 1969. *Black rage.* New York: Basic.

Hetherington, E. M. 1987. Coping with family transitions: Winners, losers, and survivors. *Child Development, 60,* 1–14.

Hill, R. 1971. *The strengths of Black families.* New York: Emerson Hall.

Hill, R. B. 1993a. Economic Forces, Structural discrimination, and Black family instability. In H. E. Cheatham and J. B. Stewart (ed.). *Black families: Interdisciplinary perspectives.* (pp. 87–105). New Brunswick, NJ: Transaction.

Hill, R. B. 1993b. *Research on the African American family.* Westport, Conn.: Auburn House.

Ho, M. K. 1987. *Family therapy with ethnic minorities.* Newbury Park, Calif.: Sage.

Hunter, G. A., and Davis, J. E. 1992. Constructing gender: An exploration of Afro-American men's conceptualization of manhood. *Gender and Society, 6,* 464–479.

Kimmel, M. S. (ed.). 1987. *Changing men: New directions in research on men and masculinity.* Newbury Park, Calif.: Sage.

Kitson, G. C. and Holmes R. 1992. *Portrait of divorce: Adjustment to marital breakdown.* New York: Guilford.

Kitson, G. C. 1982. Attachment to the spouse in divorce: A scale and its application. *Journal of Marriage and the Family, 44,* 379–393.

Kitson, G. C., Babri, K. B., and Roach, M. J. 1985. Who divorces and why: A review. *Journal of Family Issues, 6,* 255–293.

Kitson, G. C., and Langlie, J. K. 1984. Couples who file for divorce but change their minds. *American Journal of Orthopsychiatry, 54,* 469–489.

Kitson, G. C., and Morgan, L. A. 1991. The multiple consequences of divorce: A decade review. *Journal of Marriage and the Family, 52,* 913–924.

Kitson, G. C., and Raschke, H. 1981. Divorce Research: What we know; what we need to know. *Journal of Divorce, 4,* 1–38.

Kivett, V. R. 1993. Grandparenting. Racial comparisons of the grandmother role. Implications for strengthening the family support system of older Black women. *Family Relations, 42,* 165–172.

Langelier, R., and Duckert, P. 1980. Divorce counseling guidelines for the late divorced female. *Journal of Divorce, 3,* 403–411.

Leslie, L. H., and Grady, K. 1988. Social support for divorcing mothers: What sees to help? *Journal of Divorce, 11,* 147–165.

Lawson, E., and Thompson, A. 1996. Black men's perceptions of divorce-related stressors and strategies for coping with divorce. *Journal of Family Issues, 17,* 249–273.

Lawson, E., and Thompson, A. 1995. Black men make sense of marital distress and divorce: An exploratory study. *Family Relations, 44,* 211–218.

Masheter, C. 1990. Postdivorce relationships between ex-spouses: A literature review. *Journal of Divorce & Remarriage, 14,* 97–122.

McKenry, P. C., and Price, S. J. 1991. Alternatives for support: Life after divorce—A literature review. *Journal of Divorce and Remarriage, 17:* 121–133.

Milardo, R. M. 1987. Changes in social networks of women and men following divorce: A Review. *Journal of Family Issues,* 8: 78–96.

Miller A. A. 1970. Reactions to friends to divorce. In Paul Bohannan (ed.). *Divorce and after.* (pp. 56–77). Garden City, N.J.: Doubleday.

Nobles, W. W. 1974. Africanity: Its role in Black families. *Black Scholar,* 5, 10–17.

Pleck, J. H. 1983. *The myth of masculinity.* Cambridge, Mass.: MIT Press.

Randolph, S. M., African American children in single-mother families. In B. J. Dickerson (ed.). *African American Single Mothers* (pp. 117–145). Thousand Oaks, Calif.: Sage.

Reissman, C. 1990. *Divorce talk: women and men make sense of personal relationships.* New Brunswick, N.J.: Rutgers University Press.

Spanier, G. B., and Castro, R. F. 1979. Adjustment to separation and divorce: An analysis of 50 case studies. *Journal of Divorce,* 2: 241–254.

Spanier, G. B., and Thompson, L. 1983. Relief and distress after marital separation. *Journal of Divorce,* 7: 32–49.

Spanier, G. B., and Thompson, L. 1984. *Parting: The aftermath of separation and divorce.* Beverly Hills: Sage.

Staples, R. 1982. *Black masculinity: The Black male's role in American society.* San Francisco: Black Scholar.

Staples, R. 1985. Changes in Black family structure: The conflict between family ideology and structural conditions. *Journal of Marriage and the Family,* 53: 221–230.

Strauss, A. L. 1986. *Qualitative analysis.* Cambridge: Cambridge University Press.

Sudarkasa, N. 1988. Interpreting the African heritage in Afro-American family organization. In H. P. McAddo (ed.), *Black families* (pp. 27–43). Newbury Park, Calif.: Sage.

Taylor, R. J. 1986. Receipt of support from family among Black Americans: demographic and familial differences. *Journal of Marriage and the Family,* 48: 67–77.

Taylor, R. J., Chatters, L. M., Tucker, M. B., and Lewis, E. 1990. Development in research on Black families: A decade of review. *Journal of Marriage and Family,* 52: 993–1014.

Tedder, S. L. Scherman, A., and Sheridan, K. M. 1984. Impact of group support on adjustment to Divorce by single, custodial fathers. *American Mental Health Counselors Association Journal,* 6: 180–189.

Thoits, P. A. 1986. Social support as coping assistance. *Journal of Counseling and Clinical Psychology,* 54: 416–423.

Thomas, S. P. 1982. After divorce: Personality factors related to the process of adjustment. *Journal of Divorce,* 5: 19–36.

Thomas, V. G. 1990. Determinants of global life happiness and marital happiness in dual-career Black couples. *Family Relations,* 39; 174–178.

U.S. Bureau of the Census 1995. *Studies in marriage and the family* (Series P-23, No. 162; Current Population Reports. Washington, D.C.: Government Printing Office.

Vaughan, D. 1986. *Uncoupling: Turning points in intimate relationships.* New York: Oxford University Press.

Wallerstein, J. 1986. Women after divorce: A Preliminary report from a ten-year follow-up. *American Journal of Orthopsychiatry,* 56: 65–77.

Wallerstein, J. S., and Kelly, J. B. 1979. Divorce counseling: A community service for the midst of divorce. *American Journal of Orthopsychiatry,* 47: 4–22.

Wallerstein, J., and Blakeslee, S. 1989. *Second chances: Men, women, and children. A decade after divorce.* New York: Ticknor and Fields.

Weiss, R. S. 1975. *Marital separation*. New York: Basic.

Weitzman, L. 1985. *The divorce revolution*. New York: Free Press.

Weingarten, H. R. 1985. Marital status and well-being: A national study comparing first-married, currently divorced, and remarried adults. *Journal of Marriage and the Family,* 47: 653–662.

White, S. W., and Bloom, B. L. 1981. Factors related to the adjustment of divorcing men. *Family Relations, 30*: 349–360.

Wilkinson, D. 1977. The stigmatization process: The politicization of Black male's identity. In D. Wilkinson and R. Taylor (eds.), *The Black male in America* (pp. 145–158). Chicago: Nelson-Hall.

Willie, C. 1991. *A new look at Black families* (4th ed.). New York: General Hall.

Wymard, E. 1994. *Men on divorce*. Carson, Calif.: Hay House.

❀

7

Black and White Relationships

Interracial Relationships: A Convergence of Desire and Opportunity

ROBERT STAPLES

This paper reviews the literature on interracial relationships and the various sociocultural forces that promote and deter the mating of Blacks and Whites in the United States. The author notes that fewer than 5 percent of Black marriages nationally are with White spouses. Although Black male-White female is the most common pairing, the trend is toward more bonds between Black women and White men. As racial barriers in American institutions drop, we can expect an increase in marriages between different racial groups.

■

INTRODUCTION

Intermarriage among people of different races, religions, nationalities, and ethnicities would be a subject of little concern in many societies (Degler, 1971). The same should be expected of a culturally diverse society such as that of the United States. Indeed, the United States is the most racially and culturally diverse nation in the Western industrialized world. The heterogeneous composition of the United States should lend itself to a high degree of tolerance and acceptance of diversity in marriage patterns among its constituent groups (Spickard, 1989). As of the 1990s, intermarriage rates among populations defined as ethnic minorities in the United States are practically normative (U.S. Bureau of the Census, 1985). Only between Blacks and Whites has intermarriage remained such a rare practice as to still be regarded as socially deviant behavior. For that reason, this discussion of intermarriage will focus largely on those two groups.

Slavery had its greatest impact on interracial relations of the Africans brought to the United States. Most of the slaves who came in the beginning were males. The number of Black females was not equal to that of males until 1840.

Originally published in *Encyclopedia of Sociology*, E. F. Borgatta and M. L. Borgatta, editors. New York: Macmillan, 1992: 968–974.

As a result, the number of sex relations between Black slaves and indentured White women was fairly high. Some of these interracial relationships were more than casual contacts and ended in marriage. The intermarriage rate between male slaves and free White women increased to the extent that laws against them were passed as a prohibitive measure. Before the alarm over the rate of intermarriage, male slaves were encouraged to marry White women, since the children from such unions were also slaves. These children increased the property of the slavemaster (Jordan, 1968).

The end of slavery did not give the Black woman any right to sexual integrity. What slavery began, racism and economic exploitation continued to impose on the sexual lives of Black women. In the postbellum South, Black women were still at the mercy of the carnal desires of White men. According to historians, Black women were forced to give up their bodies like animals to White men at random. The literature has noted that many Southern White men had their first sexual experience with Black women. In some cases the use of Black women as sexual objects served to maintain the double standard of sexual conduct in the White South. Many White men did not have sexual relations with White women until they married. Some Southern White men were known to jokingly remark that until they married they did not know that White women were capable of sexual intercourse (Cash, 1960; Dollard, 1957).

It was the protection of the "sexual purity" of the White woman that partially justified the erection of racially segregated institutions in the South. The Southern White man assumed that Black men had a strong desire for intermarriage and that White women would be open to proposals from Black men if they were not guarded from even meeting with them on an equal level. As Jessie Bernard (1966:75) writes: "The White world's insistence on keeping Negro men walled up in the concentration camp [of the ghetto] was motivated in large part by its fear of Black male sexuality."

The taboo on intermarriage focuses primarily on Black men and White women. One reason for this is that White men and Black women have engaged in coitus since the first Black female slaves entered this country. (Some Black slave women were forced to engage in sexual relations with their White masters; others did so out of desire.) Thus, interracial sex became a prerogative of the White man, a symbol of his authority and power. Relations between a White woman and a Black man were an affront to the White man's power.

Traditionally, White fear of interracial relations has focused on the desire to avoid mongrelization of the races. Such a fear lacks any scientific basis since many authorities on the subject of racial types seriously question that a pure race ever existed on this planet. Most authorities note as an actual fact that the whole population of the world is hybrid and becoming increasingly so. At any rate, the rate of miscegenation in the past almost certainly casts doubt on any pure race theory for the United States (Day, 1972).

Since the interracial taboo focused on Black men and White women, it is not strange that these two groups have a certain curiosity about each other. Inflaming this curiosity are the sexual stereotypes mutually held by Blacks and Whites about each other as sexual partners. Just as these sexual stereotypes may stimulate the curiosity of White women, the Black male may be equally attracted by the concept of sacred White womanhood applied to all White women as far as Blacks are concerned. Especially in the South, the penalties for having sex with a White female were extremely severe. Her forbidden fruit status could only add to the natural attraction that most men have for the opposite sex. What is taken for granted by most White men became a forbidden pleasure to Black males. Regardless of the social taboos, intermarriage does take place between the races—most noticeably in the North.

Despite the problems inherent in interracial marriages, such unions appear to be increasing. Two important factors influenced this increase: the United States Supreme Court ruling of 1967 that declared all laws prohibiting marriage between members of different races unconstitutional, and the status gains for Blacks in the sixties. In 1992 there were 246,000 Black-White couples, almost four times the number there were in 1970 (Nakao, 1993). Despite this increase, Black-White marriages still account for less than 1 percent of all marriages in the United States (Spickard, 1989). Little research is available on the success of interracial marriages. Authorities who have studied the subject generally have concluded that these marriages have a fairly good chance of survival. The external pressures faced by interracial couples are often great, but they do not appear to be overwhelming (Cretser and Leon, 1982).

CONTEMPORARY BLACK AND WHITE MARRIAGE

The last two decades witnessed a significant increase in interracial dating and marriage. Among the reasons for this change in Black-White dating and marriage was the desegregation of the public school system, the work force, and other social settings. In those integrated settings, Blacks and Whites met as equals. There were, of course, other factors, such as the liberation of many White youth from parental control and the racist values parents conveyed to them (Staples, 1981).

Although no research studies have yet yielded any data on the subject, there appears to be a decline in Black male–White female couples and an increase in Black female–White male pairings (U.S. Bureau of the Census, 1985). Several factors seem to account for this modification of the typical pattern. Many Black women are gravitating toward White men due to the shortage of Black males and their disenchantment with those they have access to. In a similar vein some White men are dissatisfied with White females and their increasing and vociferous demands for sex role parity. A possible reason for the decrease in Black male–White female unions is that the pairing is no longer as fashionable as it was in the 1960s

and 1970s. Much of the attraction between Black men and White women may have been based on the historical lack of access to each other and the stereotype of Black men as superstuds and White women as forbidden fruit (Staples, 1981). Once the two groups had extensive interaction, the myths exploded and the attraction consequently diminished (Hernton, 1965).

There are, of course, relatively normal reasons for interracial attractions and matings. At the same time it would be naive to assume that special factors are not behind them in a society that is stratified by race. Given the persistence of racism as a very pervasive force, many interracial marriages face rough sledding. In addition to the normal problems of working out a satisfactory marital relationship, interracial couples must cope with social ostracism and isolation. A recent phenomenon has been the increasing hostility toward such unions by the Black community, which has forced some interracial couples into a marginal existence (Hare and Hare, 1984). It is such pressures that cause the interracial marriage rate to remain at a very low level. Less than 5 percent of all marriages involving a Black person are interracial.

There are many factors and problems associated with interracial dating. Because of the unique and historical relationships between the races, interracial dating practices often have a different motivation and character than the same behavior between members of the same race (Beigel, 1966). Heer (1974) used an analysis of census data to interpret the changes in interracial marriages in the period between 1960 and 1970. Among his major findings was the shift of such marriages from the South to the North, an increase in Black husband–White wife unions, and a fairly high rate of dissolution of such marriages.

No other issue provokes such an emotional response as that of interracial dating and marriage. If Blacks are asked if they have ever dated a member of another race, two types of responses emerge. One group is so strongly opposed to it that they give a strident no. The other group has engaged in mixed dating and is quite defensive about it. Some of the latter group would think the question was hostile and even stupid, and they would assume there is something strange about people who date across the color line. Whether strange or not, it is undeniable that, in this country at this point in time, interracial dating is a controversial activity (Staples, 1981). Male–female relationships without the racial element are a controversial topic, and race has historically been a volatile and emotional issue. It is a fact that the scars of nearly 400 years of the worst human bondage known are not healed, and disapproval by many Black and White people of interracial love affairs is one of the wounds.

Intermarriage is certainly nothing new in the United States. Its meaning and dynamics have, however, changed over the last 400 years, since Blacks entered this country. In the pre-slave era, Black male and White female indentured servants often mated with each other. During the period of Black bondage, most mixed sexual unions took place between White men and female slaves, often involving coercion by the White partner. A similar pattern of miscegenation occurred after slavery, with White men–Black women as the typical duo. When Blacks moved to larger cities outside the South, the Black male–White female pairing became more common. As is commonly known, legal unions between the races was prohibited by law in many states until 1967. Legal prohibitions were not the only deterrent to biracial unions. This country's history is replete with acts of terror and intimidation of interracial couples who violated the society's taboos on miscegenation. While Blacks and Whites came together in love and marriage over the years, it was generally at a high cost that ranged from death to social ostracism (Stember, 1976).

Around 1968, society witnessed the first significant increase in interracial dating. This was the year that Blacks entered predominantly White college campuses in comparatively large numbers. Coterminous with this event was the sexual and psychological liberation of White women. Although White society disapproved of all biracial dating, the strongest taboo was on the Black male–White female bond. Hence, Black males and White females became the dominant figures in the increments of biracial dating. The college campus became an ideal laboratory for experiments in interracial affairs. Young White women, who were not as racist as their parents, were liberated from parental and community control. Their student cohorts were more accepting or indifferent to dating across racial lines. One study revealed that as many as 45 percent of White female students had dated interracially (Willie and Levy, 1972). There were, of course, regional differences. In a national survey researchers found that 20 percent of all Americans had dated outside their race. The South had the lowest incidence of biracial dating (10 percent); the West and young people had the highest rate (one out of three) (Downs, 1971).

Those changes in interracial dating practices coincided with the civil rights movement and a greater White acceptance of Blacks as racial equals. Moreover, in the university setting, the Blacks and Whites who dated were peers. They had similar educational backgrounds, interests, and values. Along with increments in racial unions came what appeared to be a change in public attitudes toward biracial couples. A 1985 poll indicated that only a minority of White Americans would not accept their child's marrying outside his or her race (Schuman, Steel, and Bobo, 1985). This poll result could be misleading. Many people tend to give the liberal answer they think is proper or expected when asked about controversial issues such as interracial marriage. However, when confronted with the issue on a very personal level, their response is likely to be very different. Whether parents approve or not, it is clear that biracial matches have become part of the changing American scene. Mixed couples can be observed daily in the cities of the deep South and are commonplace in such liberal bastions as New York, Boston, and San Francisco. And parental approval is irrelevant to many Black and White singles who have deviated from a number of society's other norms related to sexual orientation, sex roles, sexual behaviors, marriage, and the like.

Factors in Interracial Marriages

The increase in interracial dating has as a logical result an increase in interracial marriages. Using selective data, Heer (1974) found definite evidence of an upward trend in the percentage of Blacks marrying Whites. The interracial marriage rate was particularly high in those areas where residential segregation by race was low and where there were minimal status differences between the White and Black population. However, Heer also discovered that marriages between Black men and White women are much more common than those between White men and Black women. In the western region, for example, the interracial marriage rate of Black men is 12.3 percent and of Black women, 3.1 percent (Tucker and Mitchell-Kernan, 1990).

Other factors may propel people into an interracial marriage. Some students of the subject assert that uneven sex ratios are a basic cause. Whenever a group in nearness to another group has an imbalance in sex ratio, there is a greater likelihood of intermarriage. If the groups have a relatively well-balanced distribution of the sexes, members will marry more within their own group (Guttentag and Secord, 1983; Parkman and Sawyer; 1967).

In interracial marriages, one always looks for ulterior motives. It is said that people marry interracially because of rebellion against their parents, sexual curiosity, and other psychological reasons. But many marriages that are homogeneous take place for the same reasons. There are all kinds of unconscious variances that attract individuals and lead them to marriage. Thus, people may marry "their own kind" for the most weird reasons, yet these reasons do not make each marriage suspect. Perhaps the imputation of ulterior motives to interracial couples says more about the individual making these interpretations and about the society we live in than about the men and women who intermarry.

Although the proportion of western Black men dating interracially is much higher than Black women, the difference is not so great when it comes to interracial marriages nationally. While Black women are deprived of many dates by White women, the vast majority of Black males are still available to them for matrimony. Moreover, a great number of Black women marry White men, perhaps an even larger percentage of all Blacks who date persons of other races.

In the past, many of the Black men who married White women were of a higher social status than their wives. In fact, "marrying down" was so common that sociologists formulated a theory about it. They hypothesized that the Black groom was trading his class advantage for the racial caste advantage of the White bride (Davis, 1941; Merton, 1940). But contemporary interracial marriages are more likely to involve spouses from the same social class. Furthermore, when intermarriages involved members of different social classes, there was a pronounced tendency for Black women to marry up rather than to marry down (Heer, 1974; Monahan, 1976).

Consequently, one reason that Black women marry White men is to increase their station in life. Of course, this is true of many marriages. One exception, however, are the Black female entertainers. Because they are closely associated with White males in the course of their jobs, many of them form interracial unions. Most of the celebrated cases in recent years involved famous Black women who married White men not equally famous or wealthy.

While the motivation for an interracial marriage may or may not differ from that of an intraracial marriage, there are problems that are unique to interracial marriages. When researchers studied interracially married couples, they discovered that the courtship of most of them had been carried on clandestinely and, further, that after marriage many of them were isolated from their families. The White families, in particular, frequently refused to have anything to do with children who entered into interracial marriages (Golden, 1954; Porterfield, 1982; Spickard, 1989).

Other outstanding social problems encountered by the couples involved such factors as housing, occupation, and relationships with family and peers. Several of the spouses lost their jobs because of intermarriage; others felt it necessary to conceal their marriages from their employers. The children born of such marriages identified themselves with and were accepted by the Black community. In sum, the couples had to rely upon themselves and their own power of determination to continue the marriage (Wilkinson, 1975).

As for the sociocultural factors that promote or deter interracial marriages, several explanations have been put forth to explain the variation in intermarriage patterns in the United States. Tucker and Mitchell-Kernan (1990) hypothesized that certain environments are more racially tolerant of intermarriage than are others. Their hypothesis is based on the findings from U.S. census data showing interracial marriage rates highest in the West and lowest in the South (U.S. Bureau of the Census, 1985). Similar to their explanation is the argument by Blau and Schwartz (1984): The larger the group size as a proportion of the population, the less likely it is that members will marry outside their group. Secondly, they suggested that the more heterogeneous an area's population, the more likely it is that people will marry outside their group. Both the aforementioned propositions imply that intermarriage is a function of environmental forces, not individual motivations.

SUMMARY

Interracial mating is a subject fraught with controversy. Those who oppose it often combine a hostility toward institutional racism with invidious assessments of the private thoughts and lives of interracial couples. Many men and women mate for no more complex reasons than meeting, liking each other as individuals, and choosing to transcend the societal barriers to their relationship. Only in societies similar to U.S. society does a biracial union take on any greater significance. For centuries, Latin American nations have undergone such a fusion of the races that only nationality, language, and religion remain as sources of identity. But the painful history of race relations in North America militates against the natural mixing of individuals from different races. Instead of adopting the philosophy that interracial dating and marriage are matters of personal choice, many minorities have taken up the call for racial purity so common to the White supremacists, their adversaries of the past.

Despite the opposition to biracial unions, they will continue to increase, for both Black men and women, as long as the social forces that set intermarriage into motion are extant. There is, for example, the class factor. As long as middle-class Blacks occupy token positions in the upper reaches of the job hierarchy most of the people they meet in their occupational world will be White. Considering the fact that the job setting is the paramount place for meeting mates, it is only natural that many Blacks will date and marry Whites. Those Whites will be the people they most often encounter and with whom they share common values, interests, and life-styles. Almost 40 years ago, E. Franklin Frazier (1957) predicted:

The increasing mobility of both White and colored people will not only provide a firsthand knowledge of each for the other but will encourage a certain cosmopolitanism. That means there will be a growing number of marginal people who will break away from their cultural roots. These marginal people will help create not only an international community but an international society. In becoming free from their local attachments and provincial outlook, they will lose at the same time their racial prejudices, which were a product of their isolation. Many of these marginal people will form interracial marriages because they are more likely to find suitable marriage partners in the cosmopolitan circles than within their native countries.

Not all Blacks who consort with non-Blacks will do so for noble motives. Because Blacks tend to stereotype each other in negative terms, many will cross the color line to find what they believe is absent in their own race. However, many of the alleged advantages of the White female actually result from her longer tenure and security in her class position. It is easier, for instance, to enact the traditional female role when the men in your class—and race—can fulfill the normative masculine role, and few Black males have been allowed that opportunity in a racially stratified society

Even more important is the fact that crossing racial lines does not eliminate the normal stresses and tensions that occur between men and women. The 78 percent increase in divorce for Whites during the past decade obviously indicates that they are encountering their share of problems with each other. Add to that the fact that interracial marriages have a considerably higher dissolution rate, it is clear that marrying across racial lines is no quick solution to the intractable problems of male-female conflict.

The wave of the future, however, does not seem to be the Black male–White female dyad. Increasingly, Black women are dating and marrying White males. The attention of society in general and Black women in particular has focused on Black men and White women and has overlooked the fact that the most common interracial pairing in the sixties were Black women and White men. Some studies reveal that as many as 49 percent of Black women have dated White men. As Black women ascend in the middle-class world, they too, will mate on the basis of proximity and class interests. Previously fewer Black women engaged in interracial mating because White males were not interested in them, at least not for marriage. As racial barriers drop in the society in general, especially among the middle classes, the opportunity structure will increase for Black women, and the outcome will be the same for them as for Black men. Whether their biracial unions will be any more durable may depend primarily on the trajectory of social forces in the culture at large.

REFERENCES

Beigel, H. G. 1966. Problems and motives in interracial relationships. *Journal of Sex Research, 2*: 185–205.

Bernard, J. 1966. *Marriage and family among Negroes.* Englewood Cliffs, N.J.: Prentice-Hall.

Blau, P., and J. E. Schwartz. 1984. *Crosscutting social circles: Testing a macro-structural theory of intergroup relations.* Orlando, Fla.: Academic.

Cash, W. J. 1960. *The mind of the South.* New York: Vintage.

Cretser, G., and J. Leon. 1982. *Intermarriage in the United States.* New York: Haworth.

Davis, K. 1941. Intermarriage in caste societies. *American Anthropologist, 43*: 388–395.

Day, B. 1972. *Sexual life between Blacks and Whites. The roots of racism.* New York: World.

Degler, C. N. 1971. *Neither Black nor White.* New York: Macmillan.

Dollard, J. 1957. *Caste and class in a Southern town.* Garden City, N.Y.: Doubleday.

Downs, J. 1971. Black/White dating. *Life, 28*(May): 56–61.

Frazier, E. F. 1957. *Race and cultural contacts in the modern world.* New York: Knopf.

Golden, J. 1954. Patterns of Negro-White Intermarriage. *American Sociological Review, 19*: 144–147

Guttentag, M., and P. F. Secord. 1983. *Too many women? The sex ratio question.* Beverly Hills, Calif.: Sage.

Hare, N., and J. Hare. 1984. *The endangered Black family.* San Francisco: Black Think Tank.

Heer D. M. 1974. The prevalence of Black-White marriage in the United States, 1960 and 1970. *Journal of Marriage and the Family, 35*: 246–258.

Hernton, C.. 1965. *Sex and racism in America.* New York: Doubleday

Jordan, W. D. 1968. *White over Black. American attitudes toward the Negro 1550–1812.* Chapel Hill: University of North Carolina Press.

Merton, R. 1941. Intermarriage and social structure: Fact and theory. *Psychiatry, 4*: 361–374.

Monahan, T. P. 1976. The occupational class of couples entering into interracial marriages. *Journal of Comparative Family Studies, 7*: 175–192.

Nakao, A. 1993. Interracial marriages on rise in state, U.S. *San Francisco Examiner,* February 12: p. A-1.

Parkman, M. A., and J. Sawyer. 1967. Dimensions of ethnic intermarriage in Hawaii. *American Sociological Review, 32*: 593–608.

Porterfield, E. 1982. Black-American intermarriage in the United States. In *Intermarriage in the United States,* G. A. Cretser and J. J. Leon, eds., pp. 17–33. New York: Haworth.

Schuman, H., C. Steel, and L. Bobo. 1985. *Racial attitudes in America.* Cambridge, Mass.: Harvard University Press.

Spickard, P. R. 1989. *Mixed blood intermarriage and ethnic identity in twentieth century America.* Madison: University of Wisconsin Press.

Staples, R.. 1981. *The world of Black Singles. Changing patterns of male/female relations.* Westport, Conn.: Greenwood.

Stember, C. H.. 1976. *Sexual racism.* New York: Elsevier.

Tucker, M. B., and C. Mitchell-Kernan. 1990. New trends in Black American interracial marriage: The social structural context. *Journal of Marriage and the Family, 52:* 209–218.

U. S. Bureau of the Census. 1985. *Census of the population, 1980, Volume 2, Marital characteristics.* Washington, D.C.: U.S. Government Printing Office.

Wilkinson, D. Y. 1975. *Black male/White female: Perspectives on interracial marriage and courtship.* Cambridge, Mass.: Schenkman.

Willie, C. V., and J. D. Levy. 1972. Black is lonely. *Psychology Today, 5:* 76–86.

The End of Africanity?
The Biracial Assault on Blackness

RHETT S. JONES

*Looking at the current movement to place a small seg-
ment of the American population's in a biracial category, i.e., those of mixed race heritage, the author
claims it is a thinly disguised effort to create a niche of
privilege for the small minority of Blacks with one
White parent. To deconstruct whiteness, based on racial
purity, this movement must attack the definition of
blackness. Using examples such as the Cherokee Indians and the Chinese citizens of Mississippi, he shows
that the biracial movement is not an attempt to attack
racist definitions of racial classifications but, in reality,
an effort to escape the liabilities associated with being
labeled Black in a country where race is bipolar.*

■

Black people have coped with—when they
have not overcome—slavery, racism, economic
exploitation, political oppression, and a host of
other afflictions in the United States and the thirteen colonies of British North America that preceded its formation. At present African Americans
confront the grave problems of Black-on-Black
crime, drugs, unemployment, underemployment,
and perhaps most serious of all, the disorganization of Black families.

Blacks not only survived these and many other
difficulties, but managed at the same time to create one of the most remarkable cultures in human
history. The slaves, without property, wealth, political power, full control over their own families,
or even full control over their own bodies, created a culture in which African Americans delivered respect to one another. Respect in the slave

community was not based on money or power, as
the slaves had neither, but rather on reputation,
which in turn was based on treatment of children,
respect for the elderly, belief in God, and meeting
one's responsibilities to the community.

This culture, the racial unity on which it
rests, and the idea of blackness or Africanity itself is now under attack. This paper places the assault of Africanity in historic and hemispheric
context and examines the reasons why it is being
launched at this time.

African Americans who consider themselves
to be biracial or multiracial are in the forefront
of efforts to deconstruct blackness. Like most
Black Americans these persons are of mixed
racial ancestry, but unlike most Black Americans,
they are attempting to carve out for themselves a
separate racial identity, distinct from the mass of
Blacks. They want their non-African ancestry
recognized. When asked to identify themselves
racially they do not want to call themselves
Black, instead they wish to be called biracial or
multiracial, and some even wish to list the different races from which they are descended. Some
have said they do not mind calling themselves
Black, providing they can also point out that they
are at the same time not entirely Black. Others
have lobbied state legislatures and the federal
government to establish a category of biracial or
multiracial so that on printed forms they will not
have to check Black or "other."

The biracial movement is, of course, larger
than those who are of mixed Black and non-Black

From the *Western Journal of Black Studies,* vol. 18, No. 4, 1994: 201–210. Copyright 1994 by the Board
of Regents, Washington State University, Pullman, WA 99164. Reprinted by permission.

ancestry, but it is in the African American community that it has produced most discussion. For persons of mixed White-Latino, White-Asian American, or White-Native American ancestry biracialism is not an important issue because it has a long history of being recognized and acknowledged. The rules of race in the United States permit these persons to acknowledge their mixed race ancestry, and indeed to claim to be both White and non-White. For example, in the West persons who are regarded as White may run for office and make mention of a Native American grandmother in an attempt to attract the Indian vote. And in Florida the same person may at times present herself as White, and at other times as a Latina. With the exception of Blacks, all people of color have been permitted to follow the path laid down by Europeans who migrated to the United States in that they are regarded as assimilating minorities (Davis, 1991). Their racial ancestry is of interest, and they may point out that one of their parents is not White, but this is only an issue of passing curiosity. It is understood that they are in the process of becoming White Americans.

According to a number of studies (Quan, 1982; Loewen, 1988; Wong, 1993) over the course of the twentieth century Chinese and Chinese Americans in Mississippi were able to move from being regarded as Black in the state's biracial system to being regarded as White. In the opening statement of his book, Loewen (1988: iii) quotes a conversation with a White Baptist minister in Mississippi:

> You're either a white man or a nigger, here. Now, that's the whole story. When I first came to the delta, the Chinese were classed as nigras.
> [And now they are called whites?]
> That's right!

Blacks could not follow the Chinese into whiteness. And because of the "one-drop" rule, it is impossible for a politician, otherwise thought of as White, to run for office and make mention of his Black grandmother as a ploy to attract the African American vote. The one-drop rule holds that any person of known African ancestry, regardless of his/her physical appearance, is Black. It applies only to Blacks, and is not applied to Asian Americans, Latinos, and Native Americans. The one-drop rule made it illegal in many states for Whites, and in some states Native Americans, to intermarry with Blacks. But even before anti-miscegenation laws were struck down in 1967 by the Supreme Court they were for the most part focused on African Americans. According to Fuchs (1990: 139–140):

> Japanese, Chinese, and Filipinos even escaped the antimiscegenation statues of several mainland states, probably because they were difficult to enforce, but also because they were not made to apply to them by the courts in every state. In Louisiana, for example, the state supreme court in 1938 decided that African ancestry was the only definition of color. In a subsequent decision, the court made it plain that to be a Filipino was not to be colored but white. It made no difference that some Filipinos had much darker skin color than some African-Americans. That was, of course, the whole point of caste, to confine [black] people by blood lines (not by a color alone) in a subjugated status.

Not only does the one-drop rule apply only to African Americans, but it exists only in the United States. All of the nations of the western hemisphere are multiracial, including within their borders varying numbers of people from Europe, Asia, and Africa, as well as the descendants of the original inhabitants. As is the case in the United States, race relations in these nations, and the colonies that preceded them have been characterized by miscegenation, but unlike the United States, most of these nations acknowledge racial intermixture. So, for example, in Haiti the term "mulatre" is applied to persons of mixed European and African ancestry, while the term "mulatto" is applied to the same persons in Mexico. Only in the United States is the reality of sexual relations between Whites and non-Whites denied, and then only when the non-White partner is Black. There are no mulattos in the United States, only Blacks.

Ironically, many of the biracials who are at the forefront of efforts to deconstruct blackness claim they are not primarily concerned with it, but with whiteness. As Reddy (1994) sees it, claims of white superiority in the United States rest on the idea that Whites are a pure race and not only created civilization, technology, and rational thought, but played the central role in all the achievements of mankind. Blacks, on the other hand, never created any great civilizations, this argument runs, and are fortunate to have been transported to America where they benefit from contact with Whites. By insisting that the white race is not a pure one, Reddy argues, and celebrating their mixed race ancestry, biracials undermine the idea of race purity and the racist thought it makes possible. Liem (1994) agrees, noting that biracialism disturbs conventional ideas about race and therefore challenges racism.

Zack (1993: 164) sees the person who insists on having her biracial ancestry acknowledged as claiming an identity "that looks to the future rather than to the past, an identity founded on freedom and resistance to oppression rather than immanence and acceptance of tradition." She (Zack, 1993: 164) continues:

> An American who identifies herself as mixed black and white race is a new person racially, because old racial categories do not allow her to identify herself in this way. It is such a person's very newness racially that gives her the option of racelessness. To be raceless in contemporary racial and racist society is, in effect, to be anti-race. If "authenticity" is a definition of the self in the face of oppression, then the authenticity of a person of mixed race may rest on her resistance to bi-racial racial categories—the racial authenticity of mixed race could therefore be the racial position of anti-race.

The biracials take the position that those who continue to fight *as Blacks* against racist oppression are essentially the prisoners of past conceptual categories. By refusing to abandon their Africanity and failing to insist that they are partially White, these backward looking African Americans enable European Americans to continue the ideas of race purity that make possible racism.

ELUDING AFRICANITY: RACIAL CONSTRUCTS OUTSIDE THE UNITED STATES

But ideas of race purity and the ideology of racism are not as closely linked as this argument suggests. The history of race in American nations outside the United States makes this clear. While these countries acknowledge racial intermixture in their racial terminology, they remain racist. In *Slave and Citizen: The Negro in the Americas*, the book that pioneered the comparative study of racism and slavery in the Americas, Tannenbaum (1946) argued that slaves were treated better in Latin America than in the United States for two reasons. First, the Roman Catholic Church insisted on the spiritual equality of the races, and while this did not mean that the church advocated either the end of slavery or racial equality, it did mean that Blacks were entitled to full membership in the Church, and that they therefore had the right to be baptized, to be married and to benefit from all the other sacraments. In many North American Protestant denominations there was no agreement that Blacks were human beings nor were they regarded as the spiritual equals of Whites. The second part of what has come to be known as the Tannenbaum Thesis suggests that while slavery was natural, normative, and common in Spain and Portugal, the institution had died out in Britain. When the Spaniards and Portuguese settled their American colonies they routinely imported to the New World a form of labor common in the Old. But the English settlers had to create and justify what for them was a new institution. Their rationalizations eventually evolved into racism.

In the half-century since it first appeared, the Tannenbaum Thesis has been subjected to a variety of criticisms from persons trained in a number of different disciplines. While conceding that patterns of race relations varied in different parts of the Americas, historian Greene (1942), anthropologist Harris (1964), historian McManus (1973), and folklorist Piersen (1988) concluded the explanation for this variance was demographic rather than the cultural reasons advanced by Tannenbaum. They argued that in those areas where Blacks were numerous and therefore viewed as threatening they were likely to be treated more harshly than in those areas where they were small in number. Prior to publication of Tannenbaum's book Williams (1944) had argued that economic forces shaped and determined different patterns of race relations in the Americas, an argument further developed by Aptheker (1956) and Genovese (1971, 1976).

Despite their disagreements over the causes of racial discrimination, scholars agreed that racism was a force throughout the Americas, although it manifested itself in different racial structures. The sociologist Hoetink (1967) contrasted the two-tiered system of race relations in the United States, which recognized only Blacks and Whites, with the three-tiered system of race in Latin America which recognized Whites, Mulattos, and Blacks. A number of scholars (Morner, 1967; Mellafe, 1975; Rout, 1976) provided descriptions of the elaborate racial terminologies constructed by Spanish and Portuguese settlers demonstrating thereby the many intermediate racial categories between Whites and Blacks.

In discussions of the Tannenbaum Thesis, slavery and race relations in Brazil emerged as central (Jones, 1990). Writing in an era when Jim Crow laws made racial segregation legal in the South, and *de facto* racial segregation was characteristic of the West and North, Tannenbaum viewed Brazil as the ideal to which the United States should aspire. Tannenbaum's argument was buttressed by the translation of Gilberto Freyre's massive study, *The Masters and the Slaves: A Study in the Development of Brazilian Slavery* (1946), of

slavery in his country in which he argued that the Portuguese colonizers of Brazil drew no hard and fast line between the races, and that Blacks were free to rise in the system. Many North American students of the Brazilian race relations observed that Blacks occupied high positions in church, military, education, and politics in Brazil. Elkins (1959), Klein (1967), and Morner (1967) were among the scholars influenced by these arguments, although they modified them in many significant respects. Three informative anthologies on the comparative study of race in the Americas (Foner and Genovese, 1969; Cohen and Greene, 1972; Winks, 1972) devoted considerable attention to Brazil.

Hoetink (1967, 1973) concluded that while Tannenbaum and Freyre may have been right in suggesting that some persons of African descent found the system more open to them in Brazil than did their brethren in the United States, this did not mean that the Portuguese were any less bigoted than the English. Hoetink suggested that because the Portuguese had a conception of whiteness that was darker than that held by the English, Brazil provided greater opportunities for persons of mixed racial ancestry than did the United States. These persons could approximate the "somatic norm image" of the Portuguese and hence were regarded as White. Similarly, Degler (1971) suggested that a "mulatto escape hatch" existed in Brazil which enabled those persons of African ancestry who were light-skinned and possessed European facial features to rise in Brazil society, while those who were phenotypically African could not.

In the United States where the one-drop rule determined ideas about race, most Blacks neither understood nor appreciated the Brazilian distinction between mixed-race and Black. The collection of essays collected by Hellwig (1992) demonstrates that many Blacks in the United States believed that Brazil was a racial paradise. Such otherwise shrewd observers of race relations as Oliver Cromwell Cox, E. Franklin Frazier, and Robert S. Abbott believed that Brazil provided a model of race relations the United

States would do well to emulate. More recently, however, African Americans, influenced by the writings of such Black Brazilians as do Nascimento (1989), the work of Ghanaian born Anani Dzidzienyo (1983, 1985a, 1993) and the research of Brazilian social scientists themselves, have accepted the idea that while Brazilians view race in different ways than Americans, Brazil is as racist as the United States. In both nations Blacks are discriminated against, must cope with powerful negative stereotypes, and are able to rise in the system only when their behavior demonstrates they have consciously and deliberately rejected behavioral patterns the White controlled society considers African.

In suggesting that their attacks on the purity of whiteness will undercut and discredit racism, biracials seem curiously ignorant of, or unwilling to systematically explore, the history of race relations outside the United States. Skidmore (1974) shows that Brazilians have long held a conception of whiteness that is not based on race purity, and instead have advocated a "whitening" process in which, over time, Blacks would gradually be absorbed into the White population. In a reversal of the one-drop rule, the Brazilian assumption has been that as Whites are the dominant, superior, and more powerful race they will absorb Blacks into the White race with little difficulty. The resultant race, while White, would include persons of African ancestry, and therefore would not be pure in the sense that the biracials in the United States use the term. The Brazilian example suggests that even where racists do not view Whites as constituting a pure race, they remain racists.

Zack (1993: 75) is one of the biracials who understands this:

> It has been estimated that between 70 and 80 percent of all designated black Americans have some degree of white ancestry. If Americans, like Brazilians, were racist but more benevolent toward individuals, then 70 to 80 percent of all designated black Americans could be redesignated not-black. This is not to suggest that such redesignation would

alleviate the problems of black Americans—the traditions of racial discrimination are too powerful in American life for any mere linguistic change to erase the kinds of racism that are an integral part of American life.

Why then suggest that millions of Black Americans who have sought the end of slavery, Jim Crow, and racism become not-Black? Leaving aside what this would mean for the 20 to 30 percent of "all designated Black Americans" who having no white ancestry would be separated from other Blacks by the new racial category, why do biracials such as Zack urge those African-Americans who have White ancestors to abandon Africanity?

The answer is simple. Because race in the United States is bi-polar, in order to deconstruct whiteness biracials must attack blackness. Whites and Blacks have very different reasons for opposing the biracial movement, but biracials do not always distinguish between these reasons, nor the different histories that have shaped them. Blacks and Whites are not equal and by asserting they want to be something other than Black, the biracials are not making a politically neutral statement in which they equally condemn Whites and Blacks for their shared simplistic ideas about race, but are making an anti-Black statement. To be sure, they are attacking whiteness, the glue that binds European Americans together and makes possible racism, but at the same time they are attacking blackness, the glue that binds African Americans together at a time when Black America needs the unity Africanity provides perhaps more than any other time in their history.

ESCAPING AFRICANITY: RACIAL CONSTRUCTS IN THE UNITED STATES

The issue is complicated by the fact that biracials seem to be more hostile toward Blacks than toward Whites. While at first glance this seems strange, the social scientific literature demonstrates that intermediate racial groups—and those like the biracials who would like to create an intermediate status for themselves—often vent their hostilities on the group beneath them, rather than on the group above them. It is, after all, less risky to attack the powerless than to attack the powerful, and such attacks help the intermediate group to distance itself from the lower group. This is nowhere more clear than in the evolution of racial attitudes among Native Americans.

The growth of racism in the United States and the end of Indian military power placed Native Americans on the east coast in a vulnerable position. The Indians, writes McLoughlin (1984: 254), worked to give themselves "a status superior to that of the Black man, a necessity forced upon the Indian by the slave status of Black people in America and the efforts of White Europeans to place the Indian in the same caste." As long as the Native peoples were sufficiently powerful to hold their own against the encroaching Whites, they were free to hold whatever attitudes they wished toward Blacks. Some of them freely accepted runaway slaves into their tribes, others simply ignored them, and still others returned the fugitives to their owners. Some Indians made a practice of stealing slaves or encouraging them to run away, and then selling them to other Whites. As long as they were powerful militarily the Indians decided how they would treat Blacks, just as they decided how they would treat Whites, and how they would treat one another. But as it became clear the Euro-Americans were winning the military struggle, Indian peoples prudently and practically took into consideration White attitudes toward Blacks.

Among the most watchful and adaptive of these tribes were the Cherokee. Many of the Cherokee adopted the emergent Euro-American culture to avoid the near-destruction of such coastal tribes as the Catawba and Uchee. According to McLoughlin (1986: 336):

> However, as the Cherokee gradually accepted the white man's style of plantation

agriculture and realized how whites felt about "people of color," their attitude toward Africans. . . . At first reluctantly and later without compunction, the Cherokee concluded that their survival as a nation depended upon their clearly distinguishing themselves from Africans. To treat blacks as equals would not raise the blacks in white eyes but would simply lower the red man. "Civilization" for the Cherokee became the adoption of the southern white attitude toward Black labor. To own slaves became both a source of wealth and a source of respect.

Conscious of their increasingly vulnerable position, the Cherokee quickly mastered and accepted the racial terminology of European Americans. In a 1793 letter sent by Little Turkey, one of the Cherokee leaders, to the governor of Tennessee, the Spaniards were described as "a lying, deceitful, treacherous people, and... not real white people, and what few I have seen of them looked like mulattos, and I would never have anything to say to them" (Perdue, 1979: 48). Whether Little Turkey actually believed the Spaniards were mulattos is beside the point. He clearly understood the nuances of race and sought to use his knowledge to the advantage of his people.

Like all other peoples, the Cherokee had what anthropologists term creation myths, accounts of the beginning of the world. Under contact with Whites and Blacks, these myths, which originally made no mention of race, evolved to explain racial differences and to distance the Cherokee, and other Indians, from Blacks. A Cherokee chief told a White man in the 1820s that the Great Spirit, having first created three men, one White, one Black, and one Red, then spoke to them (McLoughlin, 1984: 257):

> "White man, you are pale and weak, but I made you first, and will give you first choice; go to the boxes, open them and look in, and choose which you will take for your portion." The white man [took the box that] was filled with pens, and ink, and paper, and

compasses, and such things as your people now use. The Great Spirit spoke again and said, "Black man, I made you next, but I do not like you. You may stand aside. The Red man is my favourite, he shall come forward and take the next choice." [The red man chose] a box filled with tomahawks, knives, war clubs, traps, and such things as are useful in war and hunting. The Great Spirit laughed when he saw how well his red son knew how to choose. Then he said to the negro, "You may have what is left, the third box is for you." That was filled with axes, and hoes, with buckets to carry water in, and long whips for driving oxen, which meant that the negro must work for both the red and white man, and it has been so ever since.

In the reconstruction of their past and their treatment of Blacks, whether slave or free, the Cherokee and other eastern tribes sought to make certain that Whites understood that Indians were different from Blacks and that they should not together be regarded as people of color. To achieve this goal Native peoples had to deny and disassociate themselves from persons of mixed Black and Indian ancestry, whom Whites were now defining as Black. Prior to accepting this Euro-American conception of Blackness, Native Americans had sometimes intermarried with, adopted, and accepted Blacks into their tribes, but they now found themselves forced to reject their own kin in order to carve out a middle place for themselves between Whites and Blacks.

The notable exception to this tendency in North America, at least up through the early 19th century, were the Seminole, who, far from accepting the negative White view of Blackness, refused to abandon those Africans and descendants of Africans who had intermarried with and become part of the tribe. Bateman (1990:18) concludes that, "because the Seminole were themselves an amalgam of peoples of diverse cultural and linguistic background, the Blacks who settled and allied with them became an integral part of the Seminole people." As the Seminole

were, for much of the period of the late eighteenth and early nineteenth century, able to remain isolated from direct military and social pressure from the United States, it may be that they maintained ideas about the nature of race different from those held by Euro-Americans. Whatever may be the explanation, slavery among the Seminole "began to assume characteristics greatly different from slavery in the neighboring tribes" (Littlefield, 1977: 5). According to Katz (1986: 52), "By the nineteenth century Black Seminoles had become key advisors and valuable interpreters for the nation. They were familiar with English, Spanish, and the Muskogee or Hitchiti Seminole languages."

Unlike the Seminole, and like the Cherokee, the Chinese of Mississippi separated themselves from Blacks. The majority of Chinese who settled in the Mississippi Delta arrived between 1910 and 1930 (Wong, 1993:20). They were to work as sharecroppers and thereby provide the plantation owners with an alternative source of labor to that of Blacks. Whites feared that Blacks would leave Mississippi for the North in such large numbers that they would lack workers, but while many African-Americans did leave the state, enough remained to continue to serve as the backbone of the state's labor force. In the meantime the Chinese arrivals realized that sharecropping would not enable them to get ahead in American society. But they soon discovered a niche for themselves. In the early to mid-twentieth century close to eighty percent of the Mississippi Chinese were grocers. They were able, in this capacity, to serve both races and provide arenas in which the two races could informally meet. They rapidly prospered in ways in which those grocers who were limited to serving only Black or White clientele could not.

According to Wong (1993: 21):

The relationship between the Chinese grocers and the black members of the community grew over the years. Not only did the Chinese run businesses in the black community, but they also lived there. Therefore, they were subject to the same discrimination and prejudice that blacks received from whites. Consequently, the Chinese grocers were more friendly than white grocers toward black customers. Most Chinese grocers, for instance, "did not require the deferential courtesy forms customarily demanded by whites." The Chinese grocers were thus able to monopolize a portion of the market in the black community. For Chinese grocers, being in a position in between white and black was very rewarding, financially as well as socially.

This passage somewhat understates the relationship between the Chinese and Blacks, for not only did the Chinese live in the Black community, but they often intermarried and/or cohabited with Blacks.

As the Chinese community grew and prospered its successful members sought to take their children out of Mississippi's inferior Afro-American schools and move them to Euro-American ones. Cohn (1967: 235) argues that Whites had no objection to admitting Chinese children to White schools, but feared if the doors were open to them, children of mixed Chinese/African American ancestry would attend. To permit children of part-African ancestry to attend Euro-American schools would, of course, violate the one-drop rule. To win acceptance for their children in the school system and to provide them with better opportunities, the Chinese cut ties with the Black community. "By pressuring Chinese men to end their relationships with Black women and to abandon their biracial children, or by forcing Chinese-Black families to leave the community, the Chinese hoped to eliminate Chinese-Black American relationships (Wong, 1993: 22).

Those Chinese who were willing to abandon Black wives and children and cut social ties with Blacks, prospered and were accepted by Whites. Their children were enrolled in the schools, they joined White churches, and they became members of many White social organizations. But (Loewen, 1988: 136–137):

A vastly different fate befell those Chinese who refused to give up their Negro wives, usually because they had children in them. Even though some of them in past years were eminent in the Chinese community, their position is now extremely marginal. They do not participate to any substantial extent in the social life of any of the racial groups around them. Typically, these families have no social life whatever, beyond the nuclear family itself. One [of the "white" Chinese] put it this way: "We didn't associate at all with those Chinese. Well, we *did* associate with them but just as little as could."

This man and those like him who have escaped blackness, are accepted by Whites, and, smugly comfortable in their escape, give little thought to those Chinese who chose to remain linked with African Americans.

ATTACKING AFRICANITY: BIRACIAL STRATEGIES

The biracials' approach to race has more in common with that of the Cherokee and the Mississippi Chinese than that of the Seminole, as they attempt to distance themselves from Blacks in the hope of persuading White America that they are not Black. Like the Cherokee and the Mississippi Chinese, the biracials focus on blackness, not whiteness. While they claim to be attacking whiteness they have little to say about White people, being centrally concerned and fearful that Whites will think of them as Black.

This is nowhere more clear than in a collection of essays by undergraduates who consider themselves biracial (Anderson, 1994). Anderson's study makes it clear that while these young people are primarily interested in constructing a biracial identity, they are also interested in distancing themselves from Blacks. One student wrote, "Obviously there was no escaping the amount of pigment in my body, but I did not want to be *prejudged as Black* [emphasis mine] . . .

The most comfortable identity for me was that of a multiracial Caribbean American" (Anderson, 1994: 7). Another student observed, "Because my identity contained the elements of both sides I could relate to Asians much better than the Blacks" (Anderson, 1994: 4). This student does not explain why he had better relations with Asians than with Blacks, but does point out that while in high school he joined the Afro-Latino Society because he was expected to do so, not because he wanted to. Clearly, both students felt they were regarded as Black, that they were pressured to be Black, and that they did not want to be Black.

Attempts to escape from blackness are not limited to undergraduates. Zack (1993: xi) begins her book, *Race and Mixed Race:*

> I was born in Brooklyn in 1944. My mother was a single parent and I was an only child. She was an artist. . . If racial identification had been required, I would have identified myself as my mother had brought me up to do: I was "Jewish". . . My mother had a close friend while I was growing up who was married to someone else. He regularly drank too much and was rarely sober when he visited my mother. He seemed to be indifferent to children although—or because—he and his wife had ten. He rarely spoke to me. He faded out of our lives when I was twelve. When I was sixteen I found out that he had been my father.

The words, carefully chosen by a philosopher, while at one level merely descriptive, are revealing. Zack's White mother is an "artist." The Black man who "had been my father" drank too much. As it is not mentioned, presumably he had no occupation, or at least not one Zack's mother shared with her, or which she recalls, or cares to recall.

Zack (1993: xi) does recall that, "During my student years, race was not an issue for me: I did not have to identify myself racially on any forms, and I do not remember any official person in the New York City public school system, in college, or in graduate school asking me what race I was." Unlike most other Americans of African descent who came to adulthood over the course of the 1950s and 1960s race played no role in Zack's life. "Race did not seem to be preemininent in my life—until 1990 when I returned to academia. Between 1970 and 1990, academia has become racialized. *Now* [emphasis mine] race is a big issue" (Zack, 1993: xii).

Zack is fortunate, for historically, race has always been a "big issue" for most African Americans, and it continues to be even for those who do not want to be regarded as Black. Reddy (1994) observes that biracial students see themselves as passing for Black, by which she means that it will be assumed they are Black unless they make it clear that they are biracial. In a 1992 forum held by such students at Brown University they argued that if they do not make it clear that they have a White parent, they will have to listen to attacks being made on Whites and therefore on their parents by Blacks who assume that as they appear to be Black they will have no objection to anti-White statements. For this reason biracial students try to make it clear as soon as possible after meeting Afro-Americans that they are not Black, but biracial. But as all biracials fall within the phenotypical range of those who are regarded as Black in the United States, their pronouncements are usually received by African Americans with surprise and hostility. Most Blacks, aware of the mixed ancestry of African Americans in the United States, see the biracials as attempting to claim a privileged status for themselves.

In this they are not alone. blackness is such a despicable status in the Americas that persons of African descent have made, and continue to make, repeated efforts to escape it. Dzidzienyo (1985b), long-time student of race relations in Brazil, explained that nation's proliferation of intermediate racial categories between White and Black, with the simple explanation that in Brazil "No one wants to be Black." Zack (1993: 75) understands why Whites would not want Afro-Americans with White ancestors to be regarded as White, "But it is not clear on the face of it why a Black person . . . would want to impose a Black designation on a racially mixed person." If a person can escape from this despised position into a non–Black category, then as Zack sees it, he/she should be allowed to do so.

But in the United States only those persons who want to escape Blackness seem interested in changing America's racial categories by creating a new category of biracials. Sundiata (1994: G-22) asks, "What will be the effect of change on Asians, Hispanics and Native Americans? There is no evidence that these groups wish to have interracial offspring put within a new 'multiracial' designation." Neither the Cherokee nor the Chinese in Mississippi sought to be considered as biracial; they were content to have escaped being thought of as Black or somehow linked to Africanity. Nor is there any evidence that European Americans, many of whom might by virtue of Native American, Asian, or African ancestry claim to be biracial, have any wish to be regarded as other than White. To be sure these are a number of Euro-Americans, dubbed by unsympathetic Native Americans as "Indian wanabees," who do not want to be White. But these persons do not want to be termed biracial either; instead they wish to parlay such Native American heritage as they may possess into full tribal membership. The biracial movement is largely composed of persons of African ancestry who do not want to be Black.

A number of factors explain why the biracial assault on Blackness has emerged at this particular time. First, the end of segregation made it possible for persons of obvious African ancestry to freely move about public places. This freedom is unparalleled in the twentieth century, for less than a generation ago guide books were published for traveling Blacks indicating where they could eat, use the restroom, or rent a hotel room. There was a "gentleman's agreement" in many communities which prevented apartments being rented or homes being sold to Blacks, and often the agreement was backed up by force of law. In many states, not all of them southern, it was legal to sell property with the restriction it might not

be resold to an African American. In this era all persons of African ancestry were on the same side of a color line that was firmly and clearly drawn. But now that segregation no longer exists some biracials are emboldened to separate themselves from Blacks. Free to move about where they wish, they no longer need the Black support system created by their ancestors. For them Blackness is not only out of date, but seems likely to permanently link them to an inferior race.

At the same time the African American culture so painfully constructed by the slaves is itself in disarray. The same racial segregation which so oppressed Black Americans was a source of strength. Denied entry into the larger White society—one which rested on wealth, property, education, and political power—the slaves created a separate culture of their own (Jones, 1993: 11). Within this culture they delivered respect to one another based on how members of the slave community treated one another. As racism continued after emancipation so too did this culture, only where it had previously operated underground and hidden from Whites it now surfaced. Free, Blacks were able to establish institutions—churches, fraternal organizations, insurance groups, newspapers, women's clubs, colleges, burial societies, and schools—in which they publicly recognized, celebrated, rewarded, praised, and supported one another. By Euro-American standards these institutions had neither wealth nor political power, but they provided African Americans with a sense of achievement. The distinguished Black sociologist, E. Franklin Frazier misunderstood the purpose of these institutions when he derided the *Black Bourgeoisie* in his book by the same title (1957). Frazier ridiculed middle-class Blacks for their social pretensions, noting that most of them lacked the resources that would have made for middle class standing in the White community. But that was just the point. They were not in the White community, but the organizations they created enabled these Black Americans to give one another a sense of status, recognition, and prestige.

Integration made it possible for a tiny handful of Blacks to become vice-presidents in Fortune

500 companies, generals in the United States Army, bishops in the Roman Catholic Church, and professors in Ivy League universities, while hundreds of others achieved similar middle-rung status in other White institutions. For the first time in the nation's history, so many African Americans entered the middle-class that one sociologist (Wilson, 1978) boldly entitled his book *The Declining Significance of Race.* Social scientists differ over how many Blacks have achieved middle class status, but clearly many Black Americans believed that neither the culture that had carried their ancestors through slavery and its aftermath, nor the institutions this culture created were any longer necessary. These organizations were not allowed to silently wither away as many publicly questioned the need for Black professional organizations, sororities, colleges, publications, and other Black institutions. As the biracial movement demonstrates, it is but a short step from questioning the need for Black institutions to questioning the need for blackness.

Two other factors made this step easy to take. The end of legal segregation in housing—while covertly evaded in many areas—and the growth of the Black middle class meant that some Blacks were able to move out of Black neighborhoods. Up through the 1970s most Blacks—regardless of occupation, education, and income—lived in Black neighborhoods, a fact that reinforced African American solidarity. But now many Blacks who had been successful no longer lived in Black neighborhoods and were therefore able to enter into informal relationships with Whites that would have been both unthinkable and impossible a decade earlier. Second, and paradoxically, this same period produced the "White backlash," in which millions of Whites in their votes and in the policies they supported indicated they thought Blacks had come too far too fast. Three times, beginning in 1980, Euro-American voters elected to the presidency men whose policies sought to turn back the racial clock. Under the guise of a color-blind policy these men sought, and with considerable success achieved, the goal of restoring the "Whites first" policy that

had long been characteristic of the United States. It is against the backdrop of these events that the biracial attack on blackness is taking place.

Of course, there is no such thing as a biracial community in the United States, but with African-American culture in disarray, middle class Blacks fleeing the Black community, and a White backlash gaining force, biracials doubtless see it to their advantage to escape blackness. They face a real problem, though. Most African Americans do not care to join them.

Perhaps three-quarters of the Black American population has ancestors who are not African and therefore have as much right to claim a biracial identity as do the biracials. For while the idea of whiteness is based on race purity, the idea of blackness is not. The African-American population includes persons who are the descendants of virtually every racial and ethnic group on the face of the earth. Moreover, many Blacks know the racial identity of their non-Black ancestors, and some—especially those with Native American or White ancestors—know a considerable amount of their non-African family background. If they wish they could clearly lay claim to a biracial or multiracial status. It is instructive, however, that in their attempts to be recognized as non-Black, the biracials have not appealed to this mass of Blacks to join them and also be classified as biracial. Instead they have concentrated their energies in getting Whites to recognize biracials as something other than Black.

In order to win Black Americans to their cause biracials would need to answer a number of difficult questions. First, there is the question of the application of the term biracial. Given that those who are children of White-Latino, White-Asian American, and White-Native American parents seem little interested in being biracial, is the term to apply only to those who are the children of a Black and non-Black parent? And how far back does biraciality go? Is it only for this generation of mixed children? Or may all Black Americans claim to be biracial? And since, under the laws of the United States most of the ancestors of present day African Americans, however racially mixed they may have been, will simply be listed in the public records as Black—or its historical equivalent—how is it to be determined that present day Blacks are in fact racially mixed? Could they simply present themselves for physical inspection, relying on skin color, hair texture, lip shape, or eye color as proof of their non-Black ancestry? Or would a mere declaration of mixed ancestry suffice? And what of those who, although of "pure" African ancestry, shall attempt to pass for biracial? Shall they be legally punished or will a simple public declaration that they are Black, not biracial, be sufficient punishment and humiliation?

Biracials have not spent much time in answering these questions because their primary appeals have been made not to Blacks but to Whites. Although most African Americans qualify for biracial status, few would accept it even if it became an option. Unlike Brazil and other nations of this hemisphere, there is no tradition of escaping blackness in the United States. There is no intermediate racial tier by means which persons can acknowledge White relatives and Black, so that historically the only way in which one could escape Africanity was to pass, to cut all ties with Black kin and become White. Some African Americans have been willing to take this step, just as were some Mississippi Chinese and some Cherokee in order to obtain better opportunities for their children and themselves in a racist social order.

CONCLUSION

The biracial assault on Africanity is born out of a great deal of pain. The people who are its leaders say they resent having to choose between their parents, resent having to deny a part of themselves, and resent being forced to consider themselves Black, when they do not feel Black. They focus much of this resentment on African Americans. Ironically the very people from whom they seek to escape and the very idea they seek to deconstruct might offer them comfort and guidance.

The Black community in the United States has never had the luxury of excluding persons because of their racial ancestry, nor, to do them justice, have its members been much interested in doing so. The reason for this is while European American and African American culture have much in common they differ in their ideas as to the cause of behavior. Because most African Americans know they are of mixed racial ancestry, race does figure significantly as a causal factor in African American culture. Most, but not all, White Americans really believe that race determines behavior and that Blacks behave in ways that are different from and inferior to those of Whites because, as a degraded, despicable and inferior people, they simply cannot help themselves. If most Whites did not believe this the nation would not remain racist. Most, but not all, Black Americans really believe that moral choice determines behavior and that (some) Whites behave in racist ways because they choose to be racists.

Blacks do not believe in biological determinism which is why Black hatemongering groups have so small a following—despite considerable media attention—in the Black community. This is not to say there are no Black bigots, nor is it to say that the Black community is perfect. Jones (1977) demonstrated that at least through the mid-1970s most Blacks who wrote on African American history accepted White stereotypes of Native peoples in an attempt to demonstrate the superiority of Africans over Indians. It is to say that when Martin Luther King, Jr., looked forward to a time in the United States when people would be judged by the content of their character and not the color of their skin, he merely urged White people to do what Black people had long done: judge people by their actions, not by their race.

Armed with this belief African Americans have achieved so much in the battle against race hate *as Black people* that most are little minded to put aside blackness, on the grounds that if Whites recognize some Blacks as biracial this will undercut racism. Most Blacks have no intention of claiming a special biracial status for themselves while leaving behind those Blacks who can make no such claim. Biracials who mislike this reality may, of course, and should continue their appeals to Whites for special recognition. Those who understand it should rejoin the African American community and continue the struggle for racial justice. There will be time enough to talk about being biracial and multi-racial when that struggle is won and Whites are no longer regarded as superior to Blacks.

REFERENCES

Anderson, W. W. 1994. Structuring biracial and multiracial identities across cultures. Paper presented at Annual Meeting of the Association for Asian American Studies, Ann Arbor, Mich., April 7.

Aptheker, H. 1956. *Toward Negro freedom.* New York: New Century.

Bateman, R. B. 1990. African and Indians: A comparative study of the Black Carib and Black Seminole. *Ethnohistory,* 37 (Winter): 1–24.

Cohen, D. W. and J. P. Greene (eds.). 1972. *Neither slave nor free: The freedmen of African descent in the slave societies of the New World.* Baltimore: Johns Hopkins University Press.

Cohn, D. L. 1967. *Where I was born and raised.* Notre Dame, Ind.: University of Notre Dame Press.

Davis, F. J. 1991. *Who is Black? One nation's definition.* University Park: University of Pennsylvania Press.

Degler, C. 1971. *Neither Black nor White: Slavery and race relations in Brazil and the United States.* New York: Macmillan.

Do Nascimento, A. 1989. *Brazil: Mixture or massacre? Essays in the genocide of a Black people.* Dover, Mass.: Majority.

Dzidzienyo, A. 1983. Blackness and politics in Brazil. In R. S. Jones (ed.), *Politics and the African Legacy.* Providence: Rhode Island Black Studies Consortium.

Dzidzienyo, A. 1985a. The African connection and the Afro-Brazilian condition. In Pierre-Michel Fontaine (ed.), *Race, class and power in Brazil.* Los Angeles: Center for Afro-America Studies, University of California.

Dzidzienyo, A. 1985b. Personal communication.

Dzidzienyo, A. 1993. Brazilian race relations studies: Old problems. New ideas? *Humboldt Journal of Social Relations,* 19 (2): 109–129.

Elkins, S. M. 1959. *Slavery: A problem in American institutional and intellectual life.* Chicago: University of Chicago Press.

Foner, L., and E. D. Genovese (eds.). 1969. *Slavery in the New World: A reader in comparative history.* Englewood Cliffs, N.J.: Prentice-Hall.

Frazier, E. F. 1957. *Black bourgeoisie: The rise of a new middle class in the United States.* Glencoe, Ill.: Free Press.

Freyre, G. 1946. *The masters and the slaves: A study in the development of Brazilian civilization.* Translated by Samuel Putnam. New York: Knopf.

Fuchs, L. H. 1990. *The American kaleidoscope: Race, ethnicity, and the civic culture.* Hanover, N.H.: University Press of New England.

Genovese, E. D. 1971. *The world the slaveholders made: Two essays in interpretation.* New York: Vintage Books.

Genovese, E. D. 1976. *Roll, Jordan, roll: The world the slaves made.* New York: Vintage.

Greene, L. J.. 1942. *The Negro in Colonial New England.* New York: Columbia University Press.

Harris, M. 1964. *Patterns of race in the Americas.* New York: Walker.

Hellwig, D. J. (ed.). 1992. *African-American reflections on Brazils racial paradise.* Philadelphia: Temple University Press.

Hoetink, H. 1967. *The two variants in Caribbean race relations: A Contribution to the sociology of segmented societies.* Translated by Eva M. Hooykaas. New York: Oxford.

Hoetink, H.. 1973. *Slavery and race relations in the Americas: An inquiry into their nature and nexus.* New York: Harper & Row.

Jones, R. S. 1977. Black over red: The image of Native Americans in Black history. *Umoja,* I (Summer): 13–29.

Jones, R. S. 1990. Brazilian race relations in hemispheric perspective: Review essay. *Trotter Institute Review* 4 (Summer): 15–18.

Jones, R. S. 1993. Double burdens, double responsibilities: Eighteenth century Black males and the African American struggle. *Journal of African American Male Studies,* I (Winter): 1–14.

Katz, W. L. 1986. *Black Indians: A hidden heritage.* New York: Atheneum.

Klein, H. S. 1967. *Slavery in the Americas: A comparative study of Virginia and Cuba.* Chicago: University of Chicago Press.

Liem, R. 1994. *Discussant's comments on crossing boundaries? Interracial marriages and multiracial children.* Meeting of the Southern New England Consortium on Race and Ethnicity, Providence, R.I., February 5.

Littlefield, D. F., Jr. 1977. *Africans and Seminoles: From removal to emancipation.* Westport, Conn.: Greenwood.

Loewen, J. W. 1988. *The Mississippi Chinese: Between Black and White.* Prospect Heights, Ill.: Waveland.

McLoughlin, W. G., with W. H. Conser, Jr. and V. D. McLoughin. 1984. *The Cherokee ghost dance: Essays on the Southeastern Indians, 1789–1861.* Macon, Ga.: Mercer University Press.

McLoughlin, W. C. 1986. *Cherokee Renascence in the New Republic.* Princeton, N.J.: Princeton University Press.

McManus, E. J. 1973. *Black bondage in the North.* Syracuse, N.Y.: Syracuse University Press.

Mellafe, R. 1975. *Negro slavery in Latin America.* Translated by J.W.S. Judge. Berkeley: University of California Press.

Morner, M. 1967. *Race mixture in the history of Latin America.* Boston: Little, Brown.

Perdue, T.. 1979. *Slavery and the evolution of Cherokee Society, 1540–1866.* Knoxville: University of Tennessee Press.

Piersen, W. D. 1988. *Black Yankees: The development of an Afro-American subculture in eighteenth century New England.* Amherst: University of Massachusetts Press.

Quan, R. S. 1982. *Lotus among the Magnolias: The Mississippi Chinese.* Jackson: University of Mississippi Press.

Reddy, M. 1994. *Crossing the color line: Race, mothering, and culture.* Paper presented at the Meeting of the Southern New England Consortium on Race and Ethnicity, Providence, R.I., February 5.

Rout, L. B. Jr. 1976. *The African experience in Spanish America.* New York: Cambridge University Press.

Skidmore, T. 1974. *Black into White: Race and Nationality in Brazilian thought.* New York: Oxford.

Sundiata, I. K. 1994. How Black is Black? *Boston Globe.* June 5: G-22.

Tannenbaum, F. 1946. *Slave and citizen: The Negro in the Americas.* New York: Knopf.

Williams, E. 1944. *Capitalism and slavery.* Chapel Hill: University of North Carolina Press.

Wilson, W. J. 1978. *The declining significance of race: Blacks and changing American Institutions.* Chicago: University of Chicago Press.

Wines, R., (ed). 1972. *Slavery: A comparative perspective.* New York: New York University Press.

Wong, V. W. 1993. The Chinese in Mississippi: A race in between. *Trotter Institute Review* 7: pp. 20–23.

Zack, N. 1993. *Race and mixed race.* Philadelphia: Temple University Press.

PART THREE

The Family

The bearing of children has traditionally been a very important function in the Black community. The sacrifices of Black mothers for their children have been legendary for hundreds of years. Although children are still regarded as a strong value to Blacks, attitudes toward having large numbers of them have changed dramatically since 1965. Contributing to this change are the beliefs of many Black women that the responsibility for rearing large numbers of children is destructive to their personal freedom and job mobility, the different problems faced in raising children in urban centers, the decline in biparental households, and the necessity of raising children alone.

CHILDBEARING AND PARENTAL ROLES

Raising a Black child is not, and has never been, an easy task. In light of the obstacles they face, Black parents have done a more than adequate job. Generally, they have more children to rear, with fewer resources, than white parents do. Black parents must also socialize their children into the values of mainstream culture to adapt successfully to majority group requirements and institutions. At the same time they must teach the children the folkways of their own culture and what it means to be Black in a racist society. Given the poor social conditions under which most Black children are raised, it is not surprising that some fail in life. What is even more surprising is that so many succeed given the adverse circumstances they encounter.

Child-rearing practices do not differ significantly by race. Variations in socialization techniques are more a function of class membership. Middle-class parents, Black and White, are more likely to use verbal than physical punishment to discipline a child. Lower-class Black mothers are often regarded as ineffective parents because of their reliance on physical punishment techniques to control their children. What is not considered in that assessment is the tendency of many Black mothers to combine physical measures with very heavy doses of emotional nurturance. This combination of spankings and affection may be more beneficial for a child's development than is the middle-class parents' threat of withdrawal of love if the child does not behave correctly. Many observers of the Black family have noticed how children in the lower-class Black community are well treated and seem emotionally and psychologically healthy.

The attitudes and behavior of many Black parents are changing. Fewer children are being born per family, and there are indications that those children who are brought into this world are not as well treated. The same trend is also evident in the White community and seems to be part of the tendency of mothers to put their own wishes and goals ahead of everything and everyone else. There are also certain tensions in our society, particularly in urban areas, that affect behavior toward children. Corresponding to an increase in those tensions has been an elevation of the incidence of child abuse in Black families and a decline in the respect of Black children for their elders. Certain changes in the Black fertility pattern are responsible for some of the inadequate parenting that exists today. While there have been overall declines in the Black birth rate, there has been a significant increase in out-of-wedlock pregnancies, primarily to teenaged women. With the decline in the Black extended family system, immature mothers and one-parent households have fostered the arrogance and negativism emerging among many Black youth.

THE EXTENDED FAMILY

Kinship bonds have always been important to the Black population. In African societies, kinship was and is the basis of the social organization. During the period of slavery, many of the bondsmen were organized into an extended family system based on biological and nonbiological standards. Most research studies of Black kinship networks generally indicate that they are more extensive and significant to the Black community than to the White community. Whatever the reason, there is little doubt that kinsmen play an important role in the Black family system.

Among the valuable services provided by kin is the sharing of economic resources, child care, advice, and other forms of mutual aid. Those are acknowledged functions of a kinship network, but members of the extended family also serve to liberate children from the confines of the nuclear family unit. Children have someone other than mother or father to relate to and from whom to receive emotional nurturance. The network also helps socialize children more effectively into values that Blacks held more strongly in rural an southern settings. The function of kinship groups to Blacks is so important that many nonblood relative are referred to and regarded as kinsmen. Usually this is a special friendship in which the norms claims, obligations, and loyalties of the kin relationships are operative, such as those of godmothers or play brothers.

One of the problems the Black family is facing today is a decline in the extended family system. This has occurred, in large part, as a result of Black mobility patterns. Many Blacks have moved from their place of origin to large cities where they have few, if any, kin. Fairly large numbers of Blacks are moving to suburban areas, where they often lack friends or relatives in their immediate neighborhood or community. Changes in the attitudes of Black youth toward their elders have also weakened the role of some older kin. The antiauthority attitudes of many youth have made many of them less responsive to the wisdom and guidance of grandparents and other kin.

ADOLESCENCE AND PERSONALITY DEVELOPMENT

The period of adolescence has been generally regarded as a time of identity acquisition and liberation from parental control. For Black youth the problem of transition from adolescence to adulthood has been compounded by their unique status in the society. Many, for example, do not have carefree period in which to acquire their identity as do middle-class White youth. Because they come from relatively poor families, large numbers must find jobs to help support their families. Finding employment in today's job market is not easy task Without any special skills and with little education, the majority of Black youth are without regular employment of any kind.

Because of that high unemployment rate, Black youth are overrepresented in the crime statistics, in the volunteer army, among drug addicts, and in other negative social indexes. There has been a tendency to place the responsibility for the problems of Black youth on their disorganized family system. Although it is true that a slight majority of Black youth are now living in one-parent homes, there is reason to question that those types of families produce uneducable and delinquent children. One-parent households are generally poor families, and it is the relationship between poverty and negative youth behavior that bears watching.

SOCIAL AND ECONOMIC ISSUES

It is necessary to understand the influence of economics on Black families' lives in order to conceptualize the conditions under which they function—or fail to function—as a viable system. Ever since the release from slavery, economic deprivation has been a fact of life for Black people. Since the 1940s the rate of unemployment among Blacks has been steadily twice that of Whites. Men who cannot find work not only have trouble maintaining a stable marital and family life but often cannot find a woman willing to marry them in the first place. As incomes rise so does the number of Black men who marry.

HEALTH ISSUES

Despite the promise of greater racial equality in American life, most statistics show a widening racial gap in the 1990s. Nowhere is this truer than with regard to health conditions. From 1984 to 1997 the gap in life expectancy between Blacks and Whites continued to grow. That trend was almost entirely a function of deaths from preventable causes, such as AIDS, drug overdoses, and other drug-related factors: diseases and disabilities that kill infants in their first year; accidents, mainly those involving motor vehicles; and chronic liver diseases, including cirrhosis caused by alcoholism. Actually, this increased gap is largely a result of the high death rate of Black males—especially in their younger years. High unemployment, low self-esteem, and poor social image all contribute to a sense of despair among this group that leads to self-destructive behavior. AIDS, for example, is the leading cause of death among Black men, ages 15—30 years. It is during these years of greatest marriageability that Black men die at a rate triple that of similar Black women. Consequently, the marriage pool is considerably reduced for women who desire marriage to men in the same race. Those who are not victims of AIDS die from homicide, suicide, and drug overdoses. And, almost all of those early deaths occur in the lower socioeconomic classes.

FAMILY VIOLENCE

What has long been a feature of married life for many Americans, domestic or family violence, gained great visibility and importance during the O.J. Simpson double homicide trial. Surprisingly, the perpetrator was a Black, millionaire celebrity, and the victim, Nicole Brown Simpson, his White ex-wife. Previous studies of family violence had languished in obscurity because marital violence was perceived as a problem of the lower-income groups. Yet, those studies had revealed family violence to exist among a cross-section of socioeconomic, racial, age, and gender groups.

Certainly, the problems of poverty and low income compound the problems that result for the battered spouse, generally the female member of a marital, cohabitation, or dating relationship, in finding a sanctuary away from their violent partner. Many of the injuries to, and murder of, women occur in the context of an intimate relationship. Racial factors, though no excuse, play a role in the domestic violence of Black American families. They are more likely to be poor than the average Euro-American and, as a result, come to the attention of the police and other institutions. Additionally, racial membership brings with it a great deal of mundane stress not as often experienced by the racial majority in the United States. To address, and remedy, this issue means doing more than giving individual offenders therapy but must involve eliminating the cultural supports for violence in a country that has the highest rate of violence in the industrialized Western world.

8

The Maternal Role

The Meaning of Motherhood
in Black Culture

PATRICIA HILL COLLINS

This essay explores the relationship between the meaning of motherhood in Black American culture by addressing three primary questions. These questions concern (1) how competing perspectives intersected to form a distinctly Afrocentric ideology of motherhood, (2) what the themes contained in that ideology of motherhood are, and (3) what the effect of this ideology of motherhood is on Black mother-daughter relationships.

■

"What did your mother teach you about men?" is a question I often ask students in my courses on African-American women. "Go to school first and get a good education—don't get too serious too young," "Make sure you look around and that you can take care of yourself before you settle down," and "Don't trust them, want more for yourself than just a man," are typical responses from Black women. My students share stories of how their mothers encouraged them to cultivate satisfying relationships with Black men while anticipating disappointments, to desire marriage while planning viable alternatives, to become mothers only when fully prepared to do so. But above all, they stress their mothers' insistence on being self-reliant and resourceful.

These daughters from varying social class backgrounds, ages, family structures and geographic regions had somehow received strikingly similar messages about Black womanhood. Even though their mothers employed diverse teaching strategies, these Black daughters had all been exposed to common themes about the meaning of womanhood in Black culture.[1]

This essay explores the relationship between the meaning of motherhood in African-American culture and Black mother-daughter relationships by addressing three primary questions. First, how have competing perspectives about motherhood

An abridged version adapted from *SAGE: A Scholarly Journal on Black Women*, 4(Fall 1987): 3–10.

intersected to produce a distinctly Afrocentric ideology of motherhood? Second, what are the enduring themes that characterize this Afrocentric ideology of motherhood? Finally what effect might this Afrocentric ideology of motherhood have on Black mother-daughter relationships?

COMPETING PERSPECTIVES ON MOTHERHOOD

The Dominant Perspective: Eurocentric Views of White Motherhood

The cult of true womanhood, with its emphasis on motherhood as woman's highest calling, has long held a special place in the gender symbolism of White Americans. From this perspective, women's activities should be confined to the care of children the nurturing of a husband, and the maintenance of the household. By managing this separate domestic sphere, women gain social influence through their roles as mothers, transmitters of culture and parents for the next generation.[2]

While substantial numbers of White women have benefited from the protections of White patriarchy provided by the dominant ideology, White women themselves have recently challenged its tenets. On one pole lies a cluster of women, the traditionalists, who aim to retain the centrality of motherhood in women's lives. For traditionalists, differentiating between the experience of motherhood, which for them has been quite satisfying, and motherhood as an institution central in reproducing gender inequality, has proved difficult. The other pole is occupied by women who advocate dismantling motherhood as an institution. They suggest that compulsory motherhood be outlawed and that the experience of motherhood can only be satisfying if women can choose not to be mothers. Arrayed between these dichotomous positions are women who argue for an expanded, but not necessarily different role for women—women can be mothers as long as they are not *just* mothers.[3]

Three themes implicit in White perspectives on motherhood are particularly problematic for Black women and others outside of this debate. First, the assumption that mothering occurs within the confines of a private, nuclear family household where the mother has almost total responsibility for childrearing is less applicable to Black families. While the ideal of the cult of true womanhood has been held up to Black women for emulation, racial oppression has denied Black families sufficient resources to support private, nuclear family households. Second, the assumption of strict sex-role segregation defining male and female spheres of influence within the family has been less applicable to African-American families than to White middle class ones. Finally, the assumption that motherhood and economic dependency on men are linked and that to be a "good" mother, one must stay at home, making motherhood a full-time "occupation," is similarly uncharacteristic of African-American families.[4]

Even though selected groups of White women are challenging the cult of true womanhood and its accompanying definition of motherhood, the dominant ideology remains powerful. As long as these approaches remain prominent in scholarly and popular discourse, Eurocentric views of White motherhood will continue to affect Black women's lives.

Eurocentric Views of Black Motherhood

Eurocentric perspectives on Black motherhood revolve around two interdependent images that together define Black women's roles in White and in African-American families. The first image is that of the Mammy, the faithful, devoted domestic servant. Like one of the family, Mammy conscientiously "mothers" her White children, caring for them and loving them as if they were her own. Mammy is the ideal Black mother for she recognizes her place. She is paid next to nothing and yet cheerfully accepts her inferior status. But when she enters her own home, this same Mammy is transformed into the second image, the too-strong matriarch who raises weak sons and "unnaturally superior" daughters.[5] When she protests, she is labeled aggressive and non-feminine, yet if she remains silent, she is rendered invisible.

The task of debunking Mammy by analyzing Black women's roles as exploited domestic workers and challenging the matriarchy thesis by demonstrating that Black women do not wield disproportionate power in African-American families has long preoccupied African-American scholars.[6] But an equally telling critique concerns uncovering the functions of these images and their role in explaining Black women's subordination in systems of race, class and gender oppression. As Mae King points out, White definitions of Black motherhood foster the dominant group's exploitation of Black women by blaming Black women for their characteristic reactions to their own subordination.[7] For example, while the stay-at-home mother has been held up to all women as the ideal, African-American women have been compelled to work outside the home, typically in a very narrow range of occupations. Even though Black women were forced to become domestic servants and be strong figures in Black households, labeling them Mammys and matriarchs denigrates Black women. Without a countervailing Afrocentric ideology of motherhood, White perspectives on both White and African-American motherhood place Black women in a no-win situation. Adhering to these standards brings the danger of the lowered self-esteem of internalized oppression, one that, if passed on from mother to daughter, provides a powerful mechanism for controlling African-American communities.

African Perspectives on Motherhood

One concept that has been constant throughout the history of African societies is the centrality of motherhood in religions, philosophies and social institutions. As Barbara Christian points out, "There is no doubt that motherhood is for most African people symbolic of creativity and continuity."[8]

Cross-cultural research on motherhood in African societies appears to support Christian's claim.[9] West African sociologist Christine Oppong suggests that the Western notion of equating household with family be abandoned because it obscures women's family roles in African cultures.[10] While the archetypal White, middle-class nuclear family conceptualizes family life as being divided into two oppositional spheres—the "male" sphere of economic providing and the "female" sphere of affective nurturing this type of rigid sex role segregation was not part of the West African tradition. Mothering was not a privatized nurturing "occupation" reserved for biological mothers, and the economic support of children was not the exclusive responsibility of men. Instead, for African women, emotional care for children and providing for their physical survival were interwoven as interdependent, complementary dimensions of motherhood.

In spite of variation among societies, a strong case has been made that West African women occupy influential roles in African family networks.[11] First, since they are not dependent on males for economic support and provide for certain key dimensions of their own and their children's economic support, women are structurally central to families.[12] Second, the image of the mother is one that is culturally elaborated and valued across diverse West African societies. Continuing the lineage is essential in West African philosophies, and motherhood is similarly valued.[13] Finally, while the biological mother/child bond is valued, child care was a collective responsibility, a situation fostering cooperative, age stratified, woman-centered "mothering" networks.

Recent research by Africanists suggests that much more of this African heritage was retained among African-Americans than had previously been thought. The retention of West African culture as a culture of resistance offered enslaved Africans and exploited African-Americans alternative ideologies to those advanced by dominant groups. Central to these reinterpretations of African-American institutions and culture is a reconceptualization of Black family life and the role of women in Black family networks.[14] West African perspectives may have been combined with the changing political and economic situations framing African-American communities to produce certain enduring themes characterizing an Afrocentric ideology of motherhood.

ENDURING THEMES OF AN AFROCENTRIC IDEOLOGY OF MOTHERHOOD

An Afrocentric ideology of motherhood must reconcile the competing world views of these three conflicting perspectives of motherhood. An ongoing tension exists between efforts to mold the institution of Black motherhood for the benefit of the dominant group and efforts by Black women to define and value their own experiences with motherhood. This tension leads to a continuum of responses. For those women who either aspire to the cult of true womanhood without having the resources to support such a lifestyle or who believe stereotypical analyses of themselves as dominating matriarchs, motherhood can be an oppressive institution. But the experience of motherhood can provide Black women with a base of self-actualization, status in the Black community, and a reason for social activism. These alleged contradictions can exist side by side in African-American communities, families, and even within individual women.

Embedded in these changing relationships are four enduring themes that I contend characterize an Afrocentric ideology of motherhood. Just as the issues facing enslaved African mothers were quite different from those currently facing poor Black women in inner cities for any given historical moment, the actual institutional forms that these themes take depend on the severity of oppression and Black women's resources for resistance.

Bloodmothers, Othermothers, and Women-Centered Networks

In African-American communities, the boundaries distinguishing biological mothers of children from other women who care for children are often fluid and changing. Biological mothers or bloodmothers are expected to care for their children. But African and African-American communities have also recognized that vesting one person with full responsibility for mothering a child may not be wise or possible. As a result, "othermothers," women who assist bloodmothers by sharing mothering responsibilities, traditionally have been central to the institution of Black motherhood.[15]

The centrality of women in African-American extended families is well known.[16] Organized, resilient, women-centered networks of bloodmothers and othermothers are key in understanding this centrality. Grandmothers, sisters, aunts, or cousins acted as othermothers by taking on childcare responsibilities for each other's children. When needed, temporary child care arrangements turned into long-term care or informal adoption.[17]

In African-American communities, these women-centered networks of community-based childcare often extend beyond the boundaries of biologically related extended families to support "fictive kin."[18] Civil rights activist Ella Baker describes how informal adoption by othermothers functioned in the Southern, rural community of her childhood:

> My aunt who had thirteen children of her own raised three more. She had become a midwife, and a child was born who was covered with sores. Nobody was particularly wanting the child, so she took the child and raised him…and another mother decided she didn't want to be bothered with two

children. So my aunt took one and raised him . . . they were part of the family.[19]

Even when relationships were not between kin or fictive kin, African-American community norms were such that neighbors cared for each other's children. In the following passage, Sara Brooks, a Southern domestic worker, describes the importance of the community-based childcare that a neighbor offered her daughter. In doing so, she also shows how the African-American cultural value placed on cooperative childcare found institutional support in the adverse conditions under which so many Black women mothered:

> She kept Vivian and she didn't charge me nothin either. You see, people used to look after each other but now it's not that way. I reckon it's because we all was poor; and I guess they put theirself in the place of the person that they was helpin.[20]

Othermothers were key not only in supporting children but also in supporting bloodmothers who, for whatever reason, were ill-prepared or had little desire to care for their children. Given the pressures from the larger political economy, the emphasis placed on community-based childcare and the respect given to othermothers who assume the responsibilities of childcare have served a critical function in African-American communities. Children orphaned by sale or death of their parents under slavery, children conceived through rape, children of young mothers, children born into extreme poverty or children, who for other reasons have been rejected by their bloodmothers, have all been supported by othermothers who, like Ella Baker's aunt, took in additional children, even when they had enough of their own.

Providing as Part of Mothering

The work done by African-American women in providing the economic resources essential to Black family well-being affects motherhood in a contradictory fashion. On the one hand, African-American women have long integrated their activities as economic providers into their mothering relationships. In contrast to the cult of true womanhood where work is defined as being in opposition to and incompatible with motherhood, work for Black women has been an important and valued dimension of Afrocentric definitions of Black motherhood. On the other hand, African-American women's experiences as mothers under oppression were such that the type and purpose of work Black women were forced to do greatly impacted on the type of mothering relationships bloodmothers and other-mothers had with Black children.

While slavery both disrupted West African family patterns and exposed enslaved Africans to the gender ideologies and practices of slaveowners, it simultaneously made it impossible, had they wanted to do so, for enslaved Africans to implement slave-owner's ideologies. Thus, the separate spheres of providing as a male domain and affective nurturing as a female domain did not develop within African-American families.[21] Providing for Black children's physical survival and attending to their affective, emotional needs continued as interdependent dimensions of an Afrocentric ideology of motherhood. However, by changing the conditions under which Black women worked and the purpose of the work itself, slavery introduced the problem of how best to continue traditional Afrocentric values under oppressive conditions. Institutions of community-based childcare, informal adoption, greater reliance on othermothers, all emerge as adaptations to the exigencies of combining exploitative work with nurturing children.

In spite of the change in political status brought on by emancipation, the majority of African-American women remained exploited agricultural workers. However, their placement in Southern political economies allowed them to combine child-care with field labor. Sara Brooks describes how strong the links between providing and caring for others were for her:

When I was about nine I was nursin my sister Sally—I'm about seven or eight years older than Sally. And when I would put her to sleep, instead of me goin somewhere and sit down and play I'd get my little old hoe and get out there and work right in the field around the house.[22]

Black women's shift from Southern agriculture to domestic work in Southern and Northern towns and cities represented a change in the type of work done, but not in the meaning of work to women and their families. Whether they wanted to or not, the majority of African-American women had to work and could not afford the luxury of motherhood as a noneconomically productive, female "occupation."

Community Othermothers and Social Activism

Black women's experiences as othermothers have provided a foundation for Black women's social activism. Black women's feelings of responsibility for nurturing the children in their own extended family networks have stimulated a more generalized ethic of care where Black women feel accountable to all the Black community's children.

This notion of Black women as community othermothers for all Black children traditionally allowed Black women to treat biologically unrelated children as if they were members of their own families. For example, sociologist Karen Fields describes how her grandmother, Mamie Garvin Fields, draws on her power as a community othermother when dealing with unfamiliar children.

She will say to a child on the street who looks up to no good, picking out a name at random, "Aren't you Miz Pinckney's boy?" in that same reproving tone. If the reply is, "No, ma'am, my mother is Miz Gadsden," whatever threat there was dissipates.[23]

The use of family language in referring to members of the Black community also illustrates this dimension of Black motherhood. For example, Mamie Garvin Fields describes how she became active in surveying the poor housing conditions of Black people in Charleston.

I was one of the volunteers they got to make a survey of the places where we were paying extortious rents for indescribable property. I said "we," although it wasn't Bob and me. We had our own home, and so did many of the Federated Women. Yet we still felt like it really was "we" living in those terrible places and it was up to us to do something about them.[24]

To take another example, while describing her increasingly successful efforts to teach a boy who had given other teachers problems, my daughter's kindergarten teacher stated, "You know how it can be—the majority of children in the learning disabled classes are *our children*. I know he didn't belong there, so I volunteered to take him." In these statements, both women invoke the language of family to describe the ties that bind them as Black women to their responsibilities to other members of the Black community as family.

Sociologist Cheryl Gilkes suggests that community othermother relationships are sometimes behind Black women's decisions to become community activists.[25] Gilkes notes that many of the Black women community activists in her study became involved in community organizing in response to the needs of their own children and of those in their communities. The following comment is typical of how many of the Black women in Gilkes' study relate to Black children: "There were a lot of summer programs springing up for kids, but they were exclusive...and I found that most of *our kids* (emphasis mine) were excluded."[26] For many women, what began as the daily expression of their obligations as community othermothers, as was the case for the kindergarten teacher, developed into full-fledged roles as community leaders.

Motherhood as a Symbol of Power

Motherhood, whether bloodmother, othermother or community othermother, can be invoked by Black women as a symbol of power. A substantial portion of Black women's status in African-American communities stems not only from their roles as mothers in their own families but from their contributions as community othermothers to Black community development as well.

The specific contributions Black women make in nurturing Black community development form the basis of community-based power. Community othermothers work on behalf of the Black community by trying, in the words of late nineteenth century Black feminists, to "uplift the race," so that vulnerable members of the community would be able to attain the self-reliance and independence so desperately needed for Black community development under oppressive conditions. This is the type of power many African-Americans have in mind when they describe the "strong, Black women" they see around them in traditional African-American communities

When older Black women invoke this community othermother status, its results can be quite striking. Karen Fields recounts an incident described to her by her grandmother illustrating how women can exert power as community othermothers:

> One night . . . as Grandmother sat cro-
> cheting alone at about two in the morning, a
> young man walked into the living room
> carrying the portable TV from upstairs.
> She said, "Who are you looking for this time
> of night?" As Grandmother (described) the
> incident to me over the phone I could hear
> a tone of voice that I know well. It said,
> "Nice boys don't do that." So I imagine
> the burglar heard his own mother or grand-
> mother at that moment. He joined in the
> familial game just created: "Well, he told me
> that I could borrow it." "Who told you?"
> "John." "Um um, no John lives here. You
> got the wrong house."[27]

After this dialogue, the teenager turned around, went back upstairs and returned the television.

In local Black communities, specific Black women are widely recognized as powerful figures, primarily because of their contributions to the community's well-being through their roles as community othermothers. Sociologist Charles Johnson describes the behavior of an elderly Black woman at a church service in rural Alabama of the 1930s. Even though she was not on the program, the woman stood up to speak. The master of ceremonies rang for her to sit down but she refused to do so claiming, "I am the mother of this church, and I will say what I please." The master of ceremonies later explained to the congregation—"Brothers, I know you all honor Sister Moore. Course our time is short but she has acted as a mother to me . . . Any time old folks get up I give way to them."[28]

IMPLICATIONS FOR BLACK MOTHER-DAUGHTER RELATIONSHIPS

In her discussion of the sex-role socialization of Black girls, Pamela Reid identifies two complementary approaches in understanding Black mother-daughter relationships.[29] The first, psychoanalytic theory, examines the role of parents in the establishment of personality and social behavior. This theory argues that the development of feminine behavior results from the girls' identification with adult female role models. This approach emphasizes how an Afrocentric ideology of motherhood is actualized through Black mothers' activities as role models.

The second approach, social learning theory, suggests that the rewards and punishments attached to girls' childhood experiences are central in shaping women's sex-role behavior. The kinds of behaviors that Black mothers reward and punish in their daughters are seen as key in the socialization process. This approach examines specific experiences that Black girls have while growing up that encourage them to absorb an Afrocentric ideology of motherhood.

African-American Mothers as Role Models

Feminist psychoanalytic theorists suggest that the sex-role socialization process is different for boys and girls. While boys learn maleness by rejecting femaleness via separating themselves from their mothers, girls establish feminine identities by embracing the femaleness of their mothers. Girls identify with their mothers, a sense of connection that is incorporated into the female personality. However, this mother-identification is problematic because, under patriarchy, men are more highly valued than women. Thus, while daughters identify with their mothers, they also reject them because, in patriarchal families, identification with adult women as mothers means identifying with persons deemed inferior.[30]

While Black girls learn by identifying with their mothers, the specification of the female role with which Black girls identify may be quite different than that modeled by middle class White mothers. The presence of working mothers, extended family othermothers, and powerful community othermothers offers a range of role models that challenge the tenets of the cult of true womanhood.

Moreover, since Black mothers have a distinctive relationship to White patriarchy, they may be less likely to socialize their daughters into their proscribed role as subordinates. Rather, a key part of Black girls' socialization involves incorporating the critical posture that allows Black women to cope with contradictions. For example, Black girls have long had to learn how to do domestic work while rejecting definitions of themselves as Mammies. At the same time they've had to take on strong roles in Black extended families without internalizing images of themselves as matriarchs.

In raising their daughters, Black mothers face a troubling dilemma. To ensure their daughters'

physical survival, they must teach their daughters to fit into systems of oppression. For example, as a young girl in Mississippi, Black activist Ann Moody questioned why she was paid so little for the domestic work she began at age nine, why Black women domestics were sexually harassed by their White male employers, and why Whites had so much more than Blacks. But her mother refused to answer her questions and actually became angry whenever Ann Moody stepped out of her "place."[31] Black daughters are raised to expect to work, to strive for an education so that they can support themselves, and to anticipate carrying heavy responsibilities in their families and communities because these skills are essential for their own survival as well as for the survival of those for whom they will eventually be responsible.[32] And yet mothers know that if daughters fit too well into the limited opportunities offered Black women, they become willing participants in their own subordination. Mothers may have ensured their daughters' physical survival at the high cost of their emotional destruction.

On the other hand, Black daughters who offer serious challenges to oppressive situations may not physically survive. When Ann Moody became involved in civil rights activities, her mother first begged her not to participate and then told her not to come home because she feared the Whites in Moody's hometown would kill her. In spite of the dangers, many Black mothers routinely encourage their daughters to develop skills to confront oppressive conditions. Thus, learning that they will work, that education is a vehicle for advancement, can also be seen as ways of preparing Black girls to resist oppression through a variety of mothering roles. The issue is to build emotional strength, but not at the cost of physical survival.

This delicate balance between conformity and resistance is described by historian Elsa Barkley Brown as the "need to socialize me one way and at the same time to give me all the tools I needed to be something else."[33] Black daughters must learn how to survive in interlocking structures of race, class and gender oppression while rejecting and transcending those very same structures. To develop these skills in their daughters, mothers demonstrate varying combinations of behaviors devoted to ensuring their daughters' survival—such as providing them with basic necessities and ensuring their protection in dangerous environments—to helping their daughters go farther than mothers themselves were allowed to go.

The presence of othermothers in Black extended families and the modeling symbolized by community othermothers offer powerful support for the task of teaching girls to resist White perceptions of Black womanhood while appearing to conform to them. In contrast to the isolation of middle class White mother/daughter dyads, Black women-centered extended family networks foster an early identification with a much wider range of models of Black womanhood which can lead to a greater sense of empowerment in young Black girls.

NOTES

1. The definition of culture used in this essay is taken from Leith Mullings, "Anthropological Perspectives on the Afro-American Family," *American Journal of Social Psychiatry 6* (1986), pp. 11–16. According to Mullings, culture is composed of "the symbols and values that create the ideological frame of reference through which people attempt to deal with the circumstances in which they find themselves," p. 13.

2. For analyses of the relationship of the cult of true womanhood to Black women see Leith Mullings, "Uneven Development: Class, Race and Gender in the United States Before 1900," in *Women's Work: Development and the Division of Labor by Gender*. eds. Eleanor Leacock and Helen Safa (South Hadley, Mass.: Bergin & Garvey 1986), pp. 41–57; Bonnie Thornton Dill, "Our Mothers' Grief: Racial Ethnic Women and the Maintenance of Families," Research Paper 4, Center for Research on Women (Memphis, Tenn.: Memphis State University, 1986); and Hazel Carby, *Reconstructing Womanhood: The Emergence of the Afro-American Woman Novelist* (New York: Oxford University, 1987), especially Chapter two.

3. Contrast, for example, the traditionalist analysis of Selma Fraiberg, *Every Child's Birthright: In Defense of Mothering* (New York: Basic, 1977) to that of Jeffner Allen, "Motherhood: The Annihilation of Women," in *Mothering, Essays in Feminist Theory*, ed. Joyce Trebilcot (Totawa, N.J.: Rowan & Allanheld, 1983). See also Adrienne Rich, *Of Woman Born: Motherhood as Experience and Institution* (New York: Norton, 1976). For an

overview of how traditionalists and feminists have shaped the public policy debate on abortion, see Kristin Luker, *Abortion and the Politics of Motherhood* (Berkeley: University of California, 1984).

4. Mullings, 1986, note 2 earlier; Dill, 1986; and Carby, 1987. Feminist scholarship is also challenging Western notions of the family. See Barrie Thorne and Marilyn Yalom, eds., *Rethinking the Family* (New York: Longman, 1982).

5. Since Black women are no longer heavily concentrated in private domestic service, the Mammy image may be fading. In contrast, the matriarch image, popularized in Daniel Patrick Moynihan's, *The Negro Family: The Case for National Action* (Washington, DC: U.S. Government Printing Office, 1965), is reemerging in public debates about the feminization of poverty and the urban underclass. See Maxine Baca Zinn, "Minority Families in Crisis: The Public Discussion," Research Paper 6, Center for Research on Women (Memphis, Tenn.: Memphis State University, 1987).

6. For an alternative analysis to the Mammy image, see Judith Rollins, *Between Women: Domestics and Their Employers* (Philadelphia: Temple University, 1985). Classic responses to the matriarchy thesis include Robert Hill, *The Strengths of Black Families* (New York: Urban League, 1972); Andrew Billingsley, *Black Families in White America* (Englewood Cliffs, N.J.: Prentice-Hall, 1968); and Joyce Ladner, *Tomorrow's Tomorrow* (Garden City, N.Y.: Doubleday, 1971). For a recent analysis, see Linda Burnham, "Has Poverty Been Feminized in Black America?" *Black Scholar* 16(1985), pp. 15–24.

7. Mae King, "The Politics of Sexual Stereotypes," *Black Scholar* 4(1973), pp. 12–23.

8. Barbara Christian, "An Angle of Seeing: Motherhood in Buchi Emecheta's *Joys of Motherhood* and Alice Walker's *Meridian*," in *Black Feminist Criticism*, ed. Barbara Christian (New York: Pergamon, 1985), p. 214.

9. See Christine Oppong, ed., *Female and Male in West Africa* (London: Allen & Unwin, 1983); Niara Sudarkasa, "Female Employment and Family Organization in West Africa," in *The Black Woman Cross-Culturally* ed. Filomina Chiamo Steady (Cambridge, Mass.: Schenkman, 1981), pp. 49–64; and Nancy Tanner, "Matrifocality in Indonesia and Africa and Among Black Americans," in *Woman, Culture, and Society*, eds. Michelle Rosaldo and Louise Lamphere (Stanford, Calif.: Stanford University 1974), pp. 129–156.

10. Christine Oppong, "Family Structure and Women's Reproductive and Productive Roles: Some Conceptual and Methodological Issues," in *Women's Roles and Population Trends in the Third World*, eds. Richard Anker, Myra Buvinic, and Nadia Youssef (London: Croom Helm, 1982), pp. 133–150.

11. The key distinction here is that, unlike the matriarchy thesis, women play central roles in families and this centrality is seen as legitimate. In spite of this centrality it is important not to idealize African women's family roles. For an analysis by a Black African feminist, see Awa Thiam, *Black Sisters, Speak Out: Feminism and Oppression in Black Africa* (London: Pluto, 1978).

12. Sudarkasa, 1981.

13. John Mbiti, *African Religions and Philosophies* (New York: Anchor, 1969).

14. Niara Sudarkasa, "Interpreting the African Heritage in Afro-American Family Organization," in *Black Families*, ed. Harriette Pipes McAdoo (Beverly Hills, Calif.: Sage, 1981), pp. 37–53; and Deborah Gray White, *Ar'n't I a Woman? Female Slaves in the Plantation South* (New York: W.W. Norton, 1984).

15. The terms used in this section appear in Rosalie Riegle Troester "Turbulence and Tenderness: Mothers, Daughters, and 'Othermothers' in Paule Marshall's *Brown Girl, Brownstones*," *SAGE: A Scholarly Journal on Black Women* 1 (Fall 1984), pp. 13–16.

16. See Tanner's discussion of matrifocality 1974; see also Carrie Allen McCray, "The Black Woman and Family Roles," in *The Black Woman*, ed. LaFrances Rogers-Rose (Beverly Hills, Calif.: Sage, 1980), pp. 67–78; Elmer Martin and Joanne Mitchell Martin, *The Black Extended Family* (Chicago: University of Chicago, 1978); Joyce Aschenbrenner, *Lifelines, Black Families in Chicago* (Prospect Heights, Ill.: Waveland, 1975); and Carol B. Stack, *All Our Kin* (New York: Harper & Row, 1974).

17. Martin and Martin, 1978; Stack, 1974; and Virginia Young, "Family and Childhood in a Southern Negro Community" *American Anthropologist* 72(1970), pp. 269–288.

18. Stack, 1974.

19. Ellen Cantarow, *Moving the Mountain: Women Working for Social Change* (Old Westbury, N.Y.: Feminist Press, 1980), p. 59.

20. Thordis Simonsen, ed., *You May Plow Here, The Narrative of Sara Brooks* (New York: Touchstone, 1986), p. 181.

21. White, 1985; Dill, 1986; Mullings, 1986, note 2 earlier.

22. Simonsen, 1986, p. 86.

23. Mamie Garvin Fields and Karen Fields, *Lemon Swamp and Other Places, A Carolina Memoir* (New York: Free Press, 1983), p. xvii.

24. Ibid, p. 195.

25. Cheryl Gilkes, "'Holding Back the Ocean with a Broom,' Black Women and Community Work," in Rogers-Rose, 1980, pp. 217–231; "Going Up for the Oppressed: The Career Mobility of Black Women Community Workers," *Journal of Social Issues* 39 (1983), pp. 115–139.

26. Gilkes 1980, p. 219.

27. *Fields and Fields,* 1983, p. xvi.

28. Charles Johnson, *Shadow of the Plantation* (Chicago: University of Chicago, 1934, 1979), p. 173.

29. Pamela Reid, "Socialization of Black Female Children," in *Women: A Developmental Perspective*, eds. Phyllis Berman and Estelle Ramey (Washington, DC: National Institute of Health, 1983).

30. For works in the feminist psychoanalytic tradition, see Nancy Chodorow, "Family Structure and Feminine Personality," in Rosaldo and Lamphere, 1974; Nancy Chodorow, *The Reproduction of Mothering* (Berkeley: University of California, 1978); and Jane Flax, "The Conflict Between Nurturance and Autonomy in Mother-Daughter Relationships and Within Feminism," *Feminist Studies* 4 (1978), pp. 171–189.

31. Moody, *Coming of Age in Mississippi* (New York: Dell, 1968).

32. Ladner, 1971; Gloria Joseph, "Black Mothers and Daughters: Their Roles and Functions in American Society" in *Common Differences,* ed. Gloria Joseph and Jill Lewis (Garden City, N.Y.: Anchor, 1981), pp. 75–126; Lena Wright Myers, *Black Women, Do They Cope Better?* (Englewood Cliffs, N.J.: Prentice-Hall, 1980).

33. Elsa Barkley Brown, "Hearing Our Mothers' Lives," paper presented at Fifteenth Anniversary of African-American and African Studies at Emory College, Atlanta, 1986. This essay will appear in the upcoming Black Women's Studies issue of *SAGE: A Scholarly Journal on Black Women*. Vol. VI, No. 1.

African-American Daughter-Mother Relations
and Teenage Pregnancy:
Two Faces of Premarital Teenage Pregnancy

JOSEPH W. SCOTT

Using a sample of school age mothers enrolled in a public school program, the author tests the hypotheses that single parent families are less inclined to delay or prevent premarital pregnancies during the pre-adolescent and adolescent years and that negative daughter-mother affect will be associated with the earliest teenage pregnancies. The author consistently found that negative daughter-mother relationships during pregnancy are associated with the younger ages at first pregnancy.

■

INTRODUCTION: MOTHERS AND ADOLESCENT DAUGHTERS

By comparison to other ethnic groups in the United States, the socialization of African American daughters for womanhood is one of the most complex processes ever to be attempted (Collins, 1987). Thus, the African American daughter-mother relationship is central to understanding the lifeways of this group (Young, 1970; Aschenbrenner, 1975; Stack, 1972).

Aschenbrenner (1975) did an ethnographic study of Black families in Chicago and came to the conclusion that the relationship of mothers to daughters is at best "a difficult apprenticeship." Aschenbrenner reported: "It is doubtful that a mother has much control over whether or not her daughter becomes pregnant; other social and

environmental influences, such as the influence of peers, are probably much more important" (48).

One of the complexities of this particular apprenticeship process originates from the fact that African Americans have to be socialized to navigate through the seas of both the Afrocentric and Eurocentric cultural worlds (Collins, 1987; Young, 1974). These Black and White worlds make demands that are at once different and opposing. To be specific. the Afrocentric conception of woman contains elements that are assigned separately to males and to females in the Eurocentric world. The strict Eurocentric division of gender roles is somewhat dysfunctional in African American communities (Lewis, 1975; Bartz and Levine, 1978).

A case in point is that African American daughters are socialized to be at once independent and assertive as well as familistic and nurturant. They are socialized to be sexually assertive and yet not "forward" and not "fast." They are socialized to be as authoritative, individualistic and confident as African American sons are, and as economically self-sufficient and personally autonomous as sons are. The end result is that within African American culture, they are imbued with personal traits that are commonly divided into separate male and female gender roles within European cultures (Lewis, 1975). Consequently, African American mothers have a difficult time at best socializing their daughters to

From the *Western Journal of Black Studies,* Volume 17, No. 2, 1993: 73–81. Copyright 1993 by the Board of Regents, Washington State University, Pullman, WA 99164. Reprinted by permission.

cope and survive within an African American subsociety which itself is trying to survive within a dominant and controlling Eurocentric culture and society (Coffins, 1987).

The Afrocentric process of socialization encompasses numerous distinct values and activities. For example, African American mothers are expected to nurture and emphasize, teach and idealize, edit and criticize, interpret and chastise their daughters in the process of giving them economic independence and mutual aid training, sexuality and attractiveness training, competition and personal assertiveness training, and morals and manners training. Finding the correct balance among these is a delicate balancing act, because they must inculcate in their daughters personal traits which are presently antithetical to the Eurocentric model of woman.

Thus, African American mother-daughter conflicts are endemic. If the Black mother's messages "sink in," positive regard abounds, and it is reciprocated. If not, conflict and negative affect abound unabated.

Adolescence for youths (Udry, 1988; Steinberg, 1988) at best, is a time of hormonal changes, conflicting inner feelings, unattainable ideals, and peer expectations which conflict with parental and societal moral imperatives. Adolescence is a time of discontinuing some emotions and behaviors while at the same time continuing others. It is a time of quasi-childhood and quasi-adulthood.

On the other side, adolescence for parents at best is a time of intense social pressures on mothers to inculcate in daughters adult scripts for female goals, roles, and responsibilities, including scripts for making satisfactory adjustments to the opposite sex (Barglow et al.). Miscommunication is inevitable. Conflicts and confusion are bound to happen, and accordingly, conflict resolution is needed more during adolescence than ever (Fox, 1980: 25–27).

Virtually all studies on this subject agree that Black mothers are more closely bonded with their children than Black fathers are, even in two-parent homes. They also agree that mothers are the dominant adult figures in their daughters' lives. The expectation is that daughters can follow in their mothers' footsteps, while sons, for the most part, cannot assume their mothers' adult roles within the family or society. Role learning by imitation can be direct for daughters because mothers can be directly emulated in the ways of womanhood connected with body image, menarche, menstruation, pregnancy, nursing a baby, and economic self-support. For biosocial reasons, there are inescapably many more common experiences for mothers and daughters than for mothers and sons (Farber, 1990).

Inasmuch as same-sex imitation and suggestion is more "natural" than that of opposite-sex, mothers expect their daughters to use them as role models, role instructors, and role evaluators (Fox, 1980). At the same time that mothers expect emulation by their daughters, same-sex emulation invites invidious comparisons and personal rejection of the mothers by daughters (Anderson, 1980). As a consequence, daughter-mother relationships are, during adolescence, inordinately emotion laden. Perhaps they are more so than mother-son relationships.

Typically, mothers strive to develop in their daughters a sense of obligation to and trust in them (Fox, 1980). They do so, in part, because they are held to be more responsible for the morals and manners of their daughters, and for the public behavior of their daughters. They also do so, because in the process of training their daughters, they become the primary reward and punishment givers, and they do most of the day-to-day disciplining of their daughters. The role training and role learning rarely go smoothly. The net result is that Black mothers and daughters become locked in relationships which are impregnated with tensions and conflicts, and the resolution or non-resolution of these tensions and conflicts have great influences on the occurrence of teenage premarital pregnancy.

REVIEW OF LITERATURE: DAUGHTER-MOTHER RELATIONSHIPS

First, let the author offer a caveat: Only a few studies have reported data of any kind using samples of African Americans.

Phipps-Yonas (1980) reviewed hundreds of studies, including just a few on Blacks, and found that teenagers who became pregnant in the 1960s and in the early 1970s were more likely than not to come from homes marked by poor family relationships and that these teenagers were somewhat socially isolated and untrusting.

Zelnik et al. (1981: 39), using a national sample of mostly White teenagers, found that compared to teenagers from two-parent families, more of the teenagers from one-parent families, adoptive families, foster homes or homes with parent surrogates felt that "it is not important to be near those who raised them."

Lewis et al. (1973), conducting a clinical sample study of both Black and White pregnant teenagers, found that their relationships with their mothers were "invariably poor." They also found that the girls suffered from a deprivation of maternal closeness. Lewis (1973) found that happiness at home and not feeling close to their mother were associated with earlier ages at first intercourse, multiple sex partners and greater incidence of coital activities.

Barglow (1968), using a sample of Black adolescents 11–16 years of age and pregnant for the first time, found that ambivalent mother-daughter relations and an absent father were associated with premarital teenage pregnancy. A daughter-mother bond broken during adolescence was clearly associated with these pregnancies.

Babikian and Goldman (1971), studying a clinical sample of Blacks and Puerto Ricans, found that poor daughter-mother relationships inhibit ego development and that poor ego development in turn results in the girls acting out sexually. They also found that most of the pregnant girls had ambivalent feelings towards their mothers, and none had accepted their mothers as an ego ideal.

Scott (1986), using a case study approach, studied 22 Black women and looked into how teenage mothers drift into polygamous relationships with married men. He found that a negative daughter-mother relationship can motivate some daughters to leave home at an early age and to drift into polygamous relationships.

Scott and Perry (1990), using a sample of Black school-age mothers, found that a negative daughter-father relationship coupled with a positive daughter-mother relationship delayed the age of first pregnancy until late adolescence—if it was to occur at all. They say that a restrictive father, coupled with affective closeness (positivity) between daughter and mother from the onset of puberty and throughout adolescence, allows the mother to inculcate her values into the daughter more easily and to enforce abstinence from sex and/or to encourage contraception use" (80).

Jones and Phillber (1983), studying a Black and Hispanic sample in New York City found that consistent contraceptors who had never been pregnant "seem more likely to live with, confide in, and be closest to their mothers, both in general, and on sexual matters particularly" (242).

There are several suggestive facts among these studies: (1) Two-parent families are more effective than one-parent families in cultivating and maintaining positive daughter-mother affect; (2) compared to positive daughter-mother relationships, negative daughter-mother relationships are more correlated with sexual acting out and with the earliest teenage premarital pregnancies. Finally, (3) negative daughter-mother relationships inhibit daughters' ego development and their emulation of their mothers.

HYPOTHESES

Given these data, the author hypothesizes that, compared to two-parent families, single-parent families will be less likely to delay or prevent pre-marital pregnancies during the pre-adolescent and adolescent years. Secondly, compared to positive daughter-mother affect, negative daughter-mother affect will be associated with the earliest teenage pregnancies.

SAMPLE AND METHODOLOGY

The sample population consisted of School-Age Mothers (SAMs) enrolled in a public school program in River City (pseudonym). Young, pregnant women students voluntarily enrolled in a special alternative school for pregnant school-age women within the public school corporation of River City. From 1976 to 1981, this school program signed up approximately 277 students, of whom 239 became "active" attenders. Once per semester, from the 1976–77 to the 1980–81 school year, the students were interviewed: all of the students who were in attendance on a day selected at random were interviewed. Randomness of the dates protected against attendance biases such as the tendency for certain types of students to be absent on Mondays and Fridays. Participation was voluntary, but a stipend of $10 was offered to each participant for volunteering her time. The interview took about one hour. A total of 153 SAMs, approximately 80 percent of those in regular attendance in the special school, were interviewed.

Of the 277 SAMs, 62 percent were Black, 36 percent were White, and 24 percent were Hispanic. Our sample of 153 included 67 percent Black, 33 percent White, and only a couple of Hispanics. Whites were more apt to return to regular classrooms or to withdraw from school altogether, due to marriage.

Approximately 200 items of information were collected on each respondent by means of a structured questionnaire developed from about 30 open-ended interviews. The following questions and their subsequent answers are the foci of this study:

Q: What were your reasons for beginning sexual intercourse?

A: (1) Pressure from other girls. 6.2%; (2) pressure from boys, 15.5%; (3) curiosity about sex, 34.1%; (4) loved the boy, 42.6%; (5) to be a woman, 1.6%.

Q: At what age did you begin sexual intercourse?

A: The range is age 10 to age 18. The modal category is age 15.

Q: At what age did you become pregnant (first)?

A: The range is from age 12 to age 19. The modal category is age 16.

Q: Before the age of 10, how did you get along with your mother? (father?)

A: (1) Positively, 78%; (2) Negatively, 22%. (Mother)

A: (1) Positively, 64%; (2) Negatively, 35%. (Father)

Q: After the age of 10, how did you get along with your mother? (father?)

A: (1) Better, 33%; Same, 48%; Worse. 20%. (Mother)

A: (1) Better, 17%; Same, 63%; Worse, 19%. (Father)

Q: With whom did you spend the first 10 years of your life?

A: (1) Mother & Father, 65%; (2) Mother & Grandmother, 2%; (3) Mother only, 28%; (4) Other, 5%.

Q: Did you live with both of your parents between 10–15?

A: (1) Yes, 46%; (2) No, 52%; (3) NR, 2%.

THE ANALYSIS

For the total Black-White sample of 153 cases combined, 21 percent of the SAMs came from continuous one-parent homes, 44 percent from continuous two-parent homes; and 35 percent came from reconstituted families—those which changed from one- to two-parents and vice versa.

**TABLE 1 One- and Two-Parent Family Types by Daughter-Mother
Relations, and Mean Ages at First Pregnancy, Arrayed
Separately and Rank Ordered**

Family Types and Daughter-Mother Relationships	Means	N	Rank
Two-Parent & Pos. Daughter-mother Rel.<10 & Pos. Daughter-Mother Rel. >10	16.1	36	2
Two-Parent & Neg. Daughter-mother Rel.<10 & Pos. Daughter-Mother Rel.>10	17.5	02	1
Two-Parent & Pos. Daughter-mother Rel.<10 & Neg. Daughter-Mother Rel.>10	15.5	02	3
Two-Parent & Neg. Daughter-mother Rel.<10 & Neg. Daughter-Mother Rel.>10	15.0	03	4
One-Parent & Pos. Daughter-mother Rel.<10 & Pos. Daughter-Mother Rel.>10	15.3	13	3
One-Parent & Neg. Daughter-mother Rel.<10 & Pos. Daughter-Mother Rel.>10	16.0	02	1
One-Parent & Pos. Daughter-mother Rel.<10 & Neg. Daughter-Mother Rel.>10	15.0	05	4
One-Parent & Neg. Daughter-mother Rel.<10 & Neg. Daughter-Mother Rel.>10	15.3	06	3

For the African American subsample of 102 cases combined, 26 percent came from continuous one-parent families, 43 percent from continuous two-parent families, and 27 percent from reconstituted families. The remainder were other types.

For the White families, the comparable figures were 9 percent, 44 percent and 47 percent, respectively.

The mean ages at first pregnancy were as follows:

All White Families	15.9
All Black Families	15.7
Continuous one- & two-parent Black Families	15.8
Continuous one- & two-parent White Families	16.2

FINDINGS

In order to control for influences of reconstituted family structures, the investigator separated out continuous two-parent families and continuous one-parent families for further analysis. By contrast, the discontinuous families—those that changed from two-parent to one-parent and from one-parent to two-parent families—were omitted. Additionally, since the investigator

found that one-parent families have higher proportions of negative daughter-mother relationships and that they must resolve conflict in different ways than two-parent families, at times he analyzed them separately. See Table 1 for family types, daughter-mother relations, and mean ages at first pregnancy.

Considering all Black families together, two generalizations emerge. Negative daughter-mother relationships from age 10 onward are consistently associated with lower pregnancy ages when compared to positive daughter-mother relationships from age 10 onward. But, a negative daughter-mother relationship which begins negative before age 10 and continues to be negative into adolescence is associated with the very lowest average age at first pregnancy which is 15.3 years of age. By contrast, the highest average age at first pregnancy is 16.6 and it is associated with adolescents who lived out their lives in negative relationships before age 10 but who experienced positive relationships after age 10.

First to be considered is the continuous two-parent families. Within this category, the difference between the lowest and the highest average age at first pregnancy is even larger than all families together. For the relationships which are negative before 10 and after 10, the average age at first pregnancy is 15.0. And, for the relationships that are the negative before 10 but positive after 10 relationship, the average pregnancy age is 17.5. Just as when all of the families were considered together, as a rule, the negative relationships from age 10 onward are associated with the younger average ages at first pregnancy and the positive relationships from age 10 onward are associated with the older average ages at first pregnancy.

Next, an investigation of the continuous one-parent families. The lowest average age at first pregnancy is 15.0, and it is associated with daughter-mother relationships which started positive from age 0–10 but turned negative from age 10 onward. By contrast, the highest average age 16.0 is associated with relationships which started negative from age 0–10 but turned positive from age 10 onward. This negative-to-positive transition being associated with the older ages at first pregnancy is consistent with the patterns reported for continuous two-parent families and for all families together.

What is not consistent with the patterns above is that the positive-to-positive relationships and negative-to-negative relationships have the same average age at first pregnancy, 15.3. Notwithstanding this deviation from the pattern, the highest average age at first pregnancy 16.0 is still associated with a positive daughter-mother relationships during adolescence, even in one-parent families.

In sum, the consistent finding is that negative daughter-mother relationships during adolescence are associated with the younger ages at first pregnancy, and the positive daughter-mother relationships during adolescence are associated with the older ages at first pregnancy. The most favorable long-term relationship among both two-parent and one-parent families is one that starts out as negative during the years of 0–10 but becomes positive from 10 onward. This negative-to-positive relationship is the optimal long-term relationship for pushing up the age at first pregnancy. The daughter-mother relationship that is positive all the time is second in potency in terms of delaying or preventing adolescent pregnancy.

THE COMBINED DAUGHTER-MOTHER/ DAUGHTER-FATHER RELATIONSHIP

Among the SAMs, the great majority of those who have lived all of their lives in one-parent families and two-parent families have relationships with their biological fathers. Thus, the simultaneous daughter-father relationship might be influencing the daughter-mother relationship. To ascertain that effect, the investigator analyzed the simultaneous relationship of the daughters with both parents during adolescence.

Considering first the continuous two-parent families, the positive daughter-mother relationship coupled with either the positive or the negative daughter-father relationship during adolescence is associated with the older average ages at first pregnancy 16.0 and 16.1; by contrast, the negative daughter-mother relationship coupled with either the positive or the negative daughter-father relationship during adolescence is associated with the lower average ages at first pregnancy, 15.0 and 15.5.

On the other hand, considering the continuous one-parent families, the combined negative daughter-father/negative daughter-mother relationship is associated with the younger average age at first pregnancy, 14.8. But when the asymmetrical negative daughter-father relationship is coupled with the positive daughter-mother relationship during adolescence, the average age at first pregnancy is highest, 15.7.

What is most divergent about one-parent families is that both the positive daughter-mother relationship and the negative daughter-mother relationship are not consistently associated with either high or low ages at first pregnancy (within this particular sample size).

Notwithstanding this particular inconsistency among single-parent families only, what these data indicate overall rather clearly is that the daughter-mother relationship during adolescence is the most potent one in influencing an

**TABLE 2 Family Types, Daughter-Mother Relations, and Mean Ages
at First Pregnancy, Arrayed Together and Rank Ordered**

Family Types and Daughter-Mother Relationship	Means	N	Rank
Two-Parent & Pos. Daughter-mother Rel. <10 & Pos. Daughter-Mother Rel.>10	16.1	36	2
Two-Parent & Neg. Daughter-mother Rel. <10 & Pos. Daughter-Mother Rel.>10	17.5	02	1
One-Parent & Pos. Daughter-mother Rel. <10 & Pos. Daughter-Mother Rel. >10	15.3	02	1
One-Parent & Neg. Daughter-mother Rel. <10 & Pos. Daughter-Mother Rel. >10	16.0	02	3
Two-Parent & Pos. Daughter-mother Rel. <10 & Neg. Daughter-Mother Rel. > 10	15.5	02	4
Two-Parent & Neg. Daughter-mother Rel. <10 & Neg. Daughter-Mother Rel. >10	15.0	03	7
One-Parent & Pos. Daughter-mother Rel. <10 & Neg. Daughter-Mother Rel. > 10	15.0	05	7
One-Parent & Neg. Daughter-mother Rel. <10 & Neg. Daughter-Mother Rel. > 10	15.3	06	5

rho = .79

unmarried teenage daughter's age at first pregnancy. Furthermore, with a few exceptions, the positive daughter-mother relationship during adolescence is rather consistently associated with the older ages at first pregnancy.

A RANK-ORDER ANALYSIS

To do this analysis, the investigator permuted three variables: the one- and two-parent family types daughter-mother relationships before age 10 and after age 10. He came up with eight qualitative family types. See Table 2.

To arrive at these permutations, the investigator first correlated each of the three variables above with the reported ages at first pregnancy. He found that the positive daughter-mother relationship after age 10 is most highly correlated with the higher ages at first pregnancy. Next most highly correlated is the two-parent family structure; and the positive daughter-mother relationship before age 10 is the lowest correlated with the higher ages at first pregnancy.

Next, the investigator used these correlations to weight the three variables: A positive daughter-mother relationship after age 10 was weighted 5; a two-parent family was weighted 3; and a positive daughter-mother relationship before age 10 was

weighted 1. These weights yielded eight permutations combining the two-parent family types with positive and negative daughter-mother relations before and after age 10. Using this method, the two-parent family type, coupled with a positive daughter-mother relationship before age 10 and a positive daughter-mother relationship after age 10 is hypothesized to be the most potent family type for delaying or preventing teenage premarital pregnancy, and the one-parent family type coupled with a negative daughter-mother relationship before and after age 10 is the least potent. See Table 2.

Matching this array of family structures and daughter-mother relationship types with their average ages at first pregnancy yielded a rank-order correlation coefficient of .79. It appears that the family structure and relationship types can quite consistently predict the direction of the higher and lower average ages at first pregnancy. (A caveat: the Ns are very small but the direction is consistent. Additional research with larger samples could clarify this finding.)

BASES FOR NEGATIVE DAUGHTER-MOTHER RELATIONS

To find some bases for negative daughter-mother relations, the investigator pulled out other questions in the questionnaire. He found that 33 percent of those in negative relationships said that they began sexual intercourse for the reason of pressure from boys or pressure from girls. Moreover, those in negative relationships were influenced equally by males and by females; those in positive relationships were influenced overwhelmingly by pressure from males alone—usually their "boyfriend."

When asked, "What does a woman have to give to keep a man?" 44 percent in negative daughter-mother relationships and 67 percent in positive daughter-mother relationships said "sex"; 88 percent in the negative relationships and 100 percent in the positive relationships said "love"; 50 percent in the negative and 89 percent in the positive said "faithfulness."

Significantly higher proportions of those in positive relationships as opposed to those in negative relationships said a woman has to give money, time and trust.

When asked, "To whom do you (or would you) turn for emotional support?" zero percent in negative relationships mentioned their mother, while 14 percent in positive relationships mentioned their mother; 79 percent of those in positive relationships mentioned a family member of some type, while only 32 percent of those in negative relationships mentioned a family member of some type; 45 percent in the positive relationships mentioned siblings, while only 13 percent in the negative relationships mentioned siblings.

In short, three times as many in positive relationships mentioned other siblings, twice as many mentioned aunts and uncles; but, almost equal numbers mentioned grandparents.

What is very notable is that 40 percent of both, the positive and the negative categories, said that the father of their baby is the one to whom they would turn first. This would suggest some considerable bonding among these adolescent females with their male partners. Feelings of "love" may be more of a driving social force than first believed.

When asked, "Did your parents know when you were dating (going out on dates)?" 45 percent

in positive relationships, and 21 percent in negative relationships said "always"; on the other hand. 29 percent of those in negative relationships and 11 percent of those in positive relationships said "never." The greater part of the remainder said "sometimes."

When the investigator quantified this variable, those in positive relationships collectively had an average score tending toward "always," and those in negative relationships collectively had an average score tending towards never.

When asked, "Did your parents approve of your dating at this age?" 49 percent of those in positive relationships and 39 percent of those in negative relationships said "approved." The remainder said that their parents gave "mixed answers," "disapproved," "did not know" or "said nothing." When this variable is quantified, those in positive relationships collectively have a considerably higher average parental approval score than those in negative relationships.

When asked, "How many sex partners have you had?" those in negative relationships reported an average of 2.6 partners and those in positive relationships reported an average of 1.6. The medians were 2.0 and 1.0, respectively.

When asked, "What was your age at first dating?" those in negative relationships reported an average age of 15.1 and those in positive, an average age of 14.7. But, when it came to their age at first pregnancy, those in negative relationships became pregnant at the average at 15.1 years of age and those in positive relationships became pregnant at the average age of 15.9. Those in negative relationships became pregnant almost immediately while those in positive relationships became pregnant over a year later.

Summarizing these findings above, one finds that compared to those in positive relationships, those in negative relationships began dating at a later age, but they became pregnant at an earlier age. They had more sex partners. They had lower parental approval of dating and lower parental knowledge of their dating. Fewer of them mentioned any family members at all to whom they would turn for emotional support.

Many more were pressured into their first sexual experience by peers of both sexes, and fewer believed that they have to give sex or faithfulness to keep a man.

On the other hand, many more of those in positive relationships believed that they must give "sex" and "faithfulness" to keep a man.

TWO FACES OF BLACK ADOLESCENT PREGNANCY

There is a widely circulated belief in this society that, as a general rule, the so-called "bad girl" is the one who becomes pregnant and the so-called "good girl" does not. The girl from the so-called "high-risk" family is the one who becomes the unwed teenage mother and the girl from the so-called "low-risk" family does not.

The so-called "high risk" girl is the incorrigible one, the occasional runaway, the know-it-all, the 14-year-old-who-is-going-on–20. It is easier to forecast negative outcomes about the child who is said to be "at risk." She is the one the school counselors predict will become pregnant out of wedlock before graduating from high school.

By contrast, the "low risk" girl is the obedient one, the socially "slow" daughter, the one who loves church, the one who does not give her parents any "trouble." She is more difficult to talk about when she becomes an unmarried school-age mother. She comes as a shock to parents and counselors alike when she—the least likely girl to become pregnant—becomes an adolescent mother at 14, 15 or 16. How can one explain what would possess a young obedient daughter to engage in unprotected sexual intercourse, in her own home (of all places!), and then become pregnant and carry the pregnancy to full term?

The fact is that most of the young females becoming pregnant today are being reared in two-parent homes. They are being reported as having "troubles" with either parent or teachers. Most research on out-of-wedlock teenage pregnancy postulates negative socioeconomic forces or social psychological deficiencies to explain such

social deviation of adolescent girls from the norms of the Black community.

This section theorizes about the motivations and the behaviors which underlie the adolescent pregnancies of both the so-called "high risk" girls and "low risk" girls.

THE SO-CALLED "HIGH-RISK" GIRL

Being in a negative daughter-mother relationship seems to accelerate the probability and the timing of an adolescent pregnancy. A negative relationship seems to encourage a relatively earlier pregnancy age. One theory is that a negative relation pushes a child out of the arms of her mother and into the arms of peers where she can find comfort and support for her social and sexual impulses. As a result, she is more likely to associate with those who will support her beliefs, sentiments and values. Her associates, more than her parents, will encourage "fun and games" as well as "fun and excitement." What is more exciting than sexual activities? Given the heightened hormonally-driven impulses during adolescence, a facilitative set of friends, especially young male friends, creates the structure of social and physical opportunities for her to initiate and complete the sex act. For an adolescent female, her peers provide the affection and support that her parents, especially her mother, is not giving at this crucial time.

Her parents may be still very parentally loving at this time, but they may show it in ways that the child interprets as control, interference, meddling, and disaffection. Her parents may feel that they must be vigilant at this age of the raging hormones, at this age of peer pressure and peer conformity, in order to prevent an early unwanted pregnancy by their sons and their daughters. The parents know that their values are opposed to those of the youth culture of the streets. Unfortunately, the child generally does not see eye to eye, value to value and timing to timing with her parents about dating, sexual intercourse, and hanging out.

Under these conditions, the child is not on the same wave length with her parents. Thus, she does not seek complete parental approval of her dating; she does not turn to her mother when she needs emotional support. Controversies and conflicts abound and continue unresolved.

After so much negativism, the adolescent girl in such a daughter-mother relationship leaves home emotionally if not physically. When she leaves home emotionally, she comes under the influence of her male and female peers as well as the older, more predatory aggressive males over 20 years of age. The more negative the daughter-mother relationship, the more she is encouraged to experiment with male/female relationships, not usually out of love but for fun and excitement, and not usually out of independent goals but in order to conform with her peers and their street norms.

Her sexual experimentation is extensive; her sexual partners are also multiple. She is somewhat sexually precocious. Keeping a man in her life is uppermost, not keeping a "one and only" man in her life. The time between beginning her first dating activities and her first sexual intercourse, and her first pregnancy is relatively short. Sex and pregnancy before marriage are not major considerations either before or after the discovery of pregnancy. She is neither in pursuit of love, nor marriage, nor sexual intercourse nor childrearing within the confines of marriage. Pregnancy is "accidental" and unwanted resulting from negativism and hedonism. It results from rebellion, and the rebellion is aimed at being either more independent or more dependent.

One positive outcome is that she may feel that her baby will love her exclusively, unconditionally and perpetually—something she did not receive at home from her parents.

THE SO-CALLED "LOW-RISK" GIRL

The adolescent girl in a positive daughter-mother relationship is generally adaptive rather than maladaptive. Her parents inculcated in her the value of the love-marriage-sex-parenthood complex held out to everyone of the dominant culture persuasion. She does partly succeed in the pursuit of this culturally given sequence. However, her own parents partly assist her by inviting her boyfriend to the home. Her parents expect that she will conform in sexual matters as she has in school and other matters. Her parents trust that she will "do the right thing." They say that they "trust" her and him.

Contrary to parents, the mass media (TV and audio cassettes) and her peers together encourage sexual activities before marriage. Kissing, petting, "dirty dancing," and fondling are presented as acceptable. If they are done with genuine affection, so much the better. She learns that affection is a sufficient justification for sexual intercourse, and if the affection takes the form of love, this is the ultimate justification. She also learns that sexual activities are positive reinforcements for the continuance of a social contact with an object of her affection. Additionally, she learns that sexual activities can be bonding activities that facilitate the deepening of affection, the negotiation of commitments, the negotiation of promises of marriage, and the development of sexual compatibility.

There are many cultural scripts which tell her to "Learn to drive before getting a license," to "Road-test the car before buying it," and to "Live together before marriage to insure against incompatibility after marriage." In sum, both implicit and explicit cultural messages say that premarital sex is positively functional for successful marital relations. One of the consequences of these messages and of parent encouragement is that the adolescent girl in a positive parent-child relationship believes both her parents and her peer culture. She comes to feel justified in having sexual intercourse because she is in love and she wants, hopes and plans to marry her sexual partner in the future. She is really in pursuit of the American Marriage and Family Dream, but an accidental pregnancy interdicts the process and changes the timing of ultimate end which is parenthood within the confines of marriage.

The so-called low-risk adolescent female has an ultimate goal of marriage; she is involved in the courtship-to-marriage process with her parents' approval; her parents always know when and where she is dating (even if they do not know what she is doing on the dates). Her male friend is her one and only sex partner and he is a very important significant other—soul mate. She may be trying to become pregnant in order to insure marriage to a particular mate or she may "accidentally" become pregnant in her efforts to give sex for love and commitment to their mutual futures. She is not very sexually knowledgeable about birth control and STDs.

Her parents exercise normal discipline and control over her activities and do a good amount of talking with her. They encourage the normal courtship process. They encourage a normal progression into heterosexual courtship and on to marriage. However, two omissions are critical: First, they "trust" that she will resist both hormonal and outside influences; and she does conform to that expectation up to a certain point. Secondly, no matter how positively close she feels toward her mother (and her father), she does not discuss sexual activities with them.

Her mother, the most likely parent to know, does not know when her daughter is engaging in sexual intercourse and thus cannot prevent an "accidental" pregnancy from occurring. The mother has a daughter who turns to her for emotional support, but the mother does not tell her about handling her sexual desires and sexual foreplay with the opposite sex. What seems to be going on is that both the mother and the daughter consider sex an unshareable secret, and this secrecy contributes to an overall communication problem.

For the "low risk" girl, adolescent pregnancy occurs in the pursuit of the American marriage and family dream and does not occur out of child-parent negativism or maladaptive behavior.

The following letter is a case in point:

The most difficult obstacle to overcome as a teenager, in my opinion, is the temptation to have sex. I find that even younger kids, like 12 or 13, have the same temptation. At one time I felt sex was wrong and should be kept until you are married. But I find that, as I become older, my views are changing dramatically.

I have my first real boyfriend now, and I'm experiencing feelings I never had before. Yes, I have had other boyfriends, but they never meant as much to me as he does. We've come close to having sex many times. I love him. Can you please ask people how they feel about sex as a teenager, and their experience on the subject?" *(Parade Magazine,* p. 12, August 23, 1992.)

REFERENCES

Anderson. K. L. 1980. Educational goals of male and female adolescents. *Youth and Society* 12(2, Dec.): 173–188.

Aschenbrenner, J. 1975. *Lifelines: Black families in Chicago.* Prospect Heights, Ill.: Waveland.

Babikian. H., and A. Goldman 1971. A Study in Teen-Age Pregnancy. *American Journal Psychiatry* 128(6, Dec.): 111–116.

Barglow. P. et al. 1968. Some psychiatric aspects of illegitimate pregnancy in early adolescence. *American Journal of Orthopsychiatry* 38, 672–687.

Barnett. A. P. 1985. Sociocultural influences on adolescent mothers. In R. Staples (ed.), *The Black family: Essays and studies,* 4th ed., Belmont, Calif.: Wadsworth, 1991. Pp. 160–168.

Bartz. K. W., and E. S. Levine. 1978. Childrearing by Black parents: A description and comparison to Anglo and Chicano parents. *Journal of Marriage and the Family,* 40 (Nov.), 709–719.

Collins. P. H. 1987. The meaning of motherhood in Black culture. *SAGE: A Scholarly Journal on Black Women,* 4 (2, Fall), 3–10.

Faber, N. 1990. The significance of race and class in marital decisions among unmarried adolescent mothers. *Social Problems,* 37 (1, Feb.), 51–63.

Fox, G. L. 1980. The mother-daughter relationship as a sexual socialization structure: A research review. *Family Relations,* 29 (Jan.), 21–28.

Fox, G. L., and J. K. Inazu. 1980. Mother-daughter communication about sex. *Family Relations,* 29 (July), 347–352.

Glasser. P., and E. Navarre. 1965. Structural problems of the one-parent family. *Journal of Social Issues,* 21 (Jan.), 98–109.

Jones, J. B. and S. Philliber. 1983. Sexually active but not pregnant: A comparison of teens who risk and teens who plan. *Journal of Youth and Adolescence* 12 (3), 235–251.

Lewis, D. K. 1975. The Black family: Socialization and sex roles. *Phylon* 36:3 (Fall), 221–237.

Lewis. D. O., L. V. Klerman, I. F. Jekel, and J. B. Currie. 1973. Experiences with psychiatric services in a program for pregnant school-age girls. *Social Psychiatry,* 8, 16–25.

Lewis. R. A. 1973. Parents and peers: Socialization agents in the coital behavior of young adults. *Journal of Sex Research,* 9, 156–170.

Scott, J. 1986. From teenage parenthood to polygamy: Case studies in Black polygamous family formation. *Western Journal of Black Studies,* 10 (Winter), 172–179.

Scott J., and R. Perry. 1990. Black family headship structure, parent-child affect, communication, and delaying teenage pregnancy. *National Journal of Sociology* 4 (1, Spring), 67–84.

Steinberg, L. 1988. Reciprocal relation between parent-child distance and pubertal maturation. *Developmental Psychology,* 24 (1), 122–128.

Udry, J. R. 1988. Biological predispositions and social control in adolescent sexual behavior. *American Sociological Review,* 53 (Oct.), 709–722.

Young., V. H. 1970. Family and childhood in a Southern Negro community. *American Anthropologist,* 72, 269–287.

Young. V. H. 1974. A Black American socialization pattern. *American Ethnologist,* 1 (2), 405–413.

Incarcerated Black Mothers
and Their Children

VIDELLA WHITE & ERMA JEAN LAWSON

Women who enter prison are disproportionately poor women of color with minor children. This study examines the stressors of parenting among incarcerated Black mothers. Fifteen women between the ages of 25 and 45 from Project Transition, a residential training program for women in conflict with the law, were interviewed. The results found that imprisoned mothers confront the following issues: (1) pre-incarceration parenting difficulties caused by being raised in homes plagued by poverty, experiences of childhood sexual abuse, and exposure to parental conflict; (2) profound incarceration distress as a consequence of separation from children; and (3) problems in establishing of mother-child bonds following release from prison. These findings suggest that policies should address the following issues for Black incarcerated mothers: (1) consider the importance of children in the lives of incarcerated mothers; (2) place half-way houses and community correctional facilities for women in proximity to their children, and (3) acknowledge factors that operate differently for incarcerated women of color, such as low income and educational attainment.

■

INTRODUCTION

Women represent the fastest growing population in prison. Between 1980 and 1993, the female prison population increased approximately 313 percent compared to 183 percent for men (U.S. Justice Department, 1993). Women are especially affected as the nation moved toward punitive correctional policies, which caused the total U.S. prison population to increase to the highest incarceration rated in the world (Renzetti and Curran, 1995). Of importance, only 25 percent of women in prison are incarcerated for violent recidivist crimes compared to 50 percent of men. Additionally, 40 percent of American female inmates are physically and sexually abused before conviction (U.S. Justice Department, 1993).

Women entering prison are disproportionately women of color, overwhelmingly poor, unemployed, and are mothers of children under age 18. Compared to 50 percent of men, 70 percent of women are custodial parents to minor children prior to incarceration (U.S. Justice Department, 1993). Approximately, 167,000 of children have mothers who are incarcerated (Bloom and Steinhard, 1993). Three-fourths of all children, or more than 125,00 children are under age eighteen (Bloom, 1993; Bloom and Steinhard, 1993). Consequently, a large number of children lose their primary caretakers to the criminal justice system, which place them at risk for future involvement in crime (Maeur and Huling 1995).

This paper presents a study of incarcerated Black mothers and their children. First, it reviews the literature on incarcerated mothers and discusses the effects of imprisonment-related separation on children. The second section emphasizes the stressors of parenting prior to incarceration as well as the strain of parenting during and following imprisonment.

Previously unpublished paper, 1997. Reprinted by permission of the author.

LITERATURE REVIEW

Mothers

Three quarters of mothers in prison cared for one child before incarceration, and most will do so when released (National Women's Law Center, 1995). Thus, child custody is a salient concern for Black incarcerated mothers. For example, it is often difficult to establish and retain custody when states decide custody of children. Because courts interpret imprisonment as abandonment to justify termination of parental rights, inmate mothers are often pressured by child-care agencies to place children for adoption. Incarcerated Black mothers often never regain a relationship with their children who are left in the custody of others (Knight, 1992; Rizzo, 1996).

Black mothers confront unique situations when they enter prison. Approximately 75 percent of children with mothers in prison live with grandparents (Hunter, 1994). Black imprisoned mothers must assure that their children are cared for during their incarceration while dealing with the myriad of circumstances surrounding separation. Inmate Black mothers raise concerns that caretakers are too lenient with their children (Hunter, 1984). As a result, children are often raised with little discipline.

Female inmates also report that their children are often a financial or emotional burden for elderly parents and relatives who have their own family responsibilities. Problems associated with assuming a parenting role late in life and dealing with emotional and health problems of these children, required stamina and resources that some grandparents have difficulty providing. Research has reported that inmate mothers and caregivers perceived that children have problems primarily related to learning in school and disruptive school-related behaviors (Hunter, 1994).

Another issue Black mothers face is explaining to children reasons for their imprisonment. Studies report that mothers experience profound difficulty explaining the reasons for their absence to children (Datesman and Cales, 1995; Feinman, 1994). Some mothers tell children they are away at school or in the hospital while others simply avoid informing children of their whereabouts. Nevertheless, children provide a major motivating factor for imprisoned mothers to make behavioral and lifestyle changes (Clark, 1995). For example, Datesman and Cales found that inmates who maintain family interactions are more likely to be paroled and are more likely to perform successfully during parole.

Visitation is another important concern for Black incarcerated mothers. Most jails in the U.S. do not allow for contact visits with children, and age restrictions further eliminate children from visiting jailed mothers (Feinman, 1994). In prison, where visits are allowed, other issues surface. Because courts often support the view that prisoners have no absolute visitation rights, prison officials often decide which visitation restrictions are imposed (Knight, 1992). Consequently, letters and phone calls are the major links between inmate mothers and their children. Other visitation problems include distance from the correctional facility and lack of transportation (Center for Children of Incarcerated Parents 1992; Rizzo 1995). Therefore, Black incarcerated mothers often never see their children (Clark, 1995; Hunter, 1984).

Nevertheless, Black children benefit from visitations. Visits allow children to express their emotional reactions to the separation, which they may be unable to express elsewhere. Importantly, visitation allows children to view their parents realistically and observe mothers define new goals (Clark 1995). Visits further help to dispel stereotyped notions of prison life. Visitation is especially critical for children under the age of 12 or 13 (Unheard Voices, 1993). In fact, children expend a large amount of mental energy coping with the complexities of being mothered from prison and desire to remain connected to their mothers (Muse 1994).

Further, maintaining contact during incarceration is beneficial for Black mothers. Visitation allows mothers to receive assurance with regard to their children's physical and emotional development. Frequent interactions with children reassure mothers that their children still know them as mommy who loves and care about them (Datesman and Cales 1995). Indeed, irrespective of the pre-prison quality of maternal relationships, children are central to the identity and affectional lives of imprisoned mothers.

Children

Studies have documented that children of incarcerated parents face a number of difficulties. Estimates suggest that children of inmates are five to six times more likely than their peers to become incarcerated themselves (Barnhill and Dressel, 1991). In fact, seventy eight percent of the participants in the Center's Therapeutic Intervention Project (TIP) had a parent who was previously or is currently in jail or prison. Children of incarcerated mothers are most likely to enter the criminal justice system and demonstrate emotional reactions to the events of their lives at a very young age. Many express anger, defiance, and aggression. During preadolescence, children express negative reactive behaviors to mothers' imprisonment through class room disruptive behavior, poor academic performance, and truancy.

Data from the NCCD (1993) suggest that three major factors place children of offender mothers at risk for self-destructive behaviors: (1) They are traumatized by events relating to parental crime and arrest; (2) They experience an inadequate quality of care due to extreme poverty; and (3) they are more vulnerable to drugs and involvement with the criminal justice system as a result of separation from their parents (Bloom, 1993). The multiple negative effects of parental incarceration on children also includes, traumatic stress, loss of self confidence, aggression, withdrawal, depression, gang-activity, and interpersonal violence (Johnston, 1993). Moreover, a majority of children with imprisoned parents have experienced parents' substance abuse, domestic violence, and poverty. They have also moved a number of times and experienced multiple parental separations, and have been cared for by more than one caregiver.

While research has explored children as victims of mothers' incarceration, few studies have focused on Black mothers. Although a large number of Black women are in prison, there is an absence of studies on parenting stressors of Black women prior to incarceration, during imprisonment, and following prison release. The following section explores these issues through in-depth interviews with Black inmate mothers.

METHODS

The research subjects were recruited from Project Transition in a large mid-western city. Project Transition is a residential training program for women in conflict with the law. It provides women offenders with the necessary skills for successful reintegration into society by offering a residence away from jail or prison; G.E.D., adult and vocational education; personal and family counseling; linkages to community resources; support services; job search assistance, and discharge planning and aftercare assistance. Women 17 and over are referred to Project Transition (PT) from the courts and correctional institutions. Since PT is a residential facility, the length of remaining in the program is determined by the time on sentences and/or attainment of program goals.

The data were collected through interviews. The duration of the interviews ranged from one to two hours. Interview questions were asked using a semi-structured interview schedule. The interviews were designed to elicit the multifaceted dimensions of the incarceration experience, specifically focusing on mother-child relationships. The interviews were tape-recorded and transcribed. All the women who were asked agreed to participate.

RESULTS

Sample

The sample consists of 15 women between the ages of 25–45. Fifty-three percent were between the ages of 30 and 36. Approximately 40 percent of women had completed high school and 26.7 percent of women had some education: beyond high school. A majority of the women had never married (60 percent), 26.7 percent were separated, and 13.3 percent were divorced. A large majority of women were parents (86.7 percent) and were raised by single mothers (86.7 percent). Only two of the women were raised in a two parent household. Of those who reported work experience prior to incarceration, 87 percent reported an annual income of less than $10,000. Over half (53.3 percent) reported being affiliated with the Baptist church while a small percentage indicated no religious affiliation (26.7 percent). Overall, the sample consisted of never married parents, raised in single mother households who lived below the poverty level prior to incarceration.

Pre-incarceration Mothering

The respondents reported that prior to incarceration parenting was extremely difficult since their childhood was characterized by tension and instability. Although a majority of women stated they were loved as children, they were often raised in homes plagued by conflict as well as experiencing multiple incidents of childhood sexual abuse. Jean explained,

> My childhood was one of being responsible for my sisters and brothers. I had three under me and my second oldest brother use to have sex with me, so I am an incest victim. At age 13, 1 raised myself in the streets. When I first left home, I started selling drugs and that was my way of keeping money in my pocket and making sure I didn't have to ask anybody for anything.

Indeed, using a conservative definition of sexual abuse—actual physical contact—one-third of female children have been sexually abused by age 18 (CDC, 1996). Childhood sexual abuse has been linked to adult substance-abuse, depression, victimization, and criminal behavior (CDC, 1996). Early sexual abuse also has been related to Black women's educational and income levels. Women who have been sexually abused during childhood achieve an annual income from 3 percent to 20 percent lower than their non-sexual abused counterparts (Hampton and Newberger, 1985). Thus, a recurring theme in the narratives was "running away" from difficult situations.

Growing up in homes plagued by poverty also influenced the respondents' parenting behavior. Half of the women were raised in households headed by a single mother who desperately tried to make ends meet. The struggle for life's bare necessities and still never achieving a secure life was perceived by the respondents as a reality in which one could not easily escape. As Sharon's comments revealed,

> My mother worked all the time. She could never buy us new clothes. We always wore clothes from second hand stores and from rummage sales. I started stealing 'cause I wanted new clothes. My children had new clothes 'cause I stole so they would have nice clothes to wear. I didn't have enough money to buy them the things I thought they should have.

Sharon realized that one way to defy the various structural forces in her environment was to steal. Consequently, stealing material goods and subsequently pawning them had a high functional value. The respondents, therefore, had money to buy their children food and adequate clothing. The risk of getting caught was less important than the valued objects. The concern with possessing items by whatever means available represented a compensation for material possessions Sharon could not possess. Similarly, Ellen describes growing up in poverty and the functional aspects of involvement with the underground economy which provided needed income.

> I don't blame my mother, but it was something that I was caught in during childhood. My father had lost his job and started punishing me again. My father said, "let's move to Florida cause there is no work for me." My mother said, "no, you go ahead." When my father left, my mother couldn't take care of me. She could not give me things I wanted. I started to work and met a man who was 40-years-old and I was age 16. 1 would bring home 40 and 60 dollars a day by selling weed and bagging it up. We would also cook up cocaine and then bag it up and sell it. At 18, I was making hundreds of dollars. Most of my money went to my mother who was on welfare and I was doing everything I could for her.

Ellen further noted that she did not think of selling drugs as a crime, but a business which enabled her to provide for her mother. Because she could financially provide for her mother, participating in the underground economy increased her self-worth and set the stage for financially providing for her children.

Another stressor of parenting, prior to incarceration, related to the age of the respondents' pregnancies. Some women became "street kids," and by the time they were preteens, they had considerable experiences with the adult world. Julie, for example, who left home at age 13, and became a mother at aged 17 comments on the stressors of teenage parenthood.

> When I left home at age 13, I started selling drugs to keep money in my pocket. My daughter was born in 1972 when I was 15. In 1974, 1 had a son who died of crib death. Since I was addicted to drugs, I felt I had killed my son. I also blamed God for taking him away from me. In 1979, I lost my second son and I lost the baby's daddy. So, in 1979, I felt like I was going crazy.

Julie also noted that she was too young to adequately assume motherhood responsibilities. As a result, her mother and other family members raised her children. Similarly, Janet described the birth of her children during a young age.

> My mother was using drugs so my grandparents got custody of me, my brother, and my sister. At age 15, I got pregnant and my grandfather made me have an abortion. So, I left home at age 17 and began prostitution and using drugs. First, I used weed and then crack. As a prostitute, I was also raped. I had my son when I was 18 and my daughter at age 22.

Janet's experiences during childhood and adolescent formed part of the environment in which she raised her own children. For example, Janet and other respondents emphasized strong sibling bonds and that "children should look out for each other." As Elaine reported, "My oldest daughter protected the other kids when I was running. I didn't want my kids taken away." Strong bonds to siblings also existed beyond childhood. As Mary indicated, "It is kind of hard on my middle sister because she has taken the place of my mother. One of my brothers who recently got out of the Federal penitentiary lives with her and she has my two kids while I'm here." Moreover, the respondents stressed avoidance of separating siblings in cases of family disruptions. Indeed, during imprisonment, women expressed pride that "at least the children are together."

The respondents' perceptions of mothering was directly related to having a "good man," which was not necessarily a legal marriage, but a man who "claimed his children," accepted the respondents' children from a previous relationship, and provided financial support. Molly said, "My husband, I call him that 'cause we lived together for 13 years and two of my kids are his. All my kids call him Daddy. He had a furnished house and we moved in." Betty also recalled,

> I met a boyfriend named Bill. I stayed with him for nine years. He was a good guy

and a bus driver. I was so in love with him and my kids liked him. He had a house and I sold my furniture and moved in with him.

Men played an important and decisive role in the woman's identity as a parent. It was the male who affirmed the respondents' motherhood identity. The ability to measure up to the standards that he set for mothering was considered a major accomplishment. For instance, Celeste explained her husband's evaluation of her status.

I was a young woman involved with a man trying to help him find his dreams. I was 21 with a baby and my man was selling dope. He expected me to stay home with the baby and keep the house clean. I did that for years, but time goes on and people get tired. My old man decided to stray and to do whatever he wanted to do. He neglected my needs and it took a toll on our marriage.

Celeste also noted that initially she accepted her husband's definition of mothering. However, following a few years of marriage, she devised her own motherhood identity.

Although most respondents were introduced to drugs through involvement with men, they emphasized the importance of concealing drug-related behaviors from children. Sharon, said, "I kept my life from my children. I was turning tricks and selling dope, but my kids never knew what was going on. I set time every week to take them to eat pizza." Indeed, some mothers indicated that although they were engaged in the underground economy, their children were a priority. As Lucina said,

Although I sold drugs to provide for my children and mother, I had money to take my children places. Every week, we had an outing. My children know I love them 'cause I spent time with them.

Indeed, a frequent comment was, "My children respect me 'cause they never saw me do drugs, and my man wanted it that way."

Parenting During Incarceration

In contrast to stereotypes of Black female offenders, the respondents cared greatly for their children. They expressed love for children in the form of hopes and aspirations for the future. One mother related how she encouraged her daughter to pursue education, usually translated into "stick with the books." The mother, herself a high school dropout, had found the subject of art fascinating and she hoped her daughter would too. She encouraged her preteen daughter to perform well in school as the first step toward a more satisfying adult life. This was regarded as an expression of love and caring.

As mothers talked about their role as a parent, they linked the importance of parental love and attention to their own recollections of feeling neglected by parents. A frequent comment was, "I don't want to repeat the same mistakes as my parents." Dot, for example, described a philosophy of parenting based on her experiences.

I was sentenced two to five years for retail fraud and larceny. I had indulged in drugs. I want to raise my daughter the opposite of how I was raised. My parents worked all the time and were very strict. When I ran away from home at age 15, I was too frightened to go back cause my father would have whipped me to death. We lived in the ghetto and there were no positive role models. I wanted to raise my daughter in a better environment than where I grew up and to give her nice things. And, at the time, stealing was tax free money and the easy way out with someone with no education.

The respondents equated the importance of mothering with children acknowledging them as a parent. Because children often were raised by grandparents, older siblings, and other family members, the respondents' believe that their children's ability to recognize them were crucial to their identity. As Linda stated,

My son knows who his mother is. I took my son to live with his grandmother when he was aged 16, so he was with me until that time. He works at a car rental place, had never used drugs, and has not gotten a girl pregnant.

The stressor of mothering during incarceration also included being unable to prevent children from self-destructive behavior, including participating in street gangs, selling and using drugs, as well as engaging in criminal behavior. Consequently, incarcerated mothers worried how to prevent their children from criminal behavior. Laquita recalls concerns for her children,

> I am 40 years old and I am seriously tired. I look at my kids and I breakdown and cry every time I see them 'cause they need me to be at home. They are teenagers and getting involved with sex and drugs. My older daughter had a baby at age 14 and she is still hanging out in the streets.

Similarly, Carolyn was also disturbed when her 16-year-old son started to sell drugs. "Mom you can't do nothing for me in there," he said. Carolyn felt helpless and said,

> You can't control children from prison, you can't help them avoid drugs. The gang has taken my place. So, I worry that my son will be in prison or dead before he reaches age 20. It's hard to raise Black male children these days, and even harder when a mother is in prison.

Parenting Following Release from Prison

Re-establishing a life following release from prison is difficult. In fact, approximately, 42 percent of women released from prison return. Although Black female offenders experience similar adjustment stressors as their male counterparts, female inmates confront additional stressors. These problems include difficulty to adjust to unrealistic role expectations generated by family and children. As Kim said,

> My bothers and sisters expected me to care for my mother who had cancer when I got release. So, I bathed my mother everyday while I watched her suffer and eventually die. This got the best of me 'cause I was dealing with being back home and coping with my own addiction. My family didn't understand all the stress I was dealing with. So with all these pressures, I started stealing and caught another case.

The respondents reported that following release from prison the lack of financial resources as a profound stressor which influenced their ability to parent. As Betty stated,

> Release from prison is very hard 'cause I have to start all over after release. If I had never went to prison, I would be in a very good job. I spent three years in prison. The first time, I was 19 then got out, worked at a fast food restaurant. I quit 'cause the money was not enough for me to support my children. I started stealing and caught another case.

In addition to inadequate income, difficulties related to the re-establishment of parental bonds also surfaced. The respondents often expressed trouble with teenage children who were traumatized by parental arrest and indicated that anger was a common reaction to their imprisonment. For example, Martha explained,

> In 1990, I had two adolescents who had lived in foster care when I was in prison. When I was released, they felt that I was giving more attention to everybody, but to them. I stopped working and did things to please them. And, it got stressful for me. I couldn't deal with it. Plus, my daughters started having babies. Everything started to pile up on me again and I had no income coming in. So once again I went back to what I knew. I started selling drugs, which led me back into using, and later being in prison again.

Martha struggled to avoid returning to prison while she attempted to re-establish mother-child bonds. A host of factors conspired against her to form mother-child bonds following release from prison. One such issue was coping with her children's distrust and anger. Thelma also remarked:

It takes time for kids to trust parents after being in prison. I think of the times I lied to my daughters, so it is hard for them to trust me again. I promised them things, and never followed through. So, they don't respect me.

Indeed, the National Council on Crime and Delinquency (NCCD) found that inmate mothers had difficulty establishing close, trusting, mother-child relationships following release from prison. Consequently, the imprisonment of Black mothers often permanently threatened the mother-child relationship (McGowan and Blumenthal 1978).

DISCUSSION

This exploratory analysis examined the experience of mothering among Black inmates. It found that pre-incarceration parenting was extremely difficult. Several factors contributed to parenting difficulties. First, childhood sexual abuse often led to drug abuse and criminal behavior as adults. Second, the respondents motherhood identity was directly related to relationships with men in their lives. The respondents' early age of pregnancy coupled with their low income resulted in parenting prior to incarceration as being extremely stressful.

These data revealed that during incarceration mothers emphasized the importance of children recognizing them as parents. Relationships with children were often described as "My children know I love them." It may be that an effective time management during incarceration requires denial of the disruption experienced on children and placed their maternal identities on hold. Assuming that adequate childcare provisions have been made during the mother's absence, mothers may avoid reactions of children to imprisonment until release. This points to the need for research on the incarcerated Black woman. Especially important are studies which goes beyond profiles of offenders and explore Black women's lives, such as experiences of physical and sexual abuse. Such information will make the lives of incarcerated women understandable.

Future research is also needed on the relationship between incarcerated Black mothers and possible involvement of their children in juvenile delinquent behavior. This inquiry would explore the need for special programs and services for these mothers as a juvenile delinquency prevention measure.

Policy Implications

These findings point to the difficulties of Black women following release from prison, including childcare responsibilities with little income. Thus, it is clear that former Black female inmates must have more money available for alleviating the constant stress of insufficient income. Policies must neither provide handouts nor incentives to work, but must ensure former inmate adequate employment, as well as employment security, better benefits, and increased opportunity for personal employment satisfaction.

Indeed, Black female-headed households are disproportionately represented among the poverty population, with a poverty rate more than four times that of male-headed households (U.S. Department of Commerce 1993). Feminist criminologists assert that "economic marginalization" of minority women, has had a significant effect on their involvement in the criminal justice system. Consequently, one useful approach would be to assist Black female offenders who are on parole. Focused assistance to help Black women to enter the world of work satisfactorily at this important point would decrease recidivism.

Additionally, the percentage of women incarcerated for violent crimes has dropped from 41 percent of the prison population in 1986 to 32 percent in 1991, while the percentage of female drug convictions has increased from 12 to 33 percent. Given the cost of imprisoning women $30,000 per year to house and inmate, $20,000 for foster care, it seems reasonable that nonviolent offenders could be treated in rehabilitation programs that maintain family stability while providing cultural-specific parenting skills. Another strategy is to offer age-related information on the impact of incarceration on children during imprisonment, coordinated with university-based partnerships.

In the quest for parity, women prisoners have lost their special advantages. While some needs of women inmates are identical to their male counterparts, others are not. Therefore, women inmates deserve to receive "unequal treatment" in prison (Pollock-Byrne, 1990). The current influx of Black women in prisons might reflect a need for parity and "special treatment" during imprisonment and following release from prison.

A history of subjugation, blocked access to opportunity structures, exploitation, and domination rooted in racism and patriarchy, and legitimated by gender stereotypes has created a critical attitude toward asserting the special needs of women. Yet, men and women do not enter the prison equally, nor experience hardship equally. Although the criminal justice system does not have any legal obligation to provide services to maintain family ties, the system is morally obligated to assist female offenders with successful community reintegration as a means of reducing recidivism rates.

Moreover, the correctional system is oriented toward punishment and rehabilitation of the offender as an individual and neglects the person with familial roles and responsibilities. Yet, the most positive factor in the rehabilitation of offenders is the maintenance of family ties while in prison and upon release (Hunter 1984). It is therefore imperative that correctional officials and policy makers consider the inmate's family as a prime treatment target and recognize the need for family contacts as a major behavioral-change strategy.

As prisons address the issue of maintaining mother-child relationships a two-pronged approach is needed: 1) enabling consistent contact between mothers and their children and 2) empowering women to understand the issues that brought them to prison (Clark 1995). Additionally, the placement of more half-way houses and community correctional facilities for women in highly populated urban areas where a majority of the children of incarcerated Black mothers are located would decrease children separation distress. Public dollars for prisons should be spent on programs located in underclass communities and receive input from the people they serve.

Moreover, it is important to discover the biases that increase Black women's contact with the criminal justice system. Since Black women are characterized as overbearing, loud, and aggressive, these stereotypes place Black women more at risk for being arrested than given a warning; or being written up while incarcerated. Therefore, Black women may come into contact with the justice system not for the offense, but for such factors as demeanor and misunderstood cultural differences. Often scholars and policy makers have ignored the psychological effects of race, class, and gender on those who work in the criminal justice system. In the process, Black women have been disparaged and vilified.

REFERENCES

Barnhill, S., and P. Dressel. 1991. *Three generations at risk*. Atlanta, Ga.: Aid to Imprisoned Mothers. Unpublished.

Baunch, P. J. 1992. Critical problems of women in prison. In I. Moyer (ed.) *The changing roles of women in the criminal justice system—Offenders, victims, and professionals*. Prospect Heights, Ill.: Waveland Publishers.

Bershad, L. 1985. Discriminatory treatment of the female offender in the criminal justice system. *Boston College Law Review*, 26: 385–438.

Bloom, B. 1993. Incarcerated mothers and their children: Maintaining family ties. In *Female offenders, meeting needs of a neglected population*. Laurel, Md.: American Corrections Association.

Bloom, B., and D. Steinhard. 1993. *Why punish the children?: A reappraisal of the children of incarcerated mothers in America*. San Francisco: National Council on Crime and Delinquency.

Center for Children of Incarcerated Parents. 1992. *Report No. 6: Children of offenders.* Pasadena, Calif.: Pacific Oaks College and Children's Programs.

Centers for Disease Control (1996) (CDC). *Chronic disease reports. Morbidity & mortality weekly reports* 39, 17–22. Atlanta, Ga.

Clark, J. 1995. The impact of the prison environment on mothers. *The Prison Journal,* 75: 302–329.

Cummings, P. 1978–1979. The single mother as criminal defendant: A practitioner's guide to the consequences of incarceration. *Golden Gate University Law Review,* 9: 507–552.

Datesman, S., and G. L. Cales. 1995. I'm still Mommy: Maintaining the mother/child relationship in prison. *The Prison Journal,* 63: 142–154.

Feinman, C. 1994. *Women in the criminal justice system.* Westport, Conn.: Praeger.

Hampton, R. L., and Newberger, B. 1985. Child abuse incidence and reporting by hospitals. The significance of severity, class, and race. *American Journal of Public Health,* 75, 56–69.

Hirschi, T. 1969. *Causes of delinquency.* Berkeley: University of California Press.

Hunter, S. M. 1984. *The relationship between women offenders and their children.* Ph.D. Dissertation: Michigan State University. Ann Arbor: University Microfilms International.

Johnston, D. 1993. *Report No. 13: Effects of parental incarceration.* The Center for Children of Incarcerated Parents. Pasadena, Calif.: Pacifies Oaks College and Children's Programs.

Knight, B. B. 1992. Women in prison as litigants: Prospects for post-prison future. *Women and Criminal Justice,* 4: 91–116.

Mauer, M., and T. Huling. 1995. *Young Black Americans and the criminal justice system: Five years later.* Washington, D.C.: The Sentencing Project (October).

Merton, R. (1938). Social structure and anomie. *American Sociology Review,* Vol. 3 (October): 672–682.

McCord, J. 1991. Family relationships, juvenile delinquency, and adult criminality. *Criminology,* 29: 397–417.

McGowan, B. G., and K. L. Blumenthal. 1978. *Why punish the children? A study of children of women prisoners.* Hackensack, N.J.: National Council on Crime and Delinquency.

Michigan Women's Commission. 1993. *Unheard voices: A report on women in Michigan County jails.* Lansing, Mich.

Muse, D. 1994. Parenting from prison. *Mothering,* Fall: 99–105. Fall.

Palmer, R. D. 1978. On prisoners and parenting: Preserving the tie that binds. *Yale Law Review,* 87: 1408–1429.

Petersilia, J. 1991. The value of corrections research: Learning what works. *Federal Probation.* June.

Pollock-Byrne, J. M. 1990. *Women, prison, and crime.* Pacific Grove, Calif.: Brooks/Cole Publishing.

Renzetti, C. M. and D. Curran. 1995. *Women, men, and society.* Boston: Allyn &Bacon.

Rizzo, E. 1996. The effects of equality demands on women's prisons: A case study. Working Paper presented at the Annual Meeting of the American Society of Criminal Justice Sciences. Las Vegas, Nevada.

Taylor, D. 1996. Family and delinquency: African American female-headed households and chronic maladaptive behavior by juveniles. In A. Sutton (ed.) *African American perspectives on crime causation, criminal justice administration, and crime prevention.* Boston: Butterworth-Heinemann.

U.S. Department of Commerce, Bureau of the Census. *Statistical Abstract of the United States, 1993.* Washington D.C.: Government Printing Office.

U.S. Justice Department, Bureau of Justice Statistics. *Women in Prison, 1993.* Washington D.C.: Government Printing Office.

9

The Paternal Role

Other Fathers: An Alternative Perspective on African American Community Caring

LORA BEX LEMPERT

Through acceptance of popular cultural images of African American families as "matriarchal" and through inattention to the significant roles of African American men in their families and communities, the complex contributions of men in African American families have been effaced. This exploratory report suggests an alternative view of African American men as other fathers, that is, men who as family or community members actively engage themselves as providers, protectors, role models, and mentors in the lives of other men's children.

■

Recent public attention on African American families has focused primarily on the growing numbers of African Americans at the low end of the income distribution and particularly on inner-city, female-headed households. The attendant research on these female-headed households has developed in essentially three directions. One research strand points to the strengths of the matriarchal family in maintaining generational continuity and services to kin (Stack, 1974; Hogan, Hao, and Parish, 1990; McAdoo 1983, 1993); a second details the negative impacts of institutionalized racism—unemployment, low wages, and residential segregation—on nontraditional family forms (Martin and Martin, 1985; Massey and Denton, 1987; Hill et al., 1993) ; and the third defines these familial forms as dysfunctional (Moynihan, 1967, 1990; Murray, 1984, 1996). Each of these research lines inadvertently ignores the familial contributions of African American men by denying them research attention, or by treating them as either absent from or peripheral to the "matriarchal" family constellations. In directing the research lens almost exclusively on female-headed households, researchers have quietly eliminated the significant support provided by African American men from the complex picture of African American families.

Previously unpublished paper, 1997. Reprinted by permission of the author.

Popular culture and ideological events like the Million Man March with its theme of "atonement" have sometimes converged to further highlight the image of the "absent father" in inner-city communities (Beck, 1995; Gray, 1995; Taylor, 1995; Bragg, 1995; Murray, 1996). Such contemporary convergence, with its focus on individual responsibility, both maintains and reinforces the image of ne'er-do-well African American men and grants the negative characterizations both popular validity and social currency. Additionally, print and electronic media coverage of African American families has often charted the presumed problems relevant to families without a father, such as the negative effects resulting from the lack of a male role model and disciplinarian (Downey, 1994; Moynihan, 1990; Heiss, 1996). Such contemporary social imagery of absent African American fathers links "African American families" and "matriarchy" so successfully that the terms have become both synonymous and ubiquitous.

Data collected in the course of a study of African American grandparents raising their adolescent grandchildren challenge such unidimensional, negative African American family images and suggest instead that these communities may be sustained by *other fathers,* that is, men who assume financial responsibility, in part or in whole, for the children of other men; or who model honesty, respectability, dignity, social wisdom, and race pride; or who consistently maintain a positive, interactive presence in the lives of the children in their extended families or communities.

OTHER FATHERS

Patricia Hill Collins (1990) has identified African American grandmothers, sisters, aunts, and cousins as "othermothers," those women in African American communities who take on child care responsibilities for other women's children, providing nurturance and support under adverse social and economic circumstances. Her work thus speaks to the centrality of women in African American extended families. Importantly, however, Collins also cautions against assuming this centrality to be predicated on an absence of husbands and fathers, acknowledging, for example, that: "Men may be physically present and/or have well-defined and culturally significant roles in the extended family . . ." (Collins, 1990: 119). The research presented here supports Collins' depictions of "othermothers" while also extending consideration of the significance of men in African American family constellations to that of *other fathers,* men who, as family members and/or as community members, actively engage themselves as role models and mentors in the lives of other people's children.

Data on *other fathers* in this study suggest that the erosion of commitment to social obligations in general and to children in particular earlier identified by Coontz (1992) and Bly (1991) may now be shifting. If *other fathers* did not exist in the African American communities of the past (and that contention is highly questionable), they are certainly reported by grandparent caregivers to be present now. Comments such as these are frequent in the interview narratives (All names are pseudonyms, by and large, chosen by the grandparent respondents.)

Martha Luke: Frederick and Cirell [grandsons], they have what you call a mentor, kind of like a big brother, you know. He's a policeman for the housing authority . . . He's 35 years old. He doesn't live here. He lives in Forest Woods . . . and pretty soon they gon' go on a some little camping, you know, trip. They . . . doing basketball and all this together.

Teheira Stitt: There are uncles that would keep him [when she goes away], nephews that would keep him, he stays, he can stay anywhere . . . I have a son who's in Car City always said when are you gonna bring him for the weekend. So, probably not this one, but next weekend he'll be out there with my other son and his son.

LL: So [long time partner] acted like a father to them as well?

Sarah Peck: Yes. Very much so.

Descriptions such as these challenge the collective ethnographic portrait of ghetto-specific masculinity, which conventionally constitutes manhood in overt concerns with sexual exploits, toughness, ability to command respect, personal appearance, liquor consumption, and verbal ability (Duneier, 1992; Anderson, 1993). In contrast, this exploratory data suggest that perhaps ghetto-specific masculinity more often than not includes extraordinary "caring behavior" (Duneier, 1992), as well as commitment, responsibility, and sincerity. In her seminal research on the Black family, Stack (1974) noted that children in poor single parent or extended family households had constant and close contact with men who were members of the extended family and that, especially in the case of male relatives, those relationships lasted over several years.

Caregiving African American grandparents are cognizant of the need children have for male attention and contact, interest, and support. The grandmothers, "othermothers" (Collins, 1990), in this study readily acknowledge the importance of men in their grandchildren's lives and they work to create opportunities for consistent and continuous contact. For example, Teheira Stitt, a 60-year-old caregiving grandmother to an adolescent grandson, articulates the feelings of many other "othermothers":

> They [grandchildren] got to have some men in their lives. They have to have that. I'm not a man so there are many things about men that I don't know, you know, and men are the ones that can tell them that, not me, you know.

Nurturing and support of children is a more or less universal family function. If African American families are acknowledged as collective responsibilities, then social recognition can be accorded to "othermothers" and *other fathers*. However, when both societal and research bias favors individual accountability and responsibility, then conceptualizing fatherhood as a socially assumed (versus a biologically ordained) role is precluded.

The identification of *other fathers* in this report, those African American men assuming responsibilities traditionally associated with paternity for children not their own, is merely suggestive as it grew out of a larger study of African American grandparents raising their adolescent grandchildren. The report is necessarily exploratory and provisional. Nonetheless, the suggestive evidence is compelling as it charts the types of relationships with *other fathers* that grandparent caregivers described as meaningful in their grandchildren's lives. I draw from their stories to illustrate the complexity, ambiguity, and emotional richness involved in these relationships. In presenting this evidence, I do not however deny the destructive reality that is the life condition of many children growing up in inner city, ghetto communities. *Other fathers* may mitigate the effects of negative life circumstances, but they cannot unilaterally transform them.

In their narratives grandparent caregivers described several roles played by *other fathers* that fall outside contemporary popular cultural depictions of African American men. I characterize these roles as one step removed, stand up fathers, and stand in fathers. These characterizations are not simply a list of metaphors for relationships, rather, these three exemplars are offered as mutually reinforcing elements of the relational panorama identified as *other fathers*.

METHODOLOGY

I ground my description of these African American *other fathers* in the in-depth interview data from 32 African American grandparents who had legal or informal responsibility for raising their adolescent grandchildren. Grandparent respondents were interviewed in two regional, urban locations, Detroit and San Francisco. The specific nature of such a limited sample necessarily restricts the generalizability of the data.

Although the probe "are there any men in your grandchild's life?" was included in the open ended interview protocol, it was not the focus of the research. It did, nonetheless, often precipitate extended narrative descriptions. Suggestive, descriptive data on *other fathers* emerged as analytically salient in the process of a grounded theory analysis (Glaser and Strauss, 1967; Glaser, 1978; Strauss, 1987; Strauss and Corbin, 1990) of the grandparent narratives. My report is presented as an invitation for further research on the relevance of the category of *other fathers*.

Grandparent respondents ranged in age from 43 to 80 years old, clustering in the late 50s and early 60s. Of the 32 participants, 29 were grandmothers and 3 were grandfathers or step-grandfathers. While most of the grandmothers were widowed, 4 were divorced, 1 was separated, and 6 were currently married. All of the grandfathers were interviewed with their spouses. This study population substantially reflects McAdoo's (1990) earlier identification of the social pattern of caregiving grandparents in urban areas as African American grandmothers. It is the social construction of "caregiving" as gendered work that, I contend, contributes to the invisibility of the sustenance provided by these African American *other fathers*.

The interviews ranged in duration from 45 minutes to three and a half hours. All interviews were taped and most were transcribed. I used open-ended probes asking the grandparent respondents to tell me about the origin and the ongoing nature of their caregiving responsibilities. In the course of their narratives, all of the respondents identified kin-related or community-based men in their grandchildren's lives who provided the kind of care and/or modeling traditionally associated with fatherhood. These narratives are the basis for the suggestive category of *other fathers*.

GRANDFATHERS: ## ONE STEP REMOVED

As coercive circumstances (i.e., death, drugs, homicide, neglect, relationship dissolution, in-

carceration, eviction, and so on) destabilized the lives of young African American children and adolescents, grandparents often intervened by assuming and asserting parental rights and responsibilities. It is in these assumptive roles that grandfathers became exemplar *other fathers*, as they also enacted historical roles as the community "absorption mechanisms" (Martin and Martin, 1978: 39) for their families in times of need.

In concert with their wives, the grandfathers in this study assumed many of the primary care responsibilities typically associated with parental roles. They also reflected considerable variation—primarily as consequences of differentials in class and grandchild gender—in the ways that their second parenting was accomplished. Those grandfathers who commanded more material resources enacted many more traditional gender divisions in family work. For example, their work was more instrumental and included such responsibilities as financial providers, protectors, and primary decision-makers; while the grandmothers' work was generally more expressive and nurturant and appropriate to their role as keepers of the household. Although grandchild gender and material resource differentials affected how caregiving was enacted, all the grandfathers exhibited congruency in the very acts of assuming responsibility for the care and nurturance of their grandchildren, in the protective nature of their care, as well as in their explicit attention to lessons of race socialization.

Matthew Madison is an example of an economically advantaged grandfather. As the pastor of a church with over 1,000 members, he is able to provide his grandson with a comfortable life including private, religious school education, as well as such non-essentials as orthodontic correction for his teeth. Mrs. Madison does not work in paid employment and the family dines together each evening. Reverend Madison has assumed the mantle of "traditional father" in interactions with his grandson, Waldo, whose own father is unknown to him. Reverend Madison acknowledges the generational dilemmas inherent in second parenting:

This is difficult when, you know, we are, I'm 66 and she's 65 and you dealing with a 13-year-old kid, it's two different worlds altogether. You try to get in his world and it's no way in the world you can do it.

And he cares for his grandson in the ways he knows best. Reverend Madison assumes responsibility as the family financial provider ("It's all on me."), major decision-maker ("I said, well, we have to talk to your granddaddy about going to catholic school."), as the disciplinarian ("They know he means business."), as a role model ("I think they all [his own children and his grandson] tried to accept the responsibility of being a preacher's kid, quote PK, and all do that they can to be supportive."), as an advocate for Waldo with Mrs. Madison ("Anything he needs that she won't give him, then he comes to me and I don't know a thing about him going to her in the first place."), as the initiator of man-to-man sex education ("Not as much as I should, but we've talked . . . Enough for him to have some idea what it's all about."), and as Waldo's socializer to contemporary race relations ("If you're gonna get into those situations [mixed race competitions for opportunities], it's an individual thing. I must run faster. I must be better in everything else than everybody else who gets into those situations."). Grandfathers, like Matthew Madison, ease their grandsons through boyhood into manhood, socializing them to meet adult responsibilities by modeling, through lives of decency and commitment, responsibility to and for family and community.

Those grandfathers and step-grandfathers, who are less financially secure and who are raising granddaughters, remain as committed to their child-rearing tasks as their more advantaged brethren, but must work harder to create safety and security for their grandchildren. Olin Reed is a step-grandfather who has assumed all the traditional responsibilities of fatherhood for his wife's granddaughter, Cherie. He is retired and the family lives on a fixed social security income. Cherie has multiple physical and emotional disabilities resulting from early childhood neglect and abuse. Mr. Reed articulates the burdens he feels as the second tier parent with primary child-rearing responsibilities:

Because if I had the money, I would not be having the problems that I am having with Cherie now . . . because knowing that there was a problem, I would have enough money to put Cherie perhaps in a private school. You know, or a private situation, where she could receive professional attention. But since we don't have it, we doing what best we can because it's a problem that we do not know how to handle physically or mentally . . . if I had enough money, she could be put into a situation where she could be assisted, trained and tutored that in years to come she could be an independent person in this system . . . You know, we're not going to be here forever. What is going to happen to her? I feel inadequate because I don't think that I'm able at this time to build that foundation, you know, where she would be able to function in this society.

Committed to Cherie's present and future, Olin Reed has assumed more than a father's burden, he has also assumed a father's blame. Mr. Reed's financial limitations result in his feelings of inadequacy for failing to meet one of the primary duties of parents—preparing a child for independent living. He knows what Cherie needs, but unfortunately, he is economically unable to provide it. Thus because he has convictions about the proper behavior for a man like him, he blames himself for what he regards as the failure to live up to conventional standards of moral worthiness as a second tier parent.

Olin Reed could be a man drawn directly out of Duneier's (1992) insightful ethnography of race, respectability, and masculinity among working class, African American men. Mr. Reed epitomizes belief in personal responsibility, humility, and respectability. The depth of his own historical sense of himself as a Black man, in a social system that has "decimated" (Staples,

1992) persons with those identifiers, is evident in Mr. Reed's reasons for assuming parental responsibility for his step-granddaughter:

> He [Reed's father] loved me, you know, and I'm saying that I'm not gon' let my father be a better man than me, you know, I'm gonna do for mine like he did for me.

Although grandfathers, like fathers, are often neglected in the developmental literature as important socialization agents of children (Pearson, Hunter, Ensminger, and Killam, 1990), by mirroring traditional fathers' contributions to family, the care-giving grandfathers in this study actively transmitted expectations, values and beliefs to their grandchildren. Grandfathers, like Olin Reed and Matthew Madison, point to race as a salient factor in determining grandchildren's life chances in America. In their formulations race is a principle determinant of social organization affecting every aspect of employment, educational opportunity, health, and justice. As persons committed to responsible child-rearing, these grandfathers then employ processes of explicit racial socialization to attempt to prepare their children for the realities of being African American in America. As Matthew Madison did earlier, Olin Reed speaks to these perceptions and processes:

> It's us against the world, it's us, it always have been, you know, so like a lot of people say well, why are these people [African Americans] so resentful, you know. Everyday I wake up, I'm reminded that I'm Black, everyday that I wake up, you know. Then people, then my riders [at work], then they say, oh, you know, you're so intelligent, you're so informed and it just hurts me, you know. And my co-worker, I say what is it? I mean because you Black you have to be dumb? . . . Like I'm saying, the only thing I want is what's due me, I'm not asking for anything extra. You know, just like out there the white boy I said, you know, what have you done? What have you done to get all

these rights? . . . These is all code words for Blacks, welfare, crime, liberal, all these is code words and every time you turn around, yes, they're using them, yeah . . . Everything that this system puts out there to you is not meant for you. I said you have to be better than the white boy. I said you cannot go on the job with the same talent and credential . . . I'm telling you now, you have to be better.

While rejecting negative cultural characterizations of African Americans, these grandfathers view as a moral commitment their caregiving responsibility to prepare their grandchildren for lives in a racialized society. "You have to be better" is both an oft-repeated caution and a moral imperative.

Consistent with the second father role responsibilities identified earlier, Olin Reed is also an active participant in his step-granddaughter's life. Aside from assuming all financial obligations for her care and nurturance, he negotiates with school officials on her behalf, as well as arguing intensely for education accommodations for other similarly disadvantaged students. He is Cherie's advocate and protector and he actively strategizes to develop opportunities for her future, all the while recognizing the limits of his own situation:

> I think our biggest problem is that we don't understand. Now we're into a situation where I think people call it abnormal. And this is what, you know, we just don't know how to deal with it.

In every parental context except that of biological origins, Olin Reed assumes the responsibilities of a traditional father to Cherie.

Other grandfathers, like those in Thomas' (1986) study of gender differences in grandparenting, may provide their grandchildren with sex role models that are nontraditional, although not recognized as such. Thomas (1986) reported that grandfathers derived satisfaction from responsibilities for taking care of and helping their grandchildren. The grandchildren of these nurturing grandfathers may witness repeated examples of caring and expressivity in grandfather's behavior, which might support development of relatively androgynous conceptions of sex roles. Lawrence Sebastian, another step-grandfather who is also physically disabled civil service worker, models such nurturing behavior for the five grandchildren under the grandparent couple's care. He cooks, does the laundry, baby sits, and otherwise advises, counsels, and nurtures the children of a mother who "has like gave up on life itself."

While providing androgynous role models, these grandfathers also help to locate their grandchildren in the wider social communities of which they are a part. Another grandfather is "supervisor for the guard [crossing guards], you know, those guards that go around . . . from school to school, so everybody know his grandfather." Several study grandfathers, through participation in their grandchildren's lives, seek to create a web of community interrelatedness reflecting a pattern from a smaller town America, where everyone in the community knew everyone else and reported to one another on children's comings and goings. These grandfathers hope that children reared in communities characterized by dignified face to face contact will continue to grow into their potentials despite the absence of biological parents.

Grandfathers, one step removed in biological creation, can and do assume many of the traditional fatherhood responsibilities. They provide for their grandchildren financially and often emotionally, they advocate for their grandchildren at home and at school, they advise and counsel their grandchildren, and they socialize them to the conditions and constraints of African Americans in the United States. Sometimes their efforts are appreciated, as Rebecca Sebastian says of her husband, Lawrence:

> We [she and the grandchildren] are
> blessed. We are blessed. We are truly blessed.
> And he has his own pain and everything but

still . . . Lawrence is a responsible person. If he wasn't responsible, he wouldn't be here giving all these years to these children. You see what I'm saying?

The grandfathers in this study challenge the cultural myth that children growing up without a father is "the greatest social catastrophe facing our country. It is at the root of the epidemics of crime and drugs, it is deeply implicated in the decline in educational attainment, and it is largely responsible for the persistence of widespread poverty despite generous government support for the needy" (Davidson, 1990: 40). Some of the children growing up without biological fathers are privileged to have grandfathers who are one step removed.

STAND OUT FATHERS: FATHERING FROM PRISON

Largely because of drug prosecutions in poor, minority neighborhoods, nearly one of every three African American men aged 20 to 29 is either in prison, on probation, or on parole (Zucchino 1997). Black males make up 42 percent of jail inmates, 31.2 percent of those arrested, 34 percent of those on probation, and 50 percent of those on parole (U.S. Bureau of the Census 1996). High rates of African American male arrest and incarceration contribute to the "decimation" (Staples, 1992) of the Black male and to the demise of African American family and community structures. These men, who are removed from communities through incarceration, are also removed from opportunities to enact their parental responsibilities. Their children lose the presence of a father and the concomitant discipline, socialization, and role modeling that father's traditionally provide. Proponents of the father-absent hypothesis contend that the parental authority structure is often weaker in non-traditional families than in biological two parent families resulting in more deviant behavior by the children (Dornbusch et al.,

1985). This male-model argument contends that the presence of a father figure is necessary for certain kinds of childhood socialization to occur (Heiss, 1996)

Alternatively while fathers may be out of the household, they are not necessarily inactive in their children's lives (King, 1994; Wade, 1994; Allen and Doherty, 1996). Although physical proximity is missing, fathers under the care of the criminal justice system may, nonetheless, exert considerable influence in the lives of their children. Furstenberg, Morgan and Allison (1987) in a review of single-parent research studies found no association between father visitation and child well being suggesting that perhaps quality, not simply father–child contact, influences well-being outcomes. Incarcerated fathers, who by definition lack traditional parenting opportunities, may nonetheless create affirming relationships with their children mirroring the model of *other fathers*. Jason Lowery is such an incarcerated father. While his 16-year-old daughter, Desiree, lives with his mother, Jason Lowery has not relinquished those parental responsibilities that he can effect from prison.

Lowery, incarcerated for two years "for bothering drugs . . . he wasn't selling, he was holding it for somebody," is described by his mother as an "active parent." He calls Desiree every day. He counsels and advises her with regard to worrisome issues for parents of adolescents:

> He talks to her about her boyfriend which he [boyfriend] is not a person that's going anyplace, he's just here taking up space. He just have a job and that's all. He [Jason] talks to her about that and . . . he says well I'm a man and I was young once and, you know, I don't want you sexually active but if you are, he tell her what, you know. And your boyfriend too. What you should do [to protect] yourself. And it's not just one time he does, every time he talks to her about it.

Jason Lowery uses his own manhood and experience as a legitimate context from which to frame his concern over his daughter's choice of a boyfriend. He simultaneously communicates his high expectations of her. He also uses these telephone opportunities to express his hope that she will choose celibacy over sexual activity. Yet both sets of expectations are couched in the recognition that, through incarceration, he has lost the power as a parent to enforce his desires.

For children living with the ambiguity of a father in prison, *other fathers* and other family members may provide a reassuring contextual frame for interpretation:

> He care about you, he just in a situation right now that he can't handle or he just trying to clean it up so he can, you know, be there for you.

And this strategy seems to work. Because Jason Lowery maintains consistent contact with Desiree, because he demonstrates his care and concern, she:

> has high respect for him, even in jail she respect him highly. She don't want her daddy to know anything bad about her.

Although public norms increasingly support the greater involvement of fathers, such norms are predicated on an assumption that this involvement will have positive benefits for the children. King (1994) finds limited evidence for that assumption. More important perhaps is the quality of the time spent in interaction (Furstenberg, Morgan, and Allison, 1987), incarcerated fathers may bridge the physical gap of forced separation from their children through consistent affirmations of caring and concern.

STAND-IN FATHERS: FAMILY MEMBERS AND COMMUNITY WORKERS

In creating social safety nets for at risk children, grandparent caregivers rarely rely on a single *other father* to fill in the familial gaps created by loss of parental involvement and adverse social and economic conditions. More typically, their grandchildren are connected to a variety of men who each enact some paternal behaviors. In each grandchild's life there are then multiple *other fathers*. Some *other fathers* are family members, like uncles and cousins, others are fictive kin or in-laws, still others are church or community members, and the furthest removed are those men interacting through organizations, such as Boys Clubs or PAL (Police Athletic Leagues). All these other fathers, through intent and behavior, attempt to remedy aspects of the coercive circumstances that put some African American children at risk. Ms. Dora Webb, 62-year-old step-grandmother to an adolescent granddaughter, relates this connection,

> My son [uncle] does not live too far from here. He's crazy about her. She couldn't have gotten into a better family cause they treat her, she just, is a granddaughter, you know what I mean? . . . She depends on [uncle], he bought her a bicycle for Christmas, her birthday, you know. He likes to save up and "[uncle], I need this" you know. And 'cause [uncle] is ok with her dad . . . her dad doesn't . . . he doesn't have quite the money, you know, to help her like we do.

These *other fathers* fulfill what another grandmother, Bernice Peach, suggests is an African American cultural practice:

> . . . in the Afro-American family, there's a great belief in standing with them [children], you know, taking care of your own and stuff.

With family welfare perennially at stake (Martin and Martin, 1978), many African American community members informally adopt children into extended kin networks on either a temporary or a permanent basis (Johnson, 1934; Stack, 1974; Billingsley, 1992). *Other fathers* are part of the fabric of the communal safety nets that seek to protect and nurture at risk children by contributing to economic support, or by role modeling, or by participating in socializing them, or by being "for real."

Caregiving grandparents actively seek out appropriate males in the family and in the community with whom their grandchildren can interact positively. In identifying these *other fathers*, grandparents seek to provide their grandchildren with antidotes to the negative role modeling often existent in poor communities as well as that imposed by stereotypes in the broader culture. "Successful" men, especially those who come from the same communities, enact for at risk children the possibility of lives different than the ones they are currently living. In discussing the interactions of her son with his nieces and nephews, for example, Gwenetta Roosevelt, caregiving grandmother of five, says: "They thought Uncle Jim was rich . . . and yet he wasn't rich." Although able to travel extensively, swim, and "mix with people," Uncle Jim worked "two jobs to keep up his lifestyle." Nonetheless, to his nieces and nephews:

> They thought he had a great deal. He was doing much better than they had ever seen. It's good for them to see "the better" to see that it can be better, that is isn't, it isn't always without food to eat and, and with hardly food.

Uncle Jim is an *other father,* a successful male from their own family, an uncle who also buys presents, takes the children on day trips and out to dinner, and occasionally provides financial assistance for on-going expenses. He is both like and unlike his nieces and nephews, because although he was raised in the same family and located in the same community, he was able to change his own economic and social circumstances He attempts to motivate his nieces and nephews to do the same by exposing them to other alternatives. He models different life experiences for them.

Role modeling, socialization through advice and example, and "man kind of interactions" are presumed by these grandparent caregivers to differ in substance and kind from matriarchal forms of childrearing. Grandmothers are quick to identify *other fathers,* who fill in the familial gaps left by non-resident biological fathers and who provide entertaining, educational experiences through quality time "with the boys:"

> Sometimes my brother will come and take them, the boys to the, he's taken them to [the] Air Force Base for the air show. [Brother]'ll come and take [grandson] down to the [City] Plaza, he'll come and do things with him. I have another nephew who would come and get [grandson], spend the weekend with him, and [nephew] has a son about the same age and he'll take them out and then he'll take them to church Sunday.

Some *other fathers* combine the field trips with repeated, focused advice and concern that draws youth attention to the details, the history, the practical uses of social information, sometimes identified as "cultural literacy" (Hirsch, 1987). The intention is to help prepare children to assume successful places in the larger society. Mary Smith, at 80 years the oldest study respondent and caregiver to two adolescents, speaks to this contribution:

> My oldest son will go and get them, take them to [tourist location]. All the time he's walking with them, he's talking to them, showing them different things. Well, what is that? That's so and so, and do this to them, that to them. And it's there for a certain reason and why and all that stuff.

Such nurturing interactions by African American men embed the youths in shared ideas and cultural values, as they also promote a richer experience of community.

For most Americans education is perceived to be an avenue of opportunity enabling otherwise disadvantaged youth occasions for successful participation in the society. Consequently, some other fathers assume the daily responsibilities of encouraging academic achievement in these adolescents. Some drive children to school or pick them up after school every day; some

provide the children with school supplies. Others like Ms. Joseph's son-in-law, monitor children's academic preparedness and, thereby, inculcate standards and values:

> My son in law helps them with their homework. When they finish their homework, they always take it to him.

Most *other fathers,* however, appear to fundamentally impact the children's lives by establishing consistent, caring interactions. As a great-grandmother caregiver to two adolescent great-grandchildren, Alicia Joseph has a multigenerational pool of male extended kin to call upon in this regard:

> My grandson next door (college student) takes my great-grandson bowling, that's their date every [week] . . . they go out and have some lunch and go bowling. [Male family members] know that [father] had never spent too [much] time with them, so they kind of take up time where he left off.

Male family members recognize at risk children's needs and they attempt to meet them, as they also model appropriate male responses to familial responsibilities. That both *other fathers* and "other mothers" (Collins, 1990) are active collaborators in creating positive socialization experiences for at risk youth is obvious in Teheira Stitt's declaration: "We do a lot of together things, men and women together, you know, so that the children can see how people are supposed to get along." These experiences serve as alternative models and antidotes to the less "mannerable" models available to youths on the street.

Although family members are the first men called upon to assist in providing a social safety net for children, for a good many adolescents, whose family networks have been weakened by death, drugs, and other forms of social destruction, the men hired in community and state sponsored programs are often their primary role models. These men are often valorized by caregiving grandparents who appreciate their honesty, their "street smarts," and their willingness to work with difficult youth. Mary Smith, caregiving grandmother to an adolescent grandson, articulates the feelings of many others:

> . . . the Boys Club on [Charlton] Street . . . those are, that's a very nice place for boys because those men over there, they are all for real. And this is what I'm proud of, that they have found some way, or something to do, or some place to bring the kids and teach them what it's all about. They are very good.

Community *other fathers* familiar with the codes and values of the "street," being "for real," are invaluable resources for both grandparents and their grandchildren. From a grandparent's perspective, in their neighborhoods the "street" is both a metaphorical and a literal location that embodies danger: drugs, distrust, destabilization and decline, alienation, crime, threats from strangers, in short, all the public vulnerabilities that require personal management (Anderson, 1990). In the "street," kids are on drugs, into sex, lacking hope of a different future, and they are locked into a social condition that appears intractable (Anderson, 1990). So grandparents worry about the "street" and assail their grandchildren with reproaches and warnings. In such social contexts, they are also very cognizant of those community *other fathers* who provide positive models and alternative social locations for children to interact and grow. Martha Luke cites the work of the young men in her church as an example:

> And the people at church is so helpful . . . the young men there, they keep the kids really busy. Like Saturdays, we have a, they have a basketball team going, you know . . . so they are really involved and [grandchildren] like going to church. So I think this is what actually keep them kind of intact, keep them, you know, out of the streets.

Other fathers provide at risk children with an antidote to the negative role modeling ubiquitous in poor communities. These family members, community workers, or interested adults assume responsibilities, in part or in whole, for the children of other men. They provide economic assistance, guidance and advice, as they role model appropriate male behavior and encourage children to rise above difficult conditions.

CONCLUSION

In the more slowly changing societies of the past, tradition and precedent dictated behavioral expectations. Children learned primarily from their parents by listening, observing, seeing, and *not* being heard. With some certitude, they were able to foresee their own futures in the lives of their parents and grandparents. In such societies, values were shared and universalized because they were located in a broader social frame of reference that included both internal and external racial communities. For a myriad of reasons, many having to do with the persistent and increasing social vulnerability of African Americans, i.e., high rates of drug addiction, homicide, incarceration, early deaths from disease, and neglect and abuse, the familial safety net in African American communities is torn, but it is not destroyed.

While some African American children may be growing up without the care of their biological parents, they are not growing up without love and nurturing, protection and provision, from "othermothers" (Collins, 1990) and *other fathers*. Due to the historical and contemporary legacy of racism and discrimination, the survival of African American families in America has always been predicated on an interdependence of family members and community institutions (Stack, 1974; Jewell, 1988). These extended family accommodations, vestiges perhaps of West African culture have fortified individuals and families with a broad range of adaptive strategies with which to respond to situational constraints originating within the broader society (Hatchett and Jackson, 1993). The phenomenon of *other fathers* suggested here may be yet another permutation in the historical progression of community caring.

REFERENCES

Allen, W. D., and W. J. Doherty. 1996. The responsibilities of fatherhood as perceived by African American teenage fathers. *Families in Society,* 77 (3), 142–155.

Anderson, E. 1990. *Streetwise.* Chicago: University of Chicago Press.

Anderson, E. 1993. Sex codes and family life among poor inner-city youths. In William J. Wilson (ed.) *The ghetto underclass: Social science perspectives.* Newbury Park, Calif.: Sage.

Beck, M. 1995. Beyond the moment, what can one day do? *Newsweek,* 126, 38–39. October 30.

Billingsley, A. 1992. *Climbing Jacob's Ladder.* New York: Simon & Schuster.

Bly, R. 1991. *Iron John: A book about men.* New York: Random House.

Bragg, R. 1995. Georgia, pursuing child support, discovers potential and limits. *New York Times,* April 14, 1995. A1.

Cherlin, A. J., and Furstenberg, F. F., Jr. 1986. *The new American grandparent.* New York: Basic Books.

Collins, P. H. 1990. *Black feminist thought: Knowledge consciousness, and the politics of empowerment.* Boston: Unwin Hyman.

Coontz, S. 1992. *The way we never were.* New York: Harper-Collins.

Davidson, N. 1990. Life without father: America's greatest social catastrophe. *Policy Review,* 51 (winter), 40–44.

Dornbusch, S. M., J. M. Carlsmith, S. J. Bushwall, P. L. Ritter, H. Leiderman, A. H. Hastorf, and R. T. Gross. 1985. Single parents, extended households, and the control of adolescents. *Child Development,* 56 (2), 326–341.

Downey, D. B. 1994. The school performance of children from single mother and single father families: Economics and interpersonal deprivations? *Journal of Family Issues,* 15 (1), 129–147.

Duneier, M. 1992. *Slim's table.* Chicago: University of Chicago Press.

Furstenberg, F. F., Jr., S. P. Morgan, and P. D. Allison. 1987. Paternal participation and children's well-being after marital dissolution. *American Sociological Review,* 52 (5), 695–701.

Glaser, B. G. 1978. *Theoretical sensitivity.* Mill Valley, Calif.: Sociology Press.

Glaser, B. G., and A. L. Strauss. 1967. *The discovery of grounded theory.* New York: Aldine de Gruyter.

Gray, M. 1995. The path of responsibility. *Essence,* 26 (June): 42.

Hatchett, S. J., and J. S. Jackson. 1993. African American extended kin systems: An assessment. In H. P. McAdoo, Harriet Pipes (ed.). *Family ethnicity.* Newbury Park, Calif.: Sage, 90–108.

Heiss, J. 1996. Effects of African American family structure on school attitudes and performance. *Social Problems,* 43 (3), 246–267.

Hill, R. B., A. Billingsley, E. Engram, M. R. Malson, R. H. Rubin, C. B. Stack, J. B. Stewart, and J. E. Teele. 1993. *Research on the African-American family: A holistic perspective.* Westport, Conn.: Auburn House.

Hirsch Jr., E. D. 1987. *Cultural literacy.* Boston: Houghton Mifflin.

Hogan, D. P., L. X. Hao, and W. L. Parish. 1990. Race, kin networks, and assistance to mother-headed families. *Social Forces,* 68: 797–812.

Jewell, K. S. 1988. *Survival of the Black family: The institutional impact of U.S. social policy.* New York: Praeger.

Johnson, C. S. 1934. *Shadow of the plantation.* Chicago: University of Chicago Press.

King, V. 1994. Nonresident father involvement in child well-being: Can dads make a difference? *Journal of Family Issues,* 15 (1), 78–96.

Martin, E. P., and J. M. Martin. 1978. *The Black extended family.* Chicago: University of Chicago Press.

Martin, J. M., and E. P. Martin. 1985. *The helping tradition in the Black family and community.* Silver Springs, Md.: National Association of Social Workers.

Massey, D. S., and N. A. Denton. 1987. Trends in the residential segregation of Blacks, Hispanics, and Asians. *American Sociological Review,* 52 (6), 802–825.

McAdoo, H. P. (ed.) 1993. *Family ethnicity: Strength in diversity.* Thousand Oaks, Calif.: Sage.

McAdoo, H. P. 1983. *Extended family support of single Black mothers: Final report.* Washington, D.C.: U.S. National Institute of Mental Health.

Moynihan, D. P. 1967. The Negro family: A case for national action. In L. Rainwater and W. L. Yancey (eds.), *The Moynihan report and the politics of controversy.* Cambridge, Mass.: M.I.T. Press, 41–124.

Moynihan, D. P. 1990. Families falling apart. *Society,* 27 (5), 21–22.

Murray, C. A. 1984. *Losing ground: American social policy, 1950–1980.* New York: Basic Books.

Murray, C. A. 1996. Keeping priorities straight on welfare reform. *Society,* 33, 10–12.

Pearson, J. L., A. G. Hunter, M. E. Ensminger, S. G. Killam. 1990. Black grandmothers in multigenerational households: Diversity in family structure and parenting involvement in the Woodlawn community. *Child Development,* 61, 434–442.

Stack, C. 1974. *All our kin: Strategies for survival in a Black community.* New York: Harper & Row.

Staples, R. 1992. African American families. In J. M. Henslin (ed.) *Marriage and family in a changing society*. New York: Free Press, 51–65.

Strauss, A., and J. Corbin. 1990. *Basics of qualitative research*. Newbury Park, Calif.: Sage.

Strauss, A. L. 1987. *Qualitative analysis for social scientists*. Cambridge: Cambridge University Press.

Taylor, S. L. 1995. Mothering Solo. *Essence* 26, p.83. October 1995.

Thomas, J. L. 1986. Gender Differences in Satisfaction with Grandparenting. *Psychology and Aging,* 1 (3), 215–219.

U.S. Bureau of the Census, *Statistical Abstract of the United States: 1996.* (116th edition.) Washington, DC, 1996. No. 349, No. 351, No. 354, No. 323.

Wade, J. C. 1994. African American fathers and sons: Social, historical, and psychological considerations. *Families in Society,* 75 (9), 561–570.

"To Be, or Not to Be There": Understanding the Gap Between Adolescent Paternal Aspirations and Performance.

WILLIAM DERYCK ALLEN

Using a small group of young Black men as his sample, the author attempted to examine the young fathers' perceptions of fatherhood and their evaluation of their performance as fathers. In addition, he hoped to learn what they perceived as the main obstacles to their paternal goals and how building on those aspirations might prove useful in bettering their life experiences and those of their natal partners and their children.

■

INTRODUCTION

Sometimes, more is not better. In the study of human behavior and motivation, establishment of normative trends based on large data samples is a proven strategy. It can be useful to researchers trying to predict interpersonal responses to specific situations. It can also be a boon to service providers and clinicians working with those who face these situations in their lives. Unfortunately, this strategy is less effective at explaining the more complex and often subtle factors that shape normative trends. These underlying factors demand precise exploration and often require qualitative analysis of smaller samples.

The life experiences of adolescent mothers (and their children) have generated considerable research (Furstenberg, Brooks-Gunn, and Morgan, 1987; Hofferth and Hayes, 1987). Indeed,

most of the remedial programs related to the educational and employment needs of adolescent parents focus on the needs of the adolescent mother and her child (Dunston, Hall, and Thorne-Henderson, 1987). Although the relative amount of scholarship regarding adolescent fathers has increased dramatically in the last two decades, compared to adolescent motherhood, much less is known about these young fathers (Connor, 1988; Elster and Lamb, 1986; Freeman, 1989; Hendricks, 1983; Robinson, 1988b; Sullivan, 1986). This deficit in research carries over into practice as evidenced in the small (but growing) number of programs aimed at supporting adolescent fathers.

Much of the recent work on young fathers presents demographic and statistical information (Baffle, 1988; Parke and Neville, 1987). However, few researchers have attempted to explore the more subjective aspects of adolescent fatherhood. This is problematic in view of the tendency for subjects of multivariate analysis to end up stripped of any cultural or socio-historical context. Nowhere is this more apparent than in the case of African-American adolescent fathers, a group typically at risk due to several social problems (e.g., poverty, lack of education, problems with employment, etc.). In order to understand these fathers, we must integrate both the quantitative and qualitative aspects of these young menus experiences. A deeper understanding of the meaning of fatherhood among these

Previously unpublished paper, 1998. Reprinted by permission of the author.

young fathers might facilitate societal efforts to support them in their efforts to become good providers for their natal partners and children. It should also bolster preventative efforts focused on African-American adolescent males who have not yet become fathers by clarifying the enormous responsibilities inherent with parenthood and the complexities of effective co-parenting.

There is both empirical (Robinson, 1988a) and anecdotal (Dash, 1989) evidence that many adolescent fathers value fatherhood as a primary component of their self-identity. They also cite fatherhood as a salient role that provides a unique sense of purpose to their lives. Yet, the literature on paternal establishment and involvement over time suggests that few adolescent fathers claim their children at birth, or remain consistently connected with them throughout their childhood. In considering such contradictory evidence, several central questions arise. What do adolescent fathers mean when they use the term "fatherhood"? (Are they referring to their biological roles in reproduction, or are they incorporating contemporary social and cultural expectations of fathers emerging in the broader society?) How do these young men develop perceptions of fatherhood? And finally, what factors might explain the divergence between high paternal aspirations and low paternal involvement among so many adolescent fathers?

To begin to answer these questions, a small group of African-American adolescent fathers was interviewed. We discussed their perceptions of fatherhood and their evaluation of their performance as fathers. In addition to understanding how these adolescents defined fatherhood, we hoped to learn what they perceived were the principal obstacles to their paternal aspirations. Finally, we considered how building on aspirations might prove useful in improving the life experiences of these young fathers, natal partners and their children.

The study uses two theoretical bases: symbolic interactionism and human ecology. The first of these focuses on the connection between *symbols,* and the *interactions* that define and maintain these symbols. Although symbolic interactionism encompasses a broad range of theoretical principles and empirical approaches (LaRossa and Reitzes, 1993), this study was guided by a Blumerian interpretation of the social forces shaping adolescent fathers' behaviors (Blumer, 1969). We suspected that the young men's perceptions of fatherhood *(meanings)* would shape their paternal behavior. These perceptions would emerge from their social interactions with family and peers. Finally, the interplay of perceptions and actual paternal behavior would demonstrate the dynamic and interpretive process of meaning making. Thus, these young men's paternal performance should be shaped by their perceptions of fatherhood, particularly their perceptions of themselves as fathers.

This study also relied on two concepts from human ecology theory (Bubolz and Sontag, 1993). First, the interdependence of people and their environments suggested that both human and environmental factors interacted to determine the course and quality of these young father's lives (Westney, Brabble, and Edwards, 1988). Second, the ability (or inability) of the respondents to exert control over their environment was limited. Their transition to parenthood was heavily influenced by the context in which their family's pregnancy, birth, and neonatal experiences occurred.

It is impossible to understand either the antecedents or the consequences of adolescent fatherhood without incorporating the social, ethnic, and historic context in which these young men live (McAdoo, 1993). This study was designed to incorporate possible socioeconomic and ethnic influences on the young men in our sample (Allen, 1982). This was a major consideration in the decision to focus the present study on African-American adolescent fathers. To avoid making inappropriate distinctions attributed to ethnic differences in the sample, the study was conducted with an African-American sample. The principle investigator also was able to draw on his experience as an African-American male in designing the questionnaire and in analyzing the data.

LITERATURE REVIEW

Adolescent fathers are thought to be responsible for as many as 116,000 live births annually (Barth, Claycomb, and Loomis, 1988), though this figure may underestimate the true number. Precise estimates are difficult to ascertain because of the relatively low avowal rate of paternity by adolescent males (Wattenberg, 1990), and due to the negative social stigma attached to early child-bearing. In the introduction to their descriptive study of adolescent fathers, Barret and Robinson (1982) state that *"adolescent fathers are both under-researched and clinically under-served."* A telling example of this is that a recent issue of *Family Relations* (October 1991) focusing on "Adolescent Pregnancy and Parenting" did not include a single article on adolescent fathers.

Several explanations have been presented for the gap in the literature. Many researchers have found adolescent fathers elusive and difficult to reach (Barret and Robinson, 1982; Christmon, 1990a; Robinson, 1988b). Some young fathers seeking to escape their paternal responsibilities deny paternity. Given negative images of adolescent parents and non-custodial fathering in the popular media, it should not be surprising that they are reluctant to being associated with such images. Other adolescent fathers, involved in problematic relationships, are often purposely not identified by the mothers of their children (Hardy, Duggan, Masnyk, and Pearson, 1989).

Methodological problems have also added to our lack of understanding of adolescent fatherhood (Robinson, 1988b). Use of indirect methods of study (asking the mothers about their natal partners) leaves us vulnerable to accepting the perspective of adolescent mothers, who often have relationship problems with the adolescent fathers in question. Similarly, asking adults who were adolescent fathers to recollect their experiences may rely too much on perspectives that have subsequently been affected by unrelated influences. Even the term *adolescent father* has not always been well defined, with some researchers

applying it to men in their mid- and late twenties, who impregnate adolescent natal partners.

Studies that that combine subjects from different ethnic groups often do a poor job of analyzing the potential contribution of ethnicity in observed differences among subjects. For example, although many studies report higher levels of paternity among African-American adolescent males, relatively little analysis has been done on the influence that ethnicity may have played in these adolescents' (and their natal partners') child-bearing decisions or subsequent parenting behavior. There is good evidence that ethnic differences in adolescent fathers' preferences regarding pregnancy resolution (Marsiglio, 1989; Redmond, 1985) are important factors in differential rates of pregnancy termination among ethnic groups (Zelnik, Kantner, and Ford, 1981). As African-American adolescent males are much more likely than their European-American peers to encourage their partners to continue pregnancies to term, they are disproportionately more likely to become adolescent fathers. However, this increased likelihood is lost when ethnicity is simply reduced to being a "risk factor" associated with adolescent fatherhood.

Ethnicity is a poor predictor of risk for adolescent fatherhood if stripped of its sociopolitical and socioeconomic contexts (Howell and Frese, 1982; Taborn, 1988). It is likely that peer attitudes towards sexuality, family structure and history regarding early child-rearing, and ethnocultural socialization interact to promote adolescent fatherhood as a salient option for some African-American youth (Christmon, 1990b; Hogan and Kitagawa, 1985). Closer examination of these interactions clarifies our understanding of ethnic differences in adolescent decision making regarding paternity and paternal involvement (Parke and Neville, 1987; Sullivan, 1986).

A major influence on adolescent paternal involvement is access to (and success in) the world of employment (Redmond, 1985). Adolescent fathers who have jobs have been found to be more involved in their children's lives than those without steady employment or who are chronically unemployed (Danziger and Radin, 1990). This supports the work of Wilson (1987) and others that point to restricted employment opportunity as a chronic source of frustration to African-American males across generational and socioeconomic lines. African-American men appear particularly vulnerable to role strain and familial relationship problems resulting from unemployment and under-employment (Bowman, 1992; Hamilton, Broman, Hoffman, and Renner, 1990). As providing for the economic and material needs of their families is a significant part of the role of fathers (Comer, 1989; McAdoo, 1993; Taylor, Leashore, and Toliver, 1988), the historical lack of employment opportunities for African-American adolescent males is potentially devastating to their attempts at fulfilling paternal responsibilities (Elster and Panzarine, 1983; Marsiglio, 1989).

Through their paternal performance, adolescent fathers have both direct and indirect influences on their children (Furstenberg, 1976; Lamb and Elster, 1985; Rivara, Sweeney, and Henderson, 1986; Vaz, Smolen, and Miller, 1983). Examples of direct influence include providing food, clothing and disposable diapers for the children. Indirect influence is demonstrated by adolescent fathers' emotional and economic support of their natal partners (Klinman, Sander, Rosen, and Longo, 1986; Robinson and Barret, 1986). Such support can help the mothers cope more effectively with parenting demands, and thus indirectly influence their children.

Although many adolescent fathers do not live with either their natal partners or their children, this does not preclude the possibility of their having a positive influence on both (Kahn and Bolton, 1986; Furstenberg, 1976; Mott, 1990). Most of these adolescents maintain some level of paternal involvement (Rivara, Sweeney, and Henderson, 1986), though there is evidence that the level of such involvement decreases over time, particularly in the absence of marriage or coresidence (Furstenberg, Brooks-Gunn, and Morgan, 1987).

Remarkably little empirical attention has focused on adolescent fathers' perceptions of fatherhood, even though these may be primary influences on their paternal performance (Westney, Cole, and Munford, 1986). Several researchers have approached the subject by posing questions such as "How do you feel about becoming a father out-of-wedlock?" or "Do you think that this pregnancy will affect your life?" (e.g., Hendricks and Montgomery, 1983.) There have also been attempts to determine the relationship between the adolescent father's self-image and his willingness to assume paternal responsibilities (Hendricks and Montgomery, 1983; Robinson and Barret, 1987). Adolescents with good self-images (defined as a well-developed sense of himself and his potential in his environment) are thought to be better prepared to manage developmental tasks more typical of early adulthood, such as early fatherhood (Christmon, 1990a). Still, these young men may be caught in a developmental dilemma. As one theorist indicates, "the cognitive and emotional capacities most essential to empathic, mature parenting are likely to be those least available to adolescent boys still engaged in struggles around separation from their own parents." (Applegate, 1988).

METHODOLOGY

The Sample

Ten African-American, adolescent males from a Midwestern, urban center (Minneapolis-St Paul, Minnesota) were recruited from social services agencies to participate in this study. The investigator chose to use a qualitative approach of in-depth interviews for several reasons. It was thought that some of these young men's abilities to express themselves through conversation, might surpass either their reading or writing skills. Interviews could potentially retrieve more of the nuances of the young fathers' lives than standardized questionnaires or surveys. This qualitative approach would also facilitate the inclusion of unexpected material that emerged during the course of each interview (Rosenblatt and Fischer, 1993).

The decision to limit the sample to African-American adolescent fathers reflected the investigator's intention to avoid several methodological problems plaguing research on African-Americans. As discussed elsewhere, some of this research reflects ethnocentric biases in both research design and interpretation of results (McKenry, Everett, Ramseur, and Carter, 1989; Wilkinson, 1987). Being African-American himself, the principal investigator hoped to limit the effects of such bias, although it is was clear that this alone could not guarantee accuracy in recording, interpreting, or presenting the experiences of the participants. Moreover, as the sample size was small (n=10), meaningful comparisons between ethnic groups would have been inadvisable.

In a broader sense, exploring adolescent fatherhood with an African-American sample provided the potential for mutual benefit as a result of the research process (Boss, 1987.) While increasing the understanding of the experience of adolescent fatherhood, the participants might enhance their understanding of their paternal aspirations by discussing these ideals explicitly (Dilworth-Anderson and McAdoo, 1988.)

For the purposes of this study, an *adolescent father* was defined as a male, biological parent between the ages of fifteen and nineteen. The terms *father, mother,* and *child,* refer to the participant, his natal partner, and their child respectively. In an attempt to obtain a sample group whose paternal experiences would be roughly comparable, an effort was made to find participants whose children had been born within two years of the interview. In the case of fathers who had more than one child, the participant was asked to identify one "focal child." Questions exploring paternal involvement and responsibility referred to this child.

The non-random, snowball sample was solicited from community and school based programs for adolescent fathers. (Programs catering to adolescent mothers were also contacted for potential referrals to fathers). Participating organizations were also asked for their critique of the project, including their advice on how to maximize the amount of information gained during the interviews. Some organizations (such as schools) allowed a poster describing the project to be displayed on their premises. Staff in other organizations suggested adolescent fathers in their client base, who they believed might be willing to participate in the study. Prospective participants were then either provided with the investigator's name and telephone number, or if it was their preference, contacted by the investigator.

The Interviews

An interview script was developed to guide the in-depth interviews. After conducting a small pilot with two fathers (who were not included in the study), a preliminary interview script was refined into a three part questionnaire used in the formal study. The first section gathered demographic data on the participants, their natal partners, and their children. The second section explored the adolescent father's relationship with his child. Participants were asked to describe their feelings toward their child, and to report specific behaviors engaged in while with their children. The third section focused on each participant's perception of what fatherhood meant to him.

In this last section, the young men defined fatherhood in their own words. They discussed their views on the importance of fathers to families (if any), and described their opinions of what made someone a "good" father. The young fathers were encouraged to discuss their experiences with their own fathers and whether these matched their current ideals of fatherhood. They were also asked to evaluate themselves as they imagined others might eventually evaluate their paternal performance (e.g., "Based on what you're doing now, when your child gets to be your age, how might he (she) rate you as a dad?)." The interview concluded with the participants being given an opportunity to identify any aspects of paternal experiences that had not previously been discussed.

If a young father agreed to participate in the study, a mutually acceptable time and location for the interview was determined. The locations were selected to be convenient to the participants and to protect their confidentiality. Ironically, food concession areas of shopping malls at off-peak hours and quiet rooms in libraries turned out to be good sites. Each interview was a one-on-one dialogue between the investigator and the participant.

After introductions, the interviewer and participant searched together for a suitable space for the interview. This cooperative task provided an opportunity to establish some rapport with each other before commencing the formal interview. During the first 15 minutes of each interview, the interviewer reviewed the basic reasons for doing the study and sought the participant's written consent. Next, the interviewer progressed through the three-part questionnaire with each participant. The interviews typically took two to three hours, although one lasted over five hours. Following the interviews, each participant received a small, cash honorarium ($10.00) expressing appreciation for his willingness to participate in the study.

The Analysis

Each session was audiotaped to insure an accurate record of the participant's responses. During the interviews, the investigator also noted various "non-verbal" cues (such as body language and facial expressions). These notations were added to a set of summary notes compiled after each interview and designed to facilitate interpretation of the audiotapes. The summary notes also included the interviewer's subjective impressions and "gut" reactions to the participant's responses during the session. The summary notes and transcripts of the audiotapes were used to develop a descriptive log for each interview.

A predominant theme or set of themes was identified for each interview log. In some cases, several iterations through a log was necessary to distill the essence of the participant's perception of fatherhood. This process generated several quotes that characterized the sentiments of these young fathers and form the basis of the Results section. Through the quotes, readers may experience the wonder, pride, frustration, and bewilderment that the participants conveyed during the interviews.

After the completion of all ten interviews, the interview logs were compared to determine if any common themes between the participants' narratives emerged. A particular area of interest was understanding possible explanations for the divergence between the participants' perceptions of fatherhood and self-reports of paternal performance. Tables summarizing various demographic, evaluative, and subjective information from the group were developed. These helped us to identify common trends among the young fathers and provided a basis for discussion of the differences among them.

RESULTS

The major findings of this exploratory study emerged from the empirical process rather than from *a priori* hypotheses. Before presenting the group's subjective perceptions of fatherhood, several objective data will be summarized. Table 1 shows demographic data on the participants, their partners, and their children. The young fathers in this study ranged in age from fifteen to nineteen ($x = 16$–$1/2$). The ages of the mothers were typically similar to the participants' ages at the time of the child's birth, though in a few cases the father was 2–3 years older. The children ranged in age from six weeks to just under three years. Most of the fathers in this group had a single child. In the case of the three participants who had more than one child, the focal child tended to be the oldest. All but one of the adolescents were pursuing either a high school diploma or G.E.D. (if still in school), or entering the job market at entry level positions in blue-collar trades or the service

TABLE 1 Summary Demographics

Subject	Subject's age	Partner's age	Number of children	Focal child's age
MM	17	17	1	14 mos.
ET	17	17	1*	2 mos.
GK	18	19	1	12 mos.
TE	18	17	1	16 mos.
DC	19	17	1	30 mos.
BM	19	16–18	3	24 mos.
RJ	19	19	2	36 mos.
FQ	19	18	1	5 mos.
DJ	16	14–17	4	12 mos.
JJ	15	18	1	2 mos.

*(ET claimed that there was a child in another state that he thought of as his own, even though it was not his biological offspring.)

industries. They reported jobs paying from $200.00 to over $800.00 per month. One father reported receiving public assistance. In general, this group did not appear to be economically stressed and did not indicate that lack of money was their primary concern.

Table 2 summarizes the participants' appraisal of two key relationships: 1) their relationship with their natal partner, and 2) their relationship with the focal child. Each young father was asked to use a Likert scale (1-Not very close, 2-Close, and 3-Very close) to characterize the quality of the two relationships. The young fathers in this sample appeared to have had long-standing relationships with the mothers of their children. All participants indicated that they had been dating the mothers for at least one year prior to the pregnancy, and some had known the mothers for three or more years. Still, the post-delivery relationships for most of the participants may have become less cordial. Half of them rated their relationships with their child higher (or closer) than the relationships with the mothers. Most participants initially described themselves as being on "good terms" with the mothers, but later elaborated more complex and often problematic relationships. None of the adolescent fathers in the study were married, and only three indicated that they believed marriage to the mother was a possibility in the future.

Table 2 also summarizes the participants' living arrangements and a measure of paternal involvement. Two fathers lived together with the mothers and children (one in his parents' household, the other independently). The remainder lived with their own mothers or members of their extended families. In order to summarize the participants' responses on paternal involvement, three categories were created for Time Spent with Child: Every day, Every other day, and Once a week. Three fathers indicated that they spent an hour or more with their children "every day." Five fathers said they saw their child "every other day" on average. The remaining two saw their children infrequently, typically on a weekly basis. It is important to note that for many participants, there were occasional periods during which they did not see their child for more than a week or more. These lapses appeared to coincide with relationship difficulties between the participant and the mother. It is also significant that only one *nonresidential* adolescent father saw his child every day.

The participants used the time spent with their children in a variety of ways. The reported activities included playing indoors or outside,

TABLE 2   Involvement with Partners and Children

Subject	Relationship with partner	Living with partner	Relationship with child	Time spent with child
MM	2	No	3	Every Other Day
ET	1	No	2	Every Other Day
GK	1	No	3	Every Other Day
TE	1	No	2	Once/week
DC	3	No	2	Every Other Day
BM	2	No	3	Every Day
RJ	3	Yes	2	Every Day
FQ	1	No	2	Once/week
DJ	3	No	2	Every Other Day
JJ	3	Yes	3	Every Day

Rating system: 1 = "Not very close"
                2 = "Close"
                3 = "Very close"

watching TV, going to the park or for walks, reading to the children, eating together, fishing and swimming. In addition to such recreational activities, some of the participants spoke of routine child-care tasks such as feeding, bathing, and putting their children down for daytime naps or to sleep at night. When asked if they were specifically responsible for child care duties, the fathers' responses ranged from "no" to "I do everything that she (the mother) does."

Some of the young men expressed confidence in their ability to care for their children on their own for extended periods. Others seemed to suggest that their child-care responsibilities were contingent on what the mothers were willing to let them do. In other words, they would be *willing* to do anything that the mothers did, but were presently not providing much in the way of comprehensive child care beyond occasional baby-sitting. Several fathers indicated that they gave portions of their salaries to the mothers to provide for the material needs of their children. However, it was in the role of emotional support that they saw themselves as most effective.

Table 3 provides a summary of the four ratings of fatherhood that each father was asked to

do. In this set of ratings, participants were asked to use a ten-point Likert scale ranging from "0" for "Terrible" to "10" for "Excellent." If the participant felt unable or unwilling to do a rating, a "–" was recorded. Participants were first asked to rate their own fathers and then to rate themselves in the paternal role. The first of these ratings helped the interviewer to explore each participant's experience with his own father. The next three were designed to allow the participants to evaluate themselves as fathers, and to speculate on how others might view them. These ratings taken together formed a subject-defined measure of their paternal performance.

Major Themes

In the search for common themes in the participants' responses, comparisons of two key items in the questionnaire proved helpful. Table 4 contains one sentence paraphrases of the participants' responses to the question: "What does being a father mean to you?" This question typically came at the midpoint during the interviews, after we had discussed the young men's lives, their relationships with their partners, and their feelings toward and interaction with their children. This

TABLE 3 Ratings of Fatherhood

Subject	Rate your father	Rate yourself	Partner's rating of you	Child's rating of you
MM	—	5	—	10
ET	8	7	6	7
GK	5	10	8	10
TE	10	7	7	—
DC	0	9	8	9
BM	10	10	8	8
RJ	2	9	9	9
FQ	0	7	7	9
DJ	—	—	10	10
JJ	5	7	5	7

Rating system: 0 = "Terrible"
                 10 = "Excellent"
                 — = "Can't or don't want to rate"

response was the adolescent's first formal opportunity to subjectively express his perception of fatherhood. The most common themes to emerge from this question were responsibility, love, caring for others, and being a provider.

Table 5 shows the responses to a restatement of this central question: "What makes someone a good father?" This phrasing allowed participants to take a more objective stance in answering the question. In most cases, the young men used the opportunity to amplify their responses to the earlier question, "What does being a father mean to you?" Although responsibility and involvement with children were among the two most cited attributes, the phrase that seemed to best embody this group's perceptions about what made someone a good father was "being there."

To this group of adolescent fathers, the phrase "being there" seemed to crystallize the perception of fatherhood. They typically used this phrase in one of two related contexts: 1) paternal involvement and 2) presence at their child's birth.

The first context of the phrase "being there" referred to the participant's being physically and emotionally present in the lives of their children. In response to the question what made someone a good father, GK responded:

Being there, caring, responsibilities again. There's a lot of things you can say about how to be a good father. The most important thing? . . . being there, I would say. Being there as a father figure.

In a similar vein, FQ said,

I think the most important thing is to be there for my daughter. I need to give her love and understanding. A father is the one who make[s] you smile. Being a father means being there for everything.

The stories the young men offered as proof that they were "there" for their children were specific and often touching. When asked to describe what his son typically did when he saw his father, MM said,

When he sees me, he'll do his little thing. Like he'll smile or act like he don't see me. But if say "OK, I'm leavin' now," then he'll look back and open his arms and start runnin' to me. And when he was little, he'd always, like you know, his eyes would light up, *his whole face* would light up. He doesn't even do that when his mom picks him up.

TABLE 4 What does being a father mean to you?

Father	Response
MM	A boost in self-esteem, makes me feel proud.
ET	Makes me happy. It's a blessing from God.
GK	Responsibility, love.
TE	Being there for your kid.
DC	Responsibility and being there.
BM	Taking care of responsibilities.
RJ	Responsibility, taking care of my kids.
EQ	Being a provider. Loving and understanding.
DJ	Knowing yourself. Being connected with your child.
JJ	Taking care of somebody, responsibilities.

TABLE 5 What makes someone a good father?

Father	Response
MM	Maturity and family focus (versus individual).
ET	Being there, responsibility.
GK	Being there, caring, responsibility.
TE	Shouldering your responsibility.
DC	Being there with your kid.
BM	Spending time with your children.
RJ	Being with your family, being there for your kids.
EQ	Being there for everything.
DJ	Understanding, knowledge of yourself.
JJ	Be around and show them that you love them.

Similarly, the youngest father, JJ, recalled meeting his child for the first time:

> I didn't want to be there; I don't like blood . . . I went to the hospital from a basketball game. My cousin and his girl-friend came over and said "Your son has been born!" I said, "Oh, God!" . . . [but then] I held him, and I could tell right then I was gonna like him.

Later, JJ discussed his aspirations for the future and how having a child would affect them:

> I want to be in professional sports (a basketball player) or a lawyer. If I could do it

over, I would not be a father right now, but he's here and I'm glad he's here. Even though he's just a little baby, when he hears my voice he'll look around, and he grabs my finger.

> [What if you had to chose between him and a career?]

> Oh . . . [Thinks for a second] I think I'd choose him. Right now, I'd choose him over anything.

The second context in which these young fathers used the phrase "being there" referred to being present at the birth of their children. Some of them spoke of their participation in the delivery process. The fathers who witnessed the births echoed FQ:

> I just think that a father should be in there, to go through the experience, you know, to see what the mother goes through. And really, when you're in the operating room or the birthing room, that really starts it all. It's like you see your son or daughter come out and you're there, and that's where everything starts.

And according to DC:

> I just about faded when I saw that. That was a weird experience! It's hard to tell what you feel when you're inside that room. It was like movies at school, but being there is something else.

[Do you think it made a difference, your being with the mother?]

> Yeah, I'm sure it did. Instead of her going through it by herself holding nobody's hand, you know, she had me there.

One of the reasons the phrase "being there" may have been so significant was the diminished ability of participants to consistently provide for the material needs of their children. Eight of the ten young men interviewed were working and had money enough to contribute to their partners and the children. However, the amount and predictability of these financial resources were typically low. Since most participants did not live with their children, their opportunities to interact with the children were also limited. Therefore, the time they spent with their children took on great symbolic significance.

In addition to "being there," a second common theme that emerged was that of responsibility. Several of the young fathers in the study cited responsibility as the most significant aspect of their perception of fatherhood, as in this quote from RJ:

> Responsibility. There's a lot of responsibility with two kids. I remember going to

temporary agencies, just tryin' to get diapers for [child]. My neighbors ask me if we want to go out to the bar, but they know we can't afford to go most of the time.

In a similar vein, GK spoke about how the multitude of responsibilities was often his biggest concern:

> All the responsibilities, I would say. I didn't think there was this much responsibilities. I mean, there's *hundreds* of 'em! Some weeks I plan for me and [child] to do somethin' the whole week and it's like, and I didn't know in between he was going to wet his clothes, and now I gotta change him, and I gotta do this, and I gotta take him to the doctor.

Most of the fathers were very specific about the behaviors and level of involvement that demonstrated their sense of paternal responsibility. Their responses to questions such as "How much time do you spend with your child?" and "What do you and your child do together?" appeared to corroborate their claims of involvement. Two fathers were comparatively vague about what they actually did to live up to their definitions of good fatherhood. In response to an inquiry about the kind and frequency of his child-care responsibilities, one father began

> I want to be there whenever she need somethin'; if she drop a toy or somethin, I make sure I'll pick it up and give it back to her.

[How much time do you spend with your daughter?]
As much as my schedule permits, [but] when I bring her to my house, it's always overnight. [How often is that?]

> Well. very rarely . . . her grandmother knows I'm OK but she also knows the type of people I hang out with. So when I ask to take the baby, they want to know, "Where you takin' her?" So, I stay away as much as I can. I don't want to intrude on their comfort.

[When last were you able to take her overnight?]

(Silence.)

This apparent contradiction between this participant's intentions and his actual paternal behavior is not unique to adolescent fathers (see the discussion of the asynchrony between the culture and conduct of fatherhood in LaRossa, 1988). Part of the problem in this instance could have been the lack of clarity in the term "child care." For the purposes of this study, child care was defined as assuming a primary role in attending to the physical (and emotional) needs of the child. However, some of the fathers initially equated the term with financial support, as in "child support."

Notwithstanding such inevitable misunderstandings, it is accurate to say that most of these adolescents perceived themselves as significantly involved in the lives of their children. Many of the adolescent fathers in this study were pushing the mothers for even more time with their children, and responsibility for the children's upbringing. Typical of the strong sense of responsibility expressed by these young fathers, was this statement by MM:

> My mom and my grandmother raised me. My dad? All I know is that his name was—, and when I was about [child's] age he left my mom. So, my mindset is that I want to be everything that he wasn't to me. Meanin' I want to be *something* to my son. I want to be a [cherished] memory, I don't want to be like just a name. My mom was talkin' about finding my dad, and I was like "Well, go ahead. I don't care." I don't want to be like that with [child]. I want to be part of his life. I want him to say, "My dad is right there." I want to take him to ball games, I want to keep him strong, I want to *be* his life.

This response was typical of the adolescent fathers in this group. Many of them proudly quoted birth statistics and could be very specific about their children's current developmental progress in areas such as walking, talking, or toilet-training. All but one of the participants predicted being involved to some extent in the lives of their children in the future. Some even thought they would continue to be involved in relationships with the mothers, although most did not see the relationships evolving into marriage. Their primary sense of responsibility was to their children as opposed the children's mothers.

The adolescent fathers in this study seemed convinced that fathers were important to families. When asked why, many of the participants' responses were similar to RJ:

> Yes, I think fathers are important. Like, my mom was a single parent, and I saw what she went through. She taught me a lot of responsibility, but she could really have used some help. I think they [fathers] can help the mom and the family

Several of the participants felt that it was particularly important that male children have their father's involvement. As GK explained,

> I think fathers are important, especially for boys. Every child needs a role model; boys need fathers as a role model.

In their assessment of the importance of fathers, the group did not appear to be expressing negative evaluations of mothers. Most participants made it clear that they felt their own mothers had made heroic efforts to raise them. A few were also complimentary about their natal partners abilities as parents. The role they felt fathers played was one of augmenting rather than competing with or replacing mothers.

OBSTACLES TO BEING FATHERS

Relationships with Partners

Three categories of problems hindered this group of adolescent fathers attempts at involvement with their children. The most formidable of these was the relationship between the participant and his partner. The majority of the fathers initially described themselves as being on "good terms" with their natal partners. However, during the course of the interviews it became clear that most of them were also having problems managing their dual roles of partners and fathers. For some, there was a sense of confusion and conflict between adolescent perspectives on dating and adult perspectives on committed relationships and parenting. The problem could be summarized in one participant's question, "Am I my girlfriend's 'man' or my baby's father?" According to DJ:

It's one thing to be a boyfriend, another to be a father. Well, let me put it like this. Being a father takes you away from being a boyfriend. You have to deal with the baby and the mom. Being a boyfriend, it's just the mom.

[Could you give me an example of why that's a problem?]

Being a father, mom has a male friend over, he picks up the baby, I want him to put my baby down. Then [the mother] want to fight over who controls the baby.

Many of these relationship problems were rooted in the divergent socialization of females and males. The participants and their partners often held different and often irreconcilable perspectives on basic issues such as intimacy, trust, and approaches to childrearing. Lacking the skills to reconcile these perspectives, the participants found themselves in what seemed "unwinable" positions. If they stayed in the relationships, they faced further problems with their partners and limited access to their children. However, if they left, they faced condemnation for "taking advantage" of their partners and abandoning their children.

These relationship problems were not solely the result of conflict in gender socialization. The root problem seemed to be the stability and maturity of the relationships themselves. Though many of the fathers had been involved in long-term relationships with their children's mothers at the time of the births, the pregnancies tended to complicate the relationship dynamics. There

were now additional sources of potential disagreement and conflict for the couple. Often, these conflicts appeared as struggles for control of the children. DJ, the father quoted above, continued

Just say she gets mad at me and says, "You can't see your child." I say "I don't even want to see you no more," and then if I don't see her, I don't see my baby. And then so I say it's best that we stay away from being obligated to each other.

In another example, DC discussed how these difficulties directly affected his paternal aspirations (e.g., his desire to be involved with his son):

Well, like when me and [partner] weren't fond of each other, it kept me and my son apart. She would always [say] "I don't want to see you today," or I would want to see my son, and me and her were fightin' I would say "Well, I'm comin' over" . . . and she say "No, you don't," and leave. And I would come over there and she'd be gone.

So she was makin' me madder and madder, 'til I really got sick of it and I never came around for a long time. And then she was like, "Dang! . . . ," I mean, she knew that [child] needed a dad so she wised up and she started lettin' me get closer to him.

This particular young man, when asked how he learned about being a father, reported how he deliberately sought and found jobs in the school nursery and later at a home daycare center in order to learn how to be "good at taking care of babies." It was hard to believe that he would have gone to such lengths in the absence of a sincere desire to prepare himself for effective fatherhood. Yet, he came to see the mother (or more accurately, the relationship with the mother) as an obstacle to his paternal involvement, particularly when their relationship was strained. This situation was typically aggravated by the participant's lack of relationship management skills. As adolescents, many of them had relatively little experience practicing trust, communication, and mutual respect in the context of intimate relationships, much less to do this effectively within the crucible of early parenting.

Problems with the Natal Partner's Family

The mother's extended family could also present an obstacle to the participants' paternal aspirations. In some cases, the young man was regarded positively by the partner's family until the announcement of pregnancy. From that point on, his relationship with his partner's family seemed to become increasingly strained, hitting a low point at or around the time of delivery. More than one young father described the experience of attempting to support his natal partner on one side of the delivery table, while the partner's mother cursed at him from the opposite side. GK provided one of the most dramatic examples of this type of conflict. When asked how he got along with his partner's family, he hesitated before replying:

> Umm . . . I would say . . . I don't know . . . because, well . . . when she was pregnant, everything was going along fine until about the sixth month. Then they didn't want to have anything to do with me. It was like. on Easter me and a friend went over to her house and her brothers actually shot at us! And that stopped me from going over for about two months. Went back again and that time her dad threatened to kill me if I didn't get out of his yard, and all this . . . It's been . . . It's been like *hell* . . .

The problem could extend to friends and acquaintances of the mother (and to the participant's own family and friends). Friends who initially seemed supportive of the young couple, later were perceived to be conspiring to destroy the couple's mutual sense of trust and commitment. RJ discussed how he and his partner handled this obstacle:

> Oh, we were havin' problems even before I found out she was pregnant[. . .] Trust is

still a big issue for us. She don't have friends and I don't have friends 'cause we don't trust each other. I can trust her, but I don't trust her around her friends. She don't trust none of my friends, either. So, we have an agreement just to hang together.

Problems with Social Institutions

For some of the participants, the hospital or clinic where their baby was born was their first experience with social institutions that would play increasingly larger roles in their lives as fathers. It was heartening to hear that some participants were welcomed by the hospital staff. (Two spoke with pride of participating in the deliveries by cutting the umbilical cords of their children.) However, other institutions were not as accommodating.

Some participants felt that society generally operated in a way that hindered their attempts to be good fathers. For example, they spoke of their frustration with a family court system that demonstrated what they perceived to be bias (toward mothers) in adjudicating child custodial issues. As one participant put it, "the system is stacked against the father" (a sentiment probably shared by many older fathers in similar circumstances). In spite of these institutional obstacles, participants were willing to take extraordinary measures to care for their children, as this incident was from GK's early parenting experience shows:

> My son was 7 months old and he had a bite mark on his face. I asked [partner] who did it, she said she didn't know. I asked her did she take him [to the emergency room], 'cause at the time she was staying at a place where cats and dogs was, and I figured, Well, if a dog or somethin' bit him, he should go in for shots.
>
> So I take him to the hospital. They look at him and they document it and they tell me, "Well, maybe you oughta take him to St. Joe's [foster home agency] and let them do some documents." Well, I made it to

St. Joe's, they told me give 'em [child] and I can go. And I'm thinkin', I'm bringin' my son here, I want to know what's goin' on. They tell me, "We can't."

When I call up there or when I went back there, they tell me I can't even see my son. They took him and told me, "Even though you're the father we can't tell you nothing. We have to notify the mother, let her know her son is here, let her know who brought him." Even though I'm the one who brought him.

Later, when I asked the county about the report concerning the bite marks, they told me, "We can't tell you anything; that information is confidential."

[After a pause, with a perplexed look on his face] . . . I'm the one who made the report . . .

"Myths and Realities": Larger Social Issues That Become Obstacles

Earlier in this paper, we cited the social stigma attending adolescent fatherhood as a possible explanation for why they are such a difficult group to research. The young men in this group also spoke of negative stereotypes and images as hindering their development of positive self-identities as fathers. GK stated his paternal aspirations, definitively:

I don't want my son growin' up like I did. There's a lot of kids who don't have fathers, or if they do have fathers they're in jail or on drugs or not working or don't care about anything else . . . so what [if] they're a father.

If you look at it, there's probably more dads out there that's not doin' what they should be doin' for their children, than there is dads doin' everything they can.

GK went on to articulate a sentiment shared by most of the participants in stating his resolve that his son "see that his dad was not what he sees in society." The author believes that this was a reference to stereotypical images that depict African-American men as athletes, entertainers,

and criminals, but seldom as managers, owners, and lawmakers. Even less seldom did the participants see themselves (or African-American adult males) depicted in family settings. The result was a social reproduction of these negative images and the biases behind the images. Thus, the images became another institutional barrier to the participants' paternal aspirations.

Taken together, the obstacles to paternal involvement may over time have become incentives for the participants to move away from their children (and natal partners). When I asked GK to speculate on why there were young fathers who were "not doing what they should be doing," he replied,

They go out and they do the same thing again. They go out and they have another baby thinking it's gonna be joy and "Well, you know, I'm going to have a son, and he's gonna be just like me, grow up to look just like me . . ." And that girl or that woman does the same thing his previous relationship did, so that throws him to do the same thing he did before. You know, "Well, I'm tired of going through it; just [dump her]," and go out and do the same thing. Then you got three babies, four babies, five babies, six babies, and its on. Until maybe one day, he finally find someone who'll settle down, get married, have children, live a life.

This scenario was a chilling illustration of the potential consequences relationship problems outlined earlier. It was possible that some of the participants with more than one child had experienced this same chain of events. In particular, it brought to mind DJ, who in describing his intimate relationships articulated certain "ground rules":

I establish that with basically any females that I have a child with. I tell 'em we can't be together. They say, "Well why not? How're we gonna be a family?" I tell them we can be a family, "I can be a father to my child, regardless, and a friend to you but that's no more, no less." Then they say, "But why?" and I say, "Because, the logistics, I mean, where the—the practicality—the formality of our relationship is us bein' a couple."

We argue, we fight. Then they say, "I hate you, I don't want to see you no more." I say "I don't want to see you no more either." And then we still have this little baby, right here that needs both of us . . .

The reasons some young, unmarried adolescent males impregnate more than once is a topic that demands more in-depth research (and is beyond the scope of this paper). However, the similarity between GK's speculations about young men who father more than one baby and DJ's experiences with intimate relationships is tragically compelling.

Some of these adolescents may have engaged in unprotected, sexual intercourse as part of a larger strategy to find validation and acceptance, in addition to love and nurturing. Unlike peers who contracept, however, these young men impregnated their partners and unintentionally became fathers. Most were slow to realize the profound consequences of early pregnancy for themselves, their partners, and eventually, for their children. Usually, these consequences dawned on them during the weeks and months following the exhilaration after the birth of their children. Almost immediately, these participants saw their lives as fundamentally changed. However, some fathers (like DJ) may not have fully appreciated these consequences until after several children have been born.

DISCUSSION

This study arose in part out of curiosity about the interpretations that adolescent fathers drew from their paternal experiences. Most professional observers would expect that the enormous responsibilities of parenthood, coupled with the truncation of normative adolescent development would make adolescent fatherhood problematic. However, the investigator attempted to balance skepticism regarding the life prospects for the participant's and their families with an openness to their responses in order to avoid inadvertently injecting personal bias into the results (Miller, 1993).

The exploratory nature of this study and particularly its small sample size limit the ability to generalize the results of this study to all adolescent fathers. The study's exclusive focus on African-Americans also limits confidence that young fathers of other ethnic groups have experiences similar to those described here. The cross-sectional nature of our design leaves it vulnerable to the charge that the findings presented here are at best, only a brief snapshot of the participant's paternal experiences. This is particularly applicable to the findings on paternal involvement which if studied longitudinally, may have produced quite a different picture. Clearly, more research is needed to verify what happens to adolescent fathers as they struggle to overcome the obstacles to their paternal aspirations.

From a family systems perspective, the study's findings lack the perspective of the significant others in the young men's ecology. It would have been interesting to hear from the mothers about their perceptions of the pre- and postnatal relationship, as well as their evaluation of the participants as fathers. Similarly, watching the young fathers actually interacting with their children would have provided powerful corroborating evidence of their claims of paternal involvement. Finally, the adolescent fathers who chose to participate in this study may represent a self-selected subset of the population. Little is known of the experience and behavioral motivation of adolescent fathers who choose not to be involved with their children. Unless their perceptions can also be ascertained, discussion of this study's findings would best be limited to adolescent fathers who choose to be involved with their children.

It is hoped that this study will add to the knowledge of adolescent fathers by revealing subjective aspects of their experience. A cursory reading of the sparse literature on adolescent fathers provides little detail of their lives or rationale for their paternal aspirations. The use of in-depth interviews in this study facilitated a deeper, more nuanced understanding of the paternal experiences of this group of young fathers. Their responses demonstrated a more intimate understanding of parental challenges than their age, or co-residential status alone would suggest. The findings also provide insights into the obstacles these adolescents perceive to their involvement with their children. This should be useful to other researchers and to clinicians interested in working with adolescent fathers and their families.

A primary influence on the young fathers in this study was their ethnocultural socialization regarding the appropriate role of males in family life. Several researchers have discussed the significance of responsibility in African-American men's conceptualization of fatherhood and masculinity. A more subtle example of ethnocultural socialization was the group's consensus that they were doing better as fathers than other fathers they knew. This finding has also been documented in studies of African-American adult fathers. That responsibility and "being there" emerged from the participants in this study, might appear paradoxical in light of the fact that some of them did not have fathers in the households they grew up in. There were also divergences in the paternal aspirations of some of the participants and their actual paternal involvement. Moreover, the empirical evidence suggests less involvement by most adolescent fathers over time. This would appear to call into question the true nature of African-American values regarding fatherhood.

One conclusion that could be drawn from all of this is that African-Americans (and these adolescents in particular) do not value fatherhood or family as highly as their counterparts in other ethnic groups. This unfortunate misapprehension drives much of the negative imagery regarding African-American adolescent fathers. A more compelling hypothesis is that the conflict between strong convictions about responsibility

to family and weak ability to fulfill those responsibilities, drives African-American adolescent fathers out of relationships and away from their children. Aggravating these macro-level forces, conflicts over level of involvement and consistency of involvement appeared to manifest themselves as relationship problems between our participants and their natal partners. It was difficult to determine whether these "involvement" conflicts were the cause or the result of the couple's relationship problems.

The divergence in paternal aspirations and paternal involvement is more probably related to (and the result of) the obstacles adolescent fathers encounter early in their parenting experiences. The fact that in spite of these obstacles, some of them continue to espouse high paternal aspirations may illustrate the persistence of such aspirations as cultural ideals in the African-American community. For example, recall GK's comment paternal responsibility: ". . . there's probably more dads out there that's not doin' what they should be doin' for their children." GK held the value that fathers should be responsible for their children, but he felt he was not able to live with his own child due to relationship problems with his natal partner and her family. However, he clearly stated that his preference would have been to be living with the mother and child. Thus, the fact that he *was not* living with them did not preclude his embracing the value that he *should be* living with his "procreated" family.

IMPLICATIONS

When the participants spoke of overcoming the obstacles to "being there," one could hear their frustration, but also a sense of determination to overcome these obstacles. Their responses to the question "What does being a father mean to you?" were filled with confidence about their future, rather than doubts about the past. Most participants described the experience of becoming fathers as having changed them in some inexplicably positive way. When asked how being a father made him feel, MM said,

> It kind o' gives you, it's a . . . it's an un-explainable feeling. Like when I was in the delivery room and he came, an he was there, you know, and he looked at me . . . it was like, you're in awe. That's the best way I can say it, you're in awe! You're like, wow! He looks at you and, and your body like tingles . . . it's almost like catching the Holy Ghost or something!

This level of exuberance in at least some African-American, adolescent fathers should be cause for optimism when considering social support for adolescent fathers, and their families. If harnessed, it could provide fuel for motivating young fathers to become and stay involved with their children. It could also motivate them to acquire the relationship skills necessary for improving their relationships with their natal partners, or at least, to facilitate more effective co-parenting with the mothers. Ideally, the adolescent's family-of-origin would provide the laboratory in which to learn and practice these skills. However, lacking this, training in these family life essentials could be part of comprehensive service offerings to young fathers.

Assessment of the adolescent father's parenting skills and interpersonal relationships are important prerequisites to developing effective support services. Agencies should use multiple strategies to recruit and work with adolescent fathers. These strategies include finding clients wherever they are (e.g., "on the court") and bringing services directly to them if necessary (e.g., making home visits). An innovative approach used by a local agency was to provide dinner during group meetings as an incentive for attendance. Use of peer advisors as group leaders also promotes credibility and opportunities for service to the community. The importance of involving African-American adult men in such program development and delivery also cannot be overemphasized (Battle, 1988). The benefits to such participation accrue to both the adoles-

cents and the adults by facilitating the transmission of cultural values about the importance of fatherhood.

Streamlining the establishment of paternity is another strategy for promoting the involvement of adolescent fathers (Wattenberg, 1990). Several of the participants in this study were attempting to establish paternity as a means of securing greater access to their children. Most were unaware of their legal rights or obligations as fathers. Even those who attended the birth of their children knew little of the options for paternity establishment they might have pursued immediately after delivery.

Relatively few programs address the needs of both adolescent mothers and fathers. As many of the adolescent fathers in the present study provided assistance to their partners, direct support to these young men indirectly supported their natal partners and children. When possible, service providers working with adolescent fathers and adolescent mothers should identify the shared needs of both parents, incorporating these into more cohesive programming for these populations.

Approaches that vilify adolescent fathers, or discourage mothers from including fathers in child care decisions, decrease the possibility of father involvement when such involvement might be forthcoming. Encouraging adolescent fathers to assume supportive roles early in the pregnancies, should facilitate their becoming effective co-parents after delivery (Allen-Meares, 1984). Inclusion and participation of the adolescent father's extended family could also enhance efforts to foster paternal involvement by providing pathways for transmission of cultural ideals regarding responsible fathering (Furstenberg, Herceg-Baron, and Jemail, 1981).

SUMMARY

Looking ahead, if the young fathers we interviewed were going to realize their paternal aspirations, their definition of fatherhood might need to include becoming supportive co-parents.

This would be enhanced if they were partnered with the mothers of their children in mutually satisfying, committed relationships. Society may also need to define parenthood more broadly to include extended family and extra-familial resources to provide the widest possible safety net for parents like these adolescent fathers, and their families. Furthermore, the "net" must extend to rebuilding the communities in which these adolescents make relationship and parenting decisions. In other words, we must take to heart the African proverb that states, "It takes an entire village to raise a child." Closer attention to the social and cultural contexts in which these young men learn and make decisions about fatherhood could prevent yet another group of young African-Americans from becoming adolescent fathers in the future.

Clearly, African-American men across the lifespan have to be in a position to become positive role models for younger men and boys. This cannot happen if systemic barriers to educational and employment opportunity persist. Similarly, it may be difficult (though not impossible) for older men who have not experienced stable, supportive family relationships to provide guidance to younger men such as the adolescent fathers in the present study. These young fathers are often grappling with serious relationship and family life issues of their own. Thus, addressing the needs of adolescent fathers may require us to address the larger needs of their communities. With the appropriate support they should be able to overcome the developmental and structural obstacles to their becoming good fathers, and be truly successful at *"being there."*

REFERENCES

Allen, W. 1982. Black family research in the U.S.: A review, assessment, and extension. *Journal of Comparative Family Studies*, 9, 167–189.

Allen-Meares, P. 1984. Adolescent pregnancy and parenting: The forgotten adolescent father and his parents. *Journal of Social Work and Human Sexuality*, 3, 27–38.

Applegate, J. 1988. Adolescent fatherhood: Development perils and potentials. *Child and Adolescent Social Work Journal, 5,* 205–217.

Barret, R., and Robinson, B. 1982. A descriptive study of teenage expectant fathers. *Family Relations,* 31, 349–352.

Barth, R. P., Claycomb, M., and Loomis, A. 1988. Service to adolescent fathers, *Health and Social Work,* 13, 277–287.

Battle, S. 1988. The black adolescent father. *Urban League Review,* 12, 70–83.

Blumer, H. 1969. *Symbolic interactionism: Perspective and method.* Englewood Cliffs, N.J.: Prentice-Hall.

Boss, P. 1987. The role of intuition in family research: Three issues of ethics. *Contemporary Family Therapy,* 2, 147–159.

Bubolz, M. and Sontag, S. 1993. Human ecology theory. In P. Boss, W. J. Doherty, R. LaRossa, W. Schumm, and S. Steinmetz (eds.), *Sourcebook of family theories and methods: A contextual approach,* pp. 419–448, New York: Plenum.

Bowman, P. 1992. Coping with provider role strain: Adaptive cultural resources among Black husband-fathers. In A. Burlew, W. Banks, H. McAdoo, and D. Azibo (eds.), *African-American psychology: Theory, research, and practice* (pp. 135–154). Newbury Park, Calif.: Sage.

Christmon, K. 1990a. Parental responsibility of African-American unwed adolescent fathers. *Adolescence,* 25, 645–653.

Christmon, K. 1990b. The unwed father's perceptions of his family and of himself as a father. *Child and Adolescent Social Work Journal,* 7, 275–283.

Comer, J. 1989. Black fathers. In S. Cath, A. Gurwitt, and L. Gunsberg. (eds.), *Fathers and their families.,* pp. 365–384, Hillsdale, N.J.: Analytic.

Connor, M. 1988. Teenage fatherhood: Issues confronting young, black males. In J. Gibbs. (ed.), *Young black and male in America,* pp. 188–218. Westport, Conn.: Auburn House.

Danziger, S. and N. Radin. 1990. Absent does not equal uninvolved: Predictors of fathering in teen mother families. *Journal of Marriage and the Family,* 52, 636–642.

Dash, L. 1989. *When children want children.* New York: William Morrow.

Dilworth-Anderson, P., and H. McAdoo. 1988. The study of ethnic minority families: Implications for practitioners and policymakers. *Family Relations,* 37, 265–267.

Dunston, P., G. Hall, and C. Thorne-Henderson. 1987. Black adolescent mothers and their families: Extending services. *Child & Youth Services,* 2, 95–110.

Elster, A., and M. Lamb. 1986. *Adolescent fatherhood,* Hillsdale, N.J.: Lawrence Erlbaum.

Elster, A. and S. Panzarine. 1983. Adolescent fathers: Stresses during the gestation and early parenthood. *Clinical Pediatrics,* 22, 700–703.

Freeman, E. 1989. Adolescent fathers in urban communities: Exploring their needs and role in preventing pregnancy. *Journal of Social Work and Human Sexuality,* 8, 113–131.

Furstenberg, F. 1976. *Unplanned parenthood: The social consequences of teenage childbearing.* New York: Free Press.

Furstenberg, F., J. Brooks-Gunn, and S. Morgan. 1987. *Adolescent mothers in later life.* Cambridge: Cambridge University Press.

Furstenberg, F., R. Herceg-Baron, and J. Jemail. 1981. Bring in the family: Kinship support and contraceptive behavior. In T. Ooms (ed.), *Teenage Pregnancy in a Family Context.* Philadelphia: Temple University Press.

Hamilton, V., C. Broman, W. Hoffman, and D. Renner. 1990. Hard times and vulnerable people: The initial effects of plant closings on mental health. *Journal of Health and Social Behavior,* 31(2) 123–140.

Hardy, J., A. Duggan, K. Masnyk, and C. Pearson. 1989. Fathers of children born to young urban mothers. *Family Planning Perspectives,* 21, 163–195.

Hendricks, L. 1983. Suggestions for reaching unmarried, black adolescent fathers. *Child Welfare,* 62, 141–146.

Hendricks, L. and T. Montgomery. 1983. A limited population of unmarried adolescent father. *Adolescence,* 18, 201–210.

Hofferth, S., and C. Hayes (eds.). 1987. *Risking the future. Vol. 2.* Washington, D.C.: National Academy Press.

Hogan, D., and E. Kitagawa. 1985. The impact of social status, family structure, and neighborhood on the fertility of black adolescents. *American Journal of Sociology,* 70, 825–855.

Howell, F. and W. Frese. 1982. Early transition into adult roles: Some antecedents and outcomes. *American Education Research Journal,* 19, 51–73

Kahn, J., and F. Bolton. 1985. Clinical issues in adolescent fatherhood. In A. B. Elster and M. E. Lamb (eds.), *Adolescent fatherhood,* pp. 141–154. Hillsdale, N.J.: Lawrence Erlbaum.

Klinman, D., J. Sanders, J. Rosen, and K. Longo. 1986. The teen father collaboration: A demonstration and research model. In A. Elster and M. Lamb (eds.), *Adolescent fatherhood,* pp. 155–170, Hillsdale, N.J.: Lawrence Erlbaum.

Lamb, M., and A. Elster. 1985. Adolescent mother-infant-father relationships. *Developmental Psychology,* 21, 768–773.

LaRossa, R. 1989. In-depth interviewing in family medicine research. In C. Ramsey, Jr. (ed.), *Family systems in medicine,* pp. 227–240. New York: Guilford.

LaRossa, R., and D. Reitzes. 1993. Symbolic interactionism and family studies. In P. Boss, W. J. Doherty, R. LaRossa, W. Schumm, and S. Steinmetz (eds.), *Sourcebook of family theories and methods: A contextual approach,* pp. 135–163, New York: Plenum.

McAdoo, J. 1993. The roles of African-American fathers: An ecological perspective. *Families in Society,* January, 28–35.

McKenry, P., J. Everett, H. Ramseur, and C. Carter. 1989. Research on black adolescents: A legacy of cultural bias. *Journal of Adolescent Research,* 4, 254–264.

Marsiglio, W. 1989. Adolescent males' pregnancy resolution preferences and family formation intentions. *Journal of Adolescent Research,* 4, 214–237.

Miller, B. 1993. Families, science, and values: Alternative views of parenting effects and adolescent pregnancy. *Journal of Marriage and the Family,* 55, 7–21.

Mott, F. 1990. When is a father really gone? Paternal-child contact in father-absent homes. *Demography,* 2, 499–517.

Parke, R. and B. Neville. 1987. Teenage fatherhood. In S. Hofferth and C. Hayes, (eds.), *Risking the future: Adolescent sexuality, pregnancy and childbearing,* 2, 145–173. Washington, D.C.: National Academy Press.

Redmond, M. 1985. Attitudes of adolescent males toward adolescent pregnancy and fatherhood. *Family Relations,* 34, 337–342.

Rivara, F., P. Sweeney, and B. Henderson. 1986. Black teenage fathers: What happens when the child is born? *Pediatrics,* 78, 151–158.

Robinson, B. 1988a. Teenage pregnancy from the father's perspective. *American Journal of Orthopsychiatry,* 58, 46–51.

Robinson, B. 1988b. *Teenage fathers.* Lexington, Mass.: DC Heath.

Robinson, B., and R. Barret. 1986. *The developing father.* New York: Guilford.

Robinson, B., and R. Barret. 1987. Self-concept and anxiety of adolescent and adult fathers. *Adolescence,* 22, 611–616.

Rosenblatt, P. and L. Fischer. 1993. Qualitative Family Research. In P. Boss, W. Doherty, R. LaRossa, W. Schumm, and S. Steinmetz (eds.), *Sourcebook of Family Theories and Methods.* pp. 167–177. New York: Plenum.

Sullivan, M. 1986. *Teen fathers in the inner city: An exploratory ethnographic study.* New York: Vera Institute of Justice.

Taborn, J. 1988. Adolescent pregnancy: A medical concern. *Urban League Review,* 12, 91–99.

Taylor, R., B. Leashore, and S. Toliver. 1988. An assessment of the provider role as perceived by black males. *Family Relations,* 37, 426–431.

Vaz, R., P. Smolen, and C. Miller. 1983. Adolescent pregnancy: Involvement of the male partner. *Journal of Adolescent Health Care,* 4, 246–250.

Wattenberg, E. 1990. Unmarried fathers: Perplexing questions. *Children Today,* March–April, 25–30.

Westney, O., E. Brabble, and C. Edwards. 1988. Human ecology: Concepts and perspectives. In R. Borden and J. Jacobs (eds.), *Human ecology—Research and applications.* pp. 129–137. College Park, Md.: Society for Human Ecology.

Westney, O., O. Cole, and T. Munford. 1986. Adolescent unwed prospective fathers: Readiness for fatherhood and behaviors toward the mother and expected infant *Adolescence,* 21, 901–911.

Wilkinson, D. 1987. Ethnicity. In M. Sussman and M. Steinmetz (eds.), *Handbook of Marriage and the Family,* pp. 183–210. New York: Plenum.

Wilson, W. 1987. *The truly disadvantaged: The inner city, the underclass, and public policy.* Chicago, Ill.: University of Chicago Press.

Zelnik, M., J. Kantner, and K. Ford. 1981. Sex and pregnancy in adolescence. Beverly Hills, Calif.: Sage.

❦

10

The Extended Family

Grandmother Functions in Multigenerational Families: An Exploratory Study of Black Adolescent Mothers and Their Infants

SR. MARY JEAN FLAHERTY, LORNA FACTEAU, & PATRICIA GARVER

This qualitative study explores the functions of nineteen Black grandmothers who are engaged in the care of their adolescent daughters' infants. Interviews with grandmothers revealed seven functions related to this role: managing, caretaking, coaching, assessing, nurturing, assigning, and patrolling. Suggestions for future research with Black grandmothers are given.

their homes 2 weeks and 3 months after the births of the infants. Open-ended interviews were conducted with the grandmothers. The interview material was subjected to content analysis. Seven grandmother functions emerged from the data managing, caretaking, coaching, assessing, nurturing, assigning, and patrolling.

■

Grandparents have been the forgotten subjects in family research. They are emerging as critical figures in the literature which depicts the changing American family at the end of the twentieth century. This qualitative study explores the functions of one group of grandparents—Black grandmothers—engaged in primary care activities of infants born to their adolescent daughters. The 19 grandmothers who were selected as subjects of the research were visited in

THE CENTRAL PLACE OF GRANDMOTHERS IN POOR BLACK FAMILIES

The evidence of teenage pregnancy is so compelling that the concerns of the 1960s (Furstenberg, 1976; Ooms, 1981) have developed into complex health and social problems in the 1980s (Baldwin and Cain, 1980; Phipps-Yonas, 1980).

From *Maternal-Child Nursing Journal* 16 (Spring 1987): 61–73. Reprinted by permission. © 1987 by the School of Nursing, University of Pittsburgh. This study was supported in part by a U.S. DHHS Division of Nursing Grant, No. 1POl NU01218–01, 1983–1984, and by The Catholic University of America School of Nursing Dean's Research Grant, 1983, 1984, 1985.

Not only does the United States lead most industrialized countries in rates of teenage pregnancy (Jones, et al., 1985), the proportion of unwed mothers in the 15–17 year old group has increased from 43 percent in 1970 to 62 percent in 1980 (Ventura and Hendershot, 1984). In the present milieu, adolescent mothers bring their babies home and grandparents play critical roles in the rearing of these babies (Furstenberg, 1980; Zuckerman, Winsome, and Alpert, 1979). Kempler (1976) suggests that extended kin, especially grandparents, offer close physical and psychological connections of instrumental and psychological value. The presence of a grandparent can relieve a single parent as the sole source of affection and care.

The involvement of grandmothers in adolescent mothering is particularly significant because the family of the adolescent mother is usually the most consistent provider of care and support (Furstenberg and Crawford, 1978; Zitner and Miller, 1980). Taylor (1975) reports that 15-year-old mothers who experienced supportive relationships with grandmothers, aunts, or counselors, had increased chances of successful mothering.

The availability of alternative caretakers may be critical to adolescents' achievement of dual roles as teenager and mother. However, grandmothers and their adolescent daughters may not agree about their respective positions and responsibilities in families (Sadler and Catrone, 1983). Poole and Hoffman (1981) describe three typical family situations involving urban grandmothers: daughter fails to assume responsibility for infant care and the burden is placed on the grandmother; the grandmother feels disgraced and has responsibility for infant care; and the grandmother is available for emotional and financial support. Smith (1983) developed a similar typology using role concepts of blocking, binding, and sharing. Generally, the literature suggests that support given to adolescent mothers varies with their need for help in mothering roles (Coletta and Lee, 1983).

The central place of Black grandmothers in the rearing of their grandchildren is usually the consequence of family organization as well as historical patterns or role configurations (Burton and Bengtson, 1985). LaFargue (1980) argues that Black families survived in the urban north by developing circles of kinfolk who shared responsibilities. Classic descriptions of Black families include studies of relationships which go beyond the mother-father-child tradition (Boszormenyi-Nagy and Spark, 1973; Cohler and Grunebaum, 1981; Stack, 1974). In these families, grandmothers fulfill supportive, child-rearing functions which are integrated into daily family lives (Staples, 1971). Black family households shelter three and four generations where grandmothers mother their own children and frequently take charge of the grandchildren as well (Colon, 1980). While this generational pattern is true for all poor families, Peters (1981) suggests that poor Black families have different child-rearing priorities. They also display attitudes and patterns of behavior which have developed in response to unique cultural, racial, psychologic, and economic pressures (McAdoo, 1981; Stack, 1974). The ordinary pattern of Black families takes on added significance when adolescent family members become mothers.

The ease with which Black grandmothers assume mothering roles for grandchildren may disguise the acceptability of such arrangements. The historical portrayal of Black grandmothers as "guardians of generations" (Frazier, 1939), reflecting wisdom, leadership, and strength (Burton and Bengtson, 1985) is challenged in the 1980s by the competing demands grandmothers fill in multigenerational families.

The question of how young mothers learn to be caregivers and parents is intriguing in any culture. Normal newborns have limited repertoires of behaviors with which to engage their mothers' interests. Yet, the social, intellectual, and emotional development of infants is strongly linked to the quality of early mother-infant interactions. Mercer (1980) identifies four critical periods: the first days following birth; at one month; between the third and fourth months; and between the sixth and ninth months of life. Infants born to adolescent mothers may be at higher risk during these periods because their mothers may fail to "cue-in," an elaborate response–reaction–response pattern (Barnard, 1985).

It is not surprising that practical questions arise about what happens when adolescent mothers bring the newborns home to multigenerational families. Do the babies have two primary caregivers? Do the grandmothers allow young mothers to interpret and respond to the baby's cues? What happens to the cue–response model described by Barnard (1980) if infants are cared for by mothers and grandmothers? What part do the grandmothers play in primary prevention of common childhood diseases and in the identification of physical and developmental problems? To what extent do grandmothers participate in decision making about daily care and health care activities?

PURPOSE OF THE STUDY

The purpose of this study was to explore the functions and extent of involvement of Black grandmothers in primary care activities of infants of young adolescent mothers. Grandmother was defined as the biological mother of the adolescent mother, a girl between 12 and 18 years of age, who delivered a normal first child and lived with her mother. Primary Infant Care Activities were physical care tasks (feeding, bathing, diaper changing, sleeping), comforting tasks (cuddling, holding, talking, singing), developmental tasks (playing, teaching, encouraging motor skills), and health care tasks (immunizations, well baby clinic visits, seeking medical care when illness is present).

DESIGN OF THE STUDY

This descriptive study was initiated in two metropolitan postpartum units and continued in the homes of grandmothers when the infants were 2 weeks and 3 months of age.

There were three data collection periods in the study: (a) during the hospital stay of the adolescent mother or at the first visit of the VNA staff nurse; (b) 2 weeks postpartum; and (c) 3 months postpartum. These times were suggested by Mercer's (1980) identification of critical periods and the investigators' experience with phases of maternal adjustment.

Method

Tools used in data collection included: Demographic Data Forms and Focused Interview and Observational Field Schedules. The Demographic Data Forms (Hospital and Home Visit Forms) elicited information about grandmothers, mothers, and infants. The Hospital Form described the pregnancy history of the adolescent mother, assessment statistics for the newborn, and information needed to contact the grandmother. The Home Visit Form enabled the investigators to gather information about the daily routines of caring for the newborn, the family structure, the educational and financial status of the mother; the work history and financial status of the grandmother; and a description of the home. These forms were introduced in the hospital and completed at the first home visit.

The interview schedule, developed by the investigators, used primary infant care activities as its organizing framework. During the initial phase of the study a panel of six maternal-child experts reviewed the interview schedule for relevance and design. Their responses influenced the structure, content, and sequencing of the questions. The revised schedule was used at each home visit to elicit specific information about caregiving roles and activities, decision making, and the meaning of being a grandmother.

Interviews were planned so that the grandmothers would be interviewed alone. In practice this proved to be impossible. While privacy is desired for interviews, lack of space and family interest in the newborn made the interviews family events. At one visit the grandmother, adolescent mother, new baby, three younger brothers and sisters, the grandmother's sister, and "Uncle Jimmie" were present. Family responses to questions thought to be intrusive (income, food stamps, and involvement of the family in the Women, Infants and Children Program—WIC) confirmed literary descriptions of family solidarity. Most family members knew the family business and did not hesitate to give information.

Interviews were recorded, transcribed, and coded to assure anonymity. The tapes were then erased.

The Subjects

The purposive sample consisted of 19 Black grandmothers who met the study criteria. Adolescent mothers were identified in postpartum units and through VNA offices located in wards of a major city where adolescent pregnancy is common. At the initial meeting, mothers were invited to participate in the study and were asked to sign informed consent forms. Grandmothers were then contacted by telephone and the study was explained. The purpose and conditions of participation were reiterated at the first home visit when the grandmother was asked to sign the same consent form as her adolescent daughter. Attrition occurred at the time of the second home visit despite phone calls and letters to the families. The loss of 10 subjects limited comparative qualitative analysis.

After data collection, the tapescripts were examined for styles of grandmothering and patterns of infant care, notes were made, and preliminary labels were assigned to behavioral and cognitive processes (Patton, 1980). The unit of analysis was difficult to establish because the grandmothers in the study did not speak in sentences or discrete phrases. A thought-behavioral sequence—an identifiable interval which began with a description of thought or behavior and ended when new material appeared on the tapescripts—became the unit of analysis. Seven themes which emerged from the initial sorting of data were used to construct a coding grid. Initial categories were then established around the emergent themes. Two research assistants independently assigned thought-behavioral sequences to derived categories, achieving an interrater reliability of .90. Field notes were employed in this period to verify and clarify information on the tape-scripts. The assignment of data was then subjected to evaluation by a social scientist and a nurse scientist in maternal-child health. O'Brien (1982) suggests that categorical assignment of raw data should be validated by experts in the field.

DEMOGRAPHIC FINDINGS

The demographic data supported the descriptions of studies of poor families (Boszormenyi-Nagy and Spark, 1973; Cohler and Grunebaum, 1981; Colon, 1980). Only 3 of the 19 grandmothers in this study lived with their spouses. All grandmothers were rearing their own children (one to 18 years of age) and one or more grandchildren when the new babies were brought home. The grandmothers ranged in age from 29 to 59 years of age with a mean age of 42.

The adolescent daughters were in school (grades 8–12) when they became pregnant. Their mean and median age at the time of delivery was 15.7 years (range 14 to 18 years). Eighteen of the mothers had prenatal care. During the antepartal periods 2 of the study subjects were treated for hypertension and 2 for venereal disease. There were no postpartal complications. One baby was born prematurely; 4 children were cesarean births. The infants weighed from 3 lb. 11 oz. to 9 lb. 9 oz. ($\bar{X}$ = 7 lb. 2 oz.).

The families lived in apartments ($n = 15$) and houses ($n = 4$). Three grandmothers owned their homes; 9 families lived in subsidized housing. Family members shared bedrooms and other living spaces.

Family financial support included monthly salaries, Aid to Families of Dependent Children (AFDC) and food stamps. Eight grandmothers worked outside the home. The 6 families who qualified for AFDC received between $299–$750 ($\bar{X}$ = $457) per month. Ten families received from $126 to $431 ($\overline{X}$ = $217) per month in food stamps. In the 11 families that reported salaries, monthly incomes ranged from $338 to $1400 ($\overline{X}$ = $800). The grandmothers in the study were members of poor families.

In analyzing data obtained by the Home Visit Forms for primary infant care activities (physical care, comforting, encouraging development, and maintaining health), it was found that adolescent mothers emerged as primary caregivers. Two-thirds of the babies slept in cribs in their mothers' rooms the remaining infants slept in their mothers' beds. Two infants were being breast fed at the first visit. All infants were bottle fed at the second visit. Data obtained at the first home visit revealed that mothers were usually the persons who fed the babies during both the day (*n* = 13) and night (*n* = 15). The patterns of daytime feedings changed when the mothers returned to school. By the time of the second visit all of the mothers who remained in the study were back in school. Data from the second visit revealed that 2 mothers fed the babies during the day and 8 mothers at night. Adolescent mothers made most of the decisions about daily care activities. However decisions about medical care were made more frequently by grandmothers who also reported that they were advised in these decisions by neighbors, sisters, or their own mothers. All grandmothers gave advice to their daughters about the care of the infants and the need for medical care.

THE INTERVIEWS

The mean length of the tapescripts was 16 pages. Four grandmothers accounted for 45 percent of the thought-behavioral sequences at visit one (VI). Analysis of thought-behavioral sequence resulted in the identification of seven grandmothers functions which are defined and described in Table 1. The incidence of these functions is shown in Table 2.

Grandmothers were outspoken in their approaches to daughters and grandbabies. It is clear from the data that grandmothers expected their daughters to care for their infants. These data support the findings of Ladner and Gourdine (1984) who reported that most grandmothers in their study provided child care but did not assume primary responsibility. Grandmothers saw themselves as "backup persons." However, there was evidence in the interviews of mutual involvement in infant care as grandmothers supplemented maternal care. Grandmothers presented the reality of their families to their daughters and grandbabies: Babies must learn to eat the family's food and adjust to family ways. A common theme in the remarks was "No one wants to care for a spoiled baby," and "They have to learn early this is how it is." This realistic approach to family life was softened by the nurturing statements made by the grandmothers expressive of concern and love for their daughters and the babies.

Managing activities, the category which contained the largest number of items, presented Black grandmothers as strong managers of family life and resources. There is a conceptual link between these data and the survival tactics that LaFargue (1980) reports on the urban Black family. Survival tactics used by the grandmothers in this study included: controlling family members' behaviors; overseeing the recovery of new mothers; fitting work school, and infant care needs into schedules; safety for "their grandbabies"; and applying for government assistance (food stamps, medical care, and public housing). Although caretaking activities encompassed the second largest category the significance of this function was mediated by the constraints which grandmothers placed on these childcare activities The study subjects said, "I'll help her for now" or "until she gets back on her feet." It was clear from the transcripts that the grandmothers expect their adolescent daughter to assume most of the infant care. In discussing the mutual responsibility for the care of the infants the grand mothers saw their responsibilities as temporary. Caretaking functions were frequently associated with assigning functions, that is, attributing ownership of the baby. One grandmother said,

See, this is her responsibility and she gonna have to deal with that. And if you take it from her—if I take it from her then she's gonna feel that "my mother's raising my child, so I ain't gotta worry about it." And then she goes out and gonna get another one. And when she feels this responsibility herself, and she knows that, "hey, I don't got time to do nothing else except take care of this kid," she ain't gonna have time to go out there and get another one. Because, see, if I was to take full charge, then she's not part of her own child . . . . And then who knows what'll happen to a little kid when they feel that way? I know I did. That's how they [her children] got here. 'Cause when my mother took full charge of my son, I said "no more" and I went and got [pregnant with] her. Then it was too late. I promised myself I wouldn't make that mistake [with my daughter], because whatever decision she makes about her child, it will be her decision and hers alone. I will not try to change it.

Grandmothers supported their daughters' returning to school and hoped that their daughters would finish school without becoming pregnant again. The grandmothers, many of whom had themselves been adolescent mothers, expressed worry about their daughters' education and future career opportunities. These concerns echo national studies which report negative correlations between early pregnancy, education, and career advancement (Card and Wise, 1978; Gabriel and McAnarney, 1983; McCarthy and Radish, 1982; Moore, Hofferth, Wertheimer, Waite, and Caldwell, 1981).

Interview data also revealed the feelings and reflections of the grandmothers on the meaning of the grandmother role and offered insights about caring for the next generation. For example, one grandmother expressed her ambivalence:

It's my first time being a grandmother. I haven't even got that feeling of being a grandmother. Feel like it happened too soon.

And I don't know . . . it will be different from having my own children . . . I know the baby is in our house. Just like another child come into the family. It still doesn't feel just like my daughter have a child. In a few more months I'll be getting used to it . . . but I be no grandmother right at the moment.

Another grandmother talked about the need for having babies in the home. "I think I told Connie [the daughter] I am thinking about adopting. Because, you know, children have always been around."

Other grandmothers wanted more knowledge about caring for young babies. In the following vignettes two grandmothers explain:

It seems like to me you care for 'em different, you know. Like it's been so long since I cared for a little baby 'cause like Ellie's 16 years old, and you forget a lot of things. 'Cause like I have to call her boy friend's mother and ask her a lot of things.

I was reading the books she [the adolescent mother] brought home, and believe me, I learned a whole lot. Because when we was having our children, it was all different, not too much different, but it was different. Only thing I know is keep 'em dry, love 'em, feed 'em.

The grandmothers used a common mechanism to help them express their feelings about their roles. They compared what they had known in raising their own children to how their new grandbabies were being raised. Some decided, "It's a lot to learn if you don't know," and "I just got to get used to it all over again, you know."

DISCUSSION

This study of Black grandmothers offers insight into the functions of grandmothers in multigenerational families. Seven grandmothers' functions evolved from the data managing, caretaking,

TABLE 1 Description of Grandmother Functions

Description	Example
Managing: Arrangement of resources and activities so that they synchronize with each to meet family needs.	I didn't have no where to put the crib up . . . and I thought it would look kind of odd setting in the front room. So I told Terri I'd try to get her one of those little playpen cribs which could fit out here in the front room.
Caretaking: Direct involvement in providing primary infant activities.	. . . in the morning after I get all the other kids out to go to school, I'll go ahead and feed Cecelia, give her a bath, brush her hair and read, and she'll go to sleep, as long as she's full. Or she'll lay in the bed and play . . . and she just really fight . . . and wants me to play with her. . . .
Coaching: Role modeling or guidance about primary infant care activities or maternal role.	. . . little thing—I always tell her though, if the baby's full, make sure she's burped, or don't lay her down on her back . . . I say "Now, you have an idea how your baby acts."
Assessing: The evaluation of the mother's attitude about or competency in the maternal role.	She's doing better than I really expected that she would do. She really surprised me . . . giving the baby a bath. The baby's very clean. You know, some young girls have babies and they don't really keep 'em . . . the way that she does it.
Nurturing: Emotional support and love of the mother and grandchild.	. . . the main thing is, that's my daughter, and the second important thing this is my first grandbaby, and I love 'em both, and I wouldn't take nothing for either one of 'em.
Assigning: Expressions which suggest ownership of the baby.	Because I figure, like if I do it . . . make it too easy on her, she'll go out here again. So, I told her, I said well, this is your body and your life and your baby.
Patrolling: Overseeing and evaluating the mother's life style and personal life goals.	I took 'em to the doctor, and he told me she was still a virgin. He asked me if I wanted to put her on the pill, so I told him, "No" . . . so, between the 5th of November and sometime . . . she got this little one. And she is going on the pill though. She's going on something.

TABLE 2 Incidence of Grandmother Functions

Function	Number		Range per family		Percentage[a]	
	V1[b]	V2[c]	V1	V2	V1	V2
Managing	148	37	4–18	2–8	30	26
Caretaking	85	34	0–16	0–7	17	24
Coaching	70	14	1–15	1–5	14	10
Assessing	68	17	0–13	0–5	13	12
Nurturing	47	25	1–7	1–6	10	18
Assigning	41	10	0–10	0–4	8	7
Patrolling	34	5	0–10	0–2	7	3
	495	142			99%	100%

[a] Figures are rounded
[b] V1 = Visit 1 (n = 19)
[c] V2 = Visit 2 (n = 9)

coaching, assessing, nurturing, assigning, and patrolling. These functions emerged as the major activities which grandmothers reported in response to questions about their involvement in the every day care of their grandbabies. The data confirmed the findings of other studies (Coletta, 1981; Mercer, 1980; Smith, 1975; Wilson, 1984) that grandmothers are important persons in the lives of adolescent mothers and in the care of their infants during the early months of life.

The study also highlights the methodological problems associated with home visits with multigenerational families. The visits were difficult to arrange. Alterations in family schedules and changes in phone numbers and addresses made it impossible to locate some of the study grandmothers. Disorganization and mobility are labels often assigned to poor families. This study supported that some poor families live with uncertainty and do not stay in one place. The loss of 10 subjects 3 months after the births of the infants limited comparative qualitative analysis. It could be hypothesized that the grandmothers who were interviewed a second time represent a different population than the original sample. Barnard (1985) argues that initial studies of unexplained phenomena should use cross sectional human behavior techniques. This preliminary work with Black grandmothers suggests that studies of multigenerational families may also be enhanced by cross sectional examination.

REFERENCES

Baldwin, W., and Cain, V. 1980. The children of teenage parents. *Family Planning Perspectives, 12,* 34–43.

Barnard, K. 1975. *The nursing child assessment satellite training manual.* Seattle: University of Washington School of Nursing.

Barnard, K. 1985. Studying patterns of behavior. *MCN: The American Journal of Maternal Child Nursing, 10*(5), 358.

Boszormenyi-Nagy, I., and G. Spark. 1973. *Invisible loyalties: Reciprocity in intergenerational family therapy.* New York: Harper & Row.

Burton, I. M., and V. L. Bengtson. 1985. Black grandmothers: Issues of timing and continuity of roles. In V. L. Bengtson and J. F. Robertson (eds.), *Grandparenthood* (pp. 61–78). Beverly Hills, Calif.: Sage.

Card, J. J., and Wise, L. L. 1978. Teenage mothers and fathers: The impact of early childbearing on the parent's personal and professional lives. *Family Planning Perspectives, 10,* 199–205.

Cohler, B., and H. Grunebaum. 1981. *Mothers, grandmothers and daughters.* New York: Wiley.

Coletta, N. D. 1981. Social support and risk of maternal rejection by adolescent mothers *Journal of Psychology, 109*(2), 191–197.

Coletta, N., and D. Lee. 1983. The impact of support for black adolescent mothers. *Journal of Family Issues, 4,* 127–143.

Colon, F. 1980. The family life cycle of the multiproblem poor family. In E. A. Carter and M. McGoldrick (eds.), *The family life cycle. A framework for family therapy* (pp. 343–381). New York: Gardner.

Frazier, E. F. 1939. *The Negro family in the United States.* Chicago: University of Chicago Press.

Furstenberg, F. F. 1980. Burdens and benefits: The impact of early childbearing on the family. *Journal of Social Issues, 36,* 64–87.

Furstenberg, F. F., and A. G. Crawford. 1978. Family support: Helping teenage mothers to cope. *Family Planning Perspectives, 10,* 322–333.

Furstenberg, F. F. 1976. *Unplanned parenthood: The social consequences of teenage childbearing.* New York: Free Press.

Gabriel, A., and E. R. McAnarney. 1983. Parenthood in two subcultures: White middle class couples and black, low-income adolescents in Rochester. *Adolescence, 17:* 595–608.

Jones, E. F., J. C. Forrest, N. Goldman, S. K. Henshaw, R. Lincoln, J. I. Rosoff, C. F. Westhoff, and D. Wulf. 1985. Teenage Pregnancy in developed countries: Determinants and policy implications. *Family Planning Perspectives, 17*(2) 53–63.

Kempler, H. 1976. Extended kinship ties and some modern alternatives. *Family Coordinator, 25,* 143–149.

Ladner, J., and R. M. Gourdine. 1984. Intergenerational teenage motherhood: Some preliminary findings. *SAGE: A Scholarly Journal on Black Women, 1*(2), 22–24.

LaFargue, J. P. 1980. A survival strategy: Kinship networks. *American Journal of Nursing 80,* 1636–1640.

McAdoo, H. P. 1981. *Black families.* Beverly Hills, Calif.: Sage.

McCarthy, J., and E. S. Radish. 1982. Education and childbearing among teenagers. *Family Planning Perspectives, 14,* 154–155.

Mercer, R. T. 1980. Teenage motherhood: The first year. Part I: The teenage mother's views and responses. Part II: How the infants fared. *JOGN Nursing: Journal of Obstetric, Gynecologic and Neonatal Nursing, 9*(1), 16–27.

Moore, K. A., S. L. Hoffreth, R. F. Wertheimer, L. J. Waite, and S. B. Caldwell. 1981. Teenage childbearing: Consequences for women, families, and government welfare expenditures. In K. G. Scott, T. Field, and E. Robertson (eds.), *Teenage parents and their offspring* (pp. 35–54). New York: Grune & Stratton.

O'Brien, M. E. 1982. Pragmatic survivalism: Behavior patterns affecting low-level wellness among minority group members. *Advances in Nursing Science, 4,* 13–26.

Ooms, T. 1981. Introduction: Historical perspectives. In T. Ooms (ed.), *Teenage pregnancy in a family context* (pp. 23–30). Philadelphia: Temple University Press.

Patton, M. Q. 1980. *Qualitative evaluation methods.* Beverly Hills, Calif.: Sage.

Peters, M. E. 1981. Parenting in Black families with young children: A historical perspective. In H. P. McAdoo (ed.), *Black families* (pp. 211–224). Beverly Hills, Calif.: Sage.

Phipps-Yonas, S. 1980. Teenage pregnancy and motherhood: A review of the literature. *American Journal of Orthopsychiatry,* 50, 403–431.

Poole, C., and M. Hoffman. 1981. Mothers of adolescent mothers: How do they cope? *Pediatric Nursing,* 1, 23–31.

Sadler, L, and C. Catrone. 1983. The adolescent parent: A dual developmental crisis. *Journal of Adolescent Health Care,* 4, 100–105.

Smith, F. W. 1975. The role of grandmothers in adolescent pregnancy and parenting. *Journal of School Health,* 45, 278–283.

Smith, L. 1983. A conceptual model of families incorporating an adolescent mother and child into the household. *Advances in Nursing Science,* 6, 45–60.

Stack, C. B. 1974. *All our kin: Strategies for survival in the Black community.* New York: Harper & Row.

Staples, R. 1971. Toward a sociology of the black family: A theoretical and methodological assessment. *Journal of Marriage and the Family,* 33, 119–138.

Taylor, J. 1975. The special needs of school-age parents and their offspring. *Sharing.* Washington, D.C.: Consortium in Early Childbearing and Childrearing.

Ventura, S. J., and G. E. Hendershot. 1984. Infant health consequences of childbearing by teenagers and older mothers. *Public Health Reports,* 99(2), 138–146.

Wilson, M. N. 1984. Mothers' and grandmothers' perceptions of parental behavior in three generational black families. *Child Development,* 55, 1333–1339.

Zitner, R., and S. H. Miller. 1980. *Our youngest parents: A study of the use of support services by adolescent mothers.* New York: Child Welfare League of America.

Zuckerman, B., G. Winsome, and J. J. Alpert. 1979. A study of attitudes and support systems in inner city adolescent mothers. *Journal of Pediatrics,* 95, 122–125.

Deep Structures of African American Family Life: Female and Male Kin Networks

JOSEPH W. SCOTT & ALBERT BLACK

The authors contend that the majority of Black families are best viewed from a kin network perspective rather than from the discrete nuclear family perspective. In order to understand Black family functioning today, researchers need to look at the formation of alliances among heads of single parent households and how they pool resources, do household chores together, and carry out childcare functions in tandem. This article describes Black female-headed kin networks and how they relate, interact, and interlock with one another.

■

Black families reached milestones during the 1970s. What is striking is the growing proportion of single-parent headed families *with children under eighteen present*. Looking even more closely, one finds that a majority of single family heads are parents who *never married* at all. Given the corollary that never-married young females and males generally earn poverty wages or near-poverty wages if any wages at all, a majority of these Black women and children are living in need of the basic resources for daily comfort and sustenance.

In order to adequately understand how African American families such as these *survive* and *function,* male and female *kin* networks must be raised from the subliminal level of perception. In point of fact, the writers believe that the only way to understand how economically deprived Black families, in general, *survive and function,* female and male *kin* networks must be analyzed both as separate entities and together. How kin

networks function and contribute to Black family survival is the theme of this paper.

Given the nuclear family bias in current analyses of U.S. families, Black male and female *kin* structures are generally ignored in the current discussions of Black *family functioning.* The current analyses routinely omit consideration of female-centered, female-anchored and female-dominated *kin* networks which function in interaction with male-centered, male-anchored and male-dominated *kin* networks. Notwithstanding these omissions, the majority of Black families are best viewed from a *kin network* perspective rather than from the discrete *nuclear family* perspective. This *kin network* perspective considers both blood kin and non-blood kin as a helping network which meets the daily material and social-emotional needs of all concerned.

In the U.S. today, Black males and females are under extraordinary economic and social pressures to form close and obligatory friendships so that their basic physical needs and wants can be satisfied (*Crisis,* 1984; Staples, 1985: 1005–1015). Under these conditions, friendship becomes defined as "those you can depend on," and includes mostly those individuals one can "count on."

The "unemployment" system and the "welfare" system have combined to push Black men from the center to the periphery of *family kin networks* (Stack, 1974; Staples, 1985). Black men have been made transitory family members, that is to say, they have been made absent fathers, boyfriends, uncles, and stepfathers who live on

From *The Western Journal of Black Studies,* 13 (Spring 1989): 17–24. © 1989 by the Washington State University Press. Reprinted by permission.

the margins of the female-centered household networks (Schulz, 1969: 136–144). For the most part, single Black males have become either part-time or floating members of other people's households. Most of these single males do not own or rent their own residences and from time to time must be housed, clothed and fed by female householders (Scott, 1979), especially female-headed households composed of biological sisters, mothers, daughters or some other blood relative on whom they have come to depend.

Even though the public welfare system was initially instituted to allay starvation and destitution (utter want, poverty, indigence and deprivation), it has not provided enough jobs, job training or economic assistance to maintain Black families intact (Piven and Cloward, 1971). The net result has been that the current majority of Black marriage-age adults have been forced into non-nuclear family arrangements, that is, they have been denied sufficient jobs and incomes to support traditional married-couple families: husband-wife families with dependent children, with all family members living in their own separate households, away from their extended family relatives, with the husband-fathers as the principal providers and wife-mothers as childbearers and childkeepers.

During slavery and after, and even up to the second half of this century, the majority of Black families were husband-wife-children families (Gutman, 1977; Jones, 1985). But, the successive depressions of the 1960s, 1970s, and 1980s have forced the majority of Black adults into family arrangements which used to characterize only a minority of Black families even during slavery, reconstruction, and the mass migration and urbanization periods of the 1920s and 1940s (Staples, 1986: 150–157). These new family arrangements are single-parent families and subfamilies largely linked, tenuously, together by scarce economic means and social and emotional ties. A typical arrangement might consist of a couple of nuclear families and subfamilies, single-parent families, and single-person households communally linked together through day to day sharing of economic

resources, childkeeping and childrearing. Charles Johnson (1966), a Black social scientist, called it "mutualism," i.e., a "mutual aid" system. Mutual aid practices create and maintain the *family kin networks* (Johnson, 1966: 64–65, 85–86).

In census statistics, Black family households appear as though they are separate and discrete family households. In reality, for the most part, these families have had to unite into tight *kin networks* which share food, clothing, furniture, sleeping space, transportation, medicine, and money or its equivalent—like food stamps—in order to survive.

Occasionally, discrete non-family households headed by single males become connected to the *kin* networks which are headed by females. Female-headed and male-headed households become connected with one another at numerous points and in numerous ways depending on the economic, the sociological or the psychological ties the males and females develop among themselves. The memberships of the *kin* networks change as individuals move into and out of the male/female relationships, i.e., social-emotional and economic unions (Drake and Cayton, 1962: 570–581).

Male-headed and female-headed family networks may either be multigenerational kin units or unigenerational kin units. That is to say, some kin units may be mother-daughter-children units. Some may be father-sister-children units. Some others may be brother-sister-children units. Still others may be aunt-niece-children units, uncle-nephew-children units, and grandmother-grandchildren units. There are many other combinations (Billingsley, 1968: 15–21; Lewis, 1964: 82–113).

These units above come into and go out of existence as a result of birth, sickness, death, unemployment, divorce, desertion, eviction and migration. Childcare functions motivate the forming of these family units and kin networks like nothing else does.

In order to survive, heads of single-person households also combine resources and function collectively as though they are a single family

group. These single persons may sleep in separate households, but they may pool economic
resources and eat together, wash clothes together
and carry out occasional childcare functions together. The formation of these alliances among
single persons also occurs as a result of food-
sharing, clothes-sharing, income-sharing and
temporary childkeeping. Socioeconomic survival and mutual aid are inseparable. Networking is inescapable.

It should be clear from the foregoing that in
order to understand Black family functioning
today, family researchers need to look at Black
family life as it is played out in *kin* networks. As
previously stated, the Bureau of Census has reported that well over half of all Black families
with children are headed by female single-parents.
These families may be linked through blood-kin
ties and fictive-kin ties as related sub-families, as
unrelated sub-families, as single-person households and husband-wife-children households. An
adequate description of Black family life must
therefore, of necessity, include network analyses.

Towards this end of better understanding of
Black family functioning, the remainder of this
paper describes Black female-headed kin networks and Black male-headed kin networks and
how they relate, interact and interlock with one
another.

THE FORMATION OF
FEMALE-CENTERED NETWORKS

Well over half of *all* Black families *with* children
are headed by a single female. These women, for
the most part, are either chronically or permanently unemployed (O'Hare, 1987). Most of
these families are officially recognized as "poor"
that is to say, recognized as poverty-level families
who suffer from a scarcity of the vital necessities
of life (Stack, 1974). For them, food, clothing,
shelter, money, heating and cooking utilities and
transportation are perpetually in short supply For
them, if there is no gainful employment, they
have to engage in other forms of gainful activity

to carry out their child-care functions. This
means that every day they must seek to alleviate
their chronic scarcities of food, other household
goods and medical services. They must constantly
be looking for and finding people who may be
able to contribute money, foodstuffs, childcare
services or other resources as their needs require.
Their needs include all of the material and non-
material resources humans need for the maintenance of life. Thus, an endless network of friends
and relatives are needed. For that reason, com-
mensalistic relationships are ever-forming and dissolving among those in need of food, shelter,
transportation, money, clothing, heating fuel and
child care at one time or other (Stack, 1974).

Borrowing and lending, giving and receiving
are the instrumental gainful activities of the poor,
in lieu of regular employment. A significant part
of every day involves "hunting and gathering."
Out of exchanging goods, services and money, social networks emerge. And, this exchange process
of acquiring and transferring the vital necessities
of life (among members of the near-poverty and
poverty class) is what makes survival possible.

While all impoverished people feel pressures
to network, unemployed single mothers feel special pressures to form friendships and alliances
which can materially benefit them. Single females with children have a continuous and present need for food, shelter, clothes, etc., and thus
have a need to look perpetually to form friendship and kinship relationships which will help
supply the vital resources necessary to fulfill their
chronic needs. If single females with children feel
the most pressure to network, they also experience the most pressure to turn male and/or female friendships into kin-type relationships. This
tendency is based on the African American belief and tradition that charity begins in the family, and therefore, kin can be *expected* to assist one
another willingly and extensively

Economic and social necessity drive the motivation for kin-type solidarity. Such security can
be found in large numbers of friends and kin.
While economic reciprocity can gradually transform friendships into kinships, by the same

token, the failure to reciprocate can destroy friendships and blood-kin ties. But, since economic resources are always scarce and uncertain, paying back favors is an unreliable, uncertain state of affairs. Hence, network relationships come readily into existence, but also go readily out of existence because of failures in reciprocity involving money, food and other vital services.

As stated above, the norm of reciprocity governs network exchanges. Failure to reciprocate results in shunning, ostracism, and sometimes, violence (Borchert: 38–40). Intentional failure to repay a debt or favor is considered something akin to thievery. Intentional failures are partially disruptive, if not completely destructive, of exchange networks and, hence, non-reciprocity is severely and collectively punished. That is to say, members of networks close ranks in the face of a non-reciprocating person in the system. The members, thereby, maintain reciprocity through collective solidarity and that means by collective condemnation of intentional malfeasance. Network solidarity is "mechanical solidarity."

"Tightening up" social relationships is a constant motivation because obligation-seeking and resource-seeking are basic to the economic survival of the poor and the near-poor. The more people one has indebted to oneself, the more social and economic resources one can call upon in times of need. By expanding one's dependencies, one becomes less vulnerable in case of a loss of a job, an eviction from a residence, a death of a mate or a debilitating injury strike. Blacks survive by family ties (Hill, 1972; Manns, 1981).

BLOOD-KIN AND FICTIVE-KIN

More Black single females than Black single males become *family householders*. This is probably because Black mothers are usually the child-keepers. Moreover, because of childkeeping responsibilities, Black females have to be concerned about daily sustenance and physical comfort. They have to cultivate friendships they can "count on." For these reasons, Black female

heads of households become the anchors of *family kin networks*.

Family roles are somewhat involuntary and somewhat voluntary (Stack, 1974). Even *blood* relatives have a social choice of assuming or not assuming their ascribed roles. A *blood* relative is, therefore, only potentially a *social* relative. Blood relationships may or may not correspond to social role playing such as mother, father, brother or sister (Stack, 1974). Social recognition of certain individuals in certain status-roles depends on the quality of participation; the trades, the swaps, the transfers, and the service performed define the closeness or tightness of relationships (Stack, 1974; Drake and Cayton, 1962: 570–581).

Friends who are willing to be obligated as "kin" can "achieve" social recognition as kin—namely, as father, mother, grandmother, grandfather, uncle, aunt, sister, brother or cousin—depending on the role they assume. Anthropologically speaking, these friends are *fictive* kin. In the Black community, they are "play fathers," "play mothers" or other "play" relatives (Stack, 1974; Schulz, 1969: 136–144). Those willing to be obligated as siblings are called "sister," or "brother" and are said to "go for" "brothers" or "sisters." Neighbors and blood kin will also publicly recognize them as kin. In sum, those willing to assume the role of kin, such as uncle or aunt, are allowed to assume these designations. Blacks "make" family where they have no blood relatives.

This process of making family relationships causes some conflicts between the expectations of fictive kin and those of blood kin. Occasionally, blood kin want to assert their so-called "natural rights." They maintain that "blood is thicker than water." They say that "blood" is supposed to be synonymous with loyalty, and, therefore, blood relatives are supposed to be more loyal, more faithful and more preferred than fictive kin. But, in reality, blood relatives may not be more giving, loyal, etc., and may even refuse to be obligated. In point of fact, blood kin occasionally follow the norm: "I don't lend and I don't borrow." They want to be left unobligated. Consequently, they become subjects of gossip and derision. If they never need to "fall back" on the family network, they can remain outside of the sea of obligatory reciprocal family relationships. As isolates, they may even achieve respect for their self-sufficiency and independence, but they are hardly left free from gossip. They usually continue to be pressured into being obligated or continue to be enticed into becoming exchangers.

Despite this potential for conflicts, acquaintanceships grow into friendships and friendships into kinships. The "tightest" relationship in the Black community is kinship, and, as we said, kinship relationships are defined and measured by the nature, the extent and the voluntariness of the exchanges between individuals. For example, friends may exchange clothes, but kin exchange child-keeping rights (Frazier, 1948). Since the nature of the exchanges define the relationships, blood ties do not automatically translate into social kin relationships and vice versa. But, when they do, the kin relationship is doubly "tight."

Sociologically speaking, kinship rights are social rights which can be assumed, granted, transferred or shared (Frazier, 1948; Stack, 1974). Kinship rights grow out of the willingness to assume obligations. With the assumption of socioeconomic obligations come kinship rights and vice versa. Normatively, blood relatives are ascribed social obligations but, factually, the assumption of these obligations becomes a choice for most adults. Thus, the social kinship system among Blacks is a system of rights and obligations among both non-blood and blood kin.

Motherhood, and fatherhood are also socially assumed roles. Even these roles are chosen and allowed, and hard to force on individuals. "Fathers" are those men who *allow* themselves to be obligated, or choose to be obligated, as fathers. That is to say, they choose to become financial providers and social nurturers of children who may or may not be blood-related (Schulz, 1969:136–144). Because they choose to take on a father's obligations, they are offered the role label.

"Mothers" are childkeepers and childrearers. Such role assumption works pretty much the same way as with men. That is to say, birthing a

baby does not automatically make a woman the "mother." Motherhood also may be assumed, shared, transferred or loaned temporarily. Motherhood rights are social agreements too (Frazier, 1948: 112–113).

THE FORMATION OF MALE-CENTERED NETWORKS

When jobs paying living wages and legitimate business opportunities are absent, male street corner networks form to engage in petty entrepreneurial and semi-criminal activities for economic survival. The "unemployment" system forces Black men into an ever-present quest for money. The unemployed, disemployed and unemployable make up the street corner networks.

The Black ghettoes of our largest cities are areas where there are great concentrations of individuals without subsistence money, basic sustenance, ordinary comfort, physical protection or personal security. The economic scarcity of the ghettoes generates predatory males (and females). It makes human survival desperate. It makes homicides, suicides, and other forms of self-destruction and other-destruction abound. It makes personal security an ever-present need and self-protection a never-ending concern.

The police do not help much in Black ghettoes. Peer networks become the main salvation. Male networks are socially and emotionally vital, for the physical and mental health of the detached, the pushed out, the locked out, and the "down and out." The male networks provide sustenance and comfort when female-based family networks have pushed them out to the margins (Drake and Cayton, 1962: 570–581).

Male *kin* networks come into being too, but usually not as *family* networks. Male *kin* networks usually coexist with "street-corner societies" (Liebow, 1967; Anderson, 1978; Cohen, 1955; Whyte, 1955). The *kin* network members refer to themselves as "rappies," "drinking buddies" and "standup friends."

Typically, male kin networks begin as young adolescent cliques and gangs (Finestone, 1962; Keiser, 1969). The cliques and gangs arise from many personal needs, but foremost are the needs for physical protection, and social and economic support. Accordingly, the clique and gang members provide food, clothes, money, places to sleep and loyal friendship, among other things, to one another. In sum, then, adolescent gangs and adult cliques exist as much for sustenance and comfort as for protection (Dawby, 1973). (Adolescent isolates do not last long in the ghetto environment of organized mayhem and violence. Sometimes the violence is for good reason, sometimes the violence is for thrills. In the ghetto, fear is normal; paranoia is normal; neuroticism is normal.)

As these adolescents become young adults, they begin to function as clubs, lodges, tavern buddies and fraternity brothers. These adult networks also come into existence and are maintained in existence through exchanges of money, food, material resources and in-kind services. The adult networks also satisfy the personal needs for emotional support, physical protection and economic security. Through constant trading and borrowing, lending and sharing, the members bind themselves together in the process.

Males, like females, feel a variety of pressures to convert their friendships to kinship relations in order to maintain access to sustenance, comfort, mutual protection and emergency aid. Those who have been pushed out or locked out of their biological families of origin survive only through networking. Hence, male street corner networks, like the female home-base networks, fall back on kin roles and kin relationships in order to cope with the vicissitudes of everyday ghetto life.

Those willing to engage in unconditional exchanges of money goods or services among themselves "go for brothers." "Going for brothers" obligates one to unwavering loyalty, trustworthiness and economic support (Liebow, 1967). "Going for brothers," is an assumed role among those who are willing to be obligated in social and economic ways.

Within these kin networks, males compete for status, even in places described as "nowhere to be somebody" (Cohen, 1955; Miller, 1958). They compete for "respect" and "dignity" within the day to day dynamics of the networks. They strive for positive status so that "their credit is always good" (Hannerz, 1970: 313–327).

Male street corner societies, over time, differentiate themselves into interest groups (Anderson, 1978; Glasgow, 1981). The law-abiding job-working males gravitate together in special places in cities. They are called "slaves" or "scufflers." The alcoholics gravitate together in other places in the cities. They are called "winos." The underground "businessmen," gravitate together. They are called "hustlers." The drug addicts gravitate together. They are called "dopeheads." The men who maintain a bevy of "working girls" gravitate together (Hare and Hare, 1984: 69–91; Staples, 1973: 85–88). They are called "pimps." These network differentiations serve various functions within the ghetto context as they overlap at the margins of each of their boundaries.

THE COMPETITION BETWEEN MALE AND FEMALE NETWORKS

Male street corner networks compete with female-centered family networks for time, money, and emotional commitments of the males and females who float back and forth among them. On the whole, male street corner networks are antithetical to family networks, even though the male economic "hustlers" of one kind or other may bring in some economic support for some families (Aschenbrenner, 1973).

Notwithstanding a few exceptions, most street corner roles and activities, by their nature, exploit females. Pimps, for example, "live off" the labor of women. "Players" provide sex, companionship and protection in exchange for shelter, gifts and money. Pimps "put women to work" prostituting or hustling money in other illegal ways. "Players" corrupt the values of both family men and family women (Glasgow, 1981).

Male tavern networks are cases in point. Tavern networks can be dysfunctional for family life because they drain off time and money that fathers and brothers could be contributing to family networks. "Tavern men do not make good husbands," it is said, because their loyalties, energies and resources are overly divided. Only a few males find a functional balance between the family demands and the tavern demands (Drake and Cayton, 1962: 570–581).

Adult male street corner networks can even threaten the continuance of female-centered networks. By establishing intimate friendships with females entrenched within female-centered family networks, males sometimes draw off valuable members from these female family networks. By establishing romantic alliances with females, males entice females into leaving their family networks and, thereby, use romantic love to undermine long established family support networks among women (Aschenbrenner, 1973). For that reason, romantic alliances may be resisted by some female members of networks as they come to see male street corner networks generally threatening the economic resources of the family networks.

Adolescent male street corner networks can also destabilize family networks by turning law-abiding children into thieves, gang bangers, and drug abusers (Cohen, 1955; Miller, 1958). They can destabilize the family networks by encouraging law-abiding children to engage in sexual promiscuity, shoplifting, drug use, ostentatious displays of money and conspicuous consumption of flashy clothes and jewelry. Adolescent males do not have the choice of social and economic support without all of the above negatives attached.

THE ROLE OF THE BLACK CHURCHES

Most Black churches are conglomerations of family networks. Family networks which do not "naturally" overlap with one another are brought together by church activities.

Church "welfare" programs facilitate the transfer of goods and resources from one household to another, from one network to another. Church libraries, nurseries, preschools, Saturday schools and Sunday schools also support the family networks. Churches are linchpins which serve as master links among family networks, household networks and isolated individuals. In sum, churches function as a web of life of welfare services for family networks and individuals.

MALE AND FEMALE NETWORKS AND THE BLACK CHURCH

The Black church exists at the intersection which brings together disparate networks of needy individuals. It preserves the integrity of the existing male and female networks and, at the same time, integrates these networks into a larger whole that functions as a social and economic safety net for all.

The Black church is best viewed as a confederation of networks. The Black church has the same problems as most gender-based networks: It needs a constant flow of new members, and hence, depends on the continued recruitment of single individuals and families.

In order to maintain its charisma, the church has to continue to meet the *instrumental* needs of its members. Inner-city churches, in particular, are composed of people who live under conditions of extreme economic scarcity. As a consequence, the church must provide some subsistence to its neediest members. In this way, the church functions like a family *kin* network system.

The church ritualizes its functions for the "sick and shut-in" by soliciting regular offerings for the "less fortunate" every Sunday. Every Sunday, the church, through its pastor, informs the congregation about sister-so-and-so and brother-so-and-so who are "sick and shut-in." In this manner, the church ritualizes the most basic function of kinship networks, that of economic survival through exchange.

The Black church not only meets the *instrumental* needs of the parishioners but also meets the *expressive* needs of its members. Black church rituals reinforce the values of caring, sharing, and sacrificing. These values are reinforced through songs, prayers and theology. In so doing, the rituals encourage the essential *raison d'être* of family networks.

The church, in the end, becomes the quintessential "kin" network itself, composed of collectivities of people who commit themselves to material and emotional sharing (Hill, 1972). The church institutionalizes and ritualizes the basic values and norms of these *survival techniques.* The church is an extension of the family. It even uses family terms such as sister, brother, daddy, and mother and, thereby, terminologically reinforces the social and psychological value of familism.

The Black church not only teaches familistic values, it also ritualizes family values. It promotes activities wherein individuals are called upon to actually carry out the requirements of their faith such as visiting the shut-in and giving time and talents to "serving" as deacons, deaconesses, ushers, elders, nurses, and choir members. For example, the church offering is a ritualistic part of each and every religious service; it is also a most symbolic example of turning belief into action. Through the offering, the church addresses the basic needs of the "church family," namely, the need for social support and economic security. Through the offering, the church dramatizes the value of physical survival and ritualizes the process by which that can occur—by communally giving one to the other.

To reiterate, the church functions as the linchpin holding an array of gender-based networks together. It does this ideologically, behaviorally and structurally. The church, however, is not equally attractive to male-centered and female-centered survival networks. Most Black church congregations are disproportionately female. The reasons for this are readily apparent. Church values and norms are those of female-centered kin networks. Church values are familistic values and their norms emphasize the preservation of the home and family. The church ritualizes these familistic values and kinship relationships.

By contrast, the values of most male-centered street corner networks tend to be more associated with the concepts of physical power, easy money and the "survival of the fittest" (Staples, 1973: 85–88; Dawley, 1973; Keiser, 1969). Male-centered networks pursue materialistic and physical ends. The church values conflict with these values. If Black males cannot meet family responsibilities in the home setting, they cannot meet the familistic responsibilities of the church. The church services and rituals are constant reminders to males of their shortfalls. Because churches have the same focal concerns as do female-based family networks, street corner male networks clash with the values and practices of the church. Hence, they absent themselves from the church.

SUMMARY

The Black community should be viewed as a complex of family and kin networks. Blacks establish fictive kin in locales where they have not any blood kin. They form fictive family relationships in new situations and places, even in prisons. Their churches also organize themselves as quasi-families, and the parishioners use kinship labels to refer to one another.

Male and female networks overlap in varying degrees. They cooperate at times and compete at times. They even fight like clans at times. But most of the time, they establish some type of order with the idea of providing material physical security in a racially discriminatory society.

Because the obligations of membership in male-centered street corner networks conflict with membership in female-led, home-centered family networks, males may become part-time or floating members of these female-based networks. Balancing the demands of competing networks at the same time seems to be impossible for a number of Black males; so, they often become men "on the move." For street corner males, life is precarious, and they grow old or lame at a very early age. "They do not make good husbands." The scarcity of marriageable Black males is even more severe than initially perceived.

REFERENCES

Anderson, E. 1978a. *Place on the corner.* Chicago: University of Chicago Press.

Aschenbrenner, J. 1973. *Lifelines: Black families in Chicago.* Prospect Heights, Ill.: Waveland.

Billingsley, A. 1968. *Black families in White America.* Englewood Cliffs, N.J.: Prentice-Hall.

Borchert, J. 1980. *Alley life in Washington: Family, community. religion, and folklife in the city 1850–1970.* Urbana: University of Illinois Press.

Cohen, A. K. 1955. *Delinquent boys.* Glencoe, Ill.: Free Press.

Dawley, D. 1973a. *Nation of lords: The autobiography of the vice lords.* Garden City, N.Y.: Anchor/Doubleday.

Drake, St. Clair, and H. R. Cayton. 1962. *Black metropolis.* New York: Harper & Row.

Finestone, H. 1962. Cats, kicks, and color. *Social Problems,* 10 (Fall), pp. 3–13.

Frazier, E. F. 1948. *The Negro family in the United States.* Chicago: University of Chicago Press.

Glasgow, D. G. 1981. *The Black underclass: Poverty, unemployment, and entrapment of ghetto youth.* New York: Vintage.

Gutman, H. G. 1977. *The Black family in slavery and freedom, 1750–1925.* New York: Vintage.

Hannerz, U. 1970. "What ghetto males are like: Another look," in N. E. Whitten, Jr., and J. F. Szwed, *Afro-American anthropology,* New York: Free Press, pp. 313–327.

Hare, N., and J. Hare. 1984. *The endangered Black family.* San Francisco: Black Think Tank.

Hill, R. 1972. *The strengths of Black families.* New York: Emerson Hall.

Johnson, C. S. 1966. *Shadow of the plantation.* Chicago: University of Chicago Press.

Jones, J. 1985. *Labor of love labor of sorrow: Black women, work, and the family from slavery to the present.* New York: Basic Books.

Keiser, R. L. 1969. *The vice lords: Warriors of the street.* New York: Holt, Rinehart & Winston.

Lewis, H. 1964. *Blackway's of Kent.* New Haven, Conn.: College and University Press.

Liebow, E. 1967. *Tally's corner: A study of Negro streetcorner men.* Boston: Little, Brown.

Manns, W. 1981. Support systems of significant others in Black Families. In Harriette Pipes McAdoo (ed.), *Black families.* Beverly Hills, Calif.: Sage, pp. 238–252.

Miller, W. B. 1958. Lower class culture as a generating milieu of gang delinquency, *Journal of Social Issues,* 14(3): 5–19.

O'Hare, W. P. 1987. America's welfare population: Who gets what? *Population trends and public policy.* Washington, D.C.: No. 13. Population Reference Bureau.

Piven, F. F., and K. A. Cloward. 1971. *Regulating the poor: The functions of public welfare.* New York: Vintage.

Pratt, W. E, W. D. Mosher, C. A. Bachrach, M. C. Horn. 1984. Understanding U.S. fertility: Findings from the National Survey of Family Growth, Cycle III, *Population Bulletin,* 39(5): 15. (Population Reference Bureau, Inc., Washington, D.C.).

Scott, J. W., and J. Stewart. 1979. "The Notre Dame Report: The pimp-whore complex of everyday life," *Black Male/Female Relationships,* 1(2), pp. 4–7.

Stack, C. B. 1974. *All our kin: Strategies for survival in a Black community.* New York: Harper & Row.

Schulz, D. A. 1969. *Coming up Black: Patterns of ghetto socialization.* Englewood Cliffs, N.J.: Prentice-Hall.

Staples, R. 1973. *The Black woman in America.* Chicago: Nelson-Hall.

Staples, R. 1979. Beyond the Black family: The trend toward singlehood, *Western Journal of Black Studies,* 3(Fall): 150–157

Staples, R. 1985. Changes in Black family structure: The conflict between family ideology and structural conditions, *Journal of Marriage and the Family* 47(Nov.): 1005–1015.

Whyte, W. E. 1955. *Street corner society,* 2nd ed. Chicago: University of Chicago Press.

11

Adolescence and Personality Development

A Comparison of Trends in Living Arrangement for White and Black Youth

SHENGMING TANG

Studies on living arrangements of Whites and Blacks often use cross-sectional designs with the conclusion that differences exist between Whites and Blacks. With the information drawn from the census reports on marital status and living arrangements, this paper examines the changes in living arrangements over years for Whites and Blacks. Three types of living arrangements are studied: marriage, independent living, and co-residing with parents. Contrary to common belief, Blacks do not display entirely different living arrangement patterns when the trend is the object of study. As for Whites, the marriage trend for Blacks has been going up while the independent living trend has been going down. The co-residence trend is also similar for Blacks and Whites, but this is only true with the 15 to 24 age group. The major difference is that Black females aged 25 to 34 display an increasingly higher likelihood of co-residence than their White counterparts do. This paper suggests that the difference is better explained by the lower marriage rate and the large numbers of female-headed families characteristic of Black females rather than by the extended family norm and the higher divorce rate that also feature Blacks.

∎

INTRODUCTION

Living arrangements of White and Black Americans have been attracting more attention recently. Glick and Lin (1986) found that Blacks were more likely to live with their parents—both men and women. Hogan, Hao, and Parish (1990) reported that Black mothers were two times more likely than White mothers to live with relatives other than husbands; three times if unmarried. Tienda and Angel (1982) suggested the Black households were 14 percent more likely than non–Hispanic and White households to be extended, when female headship, in-come-poverty

From the *Western Journal of Black Studies,* Vol. 19, No. 3, 1995: 218–223. Copyright 1995 by the Board of Regents, Washington State University, Pullman, WA 99164. Reprinted by permission.

ratio, education, foreign birth, and employment were controlled.

These studies have pointed out that different living arrangement patterns from Whites do exist for Blacks. Due to the cross-sectional designs these investigations have used, they fail to inform us of racial and ethnic differences in the change in living arrangements over years. The Census Bureau does record living arrangements of American Whites and Blacks over time. However, their reports are arranged by family status. Regrouping is necessary before information on living arrangements can be extracted.

To completely understand racial and ethnic differences in living arrangements, one must not only have knowledge of the differences observed at a given point, but also the information about the differences that extend over a long period of time. This paper explores the differences over years by examining information from the Census data on living arrangements since 1976. (The Census did not record family status by race until 1976.) Because the information is drawn from the Census, it is more precise than the inferences that researchers can make based on survey data.

DATA AND METHODS

Generally speaking, for any given person there exist three basic living arrangements: child of householder, family householder or spouse, and nonfamily household or nonfamily nonhouseholder. Each adult is thus able to be assigned one of the three statuses—married, co-residing with parents, or living independently. In the Census report, no single table contains these three categories specifically. Regrouping is thus necessary. Information on married persons is directly available from the table "Marital Status of Persons 15 Years and Over, by Age, Sex, Race, Hispanic Origin, and Metropolitan Residence" (Current Population Report). Data on independent living persons are obtained from the table "Marital Status of Persons 15 Years and Over, by Family Status, Age, Sex, Race, and Hispanic Origin"

(Current Population Report) by putting together those who live alone, those who live with nonrelatives, and those who are neither householders nor live in families (specially referring to those who live in college dorms or serve in the armed forces). Since the total numbers for each age group in the two tables are exactly the same, it is then possible to compute co-residence numbers by subtracting the previous two numbers from the total numbers in an age group. Percentages of co-residence, marriage and independent living for a particular year are then calculated to facilitate comparison (see Tables 1, 2, 3, and 4).

To obtain a precise picture of living arrangements for Whites and Blacks, information on co-residence, marriage and independent living was drawn every other year between 1976 and 1992. Only two age groups, 15 to 24 and 25 to 34, were included in this study because living arrangements tend to change most for persons within this age range.

A word of caution is in order here. Since marriage is treated as an independent category, the assumption is being made that all married persons take neolocal residence. Also, as independent living persons include those who live with nonrelatives, cohabiting couples are also counted as such. The divorced and widowed are excluded from the category of married persons because their living arrangements should differ from that of the married. They either fall into the category of independent living or that of co-residence. Although reality might display more complex patterns than such simplification, the Census Data have posed restriction in terms of classification. Such arbitrary treatments seem to be necessary.

CHANGES IN LIVING ARRANGEMENTS FOR WHITE AMERICANS

Tables 1 and 2 show the percentage distribution of the three living arrangements for Whites for the age groups 15 to 24 and 25 to 34.

TABLE 1 Living Arrangements for American Whites (15 to 24 Age Group)

Living Arrangement	1976	1978	1980	1982	1984	1986	1988	1990	1992
Total	100%								
Married	23.8	22.0	23.2	22.1	20.3	19.6	17.3	16.7	16.0
Co-resident	68.1	68.4	64.6	65.7	67.8	67.4	69.2	68.9	69.4
Independent	8.1	9.5	12.3	12.3	11.9	13.0	13.5	14.3	14.6
Male	100%								
Married	17.7	16.2	17.1	16.1	14.3	14.1	12.2	11.5	11.0
Co-resident	73.8	73.9	69.7	71.3	73.4	72.5	74.1	74.0	74.4
Independent	8.5	9.9	13.2	12.6	12.3	13.5	13.8	14.5	14.6
Female	100%								
Married	29.8	27.8	29.2	28.1	26.4	25.2	22.5	21.9	21.0
Co-resident	62.4	63.0	59.5	60.1	62.0	62.3	64.2	63.9	64.3
Independent	7.8	9.2	11.3	12.0	11.6	12.6	13.2	14.2	14.7

TABLE 2 Living Arrangements for American Whites (25 to 34 Age Group)

Living Arrangement	1976	1978	1980	1982	1984	1986	1988	1990	1992
Total	100%								
Married	77.3	76.5	73.2	70.2	68.7	66.8	65.4	64.7	63.1
Co-resident	13.5	10.0	10.4	11.9	12.7	13.2	14.4	14.7	15.3
Independent	9.2	13.5	16.4	17.9	18.6	19.9	20.1	20.6	21.7
Male	100%								
Married	77.3	74.1	70.1	66.8	65.2	62.6	60.8	59.5	57.7
Co-resident	12.2	8.7	9.7	11.8	12.6	13.3	15.2	15.7	16.3
Independent	10.5	17.1	20.2	21.5	22.2	24.2	24.0	24.7	26.0
Female	100%								
Married	77.3	78.9	76.3	73.7	72.3	71.2	70.1	70.0	68.5
Co-resident	14.8	11.2	11.0	12.0	12.7	13.1	13.6	13.7	14.2
Independent	7.9	9.9	12.7	14.3	15.0	15.7	16.2	16.4	17.3

As Table 1 shows, marriage and independent living for young people under 24 display opposite trends. Marriage percentage declined steadily from 23.8 in 1976 to 16.0 in 1992, while independent living percentage increased from 8.1 in 1976 to 14.6 in 1992. Co-residence percentage fluctuated around 67 as a result of the "canceling out" effect of the other two. Since marriage and independent living form the two pathways of leaving parental homes, the ratio between staying at home and leaving home did not change much over time.

These trends held when the table was collapsed by gender. For both males and females, marriage percentage tended to decrease, independent living percentage tended to increase, while co-residence percentage remained more or less on the same level. A comparison of males and females in their home-leaving trends, however, showed that females had a higher marriage percentage, a lower co-residence percentage and similar independent living percentage. In other words, White daughters are consistently less likely to stay with parents than sons before the age of 24, marriage being the major pathway by which they leave home.

Table 2 shows the living arrangement for the age group 25 to 34. As was with the situation for the other age group, marriage percentage displayed a downward trend while independent living percentage showed an upward trend. Co-residence percentage increased since 1978 but the tendency was more manifest for males than for females.

Gender effect was not apparent for older adults at the beginning of the period, but became increasingly clear as time advanced. The marriage percentage for males and females was the same in 1976. By 1992, the marriage percentage for females was 10.8 percent higher than that for males. Also, the independent living percentage for males and females was only 2.6 percent apart in 1976. By 1992, it showed a difference of 8.7 percent. That is, the dropping of marriage percentage and the rising in independent living percentage was much sharper and stronger for sons than for daughters.

Two trends important for cross-racial comparison are thus clear: White adults aged 15 to 34 are increasingly getting married later and increasingly seeking in-dependence by leaving parental homes earlier. That more White adult children are not co-residing with their parents might be a direct reflection of their later marriage age.

CHANGE IN LIVING ARRANGEMENTS FOR BLACK AMERICANS

Tables 3 and 4 show the living arrangements for Blacks.

Table 3 shows the changes in living arrangement trends among Blacks for the age group 15

to 24. As was with the situation for their White counterparts, the marriage percentage of Blacks showed a downward trend; independent living percentage showed an upward trend with co-residence percentage showing very slight ups and downs. These trends hold true for both males and females. Since Black females had higher marriage percentage and lower co-residence percentage than Black males, they were thus less likely to stay in parental homes than Black males. This result is also in line with the situation for White females. Despite the obvious differences existing for individual cohort between Whites and Blacks in their living arrangements, the trends characteristic of White young adults are also true of Black young adults.

Table 4 displays the living arrangements of Blacks for the age group 25 to 34. The downward trend for marriage and upward trend for independent living still exists. Co-residence, however, showed a steadily upward trend rather than just fluctuating over years. This upward trend for co-residence held true for both Black homes more males and females, with the latter showing a much higher percentage for each cohort. Compared to Whites in the same age group, Blacks displayed the same downward marriage trend and the same upward independent living trend but a much stronger and sharper upward trend in co-residence. This was especially true of females since the co-residence percentage for White females hardly changed over the years. Gender effects for marriage among Blacks did not exist. The percentage of marriage for Black males and females for each year were very much alike. Black males, however tended to seek independent living more while Black females tended to stay in parental homes more.

DISCUSSION

The literature on living arrangements has been consistent in suggesting the existence of ethnic and racial differences between Blacks and Whites The tables shown here support these findings.

**TABLE 3 Living Arrangements for American Blacks
(15 to 24 Age Group)**

Living Arrangement	1976	1978	1980	1982	1984	1986	1988	1990	1992
Total	100%								
Married	16.5	12.5	13.1	11.7	9.0	9.6	9.3	8.6	7.5
Co-resident	79.2	80.3	77.8	81.0	83.5	81.1	81.8	81.4	83.0
Independent	4.3	7.2	9.1	7.3	7.5	9.3	8.8	10.0	9.5
Male	100%								
Married	12.8	9.6	9.5	8.6	5.8	5.8	5.8	5.9	5.0
Co-resident	82.3	83.0	80.9	83.3	86.9	84.2	84.4	82.6	85.0
Independent	4.8	7.3	9.6	8.1	7.3	10.0	9.8	11.4	10.0
Female	100%								
Married	19.8	15.2	16.4	14.5	11.9	12.9	12.6	11.2	9.9
Co-resident	76.3	77.8	75.0	78.9	80.3	78.4	79.5	80.3	81.0
Independent	3.8	7.0	8.6	6.6	7.8	8.7	7.9	8.6	9.1

**TABLE 4 Living Arrangements for American Blacks
(25 to 34 Age Group)**

Living Arrangement	1976	1978	1980	1982	1984	1986	1988	1990	1992
Total	100%								
Married	65.3	60.3	57.8	54.4	48.9	49.3	46.1	45.6	38.9
Co-resident	21.3	24.3	24.8	28.3	33.2	34.8	34.7	34.8	40.6
Independent	13.4	15.4	17.4	17.3	17.9	16.0	19.2	19.5	20.5
Male	100%								
Married	64.8	61.4	57.6	54.3	46.9	49.3	44.7	44.2	37.4
Co-resident	15.5	15.4	16.3	20.9	28.0	29.8	28.8	28.9	34.9
Independent	19.6	23.1	26.1	24.8	25.1	20.8	26.5	26.9	27.7
Female	100%								
Married	65.6	59.3	58.0	54.5	50.6	49.2	47.3	46.8	40.3
Co-resident	25.7	31.5	31.5	34.3	37.5	39.0	39.8	39.9	45.4
Independent	8.6	9.2	10.5	11.1	11.9	11.8	12.9	13.3	14.3

For each given cohort in Tables 1 through 4, Blacks consistently demonstrated a lower marriage percentage and a higher co-residence percentage than Whites. In terms of the changes in living arrangements over years, however, the widely believed ethnic and racial difference between Blacks and Whites were not so manifest. For the age group 15 to 24, the trends for marriage, independent living, and co-residence were very similar, suggesting that the lower marriage rate, later marriage age, and higher independent living rate affecting Whites were also exerting impact on Blacks. For the age group 25 to 34, the trends for marriage and independent living still remained similar for the two ethnic groups. The sole major difference lay in co-residence trend. The question is, why older Black daughters became increasingly more likely to co-reside with their parents over years than their White counterparts?

A ready explanation lies in the extended family norm characteristic of Blacks. Research has consistently reported that proportion of extended households is greater among Blacks than among Whites (Beck and Beck, 1989; Hofferth, 1984; Tienda and Angel, 1982). Therefore, Blacks should display higher co-residence rate than Whites. This explanation is good at clarifying the differences observed in living arrangements between Whites and Blacks at any given point, but fails to explain the differences in trend between the two ethnic groups. The extended family norm existed in 1976 as well as in 1992. No existing evidence has suggested an intensification of this norm among Blacks over time.

Since divorce is often associated with home return, one might speculate that the high divorce rate of Blacks could explain the observed difference in trend. Blacks do have higher divorce rate than that of Whites. Because the divorce rates for White and Black females have both gone up, it is difficult to explain why co-residence trend for Black females have gone up while remaining flat for White females.

Possible causes that might explain the differences are closely related to the marriage pattern and the female headed families characteristic of Blacks. As Table 4 shows, Black females aged 25 to 34 display a much sharper downward marriage trend than their White counterparts. For Black females, marriage percentage declined from 65.6 in 1976 to 40.3 in 1992—a difference of 25.3 points, while for White females, the difference was only 8.8 points, marriage percentage going from 77.3 to 68.5 during the 16-year period. That is, marriage as a pathway of leaving home became less important for Black females. Hence, more Black daughters stayed at home.

Coincident with the downward marriage trend for Black females, the numbers of female-headed families among Blacks was on the increase. In 1970, the numbers of Black female family householders was 1,349,000. This figure

had more than doubled to 3,223,000 by 1989. The percentage points had changed from 28.3 to 43.5 (Statistical Abstract, 1991, p. 53). In other words, of all Black families, more than 4 out of 10 were female-headed families. Although the impact of female-headed families on living arrangements requires further exploration, motherhood is found to promote young women's residential dependence. Young women who are themselves parents are more likely to be residentially dependent than are comparable nonparents (Goldscheider and DaVanzo, 1985; Hogan, Hao, and Parish, 1990; Aquilino, 1990). Looked at in this light, the increase in the numbers of female-headed families over the past years should result in an increase in co-residence rate during the same period.

Considering that adverse economic situations tend to increase adult children's reliance on their parents, the upward co-residence trend for Black females might be a reflection of the deteriorating situations for Black females in a dual labor market. The adverse economic situations might also account for the increased co-residence percentage for White and Black males. Unfortunately, little literature exists in this area to follow for further expansion.

REFERENCES

Aquilino, William S. 1990. The likelihood of parent-adult child coresidence: Effects of family structure and parental characteristics. *Journal of Marriage and the Family,* 52: 405–419.

Beck, Scott H., and Rubye W. Beck. 1984. The formation of extended households during middle age. *Journal of Marriage and the Family,* 46: 277–287.

Glick, Paul C., and Sung-Ling Lin. 1986. More young adults are living with their parents: Who are they? *Journal of Marriage and the Family,* 48: 105–112.

Goldscheider, Frances K., and Julie DaVanzo. 1985. Living arrangements and the transition to adulthood. *Demography,* 22: 545–563.

Hofferth, Sandra L. 1984. Kin networks, race, and family structure. *Journal of Marriage and the Family,* 46: 791–806.

Hogan, Dennis, Ling-xin Hao, and William Parish. 1990. Race, kin networks, and assistance to mother-headed families. *Social Force,* 68: 797–812.

Tienda, Maria, and Ronald Angel. 1982. Headship and household composition among Blacks, Hispanics, and other Whites. *Social Forces,* 61: 508–531.

U.S. Bureau of the Census. 1977. Marital status and living arrangements: March 1976. *Current Population Reports,* Series p–20, No. 306. Washington, D.C.: U.S. Government Printing Office.

U.S. Bureau of the Census. 1979. Marital Status and Living Arrangements: March 1978. *Current Population Reports,* Series p–20, No. 338. Washington, D.C.: U.S. Government Printing Office.

U.S. Bureau of the Census. 1981. Marital Status and Living Arrangements: March 1980. *Current Population Reports,* Series p–20, No. 365. Washington, D.C.: U.S. Government Printing Office.

U.S. Bureau of the Census. 1983. Marital Status and Living Arrangements: March 1982. *Current Population Reports,* Series p–20, No. 380. Washington, D.C.: U.S. Government Printing Office.

U.S. Bureau of the Census. 1985. Marital Status and Living Arrangements: March 1984. *Current Population Reports,* Series p–20. No. 399. Washington, D.C.: U.S. Government Printing Office.

U.S. Bureau of the Census. 1987. Marital Status and Living Arrangements: March 1986. *Current Population Reports,* Series p–20, No. 418. Washington, D.C.: U.S. Government Printing Office.

U.S. Bureau of the Census. 1989. Marital Status and Living Arrangements: March 1988. *Current Population Reports,* Series p–20, No. 433. Washington, D.C.: U.S. Government Printing Office.

U.S. Bureau of the Census. 1991. Marital Status and Living Arrangements: March 1990. *Current Population Reports,* Series p–20, No. 450. Washington, D.C.: U.S. Government Printing Office.

U.S. Bureau of the Census. 1991. *Statistical Abstract of the United States, 1991* (111th ed.). Washington, D.C.

Sex and Class Differences in the Socialization Experiences of African American Youth

CLYDE W. FRANKLIN, II

Undoubtedly, in the United States, sex and class are critical variables affecting the socialization experiences of African American youth. This is so despite the prevailing climate of racism in America which all African American youth experience either covertly or overtly, indirectly or directly.

As a model of African American youth socialization unfolds in this discussion, sex and class effects should become apparent. The effects are manifested in the ways African American youth construct social responses to their immediate social environments and to the larger society.

The writer proposes that these are direct causal links between African American youth socialization experiences and sex and class characteristics of the youths. Delineating the specific relationships between the variables is the basic aim of this paper.

■

CHARACTERISTICS OF THE AFRICAN AMERICAN FAMILY

Understanding the socialization experiences of African American youth is dependent, in part, on knowing something about the characteristics of the African American family today. It has been suggested that "no change in the African American community has been more dramatic or more fundamental than the reordering of families and family relationships (O'Hare, et al., 1991, p. 17)." Some have even stated that the African American family is in a state of crisis generally characterized by large numbers of poor, female-headed households. The crisis is reflected in the growing numbers of African American youth being reared in single parent, female-headed homes. In fact, "the share of Black children living with two parents declined from 58 percent in 1970 to 38 percent in 1990" (O'Hare, et al., p. 19).

In 1990, the Population Bureau reported that approximately 55 percent of all African American youth lived in a single parent home with 51 percent living with their single mothers. The Bureau also reported that 27 percent of all African American youth lived with mothers who had never been married—the percentage rising to 39 percent for youth under the age of six.

The consequence of such living arrangements are dire for many African American youth. O'Hare, et al., reports that the 3.8 million African American youth in two-parent households possibly fare much better than their counterparts in single parent homes. Youth from two-parent homes typically have parents who are more educated, whose earnings quadruple single parent earnings, and who are more than twice as likely to be homeowners. The problem of poverty is exacerbated for these single parent African American families since 94 percent are female headed. Generally, African American females who head families have meager economic resources, live in the central area of urban cities; and, many live in public housing.

The implications of these changes in the African American family for African American youth socialization experiences are clear as

Kasarda (1978) Connor (1988), Wilson (1987) and others have pointed out. These authors conclude that the results for the African American community and thus, the African American family as an institution are:

> deeper "ghettoization," solidification of high levels of poverty, mounting institutional problems in the inner city (e.g., poorer municipal services and declining quality of public schools), and an increase in social dislocation (joblessness, crime, female-headed families, teenage pregnancies and welfare dependency). (Wilson, 1987, p. 181)

It is not overly dramatic to say that recent changes in the African American family have been devastating for many youth. However, not all of the economic changes in the African American family have been dysfunctional ones. Since the 1960s the number of affluent African American families has grown steadily. For example, the number of affluent African American families (families earning $50,000 and over) rose from 266,000 in 1967 to over 1,000,000 in 1989 increasing from 1 in 17 (in 1967) to 1 in 7 (in 1989).

What all of this means is that the socialization experiences of African American youth are quite diverse. First of all, the 1980s were characterized by a widening of the gap between poor African Americans and affluent African Americans. In contrast to poor African Americans, affluent African Americans are well educated, own their homes and many live in suburbs. In some ways, affluent African Americans are similar to affluent Whites even though the former are far fewer in number and experience the conditional variable racism. It is the manner in which African Americans' poverty and affluence relate to aspects of the socialization experiences of African American youth that determines much African American youth behavior. Boykin and Toms (1985, p. 33) define socialization as "the preparation of children to take on the adult roles and responsibilities of society." Borrowing from Baldwin (1980), Zigler and Child (1973) and Young (1970) they point out that socialization

essentially deals with rearing children to become functioning members of society; this is accomplished through teaching and learning of conventional beliefs, values and patterns of behavior.

While Boykin and Toms do not feel that it is necessary to distinguish between the proscriptions/prescriptions of the larger society and one's immediate environment, m contrast, this writer feels that this is a critical issue when discussing the influences of sex and race on aspects of African American youth socialization. More specifically, sex and race affect African American youth as biological organisms; the variables also affect the private identities and public identities of African American youth.

AFRICAN AMERICAN FEMALES AND MALES AS SOCIALLY NEUTRAL ORGANISMS

Of the 671,976 African Americans born in 1990, 330,535 were female and 341,441 were male. Ordinarily, the organization of physiological activity is a given in discussions of children's socialization experiences. However, because many African Americans experience the effects of poverty, ignorance, racism and numerous other social dislocations, large numbers of African American infants do not enter the world as socially neutral organisms; instead they enter the world with physiological and neurological deficits, which often translate into social deficits. These social deficits render functioning in mainstream society nearly impossible for many African American youth. Edelman (1985, p. 73) pointed out in the middle '80s that Black children suffered disproportionately from downward economic trends and lack of commitments toward eradicating physiological and social problems experienced by children in general and African American children in particular.

Given that African American youth face a relatively perilous future beginning in the prenatal period, it is absurd to assume that they enter the world as socially neutral organisms. The contention is that numerous African American youth who survive early life-threatening episodes come into the world often disadvantaged both physiologically and socially. These deficits have profound implications for the private and public identities of female and male African American youth, many of whom are programmed for dysfunctional lives. Interestingly, while many African American female and male youth generally are similarly disadvantaged at birth (prior to any type of socialization), this changes quickly once social institutions begin to impact their lives.

Still, circumstantial evidence overwhelmingly support the thesis that dysfunctional socialization experiences occur for large numbers of African American youth. For example, 671,976 live African American births were reported in the 1990 Vital Statistics bulletin of which 341,441 were male and 330,535 were female. Sixty-four percent of these children were born to unmarried mothers. Of interest also is the fact that the fertility rate for African American females between the ages 15–19 was 105.9, more than double the rate for White females in the same age category (43.7)

Just as debilitating for African Americans were the relatively high infant mortality rates reported in the 1990 Vital Statistics Mortality Report. Based on a rate per 100,000 persons, the mortality rate for White infants less than one year was 832.0 while the rate for African American infants in the same age category was 1,996.6. The African American infant mortality rate more than doubles the White infant mortality rate! There is a slight decrease in the gap as one moves to the age category 1–4. Nevertheless, the African American rate (80.8) still greatly surpasses the White rate (45.7).

The significance of the above statistics and observations for African American youth socialization experiences cannot be over-emphasized. Not only are the youths' potential as social organisms negatively affected by their circumstances but other aspects of the youths' socialization process also are affected. The two other aspects

most directly affected are the youths' *private selves* and the youths' *public selves*. Youths' private selves are their cognitions about themselves, their affectivity toward themselves and their behaviors toward themselves. How the youth defines herself/himself and the meanings given those definitions constitute the essence of the youth's *private self.* Typically, the youth organizes cognitions, affectivity and behaviors toward self; and this represents his/her private self which may or may not be shared with others. Unavoidably, however, others constitute the basis for the youth's self-conception. This is due to the fact that the youth forms conceptions of self from others' definitions, cognitions, affectivity and behaviors toward the youth. This means that *socialization* involves more than the youth's self conceptions; it also involves others' conceptions—the youth's public self. The youth's public performance/public identity refers to the constellation and organization of roles assumed by the youth in his/her daily social encounters. The public self is important for the various roles assumed by the youth. The various roles assumed by the youth organizes the public self and the public self organizes the roles assumed by the youth.

THE PRIVATE AND PUBLIC SELVES OF AFRICAN AMERICAN YOUTH

The private selves of African American youth are as diverse as the socialization experiences in their lives which are affected by race, sex and class. Collier-Watson et al. (1986, p. 82) observe that sex roles in the United States are permeated by class and race biases. They reiterate the ideas that losses and gains differentially accrue to persons on the basis of how closely they approximate the physical and behavioral attributes ideal for their sex. Moreover, the authors also note that race and sex are interactive forces which operate to constrain self-actualization and conclude that race, sex and class form an interactive social stratification system.

This type of stratification system produces African American females and males who are victims of a triple and interactive system of psychological, sociological, and economic oppression.

Lewis (1975) argues that gender egalitarianism exists for African American females and males. Far fewer differences are said to exist between African American femininity and masculinity than between White femininity and masculinity. On the question of sex differences between African American boys and girls, with respect to school matters, Hare (1985, p. 145) found that African American male youth scored significantly lower than their female counterparts in mathematic ability and achievement orientation tended toward lower school self-esteem. No significant sex differences were found in home self-esteem or self-concept of ability. However, African American male youth scored higher than African American female youth on non-school dimensions of social abilities and peer self-esteem. While Hare's results are mixed on sex differences related to African American youth socialization, some differences do seem to exist. But, what do these differences mean?

Hare's findings relate directly to the private and public selves of African American youth. African American youths' public selves actually refer to how others recognize them. While these youths, like others, assume numerous social roles, the fact that they are African American provides a central focus for the social roles they play. African American female and male youths' public selves, as reflected in Hare's school related measures, support the generally more favorable identity mainstream society has of African American female youth and the less favorable identity it has of African American male youth.

African American youth do not construct these public and private selves alone. They derive the selves from messages given to them and others by socialization agencies within the African American culture and external to the African American culture. Within the African American culture, there are such socialization agencies as the family, the intersex and intrasex peer groups, the church, and other informal agencies. Also sending subtle and sometimes not so subtle messages to African American youth are the basic institutions in American culture such as the educational institution, the polity, the economic institution, the economy and the mass media. Needless to say, messages received by African American youth from the latter institutions often emphasize their inferiority and dysfunctionality resulting in negations of their self worth. Precisely how this occurs for African American girls and boys can be seen if one assumes, first of all, that race is a conditional variable for Black youth. What does it mean to be female and Black? What does it mean to be male and Black? While some would claim that there are few differences, as alluded to earlier, others would argue the point (e.g., Bell Hooks, 1984; Benjamin, 1991).

AFRICAN AMERICAN FEMALES AND THEIR PUBLIC AND PRIVATE SELVES

Sociologist Lois Benjamin contends that African American women not only encounter sexism and racism outside of the African American community, "they must also battle sexism on the homefront" (1992, p. 193). She notes that while African American female/male relationships historically have been more egalitarian than their White counterparts, African American males have accepted the patriarchal value of male dominance even though they have not been able to exercise it. Benjamin's lamenting comments echo earlier ones by Bell Hooks who stated:

> As a group, Black women are in an unusual position in this society, for not only are we collectively at the bottom of the occupational ladder, but our overall social status is lower than any other group. Occupying such a position, we bear the brunt of sexist, racist, and classist oppression. At the same time, we

are the group that has not been socialized to assume the role of exploiter/oppressor in that we are allowed no institutionalized other that we can exploit or oppress. (Hooks, 1984, p. 14)

On the other hand, Lindzey (1990) concludes in her discussion on the American Black family that gender role flexibility has helped rather than deterred the Black family and contributed to a more equalitarian pattern, particularly among the middle and working class. She contends that male dominance and restrictive male role definitions are more characteristic of Black lower class families where role sharing is not as prevalent. This is Lindzey's conclusion despite Cazenave's findings that a majority of his middle class African American male sample felt that African American women had more opportunities than African American men and were responsible in part for the low status of African American men (Cazenave, 1983, p. 341). These African American men preferred traditional gender roles for African American men and women.

A significant question which arises is what does this mean for African American female youths' private and public selves?

African American female youths' private and public selves are affected greatly by race and gender stereotypes. While African American caretakers may feel charged with the responsibility for providing their offspring with the skills and abilities they will need to succeed in the society at large, this is not an easy task for many. As a rule, however, African American female youth hear messages which stress heavily the importance of hard work (Hale-Benson, 1986). In contrast to some previously cited works, and in agreement with others, Hale-Benson found that African American children were less gender stereotyped than White children. The picture is not at all clear, however, since the results of studies by Gonzales (1982) and Price-Bonham and Skeen (1982) suggest as much and more gender stereotyping among African Americans and Latinos as among their White counterparts.

African American girls do seem to receive strong messages about motherhood, femininity, personal uniqueness and distinctiveness. Hale-Benson contends also that considerable attention is given to sexuality, body movement, appearance, etc. While there is a dearth of information about the interactive effects of class, race and sex on African American female youth socialization experiences, there is ample evidence that each one of the variables is a singularly important influence on childhood socialization (Renzetti and Curran, 1989).

Like African American male youth, African American female youth receive contradictory cultural socialization messages from these socially constructed spheres: the sex sphere, the race sphere and the class sphere. While two of the spheres are biologically based, their influences are socially constructed.

African American females learn directly and vicariously through social interaction within the African American community and in the larger society that there is a constraining influence on their interactions and social activities. In Benjamin's (1991) study several women lamented the constraining effect of race. Female youth not only receive this message but they also learn that their sex can be an impediment. However, African American female youth do receive socialization messages primarily from the African American community which are designed to prepare them to function in a racist and sexist society.

African American girls are taught by agents within the African American community (e.g., the family, older women. etc.) that they should be self-sufficient and able to take care of themselves. These socialization agents may alert the girls to the dwindling numbers of eligible African American males able and/or willing to assume a traditional provider-protector role in female/male relationships. Female youth may be exhorted to become educated and independent. Of course many female youth find themselves unable to fulfill the prescriptions because of social and economic impediments. Numerous African American female youth find themselves in the untenable position of having meager economic resources and woefully inadequate social outlets during their formative years. The availability of supportive and functional social outlets for African American females often declines with decreases in African American family income. Many female youth who have this kind of experience become vulnerable to intersex and intrasex peer group pressure to engage in behavior inimical to their welfare. Too often, these female youth succumb to peer group pressures and the results are disastrous for them and the entire African American community. Soaring school drop-out rates, pregnancy rates and increasing numbers of African American female youth on welfare rolls are evidence of dysfunctional socialization experiences characterizing the lives of these females. Who and what agencies are responsible for these youth?

The availability of adult socialization agents for African American female youth greatly influences their socialization experiences. This availability is tied intricately to family economic resources. Generally when family economic resources are adequate, the influence of the intersex and intrasex peer groups on female youth is diminished. African American female youth dependence on intersex and intrasex peer groups is lessened when there is a greater availability of other socializing agents. Class (measured by family income) affects female youths' socialization experiences because it determines the availability of numerous socialization agents thereby affecting intersex and intrasex peer group dependence. The socialization experiences of African American female youth are shaped by the number of parents in the home, the availability of economic resources, the availability of other adult socializing agents, and intersex and intrasex peer group dependence.

Frequently the number of parents in the home is related directly to the family's economic resources which in turn affects directly the availability of socializing agents for the female youth. The availability of socializing agents for the female youth is inversely related to the female youth's dependence on her inter- and intrasex peer groups. Dependence on intersex and intrasex peer groups is positively related to female youths' social constructions of behaviors inimical to their welfare (e.g. drug addiction, teenage pregnancy, dropping out of school, etc.). (Ladner, 1972; Williams and Kornblum, 1985).

When economic resources are meager in the female youth's home, a number of socially lethal variables are set into motion which can affect whom she interacts with, how many people are in her life and how influential these people are on her life. Race and sex certainly are constraining influences on African American female youths' lives, but class may be the most salient variable determining their socialization experiences which relate directly to their future. One interpretation of the Geronimus-Korenman research is that in the 1990s widespread poverty experienced by many young women, particularly African American women, is ruining the lives of these young women. Giving birth as teenagers may not be the cause of their poverty. The fact of the matter is that many feel that they have nothing better to look forward to than having a baby. At least the baby will be theirs. Thus, teenage fertility in the 1990s seems to be often an adoptive response to social reality.

Thus, African American female youths' public and private selves depend greatly on their family's economic resources. How African American female youth feel about themselves, how they define themselves and how they behave toward themselves are related in part to the class from which these youth come.

AFRICAN AMERICAN MALE YOUTH AND THEIR PUBLIC AND PRIVATE SELVES

The private and public selves of African American male youth, like their female counterparts, are functions of their race, class, and sex spheres. Moreover, social interaction between the youth and the African American culture, the mainstream culture, and the intersex and intrasex peer groups plays a critical role in self development. Socialization messages received by African American male youth from these sources frequently are contradictory, but yet influence greatly their selves and behaviors.

First of all, others' images of African American males and African American males' images of what others feel about them are related to the roles they play in their social interactions in the previously mentioned domains. Above all, however, race is the focal point in identifying African American male youth. Ironically, race has been a central focus in perceptions of African American males for some time with different perceptual results. Ellison noted in 1972:

> I am an invisible man...I am a man of substance, of flesh and bone, fiber and liquids— and I might be said to possess a mind. I am invisible, understand, simply because people refuse to see me...When they approach me, they see only my surroundings, themselves, or their imagination—indeed, everything and anything except me. (Ellison, 1973)

Ellison decried the fact that African American males seemed not to be perceived at all in American society. From Ellison's perspective, "race" rendered the African American male invisible. In the 1990s it is safe to say that African American males are no longer invisible, especially African American male youth. The socialization experiences of a growing number of African American-males under age 18 residing in poor female-headed households are decidedly negative as they struggle toward manhood without the benefit of adult male role models and other supportive resources to facilitate their passage. Moreover, as Gibbs (1988) observes, even for African American youth in intact nuclear families, economic stability and quality of life are far less predictable and certain than is the case for their White counterparts. The direct and indirect experiences of these youths with social dislocations (Wilson, 1987; Gibbs, 1988) have produced a growing number of males who are dysfunctional social beings.

African American male youth have public selves based on the numerous social ills characterizing African American male youth such as high arrest rates for personal crimes, disorderly conduct, sexual misbehavior, theft and homicide. While most African American male youth do not engage in these activities, the stigma still affects all African American male youth. In fact, the stigma is so great and the perception of African Amen-can male youth as dysfunctional so pervasive that local and national programs are springing up across the country to intervene positively in their socialization experiences. The National Council of African American Men, Inc., founded in 1990 and headquartered at The University of Kansas Center for Black Leadership, has as one of its specific goals the provision of leadership and positive role models for African American Male youth. At its 1992 Third Annual Conference in Atlanta, Georgia, in August, 1992, a youth component of the conference held panel discussions and workshops on various issues affecting African American male youth.

African American male youth counseling and manhood training programs have been started in such diverse sections of the country as Lake Charles, Louisiana; Charlottesville, Virginia; Cleveland, Ohio; Columbus, Ohio; Kansas City, Missouri; Charlotte, North Carolina; Memphis, Tennessee; and Milwaukee, Wisconsin. Calling much attention to society's perception of African American male youth, however, have been the calls in Milwaukee, Wisconsin, and Detroit, Michigan, for all African American male youth schools. The calls were made because many feel that this may be the most effective way to address the crisis facing African American male youth.

If the public selves of African American male youth are in a state of crisis, what about African American male youths' private selves? One frequently hears in the media that poor self-esteem/poor self-concepts are critical independent variables influencing some African American males' behaviors. This seems to be consistent with the fact that many of these youth live in economically and socially disadvantaged homes and experience a variety of social dislocations (violence, unemployment, female-headed families, welfare dependency, etc.). However, Hare (1985) noted, as pointed out earlier, that African American male youth show great concern about peer relationships and social abilities. The concern with peer relationships and social abilities seems greater for males than for females. Thus, it is possible that this greater concern and involvement in peer group activities may diminish the effects of increases in socioeconomic status on peer group influence. In other words, despite African American male youths' meager economic resources, intersex peer groups definitions of manhood may influence male youth selves and male youth behavior. Most of these males enjoy positive self-concepts! Hare's study reported that despite Black boys trending toward lower school self-esteem when compared with Black girls, Black boys scored higher than their female counterparts on non-school dimensions of social abilities and slightly higher peer self-esteem. Black boys also scored significantly higher than White boys on peer-related and socially related abilities.

Typically, African American male youth experience race and sex constraints which can affect various aspects of their lives (Staples, 1986). Manhood is linked closely with power—power to control others—as Staples asserts. Poor African American male youth learn early that the power to control others is a direct function of economic resources. These youth are especially sensitive to the link between money and control over others since their life experiences have reflected that link.

African American male youth intrasex peer groups control their members, not so much through the provision of economic resources as through the recognition of their social competence which is measured through sexual exploits, successful use of defense mechanisms for survival and "cool pose" signatures. The latter refers to what Majors calls "a variety of attitudes and actions the Black man performs using characterizations and roles as facades and shields" (Majors, 1986).

In the case of African American male youth, while the class variable is inversely related to intrasex peer group influence the effects are not as great because of the influence of the sex variable. Whether affluent or poor, African American male youth aspire to manhood and if the definition of manhood for many youth is determined to a considerable extent by the peer group, then the influence of the peer group remains enormous. In such cases it is not as easy to provide alternative socialization influences. In fact, providing such influences is practically impossible because of the degree of similarity between the socialization experiences of African American male youth from diverse socioeconomic backgrounds. Illegal economic resources generally can be more easily obtained by African American male youth than female youth; and, the measures of male social competence (such as sexual exploits, coolness, etc.) tend to be evaluated similarly by the youth from diverse social classes. This occurs because male youth learn to value those characteristics and traits that are considered masculine. As long as African American males learn directly and vicariously that the road to manhood is blocked because of their race, and that their sex implies that they are powerful social beings who should dominate others, the socialization crisis will continue. Violence, teenage fatherhood, crime, and other social dislocations basically are alternative responses African American male youth make to a racist, sexist and classist society.

African American female and male youth have come to a crossroads. For decades African American youth faced and overcame barriers of monumental proportions that would have stopped the progress of a less persistent and tenacious people. Yet, each generation met the challenges and survived to see succeeding generations accomplish goals that had only been wistfully thought of by preceding generations. A major reason for survival was the socialization experiences provided African American youth by the African American family and the entire African American community. These experiences, imparted to the youth by wise old African American women and men, taught the youth survival strategies. Such teachings seem conspicuously absent on a large scale in the socialization experiences of African American youth today.

As discussed earlier, African American youth today, both female and male, commonly experience situations and circumstances which are personally devitalizing. Of course, experiencing racism can impede African American youths' attainment of worthwhile goals, but racism always has existed in American society. The existence of racism historically has not produced large numbers of African American youth who have various and sundry social pathologies. As Wilson (1987, p. 21) suggests, high rates of African American crime (much of which is committed by youth), teenage pregnancy, female headed families (many of which are female youth) and welfare dependency simply cannot be accounted for in terms of racial discrimination per se, but must be seen as having complex sociological antecedents that range from demographic changes to problems of economic organization.

Essentially, a major point in this paper is that complex social psychological issues also must be the focus in discussion of African American youth socialization experiences. There are socialization experiences unique to some youth because they are African American and have meager economic resources, but are expected to assume dominant roles in society because they are male. There are other youth who experience a different kind of socialization process because they are African American poor and are expected to assume a less dominant role in their interactions with males.

The former experiences generally characterize the lives of African American male youth who frequently opt to conform to interpeer group and intrapeer group expectations. From the youth's perspective, the expectations are realistic, consistent, male dominant and viable alternative expectations to the contradicting ones held for them by racist mainstream society and a

socially and economically impotent African American community.

Many African American female youth have the latter type of socialization experiences because of their race, sex and economic standing. They experience, first of all, two kinds of oppression: oppression based on race and oppression based on sex. When race and sex are combined to oppress, the interactive effect can be, and often is, personally disastrous. In some cases, class serves to mitigate the pernicious effects of racism and sexism. Unlike their male counterparts, African American female youths' access to economic resources appears to determine greatly their life courses. African American male youth, however, seem much more vulnerable to peer group influences regardless of socioeconomic status.

REFERENCES

Baldwin, A. 1980. *Theories of Child Development*. New York: Wiley.

Benjamin, L. 1991. *The Black Elite*. Chicago: Nelson Hall.

Boykin, A. W., and F. D. Toms. 1985. Black child socialization: A conceptual framework. In H. P. McAdoo and J. L. McAdoo (eds.), *Black children: Social, educational, and parental environments*. Beverly Hills, Calif.: Sage.

Carrigan, T., B. Connell, and J. Lee. 1987. Toward a new sociology of masculinity. in H. Brod (ed.) *The making of masculinities: The new men's studies*, pp. 63–100. Winchester, Mass.: Allen & Unwin.

Cazenave, Noel A. 1983. Black male–black female relationships: The perception of 155 middle-class Black men. *Family Relations*, 32: 341–350.

Collier-Watson, B., L. N. Williams, and W. Smith. 1986. An alternative analysis of sexism: Implications for the Black Family. In R. Staples (ed.), *The black family: Essays and studies*. Belmont, Calif.: Wadsworth.

Connor, M. E. 1988. Teenage fatherhood: Issues confronting young Black males. In J. T. Gibbs (ed.), *Young, Black and male in America: An endangered species*. Westport, Conn.: Auburn House.

Edelman, M. W. 1985. The sin is so wide and my boat is so small: Problems facing Black children today. In H. P. McAdoo and J. L. McAdoo (eds.), *Black children: Social, educational, and parental environments*. Beverly Hills., Calif.: Sage.

Ellison, R. 1972. *Invisible man*. New York: Random House.

Gibbs, J. T. 1978. *Young, Black, and male in America*. Westport, Conn.: Auburn House.

Gonzalez, A. 1982. Sex roles of the traditional Mexican family. *Journal of Cross-Cultural Psychology,* 13: 330–339.

Hale-Benson, J. 1986. *Black children: Their roots, culture and learning style* (2nd ed.). Baltimore: Johns Hopkins University Press.

Hare, B. A. 1985. Reexamining the achievement central tendency. In H. P. McAdoo and J. L. McAdoo (eds.), *Black children: Social, educational, and parental environments.* Beverly Hills, Calif.: Sage.

Hooks, B. 1984. *Feminist theory: From margin to center.* Boston: South End.

Kasarda, J. D. 1978. Urbanization, community, and metropolitan problems. In D. Street (ed.), *Handbook of contemporary urban life.* San Francisco: Jossey-Boss.

Killen, O. J. 1983. *And then we heard the thunder.* Washington, D.C.: Howard University Press.

Ladner, J. A. 1972. *Tomorrow's tomorrow: The Black woman.* Garden City, N.Y.: Doubleday.

Lewis, D. 1975. The Black family: Socialization of sex roles. *Phylon,* 26: 471–480.

Lindesmith, A. R., A. L. Strauss, and N. K. Denzin. 1991. *Social psychology* (7th Ed.). Englewood Cliffs, N.J.: Prentice-Hall.

Lindzey, L. L. 1990. *Gender roles: A sociological perspective.* Englewood Cliffs, N.J.: Prentice-Hall.

Majors, R. 1986. Cool pose: The proud signature of Black survival. *Changing Men: Issues in Gender, Sex and Politics,* 17 (Winter): 5–6.

Merton, R. 1968. *Social theory and social structure,* rev. ed. New York: Free Press.

National Center for Health Statistics. 1990. Natality, 1988. *Vital Statistics of the United States,* Vol. 1, No. 90–110, Table No. 1–2.

National Center For Health Statistics. 1991. Mortality, Part A, 1988. *Vital Statistics of the United States,* Vol. 2, Tables 1–4.

O'Hare, W. P., K. M. Pollard, T. L. Mann, and M. M. Kent. 1991. African Americans in the 1990s, *Population Bulletin,* Vol. 46, No. 1. Washington, D.C.: Population Reference Bureau, Inc. July 1991.

Price-Bonham, S., and P. Skeen. 1982. Black and White fathers' attitudes toward children's sex roles, *Psychological Reports,* 50: 1187–1190.

Renzetti, C. M., and D. J. Curran. 1989. *Women, men and society: The sociology of gender.* Boston: Allyn & Bacon.

Staples, R. 1986. *The Black family: Essays and studies.* Belmont, Calif.: Wadsworth.

Williams, T., and W. Kornblum. 1985. *Growing up poor.* Lexington, Mass.: D.C. Heath.

Wilson, W. J. 1987. *The truly disadvantaged: The inner city, the underclass and public policy.* Chicago: University of Chicago Press.

Zigler, E., and I. Child. 1973. *Socialization and personality development* Reading, Mass.: Addison-Wesley.

12

Family Violence

Domestic Violence in Black American Families: The Role of Stress

ROBERT STAPLES

An overview of the role that stress, environmental forces, and social class play in the incidence of family violence among intimates and family members. Based on a review of the statistical data and other literature, the author concluded that genetics has no role in the overrepresentation of Black Americans in domestic violence and child abuse statistics. Instead, it is a function of unemployment, poverty, stress and racial devaluation that explains most of the racial differences in family violence.

■

The subject of violence in family relations has been neglected as an area of study by behavioral scientists until recent years. Most of the research has been carried out by criminologists and not family sociologists. A primary reason for this void in the family literature on family violence has been the prevailing ideology of the family as a unit characterized by affection and cooperation between its members. Yet, it has been known for some time that the largest group of homicides in the United States involve spouses, kinsmen and close friends. One of every two women will find herself in a battering relationship at sometime in her life. One fourth of all homicides are within family killings.[1]

It is difficult to discuss violence of any kind in America without noting the over-representation of Blacks in the official statistics on violent crimes. The overall rate of homicides for Blacks is five and one-half times greater than that of Whites.[2] Although there is an increase in inter-racial acts of violence, the aggressor and victim in most acts of Black violence are Black. Most of these cases of Black violence involve family and friends. It should be noted, however, that the proportion of homicides involving strangers is sharply on the increase.

Despite the fact that Blacks are over-represented in the statistics on violent crimes, the subject of family violence in that group has been almost ignored by criminologists and other behavioral scientists. Blacks are also very prominent in those groups most likely to commit acts of family violence: the lower-class, large families, and the unhappily married. Hence, it is not surprising to find that domestic violence was the leading cause of injury in Black women under the age of forty-five.[3]

STRESS FACTORS AND BLACK FAMILY VIOLENCE

My purpose in this paper is to examine the causes of Black family violence as a result of stress factors. Although it might be easy to dismiss Black violence as a result of that group's predisposition to violence, the cross-cultural evidence does not support such an assumption. Bohannon's data from African societies illustrate that cultural rather than biological factors accounted for the high homicide rate among Afro-Americans. Bohannon's studies show that African rates tended to be lower than Afro-American rates but also lower than rates for the general population.[4]

In this paper I do not uncritically accept Frantz Fanon's theory about the therapeutic effects of violence among oppressed peoples. He does provide a guideline for understanding Black violence in his supposition that the colonized man will initially be violent against his own people and that the development of violence among the oppressed colonial subjects will be proportionate to the violence exercised by the colonial regime.[5] Thus, it is understandable that the victims of Black violence are primarily other Blacks and that the White majority and its government leaders have set an example of violence by their historical acts of aggression against people of color in the United States and throughout the world.

Before looking at certain forms of family violence, we must investigate how Blacks are socialized into violence.

SOCIALIZATION INTO VIOLENCE

Blacks are socialized into violence in a number of ways, via internal and external culture processes. The role modeling of television and movie heroes has considerable impact on the impression-able minds of young Black children. The emphasis on violence in the mass media is undoubtedly related to acts of violence among Black youth. It is estimated that by age 12, the average child has witnessed 10,000 acts of violence on television alone. Because Black children watch television more often than White children, the impact of such violence is even greater.[6] Although the number of Black exploitation movies has declined in recent years, they feed Black youth a steady diet of violence that far exceeds that found in movies catering to the White majority youth.

Lower-income Black children are exposed to violence at very early ages. In housing projects, for instance, it is not uncommon for young children to have been shot at, robbed, and raped by the time they reach the age of 10. The structure of low-income public housing projects is conducive to certain forms of crime such as rapes on the stairwell, robberies in elevators, and sniper shooting from windows. Hence, children living in these areas that are relatively unprotected by the police must learn to protect themselves. Other forms of negotiating conflicts are subordinated to the display of physical skills that will prevent one from being overwhelmed by those who will test a person's toughness.[7]

The status-conferral system in Black life initiates the youth into acts of aggression. In the ghetto, the highest level of esteem and respect is often reserved for the best streetfighter in the neighborhood. Older males in this environment encourage children to develop aggressive tendencies by their philosophy that a "real man" is supposed to fight. In altercations among Black youth, older males can often be observed encouraging children to fight. Majors and Billson comment that in the ghetto, people everyone respected were the men who had beaten somebody. And, the children respected by the adults in their neighborhood were those who did not let anybody beat them.

The Black ghetto, however, is nothing but a microcosm of the entire society. Violence is endemic to the American social structure, and the United States easily deserves its reputation as the most violent country in the world. Its homicide rate is twice as high as that of any other industrialized nation. Although public officials decry violence by oppressed minorities, they eagerly support wars that so far have accounted for four million deceased Americans and a much larger number of enemy deaths. The public support for the bombing of Iraq is but one example of the cultural support for violence in this country. Americans are the most heavily armed citizenry in the world.

MARITAL CONFLICT

Homicides and assaults committed by spouses are rather pervasive in lower-class Black communities. At one time the murder of a wife constituted 34 percent of all female homicides committed in this country.[9] Family violence is primarily a crime of the lower class as reported in official crime statistics. Although domestic quarrels occur quite often in the middle and upper classes, these classes do not report domestic quarrels with the same frequency as the poor do. Despite the underreporting of spousal violence by the upper classes, it might still be more common among lower-class Blacks for reasons associated with their socioeconomic and racial status.

Contributing to spousal violence in this group is the normative expectation that some physical violence against the wife is natural or necessary. In Chicago, for instance, a good old man was defined as one who "may slap or curse his old woman if he's angry but definitely not beat on her all the time when he's sober or endanger her life when drunk."[10] The husband is expected to use his physical superiority over his wife on occasions and frequent reference is made by lower-class Black men that they are supposed to treat women roughly to keep them in line. A major class difference, without regard to race, is that physical domination by a spouse is seen as an intolerable behavior pattern by many middle-class wives. The first blow struck by a husband is taken by middle-class wives as a symbol of gross abuse, and it alone can result in a divorce action.

Among the reasons for violent marital conflict are disputes over money, jealousy, or drunken behavior. Jealousy is often the primary cause of spousal violence. Because of a community norm that encourages extramarital affairs, a liaison with another man or woman can result in a violent conflict between spouses. Black families might be particularly subject to this stress in a marriage because of the belief by Black husbands that a wife will seek sexual gratification elsewhere if relations do not go well. Men who are only living with, but not married to, a woman are even more prone to violence motivated by jealousy. Sometimes, being married to a woman is regarded as a license for physical domination of her. Some Black men feel that even though they might not be able to control how society treats them, at the very least they should be able to control "their women."[11]

An unusual characteristic of Black spousal violence is the incidence of Black female aggression. In African societies, men are almost always the aggressor in domestic homicides. But the Black American woman has a reputation for using razor blades and lye to take care of business when he pushes her too far. In an analysis of family violence, Hampton found almost one-fourth of the female inmates at one prison had been convicted of killing abusive mates.[12]

Further investigation of these family homicides indicates that these high rates for Black women can be explained as acts of self-preservation when a woman is attacked by her spouse. However, the high rates can also reflect the low status of Black men in their family relations because of their inability to find jobs or being employed at jobs that pay very low wages.

The class characteristic of individuals involved in violent marital conflict is a natural result of their racial status. High rates of unemployment and underemployment automatically consigns a large number of Blacks to the underclass and several factors influence the incidence of marital violence. In the higher social classes, both Black and White, men are able to exercise control over their wives in other than violent ways. Middle-class men have more prestige, money, and power than lower-class men do. Hence, middle-class men possess greater resources with which to achieve their aims with intimates. The balance of power in marriage belongs to the partner bringing the most resources to the marriage. In general, money has been the source of power that sustains male dominance in the family. As we might note, money belongs to him who earns it, not her who spends it, since he who earns it can withhold it.

Lower-class Black men often find themselves at a disadvantage in relation to their wives within the family. As a result of their consignment to the underclass, they are often unable to provide for their families properly and have a problem maintaining status in the eyes of their wives and children. Because they are aware of their role failure, lower-class Black men are inclined to counterattack any perceived challenge to their manhood with violence. Oliver observed that beatings and arguments precipitated by a husband seem to occur particularly when there is a discrepancy between the demands on him as a provider and his ability to meet those demands. Hence, he responds violently in a attempt to regain status and respect for this role as head of the family.[13]

Oliver suggests that the incidence of domestic violence is probably higher among Blacks than among Whites. A major reason for this racial difference is due to the strictures of racism. The internal devaluation of their self-worth as individuals that precipitates much of Black violence, violent behavior against other Blacks is often a displacement of anger toward Whites. Since many Blacks have little power to effect change, overwhelming obstacles and hopeless surrender produce high levels of frustration.[14] In the words of psychiatrist Alvin Poussaint, "Frustrated men may beat their wives in order to feel manly. These violent acts are an outlet for a desperate struggling against feelings of inferiority."[15] Only been in recent times has this rage and anger been turned against Whites.

Marital violence among Blacks is primarily related to the poverty, oppression, and cultural values found in a racially stratified society. Blacks are not predisposed toward violence any more than other groups. But, in a society which dehumanizes them as well as economically exploits them, psychological controls are broken, and violent rage against the most accessible and safest person ensues. Environmental factors places such stress on Blacks as to make the incidence of marital violence much higher than among the White majority population. Consequently, we must look to the creation of a more equitable racial and economic system for the solution of this problem.

PARENT-CHILD VIOLENCE

Parental abuse of children is nothing new. In earlier periods it was believed that children were inherently sinful and this evil must be violently exorcised. Among Americans of African descent, however, children have historically avoided much of the abuse heaped on their White counterparts. Both the African and Afro-American's mothers' love of their children are strongly documented in the historical records.[16] In recent years the increasing trend in parental injury to children has been most pronounced among Blacks.

Some of the racial differences can be attributed to reporting bias, but much of it reflects the effect of environmental stress on Black parent-child relationship.[17]

Among the factors responsible for Black child abuse are the conditions of poverty under which many children are reared. Child abuse is primarily concentrated in the lower class. These families, especially if they are Black, are much larger than middle-class families. Moreover, lower-class families have less living space in which to rear their children than do more affluent families. Many of them will be headed by a woman, who must often work outside the home and take care of her children afterward. Such a combustible set of factors frequently leads to abusive behavior toward children.

The child-rearing methods of low-income parents is cited as an important cause of child abuse. Although middleclass parents tend to use verbal reasoning and psychological techniques with their children, the lower class inevitably uses physical punishment to exact child obedience. As was true of their parents, most lower-class parents believe that the way to make a child learn is to beat the child. Although alternate forms of punishment might also be used, a beating is eventually employed to maintain their conformity to parental instructions. However, some authorities believe that middle-class child rearing techniques can be just as violent (although only verbal) and psychologically damaging to children as those in the lower class.

At any rate, the physical method of child behavior control can and does lead to excessive injuries to some children. But, in exacting child obedience, many lower-class parents are without other effective means of accomplishing this objective. They cannot offer the more effective status rewards to their children. They are unable to reward their children for good behavior because they lack the educational and social privileges of the middle class. Very few of these resources are available to Black children in the underclass.

Although most people conceive of parent-child violence as commonly involving the parent as the aggressor, there are a number of incidents in which the parent is the victim. An increasing number of violent acts, including homicide, are committed by youth under the age of 15.[18] The lack of status and economic resources among lower-class Black families means that many parents are unable to control a child's aggressive behavior toward them. An enormously high unemployment rate among Black teenagers in the inner cities is also a contributing factor. Being poor, the uneducated young Black male is in an oppressive environment without any means of escape, and having observed violence throughout his childhood, he is an explosive force that erupts in aggression against those who are physically accessible.

IMPLICATIONS FOR FUTURE RESEARCH

Based on this limited overview of race, stress and domestic violence, the implications for further research are the following:

1. To examine the particular stresses associated with status devaluation as a racial group and how that stress factor is expressed in violent behavior. Given that all Blacks will be exposed to some element of racial stress, what factors control violence in some of them and encourage it in others?

2. How do other support systems affect the incidence of family violence among lower-income Blacks. The effects of the extended family should be explored for its role in defusing family violence among its members. Among other areas of interests are residence in urban versus rural locations and the consequence of primary relationships over secondary relationships in controlling family violence.

3. The effects of class membership on family violence among Blacks. Does access to certain social values and resources tend to mitigate the need to use violence as a form of conflict resolution in the family? This, of course, is contingent on obtaining accurate data on the amount of family violence in the various socioeconomic strata.

4. We must look at how gender and parental roles are defined in the Black community. Does the more independent role ascribed to Black women lend itself to provoking assault by the husbands? How is the relationship between parent and child defined? Does the need to exercise parental authority encourage the use of excessive violence toward children?

5. We have very little information about two emerging forms of family violence: husband abuse and child violence directed against parents. There is a need for basic research studies in these two areas.

6. A most important area of future research is an analysis of employment trends and family violence. Does family violence increase as the rate of unemployment increases? What relationship exists, if any, between the type

of status of occupations and the incidence of family violence? Because the unemployment rate is so terribly high among Black youth, they should be selected as a target population for studies in this area.

SUMMARY

In this paper the author has tried to show how acts of Black family violence and environmental stress factors are inextricably linked. Although other forces operate in the incidence of family conflict that may transcend race, the crucial variable in maintaining the practice of intrafamily violence among Blacks has been their status as a devalued racial group. There is no reason to believe that the lower-class or Blacks are any more prone to violence than the middle-class or White population. Yet, Blacks are so overrepresented in the official statistics on crimes of family violence as to preclude any explanation other than racial and economic forces as responsible for the amount of violence in their family constellation.

Although the most pronounced trend is the increase in stranger assaults and homicides, this does not necessarily reflect a decrease in the number of intrafamily acts of violence. With the attendant fragility of marriages, female-headed households, and parent-child tensions, violence continues to be a primary source of conflict resolution in the family. It is a violence that was introduced to Afro-Americans in the period of slavery and has persisted throughout their existence in this country. Although a greater emphasis on family solidarity, respect for women, and value of children can do much to reduce the amount of violence within the Black family, only by eliminating the cause of, and cultural support for, violence in the larger society can we expect to live in an environment that is safe and free from harm.

NOTES

1. Psychology Today, Why do they Stay? *Psychology Today.* 25 (May–June, 1992), pp. 17–24.

2. Richard Majors and Janet Mancini Billson. 1992. Cool pose: The dilemmas of Black manhood. New York: Lexington, p. 20.

3. E. Stark. 1993. The myth of Black violence. *Journal of the National Association of Social Workers,* 38 :485–493.

4. Paul Bohannon. 1967. *African homicide and suicide.* New York: Atheneum, p. 237.

5. Frantz Fanon. 1963. *The wretched of the earth.* New York: Grove.

6. Richard J. Gelles. 1993. Family violence. In *Introductions to Social Problems,* C. Calhoun and G. Ritzer, (eds.), 553–571. New York: McGraw-Hill.

7. William Oliver. 1994. *The violent social world of African American Men.* New York: Lexington.

8. Majors and Billson, loc. cit.

9. Gelles. loc. cit.

10. St. Clair Drake and Horace Cayton. 1945. *Black metropolis.* New York: Harcourt, Brace, pp. 566–567

11. Majors and Billson, op cit., p. 17.

12. Robert Hampton. 1987. *Violence in the Black family: Correlates and consequences.* Lexington, Mass.: Lexington.

13. Oliver, loc. cit.

14. Ibid.

15. Alvin Poussaint. 1972. *Why Blacks kill Blacks.* New York: Emerson Hall, p. 72.

16. Patricia Hill Collins. 1994. The meaning of motherhood. In *The Black family: Essays and studies,* 165–173, (5th ed.) R. Staples, (ed.). Belmont: Wadsworth.

17. Robert L. Hampton. 1994. Race, Ethnicity and child maltreatment in Staples, op. cit., pp 174–186.

18. Ibid.

African American Men who Batter: Treatment Considerations and Community Response

O L I V E R   J .   W I L L I A M S

The author points out that treatment programs for men who batter do not account for race and culture. Most current theories ignore key explanations for male violence in Black partner relationships and assume that color-blind theories explain all such interpersonal violence. Williams examines theories that explain violence in the field of partner abuse and highlights those elements that are relevant to Black men who batter. Finally, he proposes race-based treatment for that group and the community response.

■

INTRODUCTION

Because of the O. J. Simpson trial, African Americans' relationship with partner abuse has received increased attention in recent years. Because of the verdict in the case, there have been some individuals in the mainstream press and community that suggest African Americans are more accepting of partner abuse and do not view it as a problem. But the fact of the matter is, few people have examined how African Americans experience this problem. Given the attention that domestic violence has received, less attention has been directed at the causes and solution for partner violence among those African American men who batter.

Issues associated with the needs of African American women and men are often marginalized in the field. Current interventions in partner abuse treatment are often defined by theories of domestic violence arising out of a singular point of view. Theories tend to promote a one-size-fits-all perspective and do not account for all of the important intersections of race, culture and violence (Williams and Becker, 1995). This is especially true regarding African American men who batter. Men of color drop out of treatment sooner and complete treatment at lower rates than their White counterparts (Sanders and Parker, 1989; Tolman and Bennett, 1990). The current theories that explain male violence in partner relationships ignore key explanations for maladaptive behavior among African American men which may account for battering behaviors. Yet, both conventional partner abuse and culturally-focused perspectives provide important information about abusive behavior in intimate partner relationships involving African American men. Therefore, it is incumbent for those who work in this field to expand the way in which they view the causes and solutions to partner abuse. This chapter will examine the theories that explain violence in the field of partner abuse and those that address maladaptive behavior among African American men. In addition, this chapter will

Previously unpublished paper, 1998. Reprinted by permission of the author.

highlight those elements that contribute to culturally congruent treatment and community responses for African American men who batter.

EXPLANATIONS FOR VIOLENCE IN PARTNER ABUSE LITERATURE

Regardless of culture, men who batter are resistant to acknowledging their responsibility in the destructive behavior of partner abuse. The opinions of men who batter often mirror the opinions held by many in society: The problem of violence is interactional, a women is as much a part of the problem as a man, battered women can provoke a man to violence, and women can be as abusive as the man who batters. The problem of violence must be addressed wherever it exists. But those who work with battered women and men who batter understand that the predominate reality is that women are overwhelmingly the victims of partner violence in heterogeneous relationships. In treatment, men who batter learn that in order to end their violence they must take responsibility for what they contribute to it. They also understand that all relationships have conflict from time to time but don't result in violence, and that conflict is not a valid justification for violence. Their recovery process depends on such points of view.

The battered women's movement has helped scholars, researchers and practitioners understand that theory and practice must be modeled around the lives of those who are most affected by violence: battered women. This grass-roots movement has raised our society's consciousness to the problem of domestic violence on many levels. It has produced battered women's shelters, informed society about the impact of family violence on children, and was instrumental in the creation of treatment for men who batter (Westra and Martin, 1981; Edleson and Eisikovits, 1996; Peled, 1996).

The battered women's movement and a feminist critique of theories of violence have shaped the explanations for male battering behavior as well. Two theories seem to stand out from this literature: structural theory as it relates to sexism, and the theory of learned behavior. From a feminist perspective of structural theory, violence toward women is explained in terms of gender inequality (Yllo and Bogard, 1988). It has been viewed as a symptom of another problem, sexism, which is the devaluation and subordination of women by men (Rothenberg, 1988). Historically, sexism has been embodied in laws and cultural norms, which have given men license to be abusive toward women physically, emotionally, economically and legally (Yllo and Bogard, 1988; Oppenlandar, 1981). In a review of mainstream history concerning partner abuse, laws have typically been a hindrance to women's capacity to address this problem; and laws implicitly and explicitly support male violence. Until recently, there have been few sanctions for partner abuse. Violence is a choice men who batter make because the benefit is control, the results are immediate, and the legal consequences, historically, have been minimal. Ellen Pence (1989) explains how men use power and control in intimate relationships. She has influenced many in the field of domestic violence through her explanation of violence toward women. Gondolf (1985) also supports that a shared characteristic among men who batter is their need to control their female partner. Although some researchers suggest that violence for certain men also can be influenced by physical illness or personality disorders, most in the field acknowledge that the abuse of women is perpetrated by men who appear, in other ways as typical of men in society (Sonkin, Martin, and Walker, 1985; Saunders, 1992; Gondolf, 1988; Holtzworth-Munroe and Stuart, 1994; Roy, 1982). From this perspective, abuse is not considered merely a random act but a behavior focused specifically on a female partner. Currently, the protection of women and development of laws that will hold men who batter accountable for their abusive behavior have been major objectives of the battered women's movement.

According to the theory of learned behavior, when a person witnesses violence they may imitate the behavior in anger, considering it a normal strategy to employ in conflict situations. Once the behavior is learned, it can be passed on from generation to generation (Bandura, Ross, and Ross, 1963; Berkowitz, 1983; Rich and Stone, 1996; Rosenberg and Mercy, 1991; and Hammond and Yung, 1993). In the field of domestic violence, scholars specifically describe what behaviors men have learned and how their abusive behavior is directed toward women (Straus, 1978; Gelles, 1979; Martin, 1976; Flynn, 1990; Steinmetz, 1987). Violence is considered a male prerogative (Straus, 1980; Williams, 1989). Much of the research suggests that partner abuse is learned within the family of origin. In batters' treatment groups, some of the themes of treatment include the following: developing alternatives to violence, increasing perpetrators' awareness of their need to control, and reducing their sexist attitudes and behavior. Often group treatment encourages personal awareness, responsibility and accountability. Although this perspective is important, and, in my opinion, must be a primary focus of treatment, scholars and practitioners must integrate such explanations with other realities, including social context and cultural experiences.

AFRICAN AMERICAN MALE PERSPECTIVES ON VIOLENCE AND OTHER MALADAPTIVE BEHAVIOR

Few theories are specific regarding partner abuse among African American men. In fact, it has typically not been discussed in the literature on domestic violence (Williams, 1994). However, among the explanations for maladaptive behaviors in African American men, two theories stand out: structural theory and interactional theory. In these theories, scholars explore the experiences of young African American men either in racist and oppressive or violent social environments. They report that an oppressive social en-

vironment encourages violence (Blake and Darling, 1994; Hammond and Yung, 1993; Hawkins, 1987; Lemelle, 1995; Oliver, 1994; Rich and Stone, 1996; Roberts, 1994; Gibbs, 1988; Williams and Griffin, 1991; and Wilson, 1991). Many African American men are uniquely affected by violent social environments. Homicide is the leading cause of death among African American men ages 15 to 34; they also have high rates of acquaintance violence and suicide. African Americans are more at risk for physical harm by other African Americans than by Whites, and vice versa (Blake and Darling, 1994; Hammond and Yung, 1993; Hawkins, 1987; Roberts, 1994; Rich and Stone, 1996).

Writers who are concerned about maladaptive behaviors in African American men attempt to discern the social realities and antecedents that produce this behavior among these men without excusing their negative behavior. There is a convergence of opinions among many scholars that African American men are not the sole cause of their destructive behaviors. In fact, many scholars imply that to understand African American male deviance, it is imperative to understand White societal oppression. An oppressive structural social context creates hostile living environments that produce a range of maladaptive reactions among some African American men. The violence that results is predictable. Staples (1982) and Taylor-Gibbs (1988) note that violence toward women may be one maladaptive behavior that results, although most of the writers in this area chronicle other forms of interpersonal violence and problem behaviors.

Structural Theory and Troubled African American Men

Staples (1982) and Wilson (1992) suggest that before one can truly understand violence perpetrated by violent African American males, there must be a critique of all African American males' experience in the United States. Violence in the lives of African Americans is allowed and even promoted because historically their lives have been devalued in American society (Hawkins. 1987). It is, therefore, imperative to recognize the types of societal violence they experience in order to understand the violence some African American men perpetrate (Wilson, 1992). Violence and oppression unleashed on African Americans every day goes unnamed (Lemelle, 1994; Gary, 1995; Staples, 1982; Taylor-Gibbs, 1988; Wilson, 1992). Wilson (1992) observes the following historical oppressions: slavery; wage slavery and peonage; economic discrimination and warfare; political-economic disenfranchisement; Jim Crowism; general White hostility; Klan terrorism; lynching; injustice and "legal lynching"; the raping of Black women and the killing of Black men by Whites which have gone unredressed by the justice system; the near-condoning and virtual approval of Black-on-Black violence; differential arrest, criminal indictments and incarceration; segregation; job, business, professional and labor discrimination; negative stereotyping and character assassination; housing discrimination; police brutality; addictive drug importation; poor and inadequate education; inadequate and often absent health care; inadequate family support, and so forth.

Lemelle (1995) states that the study of African-American male deviant behavior highlights the individual's relationship to production. A societal structure built on a dominator/subordinate model seeks to maintain the status quo where African Americans are the subordinate group and part of the underclass. In this context, the values of the dominator are to be internalized and reinforced, while the values of the subordinates are devalued and rejected (Lemelle, 1995; Roberts, 1994). Given this social-historical experience, Hawkins, (1987) notes that violence has been encouraged among African Americans by mainstream society, as long as it was directed toward other African Americans.

Within the last 20 years, the levels of violence in the African American community has increased significantly. Lockhart (1985) and Ards (1997) report that family violence is often influenced by a person's level of income; the poor are at greater risk for family violence. As a group, African Americans are disproportionately poorer than Whites. Gibb (1988) notes that because many of the social supports that had constituted buffers against social oppression for African American's have eroded within the last 20 years, many community leaders, professionals, and more affluent African Americans moved to integrated non-segregated environments. Thus fewer indigenous resources exist within the community. This created a greater gap in economic diversity, advocacy programs, role models, social supports, social networks, community leadership and a greater gap between middle-class and poor African Americans. The results created increasingly stressful community and living environments, with fewer supports and resources for those who were left behind. Furthermore, these environments were at increased risk for higher levels of poverty, stress, frustration, crime and violence.

The poor are not the only group that experience family violence. Clearly, middle-class, and upper-class African Americans experience partner abuse as well. The gap in social support could be experienced by those who left, as well as those who were left behind. African Americans with greater financial resources are not necessarily connected to enriched family or community support and advocacy. They often feel social oppression but address it in comparative isolation (Feagin, 1995). Any African American male who is not connected to a healthy nurturing support system is at risk for displaying maladaptive responses. Yet, the tension associated with social oppression may foster conditions that increase the risk for violence in many forms. Most African American men experience social oppression regardless of social status, but low-income men may feel it more intensely (Gary, 1995).

African American Men and Interactional Theory

One consequence of an oppressive societal context is stressful and violent community environments that foster violent interactions among men. Nicholson (1995) and McCall (1994) describe their experiences in violent African American community environments and explain that violence was a behavioral imperative among their peers. They further explain that to move away from violence was a personal struggle and evolution to self awareness. Rich and Stone (1996) describe the meaning of "being a sucker" for young African American male victims and perpetrators of violence. They interviewed African American men in hospital emergency rooms who were victims of violence. Respondents reported that either an unwillingness to use violence or the perception of "weakness" and vulnerability could result in more danger and increase the potential for abuse, more so than the actual use of violence. Oliver (1994) describes the tough-guy personality that develops from exposure to a violent environmental context. Violence may ensue based on one's perceptions of others within this context. Such perceptions can be triggered by verbal and nonverbal interactions with others. What is important to recognize is that most people in that environment are operating on the same set of cognitive and behavioral imperatives. Violence for some is viewed as a rule for living and/or survival. The attributions for violence are then generalized to other contexts, such as family or intimate relationships (Williams, 1994). Violent behavior, therefore, may result from either a reaction to oppression or through learned behavior from a hostile and violent community environment. Williams and Griffin, (1991) suggest that the violence that results can be directed at the self, at intimate relationships or the community.

THE STRENGTHS OF
TWO PERSPECTIVES

Separately, theories concerning partner abuse or maladaptive behaviors and African American males offer only partial explanations concerning the behavior of African American men who batter. Regarding partner abuse, sexism, male

socialization and social learning are the underlying conditions for violence; controlling and abusive behavior are the results. Legal accountability is used to sanction and control maladaptive behaviors. Group treatment is a method used to reform and educate men who batter. But with maladaptive behaviors among some African American men, societal and internalized oppression and a violent social learning environment can produce a range of maladaptive behaviors. These maladaptive behaviors can include problems such as crime, substance abuse, violence, etc. Several writers in this field suggest that such behaviors require holistic treatment. Instead of focusing on isolated behavior change with individual behavior problems, more could be accomplished through healing and teaching African American men to live a balanced life within a community of self and others (Blake and Darling, 1994; Akbar, 1985). Men who are emotionally out of balance tend to substitute one maladaptive behavior for another (Blake and Darling, 1994). Other researchers recommend that attention to African American males' social realities is imperative. Violent African American men must develop skills to negotiate racist and violent oppressive situations and environments in adaptive ways Williams (1998). Taylor-Gibbs (1988) and Wilson (1992) recommend sanctions for the negative behavior, but they also suggest providing resource and development information for men who live in highly stressed urban communities.

Treatment approaches with violent African American men must make the link between the oppression they experience and the oppression they perpetuate because violence toward women may be a result of displaced anger from their social context (Wilson, 1992; Williams, 1993). Taken together, the two perspectives from each field provide greater insight on multiple levels in understanding and responding to men who batter. A broader, integrated perspective on violence encourages the development of more effective treatment intervention. Presently, there is no language to discuss the integration of these perspectives. Those who write about domestic violence usually do not refer to the work of scholars of African American maladaptive behaviors, and vice versa. In order to effectively confront male battering in this population, practitioners and researchers must become familiar with the literature of both fields. Models of practice with African American men who batter must emerge from these combined theories. For change to occur, it is imperative that we don't get caught in a zero-sum perspective. Williams (1998) recommends that a common philosophy emerge among scholars, practitioners and community activists in the partner-abuse field and African American male violence field. The debate must center on how to enhance treatment approaches that engage, confront, heal and hold the man who batters accountable for his behavior. It should also focus on how to protect African American and other battered women.

AN ENHANCED TREATMENT PERSPECTIVE WITH AFRICAN AMERICAN MEN WHO BATTER

Societal oppression, internalized racism, violent social learning environment, sexism and male socialization are some of the influences that may result in partner abuse by African American men. Increased awareness concerning the influence of these factors on abusive behavior should encourage African American men to behave differently. An additional consideration for African American men who batter is to increase their capacity to address societal or environmental challenges in adaptive, nondestructive ways. Accordingly, these men must learn how to reframe problems and increase their problem-solving skills. Treatment groups are most frequently used with men who batter to re-educate and resocialize them. It also can be a healthy supporting environment for learning non-violent strategies. It is imperative, however, for group leaders to address issues that may be of particular significance to African American men.

Increasing Problem-Solving Skills

In current approaches to domestic violence treatment, men who batter learn about the dynamics of sexism and how he uses it to justify his violence toward women. Present models of treatment also encourage batterers to examine when they use power and control against their partners. Several, noted traditional batterer treatment models are available. These include: the Duluth, Minnesota model developed by Ellen Pence and Michael Paymar; the Domestic Abuse Project model in Minneapolis, Minnesota; the Wilder Community Assistance Project in St. Paul, Minnesota; and David Adam's Emerge Program model in Boston, Massachusetts. Although these models have utility with any man who batters, there are few models available that emphasize the particular needs of men of color. Group workers who conduct groups with African Americans must be especially cognizant of the types of content that they may present in treatment. African American men may discuss material associated with their social realities and experiences. Among the themes that could emerge with some of these men are their experiences with racism—both personal and institutional—and themes associated with stressful or violent living environments. Group work leaders must create treatment environments that address these authentic experiences of African American men.

For example, in a court-mandated treatment group I co-facilitated recently, a client described his experience being humiliated on his job. He explained he is the only African American in his department. He says his supervisor continuously makes an example of him to fellow employees. The supervisor yells and degrades him at every opportunity. In a particular instance, the client had completed a task and then was approached by his supervisor who challenged that he had in fact completed the task. The supervisor, again, began to criticize him on what seemed to be a personal level. A White women, whom he worked with and considered a friend, witnessed the verbal abuse. After the supervisor left, he approached his coworker and yelled at her for not confronting his boss for his verbally abusive behavior . . . the client admitted later, "I went home and explained the situation to my wife . . . She asked, 'why did you yell at your coworker?,' then I slapped her . . ." As the client described the scenario and his actions, in this case, the group worker and the other men in the group were able to acknowledge and support his feeling around the racism. They acknowledged that this type of behavior does occur to African American men. In contrast, the group worker and the other men in the group confronted him concerning his behavior toward his female coworker and his partner. Regarding his coworker, they asked, "Why did he yell at her?" They also asked, "why did he think it was her responsibility to handle the situation?" Further, they pointed out that his behavior toward her was misplaced. They suggested that instead of being angry at his friend and coworker, perhaps he should find an appropriate way to confront his supervisor. Concerning the battered women, the group asked the client, "what were your interactions with your partner, which lead up to the abuse?" The batterer replied, "I was in a bad mood, and I wanted to go off on somebody." From this discussion, the group presented to this man that he was an accident waiting to happen. He noted he was "very short with her, then he got into an argument with her." The group explored whether the argument was due to a real conflict or because of what happened on the job. The client and group concluded his actions toward his partner was a result of his frustration on the job. The group then confronted him concerning his maladaptive reaction to racism—to blame his friend and partner.

Neither his coworkers nor his partners should endure his abuse. His experiences and frustrations at work were real, but others should not have to suffer the consequences. Although there is no guarantee of resolution, the appropriate course would have been to channel his frustration, in appropriate ways, to address the conflict with the supervisor. Other questions the group explored together included: Why did he choose women to be angry with instead of confronting his boss? The group worker and the treatment group made the link between this man's real life experiences with racism and how he displaced his anger to his coworker and partner—to women. Traditional themes of sexism were explored, but cultural contextual themes of scapegoating African American women were explored as well (Williams, 1998). Also important was that his experience with racism were acknowledged but not used to *excuse* his aggressive hostile, abusive or violent behavior. With regard to racism, the men in the group helped this client examine appropriate ways to confront his supervisor. In addition, the men explored appropriate ways to inform his partner about his state of being when he arrived home. Finally, the men discussed appropriate, nonviolent approaches to handling his feelings and behavior when he is at home with his family or partner.

In a second case example, while I co-facilitated a prison group for men who batter, the men in the group were asked to describe a situation where they handled a problem without the use of violence. One client mentioned the following situation. "There was a drug dealer who lived down the street from me, and he kept running through my backyard trying to get away from somebody . . . Well, one day I confronted him and said, 'Don't run through my yard. I got people in my house and they have nothing to do with your business . . . I don't want them hurt behind your stuff.' He agreed not to go through my yard again . . . The next day he did the same thing and I went out to ask him nicely again . . . don't run through my back yard . . . The very next day he did it again, and I did not do anything . . . Finally, when he came through the last day . . . I was wearing a gun and asked him . . . 'What's up!' . . . That was the last time I had a problem with him." The client was convinced that what he did was the most effective approach to handle the problem.

The men in the group validated his concern over his family's safety. Then the men began a discussion about the consequences of his actions.

Some men noted that "if he shot the man he could land in jail for life . . . then who would support his family?" Another man noted that "he could have killed you!" Another man said, "Even if you killed him, his boys could have come back and killed you and your family!" The group noted that although no violence occurred, his approach was not really nonviolent. The group leaders then asked the other men in the group to identify other ways to discourage the man from running through the backyard. They suggested get a fence, get a pitbull, organize a neighborhood watch, or move. The point of the exercise was to identify alternative approaches and thought processes to cope with a conflict situation. This approach challenged the man's way of looking at the world. But the group also examined how such a situation affected his behavior with his partner and other family members. What happened after each episode with the drug dealer? In contrast, how does he relate to his partner when there is conflict with others? They also explored how the man viewed nonviolent conflict when it occurred between himself and his partner. Given the previous situation, it's apparent that the client has problems identifying what is or is not nonviolent or abusive behavior.

Reframing Group Treatment Models

What kind of group treatment environment allows for the exploration of the above content? Williams (1995) found that only certain treatment environments encourage the discussion of authentic experiences of African American men. Accordingly, some African American men may be more engaged in treatment while others disconnect. (See Model 1.) Colorblind treatment groups do not encourage the exploration of African American male content. These groups tend to be racially mixed. Group workers tend to discourage any discussion of content that is not directly related to partner violence. Topics associated with racism and hostile living environments are discouraged as much because the worker is uncomfortable with the content as it is his perception of relevance. In these groups, workers believe that "differences" don't make a difference. Healthy heterogeneous groups are racially mixed, as well, but the group worker makes an attempt to be both culturally competent and inclusive. He/she makes every attempt to explore culturally different realities without losing sight of the purpose for the group, which is to end partner abuse. In culturally specific milieu group environments, these groups are racially homogeneous, yet group workers are still either unwilling or unprepared to address culturally specific content brought up by men in the group. Culturally focused and/or culturally centered treatment groups are racially homogeneous, and group workers are very familiar with the content of the client group and plan for it as a part of a treatment strategy (Williams, 1998).

What follows are some additional elements to include in these groups. Very often, African American clients, who live in stressful and violent community environments, also live in poverty. In fact, several urban court-mandated programs, anecdotally report that a disproportionately high number of poor African American men are referred to treatment. Group workers bring other types of information and resources to groups in order to respond to the needs of these men and to increase the perception that the group is a resource. Information associated with poverty, substance abuse, unemployment, homelessness, parenting, nutrition, education, and child abuse and neglect are explored in treatment. Certainly these other issues are influenced by a lack of resources, information and service delivery. Providing information on a group bulletin board concerning access to food, housing, employment, training and educational opportunities is also useful.

Healing and restoration is also planned for in the treatment process. The idea of healing and restoration is based on the reality that there are powerful positive models of African American manhood that all African American men must strive toward. Havenaar (1990) states that

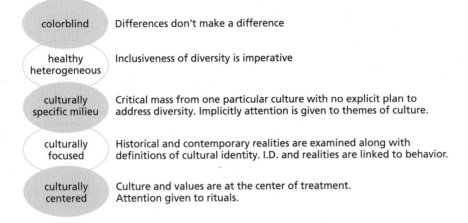

colorblind	Differences don't make a difference
healthy heterogeneous	Inclusiveness of diversity is imperative
culturally specific milieu	Critical mass from one particular culture with no explicit plan to address diversity. Implicitly attention is given to themes of culture.
culturally focused	Historical and contemporary realities are examined along with definitions of cultural identity. I.D. and realities are linked to behavior.
culturally centered	Culture and values are at the center of treatment. Attention given to rituals.

Model 1 Levels of focus on diversity of batterer treatment groups.

psychotherapy models can provide healing if they are based on the morals, cultural values and realities of a client group. He notes that every culture has its own set of cultural values that is used to resocialize and heal its people. Unless African American men have healthy definitions of manhood, based on what can be described as an African American set of values, problems will occur (Asante, 1981; Akbar, 1985; Madhubuti, 1984; Roberts, 1994). hooks (1995) and Roberts (1988) state that African American men must define themselves based on a healthy definition of masculinity, rather than based on a destructive, sexist or borrowed definition. Hooks (1995) reminds African American men not to recreate the power and control paradigm that scapegoats and oppresses women. She reminds us that oppression is destructive to everyone. Asante (1981), Akbar (1985) and Roberts (1994) describe a set of enduring values that characterize African Americans. These include the importance of group and community above competition and individual aspirations. Furthermore, sharing, respect and reciprocity are valued in interpersonal relationships. Madhubuti (1984) suggests in a poem entitled, "Black Manhood: Toward a Definition," which suggests that an African American man must live a life of balance. Akbar (1989)

expands on this theme and encourages African Americans to live in balance within a community of self and others. Waldram (1993) suggests that for one to attain balance and healing he/she must actively focus on behaviors and action steps. To transform African American men who batter, these men must have accurate information about their history as healthy (nondysfunctional, nonpathological) people. They must meet and interact with healthy models. Men who batter must be taught the rules for African American male health, which include: living in balance, learning how to negotiate life's challenges adaptively and without violence, and being respectful and inclusive of African American women and children. Finally, as they follow the action steps, they must strive to become models themselves.

Group Counselor Characteristics

If group workers are predisposed to ignore the realities of African American group members poor outcomes can be predicted. Bell (1996), in an article addressing African American men's treatment issues, recommends the following characteristics for counselors who work with African American men:

- Therapists who confront anxiety surrounding race and who explore their own issues pertaining to race.

- Therapists who understand and are sensitive to issues of culture, class, family structure, educational levels and social activities, and thereby avoid stereotyping.

- Therapists who understand barriers and frustrations about denied access, as well as the need to achieve and be upwardly mobile.

- Therapists who understand the need for strong racial and class identity, as well as for group identification and mutual dependence.

- Therapists who understand why some African American men might feel vulnerable and inferior, as well as a need to be submissive and passive.

- Therapists who understand why some African American men would be distrustful of people in authority, as well as have transient paranoid, persecutory and suspicious feelings.

- Therapists who understand the special issues of establishing rapport with African American men.

- Therapists who understand that some African American men will have a continuous, torturous struggle with self-identity and self-determination, and will be confused about various aspects of racism.

- Therapists who understand the difficulties of working with African American men, depending on whether the therapist is African American or White.

Cautions with Cultural Content

Just as social learning, male socialization and sexism are explanations for male violence, social oppression and environmental codes are added explanations for violence among African American men. All men who batter, regardless of culture, are 100 percent responsible for their violent and abusive behavior. It is important to stress that the aforementioned are explanations not excuses for violence. At times statements concerning racism or oppression of African American men must be challenged, as well, but a culturally competent group worker would know when to confront and when to acknowledge such issues. Accordingly, group workers must prevent collusion among group members on such issues. African American men must be cautioned against attending to racism and oppression to the exclusion of the primary purpose of the group, which is to end violence against women. Group workers must have as much information about the topic of men who batter as they do about cultural diversity.

They must always consider when they confront inappropriate thinking and actions when to acknowledge racism or when they are colluding on one issue to the exclusion of other important issues (see Model 2). An imbalance on either issue may result in dire consequences: Battered women may be more at risk because group workers have not provided clients with critical information to change behavior, or African American men may disengage from the treatment process due to cultural incompetence on the part of the group worker. For example, in the first case study above, an appropriate way to address the situation would be to acknowledge the racism, then to confront the abusive actions of the client. Whenever such material is brought to a group, workers must employ this paradigm of inquiry.

SAFETY AND PROTECTION OF BATTERED AFRICAN AMERICAN WOMEN

African American women know that Black men's oppression is real. Moreover, Asbury (1989) describes the double-bind many African American women and families face—being concerned about how their men will be treated in a legal system that historically has been unjust. At the same time, they hate being victimized by

Balance:

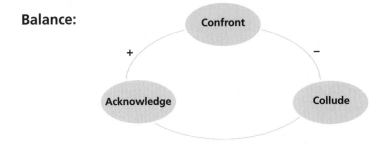

Model 2 In considering methods to engage men and address their reality, it is important that practitioners and group members don't collude! They must always question themselves and confront or acknowledge a reality. They must never collude.

his violence. So, often, women endure these hostile, violent relationships to support their partner (or family member) in order to keep the family together, or because she believes she can heal him and/or he will change. Richie (1995) in her gender entrapment theory encourages us to examine what African American families do to deny sexism and abusive behavior. She encourages the community to consider how women are sacrificed in order to protect male perpetrators. For safety's sake, African American battered women must not accept this rationale as a reason to stay with someone who is out of control. She must be informed that she is at risk for violence if she stays or if she leaves. She, alone, cannot heal his pain through loyalty because he must heal himself. Further, change from abuse to recovery takes time. Women who remain in such relationships, waiting for change (if it occurs at all) risk further injury and harm. Battered women should be informed about the limits of treatment; it is not a guarantee of change for everyone. And predicting who will succeed in treatment and who will not is unclear. Whether or not a woman chooses to remain in her relationship, it is the responsibility of batterers treatment programs and other domestic violence programs to promote her safety. This must be a priority consideration of men's treatment programs. Group workers must determine if the battered women has a safety plan, that is, a planned

course of action in the event she needs to leave the relationship because of her partner's abuse. Among the things included in this plan should be the following: places to go, people to inform, clothing and financial resources. She should be connected to battered women s shelter services. If she does not have a safety plan, someone in the agency should collaborate with battered women's services programs and help her to develop one. Programs must also put into policy the responsibility to inform. That is, women must be informed if her partner is ever determined to be a threat to her or himself.

Reduce the Sexist Attitudes and Behavior of African American Men Who Batter

hooks (1987) and Richie (1995) caution African American men not to become overly romantic regarding African Americans' historically egalitarian attitudes toward African American women. The past and present history demonstrates that sexism is alive and well in the African American community. Sexism gives all men who batter a license to abuse. This is a common phrase in the field and is as true for African American men as for any other racial or cultural group. Further, hooks (1995) cautions White women not to be overly romantic about the commonness of all womanhood around sexism. Efforts to confront sexism have often been exclusionary of African American women. And the dynamics around feminism, sexism and power between African American women and men differ in several aspects compared to those relationships between White women and men (Hooks, 1995; Staples, 1982). African American men must be confronted about their own specific brand of sexism, rather than using the models for White male-female relationships (Staples, 1982). Clearly, power and control are a part of the manifestation of sexism, but historical circumstances and role expectations also contribute. The primary similarity throughout definitions of sexism is that women are expected to be in the subordinate position.

COMMUNITY RESPONSIBILITY

In the African American community, our infrastructure and standards must be strong enough to protect women and to confront the men who batter (Williams, 1993). As a collective community, we have been reluctant to examine our association with this problem. Although there are several nationally known scholars and practitioners who work to create change in our community, our community's inattention to the issue slows our capacity to respond and resolve this problem. If change is going to occur in the African American community, the following must occur. First, we must openly admit there is a problem. Second, we must develop a deeper understanding about the problem and how other African Americans experience it. This subject should be discussed through the African American media (TV, radio, newspapers, magazines and the like). This topic should be discussed through professional organizations, clubs, fraternities, sororities, lodges and community organizations. It should be discussed in the church; ministers must preach about the problem and provide information that concretely protects women and confronts the man who abuses. The community must stand behind battered women and support

their safety. Third, we must increase our communities' capacity to turn to ourselves to address this problem. African Americans have traditionally turned to themselves in times of crisis. This has been one of our strengths. Because natural support systems are overwhelmed or it's unclear how to confront such a problem, abuse is an unresolved issue among us. More attention and resources must be directed by both formal and informal institutions in the African American community. We must develop our own helping networks both to protect battered women and confront men who batter. Although African Americans don't like to put their business in the street, we tend to have greater trust in indigenous formal and informal helping systems than in mainstream organizations. Finally, the community must build bridges with mainstream domestic violence organizations. The African American community and traditional domestic violence organizations have much to learn from each other. Further, although, as a group, African American men and women are underserved and many lack trust for such organizations, the fact is that many African Americans are also served by these institutions. Men who batter are forced into treatment through the legal system, and battered women may use shelters because this is the only available resource for them. Other bridges should be built as well with researchers and law enforcement.

SUMMARY

An enriched perspective retains the beliefs presently held in the field of partner abuse, but it differs because African American male perspectives are included as ingredients that shape the treatment content and design. These experiences include personal experience with oppression, and often with poverty and violence. Treatment interventions must incorporate these explanations and make the link between these explanations and African American men s behavior.

Violent African American men must learn how to negotiate life challenges due to social context and environment. In domestic violence treatment groups and in the African American community, it is essential to address healing, identity and community responsibility.

Engaging and confronting African American men who batter requires the capacity to respond to the dual realities of battered women and African American men who batter. First and foremost, we must protect women from abuse. We must also develop a language to talk about alternative perspectives to confronting domestic violence. We must expand the current perception of the causes and solutions of violence. We must enrich present methods of treatment to be more inclusive: A one-size-fits-all approach is not always appropriate. Scholars and practitioners who study African Americans and those in the domestic violence community must talk to each other, work with each other and learn from each other. Finally, African Americans are caught in a peculiar predicament. Racism and oppression shape their experiences, perceptions and interactions in profound ways that continue to endure. Some survive oppression better than others. Those who don't may turn against themselves through destructive responses to self, to those they profess to love and to the community. Such destructive behavior can be seen as another tool of racism—internalized oppression. There must be legal sanctions to protect women from abuse, but there must also exist community sanctions appropriated by African Americans, which protect women and confront men who batter. Violence erodes a community's capacity to care for itself. The domestic violence field and the community of African Americans must collaborate in affirming and healing gestures to reduce this problem in this community. To end this problem in all diverse communities, African American, White, Latin, Asian, Native American, etc., we must value our similar and unique realities with this problem and support our communities' recovery efforts.

REFERENCES

Akabar, N. 1985. Our destiny: Authors of scientific revolution. In H. P. McAdoo and J. L. McAdoo (eds.), *Black children: Social educational. and parental environments*. Beverly Hills, Calif.: Sage.

Ards, S. 1997. Proceedings of the Institute on Domestic Violence in the African American Community, Atlanta, Ga.

Asante, M. 1981. Black male and female relationships: An Afrocentric context. In L. Gary (ed.), *Black Men*. Beverly Hills, Calif.: Sage.

Asbury, J. 1987. African American women in violent relationships: An exploration of Cultural differences. In R. Hampton (ed.), *Violence in the Black family: Correlates and Consequences* (pp. 89–106). Lexington, Mass.: Lexington.

Bandura, A., D. Ross, and S. A. Ross. 1963. A comparative test of status envy, social power, and secondary reinforcement theories of identificatory learning, *Journal of Abnormal and Social Psychology*, 67: 527–534.

Bell, C. 1996. Treatment issues for African American men. *Psychiatric Annals*. January 26(1): 33–36.

Bell, Y. R., C. L. Boule, and J. A. Baldwin. 1990. Afrocentric cultural consciousness and African-American male-female relationships, *Journal of Black Studies*, 21 (2, December): 162–189.

Berkowitz, L. 1983. The goals of aggression. In D. Finkelhor. *The dark side of families*. Beverly Hills, Calif.: Sage.

Blake, W. M. and C. A. Darling. 1994. The dilemmas of the African American male. *Journal of Black Studies*, 24(4, June): 402–415.

Chestang, L. W. 1976. Environmental influences on social functioning: The Black experience. In Pastoral Cafferty and Leon Chestang (eds.), *The diverse society: Implications for social policy*. New York: Association Press.

Cicone, M., and D. Ruble. 1978. Belief about males. *Journal of Social Issues*, 34(1): 5–15.

Edleson, J. L. 1984. Working with men who batter. *Social Work*, May/June: 237–241.

Edleson, J. L. and Z. C. Eisikovits (eds.). 1996. *Future interventions with battered women and their families*. Beverly Hills, Calif.: Sage.

Feagin, J.R., and Sikes, M.P. 1994. *Living with racism: The Black middle-class experience*. Boston: Beacon.

Flynn, C. P. 1990. Sex roles and women's response to courtship violence. *Journal of Family Violence*, 5: 83–94.

Gary, L. E. 1995. African American men's perceptions of racial discrimination: A sociocultural analysis. *Social Work Research*, 19 (4, December): 207–217.

Gibbs, J. 1988. *Young, Black, and male: An endangered species*. Dove, Mass.: Auburn.

Gondolf, E. W. 1988. Who are those guys? Toward a behavioral typology of batterers. *Violence and Victims*, 3: 187–203.

Gondolf, E. W. 1985. *Men who batter: An integrated approach for stopping wife abuse*. Learning Publications.

Hammond, R. W., and B. Yung. 1993. Psychology's role in the public health response to assaultive violence among young African American men. *American Psychologist*, 48(2): 142–154.

Havenaar, J. M. 1990. Psychotherapy: Healing by culture." *Psychotherapy & Psychosomatic*, 53(1–4): 8–13

Hawkins, D. F. 1987. Devalued lives and racial stereotypes: Ideological barriers to the prevention of family violence among Blacks. In R. L. Hampton (ed.). *Violence in the Black family: Correlates and consequences*. Lexington, Mass.: Lexington.

Holtzworth-Munroe, A., and G. Stuart. 1994. Typologies of male batterers: Three subtypes and the differences among them. *Psychological Bulletin*, 116 (3): 476–497.

hooks, b. 1995. *Killing rage: Ending racism*. New York: Owl.

Lemelle, A. J. 1995. The political sociology of Black masculinity and tropes of domination. *Journal of African American Men*, 1 (2, Fall): 87–101.

Lockhart, L. L. 1985. Methodological issues in comparative racial analysis: The case of wife abuse. *Social Work Research and Abstracts*, 21 (2): 35–41.

Madhubuti, H. R. 1984. *Earthquakes and sun rise missions: Poetry and essays of black renewal 1973–1983*. Chicago: Third World.

Madhubuti, H. R. 1990. *Black men obsolete, single, dangerous? The Afrikan family in transition*. Chicago: Third World.

McCall, N. 1994. *Makes me wanna holler: A young Black man in America*. New York: Random House.

Nicholson, D. 1995. On Violence. In D. Belton (ed.), *Speak my name: Black men on masculinity and the American dream*. Boston: Beacon.

Norton, D. 1978. The Dual Perspective. In *The dual perspective: Inclusion of ethnic minority content in social work curriculum*. New York: Council on Social Work Education.

Oliver, W. 1994. *The violent social world of African American men*. New York: Lexington.

Oppendlander, N. 1981. The evolution of law and wife abuse. *Law and Policy Quarterly*, 3(4, October): 382–405.

Peled, E. 1996. Secondary victims no more: Refocusing interventions with children. In J. L. Edleson and Z. C. Eisikovits (eds.). *Future Interventions with battered women and their families*. Thousand Oaks, Calif.: Sage.

Pence, E. 1989. Batterer programs: Shifting from community collusion to community confrontation. In P. L. Caesar and L. K. Hamberger (eds.), *Treating men who batter: Theory, practice and programs*. New York: Springer.

Pleck, J., and E. Pleck. 1980. *The American man*. Englewood Cliffs, N.J.: Prentice-Hall.

Rich, J. A., and D. A. Stone. 1996. The experience of violent injury for young African American men: The meaning of being a sucker. *Journal of General Internal Medicine*, 11: 77–82.

Richie, B. 1995. *Gender entrapment: When battered women are compelled to crime*. Proceedings, National Institute on Domestic Violence in the African American Community. U.S. Department of Health and Human Services. Administration for Children and Families. Office of Community Services.

Roberts, G. W. 1994. Brother to brother: African American modes of relating among men, *Journal of Black Studies*, 24(4, June): 379–390.

Rosenberg, M. 1990. Change to participants: From analysis to action. *Public Health Reports*, 106: 233–235.

Rosenberg, M., and J. Mercy. 1991. Assaultive violence. In M. Rosenberg and J. Mercy (eds.), *Violence in America. A public health approach*. New York: Oxford University Press.

Rothenberg, P. S. 1988. *Racism and sexism: An integrated study*. New York: St. Martin's Press.

Roy, M. (ed.) 1982. *The abusive partner: An analysis of domestic battering*. New York: Van Nostrand Reinhold.

Saunders, D. G. 1992. A typology of men who batter women: Three types derived from cluster analysis. *American Orthopsychiatry*, 62: 264–275.

Saunders, D. G., and J. C. Parker. 1989. Legal sanctions and treatment follow-through among men who batter: A multivariate analysis. *Social Work Research and Abstracts*, 25(3): 21–29.

Sonkin, D. J., D. Martin, and L. E. Walker. 1985. *The male batterer: A treatment approach*. New York: Springer.

Staples, R. 1982. *Black masculinity: The Black male's role in American society*. San Francisco: Black Scholars.

Staples, R. 1976. Race and family violence: The internal colonialism perspective. In L. E. Gary and L. P. Brown (eds.) *Crime and Its Impact on the Black Community*. Washington, D.C.: Howard University, Institute for Urban Development Center.

Steinmetz, S. 1987. Family violence. In M. Sussman and S. Steinmetz (eds.), *Handbook of marriage and the family*. New York: Plenum.

Straus, M. 1980. Victims and aggressor in marital violence. *American Behavioral Scientist*, 23(5, May/June): 681–704.

Tolman, R. T., and L. Bennett, L. 1990. A review of quantitative research on men who batter. *Journal of Interpersonal Violence*, 5(1): 87–118.

Waldram, J. B. 1993. Aboriginal spirituality: Symbolic healing in Canadian prisons. *Culture. Medicine & Psychiatry*, Sept. 17(3): 345–362.

Westra, B., and Martin, H. 1981. Children of battered women, *Maternal and Child Nursing*, 10: 41–53.

Williams, O. J. 1994a. Group work with African American men who batter: Toward more ethnically-sensitive practice. *Journal of Comparative Family Studies*, 25(1), 91–103.

Williams, O. J. 1994b. Treatment for African American men who batter. *CURA Reporter*, September 25(3),6–10.

Williams, O. J. 1993. Developing an African American perspective to reduce spouse abuse: Considerations for community action. *Black Caucus: Journal of the National Association of Black Social Workers.* 1(2), 1–8.

Williams, O. J. 1992. Ethnically sensitive practice in enhancing the participation of the African American man who batters. *Families in Society: The Journal of Contemporary Human Services,* 73(10): 588–595.

Williams, O. J. 1990. Spouse abuse: Social learning, attribution and interventions. *Journal of Health and Social Policy* 1 (2): 91–109.

Williams, O. J. (1998). Working in Groups with African American Men Who Batter. In L. D. Davis (ed.), *A guide to working with African American men.* Thousand Oaks, Calif.: Sage.

Williams, O. J. (1998). Healing and confronting the African American man who batters. In Ricardo Cerrio and Jerry Tello (eds.), *Healing the male spirit: Men of color and domestic violence.* New York: Springer.

Williams, O. J., and Becker, L. R. 1994. Domestic partner abuse treatment programs and cultural competence: The results of a national study. *Violence and Victims,* 8(3): 287–296.

Williams, O. J., and L. W. Griffin. 1991. Elder Abuse in the Black family. Pp. 117–127 in R. L. Hampton (ed.), *Black family violence: Current research and theory.* Lexington, Mass.: Lexington.

Wilson, A. N. 1991. *Understanding Black adolescent male violence: Its remediation and prevention.* New York: Afrikan World InfoSystems.

Yllo, K. and M. Bogard, (eds.) 1988. *Feminist perspectives on wife abuse.* Newbury Park, Calif.: Sage.

13

Social and Economic Issues

Patterns of Change in the Postindustrial Black Family

ROBERT STAPLES

Reviewing the changes in Black and White families over the past forty years, Staples looks at how racial and economic factors have contributed to those changes. Ultimately, the Black family has had those changes imposed on it by the forces of racism and an exploitative economy, not by free will nor the results of its own family ideology. Dysfunctional aspects of the family are particularly visible in the lower income groups and among women. The one group, or segment, of the Black family not vulnerable to those forces, college-educated Black males, have a family structure and lifestyle that conforms with that of the racial majority.

Many changes have occurred in this country since 1954, covering a wide array of personalities, values, and institutions and bringing about a marked change in the functioning of society as a whole. These changes have been most dramatic within the institution of the family where they have had a most telling effect on our personal lives. We are all, to some degree, affected by increasing sexual permissiveness, changes in sex role expectations, a declining fertility rate, altered attitudes toward child bearing and rearing, a continuing increase in the divorce rate, and the like.

One would not expect Black families to be immune from the forces modifying our family forms. There is ample evidence that they are not. At the same time, their special status as a racial minority, with a singular history, continues to give the Black marital and family patterns a unique character. Despite what many allege to be the positive gains of the sixties and seventies, the problems of poverty and racial oppression continue to plague large numbers of Afro-Americans. Black Americans are still spatially segregated from the majority of the more affluent White citizenry and certain cultural values distinguish their family life in form and content from the middle-class, White Anglo-Saxon model. Nevertheless, the commonality of the two may be greater than the differences. We lose nothing by admitting this. Moreover, the variations within the Black population may be greater than the differences between the two racial groups. Therefore, it becomes even more important to view the Black family from the widest possible perspective.

In attempting to understand where Afro-American families are in the year 2000, it is necessary to begin by defining and classifying the concept of a minority group. The term minority would appear to be a misnomer since it generally applies only to groups physically distinctive from the Euro-American majority in the United States. Black Americans, for instance, are not regarded as a "minority" solely because of their numbers but are differentiated from White ethnic groups based on physical traits such as skin color and hair texture. No serious student of race and ethnicity would suggest that the status of Blacks can be legitimately compared to that of White American ethnic groups (for example, Jews, Italians, Irish).

Yet, a larger number of Black Americans can identify their ancestry to Africa than any White group, except Germans, can identify their ancestry with a single country.[1] Obviously, the concept of "minority" is based on much broader phenomenon than the relative size in the population. Ethnicity, for example, refers to a national identity and distinctive culture and language whereas minority status connotes a history of discrimination, social stratification, and phenotypic characteristics.

The last fifty years have witnessed changes such as international migration, booming fertility rates, and volatile economic systems that have challenged the use of national borders to define a group as a minority. The geopolitical changes of the last century have resulted in the decline of population in the largely white nations from 30 percent of the world's population to 15 percent in 1995. Thus, the groups that North America defines as minorities constitute about 85 percent of the world's population and is rising. In almost every predominately white nation—Marxist, socialist, and capitalist—the downturn in fertility rates has resulted in zero population growth while 90 percent of population growth has occurred in nonwhite societies.[2] Of greater significance, with significant policy implications, is the fact that immigration patterns and fertility rates will irreducibly alter the racial composition of the largely white nations. Demographic projections are that the ten most populous countries in the year 2100 will have majority nonwhite populations. This includes the former Soviet Union and the United States. By the year 2050, if current immigration and birthrate trends hold, slightly less than half of all Americans will be non-Hispanic Whites.[3]

VARIATIONS WITHIN FAMILIES OF COLOR

For classificatory purposes, the minority groups are regarded as American Indians, Black Americans, Asian-Americans, and Latinos. Although most of the groups and subgroups will deviate from the phenotypic norm and have a shared history of racial discrimination by the Euro-American majority, many individuals in those groups will share none of these characteristics. Some Latinos, for instance, have the same phenotypical traits as the Euro-American majority and, depending on their country of origin, will have been members of the upper classes in those societies. The discrimination they still face will be based on their cultural difference and not their socioeconomic status or physical traits. Conversely, Japanese-Americans have one of the highest educational and economic attainment rates in the United States. Although one of the most acculturated groups in North America, they still have to confront current attitudes and practices of racial discrimination based on their physical differences. Black Americans and American Indians represent a special case since they, first, had involuntary entry into and, second, were indigenous, to this White settler nation. While having the longest tenure of all the racial "minorities," Black Americans and American Indians are disproportionately subjected to poverty status and institutions insensitive or hostile to their aspirations.

Class differences exist in all the racial "minority" groups and are said to be more of a fundamental barrier than race to structural integration into American society. Yet the basic problem is that the Euro-American majority sees people of color as monolithic, independent of the minority groups' socioeconomic status. Much attention has been paid to the Black American family, not as a unique cultural institution but as the focus of social problems such as welfare dependency, teenage pregnancy, illegitimacy, and female-headed households. Yet 15 percent of all Black families earn more than $50,000 a year and are not the concern of any public policy.[4] It is obvious that there are economic, not racial or cultural, factors behind those social problems. However, Black Americans of all social classes find themselves identified with the lowest members of their group while Euro-Americans are identified with the highest achieving members of their group

RACISM AND THE AFRICAN-AMERICAN FAMILY

As scholars and practitioners involved with families, we are all aware and concerned about the alleged deterioration of the Black family. The rising tide of female-headed households and out-of-wedlock births has reached dramatic proportions and taken a deadly toll on the society in terms of high school dropouts, increased crime rates, and spiraling welfare loads. Although the effect is known, the causes are generally reduced to those of promiscuous sex and Black family values—or the lack of such values—as a strong work ethic and belief in the monogamous nuclear family. Those who subscribe to these cultural generalities tend to ignore the fact that the statistics on Black family "pathology" reflect economic more than race-bound promiscuity and values. Whereas Black middle-class women have an above-average divorce rate and might be sexually active before marriage, they are not a cause for concern. Like middle-class Whites, they remarry or are self-supporting in the event of a divorce. If their nonmarital sexual activity culminates in a pregnancy, they follow the White model and get an abortion or marry the father.

In other works I have attempted to explain the causal link between structural conditions and Black family.[5] What I, and most other family scholars, did not explore fully was the role race plays in creating and maintaining those structural conditions. Just because class is an important variable in explaining contemporary Black family structure does not mean race or racism has disappeared from American life. As Alice Kahn wrote, "After 30 years, I'm still sitting in what is essentially a Black nightclub in a Black neighborhood, perhaps on the brink of an era of resegregation. The problems between Black people and White people never got solved, we just stopped talking about them."[6]

When Richard Reeves, the nationally syndicated columnist took his panoramic survey of America, he concluded that the major issue is race. Why, then, such little attention to such a paramount, and divisive, issue. One, the development of a substantial Black middle class has led many to generalize about Black progress. On the basis of that premise, it is easy to reject the notion that race makes a difference in the individual's life chance. Another factor is that the comparatively high levels of interracial contact, particularly in work and public settings, make it difficult for the White majority to even think about racism as a pervasive phenomenon. In the abstract, most Americans subscribe to the myths of harmony and brotherhood. On the concrete level, race shapes, in part, almost every aspect of life in contemporary America.

The most important aspect of racial membership is socioeconomic status. Increasingly, being poor and non-White are synonymous traits. The 56 percent of income received by Afro-American families is a generally known measure of Black wealth in relation to Whites. In the 1980s we were told by the Census Bureau that Whites have almost 12 times more assets than Blacks. Almost one-third of Blacks, compared with 8 percent of Whites, have no wealth at all; their debts equal or exceed their assets. As we all know, wealth is measured in many ways. During periods of high inflation, cold cash can be less valuable than commodities, property, stocks and bonds, and so forth. Most White assets are more readily convertible to cash (for example, savings, stocks) while three-quarters of Black wealth consists of equity in a house or car. Because American income and inheritance tax laws lend themselves to the perpetuation of income inequality, this racial gap in wealth will persist over generations.[7]

Those wealth and income disparities, based on race, may largely explain why Americans of the dominant racial group no longer discusses race. It is easy and comforting to believe that they possess 99 percent of the nation's wealth because they were more qualified, hard working, frugal, and deserving. This world view is not shared by many Blacks.

Even middle-income Blacks realize that race is an ever present element in their life. Writing in the New York Times, famous and wealthy, the late tennis star Arthur Ashe revealed, "Early on, I learned that White society would tolerate only so many of us in one group at any time; only so many or none in some places—"nice Negro families" in a previously all-White suburban neighborhood; only so many in certain public schools; only so many in White colleges. When I got in any of these, I was supposed to feel lucky."[8]

He goes on to say that middle income, professional Blacks pay a heavy price if beholden to the myth that success in America is independent of race. Many of them, he notes, are barely able to tolerate the stress. Nearly all of them are hypertensive and some are even visiting psychiatrists. He might have mentioned that one of the highest incidences of cardiac arrests can be found among Black professionals and managers in their forties.[9]

One need not attribute malevolent motives to the majority of Whites for wanting to think we have reached a racial millennium. After all, *Cosby* was the number one TV show, Michael Jackson sold the most records in history, and Blacks dominate the major sports and earn huge sums of money. They, of course, account for less than one percent of the Black population. Meanwhile, 43 percent of adult Black males are not in the labor force; Blacks account for 41 percent of the AIDS victims, are forced into the "volunteer" army,

make up a plurality of those in prison, are dying in large numbers from cancer, and are beset by an epidemic of drug and alcohol related problems.[10] The condition of the majority of Blacks is best described by Theodore Cross in his book on racial inequality in America, "Almost without exception Black people in the United States are born into a state of powerlessness. Even when their professional, management, or business attainments are very great, individual Blacks in the United States are seldom in a position where they are feared, obeyed, or greatly respected by Whites."[11]

To those who demand documentation of my contention that racism is alive and well in 1990s America, we can start by looking at the political arena. Beginning at the top, it is not clear how much of the Republican party's landslide electoral victories and continued popularity is due to racial factors. What we do know is that it has made strident attacks on affirmative action, proposed tax exemptions for racially segregated schools, limited service to immigrants, and held numerous positions regarded as hostile to minorities and women. We also know that it has received a majority of the White male vote and 10 percent of the Black vote in the South. The new Democratic senators from the South generally received a minority of the White vote, a fact that must be attributable to the 25 percent of White Southerners who believe the Democratic party pays too much attention to Blacks. Other examples are abundant. In districts with a 90 percent Democratic registration, Black Democratic candidates lose. Among White voters, Black candidates have received fewer votes than a transvestite, a dead candidate, or one under indictment for a felony, leading to the conclusion that skin color is deeper than party affiliation or any other variable. [12]

In a truly color blind society, it is unlikely that 75 percent of the population would live in neighborhoods with members of the same racial group. We should be clear that residential segregation by race represents no bilateral racial agreement. The number of reported—and many are not reported—instances of claimed housing discrimination cases are at an all time high. No area or class is immune to these forces. The Black former Speaker of the California State Assembly, the state's second most important political official, received an out-of-court settlement for being discriminated against in the purchase of a condominium in "liberal" San Francisco. In Philadelphia, Chicago, and Los Angeles, Blacks have suffered harassment when they moved into neighborhoods that were previously all White.[13] These racial barriers, in turn, affect Black wealth and, by implication, Black family structure. Because Blacks are consigned to all-Black neighborhoods where the primary demand for their homes is from other Blacks, who typically have below average incomes, Black-owned homes are not likely to appreciate as rapidly as are White owned homes, which are sought by other Whites and higher income Blacks. Public school attendance largely follows housing patterns, so the majority of urban school districts are mostly mono-racial in composition.

The aforementioned racial factors are not accidental correlates of socioeconomic status or mere aberrations. They form the basic fabric of American life. They are not exclusive to Blacks. American Indians are even further down the socioeconomic strata. Asian Americans, the "model minority" are increasingly targets of racially motivated attacks because of economic competition from Pacific Rim countries. The increasing American preoccupation with illegal immigration and English as an official language seems to coincide with an era where 80 percent of the immigrants to this country are non-White.[14]

In other White settler nations, where indigenous non-Whites were uprooted, the statistical variables on education, employment, housing, crime, and income are almost identical to those for Black Americans. In Australia and New Zealand, for instance, the same color blind ideology exists, and, for the major minorities, the Aboriginals and Maoris, the reality of massive and pervasive racial inequality is the same as in the United States.[15]

It could be argued that the White majority has a vested interest in not addressing race-based issues. Such a view would fly in the face of two parallel trends. One is the increasing number of non-Whites in American society as a result of immigration and higher birth rates. On the practical level, it means that a largely non-White group of younger workers will be asked to support an aging White population on social security. Unless some sort of apartheid system is erected, it means that the twenty-first century will witness non-White voters deciding on a public policy that affects aging White Americans. According to the government statistics if illegal immigration remains high and annual immigration averages 1 million, the non-Hispanic White population would drop to just under 50 percent in 2050.[16] The other trend is the downward mobility of the White middle class. In the 1990s the extremes of wealth have grown further apart and the middle class could disappear altogether, leaving the United States in the position of a two-tiered society—an affluent minority and a horde of desperately poor.

It will be necessary to advance a public policy to reverse the trend toward an upward redistribution of wealth. Yet, when asked whether the federal government should see to it that every person has a job and a good standard of living, Whites are inclined to give more support to the idea of individuals "getting ahead on their own" versus government intervention.

Again, there is an association in the White consciousness that government programs only encourage indolent minorities.[17] In the more racially homogenous countries of Europe, public policy has long been used to support an equalization of wealth. In 1986 in the U.S.A., the poorest one-fifth of families received 7.4 percent of the total income for all families. By 1992 their share was only 4.8 percent, a reduction of one-third.[18]

Finally, it would be instructive to note that the direction of change is the same for all families in the United States. Where Black families were in 1960, White families are in 1998. The trend toward out-of-wedlock births, female-headed households, and other changes in family structure are an artifact of the changing economic base of family life. Instead of relying on racial stereotypes as an explanation for a group's family structure, we need to understand that they are only further down a road we are all traveling.

BLACK FAMILIES IN THE VANGUARD

Since the publication of the Moynihan Report, all American families have come to resemble the Afro-American families Moynihan described as pathological in 1965. Two of his major indexes of family pathology, more than 30 years ago, were the 22 percent of Black families headed by a single parent and the 22 percent of Black children born out of wedlock.[19] A statistical portrait of all American families in 1991 reveals that there were 10.1 million single parent families in the United States, almost 30 percent of all families with children.[20] Among the most dramatic changes in the last 30 years, was the sharp increase in unmarried mothers among the child bearing population. Within the White female population, the percentage of unmarried mothers more than doubled. By 1992, 25 percent of women had become mothers without marrying, up from 15 percent in 1982.[21]

With his two major indexes of family instability, single parent households and out-of-wedlock births, now exceeded by Americans of all races in 1992, Moynihan has conceded that the American family is in trouble.[22] Yet the alarmist responses that greeted his report on Afro-American families has not sounded when the news of changes in all American families was heard. And those were not the only changes in marital and living arrangements among Americans in the 1990s. The number of cohabiting couples increased from 523,000 in 1970 to 3 million in 1991, and 40 percent of those couples have children. Another 2 percent of all families were same sex households with 5 percent of them containing children. And, a startling 30 percent of all households consist of one person. The changes in American family life styles is dramatized in the

statistic that out of a total population of 250 million people, 82 million adults are not married and living with a spouse.[23]

With the Afro-American family acting as a vanguard of these family patterns, their own minority family pattern evolved into a majority pattern for people of African ancestry. Around the beginning of the 1990s, we found that married couple families composed about 4 million or 50.2 percent of all Black families in contrast with 47 million or 83 percent of all White families. The significance of such a low percentage of Blacks embedded in such unions is that they are the most affluent Blacks in the United States. In 1996, the median income of Black married couples was $41,968, while White husband-wife couples earned $50,190. In the Northeastern region of the United States, Black married couples almost attained earning parity with their White counterparts.[24]

As has been historically true, the higher income of Black married couples is due to the dual employment of husbands and wives. More than 56 percent of Black women, between the ages of 18 and 44 contribute from 30 to 70 percent of the family income, compared with 47 percent of White wives. While most Black women do not earn as much as their husbands, 22 percent actually earn more than their husbands and 7 percent provide more than 70 percent of the family income. In Black families with only a female head, 44 percent earned less than $10,000 a year—below the poverty level—while only 10 percent of husband-wife households had incomes below that level. However, those husband-wife couples were at high risk for family breakup because of those low incomes. According to the U.S. Census Bureau, poor two parent families were about twice as likely to break up as were two-parent families not in poverty. Among Black two-parent families, 21 percent of those who were poor broke up within two years, contrasted with only 11 percent of those who were not in poverty.[25]

The other side of the rosy picture of Black married couples is that most Black adults are not in a viable marital union. In 1990, among Blacks

15 years and over, only 38.8 of the males and 31.4 of the females were recorded as married, spouse present. Or, to state it most succinctly, 65 percent were single, a much larger percentage than the 42 percent of their White counterparts.[26] Whereas a larger percentage of Black than White women had historically been listed as ever married, in 1990 the census bureau found only 75 percent of Black women had married by their late thirties, compared with 91 percent of White and Hispanic women.[27]

Although a majority of Black women over age 15 are separated, divorced, or widowed, the Census Bureau reports that in 1992, 39.1 percent of Black women, 15 years and older, have never married. The obvious explanation for this bleak picture is the shortage of eligible Black men who are employed, drug free, and nonviolent. Although there has been an increase in interracial marriages during the last three decades, less than 2 percent of Afro-American women are married to non–Black men.[28]

Gender is just as important a factor as socioeconomic status. Even middle-class Black women face a severe shortage of available mates. A big reason is the ratio of 2 women to one man among Black college graduates. Indeed, the more educated and successful a Black women is, the less likely she is to find a comparable mate. Conversely, a high educational and income level among Black men ensures them of a large pool of eligible women. That is why they have the highest marriage rate of all segments of the Afro-American community, as high as 90 percent in some regions of the United States.[29]

A severe shortage of desirable Black men has created a new form of the Black family. In 1992, about 59 percent of all children born to Black women were out of wedlock. Many women resign themselves early to raising children alone, given the dismal prospects of finding a decent husband and father among the Black men available to them. The powerful impact of gender membership is illustrated by the fact that 22 percent of never-married Black women with incomes more than $75,000 a year have children.[30]

At least those women have the skills and resources to transmit their social class standing their children. Overall, 54 percent of Black children in single parent families are poor, in contrast with only 13 percent of such children in married-couple families.[31]

Unless there is a reversal of present trends in postindustrial America, the Black family of the twenty-first century will be a unit headed by women and children trying to survive on an income below the poverty line. The man she might have married has been institutionally decimated, by the forces of racism and a chaotic, exploitive economy. Thus, he is in prison, the military, ravaged by drugs and alcohol, or gone to an early grave. Any male child she bears faces a similar fate. Although those same economic forces are directing White families into a similar form, many of the causes are as much cultural as economic. A substantial number of White women have defined the traditional nuclear family as oppressive and have achieved the economic independence to explore alternative forms. Blacks simply find themselves in a struggle between their aspirations to have a traditional family life and the structural conditions that render those hopes futile.

A BEST AND WORSE CASE SCENARIO

The future of the Black family is inextricably tied up with the current and future status of the Black male. One study revealed that 43 percent of Black males between the ages of 16–62 were not active participants in the American labor force in 1993, a figure closely associated with the 48 percent of Black families headed by women and the 52 percent of Black children born out of wedlock in that same year.[32] If the employment rate of Black men does not improve, demographic projections are that 59 percent of Black families will be headed by women by the year 2000 and that only 8 percent of Black children born in the year 1980 will spend all their childhood lives with two parents.[33]

Unless unforeseen social forces reverse current trends, the future is likely to bring one of the first cases in history where women have achieved superiority over men in the vital areas of education, occupation, and income. Already Black women are more educated than Black men at every level, including the doctorate. The 1990 census reveals that 18.8 percent of Black women are managers and professionals compared with 13.4 percent of Black men. College-educated Black women currently earn 90 percent of the income of college-educated Black men.[34] As Black women gradually move ahead of Black men, a role reversal might take place. If Black women will not need to marry a man to attain a decent standard of living, many of them might begin to select dating partners and husbands on the basis of sex appeal rather than the traditional criterion of socioeconomic status.

The shortage of Black men who are desirable and available for marriage will continue into the twenty-first century. Black women might adapt to their situation by a variety of means. Bisexuality might increasingly be viewed as a viable option by women who want their affectional and companionship needs met. Among the women who experience the greatest shortage of men, those older than 60, a kind of grey lesbianism might emerge in response to the unavailability of men. In the college-educated segment of the Black female population, out-marriages to men of different races might become one of their adaptive responses to the male shortage. Some women might seriously consider a more formalized participation in polygamous relationships or liaisons with married men instead of remaining celibate and childless.

For the vast majority of Black women, there will continue to be some involvement with Black men. Chances are that many will continue to be sexually active at an early age, to bear children out of wedlock and rear them with assistance of a female-based kin network. Black women will likely have varying periods of cohabitation with a man but legal marriage rates will continue to decline except for college-educated Black males, the one subgroup in the Black community not plagued by low income, high rates of unemployment, and a shortage of compatible mates.

As for Black men, their employment chances will rise or fall with changes in the economy and other demographic changes in American society. If the economy continues its transformation from a goods-production to a service-dominated economy, Black men's participation rate in the labor force might decline because the latter type of economy favors female workers. That will mean Black men's continued dependence on the underground economy, their cohabitation with a woman of some means, or their living at home with their parents. One countervailing force could be the shortage of young workers predicted by the year 2000, when large numbers of the baby boom generation reach retirement age. Demographic projections show that by the year 2000, 40 percent of the school population graduating into the work force will be Black.[35] Given a substantial improvement in their employment situation, Black men will likely have an increase in marriage rates and a decline in out-of-wedlock birth rates.

However, these demographic changes are already being manifested in many parts of the United States, with no discernible improvement in the employment prospects for young Black males. While employers in low wage industries, such as fast food outlets, are complaining of an inability to fill job vacancies in the affluent suburbs, there are still more young workers than jobs in the central cities. Young White workers are often obtaining part-time and summer work at wages of $9 an hour, while Black teenagers find it difficult to secure minimum wage jobs at $4.50 an hour. Even when available, many Black teenagers perceive, rightfully, fast food and other minimum wage jobs as dead-end positions that have no long-term payoff. Other barriers to employment remain. These teenagers often find themselves competing with their older neighbors for such jobs. This sharp distinction between summer job prospects in central cities and the suburbs belies the rosy projections for young workers in the twenty first century.

A best case scenario for Black families would be the election of an enlightened government that would provide the conditions for the strengthening of Black family life. First, and foremost, would be the implementation of a full employment policy. This would require a substantial redistribution of income from the relatively affluent to the poor through a rigidly enforced system of progressive income taxation and the reduction of military expenditures to the bare minimum necessary to defend the country from an attack by foreign nations. This would not mean the creation of a huge federal bureaucracy because the government would only need to fund already existing projects and agencies such as highway construction, housing, education, the postal service, water conservation, public parks, child care, and the like. There is no reason to make it racially based because Blacks would automatically share in the benefits of a full employment economy. Some government financed training programs, in community based institutions, would be necessary to develop and improve skills of some undereducated workers.

Another governmental act would be the formulation of a family allowance plan, already in effect in most western nations. This family allowance should be set at the level most economists agree is a "good" standard of living, not at the poverty level, which only permits families to exist at the lowest standard of misery. The family allowance would be provided to all American families, reducing the stigma of current welfare programs, and the rigid system of progressive income tax rates would retrieve it from more affluent families. A family allowance plan would permit all families to have a decent income and to work out other difficulties in their relationships as best they can. Although it will work to the advantage of most American families, it should benefit Black families most by lifting their ability to create and maintain a family from under the scourge of economic pressure.

NOTES

1. Bureau of the Census, 1992. *Statistical abstract of the United States.* Washington, D.C.: U.S. Government Printing Office, pp. 24–25.

2. Richard T. Schaefer. 1993. *Racial and ethnic groups.* New York: Harper-Collins.

3. Bureau of the Census. 1993. *Population projections of the USA by age, sex, race and Hispanic origin 1995 to 2050.* Washington, D.C.: U.S. Government Printing Office.

4. Andrew Hacker. 1992. *Two nations: Black and White, separate, hostile, unequal.* New York: Ballantine.

5. Robert Staples and Leanor Boulin Johnson. 1993. *Black families at the crossroads: Challenges and prospects.* San Francisco: Jossey-Bass.

6. Alice Kahn. 1986. Still doo-wopping. *San Francisco Chronicle,* Sunday Punch Section, November 23, p.1.

7. *New York Times.* 1986. Wealth in Black and White. *New York Times.* November 20, p. A–3.

8. Arthur Ashe. 1996. No More Zero-Sum Game. *New York Times Magazine,* August 31, p.26.

9. Ronald Braithwaite and Sandra E. Taylor. 1992. *Health issues in the Black community.* San Francisco: Jossey-Bass.

10. Center for the Study of Social Policy. 1994. *World without work: Causes and consequences of Black male joblessness.* Washington, D.C.: Center for the Study of Social Policy.

11. Theodore Cross. 1984. *The Black power imperative.* New York: Faulkner, p. 34.

12. Thomas B. Edsall and Mary B. Edsall. 1991. *Chain reaction: The impact of race, rights and taxes on American politics.* New York: Norton.

13. Douglas S .Massey and Nancy A. Denton. 1993. *American apartheid: Segregation and the making of the underclass.* Cambridge, Mass.: Harvard University Press.

14. Bureau of the Census. 1993. *Statistical Abstract of the United States 1993.* Washington, D.C.: U.S. Government Printing Office, Table 5.

15. Robert Staples. 1993. A comparative analysis of Afro-American/Maori families: The Subtext of minority status. *ABNF Journal,* 4 (Winter): 5–9.

16. Bureau of the Census. 1993. *Population projections of the USA by age, sex, race and Hispanic origin 1995 to 2050.* Washington, D.C.: U.S. Government Printing Office.

17. Edsall and Edsall, *Chain reaction.*

18. Ramon G. McLeod. 1993. More Americans living in poverty than at any time since 62. *San Francisco Chronicle,* October 5, p. A–4.

19. Daniel P. Moynihan. 1965. *The Negro family: The case for national action.* Washington, D.C.: U.S. Government Printing Office.

20. Bureau of the Census. 1994. *Marriage, divorce and remarriage in the l990s.* Washington, D.C.: U.S. Government Printing Office.

21. Amara Bachu. 1993. *Fertility of American women.* Washington, D.C.: U.S. Government Printing Office.

22. Daniel P. Moynihan. 1986. *Family and nation.* New York: Harcourt, Brace and Jovanovich.

23. Bureau of the Census. 1994. *Marriage, Divorce and Remarriage in the 1990s.* Washington, D.C.: U.S. Government Printing Office.

24. Ramon G. McLeod. 1998. Gains for Black married couples. *San Francisco Chronicle,* July 30, 1998, p. A-2.

25. Robert Pear. 1993. Poverty is cited as a divorce factor. *New York Times,* January 15, 1p. A-7

26. Bureau of the Census. *Marriage, divorce and remarriage in the 1990's.* Washington, D.C.: U.S. Government Printing Office.

27. Gregory Lewis. 1993. Black women: Where are the men? *San Francisco Examiner,* October 17, p. A-1

28. Bureau of the Census. *The Black population in the United States, March 1990 and 1989.* Washington, D.C.: U.S. Government Printing Office.

29. Why the large and growing gender gap in African-American higher education? *Journal of Blalcks in Higher Education,* 7 (Spring 1998), pp. 34–35.

30. Endangered family, *Newsweek,* August 30, 1993, pp. 17–29.

31. Federal Interagency on Child and Family Statistics. *America's children: Key national indicators of well-being.* Washington D.C., U.S. Government Printing Office, 1997.

32. Center for the Study of Social Policy. *World without work.* Washington D.C., 1994.

33. Federal Interagency on Child and Family Statistics, *loc. cit.*

34. The growing gender gap in Black higher education, *Journal of Blacks in Higher Education,* 3 (Spring 1994), pp. 50–56.

35. Lewis, *loc. cit.*

World Without Work: Causes and Consequences of Black Male Joblessness

CENTER FOR THE STUDY OF SOCIAL POLICY

The central theme of this report is that Black males have a much higher rate of unemployment than White males and this gender-race discrepancy has a strong correlation with a variety of negative outcomes for the entire Black population, such as the increase in female-headed households, deepening poverty, increasing substance abuse and crime rates, lower levels of educational achievement and high levels of mental and health problems. The proportion of Black men absent from the work force is extremely high and may result in alienation and dislocation from mainstream society.

■

This monograph was supported by a grant from The Annie E. Casey Foundation.

THE ECONOMIC AND SOCIAL ALIENATION OF BLACK MEN

The alarming rise in Black families headed by single mothers, and its consequences for poverty among children, are subjects much talked about today in the press and on television and radio talk shows nationwide. Less often noted, however, is the disturbing "flip-side" of this phenomenon: the disappearance of Black men from the productive workforce. By itself, the proportion of Black men absent from the labor force is shocking, let alone when it is compared to that of White men. Statistics indicate that Black men face markedly higher unemployment than Whites and are significantly more likely to be absent altogether from the labor force.

A number of scholars have recently drawn attention to the fact that the economic and social isolation of Black males may be strongly correlated with a variety of negative outcomes for the Black population, among them the rise of single female-headed families, deepening poverty, increasing substance abuse and crime rates, decreasing levels of educational achievement, and high levels of health and mental health problems.

These associations underscore the importance of employment and economic self-sufficiency in the advancement of Black men and the stabilization of Black families. In addition, they suggest that the consequences of joblessness among Black men are not limited to economic instability alone. Involvement in the workforce provides not only economic support, but also a meaningful identity and opportunities for socialization. Without these elements, Black men may not only be isolated from the workplace, but also dislocated from the greater society as well.

Joblessness and Absence from the Labor Force

The sharp rise in joblessness among Black males in the past three decades is one of the most serious problems facing the Black community and

American society as a whole. In 1993, a startling 43 percent of working age (ages 16–64) Black men were not working. The sheer magnitude of this number is cause for alarm. Furthermore, despite the significant gains made by Blacks since the civil rights movement, the disparity between the labor force status of Blacks and Whites continues to grow, especially among men.

Figure 1 shows the employment status of Black and White men in 1993. The proportion of Black men who were not gainfully employed is double that of White men. Forty-three percent of Black men were either unemployed, out of the labor force, institutionalized, or their labor force status could not be determined (because they were missed in the 1990 decennial census) as compared to only 21 percent of White men. These statistics would be higher in inner-city urban areas where many Blacks live and where unemployment is often particularly severe.

Two categories in Figure 1 reflect gainful employment: employed and in the military. In 1993, only 54.5 percent of working-age Black men were employed, as compared to 77.6 percent of White men.[1] In contrast, a greater proportion of Black than White men are in active duty in the military: 2.3 percent of Black men compared to 1.5 percent of White men.[2] This may reflect the fact that fewer Black men can find work in the labor force and thus turn to the armed forces for gainful employment.

Four categories shown in Figure 1 reflect non-work. These are: unemployed, out of the labor force, incarcerated, and undetermined labor force status due to the census undercount.

- Individuals classified as unemployed include those who were actively seeking employment in the month prior to the census interview, but remained unable to find work. In December of 1993, 8.8 percent of all working-age Black men were unemployed, compared to 5.3 percent of all working-age White men.[3]

- Official unemployment rates alone do not convey the full extent of non-work among Black men, however, since they include only those individuals who are actively seeking work and do not count those "out of the labor force" because of disability, school attendance, or because they are discouraged and have given up looking for a job. In 1993, 20.6 percent of working-age Black men were out of the labor force, compared to only 12.9 percent of White men.[4]

- Neither unemployment nor labor force data include men in correctional facilities, who are also considered as "not working." This category—counted only in the decennial census—includes those in federal and state prisons, local jails, and other non-juvenile penal facilities. Using 1990 figures, 4.4 percent of all Black men were in correctional facilities, compared to less than one percent (0.66 percent) of all White men.[5] The absolute number of Black men in correctional facilities (469,451) was actually *higher* than the number of incarcerated White males (466,831), despite the fact that White males outnumber Blacks in the general population by more than seven to one.

- Finally, the Census Bureaus official count of the population misses a significant portion of Black men due to undercounting. Analysis of demographic information from the 1990 Census shows that 996,000 Black men and 1,498,000 White men aged 16–64 were not counted in the census.[6] This translates into a 2.1 percent undercount for White men and a 9.3 percent under-count for Black men—a much higher proportion than for any other demographic group.[7] Studies performed by the Census Bureau indicate that these "missing" men likely have unstable or transient household attachments, and generally occupy marginal positions in the economy and in society, making it unlikely that their labor force status would match the distribution of the identified population.[8]

Taken together, these numbers paint a grim portrait of the employment status of Black men in America. The enormous proportion of Black

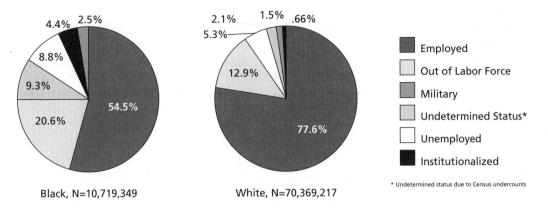

FIGURE 1 Components of U.S. Resident Population, 1993,
Working-Age Men (Age 16–64)

men out of work has grave consequences not only for the men themselves, but also for their children, the women they live with or are married to, and for the whole of our society as well.

Structural Economic Changes and Causes of Non-Work

The disappearance of Black men from the workforce is a consequence of fundamental changes in the U.S. economy and society that have affected, in varying degrees, the employment prospects of all Americans. Blacks have historically occupied a precarious position in the economy; as shown in Table 1, the unemployment rates of Black men have consistently been at least twice the unemployment rates of White men. In addition, Blacks have been severely affected by changes that occurred in the 1970's and 1980's, a period of high inflation, consecutive recessions, and major shifts in industry The fact that the industries most affected by economic changes had high proportions of male workers, and that the workers last to be hired were often first fired, contributed to a "cyclical unemployment" among Black men, who were particularly likely to lose their jobs: Blacks were disproportionately affected by other structural economic changes as well, such as the influx in immigrants, the

suburbanization of economic opportunity, and shifts in the type of available jobs.

At the same time, the legacy of unequal schooling has left a disproportionate number of Blacks without the skills or education needed to advance in an economy driven by new technologies. These factors, combined with persistent racial and cultural barriers, high rates of involvement with the underground economy and criminal justice system, and pervasive substance abuse and chronic health problems, have hindered the full participation of Black men in the labor force.

De-Industrialization

The American economy has undergone tremendous shifts in its labor markets in the past three decades. As global markets have pushed production to less costly labor markets abroad, technology and trade have forced the downsizing of the manufacturing economy of the past. Since 1979, the US. manufacturing sector has shrunk rapidly, ceding an ever larger share of the economy to service industries.[10]

While de-industrialization and accompanying changes in the economy affected many Americans, they had a disproportionate effect on the place of Black men in the labor force. In part this is because the manufacturing industries that experienced the greatest job losses were those in

TABLE 1 Unemployment Rates for Black and White Men (Numbers reflect percent of men 16 years and older in the civilian labor force)

Year	Unemployment Rate	
	Black Men	White Men
1948	5.8	3.4
1950	9.4	4.7
1955	8.8	3.7
1960	10.7	4.8
1965	7.4	3.6
1970	7.3	4.0
1980	14.5	6.1
1983	20.3	8.8
1985	15.3	6.1
1990	11.8	4.8
1993	13.8	6.2

Sources: U.S. Department of Labor, Bureau of Labor Statistics. *Employment and Earnings,* January 1994. Table 3, p. 186.

U.S. Department of Commerce, Economics and Statistics Administration, Bureau of the Census. 1991. *The Black Population in the United States: March 1990 and 1989,* Table E, p. 9.

U.S. Department of Commerce, Bureau of the Census. *Historical Statistics of the United States: Colonial limes to 1970,* September, 1975. Series D87–101, p. 135.

which Black male workers were over-represented, such as auto, steel, and rubber.[11] For example, in 1973, 37.5 percent of employed Black males ages 20–29 were employed in the manufacturing sector; by 1987 only 20 percent were in the manufacturing sector.[12]

The manufacturing industry, which once provided relative prosperity for a broad middle class of unskilled and semiskilled workers, has been replaced by a service economy that has increasingly generated either low paying jobs without benefits, or higher paying jobs that demand advanced education and skills.[13] Workers without such education or skills are typically left with low-paying, "low-skill" jobs that lack benefits.[14] Even in traditional low-skill industries, the number of workers with college degrees has nearly

doubled since 1968.[15] One study of employment in urban areas indicates that since 1970, major cities of the Northeast and Midwest have experienced significant declines in the number of jobs requiring only a high school education or less, while the number of jobs requiring some form of higher education has increased (see Table 2).[16] This shift in the educational needs of the labor market has significantly impacted Black male labor force participation as a far larger proportion of Black men do not have college degrees when compared to White men (see Section entitled Education, Skills and Unemployment and Table 3).

Increases in Immigration

As employment opportunities for low-skilled urban workers have declined, trends in immigration in recent years increase the competition for these disappearing positions. Black males often fare poorly in this competition.

Between 1981 and 1990, over 7.3 million immigrants were legally admitted to the United States—a figure almost equal to the total number of immigrants admitted between the years 1931 and 1970.[17] The number of arrivals accelerated in the late 1980's: in 1990 alone, over 1.5 million immigrants entered the United States, more than one-half of whom came from Mexico and Central America.[18] Because many immigrants have limited education and English language ability,[19] they compete for low-skilled jobs, the same jobs often sought by urban Black males.

While research suggests that the impact of immigration on the Black labor force as a whole is negligible, immigration does negatively impact less-skilled Black workers and Black workers that live in areas with stagnant economies and large immigrant populations.[20] Blacks are also negatively impacted by immigration during economic recessions.[21] In addition, while immigration increases the percentage of employed persons overall, it reduces the weekly earnings of less-skilled Black persons.[22] Finally research shows that some employers prefer to hire immigrants over Blacks for low-skilled jobs.[23]

TABLE 2 Number of Central City Jobs, in Industries Classified by Average Educational Attainment of Employees

City/Class of Industry by Average Education Attainment of Employees	Number of Central City Jobs in Each Industry Class (thousands)			Percent Change
	1959	1970	1984	1959-1984
New York				
Less than high school	1449	1445	953	-34.2
Some higher education	682	1002	1241	82.0
Philadelphia				
Less than high school	434	396	224	-48.4
Some higher education	135	205	244	80.7
Boston				
Less than high school	176	168	124	-29.6
Some higher education	117	185	252	115.4
Baltimore				
Less than high school	215	187	114	-47.0
Some higher education	59	90	105	78.0
St. Louis				
Less than high school	207	197	108	-47.8
Some higher education	61	98	96	57.4

NOTE: In this tabulation, jobs in central cities are counted by industry, and classified according to the average educational attainment of employees in each industry. Although this does not fully represent the education requirements of each industry, it is the best proxy available to illustrate the shifts over time.

SOURCE: John D. Kasarda, "America's Urban Dilemma," in *The Metropolis Era: A World of Giant Cities,* edited by Mattei Dogan and John D. Kasarda (New York: Russell Sage, 1988), p. 70. Additional calculations by the Center for the Study of Social Policy.

Suburbanization

Shifts in the labor market and increases in the value of schooling and basic skills have been accompanied by equally dramatic changes in the nation's economic geography. The movement of jobs away from central cities has accelerated in the past two decades, leaving those areas largely isolated from opportunities for economic growth. This trend has dramatically affected the economic plight of urban Blacks. Between 1976 and 1986, for instance, 20 of the nation's largest metropolitan areas—including Chicago. Philadelphia. Detroit, Washington, and Los Angeles—had at least three-quarters of their employment growth occur outside of urban centers. In some areas, the growth in suburban jobs exceeded the growth of the suburban population, often by a factor of three or more.[24]

Despite the growth of suburban employment opportunities, most Blacks live in urban areas. According to the 1990 Census, 58 percent of all Blacks lived in the central city of an urbanized area, compared to only 26 percent of Whites.[25] It has been suggested that Blacks remain confined in urban areas for a variety of reasons, among them limited mobility and persistent residential segregation.[26]

Cumulatively, the shifts in the types of jobs available, dramatic increases in immigration and the movement of jobs outside the central city have left many Black men outside the mainstream labor force. The fact that 43 percent of all working-age Black men are not employed may be at least partially explained by these national exogenous forces.

TABLE 3 Trends in Educational Attainment of 25- to 29-Year-Olds, by Race, 1965–1989 (Percent)

Attainment, Year	Black Males	White Males
Completed 4 years of high school or more		
1965	50.3	72.7
1970	54.5	79.2
1975	72.2	85.7
1980	74.8	86.8
1985	80.8	84.4
1989	80.6	84.8
1990	81.5	84.6
1991	83.5	85.1
Attainment, Year	**Black Males**	**White Males**
Completed 4 years of college or more		
1965	7.3	16.4
1970	6.7	21.3
1975	11.4	26.3
1980	10.5	25.5
1985	10.3	24.2
1989	12.0	24.8
1990	15.1	24.2
1991	11.5	24.1

SOURCE U.S. Bureau of the Census, CPS Series P-20, No. 451, Table 18; CPS Series P-20, No. 462, Table 18.

EDUCATION, SKILLS, AND UNEMPLOYMENT

Educational achievement among African Americans continues to lag behind that of all other racial and ethnic groups, despite numerous examples of individual accomplishments under segregated circumstances. Inadequate preparation in unequal schools and continued racial prejudice have trapped more than a third of African Americans in a cycle of poverty…

Shirley McBay. "The Condition of African American Education: Changes and Challenges" in *The State of Black America 1992.*[27]

The demographic and workforce changes discussed above have accentuated the value of skills acquired through formal education as criteria for success in the job market; many workers who lack such skills have found their employment opportunities and earnings ability severely restricted.

Blacks have made great strides in education in the past three decades. By 1990, Black youth were as likely as Whites to be enrolled in school and nearly as likely to graduate from high school.[28] In 1965, only 50 percent of Black males compared to 73 percent of White males aged 25–29 had graduated from high school. By 1991, this gap had virtually closed: 83.5 percent of Black males and 85.1 percent of White males had graduated from high school.[28] Despite this gain, Black males remained only half as likely as their White peers to complete four or more years of college. In 1991, only 11.5 percent of Black males ages 25–29 had completed four years of college, compared to 24.1 percent of White males in that age group (see Table 3).[29]

Advances made by Blacks in high school completion rates have been offset by the diminishing value of a high school education in the labor market. A high school diploma alone, in the absence of higher education, no longer assures passage to middle-class security, and is only marginally helpful in Black youths' search for employment. In 1991, for instance, young Black high school *graduates* were only slightly more likely to be employed than were young White high school *dropouts:* 57 percent as compared to 51 percent.[30]

The value of a high school diploma is further diminished by inconsistencies in the quality of education provided to youth. Gross disparities between urban and suburban schools, and between individual schools in the same districts, have made a high school diploma alone an inadequate measure of skill competency.[31] As a result, school completion rates do not provide an accurate portrait of the disparity in education between Blacks and Whites.

Racial differences in performance between Black and White students are stark across all subject areas and grades, with the most severe gaps between Black and White males. For example, Black male students were over twice as likely as their White peers to fall two or more grades behind the modal grade in school; in 1990 over 10 percent of Black male students ages 10–13 were two or more grades behind, compared to only 4 percent of White male students.[32]

Disparities also exist between the measured skill levels of Black and White students. Results of the 1990 survey of the National Assessment of Educational Progress (NAEP) indicated that only 12 percent of Black male twelfth graders, compared to 40 percent of White males, could "find, understand, summarize, and explain relatively complicated literary and informational material." In the same year only 20 percent of Black male and 54 percent of White male twelfth graders could compute decimals, simple fractions and percents.[33] Thus, while the rate of high school completion is comparable among Blacks and Whites, alarming disparities in skill levels remain prevalent among high school graduates.

CHALLENGES TO BLACK MEN IN THE LABOR FORCE

Criminal Records

The overriding reality is that long-term imprisonment as the sanction of choice has grown exponentially as the proportion of Blacks being arrested has increased. Prison and jail populations have skyrocketed apparently not so much in response to increases in violent crime, as to the fact that those being arrested are increasingly Black or brown. As the color of the arrestee (for whatever crime) gets darker, the sentences get longer, and the political rhetoric more strident.

Jerome Miller, National Center of Institutions and Alternatives[34]

While education and skill deficits are formidable barriers to employment for many young Black men, involvement with the criminal justice system presents an even greater problem for many youth,

inflicting enormous damage on their employment prospects. A 1989 study reported that on any given day nearly one of four—23 percent—of Black men between the ages of 20 and 29 were either in prison, jail, on probation, or on parole.[35] A 1992 study of Black males in Washington, D.C., concluded that 70 percent of young Black men living in Washington would be arrested and jailed at least once before reaching age 35, with a lifetime risk of up to 80 to 90 percent.[36]

The growing Black prison population reflects these statistics: the proportion of Black inmates in state and federal prisons (95 percent of them men) has increased from 21 percent in 1926 to an estimated 49 percent in 1991 (see Table 4). This tremendous increase took place in a period of time in which prison populations grew exponentially while the racial composition of the general population remained roughly constant.[37]

Between 1980 and 1992 alone, rates of incarceration of Black men more than doubled, rising from 1,111 incarcerated Black men per 100,000 in the population in 1980 to 2,678 per 100,000 in 1992. Rates of incarceration among White males rose as well, but the absolute figures were significantly lower: in 1980, 168 White males were incarcerated per 100,000 in the population, rising to 372 incarcerated White males per 100,000 in 1992.[38]

Contrary to public perception, the vast majority of arrests of Black men are for non-violent offenses.[39] For a large segment of young Black men—perhaps the majority in urban areas—arrest and incarceration have become a modern rite of passage.[40] But while such experience may bring an adolescent peer recognition, it later leads to ostracism from the labor market and other segments of society. Men with criminal or prison records may find themselves viewed as undesirable, both as workers and as husbands.[41] This ostracism—especially when coupled with low levels of social support and skill—may in turn feed a continuing cycle of self-destructive behavior and crime.

Incarceration not only affects the male inmate, but has far reaching economic, social, and psychological repercussions on the mans family.

Upon incarceration, any income the man may have been able to earn ceases. Wives, girlfriends and children may feel the emotional anxiety, stress and abandonment that often accompanies imprisonment of a family member. In short, the imprisonment of Black males strains the entire structure of the Black family.

The Attraction of the Underground Economy

As a result of changes in the labor force, large numbers of African American men find themselves unemployed with little or nothing society deems as productive to do. Many of them have resorted to such alternative methods of survival as drug dealing, panhandling, or hustling odd jobs.

John Wilson, Joint Center for Political and Economic Studies.[42]

Shifts in the economy and the difficulty of finding work have contributed to the widespread participation among Black men in underground— or "informal"—economies. Many low-income minority communities have come to rely heavily on informal economies as a means of supporting their families when they are unable to find "decent" jobs. The activities of informal economies range from income generated from a child's babysitting job, to "under the table" labor work (such as construction or garment manufacturing), to a range of illegal activities such as robbery, drug dealing, or other organized crime.[43]

Participation in the underground economy is often a response to limited opportunities in the formal economy. As the legal economy has become increasingly inaccessible to Black men, they have become more dependent on informal economies both as an important source of revenue as well as for a sense of self-esteem.[44] In fact, some scholars have suggested that among Black males participation in informal economies carries little stigma. Those who have earned money and prestige, even through illegal activities, are role models to younger Blacks and have replaced the hard worker, who labors for hours

TABLE 4 Percent of State and Federal Prison Admissions by Race, 1926-1992

Year	White	Black	Other
1926	79	21	1
1930	77	22	1
1935	74	25	1
1940	71	28	1
1945	68	31	1
1950	69	30	1
1960	66	32	2
1964	65	33	2
1974	59	38	3
1978	58	41	1
1981	57	42	1
1986*	40	45	15
1991**	35	49	16

*When Hispanic inmates were broken out in 1986, the percentage of White inmates dropped precipitously.

**Estimated

Source: Miller, J. (1993). "African American Males in the Criminal Justice System."

each day only to bring home a meager paycheck.[45] As Hagan notes:

. . . These youth have substituted investment in subcultures of youth crime and delinquency for involvement in a dominant culture that makes limited structural or cultural investment in their futures. Their subcultural adaptations are investments for short-term economic gains.[46]

Black youths' lack of legitimate opportunities for success is alone sufficient to cause despair. The sense of hopelessness is reinforced by the threat of an early and violent death for a significant number of Black men. Homicide is the leading killer of Black males aged 15 to 24 and the second leading killer of Black males aged 25–44.[47] All of these factors can contribute to a lack of faith in a future, which may further the tendency to engage in illegal activities.

Health and Disability

Unable to realize their roles as providers, some African American men have come to rely on alcohol and drugs to relieve the anxiety and depression that accompanies their sense of uselessness.

John Wilson, Joint Center for Political and Economic Studies.[48]

The ability of Black men to participate in the labor force is also limited by high levels of disability, health, mental health, and substance abuse problems in the Black population. These problems—which are often further exacerbated by a lack of health insurance—may be a significant factor in the weak labor force attachment of many Black men.[49]

A significant portion of Black men are not working due to health reasons. For example, 18 percent of young Black males (ages 20–29) with no paid employment during 1992 reported that illness or disability was their "main reason" for not working. Among sub-groups of the population, these rates are even higher: 26.6 percent for Black high school dropouts, 21.9 percent for Black high school graduates, and only 2.4 percent of Blacks who bad received some college education.[50]

In general, young Black males are significantly more likely than their White counterparts to not be working due to health problems or disabilities. For example 5 percent of 20–29 year old Black men reported that they could not work at all in 1992—or could not work or look for work on a year round basis—due to an illness or disability. This ratio was twice that for White men ages 20–29 (2.6 percent). In 1992, fully 8 percent of Black men ages 20–62 did not work due to health related reasons.[51]

Black men are particularly vulnerable to health problems. The National Center for Health Statistics reports that Black men are the most likely to die from heart disease, homicide and AIDS. Black male mortality rates for these killers are far higher than those for White males (see Table 5).[52]

The prevalence of health problems among Black men may be, at least partly due to their

TABLE 5 Deaths per 100,000 Resident Population in 1991

	Heart Disease	Homicide	Aids
Black Males	272.7	72.5	52.9
White Males	196.1	9.4	16.7

Source: National Center for Health Statistics, *Health, U.S., 1993*, Tables 42, 48, and 51.

low rates of insurance coverage, since health conditions among the uninsured are, likely to go untreated until they have progressed to severe or chronic stages. In 1993 only 53 percent of Black men ages 20–29 had health insurance compared to 71 percent of White men in the same age group. Forty-three (43) percent of these young White men had employer-provided insurance, as compared to only 27 percent of young Black men. For Black high school dropouts, the figure drops to 18 percent.[53]

A number of studies have suggested that both substance abuse (especially heavy drinking and alcoholism) and clinical depression are major problems among the Black community.[54] Black males in particular may be at high risk for developing severe problems: they tend to become heavy drinkers and their mental health problems are often unaddressed until after their health has significantly deteriorated.[55]

Within the Black population the highest incidence of mental disorders occurs for young men ages 15–24, who are hospitalized at a rate of 509 per 100,000; this compares to 213 per 100,000 for White males. Black females are hospitalized at a rate of 248 per 100,000 and White females at 110 per 100,000. As a group, Blacks under 44 years of age are hospitalized at three times the rate of Whites in the same age group.[56]

There is a different pattern of suicide between Black and White males as well. Black males are more likely to end their lives as they are entering adulthood, the prime period for entry into the labor force and beginning a career. White males, on the other hand, are more likely to end their lives at the end of their careers.[57]

Racial or Cultural Barriers

Little empirical evidence exists in the research literature to explain the impact of racial or cultural barriers on employment. Few would argue, however, that racial discrimination does play a part in contributing to the underemployment of Black men. Many employers view Black men as dishonest, lazy, and poorly educated. The high rates of incarceration among Black men, their participation in the underground economy, their lower skill and college education levels—all these factors reinforce fears and the worst stereotypes. Cumulatively, these images perpetuate the cycle of institutional racism.

> The restructuring of the economy will continue to compound the negative effects of perceptions of inner-city Black males. Because of the increasing shift to service industries, employers have a greater need for workers who can effectively serve and relate to the consumer. Black males are not perceived to have such qualities.
> William Julius Wilson[58]

> In fact, interviews of a representative sample of Chicago-area employers … show that many consider inner-city Blacks—especially young Black males—to be uneducated, unstable, uncooperative, and dishonest.
> William Julius Wilson[59]

CONSEQUENCES OF JOBLESSNESS

Income Differentials

> White men with less education have earnings that are equal to or greater than Black men with more education.
> Robert Hill, Institute for Urban Research, citing US. Bureau of the Census data[60]

Fundamental shifts in the economic landscape have left a disproportionate number of Black men unprepared for the labor force, unable to work, without a job, or with only part-time or low-paying jobs. These conditions have not only left Black men underrepresented in the workforce, but have resulted in the structural displacement of Black men from the mainstream economy altogether. Comparisons of Black and White incomes reflect the deepening poverty in the Black community, and highlight the growing disparity between the incomes of Blacks and Whites as well as between various segments within the Black community itself.

Real annual earnings are a good indicator of the economic well-being of young Black men. After nearly three decades of progress in improving the real earnings and incomes of young males and their families, the disparity between Blacks and Whites once again began to grow in the 1970s and 1980s.[61] Of all demographic subgroups, young men (ages 20–29) suffered the largest absolute and relative declines in annual earnings since 1973; within this group, young Black males—particularly those with little or no formal schooling—have fared the worst.[62]

The relative decline in real earnings for Black men was 24 percent, compared to 14 percent for Whites. Between 1973 and 1989, the mean earnings of Black male high school dropouts fell by nearly one-half compared to only one-third for White male high school dropouts. The earnings of Black male high school graduates fell by one-third compared to one-fifth for White male high school graduates, and the earnings of Black male college graduates fell by 16 percent compared to a slight increase (.3 percent) in real earnings among White male college graduates (see Figure 2).[63]

Part of the source of declines in mean real annual earnings may be the rise in the proportion of men who did not work at all in any given year. Almost one in five young Black men reported zero earnings in 1992 compared to less than one in 13 White males. This included 32 percent of Black male high school dropouts who had no earnings at all compared to 14 percent of White male high school dropouts; 16 percent of Black male high school graduates compared to 5 percent of their White peers; and 9 percent of Black males with

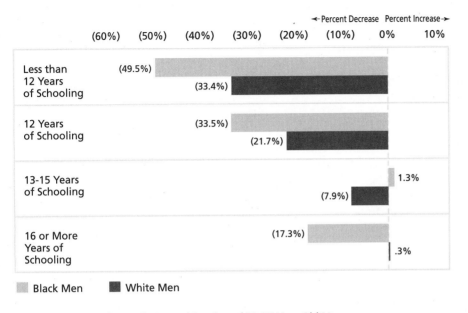

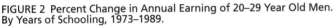

FIGURE 2 Percent Change in Annual Earning of 20–29 Year Old Men.
By Years of Schooling, 1973–1989.

some college education compared to 3 percent of White males with some college education.[64]

Many of the Blacks who did report earnings reported very low wages. In 1990, 22.4 percent of Black men who worked full-time for the entire year earned wages below $12,195, that year's poverty threshold for a family of four. For White full-time male workers, the figure was 13 percent. The proportion of men with low earnings has increased dramatically since 1974, when only 13.8 percent of Black male full-time workers had low earnings by this definition.[65]

These trends clearly have implications for differential family income levels. A disaggregation of family income by quintiles for Blacks and Whites reveals disturbing imbalances and diverging trends (see Table 6 and Figures 3 and 4).[66] Although income inequality has increased dramatically for the United States as a whole, this gap is substantially greater for Blacks.[67] (We define income inequality as the distance between

the earnings of the highest and lowest quintiles of earners.) For example, the top fifth of Black families has made remarkable gains, with income growth approaching that of the highest-income Whites. At the same time, however, the lower two quintiles of Black families have experienced significant economic decline. From 1971 to 1991, the mean income of the top fifth of Black families increased by 24.6 percent, a figure which was close to the 27.4 percent increase for the top fifth of White families. The mean income for the bottom quintiles of Blacks, however, decreased by 26.2 percent; the mean income for the bottom quintiles of Whites *increased* 4.3 percent in the same period of time.[68]

These figures indicate that the average Black family in the second quintile had about the same income as the average White family in the lowest *quintile* (see Table 6). The typical family in the bottom income quintile for Blacks had an income of only $4,369 in 1991, putting them at

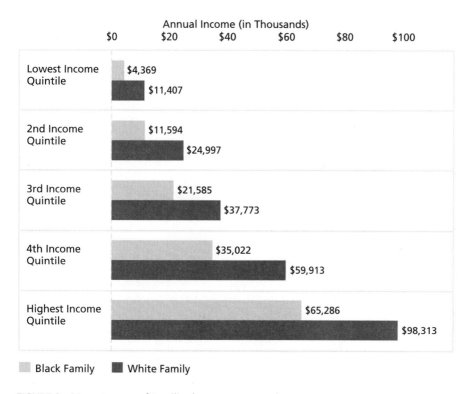

FIGURE 3　Mean Income of Families by Income Quintile, 1991.

only 39 percent of the federal poverty standard, taking into account cash income and family size.[69] These circumstances are reflected in the nations 1992 poverty rates: 33.3 percent of all Blacks were poor, compared to only 11.6 percent of Whites.[70]

The income disparity within the Black community is equally stark. While the highest quintile of Black families had a mean income of $65,286 in 1991, the mean income of the bottom quintile of Black families was approximately one-fifteenth this sum (at $4,369).

Decline in Two-Parent Families

As long as young (Black) men continue to be marginalized, the prospects for increasing the share of Black families with male heads seems remote. Strengthening female-headed families, while obviously beneficial in the short run, offers little hope for reducing the earnings gap further. Since the culprit in this link remains the deteriorating position of young Black males with little training or education beyond high school, the solution must lie in salvaging what otherwise could be a lost generation of men.

William Darity and Samuel Myers. "Racial Earning Inequality Into the 21st Century" in *The State of Black America 1992*.[71]

The relationship between the economic well-being of Black men and the stability of the Black family is complex and, most likely, reciprocal.

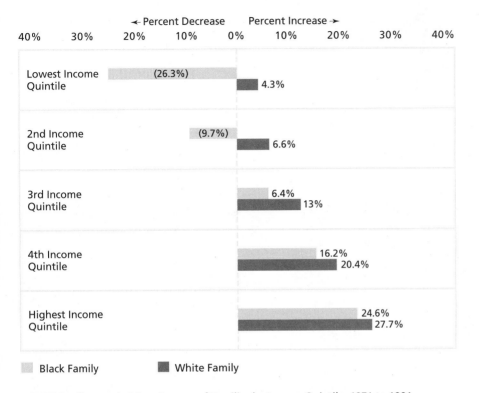

FIGURE 4   Changes in Mean Income of Families by Income Quintile, 1971 to 1991.

Some theorists have speculated that the increasing economic instability of Black males has reduced their ability and willingness to form independent households and to marry.[72] Others have noted that nonresident fathers are more involved with their children when they can provide financial support, but may choose to terminate contact with the child when economic stresses increase.[73] The connection between the disappearance of Black men from the workforce and the simultaneous rise of poor, single-mother families, however, remains for the most part unaddressed in discussions about the decline in two-parent families and increase in family poverty within the Black community.

The correspondence between Black male joblessness and the rise of female-headed households is striking. Between 1960 and 1992, the same period of time in which joblessness among Black men was rising, the number of Black female-headed households more than doubled, reaching over 46 percent of all families by 1992. While the number of White female-headed families also increased dramatically during this time, they represented a far smaller proportion of the overall White population (13.5 percent in 1992).[74]

Research suggests an association between income and the likelihood of marriage for all rates. The high proportion of Blacks in low income situations, however, makes this trend particularly relevant. Among Black men, only 5 percent of those in the bottom income quintile were married, compared to 47 percent of Black men in

TABLE 6 Mean income of Families by Income Quintile, 1971 and 1991

	Lowest	2nd	3rd	4th	Highest
All Races					
Mean income, 1991	$9,734	23,105	35,851	51,997	95,530
Mean income, 1971*	$9,999	22,020	32,217	43,631	75,150
% change since 1971	−2.6	3.8	11.2	19.1	27.0
White					
Mean income, 1991	$11,407	24,997	37,773	59,913	98,313
Mean income, 1971*	$10,931	23,448	33,424	44,788	76,958
% change since 1971	4.3	6.6	13.0	20.4	27.7
Black					
Mean income, 1991	$4,369	11,594	21,585	35,022	65,286
Mean income, 1971*	$5,925	12,836	20,281	30,128	52,416
% change since 1971	−26.3	−9.7	6.4	16.2	24.6

*1971 mean income is in 1991 dollars, calculated on the basis of the CPI-U-X1 inflation series.

Source: Bureau of the Census, CPS Series P60, No. 180, Table B-7. Additional calculations by the Center for the Study of Social Policy.

the uppermost income quintile.[75] In 1987, only 3 percent of Black men (ages 18–39) with no earnings were married. The percentage of married men increases to 7 percent among Black men with annual earnings of $1,000 to $5,000, to 29 percent for those with earnings between $15,000 and $20,000, and to over 50 percent for those with annual earnings over $20,000.[76]

At the same time, fewer Black adults are marrying than ever before. While the last 20 years have seen an increase in the number of never-married adults in all races and age groups, the rate of change is greatest among Blacks.[77] Between 1970 and 1991, the percentage of Black adults who never married rose from 20.6 percent to 37.1 percent—an increase of 80 percent. The equivalent increase among Whites was only 32 percent, from 15.6 percent to 20.5 percent.[78]

The increase in female-headed households and decrease in marriage rates have been accompanied by a dramatic rise in the rate of out-of-wedlock births. For example, in 1960 the chances of a Black child being born to an unmarried woman was about one in five (22 percent), while the chance of a White child being born to an unmarried woman was about one in fifty (2.3 percent). By 1990 these figures had risen to over three in five (65 percent) for Black children, compared to one in five (20 percent) for Whites.[79] Thus, while out-of-wedlock births among Whites have increased at a rapid pace, the rate of out-of-wedlock births among Blacks remains three times that for Whites.

Increase in Family Poverty

The problems associated with father-absence become acute for families that have been victimized by chronic, intergenerational poverty, particularly African American and other families of color that are equally victimized by discrimination. In short, the loss of income resulting from father absence reduced the capacity of single parents to be supportive, consistent, and involved in childrearing.

Vivian Gadsden, National Center on Adult Literacy[80]

TABLE 7 Median Income by Family Type and Race (in 1992 Dollars)

	1967	1970	1980	1990	1992	Increase 1967–92
Married Couple Families						
Black	22,626	26,552	31,696	36,265	34,196	51.1%
White	33,351	36,427	40,063	43,293	42,738	28.1%
Female-Headed Families						
Black	11,653	12,148	12,658	13,016	11,956	2.6%
White	18,857	19,547	20,,300	20,962	20,962	6.7%

Source: U.S. Bureau of Census, CPS Series P-60, "Money Income of Households, Families & Persons in the U.S.": 1992, Unpublished Work Table F-5.

Increases in Black single-mother families, combined with the economic disenfranchisement of numerous Black men, has contributed to an explosion of Black families living in poverty. By 1991, over 55 percent of Black children lived in female-headed households, compared to only 16 percent of White children.[81] Of all Black children living in homes headed by a single woman, an astonishing 68.2 percent lived in poverty and this figure jumps to 71.3 percent for children under age six.[82]

Black two-parent families have made dramatic economic gains in the past two decades: the median income of Black married-couple families rose 51 percent between 1967 and 1992—from $22,626 to $34,196 in 1992 dollars. In contrast, the median income of single-mother families rose only 2.6 percent and remained much lower: it was $11,653 in 1967 (translated into 1992 dollars) and $11,956 in 1992.[83] Of the 1.56 million Black children whose families had incomes below $5,000 in 1991, almost 90 percent—1.4 million—lived in single-mother families.[84]

Table 7 shows the changes in the median incomes of female-headed families and married-couple families from 1967 to 1992. Black married-couple families made the greatest gains (51 percent as noted above.) But their median income was still only $34,196, approximately the level for White married-couple families in 1967 ($33,351). By 1992, White married-couple median income had risen to $42,738. In contrast,

White female-headed families made greater income gains than Black female-headed families over the same period. The median income for Black single-mother families stayed virtually constant ($11,653 in 1967 and $11,956 in 1992) while the comparable figure for White single-mother families rose 6.7 percent (from $18,857 to $20,130).

Father absence has a variety of additional effects that go beyond income deprivation. Although research on the effects of father absence on child development is inconclusive, studies of the effects of father absence when coupled with family poverty are definitive.[85] A number of studies suggest that families in poverty are more likely to experience chronic stress resulting from low income and low levels of social support, and are more likely to experience highly stressful life events.[86] Numerous studies have found poor academic achievement, problems in socioemotional development, low self-esteem, and a host of behavioral problems to be strongly associated with poverty.[87] As Gadsden notes in her research, the legacy and culture of poverty in some communities may create an intergenerational sense of hopelessness about the ability to ever "make it."[88]

CONCLUSION

This report paints an alarming picture of the status of Black males in American society. The gulf between the employment prospects for Black males and those for White males is staggering, and growing larger. Black males have fewer opportunities in the job market, are employed far less frequently, and gain much less from their work effort than do their White counterparts. Fully 43 percent of Black men of employment age were not in the labor force in 1993. For the diminishing number of Black men who do work full-time, the rewards for doing so are less than for White men, as illustrated by the fact that the average earnings for a Black male who is a college graduate are not much more than the average earnings for a White male with only a high school diploma.

Black male joblessness directly affects the financial security of the Black family. The diminished economic condition of Black males is a factor in the increasing number of Black women who are raising children in single-parent households; and such families are likely to live in or near poverty. As the number of female-headed households has grown among Blacks, the likelihood that a Black child will grow up experiencing poverty has accelerated rapidly. Fully 46 percent of all Black children are poor today. and 68 percent of Black children in female-headed households live below the poverty line.

Bleak as is the economic picture, it is only part of a larger portrait of the increasing dislocation of Black men from the mainstream of American society. The health of Black men is worse than that of their White peers, particularly as health affects employment status. Over 8 percent of Black males cannot work because of disabling conditions, compared to less than 4 percent of White men. Black males also face more severe substance abuse and mental health problems than White men. Educational achievement for Black men is less on average than for White men. Despite substantial gains in the past twenty years in the number of Black men finishing high school, comparatively few go on to college.

The sheer repetition of these trends is numbing, and often obscures the human tragedy that underlies them. The diminished prospects for Black men are a blight on individual lives and an obstacle to the well-being of many communities. The resilience that abounds among the many Black men who "make it," despite the odds, should not lure us into disregarding the lack of opportunities for those who do not. The potential consequences of their reality have grave repercussions for everyone.

The causes that account for the current circumstances of many Black men lie deep in our nation's history and social fabric. Remedies will have to be equally profound. A rush to find simplistic and superficial solutions is only a slight improvement over the current posture of ignoring the situation. A laundry list of new federal and state programs is not what is needed, though governmental action is an essential part of the solution. Nor can the private sector alone be relied upon to redress these disparities; private enterprise by itself is clearly not providing the necessary rewards and equal opportunities for Black males. Public sector leadership *must* be blended with changes in private and public institutions, including schools, job markets, *and* public and private colleges and universities, which are the main avenues for providing opportunities for everyone.

If the trends affecting Black men are to be reversed, a new national agenda must be developed. Before that can happen, the people of this nation must recognize how fundamental the dislocation of Black males from mainstream American economic life has become. We are losing not just one generation of Black men, but many generations to come. Understanding the depth of the problem and its causes is the essential first step toward change. This report only scratches the surface of the information that must be compiled and absorbed in this process. There is much more that has to be understood.

Once the serious nature of the situation is realized, we must formulate an action agenda that combines public will with private enterprise to alter the prospects for Black men. An entire subgroup of Americans is being locked into economic segregation that is as egregious as segregation in housing, schools, and other public accommodations. Changing this course requires an array of solutions that is more powerful than the solutions brought to bear in the past. The outlines of that agenda can emerge only as the problem is recognized and discussed at the highest levels of national discourse as well as in every community where its effects are felt by individuals and families.

NOTES

1. U.S. Department of Labor, Bureau of Labor Statistics, *Employment and earnings,* Vol. 41, No. 1, January 1994, Table 3, pp. 184–186. This report shows 5,838,000 Black men aged 16–64 employed in 1993. This number was divided by the total universe of Black men aged 16–64 (10,719,349) to get the percentage employed of 54.5 percent There were 54,579,000 White men employed between the ages of 16–64, which when divided by the total universe of White men age 16–64 (70,369,217) yields a percentage of 77.6.

2. U.S. Department of Defense, Defense Manpower Data Center. *Distribution of Active Duty Forces by Service, Rank, Sex, and Ethnic Group,* March 31, 1994. These figures are not broken down by age, but by definition, few if any men under age 16 and over 64 are included in the military According to these data, the total number of Black men in active duty was 262,898 which was then divided by the universe of Black men age 16–64 (10,719,349) to produce the percentage of 2.5. The total number of White men in active duty was 1,038,386 which was then divided by the universe of White men age 16–64 (70,369,217) to produce the percentage of 1.5.

3. U.S. Department of Labor, Bureau of Labor Statistics, *Employment and earnings,* Vol. 41, No. 1, January 1994, Table 3, pp. 184–186. This report shows 947,000 Black men aged 16–64 officially unemployed in 1993. This number was divided by the total universe of Black men aged 16–64 (10,719.349) to get the percentage unemployed of 8.8 percent. There were 3,698,000 White men unemployed between the ages of 16–64, which when divided by the total universe of White men age 16–64 (70,369,217) yields a percentage of 5.3. These percentages are somewhat different from the official unemployment rates generally found in the literature and the press because they use as their denominator the entire universe of Black men age 16–64. Traditional unemployment rates use only a portion of this population as their denominator: they use only the civilian non-institutional population which excludes those in the military, in prisons and those not found in the decennial census.

4. U.S. Department of Labor, Bureau of Labor Statistics, *Employment and earnings,* Vol. 41, No. 1, January 1994, Table 3. pp. 184–186. This report shows 2,206,006 Black men aged 16–64 out of the labor force in 1993. This number was divided by the total universe of Black men aged 16–64 (10,719,349) to get the percentage out of the labor force of 20.6 percent. There were

9,089,000 White men out of the labor force between the ages of 16–64, which when divided by the total universe of White men age 16–64 (70,369,217) yields a percentage of 12.9.

5. U.S. Bureau of the Census, *1990 Census of Population: General population characteristics of the U.S.,* CP-l–1, November 1992, Table 35. This document shows there were 469,451 Black men and 466,831 White men of all-ages in correctional facilities in 1990. Unpublished data from the Census Bureau shows that approximately 99 percent of the total population in correctional facilities fall between the ages of 16–64, so we can use these numbers as close approximations of the number of men aged 16–64 in prison. Dividing the number of Black men in prisons, 469,451 by the universe of Black men 16–64 (10,719,349) produces a percentage of 4.4. The 466,831 White men in correctional facilities constituted less than one percent (.66 percent) of all White men (70,369,217).

6. Robinson, J. G. et al. 1993. Estimation of population coverage in the 1990 United States census based demographic analysis. *Journal of the American Statistical Association,* Vol. 88, No. 423, pp. 1061–1079. The undercount analysis is based on estimates of births, deaths, immigration and emigration.

7. Robinson, Bashir, and Ahmed. 1993. Estimation of population coverage in the 1990 United States census based demographic analysis, op. cit. The 996,000 Black men aged 16–64 not counted in the 1990 census is divided by the universe of Black men aged 16–64 (10,719,349) to get a 9.3 percent undercount. The 1,498,000 White men aged 16–64 not counted in the 1990 census is divided by the universe of White men (70,369,217) to get a 2.1 percent undercount.

8. Robinson, Bashir, and Ahmed. 1988. *Perspectives on the completeness of coverage of population in the United States decennial census.* Unpublished paper presented at the April 1988 meeting of the Population Association of America, New Orleans, LA. See also Kearny, A. T. (1993). *Coverage improvement from experimental residence questions.* Unpublished paper, Bureau of the Census, Washington, D.C. A large share of the Census undercount of Black males is believed to be comprised of men who have unstable or transient household attachments. Other uncounted males may "unofficially" reside with low-income women who are receiving public assistance and may be unwilling to report the presence of men in their homes.

9. Hill, R. B. 1993. *The labor force and income status of African American males: Policy implications.* Paper presented at the Policy Roundtable on Labor Force Participation and Family Formation sponsored by the Center for the Study of Social Policy and the Philadelphia Children's Network, November, 1993, Washington, D.C.; and, Hill, R. B. (1981). *Economic policies and Black Progress.* Washington, D.C.: National Urban League Research Department.

10. Wilson, J. W. 1987. *The truly disadvantaged: The inner city, the underclass, and public policy.* Chicago: University of Chicago Press; and, *1992 Economic Report of The President,* Table B-41.

11. Hill, R. B. 1993. The labor force and income status of African American males: Policy implications, op. cit.; and, Sum A. and Fogg, N. (1990). The changing economic fortunes of young Black men in America. *Black Scholar,* January-March, 1990, pp. 47-55.

12. Sum, A. and Fogg, N. (1990). The changing economic fortunes of young Black Men in America. *Black Scholar,* January-March, 1990, pp. 47–55.

13. Reich, R. B. (1991). *The work of nations,* New York: Vintage Books, pp. 208–224; and, Johnston, W. B. and Packer, A. E. (1987). *Workforce 2000: Work and workers for the 21s century,* Indianapolis: Hudson Institute, pp. 20–29.

14. Reich, R. B. (1991). *The work of nations,* op. cit.; and, Johnston, W. B. and Packer, A. E. (1987). *Workforce 2000: Work and workers for the 21st century,* op. cit.

15. *1992 Economic Report of the President, op. cit.* Workers in this category increased from 9 percent to 17 percent from 1968 to 1988.

16. Kasarda, J. D., (1988). America's urban dilemma, in *The new metropolitan era: A world of giant cities,* Dogan, M. and Kasarda, J. D. (Eds.), New York: Russell Sage, p. 70.

17. U.S. Bureau of the Census, *1992 Statistical abstract of the United States,* Table 5. The total number of immigrants for the period from 1981 to 1990 is 7.34 million; for the period from 1931 to 1970 the cumulative total is 7.40 million.

18. U.S. Bureau of the Census, *1992 Statistical abstract of the United States,* Table 8. Of the total of 1,536,500 immigrants who entered the U.S. in 1990, 679,000 were from Mexico and 146,200 were from Central America. Just over 1 million of the total were from Latin America and the Caribbean. Some portion of this rise can be attributed to the Immigration Reform and Control Act of 1986, which granted amnesty to undocumented persons who had been in the U.S. since 1982, and to certain migrant farm workers.

19. *l992 Economic Report of the President, op. cit.,* p. 88.

20. Fix, M. & Passel, J. S. 1994. *Immigration and immigrants: Setting the record straight.* Washington, D.C.: Urban Institute.

21. Bean, F. D., Fossett, M. A, and Park, K. T. 1993. Labor market dynamics and the effects of immigration on African Americans. In Gerald Javnes (ed.) *Blacks, immigration, and race relations.* New Haven, Conn.: Yale University. Cited in Fix, M. and Passell, J. S., 1994.

22. Altonji, J. G. and Card, D. 1991. The effects of immigration on the labor market outcomes of less-skilled natives. In John M. Abowd & Richard B. Freeman (eds.) *Immigration, trade, and the labor market.* Chicago: University of Chicago Press. Cited in Fix, M. and Passel, J. S., 1994.

23. Kirschenman, J. and Neckerman, K. M. 1994. We'd love to hire them, but, op. cit.: The meaning of race for employers. In Christopher Jencks & Paul E. Peterson (eds.) *The urban underclass.* Washington, D.C.: Brookings Institution. Cited in Fix, M.& Passel, J. S. (1994).

24. Hughes, M. A. and Sternberg, J. 1993. *The new metropolitan reality: Where the rubber meets the road in anti-poverty policy,* Washington, D.C.: Urban Institute, pp. 10–16. Data used in this study refers to central and outer postal zones in the 60 largest Primary Metropolitan Statistical Areas (P.M.S.A.), using a data set developed by Anita Summers and Peter Linneman of the Wharton School of the University of Pennsylvania.

25. U.S. Bureau of the Census, *1990 census of population: General population characteristics, United States,* Tables 6, 53, 103. In the northeast, 74 percent of Blacks versus 24 percent of Whites lived in central cities; in the Midwest these figures are 77 percent of Blacks and 23 percent of Whites. Although it is difficult to distinguish between "urban" and "suburban" in summary Census data, these figures serve as useful comparative proxies.

26. Massey, D. and Denton, N. (1993). *American apartheid: Segregation and the making of the underclass,* Cambridge, Mass.: Harvard University Press.

27. McBay, S. (1992). The condition of African-American education. In *The State of Black America* 1992. New York: National Urban League, Inc.

28. U.S. Bureau of the Census (1992). *School enrollment-social and economic characteristics of students, October 1990,* CPS Series P-20, No. 460, Table AA.

29. Children's Defense Fund, (1993). *Progress and peril: Black children in America,* Washington, D.C.: Children's Defense Fund; and U.S. Bureau of the Census, CPS Series P-20, No. 451, Table 18.

30. Children's Defense Fund, 1993. *Progress and Peril, op. cit.*

31. Ferguson, R. F. 1991. Paving for public education: New evidence on how and why money matters. *Harvard Journal on Legislation,* 28 (Summer): pp. 465–98; and Ferguson, R. F. (1991). Racial patterns in how school and teacher quality affect achievement and earnings. *Challenge: A Journal of Research on Black Men,* Vol. 2: pp. 1–35.

32. U.S. Bureau of the Census (1992). *School enrollment-social and economic characteristics of students, October 1990,* CPS Series P-20, No. 460, Table 3; and, Children's Defense Fund (1993). *Progress and Peril,* op. cit.

33. National Assessment of Educational Progress (September, 1993). Educational Testing Service, unpublished data.

34. Miller, J. 1993. *African-American males in the criminal justice system.* Paper presented at the Policy Roundtable on Labor Force Participation and Family Formation sponsored by the Center for the Study of Social Policy and the Philadelphia Children's Network, November 1993, Washington, D.C.

35. Mauer, M. 1994. A generation behind bars: Black males and the criminal justice system. *The American Black male: His present status and his future,* R. G. Majors and J. U. Gordon (eds.), Chicago: Nelson Hall; and Mauer, M. (1990). *Young Black men and the criminal justice system: A growing national problem,* Washington. D.C.: The Sentencing Project.

36. National Center on Institutions and Alternatives (1992). Hobbling a generation: African American males in the District of Columbia's criminal justice system, as referenced in Miller, J. (1993). *African American males in the criminal justice system.* Paper presented at the Policy Roundtable on Labor Force Participation and Family Formation sponsored by the Center for the Study of Social Policy and the Philadelphia Children's Network, November, 1993, Washington, D.C.

37. Miller, J. 1993. *African American males in the Criminal Justice System*. Paper presented at the Policy Roundtable on Labor Force Participation and Family Formation sponsored by the Center for the Study of Social Policy and the Philadelphia Children's Network, November, 1993, Washington, D.C.

38. Washington Post, Population explosion in prisons, June 2, 1994, A3.

39. Miller, J. 1993. African American males in the criminal justice system, op. cit.

40. Miller, J. 1993. African American males in the criminal justice system, op. cit.

41. Mauer, M. 1994. A Generation Behind Bars. op. cit.

42. Wilson, J. 1993. *Unemployment, mental health, and substance abuse: Joblessness and African-American men*. Paper presented at the Policy Roundtable on Labor Force Participation and Family Formation sponsored by the Center for the Study of Social Policy and the Philadelphia Children's Network, November, 1993, Washington, D.C.

43. Greenfield, H. I. 1993. *Invisible, outlawed, and untaxed: Americas underground economy*. New Haven, Conn.: Praeger; and, Henry, S. (1982). The working unemployed: perspectives on the informal economy and unemployment. *Sociological Review*, 30, pp. 460–477.

44. Anderson, E. 1990. *Streetwise: race, class, and change in an urban community*. Chicago: University of Chicago Press.

45. Anderson, E. 1976. *A Place on the Corner* Chicago: The University of Chicago Press; Anderson, E. (1980). Some observations of Black youth employment. In *Youth Employment and Public Policy*, Anderson, E. and Sawhill, I. (eds.), Englewood Cliffs, N.J.: Prentice Hall.

46. Hagan, J. 1993. Structural and cultural disinvestment and the new ethnographies of poverty and crime. *Contemporary Sociology*, 22(3), pp. 327–332.

47. National Center for Health Statistics, US Department of Health and Human Services, "Health United States, 1993." Tables 42, 48, and 51.

48. Wilson, J. 1993. *Unemployment, mental health, and substance abuse: Joblessness and African-American men*. Paper was presented at the Policy Roundtable on Labor Force Participation and Family Formation sponsored by the Center for the Study of Social Policy and the Philadelphia Children's Network, November, 1993, Washington, D.C.

49. Sum, A., Fogg, W. N., Fogg, N. P. Williams, R. B. 1991. *The changing economic fortunes of America's Young Black men: An assessment of their labor market progress and problems over the 1973–1989 period*. Boston: Center for Labor Market Studies, Northeastern University.

50. Sum, A., Heliotis, J., and Fogg, N., 1993. *Health insurance coverage rates, the incidence of health problems, and the labor market status of young African American men in the U.S*. Paper prepared for the Policy Roundtable on Labor Force Participation and Family Formation sponsored by the Center for the Study of Social Policy and the Philadelphia Children's Network, November, 1993, Washington, D.C.

51. Sum, et al. 1993. Health Insurance Coverage Rates, the Incidence of Health Problems, and the Labor Market Status of Young African American Men in the U.S., *op. cit*. This statistic is based on the civilian noninstitutional population.

52. National Center for Health Statistics, US Department of Health and Human Services, "Health, United States, 1993," Tables 42, 48, and 51.

53. Sum, Heliotis and Fogg (1993). Health insurance coverage rates, the incidence of health problems, and the labor market status of young African American men in the U.S.

54. Wilson, J. 1993. *Unemployment, mental health, and substance abuse: Joblessness and African American men*. Paper presented at the Policy Roundtable on Labor Force Participation and Family Formation sponsored by the Center for the Study of Social Policy and the Philadelphia Children's Network, November, 1993, Washington, D.C.

55. Gay, J. E. 1981. Alcohol and metropolitan Black teenagers. *Journal of Drug Education*, Vol. 11(1) as quoted in Wilson, J. (1993). Unemployment. mental health, and substance abuse: Joblessness and African American men, op. cit.

56. Majors. R. and Mancini-Billson, J. 1992. *Cool pose: The dilemmas of Black manhood in America*. New York: Lexington Books, as quoted in Wilson, J. (1993). Unemployment, mental health, and substance abuse: Joblessness and African American men, op. cit. The statistics presented here reflect age-adjusted rates.

57. Smith, J. A. and Carter, J. H. 1986. Suicide and Black adolescents: A medical dilemma. *Journal of the National Medical Association*. Vol. 78, No. 11 as quoted in Wilson, J. (1993). Unemployment, Mental Health, and Substance Abuse: Joblessness and African American Men.

58. Wilson, J. 1993. *Unemployment, mental health, and substance abuse: Joblessness and African-American men*. Paper presented at the Policy Roundtable on Labor Force Participation and Family Formation sponsored by the Center for the Study of Social Policy and the Philadelphia Children's Network, November, 1993, Washington, D.C.

59. Wilson, J. 1993. *Unemployment, mental health, and substance abuse: Joblessness and African-American men*. Paper presented at the Policy Roundtable on Labor Force Participation and Family Formation sponsored by the Center for the Study of Social Policy and the Philadelphia Children's Network, November, 1993, Washington, D.C.

60. Hill, R. B. 1993. *The labor force and income status of African-American males: Policy implications*. Paper was presented at the Policy Roundtable on Labor Force Participation and Family Formation sponsored by the Center for the Study of Social Policy and the Philadelphia Children's Network, November, 1993, Washington, D.C.

61. Sum, A. M. and Fogg, W. N. 1990. The changing economic fortunes of young Black men in America, *op. cit*.

62. Sum, K. M. and Fogg, W. N. 1990. The changing economic fortunes of young Black men in America, *op. cit*. It is important to note that although mean annual real earnings have risen for all young men since 1982, they still remain below the 1973 earnings peak, particularly among young Black males.

63. Sum et al. 1991. The changing fortunes of America's young Black men: An assessment of their labor market progress and problems over the 1973–1989 period. *op. cit.* These differences among young Black men by years of schooling reflect a variety of forces such as differences in employment rates, annual weeks and hours of employment, and mean hourly earnings. It also may reflect the number of men who reported no annual earnings; even when this was factored out, however, mean real earnings dropped significantly.

64. Sum et al. 1991. The changing fortunes of America's young Black men: An assessment of their labor market progress and problems over the 1973–1989 period.

65. U.S. Census Bureau, CPS Series P-60, March, 1993. Because low earnings tend to reduce or forestall family formation, the number of Black male workers with low earnings who actually lived in poverty was less than the percentage that had zero earnings.

66. One important caveat for analysis of income quintiles over time is that these figures do not account for economic mobility, that is, the ability of a given family to move from one quintile to another. In other words, a change in the income of a quintile as a whole does not necessarily reflect the trends that occur at the level of individual families.

67. U.S. Bureau of the Census, CPS Series P-60, No. 180, Table B-7. A common measure of overall income inequality is the Gini coefficient, where 0 represents perfect income equality and 1 represents perfect inequality. The 1991 Gini ratio for all families was 0.397; for Blacks it was 0.448. (The 1971 ratios were 0.355 for all families and 0.385 for Blacks).

68. U.S. Bureau of the Census, CPS Series P-60, No. 180, Table B-7. Percentage changes from 1971 to 1991 were calculated in constant dollars using the CPII-U-XI price deflator.

69. U.S. Bureau of the Census, CPS Series P-20, No. 180, Table B-8. The typical family in the lowest quintal of White families lived at 112 percent of the poverty standard. This percentage is converted from average income-to-poverty ratios, which are calculated on the basis of mean income and mean poverty thresholds for each quintal.

70. U.S. Bureau of the Census, CPS Series P-60, No. 185, *Poverty in the United States: 1992,* Table 1.

71. Darity W. and Myers, S. 1992. Racial earning inequity into the 21st century. In *The state of Black America 1992.* New York: National Urban League, Inc.

72. See, inter alia, William Julius Wilson, *The truly disadvantaged: The inner city, the underclass, and public policy* (Chicago: University of Chicago Press, 1987), pp. 63–106 and passim.; Gerald D. Javnes and Robin M. Williams, eds. *A common destiny: Blacks and American Society* (Washington: National Academy Press, 1989), pp. 301-312 and passim.; Gerald D. Jaynes, The labor market status of Black Americans 1939-1985, *Journal of Economic Perspectives,* Vol. 4, No. 4 (Fall 1990), pp. 9-24; David T. Ellwood and Jonathan Crane, Family change among Black Americans: What do we know?, *Journal of Economic Perspectives,* Vol. 4, No. 4 (Fall 1990), pp. 65-84; and Robert I. Lerman and Theodora Ooms eds., *Young unwed fathers: Changing roles and emerging policies* (Philadelphia: Temple University Press, 1993).

73. Seltzer, J. A. 1991. Relationships between fathers and children who live apart: The fathers role after separation. *Journal of Marriage and the Family,* 53, pp. 79-101; as quoted in Gadsen, V. (1993). *The absence of father effects on children's development and family functioning.* Paper presented at the Policy Roundtable on Labor Force Participation and Family Formation sponsored by the Center for the Study of Social Policy and the Philadelphia Children's Network, November, 1993, Washington, D.C.

74. U.S. Bureau of the Census, *Historical abstract of the United States: Colonial Times to 1970,* Series D-46 and 94; U.S. Bureau of the Census, CPS Series P-20, No. 464, *The black Population in the United States: 1991,* Table E; and U.S. Bureau of Census, CPS Series P-20. No. 471, Tables E and E.

75. Sum et al. 1991. The changing fortunes of America's young Black men: An assessment of their labor market progress and problems over the 1973-1989 period, *op. cit.*

76. Sum and Fogg 1990. The changing economic fortunes of young Black men in America, *op. cit.* This research indicates that real annual earnings of young Black men are more strongly correlated with their marital status than any employment variable over the past 15 years.

77. Wilson, J. W. 1987. *The truly disadvantaged: The inner city, the underclass, and public policy, op cit.*

78. U.S. Bureau of Census, CPS Series P-20, No. 468, *Marital status and living arrangements: March 1992,* Table A.

79. Lerman, R. I. and Ooms, T. J. 1993. Evolution of unwed fatherhood as a policy issue. In *Young unwed fathers,* K. Lerman and T. Ooms (eds.), Philadelphia, PA: Temple University Press, pp. 1-24: and U.S. Bureau of the Census, *Statistical Abstract of the United States, 1993,* Table 101.

80. Gadsden, V. 1993. *The absence of father: Effects on child development and family functioning.* Paper presented at the Policy Roundtable on Labor Force Participation and Family Formation sponsored by the Center for the Study of Social Policy and the Philadelphia Children's Network, November, 1993, Washington, D.C.

81. Children's Defense Fund. 1993. *Progress and peril: Black children in America, op. cit.*

82. U.S. Bureau of the Census, CPS Series P-60, No. 181, *Poverty in the United States,* Table 5.

83. U.S. Bureau of Census, CPS Series P-60, Money Income of Households, Families and Persons in the United States, 1992, Unpublished Work Table F-5: "Type of Family by Median and Mean Income, Race and Hispanic Origin of Householder: 1947 to 1992."

84. U.S. Bureau of the Census, CPS P-60, No. 180, Table 18.

85. Gadsden, V. 1993. The absence of father: Effects on children's development and family functioning, *op. cit.*

86. McLanahan. 1983. Family structure and stress: A longitudinal comparison of two-parents and female-headed families. *Journal of Marriage and the Family,* 45: pp. 347–357, as quoted in Gadsen, V. (1993). The Absence of Father: Effects on Children's Development and Family Functioning, *op. cit.*

87. Gadsden, V. 1993. The absence of father: Effects on children's development and family functioning, op. cit.; Lerman, R. I. and Ooms, T. J. 1993. *Young Unwed Fathers, op. cit.;* Vostler, N. R. and Proctor, E. R., 1991. Family structure and stressors in a child guidance clinic population. *Families in Society,* 72, pp. 164–173; Children's Defense Fund (1993). *Progress and peril: Black children in America, op. cit.;* Kelly, R. F. and Ramsey, S. H. 1991. Poverty, children, and public policies, *Journal of Family Issues,* 12, pp. 388–403; National Commission on Children, (1991). *Beyond rhetoric: A New American agenda for children and families,* Washington, D.C.: National Commission on Children.

88. Gadsden, V. L, 1993. *Persistence, learning and schooling: The intergenerational transfer of meaning in African-American families.* Paper presented at the meeting of the National Academy of Education and the Spencer Foundation, University of Michigan, Ann Arbor; and Gadsen, V.L (1993). The Absence of Father: effects on children's development and family functioning, *op. cit.*

14

Health Issues

Low Birth Weight and Infant Mortality in the African-American Family: The Impact of Racism and Self-Esteem

NANNY L. GREEN

This paper is a discussion of the implications of racism and low self-esteem in regard to the comparatively high rate of infant mortality in the Afro-American community. The author argues that racism produces inferior health care for and low self-esteem in pregnant Afro-American women. These factors result in low-birth weight children whose chances to live are diminished by the same factors.

■

There is a state of siege in North America. In the United States, African American babies are dying at twice the rate of white babies (Binkin, Rust, and Williams, 1988; Johnson, 1987; Schoendorf, et al., 1992). Infant mortality, the death of a live-born infant before the first year of life per thousand live births, is a national and international health indicator. The United States ranked twenty-first in worldwide infant mortality rates (United Nations, 1990). A critical factor in the poor U.S. ranking was the two-fold disparity between African American and White infant mortality

Low birth weight is a major determinant of infant mortality. Low birth weight can result from preterm labor and delivery, intrauterine growth retardation, or a combination of both of these. If babies are born too soon (prior to 37 weeks gestation) or too small (less than 2,500 grams, or 5 1/2 pounds), they are at greater risk for morbidity or mortality (Institute of Medicine, 1985). Low-birth weight rates for African American childbearing women remain approximately twice the rate for White women (Department of Health Services, Health and Welfare Agency State of California, 1990). The high incidence of African American low birth weight is a precursor to the high infant mortality rate.

Data from birth records and other vital statistics were analyzed. The data included variables such as age, race, income, marital status, and obstetrical conditions (Gould and Leroy 1988;

Previously unpublished paper, 1993. Printed by permission of the author.

Klebanoff and Yip, 1987). Although relationships between these variables and low birth weight were demonstrated, they did not account for the dramatic differential between African American and White rates. Despite a multitude of studies, racial differences in low birth weight and infant mortality remain unexplained. This paper proposes racism and self-esteem as factors to be considered in the high low-birth weight and infant mortality rates in the African American childbearing family.

DEFINITIONS

Baughman (1971:90) states "one cannot examine Blacks psychologically without concluding that the effects of oppression are to be found in almost all sectors of their lives." These effects result from policies of public and private institutions as well as the philosophies that direct these institutions. Racism in the United States is linked with oppression and the mental and physical dehumanization of the slave (Aptheker, 1969; Fanon, 1963; Franklin, 1974; Kovel, 1970). Van de Berghe (1967:11) defined racism as:

> An ideology which considers a group's unchangeable physical characteristics to be linked in a direct causal way to psychological or intellectual characteristics, and on this basis distinguishes between superior and inferior racial groups.

When racism exists there is evidence that:

1. One group receives differential treatment (for example, health services) in terms of
   a. Availability of services
   b. Attitudes of service providers
   c. Quality of care provided
2. One group demonstrates belief in the inherent superiority over another group by means of
   a. Principal leadership maintained
   b. Guidelines articulated for the oppressed group

Racism is proposed as a factor in the poor birth outcomes of African Americans. Research related to the effects of racism on low birth weight and infant mortality is minimal (David and Collins, 1991). Yet the effects of racism mandate research and action (Essed, 1991).

Self-esteem can be defined as the self-evaluation of worth (Rosenberg and Simmons, 1971). Self-esteem, a mirror of society's image of the African American woman, is demonstrated in:

1. Negative societal judgments about the African American family

2. The greater number of positive images about Whites than positive African American images

3. The fact that the North American standard of beauty is incongruent with the physical features of African women

4. Compared to indices for Whites, less positive indices regarding evaluation of African American self-esteem

It is proposed that self-esteem, a vision of one's self and one's position in the world, has a relationship with health outcomes, specifically low birth weight and infant mortality.

RELATED LITERATURE

Racism

Katz (1976) described three different interpretations of race issues:

1. Things are now better than ever.
2. Things may look better but basic attitudes have not actually changed—only verbalization has.
3. Things may be better now, but there is still a long way to go.

A fourth interpretation is that things are not better now (Wilson, 1987). Delany (1968:381) described racism as including a chronic blaming process and states that this transference of blame is "a common characteristic of racism in this nation." Coleman (1971) discussed the characteristics and disadvantages of U.S. society. A liability for African Americans is that Whites act differently toward them than to other Whites. This racism combines with lack of freedom in social action and compromises economic and political resources. Essed (1991:3) presented everyday racism as involving "systematic, recurrent, familiar practices."

Griffith and Griffith (1986:71) stated that "health professionals have not studied the psychological effects of racism in much detail." However he held that willful racial conduct has, in the courts, given the plaintiff a reasonable claim to damages. Allen (1986:60) discussed post-traumatic stress disorder among African American Vietnam veterans. The disorder has a high incidence in the community. He stated that this condition manifests as a "profound alteration in the patient's basic sense of trust" and that societal racial stress further intensifies the disillusionment. The African American unemployment rate, which is more than double the rate for White veterans, reflects the fact that "the door to the Great Society has been shut."

Deficits in access to health care among African Americans in comparison with Whites was demonstrated in a national survey of U.S. health services (Blendon et al., 1989). Data from a national survey ($N = 10,130$) revealed differences in access to care between African Americans and Whites. African Americans were less satisfied with care from their last hospitalization and were more likely than Whites to wait for more than one-half hour to see a provider on their last hospital visit. African Americans above the poverty level experienced a disparity in access to health care in comparison with their White counterparts.

Lawson (1986) stated that though, in the past, research findings relating to racial issues have been used to support concepts of inferiority, racial and ethnic factors have recently been ignored. He pointed to differentiation in racial groups in the presentation of psychiatric disorders.

This differentiation has ramifications for diagnosis, treatment, and research. Leigh (1986:57, 64) replicated a previous finding indicating "that a disproportionate number of Blacks are found in dangerous jobs." He concluded that policymakers should view "the risk and time preferences of the poor and non-Whites as negative externalities resulting from a maldistribution of income and racial discrimination."

The literature on racism is limited in terms of empirical studies of what exists; the whys have not been investigated. Leigh (1986), in his replication study of risky jobs, attempted to operationalize the effects of racism. Hypothesized explanations for the selection of risky jobs included discrimination forcing people of color into this employment. Another hypothesis was that people of color have less to lose and are more willing to accept risk. This study though not related directly to childbearing, does relate to the conception of racism. As the major literature on racism must be obtained from statistical surveys and from sociological and psychological discussions of specific findings, we are left with combining historical data and operationalizing racism. This lack may also be viewed as an operational function of racism.

Self-Esteem

Self-esteem incorporates society's image with the self-image of the African American woman and her family. Mays (1986:592, 593) reviewed history since slavery and concluded "more important than economic or education achievements is the struggle for a definitive experience of one's individual self." It is the struggle to define self that is present in the "ambivalences surrounding their identities today."

Spurlock (1986), in a review of the literature on the self-concept of African American children, stated that "studies in self-concept in Afro-American children differ in the findings according to whether the research was conducted before or after the civil rights movement of the 1960s." Earlier studies reported lower self-esteem among

African Americans than Whites, but studies conducted after the civil rights movement do not support that finding. Barnes (1980: 106) wrote:

> It is obvious that we who are concerned about Black children must think about them in relation to Black families and the Black community never forgetting that this entire configuration is embedded in a society that devalues everything Black.

The classic doll study (Clark, 1947) reported White preference as measured by doll selection in elementary-school children. Subsequent studies contradicted these findings (Hraba and Grant, 1970). Housley, Martin, and McCoy (1987) demonstrated that urban African American adolescent females had higher self-esteem than Whites. Lack of consensus does not negate the viability of self-esteem as a factor in health outcomes, specifically low birth weight and infant mortality in African Americans. Critical questions can be raised. What is the relationship of positive or negative self-esteem with health outcomes? Does high or low self-esteem have a relationship with racism? What is the nature of the relationship? What are the ways in which self-esteem can be effectively measured? These questions support the consideration of self-esteem as a factor in low birth weight and infant mortality in African American childbearing women.

LOW BIRTH WEIGHT AND INFANT MORTALITY: A RACIAL DISPARITY

Statistics (Hughes et al., 1989) document a higher infant mortality and low birth weight rate for African Americans than Whites (Table 1). Binkin et al. (1985) concluded there was (1) the need for reduction of low-birth-weight infants if there is to be a decrease in African American infant mortality rates; (2) the need for increased survival of optimal-weight infants; and (3) the need for better physician estimates of viability,

TABLE 1 U.S. Infant Mortality and Low Birth Weight: A Racial Comparison

	African American	White	All Races
Infant Mortality 1986	18.0	8.9	10.4
Low Birth Weight 1986	12.5	5.6	6.8

which would allow physicians to delay labor if infant survival is not possible.

Racial and ethnic categories may vary. As the Department of Health Services, Health and Welfare Agency, State of California (1986:278) explained, the Census Bureau denotes self-identification as the most important factor in categorization.

> Whether a Black person is self identified as Hispanic or non-Hispanic, Black still takes preference. Current rules require that the Black race designation always takes preference over all racial groups. A birth to a Black parent is always classified as Black regardless of the race/ethnicity of the other parent.

Binkin, Rust, and Williams (1988) reaffirmed the increase in the number of low-birth-weight African American babies. Higher infant mortality was related not only to an increased number of low-birth-weight babies, but an increased number of deaths of babies of optimal weight. Gould et al. (1989) found a significant difference between each income strata and infant mortality rates. Low birth weight at a specific income level for African Americans was approximately twice the rate for Whites at the same level. Neonatal mortality for the highest-income African Americans was approximately twice the rate for Whites at the same income strata. The study supports the concept that factors in addition to income are predictors of poor birth outcome in the African American childbearing family

Kleinman and Kessel (1987:752), in an attempt to identify risk factors responsible for birth-weight difference between African Americans and Whites, investigated age, parity marital status, and education on rates of low birth weight. They concluded that:

> Blacks had higher rates than Whites for every combination of maternal characteristics. In fact, the black-white race ratios were even larger among women at low risk (no risk factors) than among those at high risk (multiple risk factors). The racial disparity in birth weight is increasing.

These conclusions match findings of the Institute of Medicine report (1985). Though low-birth-weight rates declined, African Americans remain at increased risk for low birth weight. The gap between African American and White continues.

Baldwin (1986) summarized the twofold increased risk for African Americans compared with Whites and stated that other groups, such as Asians, tend to have a risk distribution similar to that of Whites. However, Puerto Ricans are at greater risk than Whites. Baldwin (1986:88) stated, "it is the unacceptably large numbers of low-birth weight babies born to Blacks and the higher risk of death among the normal-weight babies that result in their disadvantaged position." Genetic differences among racial or ethnic groups were postulated in this article as reasons for the racial differential. At a time when societal differences have not been fully investigated, biological differences as rationale for the racial disparity are not acceptable. Associated risk factors—maternal age, prenatal visits, residence, education, and month of onset of prenatal care—have been identified (Geronimius, 1986; Institute of Medicine, 1985). However, these known risk factors do not explain the high rate of African American low birth weight and infant mortality.

Schoendorf et al. (1992) found higher mortality in infants born to college-educated African American parents than in a comparable group of White infants. This difference was due to higher rates of low birth weight and supports the concept that other factors are involved. From this analysis of a well-educated sample, specific questions can be raised. What was happening in the lives of those families that was not occurring in the comparative white sample? What factors could have affected premature onset of labor? What factors could have contributed to decreased intrauterine growth? What societal issues could have played a role? Racism is proposed as a factor (Hogue and Hargraves, 1993).

SUMMARY

The literature about low birth weight and infant mortality confirms that, though infant mortality is at the lowest level, the risk for African Americans is two times that for Whites (Institute of Medicine, 1985). Low birth weight is a prime risk for infant mortality (Baldwin, 1986; Institute of Medicine, 1985; Kleinman and Kessel, 1987). And, most significantly, the gap between African American and white rates is not narrowing (Joyce, 1987). The disparity between African American and white rates, both for infant mortality and low birth weight, is well documented. The literature provides answers to the question What is happening? The "why" questions remain: Why is the incidence of low birth weight and the resultant infant mortality higher among African Americans than Whites? Why does this disparity exist, and why is it increasing?

Baldwin (1986) speculated about such variables as nutrition, higher labor force rates, and lower-status employment as conditions that could impinge on outcome for the African American woman and her family Baldwin (1986:88) asked two questions: "Does a college education give a Black woman the same access to health care resources as to a White woman? Does the same income buy the same level of living and safety of environment for Whites as Blacks?" The disparity persists when education is held constant, indicating that other determinants are involved.

Racism and self-esteem are proposed as factors related to the disparity in low birth weight and infant mortality in this nation. Racism compromises to available benefits of United States society. It is proposed that, if the antecedents of racism remain stationary or increase, then the poor outcomes of birth (that is, low birth weight and the resultant infant mortality) will remain stationary or increase.

Self-esteem, a mirror of society's image of the African American woman, is proposed to have negative relationships with racism. If the manifestations of racism are high, self-esteem will be low. Relationships with self-esteem and health outcomes have been demonstrated (Antonucci, Peggs, and Marquez, 1989). Few studies have examined relationships of self-esteem with health outcomes in African Americans. Green (1991) examined the relationships of stress, self-esteem, and racism in a sample of African American childbearing women. No significant relationships with newborn birth weight were found, but significant relationships were demonstrated between stress and racism and between self-esteem and stress. These findings support continued investigation.

A concept of self must be viewed in the context of society's definition intertwined with the individual's definition. Society's statement, unfortunately, is the definition of the ruling class; it does not embody the definitions of the oppressed. History is viewed from the vantage of the powerful, not the powerless (Fanon, 1963; Rodney, 1974). The pregnant African American woman and her family are defined as negative and powerless. In this context, self-esteem is justifiably proposed as a factor related to health outcomes, specifically low birth weight and infant mortality.

Gates-Williams et al. (1992) determined that there was a conceptual error in focusing on individual behavior and blaming African American women for outcomes such as low birth weight and infant mortality. Research and interventions related to health outcomes—specifically, low birth weight and infant mortality outcomes—need to be continued and reframed. Factors such as racism and self-esteem must be considered and investigated to mandate change in policy, government, and society—change that will affect the lives of African American women and their families.

REFERENCES

Allen, I. 1986. Post-traumatic stress disorder among Black veterans. *Hospital and Community Psychiatry,* 37(1): 55–60.

Antonucci, T. C., J. F. Peggs, and J. T. Marquez. 1989. The relationship between self-esteem and physical health in a family practice population. *Family Practice Research Journal,* 9(1): 65–72.

Aptheker, H. 1969. *American Negro slave revolts.* New York: International.

Baldwin, W. 1986. Half empty, half-full: What we know about low birth weight among Blacks. *American Medical Association Journal,* 255(1): 86–88.

Barnes, E. J. 1980. The Black community as the source for positive self-concept for Black children: A theoretical perspective. In *Black Psychology,* R. L. Jones, editor, pp. 106–130. New York: Harper & Row.

Baughman, E. E. 1971. *Black Americans: A psychological analysis.* New York: Academic.

Binkin, N. J., K. R. Rust, and R. L. Williams. 1988. Racial differences in neonatal mortality: What causes of death explain the gap? *American Journal of Diseases of Children,* 142(4): 434–440.

Binkin, N. J., et al. 1985. *Reducing Black neonatal mortality: Will improvement in birth weight be enough? American Medical Association Journal,* 253(3): 372–375.

Blendon, R. J., et al. 1989. Access to medical care for Black and White Americans. *American Medical Association Journal,* 26(2): 278–281.

Clark K. B., and M. K. Clark. 1947. Racial identification and preference in Negro children. In *Readings in social psychology,* T. Newcoomb and E. Hartley, eds. New York: Holt.

Coleman, J. S. 1971. *Resources for social change: Race in the United States.* New York: Wiley-Interscience.

David, R. J., and J. W. Collins. 1991. Bad outcomes in Black Babies: Race or racism? *Ethnicity & Disease,* 1(3):236–244.

Delany, L T. 1968. The other bodies in the river. In *Black psychology,* R. R. Jones, ed., pp. 376–383: New York: Harper & Row.

Department of Health Services, Health and Welfare Agency, State of California. 1986. *Vital statistics of California, 1984.* Washington, D.C.: U.S. Government Printing Office.

Department of Health Services, Health and Welfare Agency, State of California. 1990. *Vital statistics of California, 1988.* Washington, D.C.: U.S. Government Printing Office.

Essed, P. 1991. *Understanding everyday racism.* Newbury Park: Sage.

Fanon, R. 1963. *The wretched of the earth.* New York: Grove Press. (Original work published in 1960.)

Franklin, J. H. 1974. *From slavery to freedom: A history of Negro Americans* (4th edition). New York: Knopf.

Gates-Williams, J. G., et al. 1992. The business of preventing African-American infant mortality, *Western Journal of Medicine* 157(3): 350–356.

Geronimius, A. T. 1986. The effects of race, residence, and prenatal care on the relationship of maternal age to neonatal mortality, *American Journal of Public Health,* 76(2): 1416–1421.

Gould, J. B., et al. 1988. Socioeconomic status and low birth weight: A racial comparison: *Pediatrics* 82(6): 896–904.

Green, N. L. 1991. Stress, self-esteem and racism as factors associated with low birth weight and preterm delivery in African-American childbearing women. *Dissertation Abstracts International,* 52, 91–37398 (Microfiche: University of California, San Francisco, Thesis 795).

Griffith, E., and E. Griffith. 1986. Racism, psychological injury and compensatory damages. *Hospital and Community Psychiatry,* 37(1): 71–75.

Hogue, C. J., and M. A. Hargraves. 1993. Class, race and infant mortality in the United States. *American Journal of Public Health,* 83(1): 9–12.

Housley, K., S. Martin, and H. McCoy. 1987. Self-esteem of adolescent females as related to race, economic status, and area of residence. *Perceptual and Motor Skills,* 64: 559–566.

Hraba, J., and G. Grant. 1970. Black is beautiful: A reexamination of racial preference and identification. *Journal of Personality and Social Psychology,* 16(3): 398–402.

Hughes, D., et al. 1989. *The health of America's children.* Washington, D.C.: Children's Defense Fund.

Institute of Medicine, Committee to Study the Prevention of Low Birthweight. 1985. *Preventing low birthweight.* Washington, D.C.: National Academy.

Johnson, J. H. 1987. U.S. differentials in infant mortality: Why do they persist? *Family Planning Perspectives,* 19(5): 227–232.

Joyce, T. 1987. The demand for health inputs and their impact on the Black neonatal mortality rate in the U.S. *Social Science Medicine,* 24(11): 911–918.

Katz, P. A. 1976. Racism and social science: Towards a new commitment. In *Toward the elimination of racism,* P. A Katz, ed., pp. 3–17. New York: Pergamon.

Kessel, S. S., et al. 1984. The changing pattern of low birth weight in the United States. *American Medical Association Journal,* 257(15): 1978–1982.

Klebanoff, M. A., and R. Yip. 1987. Influence of maternal birth weight on rate of fetal growth and duration of gestation. *Journal of Pediatrics,* 111(2): 287–292.

Kleinman, J. C., and S. S. Kessel. 1987. Racial difference in low birth weight. *New England Journal of Medicine,* 317(12): 749–753.

Koval, J. 1970. *White racism: A psychohistory.* New York: Random House.

Lawson, W. B. 1986. Racial and ethnic factors in psychiatric research. *Hospital and Community Psychiatry,* 37(1): 50–54.

Leigh, P. J. 1986. Who chooses risky jobs? *Social Science and Medicine,* 23(1): 57–64.

Mays, V. 1986. Identity development of Black Americans: The role of history and the importance of ethnicity, *American Journal of Psychotherapy,* 40(4): 582–593.

Nobles, W. W., and C. M. Nobles. 1976. African roots in Black families: The social-psychological dynamics of Black family life and implications for nursing care. In *Black awareness: Implications for Black patient care,* D. Luchraft, ed. New York: American Journal of Nursing.

Rodney, W. 1974. *How Europe underdeveloped Africa.* Washington, D.C.: Howard University Press.

Rosenberg, M., and R. Simmons. 1971. *Black and White self-esteem: The urban school child.* Washington, D.C.: American Sociological Association.

Schoendorf, K. C., et al. 1992. Mortality among infants of Black as compared with White college-educated parents. *New England Journal of Medicine,* 326(23): 1522–1526.

Spurlock, J. 1986. Development of self-concept in Afro-American Children. *Hospital and Community Psychiatry,* 37(1): 66–70.

United Nations. 1990. *Demographic Yearbook, 1988.* New York: United Nations.

U.S. Department of Commerce. 1986. *Statistical abstract of the United States, 1986.* Washington, D.C.: U.S. Government Printing Office.

Van den Berghe, P. L. 1967. *Race and racism.* New York: Wiley.

Wilson, J. L. 1987. *The truly disadvantaged: The inner city, the underclass, and public policy.* Chicago: University of Chicago Press.

Social Correlates of Black Women's Health Status

ERMA J. LAWSON & LA FRANCIS RODGERS-ROSE

In the past decade, social scientists, clinicians, and pol-icy-makers have recognized the health disparities be-tween Black women and their White counterparts. This article addresses the social influences that have historically affected the health of Black women. First, it considers the impact of race-based social inequality, residential location, and occupational factors to explain the current health status of Black women. Each of these issues are discussed in the context of three historical pe-riods, slavery, post-slavery, and the late twentieth cen-tury. Second, to explore those factors, we present a health survey of 323 Black women between the ages of 18 and 65 which allowed open-ended responses to the survey questions. Results indicate that race-based social inequality correlated with medical treatment of yeast infections, pregnancy related problems, allergies, and pelvic inflammatory disease. Residence in high density areas and occupational factors are significantly correlated with treated medical conditions. We suggest that research design and analyses must recognize the historical and structural conditions that have adversely affected the health of Black women.

■

INTRODUCTION

Black women suffer a disproportionate risk of ill-health (U.S. DHHS, 1991). Compared to White women, Black women experience a greater num-ber of undetected diseases, high illness rates, and more chronic diseases (U.S. DHHS, 1991). For example, the incidence and prevalence of hyper-tension, cancer, and AIDS exceed those of White women (U.S. DHHS, 1991). Additionally, dia-betes is the third leading cause of death among Blacks and among Black women, it can be defined as an epidemic (U.S. DHHS, 1991). Moreover, the life expectancy at birth for White females is 79.8 compared to 73.5 for Black females (U.S. DHHS, 1991). The life expectancy gap between Black and White women is widening. For exam-ple, the difference between Black and White women's life expectancy increased by one year be-tween 1984 and 1992 (Office on Women's Health, U.S. Public Health Service, 1997).

While there has been a plethora of research on the incidence and prevalence of illnesses among Black women, there exists a significant void in the literature on social factors that have historically influenced their health. We suggest that from a public policy, theoretical, and methodological perspective, it is important to consider historical and environmental factors to explain the health status of Black women. This is especially significant where reliance on individ-ual characteristics to explain health status often leads to simplistic behavioral interventions and erroneous conclusions. Consequently, the iden-tification of environmental factors which main-tain and perpetuate ill-health among Black women has been limited by the dominant em-phasis on individual characteristics.

This article addresses the social influences that have historically affected the health of Black women. First, it considers the impact of race-based social inequality, residential location, and occupational factors to explain the current health

Previously unpublished paper, 1998. Reprinted by permission of the authors.

status of Black women. Each of these issues are discussed in the context of three historical periods, slavery, post-slavery, and the twentieth century. Second, to explore those factors, we present a health survey that allowed respondents to provide open-ended responses to the survey questions. Whereas the quantitative data suggest the association between variables, the qualitative data provide clarification of the closed-ended questions and illustrates how social factors may be conducive to the ill-health of Black women.

SLAVERY

Race-based Social Inequality

Studies have reported that slave women confronted numerous obstacles in obtaining adequate medical care (Jones, 1985; Savitt, 1975). One such barrier involved receiving medical care based on a racist ideology to support the genetic inferiority of Black women (Kiple and King, 1985). For instance, Cartwright, a leading medical physician of the antebellum South, believed that sick Black women should be treated as savages exposed to open air since they were physically and mentally inferior due to the improper atmospherization of "Negro blood" (Cartwright, 1852). He concluded that Black women were susceptible to diseases due to their inferior intellect, small lungs, and a sluggish circulation. Consequently, slavery was necessary to prevent Black women from "relapse into barbarism" (Cartwright, 1852).

The surgical experimentation of slave women also posed a health threat (Kiple and King, 1981; Savitt, 1978). Because contemporary physicians believed that Black women endured surgical treatment better than White women, they practiced surgical procedures initially on slave women (Kiple and King, 1981). For instance, Marion Simms perfected his operation of vesicovaginal fistulas on slave women before performing the procedure on White women (Kiple and King, 1981; Savitt, 1978). Similarly, Francois Marie

Prevost practiced fifteen cesarean sections on slave women prior to operating on White women (Savitt, 1978). Although the surgical procedures were major medical discoveries, the excessive surgical experimentation of slave women played an important role in their morbidity and mortality (Kiple and King, 1981; Savitt, 1978).

Residential Location

Slave women resided in squalid conditions, which compromised their health (Kiple and King, 1981; Jacobs, 1987; Jones, 1985). Floors made of dirt, lack of proper ventilation, cramped living quarters, and poor sanitation produced intestinal disorders, respiratory illnesses, and death (Jones, 1985; Rene, Jones, and Moore, 1992). While an illness in White households affected only the sick individual, the health of Black women was threatened by illnesses in their immediate households and the surrounding slave quarters (Rene et al, 1992; Savitt, 1978).

The overcrowding of two or more slave families in one cabin resulted in the rapid transmission of diseases (DuBois, 1972; Jones, 1985; Savitt, 1978). In one household, two members died of scarlet fever after a young slave contracted the illness while five members of this household became ill with sore throats (Tebault, 1861). Moreover, unsanitary conditions around the slaves' cabins often caused diseases (Kiple and King, 1981; Savitt, 1978). Because drinking water was also used for the deposit of human and animal bodily waste materials, female slaves often died from drinking contaminated water (Kiple and King, 1981; Savitt, 1978; Shyrock, 1966).

Occupational Factors

The working conditions of slave women also produced illness and death (Genovese, 1976; Meier and Rudwick, 1970). For example, they experienced chronic muscle pain and internal organ damage from whippings that resulted from low field work productivity (Genovese, 1976; Savitt, 1978). Bondwomen were also injured from such work-related accidents as animal kicks and overturned wagons (Savitt, 1978). Working around farm animals also posed health risks to bondwomen since they frequently died of meningitis and septicemia from handling infected animals (Savitt, 1978).

The tendency of slave owners to exploit the labor of bondwomen also increased their susceptibility to illnesses (Jones, 1985). Estimates reveal that in the 1850s 90 percent of all female slaves sixteen years of age and older worked more than 261 days per year, eleven to thirteen hours each day (Jones, 1985). They worked without proper foot attire which increased their susceptibility to tetanus (Lockjaw) and hookworm infections, diseases which were often fatal (Jones, 1985; Rene et al., 1992). Additionally, female slaves experienced skin and face rashes from tobacco leaves and their fingers were deformed by working in cotton fields (Savitt, 1978).

Moreover, slave women often self-inflicted injuries as acts of rebellion against an oppressive system that perpetuated a racial status hierarchy (Jacobs, 1987; Sterling, 1984). According to Sterling (1984), female slaves often jumped into rivers to drown in order to escape strippings and whippings (Sterling, 1984). They also disfigured their breasts to avoid suckling White children and often cut off fingers to avoid being sold (Jacobs, 1987; Sterling, 1984).

POST-SLAVERY

Race-Based Social Inequality

Social historians have pointed to Black's mortality rates following the Civil War as an indicator of their health status (Legan, 1973; Meier and Rudwick, 1970). The Black mortality rate increased and remained considerably higher for Blacks than that of Whites (Litwack, 1979). The health crisis of former slaves justified a racist ideology in which medical journals portrayed Blacks as a disease menace to Whites. Additionally White physicians called for the sterilization of

the Black male population by vasectomy. According to these physicians, "This would solve the greatest menace of all ages" (Allen, 1915; Raphael, 1972).

The attitudes of White physicians toward ex-slaves influenced the quality of care Black women received. One writer described the physicians who worked for the Freedmen's Bureau: "Former slaves are attended to by young, inexperienced, White physicians. They have inherited traditions of their elders, and let Black patients die. Physicians heave a great sigh of relief that one more source of contagion is removed" (Dubois, 1977). In fact, a missionary complained in 1866, "White doctors have but little sympathy for freed women" (Raphael, 1972). As a result, Black women were discouraged from seeking medical care due to White racial beliefs, attitudes, and customs which were reinforced by clinical practices and theories.

Residential Location

Similar to slavery, the living conditions of post-slavery continued to influence the health status of Black women (Hine, 1989; Jones, 1985). For instance, they often lived in houses that lacked running water, sanitary facilities, and adequate insulation and ventilation (Jones, 1985). The Freedmen's Bureau in Kentucky reported the following, "The conditions of tenements occupied by ex-slaves were old dilapidated miserable shanties, crowded with half starved men, women, and children" (Raphael, 1972). These cabins measured fifteen or twenty square feet. They lacked screens and sanitary facilities. Eating, sleeping, and bathing often occurred in one room (Jones, 1985). These cabins provided ideal conditions for respiratory epidemics (Jones, 1985). As a result, Black women contracted pneumonia, influenza, colds, and streptococcal infections (Raphael, 1972; Legan, 1973). Moreover, they experienced injuries and deaths from house fires (DuBois, 1977). Inadequate housing also placed Black women at risk for tuberculosis, pneumonia, typhoid fever, and whooping cough (Hine, 1989). Poor facilities for storage of food and inadequate washing facilities caused enteritis and digestive disease (DuBois, 1977; Jones, 1985). Poorly equipped kitchens, faulty electrical connections, and badly lighted stairs increased the rate of home accidents (Clark, 1967; Jones, 1985).

Substandard housing also provided ideal conditions for cholera (Kiple and King, 1981). The houses of Black women often had inadequate food storage and lacked proper food preparation facilities. Thus, flies transported this fatal bacterial disease through food and water in Black households (Kiple and King, 1981). The White fatality rate was ten deaths of every twenty-four cases, while Blacks died at a rate of ten for every sixteen cases.

Occupational Factors

Participation in the paid labor force influenced the health status of Black women. For example, to the Freedman's Bureau they reported numerous beatings from their employers. In Athens, Georgia, Margaret Martin was beaten and choked when she returned to work after visiting her sister (Sterling, 1984). Several Black women appeared before a North Carolina Freedmen's Bureau and reported that employers knocked them down when they demanded wages (Sterling, 1984). These assaults were described as beatings with clubs, hoes, and ropes (Jones, 1985). As a result of their working conditions, Black women experienced multiple head injures, chronic pain, and death (Jones, 1985).

THE LATE TWENTIETH CENTURY

Race-Based Social Inequality

According to Cornell West (1993), race matters in the late twentieth century. Racist behaviors are discriminatory acts directed toward individuals because of visible biological characteristics (Essed, 1991; West, 1993). Racism, as a system of structural inequalities, is created and maintained through routine medical clinical practices (Essed, 1991; Schwartz, Kofie, Rivo, and Tuckson, 1990;

Wennecker and Epstein, 1989). For example, Mayer and McWhorter (1989) reported that Black women with breast cancer had less aggressive therapy than did White women. In fact, they were more likely than White women to be treated nonsurgically or to have no cancer-directed therapy. These treatment differences affected five-year survival.

Similarly, Harris, Andrews and Elixhauser (1997) found that of all diseases of the female reproductive system, Black women had a significantly lower rate of therapeutic procedures than White women. Controlling for hospital characteristics and demographic variables, and payment status, race and gender remained significant predictors of medical treatment among hospitalized Blacks for a number of disease categories. The authors suggest that racial medical treatment disparities result from physicians' racial and gender stereotypes. Additionally, the hospital experience of Black women differs from that of White women. Compared to White women, Black women tend to have shorter stays in private general hospitals and to spend more days per year in public mental hospitals and in institutions for the retarded (Weddington and Gabel, 1992).

Race-based social inequality contributes to the health status of Black women in several ways. First, structural racism creates barriers to obtaining adequate access to medical care (U.S. DHHS, 1991). Second, coping with racial stereotypes contributes to stress-related health problems such as hypertension (Anderson, McNeilly and Myers, 1991)

Residential Location

A large number of Black women live near municipal landfills, abandoned toxic waste dumps, and Superfund sites cleanups which have adversely affected their health (Bullard, 1994). Consequently, the impoverishment of a large number of Black communities has resulted in Black residential areas becoming the dumping grounds for health-threatening toxins and industrial pollution (Bullard, 1994). In fact, the public health community has insufficient information to explain the magnitude of air pollution-related health problems among Black women (Bullard, 1994). Persons suffering from asthma are sensitive to the effects of carbon monoxide as well as various toxic substances, and Black women have a high prevalence of asthma and allergies (U.S. DHHS, 1991).

In many low income areas, there are often deteriorated plumbing, numerous electrical repairs, and inadequate sanitation facilities which reduce the quality of life and permit the transmission of disease. The streets are often cluttered with drug paraphernalia, and the street lights are non-functioning which increase the risk for accidents and injuries. Moreover, the services of the fire department and hospital ambulances are often delayed and unavailable in low income communities, which increases the risk of death in a medical emergency (U.S. DHHS, 1991).

Proportionately more Black than White women live in the inner city with high crime and drug rates (U.S. DHHS, 1991). In central cities, Black women are more likely to be victims of aggravated assaults and household burglary, regardless of age or family income, compared to White women (NCHS, 1996). Black women also are more likely to be injured in violent crimes and sustain serious injuries compared to their counterparts (Centers for Disease Control, 1996). Moreover, The stress associated with living in high crime and drug infected neighborhoods influences the physical and mental health of Black women. For example, the fear of crime has often affected the propensity of Black women to attend health screening and prevention services (Leigh, 1995; Murrell et al., 1996). In fact, poverty residential areas represent a new independent risk factor for Black women's adverse health outcomes (U.S. DHHS, 1991).

Occupational Factors

Black women continue to work in high health-risk occupations (U.S. DHHS, 1991). Work-related injuries included musculoskeletal injuries and occupational cancers. The largest number of injuries occur in such industries as nursing homes, department stores, and hotels/motels which are over-represented by Black women. Although the employment of Black women in civil service -collar and semi-skilled positions has increased, they are over-represented in jobs that are considered high health-risk occupations (U.S. DHHS, 1991). A high proportion of Black women work in the cosmetology industry, which has a dangerous chemical environment. Beauticians are at high risk for cancer, particularly of the uterus. Bladder disorders and respiratory infections can result from exposure to dyes, solvents and can propellants (U.S. DHHS, 1991).

Occupational stressors, including low income has characterized the life experiences of a large number of Black women. For example, 48 percent of Black female-headed households have incomes below the poverty level (Pinkney, 1994). Further, the annual income of full-time women workers in 1990 was $20,700 for Black women compared to $22,900 for women, $32,000 for men, and $24,000 for Black men, resulting in Black women as the lowest paid among the four racial/gender groups, controlling for all work full-time (Hacker, 1992; Hill, 1993).

The relationship between socioeconomic status and morbidity and mortality rates has been extensively documented (Adler et al., 1993; Krieger, Rowley, Herman, Avery and Philips, 1993; Williams, 1990). This relationship extends to a variety of health problems, including heart disease, cancer, stroke, diabetes, hypertension, infant mortality, arthritis, back pain, and kidney disease. Studies also have shown an inverse relationship between socioeconomic status and illness prognosis, suggesting that those in lower income groups tend to die earlier following a medical diagnosis compared to their middle-class counterparts (Adler, 1993; Adler, 1994; Carroll et al., 1993).

The previous discussion has highlighted both the cultural conditioning to racial beliefs and the adverse historical structures that have affected the health status of Black women. This process has allocated differential social privileges and economic rewards to Black women which in turn has influenced their spatial living arrangements, employment opportunities, and health outcomes. In this context, the following survey emphasizes the multidimensional facets of social health risks by integrating correlational analysis with open-ended responses. Thus, the combination of quantitative and qualitative approaches draws on the strengths of two methodologies to examine the social conditions that adversely affect the health of Black women.

METHODS

Data were collected in conjunction with the International Black Women's Congress Health Conference. Newspaper advertisements and flyers announcing the study were posted in Black organizations, Black professional organizations, Black newspapers, and community organizations. Black churches also announced the study during services. Public service announcements were made on local Black radio stations emphasizing the importance of the study as well as the significance of research on Black women's health.

Procedures

As women registered for the conference, they were asked to complete a 30 minute self-administered questionnaire. Following a brief script describing the project, assuring confidentiality, and informed consent, each participant was given a survey and comment sheets for open-ended responses to each survey question. The respondents' comments contained relevant information about why social factors were problematic in the maintenance of adequate health. In each conference session, women were encouraged and allowed time to complete the survey. Approximately 90 percent of the women who attended the conference completed the survey.

Measures

The selection of the questionnaire was made with special concern about the necessity for women to complete the survey with ease. The questionnaire was adapted from the Essence health survey (1992) and the University of Kentucky Annual Health Survey (1994). Race-based social inequality was determined by inquires about the extent to which respondents experienced any event of racial discrimination in the past year. Racism was defined as overt acts of discrimination based on skin color. Racial discrimination was measured by asking: "Have you ever been discriminated against in any way because of your race." Respondents rated the frequency they experienced such incidents on a 5-point Likert scale ranging from (1) not at all to a great deal of time (5).

Demographic characteristics included age, ethnicity, education, income, marital status, and residential location, based on population density. The instruments chosen and developed had been used with minority populations.

Analysis

First, the Pearson Correlation determined the bivariate relation between socioeconomic status and race-based social inequality. Second, we provide qualitative data to provide insight into the quantitative data. The survey data analyzed in this study are well-suited to addressing overall patterns of ill-health, however, they do not help us understand why a health condition may exist. The strength of quantitative methods lies in their ability to ascertain patterns in a population. However, to assess the subjective meaning and dynamic processes associated with those patterns, qualitative data are needed (Williams, 1991).

RESULTS

Sample

The current sample consisted of 323 women ranging in age from 18 to 65 (M = 46.2, SD = 2.2) and 50 percent had 16 years of education. Racially, the sample was primarily Black (91.6 percent), with smaller percentages of women

TABLE 1 Characteristics of the Sample (N = 323)

Variables	Number	Percent
Age		
18–39	10	3.1
40–49	174	53.9
50–59	129	39.9
60–65	10	3.1
Marital Status		
Single	93	28.8
Married	98	30.3
Divorced	102	31.6
Separated	7	2.2
Widowed	23	7.1
Years of Education		
Less than 12	4	1.2
12 years	35	10.8
13–15	123	38.0
16 or more	161	50.0
Race		
Black	269	91.6
White	1	.3
Multicultural	26	8.1
Household Income		
< $20,000	20	6.2
$20,000–$29,000	88	27.3
$30,000–$39,000	63	19.5
$40,000–$49,000	98	30.3
> $50,000	54	16.7
Number of Children		
No Children	70	21.7
One Child	69	21.4
Two Children	109	33.7
Three Children	50	15.5
Four or more	25	7.7

identifying themselves as multicultural (8.1 percent). Approximately 48 percent of the respondents lived in a large city, 29 percent lived in suburban areas, a small percentage lived in a small town (13 percent), and a smaller percentage lived in rural areas (8.7 percent).

The majority of women earned between $30,000–$39,000 annually (57 percent) and 92 percent of the sample reported private health insurance (through employer or purchased independently). Of importance, only six of the respondents (2 percent) were covered by Medicare and seven (2 percent) were covered by Medicaid. Twelve of the respondents (4 percent) lacked health insurance. Fifty-five percent of women were divorced and had two children (70 percent). Table 1 shows that the sample consisted of middle-age, college educated, Black divorced women.

Race-based Social Inequality

Seventy percent of women reported that they experienced racism all the time; 20 percent experienced racism sometimes, and a small percentage (10 percent) of women reported never being a victim of racism. Experiencing racism in the past year was positively correlated with treatment of yeast infections ($r = .27$ $p = <.01$), pregnancy-related problems ($r = .27$, $p <.01$), allergies ($r = .13$, $p = <.05$), and pelvic-inflammatory disease (PID) ($r = .17$, $p < .01$). Thus, women who reported more incidents of race-based social inequality were more likely to be treated for yeast infections, pregnancy-related illnesses, allergies, and PID.

The following is a response from a woman who described how racial discrimination affected her health, which resulted in hypertension.

> Why is it a mystery that racism is a health risk? I was passed over for a job promotion and still fighting a racial discrimination suit. I trained people who were less capable than I was, and they were promoted. I have not slept worrying about the suit. Last month I was diagnosed with high blood pressure.

A 46-year-old college professor also explained:

> I was looking for an apartment and discovered how much racism in housing still exists. I answered an ad for an apartment for

$700 a month. When I met the landlords, an elderly couple, I was told that the apartment rented for $1,200 per month. Since they could not tell I was Black over the phone, they provided directions to the house, plus I told them that I was a college professor. When I confronted them that the price was different than that offered in the newspapers, they said that the "Blacks" lived down the street in the cheaper housing. I worried and worried over this incidents for days, my blood pressure went up to 220/140, 1 had migraine headaches. The stress made me depressed 'cause I am a citizen of this country and pay taxes, but yet I can't live where I want to. This ugly incident flashed through my mind for months and cut through my soul like a knife. Finally, I was placed on medication for my nerves.

Other women expressed profound mental distress over being denied a mortgage although they had excellent credit histories. The respondents also reported discrimination during medical encounters, bank transactions, and hotel accommodations, which resulted in depression, anxiety, and mental fatigue as well as eating and sleeping disorders.

Residential Location

Residential location was positively related to depression (r = .14, p = <.05) and pelvic inflammatory disease (r = 23, p = <.01). Thus, women who lived in high density areas were more likely to be depressed and treated for pelvic inflammatory disease. A 42-year-old mother clarified the relationship between residential location and overall physical health status.

> Drugs, weapons, and prisons are all new forms of slavery. I live everyday in fear. I live in a war zone. I can't let my kids go out and play. I walk around nervous and have migraine headaches. I live in fear of being mugged, robbed, and even killed which makes me depressed and anxious.

A 55-year-old woman who lived in Washington, D.C., also explained:

> I believe it's the pollution where I live that has killed most of my friends. The woman next door has brain cancer, the man down the street died of intestinal cancer. On my block of about 10 people, 6 have died of cancer. They were middle-class, church going people, so I believe we live near a toxic waste-dump and nobody wants to tell us. I get depressed thinking I might be sitting on a time bomb waiting for cancer.

Indeed, unlike White women, many Black women live near hazardous-waste landfills, toxic waste dumps, incinerators, and industrial plants that pose a threat to their health (Bullard, 1994). The stress of residential location was also illustrated by written comments concerning fears about children exposure to drugs and street gangs, which resulted in the respondents being treated for headaches, depression, and anxiety.

Occupational Factors

A large majority of respondents reported that income was a major stressor a great deal of the time (56 percent). Socioeconomic status was negatively correlated with treatment for allergies (r = -.43, p = <.05) and pelvic inflammatory disease (PID) (r = -.27, p <.01), suggesting that women who reported less economic resources were more likely to be treated for allergies and PID. The open-ended questions revealed several types of economic stressors that influenced the health of women. A 35-year-old woman noted:

> My health has declined over the last three years with not getting paid enough, I have too little money. Plus I can never save enough as a result of the tax burden, I am a single female. I have no tax deductions and 35 percent of my gross pay is taken up in taxes. Can you imagine that I bring home very little money from my check. I worry about paying bills.

A 48-year-old respondent also explained how limited financial resources affected her health:

> Is there ever a time without money problems being a Black woman. I changed jobs and got behind in my rent. So I was stressed with bills coming in without money to pay for them. My allergies got worse and I had frequent colds. The stress of bills took a toll on my immune system.

Although the lack of adequate financial resources affected the health status of the respondents, the comments indicated that periodic unemployment and tax liabilities also undermined their health. Women also reported that occupational stressors such as underemployment, and unemployment as well as coping with occupational racial stereotypes compromised their health status.

DISCUSSION

This review of pertinent literature on the historical and social perspectives of Black women's health has placed emphasis on race-based social inequality, occupational factors, and residential location during slavery, post-slavery and the late twentieth century. We consider each in turn.

Race-Based Social Inequality

The results demonstrate the need to address race-based social inequality as a health issue. The contention here is that raced-based social inequality symbolized social location, structural constraints and structural power that make the experiences of Black women distinct, which ultimately influence their health. Experiencing race-based social inequality is positively correlated with treatment of yeast infections, pregnancy related problems, allergies, and pelvic-inflammatory disease. This finding suggests that not only discrete acts of racism may affect health, but also the aftermath of dealing with housing and employment discrimination may adversely influence the health status of Black women. Although chronic stressors have

been associated with hypertension among Blacks, socioecological stress has little influence on the blood pressure of Whites (Anderson, 1988; Anderson et al., 1989; Barber, 1990).

In the context of a racial hierarchy, race-based social inequality influences various health conditions other than hypertension. In other words, racism adversely affects the health and well-being of Black women. Because the history, structure, and socialization processes of American society are characterized by an almost universal tendency to unconscious racial bigotry, it is important for health researchers to address discrimination in the lives of Black women, which may influence their visits to health care facilities as well as physical and psychological symptoms.

Occupational Factors

The results show a negative correlation between occupational factors, specifically socioeconomic variables, and treatment of allergies, pelvic inflammatory disease, and pregnancy-related conditions. Unlike previous research, the qualitative data indicate that not only the lack of income increased the morbidity of Black women, but large tax liabilities and intermittent unemployment increased the likelihood of allergies and pelvic inflammatory disease. The finding suggests that future research should address the various types of economic stressors that may adversely affect the health status of Black women. Divorced Black women with few tax deductions may bear a greater tax liability than do married women. To the extent that taxes are disproportionately shifted to single women, they may be the working poor, which increases stress and adversely affect their health.

Sociological analyses have consistently demonstrate a correlation between low income and ill-health. But, in view, of this discussion, relationships ascertained between the two variables must be considered within the context of the racial stratified system and its concomitant supporting beliefs and processes. The occupational system is thus stratified on the basis of color and gender, and has sustained and legitimized economic disenfranchisement for innumerable Black women, which has had an ill-health producing effect.

Residential Location

Residential location was strongly positively correlated with depression and pelvic inflammatory disease, suggesting that living in a large city with the potential for drug-inspired crimes may be an independent health risk factor that influence the morbidity and mortality of Black women. In fact, Smith (1982) found that Blacks report less satisfaction with their housing quality than Whites with similar socioeconomic status, including dissatisfaction with police protection, quality of schools, and environmental quality.

Additionally, a large number of Black women reside in industrial corridors, live in communities where contaminated fish is consumed and dwell in neighborhoods that are dumping grounds for health-threatening toxins (Bullard, 1994). The negative health outcomes are numerous, including higher rates of emphysema, chronic bronchitis, accidents, and death.

Implications for Research

There are several methodological limitations to this study. First, this study was based on a convenience sample of women. Second, we have a cross-sectional survey, from which we cannot assess causality in relations between socioeconomic status, race-based inequality, occupational factors and physical health. Third, there may be bias in responses due to retrospective recall issues. Despite these limitations, this study provides new results concerning the effects of race-based social inequality, residential location, and occupational factors on the health status of Black women. Thus, research designs and health interventions must conceptualize health as a complex interaction between social risks that have a profound effect on the health status of Black women. Future studies of the health status of Black women would be greatly improved if researchers: (1) recognize the social conditions that influence health outcomes, (2) investigate residential location, explore neighborhood quality, and consider occupational conditions, and (3) systematically probe beyond individual demographics to explain ill-health among Black women. Health care practitioners and researchers can no longer afford to ignore the relationship between Black women's physical health and their social experiences.

REFERENCES

Adler, N., Boyce, T., Chesney, M. et al. 1993. Socioeconomic inequalities in health: No easy solution. *Journal of American Medical Association,* 269, 3140–3145.

Adler, N., Boyce, T., Chesney, M. et al. 1994. Socioeconomic status and health: The challenge of the gradient. *American Psychologist,* 49, 15–24.

Allen, L. C. 1915. The Negro health problem. *Journal of Public Health,* 5, 194–201.

Anderson, N. B. 1988. Aging and hypertension among Blacks: A multidimensional perspective. In J. S. Jackson (ed.), *The black elderly,* (pp. 190–214). New York: Springer.

Anderson, N. B., Lane, J. D., Monov, H., Williams, R. B., Jr., Houseworth, S.S. 1988. Racial differences in blood pressure and forearm vascular responses to the cold face stimulus. *Psychomatic Medicine,* 5, 161–164.

Anderson, N. B., Lane, J. D., Taguchi, F., Williams, R. B. 1989. Patterns of cardiovascular responses to stress as a function of race and parental hypertension in men. *Health Psychology,* 8, 525–540.

Anderson, N.B., McNeilly, M. and Myers, H. 1991. Autonomic reactivity and hypertension in Blacks: A review and proposed model. *Ethnicity and Disease,* 1, 154–170.

Anderson, N.B., Myers, H., Pickering, T., and Jackson, J. 1989. Hypertension in Blacks: Psychosocial and biological perspectives. *Journal of Hypertension,* 7, 161–172.

Barber, J. 1990. Black Americans in crisis. *Journal of National Medical Association,* 82, 644–666.

Berkowitz, R., Lapinski, R., Wein, R. and Lee, D. 1992. The role of race/ethnicity in gestational diabetes. *American Journal of Epidemiology,* 134, 741–742.

Brewer, R. M. 1993. Theorizing race, gender, and class. In S.M. James and A.P. Busia (eds.), *Theorizing Black feminism* (pp. 13–30). New York: Routledge.

Bullard, R.D. 1994. *Dumpin in Dixie: Race, class, and environmental quality* (2nd ed.). Boulder, Colo.: Westview.

Cartwright, S.A. 1852. Philosophy of the Negro Constitution. *New Orleans Medical and Surgical Journal,* 9, 199.

Clark, K. 1967. *Black Ghetto.* New York: Harper and Row, Inc.

Carroll, D., Bennett, P., and Davey, S. G. 1993. Socioeconomic health inequities: Their origins and implications. *Psychology Health,* 8, 295–316.

Centers For Disease Control 1996) CDC. *Chronic disease reports: Morbidity and Mortality Weekly Reports,* 39, 17–22. Atlanta, Ga.

David, R. J., and Collins, J. W. 1991. Bad outcomes in Black babies: Race or racism? *Ethnicity and Disease,* 1, 236–244.

Dressler, W. W. 1991. *Stress and adaptation in the context of culture.* Albany: University of New York Press.

DuBois, W. E. B. 1977. *Black reconstruction in America,* (7th Ed.). New York: Athenum.

Essed, P. 1991. *Understanding everyday racism: An interdisciplinary theory.* Newbury Park, Calif.: Sage.

Genovese, E. D. 1976. *Roll Jordon roll. The world the slaves made.* New York: Random House.

Green, N. 1990. Stressful events related to childbearing in African American women. *Journal of Nurse-Midwifery,* 35, 231–236.

Hacker, A. 1992. *Two nations. Black and separate: Hostile, unequal.* New York: Charles Scribner's Sons.

Harris, D. R., Andrews, R., Elixhauser, A. 1997. Racial and gender differences in use of procedures for Black and hospitalized adults. *Ethnicity & Disease,* 7, 91–105.

Hemmons, W. M. 1995. The impact of the law on single mothers and the innocent. In B. J. Dickerson (eds.), *African American single mothers* (pp. 94–116). Thousand Oaks, Calif.: Sage.

Hill, R. 1993. Economic forces, structural discrimination, and Black family instability. In H. E. Cheatham and J. Stewart (eds.), *Black families: Interdisciplinary perspectives* (pp. 87–105), New Brunswick: Transaction.

Jewell, K. S. 1988. *Survival in the Black family. The institutional impact of U.S. social policy.* New York: Praeger.

Jacobs, H. 1987. *Life of a slave girl.* Cambridge, Mass.: Harvard University Press.

Jones, J. 1985. *Labor of love, labor of sorrow. Black women, work, and the family from slavery to the present.* New York: Basic Books.

Kiple, K. F. and King, H. 1981. *Another dimension to the Black diaspora, diet, disease, and racism.* New York: Cambridge University Press.

Krieger, N., Rowley, D. L., Herman, A. A., Avery, B., and Philips, M. T. 1993. Racism, sexism and social class: Implications for studies of health, disease, and well being. *American Journal of Preventative Medicine,* 9, 83–122.

Landry, B. 1987. *The new Black middle class.* Berkeley: University of California Press.

Legan, M. S. 1973. Disease of the Freeman in Mississippi during Reconstruction. *Journal of the History of Medicine and Allied Sciences,* 28, 257–67.

Leigh, W. A. 1995. The health of African American women. In D. Adams (ed.), *Health Issues for women of color: A cultural diversity perspective* (pp. 112–131). Thousand Oaks, Calif.: Sage.

McCord, C., and Freeman, H. P. 1990. Excess mortality in Harlem. *New England Journal of Medicine,* 322, 173–177.

McWhorter, W. P., and Mayer, W. J. 1987. Black/differences in type of initial breast cancer treatment and implications for survival. *American Journal of Public Health,* 12, 1514–1517.

Meier, A. and Rudwick, E. 1970. (2nd ed.). *From plantation to ghetto.* New York: Hill and Wang.

Murrell, N., Renee, S., Gill, G., and Oxley, G. 1996. Racism and health care access: A dialogue with childbearing women. *Health Care for Women International,* 17, 149–159.

National Center for Health Statistics (NCHS). 1996. *Health, United States, 1995.* Hyattsville, Md.: Public Health Service.

Office of Minority Health Resource Center. 1988. *Closing the gap: Diabetes and minorities,* (pp. 1–4). Office of Minority Health, Public Health Service, U.S. Department of Health and Human Services, Washington, D.C.

Office on Women's Health. 1997. *The Health of Minority women,* (pp. 5–6). Office of Women's Health. U.S. Public Health Services. U.S. Department of Health and Human Services, Washington, D.C.

Pinkney, A. 1993. (4th ed.). *Black Americans.* Englewood Cliffs, N.J.: Prentice-Hall.

Raphael A. 1972. Health and social welfare of Kentucky Black people, 1865–1870. *Societas,* 2, 143–157.

Reiss, J., Mills-Thomas, B., Robinson, D., Anderson, V. 1992. An inner-city community's perspective on infant mortality and prenatal care. *Public Health Nursing,* 9, 248–256.

Rene, A., Daniels, D., Jones, W., Jr., and Moore, F. 1992. Mortality in the slave and populations of Natchioches Parish, Louisiana, 1850. *Journal of the National Medical Association,* 84, 805–811.

Rodgers-Rose, L. F. 1980. The Black women: A historical overview. In L. F. Rodgers-Rose (Ed.), *The Black women* (pp. 15–25). Beverly Hills, Calif.: Sage.

Savitt, T. L. 1978. *Medicine and slavery. The diseases and health care of Blacks in antebellum Virginia.* Chicago: University of Illinois Press.

Schwartz, E., Kofie, V. Y., Rivo, M., and Tuckson, R. V. 1990. Black comparisons of deaths preventable by medical intervention: United States and the District of Columbia 1980–1986. *International Journal of Epidemiology,* 19, 591–598.

Smith, B. 1982. Racial composition as a neighborhood amenity. In D. Diamond and G. Tolley (eds.), *The economics of urban amenities* (pp. 184–200). New York: Academic.

Sterling, D. (ed.). 1984. *We are your sisters: Black women in the nineteenth century.* New York: Norton.

Shyrock, R. H. 1966. *Medicine in America: Historical essays.* Baltimore: Johns Hopkins Press.

Taylor, R., and Chatter, L. 1988. Correlates of education, income, and poverty among aged Blacks. *Gerontologist,* 28, 435–441.

Tebault, A. G. 1861. Papers, Lecture Notebook #3, p.1 17, University of Virginia Alderman Library, University of Virginia, Charlottesville, Va. (#9926).

Thomas, V. 1992. Explaining health disparities between African American and populations: Where do we go from here? *Journal of the National Medical Association,* 84, 837–839.

U.S. Department of Health and Human Services. 1991. (3rd ed.). *Health Status of Minorities and Low-income Groups.* Washington, D.C.: U.S. Government Printing Office.

Weddington, W. H., and Gabel, L, L. 1992. Racial differences in physicians and patients in relationship to quality of care. *Journal of National Medical Association,* 569–572.

Wenneker, M. B., and Epstein, A. M. 1989. Racial inequalities in the use of procedures for patients with ischemic heart disease in Massachusetts. *Journal of the American Medical Association,* 26, 253–257.

West, C. 1993. *Race matters.* Boston: Beacon.

Wilkerson, I, and Mitchell, A. 1991. Staying alive: The challenge of improving Black Americans health. *Emerge* (Sept), 24–26.

Wilkinson, D. 1986. Minority women: Social and cultural issues. In A. Brodsky and R. Haremustin (eds.), (pp. 284–304). *Women and Psychotherapy.* New York: Guilford.

Williams, C. L. 1991. Case studies and the sociology of gender. In J. Feagin, A. Orum, and G. Sjoberg (eds.), *A case for the case study* (pp. 224–243). Chapel Hill: University of North Carolina Press.

Williams, D. R. 1990. Socioeconomic differentials in health: A review and redirection. *Social Psychology Quarterly,* 32, 81–99.

PART FOUR

Black Families
and the Future

ALTERNATIVE LIFESTYLES

Making predictions about the future nature of any group's family life is a risky endeavor. Few, for instance, could have projected what has happened to the American family as a whole since 1970. Certainly there were trends leading us in certain directions, but it was the acceleration of those trends that caught many of us by surprise. In the case of the Black family, the research literature is still so sparse and biased that we have practically no attempts to analyze Black families of the future or alternative family life-styles. Certain barometers of the future can be seen in light of the existing social conditions for Blacks and the trends in sexual behavior, fertility patterns, sex role changes, and marital adjustments.

Some adaptations to alternative life-styles will occur because large numbers of Blacks, especially in the middle class, are taking on the values of the majority culture. Family relations in the majority culture are changing and many Blacks will follow their trends. However, Blacks as a group will continue to face certain problems that may not be unique to them except to the extent of their prevalence. The continuing high unemployment rate among Black men and women will still have serious ramifications for the kind of family life they will have. That will primarily be a problem of the lower-class group, but all classes will have to adapt to the increasing critical problem of a male shortage and the consequences thereof.

Up to this time the problem of the male shortage has been handled by a type of serial polygyny whereby Black men have more than one wife in a lifetime but not at the same time. Some men remain married but are free-floating in their relations with other women. This kind of male-sharing may be necessary for a group with such an imbalanced sex ratio. It, however, gives rise to many conflicts between men and women who are strongly socialized into monogamous values. The instability of many Black marriages can be accounted for by this factor as well as by the general range of forces that cause marital disruption. In the future alternative family life-styles should be well thought out and implemented in ways conducive to individual and group harmony.

PUBLIC POLICY AND BLACK FAMILIES

According to Bell and Vogel (1968), the family contributes its loyalty to the government in exchange for leadership, which will provide direct and indirect benefits for the nuclear family. Although there is little doubt that Black families have been loyal to the political state in the United States, it appears that they have derived few reciprocal benefits in return. Although the political system has the power to affect many of the conditions influencing Black family life, it has failed to intervene in the service of the Black population and, in fact, has been more of a negative force in shaping the conditions under which Black families must live. As Billingsley (1968: 177) has stated, "no subsystem has been more oppressive of the Negro people or holds greater promise for their development."

Historically, we find that state, local, and federal governmental bodies have been willing collaborators in the victimization of Black families. Under slavery, marriages between slaves were not legal because the slave could make no contract. The government did nothing to ensure stable marriages among the slave population or to prevent the arbitrary separation of slave couples by their owners. Moreover, the national government was committed to the institution of slavery, a practice that was most inimical to Black family life (Frazier, 1939).

One function of government has been to protect the sexual integrity of the female population. Until recently, the government has not provided legal or physical protection for the Black woman against sexual advances of White males. Many Black women were forced to engage in intercourse with White males because there was no law that prevented their involuntary seduction. Some state governments passed laws that held that no White man could be convicted for fornication with a Black woman. Other states required a White person as witness to any act of rape against a Black woman (Berry, 1971).

However, the government did pass, and strongly enforce, laws against interracial marriage, which were mainly designed to prevent the mating of Black men and White women. These laws ostensibly were passed to prevent racial amalgamation; but, as Heer (1974) noted, antimiscegenation laws served other functions. The requirement of racially homogamous marriages prevented Blacks from inheriting wealth from any White person through marriage into a family of means. The ban on interracial marriages denied Blacks a chance to become familiar with the White world and to obtain jobs requiring such familiarity. Their class mobility was also restricted by the lack of informal social contacts with Whites that can facilitate their entrance into certain jobs, which are acquired through pull and connections.

In more recent years, state governments have tried to impose middle-class values on lower income families, many of whom are Black. Various state legislatures have passed laws designed to reduce or eliminate welfare benefits to women who have given birth to a child out-of-wedlock. A few states have even attempted to pass laws sterilizing women on welfare who have had more than one "illegitimate" child.

For reasons that may be related to the sacrosanct nature of the family in the United States, this country has rarely had any clearly defined plans or policy concerning the family. The closest thing to it has been the welfare system, which actually worked to disrupt more families than it did to keep them together. In light of the continuing decline of the extended family, which once provided valuable backup services to the nuclear family, some sort of family support system seems necessary. Although the Black family has an extended family character, there is some decline in its viability as a support force. At the same time the central problems facing Black families require to a much greater extent some kind of remedy by a well-formulated public policy and action program addressed to their needs.

Scott (1978) delineated what those needs are in relation to Black women in our society. She described them, most accurately, as a lower-income group with high rates of unemployment and densely concentrated in low-level service-relate jobs. Even if employment were offered to Black women who are unemployed, they would have problems because quality day care centers are not often available to them. Some critics of day-care program expansion argue that taking care of children is a function of the family, not of the government. Such arguments ignore the realities of today's families, which necessitate either low-cost, government-supervised care of children or the relegation of women to a permanent category of second class citizens.

Those same critics are advocates of involuntary birth control and sterilization programs to prevent women from having "too many" children. This is especially imposed on low-income Black women who are stereotyped as irresponsible breeders of children. Scott (1978) noted that birth control and sterilization program often have a higher priority than prenatal health services and sex education programs for Black adolescents. She suggested a number of programs that would assist Black women to maintain healthy families. Elevating their pay and status in the work force is a key one, along with the development of quality day-care facilities and promotion of research activities on the mental and physical health problems of Black women, the needs of the Black aged woman, the role of women in the media and other areas.

In an early article on "Public Policy and the Changing Status of Black Families," Staples (1973) reviewed the past relationship of government to the structure of Black family life. In general, the government's efforts, few as they have been, were sporadic, misguided, and ineffective. Because future trends are in the direction of increasing numbers of female-headed households, which are characterized by a below-average income and above-average number of children, Staples suggested the specific contents of a public policy relevant to Black families. It includes a universal family allowance, elimination of sex discrimination in employment, community controlled day-care centers, a child development program, and expanded government employment. Only through a combination of these measures will Blacks have a choice of family arrangements.

FUTURE POLICY ISSUES

In recent years, the Federal government has undertaken a draconian overhaul of the Aid to Families with Dependent Children program (AFDC) which does little to address the real needs of female-headed families. Even during a period of "relative prosperity," the costs of child care, health services and transportation far exceed the meager wages these women can earn at the minimum wage jobs available. Moreover, very few Black men have been able to secure jobs that will allow them to become participating partners in their families support. Because many of these low-income Blacks have very little education thus few skills to offer in the job market, their greatest need is for job training and education. Many of the long term AFDC recipients also have mental and substance abuse problems for which the services available are limited.

As we look at the twenty-first century, certain economic features of American society will likely continue. Over the last twenty years there has been a redistribution of wealth upward, with the rich getting richer and the poor poorer. The United States has the greatest inequality of income of all the Western industrialized nations and the only government proposals for tax reform, such as a flat tax or reducing the capital gains tax will only aggrandize the wealth of the already wealthy. Some middle class families, both Black and White, have maintained a decent standard of living by both men and women working full-time to achieve a lifestyle once sustained by the employment of only the male. Because almost two-thirds of Black women and children are not located in nuclear families, they make up a disproportionate number of the poor.

Reviewing the future prospects of Black Americans, we see that the only segment of the Black population not adversely impacted by these future economic trends are college-educated males. They do not, as their female counterparts, face a shortage in the available pool of marriage partners, have a lower unemployment rate than their less educated counterparts and earn a higher income. The long overdue income parity of college educated Black women means they will approach a comfortable standard of living but increasingly face a life without a husband, leaving them with the undesirable prospect of living a life without the tranquilizing effects of a monogamous soul mate or forced to raise a child alone. Nothing in our reading of future economic trends foretells a different future for most of them.

REFERENCES

Bell, N. and E. Vogel. 1968. *A modern introduction to the family.* New York: Free Press.

Berry, M. 1971. *Black resistance—White law: A history of constitutional racism in America.* New York: Appleton-Century-Crofts.

Billingsley, A. 1968. *Black families in White America.* Englewood Cliffs, N.J.: Prentice-Hall.

Dickerson, B. J. 1995. *African American single mothers: Understanding their lives and families.* Thousand Oaks, Calif.: Sage.

Frazier, E. F. 1939. *The Negro family in the United States.* Chicago: University of Chicago Press.

Gans, H. 1995. *The war against the poor.* New York: Basic Books.

Scott, P. B. 1978. Black female liberation and family action programs: Some considerations. In *The Black family: Essays and studies* (2nd ed.), R. Staples, ed., pp. 260–263. Belmont, Calif.: Wadsworth.

Sidel, R. 1996. *Keeping women and children last: America's war on the poor.* New York: Penguin.

Staples, R. E. and L. B. Johnson. 1993. *Black families at the crossroads: Challenges and prospects.* San Francisco: Jossey-Bass.

Wilson, W. J. 1997. *When work disappears: The world of the new urban poor.* New York: Vintage.

🐚

15

Alternative Life Styles

From Teenage Parenthood to Polygamy: Case Studies in Black Polygamous Family Formation

JOSEPH W. SCOTT

In this article the author describes a type of polygamous family formation in the Black community that develops when a single female parent becomes sexually involved with a married man and reaches a stage of sharing him with his wife on a regular and continuing basis. The author defines polygamy as a situation in which legally married men and never married women become permanently invested in children and other aspects of family life.

■

INTRODUCTION

Polygamy in the United States has been virtually forgotten as a subject of serious study by American behavioral scientists. The writer surveyed the various journals in sociology, anthropology, and marriage and the family, and was not able to find any systematic research other than his own (Scott, 1976; Scott, 1977) on the practices in the United States of polygamy outside the early studies of Mormons (Muncy, 1974) and later studies of Puerto Ricans in Puerto Rico (Stewart, 1956).

If one accepts the subjective understanding of the people one observes and if one accepts the efficacy of the consensual agreements they make, polygamy is indeed a growing family form in the United States, and, in addition, the practice is not new.

What has happened is that generally social scientists who study family relations in the United States have come across polygamous families among their cases, but they systematically treat them as "extramarital" affairs or "illicit" relations. As a result the polygamous families in the United States have been ignored with the consequence that the researched picture of American family life—especially that outside the law—has been quite incompletely reported (Schulz, 1969;

From the *Western Journal of Black Studies* 10 (Winter 1986): 172—179. Copyright 1986 by the Washington State University Press. Reprinted by permission.

Hertz and Little, 1944; Staples, 1973; Liebow, 1967; Pope, 1967).

This study is a first step in an attempt to give a more complete picture of American family life without imposing value judgments of policy implications about the phenomenon in question.

REVIEW OF LITERATURE

The Black American family has been the subject of many articles in recent years—especially since the Moynihan Report (Moynihan, 1965). Nearly all of these discussions, however, ignore the fact that the Black family has been changing in the same ways as White families have been changing—although at a faster rate. Research indicates that matrifocal Black families are the result of more and more destabilizing forces pressing upon the Black nuclear family, rather than the result of Black males and females of marriage age giving up on the *value of* marriage (Young, 1970; Aschenbrenner, 1973; Stack, 1972; Belcher, 1967). Demographic and economic forces within the larger political economy have been pressing upon the Blacks contributing to their growing number of single-parent female-headed households in contrast to the typical husband-wife headed family.

To speak of the single-parent family as a growing family form is also to beg questions of *Black family formation processes,* in general. In Black America there are many types of families: for example, couple-headed families, single-parent headed families and polygamous families....

Although increases in female-headed households have been caused by divorce, separation and widowhood, female-headed households increased in great number largely because *single women of marriage-age have been setting up their own independent households in greater number,* largely because single never-married women have been becoming mothers with the benefits of husbands.. . . Furstenberg (1978: 324) found, in fact, that out-of-wedlock births to single Black females did

contribute to young mothers leaving their parental homes to set up their own households earlier than other young women their age in their socioeconomic circumstances. In addition to biological events such as out-of-wedlock births, this author also thinks that socioeconomic stresses in many poor families have operated as "pushes" causing many young women to leave their parental homes around age 18 in order to set up independent households to relieve the burdens on their parents by living on public assistance. Black women, aged 20–24, who once largely were married by this age are remaining single.. . . While they are remaining single, they are not remaining childless.. . .

Black Polygamous Family Formation

The foregoing discussion now enables one to begin to understand polygamous family formation in the United States. This research indicates that such families grow out of the increasing single female parents in the Black community. Polygamous families may be formed in a number of ways: One style of polygamous family is a female-headed family combined with a second female-headed family, with the two females sharing the never-married father of their children between them. Another style is for a legally married man and an unmarried female to begin an extramarital courtship which eventually grows into a full-fledged familial relationship with children and patterns. In this latter type of polygamous family formation, the consensual "wife" is often a never-married mother living independently who began as a teenage parent and for various social, sexual and economic reasons became sexually involved with a married man and came to the point of sharing him with his legal wife on a regular and continuing basis.

This article describes the latter type of polygamous family formation: the families involving legally married men and never-married women who became "permanently" invested in children and other aspects of family life.

The Sample

The first sample is an availability-snowball one of Black women between the ages of 18 and 32. Interviewed were a total of 22 young Black women, one-hall of whom were married and one-half of whom were single. No interviews were completed with any *two* women who were knowingly sharing the *same* man between them. The sample of 22 women consented to open-ended interviews recorded on tape. All of the women were either still in a polygamous relationship or had recently been in that situation for some considerable period of time prior to the interview These relationships had lasted from about 2 years to over 12 years.

In a separate paper, published elsewhere, the views and life experiences of the *consensual* "wives" are compared to those of the *legal* wives (see Scott, 1980). This paper deals exclusively with the consensual "wives" and the process by which they became attached to married men on a routine basis.

All eleven consensual "wives" in this subsample were of lower socioeconomic status, although some had started college. Most were regularly unemployed, although a few were employed. Generally, they had childhoods typical for their socioeconomic status in the sense of having been more-or-less close to both of their parents up to the age of 10 and thereafter from 10–15 they became less close to their parents, most particularly less close to their fathers due to parental separations and divorces. However, the usually remained close or very close to their mothers, but these parent-child relationships were not without their problems too.

On the whole, these single females started "seeing" young males at an early age—usually 14 or 15; that is, they were "receiving company" about this age, sometimes with and sometimes without parental permission. About seventy percent of them became sexually active between 16 or 17 and hence, as one would expect, became pregnant usually at 17 or no later than about 18.

As a result of these early sexual involvements and pregnancies, they had their first babies out-of-wedlock. For the majority, these babies were unwanted, unplanned and untimed. In addition, socially and educationally, these young teenagers were not ready for motherhood.

Given the secretive nature and the antagonistic nature of these triadic relationships, the writer has not interviewed (as yet) any of the men involved with these particular women. The immense cooperation of openness required to interview all corners of these triadic relationships are being cultivated. Hence, the demographics on the male role players are still unattainable.

The woman legally married to the man who is being shared is called the legal wife; the woman not legally married to the married man being shared is called the consensual "wife." The word "wife" is preferred because of the familial nature of these relationships and because some respondents used the term to refer to themselves. This is an ethnographic study, using life histories.

FROM TEENAGE PARENTHOOD TO POLYGAMY

The typical women in this sample came from the lowest socioeconomic levels in the community, and their families of orientation were typically headed by a single mother who was either separated, divorced or never married. Family background was described in these words:

> My mother and father separated when I was twelve years old. He would come to visit us every once in a while, but my mother mostly raised us from then on. She was understanding and she was lovable; and she tried to give us the things that we needed, more so than the things that we wanted. With several kids, you can't give them too much. She wasn't working. We were on welfare.

For the most part, they had trouble with their mothers and felt it necessary to leave home in late adolescence. They were usually fifteen through eighteen years of age, still in school and still relatively unsocialized as to adult statuses when they left.

Leaving home was described this way:

> I left home because I felt that I should have more freedom than my mother wanted to give me and I realized that I had to give her respect. . . .
>
> . . . my biggest problem was getting away from her. You know, 'cause I was a teenager going to school. I didn't have nice things like other girls so l had to come home and cook and iron; she didn't even give me lunch money. So the most thing I dreamed was getting away from home.

More often than not, upon leaving, they got pregnant and had to leave school too. (Schools for the most part did not have provisions for school-age mothers.)

During this period they had their first sexual experiences. To be more precise, they had their first continuous sexual relations which as one would expect soon led to their first pregnancies. Almost all of them became pregnant by their first lovers or their first regular sexual companions largely because they were ignorant of and inexperienced in this most critical aspect of adult socialization—sexual intercourse. Leaving home (and not sex) was uppermost in their minds:

> All I ever thought about was getting away from home. You know what, I never did think about babies or anything. I figured that one day I would get pregnant, but I wasn't thinking about babies then. I was thinking about getting away from Mama.
>
> My first (sex intercourse) was at his house . . . I was just doing something cause he asked me to. I didn't even know what feeling I was supposed to get; that is a shame. I didn't know no better and I didn't care, I guess . . . I just didn't feel anything about it. I didn't know if I should like it or not. He was telling me this is the normal thing to do and

this is the only way we are going to go together and all this kind of stuff; he said that I had to understand and the fact that he was a man and he can't just be kissing and patting and stuff like that, you know.. . . When it happened I could have died; when it was over and it was very painful, very painful.. . . He was about 17 'cause I was 15.

Not having had much formal or informal instruction in the art of sexual intercourse and in the technology of birth control they were destined to get pregnant, barring any congenital maladies.

When asked if they were trying to get pregnant most said they did not want to get pregnant or become school-age mothers, even though they wanted to become mothers at some point in the future.

The first out-of-wedlock pregnancy was usually immediate:

> Well, I had my first child when I was fifteen. And I didn't go back to school because I had the baby. And by my mother having all my other brothers and sisters, I couldn't very well have her take care of my baby. And I wasn't going to have her adopted. I wasn't married.

Once they became pregnant their personal values, scripted from their mothers, prevented them from getting abortions or even considering giving up their children for adoption. The traumas of out-of-wedlock pregnancies were not enough to change their minds or their behaviors.

After confirming their pregnancies, a few considered marriage, but most did not. Even though most of their male friends offered to marry them, the girls refused them pretty much to the man. The women responded with a wholesale rejection of the institution of marriage. As they saw it, marriage was not necessarily an adequate coping mechanism for teenage pregnancies. Neither were motherhood and marriage necessarily to be combined. They had grown up under an existential pattern concerning motherhood and marriage that males and females could live happily compartmentalizing these two activities. The disjunction between motherhood and marriage had long been forced upon their friends and relatives by societally imposed socioeconomic circumstances.

Early in their childhoods as girls, they, like others in this society had held the American family dream: individually, they had expected to have a marriage, a husband, about three children, a home and a stable income. However, they were soon to learn that these simple goals held out to everyone were not materially or institutionally possible for everyone.

They had held these ideas up to the time of their pregnancies, and now their pregnancies and attendant problems caused these ideals to slowly slip out of their grasps. When asked for their hands in marriage the women had said "no" because they knew that neither they nor their male friends could even remotely come close to supporting a house and a family They must have sensed that their physical, emotional, and social immaturity were prohibitive too.

That immaturity comes through in these statements:

> Well you know—another reason I didn't want to get married was because I felt sexually I wanted to branch out, have me some more fellows. That is a sad way to think about it, but I wanted to look and see if this was really what I wanted to be stuck with the rest of my life. I wanted to find out if this was the right one. So, this is why I didn't want to just jump up and marry, you know.

Even though the women refused to marry them—usually for a good reason—the fathers nevertheless continued regular visitations and ties. Contrary to the mythologies surrounding Black males, they did not desert these women at the outset of pregnancy or at the births of the babies. At birth most started to make financial contributions within the limits of their meager incomes. For those out of school with sporadic employment, they made contributions up to the level of financial responsibility they could assume. But

one must remember that the young teenage Black males have been the main "rejects" of this money economy.

Most of the fathers reportedly wanted to make contributions in order to be able to have paternity rights and visitation rights without marriage and its attendant contractual rights. But, even though they were *willing* to contribute more than they did, they were not able to do so because of either their lack of employment or their low income from the employment they could find. They understood the rejection by the women very well. The American family ideal was more remote than it seemed at first glance, through the eyes of all these young adolescents.

The out-of-wedlock pregnancies and births caused their American family dreams to fade fast, and caused the realities of their situations to dominate: Matters of coping with stigma, with economic self support and child support, with socially and emotionally stunted men became the most pressing realities.

The unavailability of "good men" highlighted their problems:

> I feel that the good men are getting scarce. The good ones out here now are the hustlers and the so-called pimps. Even what you call the professional ones, they are doing the same thing; they are hustling but they are doing it a little more discreetly. They are getting that money from those girls and having different kinds of girls, and if they don't do certain things or if they don't give them money they don't want to be bothered with them, you know. Fellows are staying with the ones are giving them the money.

What of marriage? Marriage to immature, financially insolvent men was hardly a solution. Marriage to "legitimize" the births in the eyes of Whites was hardly a solution: that type of "legitimacy" did not matter to most members of the Black community. Marriage to convey upon them an adult status was hardly a solution; in point of fact, motherhood without marriage not only conveyed an adult status, but it also conveyed adult rights and privileges, and qualified them for public child support at a time when private child support was not at all certain. Most commonly, therefore, the women opted for motherhood without marriage.

Motherhood without marriage was a sort of decision they drifted to:

> I dreamed, you know, I wanted to be married have a nice husband and children, although I didn't get married to the one I wanted to. I wanted to get married someday but I'm glad I didn't get married. I was too young in the first place. Getting married at fifteen, even though you have a baby, that was too young.
>
> Now, marriage is not the right thing to do—it is just a piece of paper that both of you have an agreement. You can also get that by means of an understanding. You can also get that understanding without that piece of paper. That piece of paper cost you very little to get it but costs you a hell of a lot of money to get rid of it. You don't have to have that piece of paper to have that under-standing. I never thought of living my life without a husband. But if that is what is in store for me, that is what I accept.

The prior socialization for adulthood now loomed larger than ever. Ignorance of birth control and its uses clearly become a most serious omission in the socialization of school-age moth-ers because their out-of-wedlock pregnancies and births subsequently forced most of these women into several self-defeating decisions. Early motherhood had the effect of rearranging the shapes of their lives. For example, pregnan-cies and births made them dependent upon those same mothers and relatives from whom they wanted to be independent. These same pregnan-cies and births made them dependent upon pub-lic agencies which put them through continuous degradation rituals. Finally, these pregnancies and births made them dependent upon male com-panions who pressured them to do things they may not have wanted to do.

How men shaped their lives is illustrated as follows:

> A lot of men don't want to get married, especially if you have a child. Well, men don't want to be bothered with another man's child. It's hard to find a man who would take a woman on with children. The children's fathers are always somewhere in the background. . . coming, knocking and going through all these changes. Some men just don't feel like being bothered with all that. If I were a man and I married a woman, I wouldn't want her ex-husband or ex-man to come knocking on the door, saying, "Can I see my kids?" But that's the problem. You have to face it.

What all of this suggests is that these out-of-wedlock pregnancies and births reduced their options very considerably and made them more dependent upon those on whom they did not want to be dependent.

As if these reduced options were not enough, the women found that they had fewer options in the marriage marketplace too. They found an abundance of companionship from men who were the least likely to be employed and emo-tionally stable. They found that while they were not sexually "loose," they were considered sexu-ally "experienced" and many males believed them to be sexually "available."

The confusion that out-of-wedlock babies caused was revealed in these words:

> After you have a baby, then you have all kinds of suitors knocking at your door They feel that if a woman has had a baby she is easy for everybody else. That's not true for a lot of women or a lot of girls. I mean, if you make a mistake and have a baby, it's not saying that everything is open for everybody else. It's not like that. But I have had a lot of offers. But I'm the kind like this: I don't believe in a whole bunch of men even though I'm single.

Their pregnancies and births were indicative of a brief sexual experience but many males assumed more and acted on it. By contrast the school-age females who had not had any out-of-wedlock births did not give the appearance of being sexually active or available, and hence males who were looking for sexually active and available women looked for those of demonstrated experience . . . the school-age mothers.

For most of these mothers, their first out-of-wedlock pregnancies often led to second out-of-wedlock pregnancies and with these their options became still further reduced. Their semipermanent dependency on parents, public agents or male friends was now complete. More often than not the men who now came around were either single men looking for sex and money without familial attachments or married men looking for sex as a permanent consensual arrangement.

The difficulty of finding a "good" man was described this way:

> Nowadays, you can forget about having a man all to yourself. If he is going with you, you can take for granted that he has at least one more somewhere else. If it ain't nothing but where he works at, he got somebody. Nowadays he is going for everything that he can get. He is going for sex; he is going for money; if you got a car he'll take that. The first thing that they ask you is "Do you have a job?" "You working?" If you ain't working they ain't got the time.

The stable employed men who were marriageable were not looking for women who have had one or more children out-of-wedlock. Thus, one time, these women were forced to drift towards married men—into polygamous relationships. The drift was more by circumstance than by plan, but it was definitely in the direction of married men.

The women usually became consensual mates while their men were still married and living with their wives. Sometimes they became consensual mates of men who were married but separated from their wives. Rarely did these women ever find their men free and clear of other conjugal relationships. The men who were "free and clear" were usually either habitual drug users, or criminals, or homosexuals, and none of these types, the women maintained, were desirable as mates, especially, as father figures. In point of fact they could be neither stable husbands, father figures nor lovers. The men most available and most desired were married men:

> Most of the available single men have either been killed in the war or they have been put in prison, or they are queers or funnies. You're damn right there is a shortage because when you run across a good one that wants to give you something and has got something, nine out of ten times he is married. He is married; you better believe it.
>
> I rather go with a single man. But it is hard to find a good single man. But most of those married men are good, better than those single men. You find women today that won't go with nothing but a married man because they can't stand no static.

Considering the choices, married men turned out to be the more sought after. Because the married men were more accepting of maternal situations, they were also more desirable. Being kinder in demeanor, more stable in lifestyle, more frugal in spending habits and more reliable in visitation habits also made married men more desirable. Married men revealed themselves to be more knowledgeable than single men about the psycho-sexual satisfaction of women and about all other aspects of their lives. That consideration was compared in these words:

> As far as a single man and a married man is concerned, if you find a nice single man that really has himself together it is nice; hut if you don't find that kind, you are just about as well off with a married man. If it like this, some married men will do all they can possibly do for you. . . .
>
> A single man don't have the patience, nor understanding. If things don't go like they want them to, then they are mad. They are

ready to fight. Like if they make a date. They say: "Well, I'll be at your house tonight at eight o'clock." If you got kids, and your child gets sick and you can't make it he's going to say: "Well so-and-so and so-and-so." And he's going to get mad and Bam: He's gone. But now a married man, if he's got a family and your child gets sick, he says: "Well, I understand. Let me know how everything works out." Even when it comes down to sex, a married man respects a woman more than a single man, because he wouldn't want nobody to curse his wife out or curse in front of her. Whereas a single man, he might be used to cursing a woman out.

When these women found married men whom they like sexually and personally, they did not break off the relationships with the men because they turned out to be married. They took no great steps to avoid sexual and personal involvement with them perhaps because they thought they could eventually "tighten up" the relationships and make them exclusive. Hope springs eternal and hope caused these women to stay in these relationships and get deeper and deeper into them. They neither wanted to nor did they plan to share these men with anyone else permanently. Sharing married men turned out to be one of the pitfalls of the rating and dating game for unwed mothers. As the contradiction became apparent they felt further trapped, but still hopeful. When questioned about the contradiction, the women believed that they had no other real choice given their circumstances. They had to stay in these relationships to have any at all.

In the final analysis, *drifting into polygamy* has been for these women and to outside observers who know the socioeconomic facts of this society, a forced choice. School-age pregnancies and births without provisions for the adequate economic support reduced their subsequent choices to largely forced ones. Educationally, familially, occupationally and financially they generally came out of compelling circumstances and continued to get mired in even more compelling circumstances. Having babies out-of-wedlock clearly restricted their subsequent choices with regard to marriage and the family, and resulted in their social, emotional and economic dependency on married men.

Their dependency on married men finally produces a polygamous arrangement:

> I have to share him, which I am doing . . . I thought about this. I really cried when he went back. It broke me up; but like my girlfriends said, "Well, let him make up his own mind and go on like you've been doing and just don't drop out of the picture right now because he definitely wouldn't have a choice." So I think my choice would be to go on and stay with him until he leaves her and treat him like I have been treating him. He is not really married, so he can't stay with her forever . . .
>
> As far as leaving him, I feel like—there is not enough men to go around . . . I mean somebody that really wants to do thing for me. It would give me hard time to try to find somebody else; although, I know I could, it would be hard. As far as leaving . . . I don't think I would.
>
> You can say you'll let him go before you share him, but then you let him go today and meet one tomorrow, well, that is the same problem. So, I don't know what choices we would really have . . . other than not to share him.

Married men turned out to be the ones with whom these women could not put together some semblance of family lives even if only consensual rather than contractual family lives. So, even though their married men had family and paternity commitments elsewhere, these women allowed themselves to become involved. Man-sharing was not the choice the women most wanted. Though polygamy was less than a desired choice, it became a tolerable choice within the social, economic and personal choices they had.

TOWARDS A THEORY OF POLYGAMOUS FAMILY FORMATION

Developmental Task Theory seems applicable. Magrabi and Marshall (1965: 454–459) postulate that a failure to perform satisfactorily the developmental tasks at one particular stage will result in difficulty with the performance of later developmental family tasks. For example, the lack of successful use of contraception in premarital sexual intercourse is likely to lead to difficulty in planning the family size in the future stages. Even though one cannot say with certainty what behaviors or activities contribute most to later future accomplishments, the evidence of the eyes suggests that there is a relationship between behavior at one stage and success at tasks at later stages.

If one were to follow these women through the transition from virginity to sexual activity, from that to contraception use, from that to pregnancy from that to childbirth or abortion or without marriage and so on, one could see that the behaviors and activities at one stage precondition the accomplishments at the next stage.

Throughout this study the author has used the terms "forced choice" to refer to the limited skills, knowledges and performances available to these teenage subjects. The author has also intimated that these limitations preconditioned their subsequent choices and influenced the future stages they could arrive at (without extraordinary assistance). The author therefore reasoned that these women mostly "drifted" into polygamy

It seems abundantly clear that over "time" certain "tasks" such as child-rearing and income maintenance grow out of certain "situations" such as teenage parenthood, calling for the successful performance of tasks before advancement to a next stage can occur. If one were to identify the stages and activities required for passage to a new level and compare these to those options actually available at each stage, one would conclude that polygamous relationships could be possible and discernible outcomes of a teenage parenthood.

Developmental Task Theory suggests that there are tasks arising at a certain stage in the life of a family which, if successfully performed, leads to satisfaction as well as success with later tasks. On the other hand the inability or incapacity to accomplish these developmental tasks leads to either failure, or difficulty with later tasks if not to disapproval by the society at large. The drift into polygamous relations is explained very well by Developmental Task Theory.

REFERENCES

Aschenbrenner, J. 1973. Extended families among Black Americans. *Journal of Comparative Family Studies,* 4: 256–269.

Belcher, J. 1967. The one person household: A consequence of the isolated nuclear family. *Journal of Marriage and the Family,* 29(Aug.): 584–590.

Farley, R. 1984. *Blacks and Whites: Narrowing the gap?* Cambridge, Mass.: Harvard University Press.

Furstenberg, F., and A. Crawford. 1978. Family support: Helping teenage mothers to cope. *Family Planning Perspective,* 10(Nov./Dec.): 322–333.

Hertz, H., and S. Little. 1944. Unmarried Negro mothers in a Southern urban community, *Social Forces,* 23(Oct.): 73–79.

Intercom. 1977a. Vol. 5 (Feb.): 11.

Intercom. 1977b. Vol. 5 (Sept.): 5.

Liebow, E. 1967. *Tally's Corner.* New York: Little Brown.

Magrabi, F., and W. Marshall. 1965. Family developmental tasks: A research model. *Journal of Marriage and the Family,* 27 (Nov.): 454–459.

Matney, W. C., Jr., and D. L. Johnson. 1983. America's Black population: 1970 to 1982, a statistical view, *Crisis,* 90(10): 10–18.

Moynihan, D. 1965. *The Negro family: The case for national action.* Washington, D.C.: U.S. Department of Labor.

Muncy, R. 1974. *Sex and marriage in utopian communities.* Baltimore: Penguin.

Pope, H. 1967. Unwed mothers and their sex partners. *Journal of Marriage and the Family,* 29(Aug.): 555–567

Schultz, D. 1969. Variations in the father role in complete families of the Negro lower class. *Social Science Quarterly,* 49(Dec.): 73–79.

Stack, C. 1972. Black kindreds: Parenthood and personal kindred among urban Blacks. *Journal of Comparative Family Studies,* 3: 194–206.

Staples, R. 1973. *The Black woman in America.* Chicago: Nelson-Hall.

Stewart, J. B. and J. W. Scott. 1978. The institutional decrimation of Black American males. *The Western Journal of Black Studies,* 2(Summer): 82–92.

Stewart, J. and Associates. 1956. *The people of Puerto Rico.* Urbana: University of Illinois Press.

Young, V. 1970. Family and childhood in a Southern Negro community. *American Anthropologist,* 72: 269–288.

Sociocultural Facets of the Black Gay Male Experience

SUSAN D. COCHRAN & VICKIE M. MAYS

This article reviews the literature on Black gay and bisexual men. It reports on the development of a Black gay identity, the integration of Black gay men into the Black heterosexual world, some of their sexual practices, behavior that places them at risk for AIDS and alcoholism, and their social networks. The authors caution that the experiences of Black gay men cannot be interpreted in terms of a White gay male standard.

■

Prior to the appearance of AIDS in this country, studies on the sexual preferences and behaviors of gay men generally ignored the specific experiences of Black men (Bell, Weinberg, and Hammersmith, 1981). With the press of the AIDS epidemic to develop baseline information on men's intimate behaviors, this tendency rarely to study Black gay men, or do so in the same manner as White gay men, persists. While many researchers may recognize the importance of possible cultural differences, their approach has been to assume that Black gay men would be more like White gay men than Black heterosexuals. Questionnaires, sampling procedures, and topics of focus have been more consistent with White gay men's experiences (see Becker and Joseph, 1988, for a comprehensive review of behavior change

studies). This proclivity has resulted in an emergence of comparisons between Black and White men using White gay standards of behavior that may be obscuring our understanding of important psychosocial determinants of sexual behaviors in Black gay men. Given the differences that have been observed in family structure and sexual patterns between Black and White heterosexuals, there is no empirical basis upon which to assume that Black gay men's experience of homosexuality would perfectly mimic that of Whites (Bell, Weinberg, and Hammersmith, 1981). Indeed, very little is known empirically about the lives of Black gay men (Mays and Cochran, 1987), though there are some indications, discussed below, that they are more likely to engage in activities that place them at greater risk for HIV infection.

In the absence of any data we need to proceed cautiously with assumptions that imply anything other than [that] same-sex *activities* of Black gay men resemble those of White gay men. This caution is particularly true for AIDS studies that purport to study psychosocial behavior. Studies of this type report not only on behavior but also attempt to describe motivations and circumstances that led to the behavior. In the absence of a set of

An abridged version of the article "Epidemiologic and Sociocultural Factors in the Transmission of HIV Infection in Black Gay and Bisexual Men" printed in *A Sourcebook of Gay/Lesbian Health* Care (M. Shernoff and W. A. Scott, eds.) Washington, D.C.: National Gay and Lesbian Health Foundation, 2nd ed. Copyright 1988 by the National Gay and Lesbian Health Foundation. Reprinted by permission. Support for this chapter was provided by a grant from the National Institute of Mental Health to both authors—a California State University, Northridge Foundation grant to the first author, and a USPHS Biomed grant from the University of California, Los Angeles, to the second author. Work on this chapter was completed while the second author was a National Center for Health Services research fellow at the Rand Corporation, Santa Monica, California.

questions or framework incorporating important cultural, ethnic, and economic realities of Black gay men, interpretations emanating from a White gay male standard may be misleading.

DEVELOPMENT OF A BLACK GAY IDENTITY

In recent years, researchers (Spanier and Glick, 1980; Staples, 1981; Guttentag and Secord, 1983) have noted differences between Whites and Blacks in their intimate heterosexual relationships. Differential sociocultural factors presumably influence the development and specific structure of sexual behavior within Black heterosexual relationships. These factors include the unavailability of same ethnic group partners, fewer social and financial resources, residential immobility, and lack of employment opportunities. Many of these same conditions may surround the formation, maintenance and functioning of Black gay male relationships.

Popular writings in past years by Black gay men describe the difficulty in finding other Black gay men for potential partners, the lack of a visible Black gay community, an absence of role models, and the dearth of Black gay male social or professional organizations (Soares, 1979; Beame, 1983). While gay bars, gay baths and public places existed where White gay men gathered, some of these were off limits to Black gay men either due to actual or perceived racism within the White gay community or the danger of passing through white neighborhoods in order to participate in gay community activities. Thus, expectations that the experiences of Black gay men are identical to those of White gay men seem unwarranted.

In examining differences between Blacks and Whites in the emergence of a homosexual orientation, Bell, Weinberg, and Hammersmith (1981) found that, for the White males, pre-adult sexual feelings appeared to be very important. In contrast, among Black males, childhood and adolescent sexual activities, rather than feelings,

were stronger predictors of the development of adult homosexual sexual orientation. Thus Blacks started to act at an earlier age on their sexual inclinations than Whites did (Bell, Weinberg, and Hammersmith, 1981). This would be consistent with Black-White differences in the onset of heterosexual sexual activity if socioeconomic status is not statistically controlled for (Wyatt, personal communication).

The typical conceptualization of sexual orientation is that individuals are located in terms of their sexual feelings and behaviors on a bipolar dimension where one extreme is heterosexuality, the other is homosexuality, and lying somewhere in between is bisexuality (Bell and Weinberg, 1978). This definition does not include ethnicity or culture as an interactive factor influencing the expression of sexual behavior or sexual orientation. For example, Smith (1986) makes a distinction between Black gays and gay Blacks complicating the demarcation between homosexuality and bisexuality:

> Gay Blacks are people who identify first as being gay and who usually live outside the closet in predominantly White gay communities. I would estimate that they amount to roughly ten percent of all Black homosexuals. Black gays, on the other hand, view our racial heritage as primary and frequently live "bisexual front lives" within Black neighborhoods. (p. 226)

These two groups are probably quite different in both social activities and sexual behaviors. The Black gay man, strongly identified with Afro-American culture, will often look and behave much like the Black heterosexual man except in his sexual behavior. The extent to which his same-sex partners are integrated into his family and social environment may be a function of his class status (Soares, 1979). It has long been noted by Blacks that there are differences, both in values and behaviors, between middle-class and working-class Blacks. There is no reason to assume that within the Black gay community such diversity would not persist. While Smith

(1986) has described the Black gay community in only two dimensions we would be remiss if we stopped here. There is a growing population of Black gays who have forged an identity acknowledging both statuses:

> At times I cried just remembering how it is to be both Black and gay during these truly difficult times. But here we are, still proud and living with a culture all our own. (Sylvester, p. 11, 1986)

We know less about the behavior of Black men who identify as bisexual and least about those Black men who engage in same-sex sexual behavior but identify as exclusively heterosexual. When the factor of social class is added the distinction between homosexuality and heterosexuality may become even more blurred. Among lower socioeconomic Black men, those engaged in same-sex sexual activities, regardless of their sexual object choices, may appear on the surface no different from Black heterosexuals. If the support systems of Black gay men are like those of Black lesbians (Cochran and Mays, 1986), fewer economic resources result in a greater reliance on a Black social network (both gay and heterosexual) for tangible and emotional support, a strong tendency to live in predominantly ethnic neighborhoods, and the maintenance of emotionally and economically close family ties.

This extensive integration into the Black heterosexual world may not only be a function of fewer economic resources, but also of ethnic identification. The culture of gay life, generally perceived to be White, may not be synonymous with the norms of Black culture. Choices of how to dress, what language to use, where to live, and whom to have as friends are all affected by culture. The White gay community, while diverse, has developed norms concerning language, social behavior, and other demarcations (Warren, 1974) that may not mesh well with certain subgroups of Black gays. For example, in the past there has been a heavy emphasis in the gay White community (except among the middle-aged, middle-class closeted gay men) on socializing in public

places—bars, beaches, and resorts (Warren, 1974). In contrast, the Black gay community places greater emphasis on home entertainment that is private and not public, perhaps as a holdover from the days when discrimination in many public places was common. This pattern of socializing would facilitate the development of a distinct Black gay culture (Soares, 1979).

It is perhaps this difference in socializing that has frustrated health educators attempting to do AIDS education through the social network in gay bars. Generally, they have found that they do not reach a significant number of Black men using this technique. An understanding of the Black gay community makes salient that risk reduction strategies should focus on "risk behaviors" and *not* "risk groups. Emphasizing risk reduction strategies that rely on group membership requires a social and personal identification by Black men that for many may not be relevant.

SEXUAL BEHAVIOR

Bell and Weinberg, in a 1978 study comparing sexual activities of White and Black gay men, found that Blacks were more likely to report having engaged in anal sex, both passively and actively, than White gay men. In terms of our current knowledge of AIDS, this appears to be one of the highest risk factors for contracting the HIV virus (Friedland and Klein, 1987).

A second aspect of Black gay men's sexuality is that they may be more bisexual in their behaviors than White gay men. Evidence for this comes again from Bell and Weinberg (1978) who reported that Black gay men were significantly more likely to have engaged in heterosexual coitus (22 percent) in the previous twelve months than White gay men (14 percent). This seems to be borne out nationally by the AIDS statistics. Among male homosexual/bisexual AIDS patients, Black men are more likely than White men to be classified as bisexual (30 percent versus 13 percent) rather than homosexual (70 percent versus 87 percent). Due to the intense homophobia in the Black community and the factors we discussed above, men may be more likely to remain secretive regarding their homosexual activities (Mays and Cochran, 1987). This may provide a mode of transmission of the AIDS virus outside of an already identified high risk group.

There are several other differences between Black and White gay men noted in the Kinsey Institute data that have implications for contracting the HIV virus. Looking at sexual behavior both pre- and post-Stonewall, Black gay men, in comparison to White gay men, were more likely to be sexually active across ethnic boundaries and less likely to report that their sexual partners were strangers (Gebhard and Johnson, 1979; Bell and Weinberg, 1978). Sexual practices post-Stonewall underwent profound change in the gay community. Black gay men were a part of that change (Gebhard and Johnson, 1979; Bell and Weinberg, 1978). However, these differences in meeting partners or choice of partners remain. They are apparently less malleable to change than specific risk-related sexual behaviors.

While the 1978 Bell and Weinberg study was conducted on a small sample in the San Francisco area, it is suggestive of the need for further research to assess the prevalence of risk behaviors and strategies most effective for decreasing risk. Indeed, a recent report of ethnically based differences in syphilis incidence rates (Landrum, Beck-Sague, and Kraus, 1988) suggests Black gay men are less likely than White gay men to be practicing "safer sex." Sexual behavior has multiple determinants and it is important that variables such as culture, ethnic identification, and class be incorporated into health education programs designed to promote sexual behavior change by Black men.

INTRAVENOUS DRUG USE

IV drug use is more common in the Black community (Gary and Berry, 1985), which may explain the higher than expected prevalence of Blacks in the co-categories of IV drug user and homosexual/ bisexual male. HIV infection is endemic among IV drug users in the urbanized Northeast who themselves are most likely to be Black (Ginzburg, MacDonald, and Glass, 1987). Ethnic differences exist between the percentage of homosexual/bisexual men with AIDS who are also IV drug users; for White gay and bisexual men with AIDS, 9 percent have histories of IV drug use, while for Blacks the figure is 16 percent. Black gay and bisexual men who do not use IV drugs may also be at increased risk because they are more likely than Whites to be sexual partners of Black men who are IV drug users. In the Bell and Weinberg study (1978), 22 percent of White men had never had sex with a Black man, whereas for Black respondents, only 2 percent had never had sex with a White man.

ALCOHOL AS A COFACTOR

Recently, alcohol use has been implicated as a cofactor facilitating the occurrence of high risk sexual behavior among gay men (Stall, McKusick, Wiley, Coates, and Ostrow, 1986). In predicting alcohol use among Black gay and bisexual men, one might expect that normative use patterns will be influenced by what is common behavior in both the Black community and gay community.

Norms for alcohol use in the Black community reflect a polarization of attitudes, shaped on the one hand by traditional religious fundamentalism and rural southern heritage and on the other by a focus on socializing in environments where drinking is common, such as bars, nightclubs, and home parties (Herd, 1986). This latter norm is more prevalent in urban Black communities. Blacks and Whites vary in small ways in their drinking patterns, although Blacks are more likely to suffer negative consequences, including alcohol-related mortality and morbidity, from their drinking than are Whites. Current rates of mortality due to liver cirrhosis indicates that rates are 10 times higher in Black men aged 25—34 as compared to White males. While drinking is found across all socioeconomic groups of Blacks, health and social problems associated with drinking have been found more often in low income urban Blacks (Lex, 1987). Similarly, for this group it was found that Black males 30—59 were most likely to use alcohol to face the stress of everyday life situations. This is the group most affected by HIV infection.

Within the gay male community, alcohol abuse is a serious problem (Icard and Traunstein, 1987). This may result from both the sociocultural stress of discrimination and the tendency for gay-oriented establishments to be drinking establishments as well. Thus, gay men frequently socialize in environments where alcohol consumption is normative.

Black gay and bisexual men, depending upon their relative identification with the Black or gay community, would be expected to demonstrate behavior consistent with these norms. For some, this might mean a high level of abstinence apart from social drinking consistent with other Black Americans; for others, alcohol consumption might more closely resemble that of White gay men with concomitantly higher rates of alcohol dependency.

CROSSING TRADITIONAL RISK GROUPS' BOUNDARIES

Early AIDS epidemiologic tracking programs conceptualized the disease as a result of the gay lifestyle (Mays, 1988). Indeed, now discarded names for different manifestations of the illness included Gay-related Immunodeficiency Disease and Gay cancer. This focus on discrete risk factors continues to the present, although the additional populations of IV drug abusers, hemophiliacs, persons born in Haiti and Central Africa, and recipients of blood transfusions after 1978 have been added to the list. For Whites, this approach is highly successfully, describing the presumed HIV transmission vector in 94 percent of cases; for native-born Blacks, the percentage

of cases accurately labeled by a single risk factor (including the combination of IV drug use and male homosexual sexual contact) drops to 88 percent (Cochran, 1987). This underscores the reality that sociocultural factors varying across ethnic groups strongly influence individuals' behavior, and by this their risk of contracting HIV

For Black gay and bisexual men, the reliance on highly specified risk groups (or factors) ignores the fundamental nature of their behavioral location in society. The multiplicity of their identities may indirectly increase their risk for HIV infection by exposing them to more diverse populations (Grob, 1983).

First, as Blacks, they are behaviorally closer to two epicenters of the AIDS epidemic: IV drug use and foreign-born Blacks (primarily those from Haiti and Central Africa where HIV infection is more common). Social and behavioral segregation by ethnic status is still a reality of the American experience and Black gay and bisexual men suffer, like other Blacks, from pervasive racism. As we noted above, if their social support systems are similar to what we know of Black lesbians (Cochran and Mays, 1986), extensive integration into the Black heterosexual community is common. Behaviorally, this may include both IV drug use and heterosexual activity with HIV infected individuals. Thus Black gay and bisexual men are at increased risk for HIV infection simply by virtue of being Black.

Second, as men who have sex with other men, Black gay and bisexual men are often members of the broader gay community in which ethnicity probably reflects the general U.S. population (84 percent White). Black gay and bisexual men may have relatively open sexual access to White men, although racism in the community may preclude other forms of socializing (Icard, 1985). Data from the Bell and Weinberg study (1978) suggests several interesting differences, as well as similarities, between White and Black gay men. Blacks reported equivalent numbers of sexual partners, both lifetime (median = 100–249 partners) and, in the previous 12 months (median = 20–50), as

Whites. Although they were significantly less likely than White gay men to engage in anonymous sexual contacts (51 percent versus 79 percent of partners), more than two-thirds reported that more than half their sexual partners were White men. In contrast, none of the White respondents reported that more than half their partners were Black. It should be kept in mind, however, that a greater percentage of the White sample (14 percent) was recruited at bath houses than the Black sample (2 percent). Nevertheless, at least sexually, Black gay men appear to be well integrated into the gay community. Therefore, Black gay and bisexual men are also at higher risk for HIV infection because they are behaviorally close to another epicenter of the AIDS epidemic: the gay male community.

Third, as a social grouping unto itself, the Black gay and bisexual male community may be more diverse than the White gay community (Icard, 1985). Some men identify more closely with the Black community than the gay community (Black gay men); others find their primary emotional affinity with the gay community and not the Black community (gay Black men). To the extent that this diversity of identity is reflected in behavioral diversity as well, HIV transmission may be greatly facilitated (Denning, 1987).

Thus Black gay and bisexual men are individuals often located behaviorally at the crossroads of HIV transmission. Their multiple social identities make it more likely that the practicing of high risk behavior, whether sexual or needle-sharing, will occur in the presence of HIV.

PERCEPTIONS OF RISK

There may be a reluctance among Black gay and bisexual men to engage in risk reduction behaviors because of the perception by some members of the Black community that AIDS is a "gay White disease" or a disease of intravenous drug users (Mays and Cochran, 1987). In addition, many risk reduction programs are located within outreach programs of primarily White gay organizations. These organizations often fail to attract extensive participation by Black gay men.

Research findings suggest that the personal perception of being at risk is most often influenced by accurate knowledge of one's actual risk and personal experiences with the AIDS epidemic (McKusick, Horstman, and Coates, 1985). There may be a variety of reasons why Black gay and bisexual men do not see themselves as at risk. These include the notion of relative risk and a lack of ethnically credible sources for encouraging risk perceptions (Mays and Cochran, 1988). Relative risk refers to the importance of AIDS in context with other social realities. For example, poverty, with its own attendant survival risks, may outweigh the fear of AIDS in a teenager's decision to engage in male prostitution. Economic privilege, more common in the White gay community, assists in permitting White gay men to focus their energies and concerns on the AIDS epidemic. For Black gay men of lesser economic privilege other pressing realities of life may, to some extent, diffuse such concerns. Credible sources relate to the issues that we have presented here of ethnic identification. Black gay men who are emotionally and behavioral distant from the White community may tend to discount media messages from White sources.

REFERENCES

Acquired Immunodeficiency Syndrome (AIDS) Weekly Surveillance Report, United States AIDS Activity, Center for Infectious Diseases, Centers for Disease Control, April 4,1988.

Bakeman, R., J. Lumb, R. E. Jackson, and P. N. Whitley. 1987. The incidence of AIDS among Blacks and Hispanics. *Journal of the National Medical Association,* 79: 921–928.

Beame, T. 1983. Racism from a Black Perspective. In *Black men/White men: A gay anthology.* M. J. Smith, ed. San Francisco: Gay Sunshine.

Becker, M. H. and J. G. Joseph. 1988. AIDS and behavioral change to reduce risk: A review. *American Journal of Public Health,* 78: 394–410.

Bell, A. P. and M. S. Weinberg. 1978. *Homosexualities: A study of diversity among men and women.* New York: Simon & Schuster.

Bell, A. P., M. S. Weinberg, and S. K. Hammersmith. 1981. *Sexual preference: Its development in men and women.* Bloomington: Indiana University Press.

Bureau of the Census. 1983. *General population characteristics, 1980.* U.S. Department of Commerce: U.S. Government Printing Office.

Centers for Disease Control. 1987. Human Immunodeficiency Virus Infection in the United States: A review of current knowledge. *Morbidity and Mortality Weekly,* 36 (Suppl. no. S-6): 1–48.

Cochran, S. D. 1987. *Numbers that obscure the truth: Bias in data presentation.* Paper presented at the meetings of the American Psychological Association, New York, August.

Cochran, S. D. and V. M. Mays. 1986. *Sources of support among Black lesbians.* Paper presented at the meetings of the American Psychological Association, Washington, D.C., August.

Cochran, S. D., V. M. Mays, and V. Roberts. 1988. Ethnic minorities and AIDS. In *Nursing Care of Patients with AIDS/ARC,* A. Lewis ed., pp. 17–24. Maryland: Aspen.

Denning, P. J. 1987. Computer models of AIDS epidemiology. *American Scientist,* 75: 347–351.

Friedland, G. H. and R. S. Klein. 1987. Transmission of the Human Immunodeficiency Virus. *New England Journal of Medicine,* 317: 1125–1135.

Friedman, S. R., J. L Sotheran, A. Abdul-Quader, B. J. Primm, D. C. Des Jarlais, P. Kleinman, C. Mauge, D. S. Goldsmith, W. El-Sadr, and R. Maslansky. 1987. The AIDS epidemic among Blacks and Hispanics. *Milbank Quarterly,* 65, Suppl. 2.

Gary, L. E. and G. L Berry. 1985. Predicting attitudes toward substance use in a Black community: Implications for prevention. *Community Mental Health Journal,* 21: 112–118.

Gebhard, P. H. and A. B. Johnson. 1979. *The Kinsey data: Marginal Tabulations of the 1938–1963 interviews conducted by the Institute for Sex Research.* Philadelphia: W B. Saunders.

Ginzburg, H. M., M. G. MacDonald, and J. W. Glass. 1987. AIDS, HTLV-III diseases, minorities and intravenous drug abuse. *Advances in Alcohol and Substance Abuse,* 6: 7–21.

Gottleib, M. S., H. M. Schanker, P. Fan, A. Saxon, J. D. Weisman, and I. Posalki. 1981. Pneumocystic Pneumonia—Los Angeles. *Morbidity and Mortality Weekly Report,* 30: 250–252.

Grob, G. N. 1983. Diseases and environment in American history. In *Handbook of health, health care, and the health professions,* D. Mechanic, ed., pp. 3–23. New York: Free Press.

Guttentag, M. and P. E. Secord. 1983. *Too many women: The sex ratio question.* Beverly Hills, Calif.: Sage.

Herd, D. 1986. A review of drinking patterns and alcohol problems among U.S. Blacks. In *Report of the Secretary's Task Force on Black and Minority Health:* Volume 7, M. Heckler, ed. USDHHS.

Icard, L. 1985. Black gay men and conflicting social identities: Sexual orientation versus racial identity. *Journal of Social Work and Human Sexuality,* 4: 83–93.

Icard, L. and D. M. Traunstein. 1987. Black, gay, alcoholic men: Their character and treatment: *Social Casework,* 68: 267–272.

Landrum, S., C. Beck-Sague, and S. Kraus. 1988. Racial trends in syphilis among men with same-sex partners in Atlanta, Georgia. *American Journal of Public Health,* 78: 66–67.

Lex, B. W. 1987. Review of alcohol problems in ethnic minority groups. *Journal of Consulting and Clinical Psychology* 55(3): 293–300.

Macdonald, D. I. 1986. Coolfont Report: A PHS plan for the prevention and control of AIDS and the AIDS virus. *Public Health Reports,* 101: 341–348.

Mays, V. M. 1988. *The epidemiology of AIDS in U.S. Blacks: Some problems and projections.* Unpublished manuscript.

Mays, V. M. and S. D. Cochran. 1987. Acquired Immunodeficiency Syndrome and Black Americans: Special Psychosocial Issues. *Public Health Reports,* 102: 224–231.

Mays, V. M. and S. D. Cochran. 1988 Issues in the perception of AIDS risk and risk reduction activities by Black and Hispanic women. *American Psychologist,* 43: 11.

McKusick, L, W. Horstman, and T. J. Coats. 1985. AIDS and sexual behavior reported by gay men in San Francisco. *American Journal of Public Health,* 75:493–496.

Morgan, W. M. and J. W. Curran. 1986. Acquired Immunodeficiency Syndrome: Current and future trends. *Public Health Reports,* 101: 459–465.

Samuel, M. and W. Winkelstein. 1987. Prevalence of Human Immunodeficiency Virus in ethnic minority homosexual/bisexual men. *Journal of the American Medical Association,* 257: 1901 (letter).

Smith, M. C. 1986. By the year 2000. In *In the life: A Black gay anthology,* J. Beam. ed. Boston: Alyson.

Soares, J. V. 1979. Black and gay. In *Gay men: The sociology of male homosexuality,* M. P. Levine, ed. New York: Harper & Row.

Spanier, G. B. and P. C. Glick. 1980. Mate selection differentials between Whites and Blacks in the United States. *Social Forces,* 58: 707–725.

Stall, R. S., L. McKusick, J. Wiley, T. J. Coates, and D. G. Ostrow. 1986. Alcohol and drug use during sexual activity and compliance with safe sex guidelines for AIDS: The AIDS Behavioral Research Project. *Health Education Quarterly,* 13: 359–371.

Staples, R. 1981. *The changing world of Black singles.* Connecticut: Greenwood.

Sylvester. 1986. Foreword. In *In the life: A black gay anthology,* J. Beam, ed. Boston: Alyson.

Warren, C. A. B. 1974. *Identity and community formation in the gay world.* New York: John Wiley.

16

Public Policy and Social Problems

Racial Inequality, Welfare Reform and Black Families: The 1996 Personal Responsibility and Work Reconciliation Act

GRACE J. YOO

This paper describes the development of the U.S. welfare state in relation to Black families. Racism, patriarchy and classism have influenced past and current U.S. welfare state backlashes. Because of the increasing numbers of Black recipients, the Aid to Families with Dependent Children (AFDC) cash assistance program has been under constant attack. The use of racist and demeaning constructions of AFDC recipients helped in the passage of the 1996 federal welfare reform law. This law has major implications for poor families. No longer is AFDC a federal entitlement, but a state block grant—Temporary Assistance for Needy Families. This paper investigates the implications of welfare reform on poor Black families.

■

INTRODUCTION

On August 22, 1996, President Clinton signed into law the Personal Responsibility and Work Opportunity Reconciliation Act (PRWORA) also known as welfare reform. President Clinton's electoral campaign was to "end welfare as we know it." No longer are poor families entitled to a federal safety net. Overall, this act saves $70 billion over the next five years. Welfare reform drastically changes the eligibility criteria for federal means-tested programs by barring aid to legal immigrants and placing time limits on cash and food assistance. Moreover under welfare reform, AFDC is no longer a federal entitlement but a block grant—Temporary Assistance for Needy Families (TANF). Federal law limits eligibility to TANF to a lifetime limit of 5 years and bars cash assistance to unwed minor mothers or children born to mothers on welfare. Because of welfare reform state and local officials are now accountable for meeting work participation rates and ensuring that recipients are in work activities within two years of their initial receipt of assistance. This paper examines the history of welfare in the United States, welfare state backlashes, welfare reform, and the implications of

Previously unpublished paper, 1998. Reprinted by permission of the author.

welfare reform on poor Black families in the United States.

HISTORY OF WELFARE IN THE UNITED STATES

The Social Security Act enacted in 1935 commenced the start of America's welfare programs. This act created three programs: Old Age Assistance (OAA), Aid to the Blind (AB), and Aid to Dependent Children (ADC). These provisions provided means tested entitlements to low-income elderly, the blind, and poor children with absent fathers. Although Franklin D. Roosevelt laid the groundwork for a welfare state, he did not address racism and racist inequality that was so widespread in the USA (Quadagno, 1994). In 1935, most Blacks resided in the south and many sharecropped. In order to pass the Social Security Act, Roosevelt needed the support of southern congressman. However, southern congressmen opposed any federal legislation that would give direct cash to Blacks (Quadagno, 1994). They feared that direct cash would destroy the plantation industry. Instead, southern legislators lobbied for the states to have the right to determine eligibility (Quadagno, 1994). Since the states determined eligibility, many Blacks who were concentrated in the agricultural and domestic industries—were denied the major programs of the Social Security Act (Quadagno, 1994). Moreover, the states standard for ADC eligibility was based on adherence to traditional marital and family arrangements (Abramovitz, 1996). Poor Black mothers who were not married, divorced or separated—were disqualified from receiving ADC. At the time, eligibility for ADC were for widows only and most of the recipients were White (Mink, 1995). In 1931, ADC recipients were 96 percent White, 3 percent Black, and 1 percent other (Bell 1965). In addition to limiting eligibility, the same southern legislators also opposed a national benefit standard to the Aid to Dependent Children (ADC) program. They wanted the states to have the right to limit pay-

ments below the standard of minimum need (Bell 1965; Abramovitz 1988).

Initially, the states were given the right to set eligibility and payment standards. Later, federal eligibility rules and standards were constructed to prevent discriminatory practices of the state and local welfare agencies (Abramovitz, 1996). This allowed poor mothers, who were not widows, to apply for ADC. The Social Security Act amended in 1939 also strengthened the Old Age Insurance (OAI) and included eligibility for widows and their children. However, the shift of widows to the old age insurance program (OAI) from ADC exacerbated the racial divide and increased the stigmatization of ADC recipients (Abramovitz, 1996). ADC now served divorced, never-married and separated single mothers. Since Black men could not qualify for social security benefits, their widows and children could not qualify for OAI, and many had no other option but to apply for ADC (Abramovitz, 1996). "Transfer of White widows to OAI ensured that in the future non-widowed and non-White single mothers would become overrepresented on ADC, leaving the program open to hostility from a public that continued to denigrate the poor, women and people of color (Abramovitz, 1996, 65)."

Because of the civil rights movement and increasing consciousness about racial inequality, the 1964 Economic Opportunity Act was passed. Unlike other previous welfare laws passed, this act provided community development, job training and housing. Moreover, there was a serious fight against the root causes of poverty (Blaustein 1982). According to Quadagno (1994), White backlash against the welfare state began to develop at this time. The programs of the 1964 Economic Opportunity Act became associated with the civil rights struggle through the large visible numbers of Black recipients and this also exacerbated racial tensions.

In 1988 Congress enacted the Family Support Act—an early effort to reform welfare. It created a new program called Job Opportunities and Basic Skills (JOBS) which required welfare recipients to participate with the anticipation of moving people into jobs. Even though the Family Support Act preceded the 1995 welfare reform law, there was a resemblance in the way welfare and its recipients were presented. Both of these acts constructed welfare recipients in a negative fashion and argued that public assistance contributed to the following: (1) encouraged intergenerational public assistance, (2) eroded any sense of work ethic, (3) caused family break-up, and (4) discouraged fathers from providing for their families (Naples, 1997). During the 1996 welfare reform debate, politicians of varying perspectives echoed these similar sentiments. In fact, before Bill Clinton became president he was a strong proponent of the Family Support Act. However, as he campaigned for the presidency, his attitude towards welfare changed as he pledged to "end welfare as we know it (Sawhill, 1995)."

UNDERSTANDING WELFARE STATE CUTBACKS

The Class Conflict Perspective

Piven and Cloward (1982) explain how gains are made in terms of public provisions, but they also illustrate how cuts and rollbacks to the welfare state also emerged. In *The New Class Wars,* they discuss the Reagan legacy and cuts made to several federally subsidized programs. They argue that these cuts were done purposively to aid in the development of capital. Cash assistance programs were helping large numbers of persons and this affected the labor market by keeping wages strong. Piven and Cloward (1982) describe in detail the reasons why the powerful and wealthy elite have targeted such programs. The power of huge employers diminishes to the extent that the state offers an alternative like a cash assistance program which indirectly stabilizes workers' wages, and have "weakened capital's ability to depress wages by means of economic insecurity, especially by means of manipulating the relative numbers of people searching for work" (Piven and Cloward 1982: 31). Since there have been no downward pressures on wages, massive unemployment would

result in the lowering of wages. Because of the availability of a safety net, "unemployment has lost some of its terrors, both for the unemployed and for those currently working (Piven and Cloward, 1982: 31)."

According to Piven and Cloward (1982), the most effective way to "regulate the poor" in the labor market is to offer no viable option for subsistence. Because there are no other mechanisms for survival, workers are much more productive, docile and inexpensive. On the other hand, if workers have many options for subsistence, workers are more costly, less compliant, and less productive. For example, cuts in cash assistance programs means that workers would have to accept and be susceptible to oppressive working conditions and to accept below average wages in the face of inflation. With cuts to cash assistance, economic insecurity will be exacerbated, and those on cash assistance would be forced to become part of the larger pool of unemployed persons. For example, if AFDC recipients find that they are ineligible for continued assistance because of the time limits, more individuals will be looking for work, which in turn would lower wages and increase unemployment.

On the one hand, a safety net—that provides cash, food and health assistance—weakens capital, but at the same time these benefits also "contribute to profitability by lowering the costs to employers of maintaining a healthy and skilled labor force" (Piven and Cloward, 1982: 30). Without public assistance, employers would be burdened with paying the costs for health education, and other benefits and services, or increase wages so workers could afford to pay for these needed services. Second, public assistance aids capital because it pacifies those who are angry with the system, especially those without work. According to Piven and Cloward, this is seen as a strategy by the ruling class to silence the poor by offering cash assistance, political organizing diminishes and "with the expansion of these programs, the body politic presumably grows more compliant, listless and enfeebled" (Piven and Cloward, 1982: 29).

The Ideology of Individualism

Opposition to welfare has arisen out of class-based economic self interest or individualistic ideology (Giles, 1995, Feagin, 1975). Welfare is unpopular because of two major reasons. First, middle-class Americans end up paying for services used by the poor (Giles, 1995). Second, Americans value individualism and individual responsibility (Giles, 1995, Feagin, 1975). Laissez-faire economic ideologies are part of the United States and inherent in this belief is that all people are rational and self interested. Because of this type of ideology, those who do not succeed can be blamed and judged. This can be interpreted to mean that the poor are lazy and lack a work ethic, and deserve their fate, while those who are rich are entitled because of their hard work. These misconceptions arise out of an individualist explanation of the causes of poverty. Feagin (1975) describes how there are three different explanations to explain poverty: individualistic, structural and fatalistic. Individualistic explanations—which most Americans subscribe to—place the blame on the individual. Structural explanations attribute poverty to social and economic circumstances, and fatalistic explanations place responsibility on fate (Feagin, 1975). Based on the individualistic interpretation, if one spends recklessly, lacks effort, or is immoral, she is undeserving of public support.

Constructing Welfare Recipients: The use of racism

Herbert Gans (1995) in his book, *The War Against the Poor*, discusses how myths of welfare recipients are constructed to justify cutbacks on the poor. The basis of ideology construction is to condemn the poor. There are two uses for this type of social construction. First, this social construction allows the undeserving poor to be scapegoated for the country's economic problems. Recipients are seen as the cause of high taxes and the budget deficit. The second use of this social construction is to label the poor and coerce them out of the labor market, so employment can be preserved for worthy citizens. "People assigned to the underclass may be forced out of the economy on the grounds that they are biologically unable to perform as workers (Gans, 1995: 8)." Gans (1995) outlines how this ideology is facilitated. First, if poor people don't abide by mainstream principles, then they are classified as undeserving. They are undeserving because they are not compliant to the values of the majority and deliberately do not want to assimilate into mainstream America. Another premise is that poor men are inherently lazy and lack a work ethic. They are incapable of understanding the merit of hard work, and hence develop into criminals or non-contributing members of society. On other hand, women who make-up the undeserving poor are depraved for having children out of wedlock. Moreover, if the undeserving poor do not change their behavior to comply with mainstream standards, "they must be forced to do so, for example, by ending welfare payments (Gans, 1995: 7)."

Cook and Barrett (1992) speculate that support for social welfare is also based on the public's perceived self-interest: "How will the policy in question affect me?" Cook and Barrett's study neglects how racial attitudes may generate opposition to welfare. In fact, most studies examining popular attitudes and welfare ignore how racial attitudes may effect these views (Giles, 1995). Giles found that Whites who attribute racial inequality to Blacks' lack of effort are more likely to oppose welfare than those who blame social conditions. According to Giles (1995), even though attitudes have changed and there is increasing racial tolerance, views on welfare and welfare recipients are racialized and racist. For example, he found that racist attitudes such as Blacks lacking commitment to the work ethic were common among many White Americans, and were most often associated with those who oppose means-tested entitlements. Giles argues that advocates involved with means-tested entitlements are moving away from using race to depict welfare recipients and utilizing class. However, most White Americans still associate welfare recipients with Blacks, and those who oppose such entitlements, usually also have negative perceptions of Blacks. "Any anti-poverty policy will have to face the very substantial skepticism of White Americans toward deservingness of the Black poor. Whether race-specific or race-neutral, anti-poverty policy in this country has become hostage to White American's cynicism toward poor Blacks and specifically to the belief that Black's economic problems are of their own making" (Giles, 1995: 1011).

Edsall and Edsall (1992) discuss the growing discontent among California voters desiring tax relief. As early as 1978, the tax revolt was highly organized in California. Proposition 13 passed and proposed to cut property taxes. "The tax result opened up a new schism in American politics, pitting taxpayers against tax recipients" (Edsall and Edsall, 1992). The division was between tax payers and tax recipients and was connected to racial divisions: non-Whites were constructed as the primary recipients of public assistance. Utilizing the race card became a strategy by conservatives in dismantling the welfare state (Edsall and Edsall, 1992). High taxes became associated with racialized tax recipients. Similar race-coded constructions were used in the passage of welfare reform. These race-coded messages about welfare recipients appeased the White majority, but at the expense of poor Black Americans (Aaronson, 1996). The use of these constructions gave the perception that poor Black families were the bulk of AFDC recipients which fueled the public backlash against the program (*CQ researcher,* 1992).

BLACK FAMILIES AND PUBLIC ASSISTANCE

Poverty, AFDC and Black Families

In 1993, the nation had 3.8 million mothers receiving AFDC. An additional .5 million women over 45 years old and .3 million fathers living with the dependent children also received AFDC (U.S. Department of Commerce, 1995).

Stereotypes about AFDC as a program primarily benefiting Black women are used to hide the fact that large numbers of AFDC mothers are White, but also is used to divide women from each other (Abramovitz, 1988). Black women do represent large numbers on welfare, but they are also overrepresented among the poor. In 1993, Black families maintained by women with children had a median income of only $10,380. On the other hand White families headed by a woman with children had a median income of $17,890 (U.S. Bureau of the Census, 1993). Moreover, the poverty rate for Blacks is approximately two and half times greater than of Whites (see Table 1) (U.S. Bureau of the Census, 1996).

In 1993, 1 in 4 Black mothers of childbearing ages were AFDC recipients, higher than the 7 percent of corresponding White mothers. Despite these differences in recipiency rates, Black AFDC mothers did not have significantly more children than their White counterparts (U.S. Bureau of the Census, 1993). In 1995, AFDC recipients by race of parent broke down as follows: 35.6 percent White families, 37.2 percent Black families, 20.7 percent Hispanic families 20.7 percent, Asian families 3.0 percent and native American families 1.3 percent (see Table 2).

Black Women on AFDC

Black women represent 94.2 percent of all Black AFDC recipients (U.S. Bureau of the Census, 1996). Black men comprise 5.8 percent of all Black AFDC recipients. A majority of Black women on AFDC have never married (68.5 percent), and a large number (39 percent) have less than a high school education (see Table 3). On the other hand, White women on AFDC were currently married or had been married (e.g., divorced, widowed, separated) (66 percent) (U.S. Bureau of the Census, 1996). Like Black women on AFDC, the majority of White women on AFDC had less than a high school education (42 percent) (U.S. Bureau of the Census, 1996).

Although the annual high school drop out rate for young Blacks in the USA has declined (US

TABLE 1 Poverty rates by race, 1996. Source: U.S. Bureau of Census, 1996. March Current Population Survey, 1996. Washington DC: General Accounting Office.

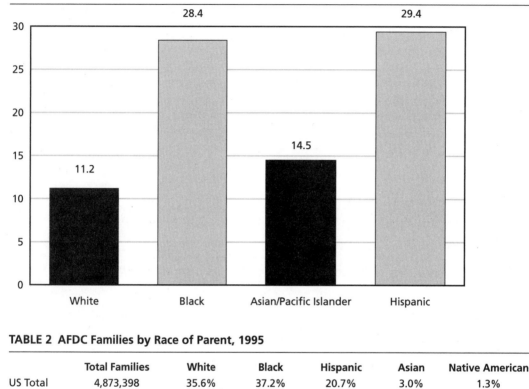

TABLE 2 AFDC Families by Race of Parent, 1995

	Total Families	White	Black	Hispanic	Asian	Native American
US Total	4,873,398	35.6%	37.2%	20.7%	3.0%	1.3%

Source: U.S. Administration to Children and Families. 1995. Characteristics and Financial Circumstances of AFDC Recipients, FY 1995: Washington D.C.: Office of Family Assistance.

Bureau of the Census, 1994), the economic prospects for Blacks who do drop-out of high school remains bleak. Young Black women who do not complete high school face the enormous economic hardships. Over the last 20 years, the most severe wage loss was for Black women with less than a high school education whose hourly wages fell by over 20 percent (Mishel and Burtless, 1995). In addition to suffering a major wage loss, Black women with less than a high school education also faced the highest unemployment rate (Bernstein, 1997, see Table 4). Overall, the employment rate for Blacks continues to be higher than for Whites.

The employment rate for Blacks is almost twice that of Whites (U.S. Bureau of the Census, 1994).

Black Women, AFDC and the Racist Welfare Backlash

The Aid to Families with Dependent Children program symbolizes the racially divisive character of the American welfare state. Compared to any other federal means-tested entitlement, AFDC has been under constant attack by conservatives. AFDC is misperceived and associated with rewarding laziness and discouraging family formation.

TABLE 3 Characteristics of Black Women on AFDC

	Percent
Age	
Teenager	8%
20-24	21
25-34	42
35-44	21
45+	8
Education	
Less than High School	39.0
High School Graduate	35.2
Some College	25.9
College Graduate	1.0
Marital Status	
Married	8.6
Widowed	1.7
Divorced	7.7
Separated	13.5
Never Married	68.5

Source: U.S. Census Bureau. 1996. March 1996. Current Population Survey. Washington D.C.: General Accounting Office.

TABLE 4 Unemployment Rates by Race/Ethnicity, Gender and Education, 1996

	Males	Females
All	5.4	5.5
Race/Ethnicity		
White	4.3	4.1
Black	11.2	10.0
Hispanic	8.1	10.3
Other	5.9	6.3
Education (by race)		
Less than High School		
All	11.6	13.6
White	10.4	10.8
Black	20.3	20.9
Hispanic	10.2	15.9
Other	13.7	12.2
High School		
All	5.9	5.7
White	4.6	4.3
Black	11.8	11.1
Hispanic	7.8	9.4
Other	7.7	7.8
Some College		
All	4.7	4.6
White	4.0	3.8
Black	8.5	8.2
Hispanic	6.0	6.8
Other	6.0	5.0
College		
All	2.3	2.6
White	2.1	2.4
Black	3.9	3.0
Hispanic	3.8	4.3
Other	2.5	4.3

Source: Bernstein, Jared. 1997. Data derived from the Current Population Surveys. 1996 panel.

Messages about its' recipients and their behavior have been coded by race. The problems with the AFDC program and its' recipients have come to simultaneously mean problems of Black families (Quadagno, 1994). Federal policy discussions to reform welfare do not discuss structural constraints that low-income Black families face in terms of low wages, institutional racism, underemployment and unemployment (Naples, 1997). Rather the policy discussions about Black families and welfare have been about behavioral and individualist frames and Black women have been blamed for long term intergenerational dependency on welfare (Mink, 1995, Naples, 1997). The number of Black recipients on AFDC have increased and this may explain why AFDC has come under attack in the last 10 years.

The backlash against Black women on AFDC is not surprising. It reflects the racist and sexist history that Black women have faced in this country. The work Black women do for their young children is not valued, rather the work that Black women do caring for White families is highly regarded and seen as beneficial. According to Nakano-Glenn (1985), the caretaking responsibilities or reproductive roles of racial ethnic women are never visible and seen as important, rather their roles as workers are much more recognized by society. The conception of motherhood confined to the home never applied to Black women (Roberts, 1994). There are no popular images of Black mothers taking care of their children, rather there are American images of Aunt Jemima dressed in an dress, apron and scarf and "working in someone else's kitchen (Roberts, 1994: 876)." Because of these images, the growing numbers of Black women on AFDC resulted in reactionary racist tactics to curtail public assistance. The image of the young, single Black mother had become synonymous with welfare dependency (Fraser and Gordon, 1994) and the American public felt it was time to put poor Black mothers back to work—even if it meant leaving their children for work (Roberts, 1994).

Black Males, Children and Joblessness

The impoverishment of Black women does not necessarily translate into affluence for Black men. Rather, there is a strong correlation between the rapidly rising numbers and increasing proportion of Black female headed households and the declining labor-force participation of Black men (Smith and Joe, 1994, Burnham, 1986). Unfortunately, the percentage of Black adults who never married rose from 20.6 percent to 37.1 percent between 1970 and 1991 (U.S. Bureau of the Census, 1992). In view of the poverty and unemployment that Black men face, marriage and family life becomes more difficult and supporting a family becomes a more daunting task. Moreover, Black men are also more likely than White men to die or to be sent to prison at a young age (Smith and Joe, 1994).

Because of the structural and economic transformations that the United States has gone through, less educated workers have a harder time finding employment and receiving an adequate

wage (Danziger and Lehman, 1996). Black men have been the group most severely affected by these changes. The large numbers of Black males facing joblessness is a chronic and persistent problem. In 1993, 43 percent of working age (ages 16–64) Black men were not working (Smith and Joe, 1994). The proportion of Black men unemployed is double that of White men. In 1993, only 54.5 percent of working-age Black men were employed, as compared to 77.6 percent of White men (Smith and Joe, 1994). The lack of education among poor Black men (see Table 4) contributed to higher rates of unemployment. Those with less than a high school education faced an unemployment rate double that of Whites and other races (Bernstein, 1996).

In *When Work Disappears: The World of the New Urban Poor,* William Julius Wilson (1996) discusses the implications of unemployment on the lives of poor Black families:

The evolving patterns may be seen in the sharing of negative outlooks toward marriage and toward the relationships between males and females in the inner city, outlooks that are developed and influenced by an environment plagued by persistent joblessness. This combination of factors has increased out-of-wedlock births, weakened the family structure, expanded the welfare rolls, and, as a result, caused poor inner city Blacks to be even be more disconnected from the job market and discouraged about their role in the labor force (106).

The structural constraints—institutional racism and unemployment—place stress on the lives of poor Black families. Ultimately, the lives of young children are also affected and their hopes for a promising future. Approximately half of all poor Blacks were children under 18 years (U.S. Bureau of the Census, 1993). Among all poor children, Black children were overwhelmingly (40 percent) over-represented compared to White children (16 percent) (U.S. Bureau of the Census, 1996). The lack of financial resources affects the status of children, and it also affects relations with fathers. Non-resident fathers are more involved with their children when they can contribute financial assistance, but may discontinue contact with a child when facing financial hardship (Smith and Joe, 1994).

IMPLICATIONS: BLACK FAMILIES AND WELFARE REFORM

A five year limit on AFDC without guarantees of an adequate wage, child care and health insurance is an unrealizable goal. In the next decade, service providers and community leaders in all low-income communities will face an enormous challenge finding employment for welfare recipients. Pavetti et al. (1996) documents that many families receiving welfare face a number of personal and family challenges that may affect their ability to find employment, but also to stay employed. They found that low skills are the most common potential barrier to employment among welfare recipients followed by alcohol and drug use, depression, and health problems.

On the other hand, William Julius Wilson (1996) suggests that those disabled by mental health, medical or substance problem are a minority and many recipients in the inner city are "ready, willing, able, and anxious to hold a steady job (238)." He dispels the myth that welfare recipients are lazy and do not want to work. Rather Wilson proposes that the long term solutions to poverty are to generate good jobs, decrease the wage inequality and find solutions to the inequalities persistent in education and employment. Currently, there are not enough jobs to employ parents wanting to leave welfare (Deparle, 1997). A recent report states that there were 23 applicants for every low-skilled job that paid at least $12,278 annually, 66 candidates for jobs that paid at least $18,417 and 100 job-

seekers for every low-skilled job that paid $25,907 (Children's Defense Fund, 1997).

Because of welfare reform, welfare case loads have dramatically decreased (Deparle, 1997). Although recipients are being dropped, this does not necessarily mean that recipients are successful at finding work. According to a Institute for Women's Policy Research (1997) report, the significant factors that increase an AFDC recipients' likelihood of working include the following: not having infants or toddlers, having only one child, another earner in the household, able-bodied, a high school diploma, work experience, job training, residing in states with a low unemployment rate (3.5 percent). Moreover, the factors that improve the possibilities of fleeing poverty include the conditions mentioned above, but also include stable work and union coverage. In addition, a high welfare benefit also contributes to an AFDC recipients prospect of leaving poverty (IWPR, 1997).

CONCLUSION

Welfare reform has major implications for poor Black families. The current welfare reform law is an outgrowth of years of racism. As the numbers of Black AFDC recipients has increased, so has the racist backlash. Stereotypes and myths about poor Black families on AFDC have surfaced and gone unchallenged. Statistics further validates the changing composition of AFDC recipients. Federal policy discussions failed to discuss the structural constraints that low-income Black families face in terms of low wages, institutional racism and unemployment. As a result, poor Black families became constructed as "undeserving" and individualistic explanations were used to justify their unworthiness. The passage of the welfare reform act was meant to appease White voter angst, but has been paid at the expense of poor Black families. Although there are statistics and figures on demographics, there are a lack of studies on the implications of welfare reform on

Black families. Further research on the ramifications of welfare reform on poor Black families needs to be undertaken so inequalities can be addressed and racist stereotypes contested.

REFERENCES

Aaronson, M. N. 1996. Scapegoating the poor: Welfare reform all over again and the undermining of democratic citizenship. *Hastings Women Law Journal,* 7(2): 21 3–256.

Abramovitz, M. 1988. *Regulating the lives of women.* Boston: South End.

Abramovitz, M., and F. Newdom. 1995. *Fighting back! Challenging AFDC myths with the facts.* [http://www.hartford-hwp.com/archives/45/029.html]

Abramovitz, M. 1996. *Under attack, fighting back: Women and welfare in the United States.* New York: Monthly Review Press.

Albelda, R., N. Folbre, and Center for Popular Economics. 1996. *The war on the poor: A defense manual.* New York: New Press.

Bell, W. 1965. *Aid to Dependent Children.* New York: Columbia University Press.

Bernstein, J. 1997. *The challenge of moving from welfare to work.* Washington D.C.: Economic Policy Institute.

Bernstein, J. and L. Mishel. 1995. *Trends in the low-wage labor market and welfare reform.* Washington D.C.: Economic Policy Institute. [http://epn.org/epi/epiwelf.html]

Blaustein, A. 1982. *The American promise.* New Brunswick, N.J.: Transaction.

Burnham, L. 1986. Has poverty been feminized in Black America? In *For crying out loud: Women and poverty in the United States,* ed. R. Lefkowitz and A. Withorn, 69–83. New York: Pilgrim.

Children's Defense Fund. 1997. *The new welfare law: One year later.* Washington D.C.: Children's Defense Fund. [http://www.childrensdefense.org/fairstart_oneyr.html]

Cook, F. L., and E. Barrett. 1992. *Support for the American welfare state.* New York: Columbia University Press.

CQ Researcher. 1992. The welfare backlash. *CQ Researcher,* 2(14): 320.

Danziger, S., and J. Lehman. 1996. How will welfare recipients fare in the labor market? *Challenge,* 39(2) March–April: 30.

Deparle, J. 1997. Welfare reform creates hardship in Mississippi. *New York Times* (on the Web). October 16.

Deparle. J. 1997. Tougher welfare limits brings surprising results. *New York Times* (on the Web). December 30.

Edsall, T. B., and M. D. Edsall. 1991. *Chain reaction: The impact of race, rights and taxes on American politics.* New York: Norton.

Feagin, J. 1975. *Subordinating the poor.* Englewood Cliffs, N.J.: Prentice Hall.

Fraser, N., and L. Gordon. 1994. A genealogy of dependency: Tracing a keyword of the U.S. welfare state. *Signs.* 19(Winter).

Gans, H. 1995. *The war against the poor.* New York: Basic Books.

Gilens, M. 1995. Racial attitudes and opposition to welfare. *Journal of Politics.* 57(November): 994–1014.

Glenn, E. N. 1985. Racial ethnic women's labor: The intersection of race, gender and class oppression. *Review of Radical Political Economics,* 17(3): 86–108.

Institute for Women's Policy Research. 1997. *Welfare that works: The working lives of AFDC recipients.* Washington D.C.: IWPR. [http://www.iwpr.org/wtwrib. html]

Mink, G. 1995. *The wages of motherhood: Inequality in the welfare state, 1917–1942.* Ithaca, New York: Cornell University Press.

Mishel, L., and G. Burtless. 1995. *Recent wage trends: The implications for low wage workers.* Washington D.C.: Economic Policy Institute [http://epn.org/epi/epiwage.html]

Naples, N.. 1997. The "new consensus" on the gendered "social contract": The 1987–1988 U.S. Congressional hearings on welfare reform. *Signs,* 22(4): 907–945.

Pavetti, L., K. Olson, D. Nightingale, and A. E. Duke. 1996. *Welfare-to-work options for families facing personal and family challenges: rationale and program strategies.* Washington D.C.: The Urban Institute.

Piven, F. F., and R. Cloward. 1982. *The L.* New York: Pantheon.

Piven, F. F., and R. Cloward. 1993. *Regulating the poor: The functions of public welfare.* New York: Vintage.

Quadagno, J. 1994. *The color of welfare.* New York: Oxford University Press.

Roberts, D. E. 1995. Race, gender and the value of mother's work. *Social Politics,* 2(2); 195–207.

Roberts, D. 1994. The value of Black mothers' work. *Connecticut Law Review,* 26(Spring).

Sawhill, I. 1995. *Welfare reform: An analysis of the issues.* Washington D.C.: Urban Institute

Sidel, R. 1996. *Keeping women and children last: America's war on the poor.* New York: Penguin.

Smith, R., and T. Joe. 1994. *World without work: Causes and consequences of Black male joblessness.* Washington D.C.: Center for the Study of Social Policy.

U.S. Administration to Children and Families. *Characteristics and financial circumstances of AFDC recipients report—FY 1995.* Washington D.C.: Office of Family Assistance.

U.S. Bureau of the Census. 1992. *Statistical abstracts of the United States.* Washington D.C.: U.S. Government Printing Office.

U.S. Bureau of the Census. Current Population Reports, Series P20–480, *The Black Population in the United States: March 1994 and 1993.* Washington D.C.: U.S. Government Printing Office.

U.S. Bureau of the Census. 1996. *1996 March current population survey.* Washington D.C.: U.S. Government Printing Office.

U.S. Department of Commerce, Economics and Statistics Administration. 1995. *Statistic Brief—Mothers who receive AFDC.* Washington D.C.: U.S. Government Printing Office.

Wilson, W. J. 1996. *When work disappears: The world of the new urban poor.* New York: Vintage.

Social Inequality and Black Sexual Pathology: The Essential Relationship

ROBERT STAPLES

The author provides a wide-ranging discussion of the social origin of Black sexual pathology from prostitution to sexual aggression to AIDS. All these pathologies reflect and are a cause of the social inequality of Blacks in the United States. Staples concludes that only by the elimination of poverty and the provision of employment opportunities will men and women develop healthy forms of sexual communication and interaction.

■

In looking at the painful history of race relations in American society, it seems clear that much of the discrimination that Afro-Americans have encountered is due to the existence of White American stereotypes about their moral character. As a number of polls have revealed, a large number of White Americans see Blacks as a morally loose group. In fact, the sexual stereotypes about Blacks become the ultimate *raison d'être* for their exclusion from White schools, jobs and neighborhoods.

To a certain extent, many of the ideas held about Black sexuality are exaggerated versions of general attitudes toward the poor. American society was founded upon the Protestant ethic, which equated poverty with sinfulness, idleness, vice and indulgence. The image of Blacks as sexual beings is deeply rooted in American history culture, and religion and is too complex to delineate here.

In the early part of the twentieth century respected scholars imputed a genetic basis to the allegedly hotter sexual passions and richer fertility of the Black population. Subsequent research has done little to invalidate the earlier generalizations about Black sexual drives or to illuminate the sociocultural forces that differentiate Black from White sexual behavior. The result has been the fostering and reinforcement of White stereotypes about Black immorality and hypersexuality. Such false images fuel the fears of those people who remain psychologically wedded to Americans' puritanical view of sexuality and galvanize their resistance to Black demands for equal opportunity in American life.[1]

During the period of slavery, the Black woman's body was forcefully subjected to the carnal desires of any male who took a fancy to her, including the slavemaster, his overseer, or any male slave. If she was permitted a husband, he was not allowed to protect her. Essentially she was left defenseless against sexual onslaught by males on the plantation. This was especially true of her relations with the White slavemaster. It appears that coercion, as well as desire, was an important element in her sexual relations with White men during that time.[2]

Though the experience of slavery pronounced alterations of Black sexual behavior took place. Whereas community and kinship groups regulated sexual relations in Africa, the major control over the sexual impulse among Blacks during the American slave era was that exercised by the White slavemaster. The attitude of most White slaveowners toward bondsmen was that they were property, a commodity to be bought and sold. During this period, reproduction among the slaves had a certain value to the

From *The Black Scholar*, Volume 21, No. 3 (Summer) 1991: 29–37.

slaveowners, and free sex practice was tolerated. In some cases Black females, at the onset of puberty, were mated as the stock of the plantation were mated. Black women were compelled to breed children—to be the breeder of human cattle for the field or auction block.[3]

This practice of human breeding was one factor that encouraged permissive sexual conduct among slaves. Where there was no coercion, free sex practice was followed as an end in itself. More important, the nexus between sex and marriage was attenuated among Americas Black population. Although some slaveowners permitted and encouraged the legal union of their slaves and regarded marriage as a permanent association, many others expected slaves to mate without the formality of a marriage ceremony and did not regard the union as necessarily permanent. With this attitude of the slave-masters and the peculiar conditions of slave life, a permissive type of sexual behavior developed.[4]

After emancipation the permissive sex life of Afro-Americans still remained. One central reason for the continuation of their free sex life was the compulsive character of sex relations between Black women and White men. According to Hernton, "Negro women were forced to give up their bodies like animals to White men at random."[5] Others have also noted that White males used Black women to satisfy their carnal desires. Many Southern White males had their first sexual experience with Black women. In some cases the use of Black women as sexual objects served to maintain the double standard of sexual morality in the White South. Many White men did not have sexual relations with White women until they married.[6]

Since the degree of sexual relations is frequently contingent on the limits set by women, the Black culture became a sexually permissive one. By virtue of their caste status, Black women were denied the right to preserve their virginity until marriage. It was Hernton's belief that

> Ultimately, after experiencing the ceaseless sexual immorality of the White South

the Negro woman became "promiscuous and loose," and could be "had for the taking." Indeed she came to look upon herself as the White South viewed and treated her, for she had no other morality by which to shape her womanhood as far as the White South was concerned.[7]

In the post-bellum South, working in a White household as a domestic was rife with danger to the Black woman's dignity. As Du Bois once said of domestic servants, "The personal degradation of their work is so great that any White man of decency would rather cut his daughter's throat than let her grow up to such a destiny."[8]

In the same essay, Du Bois describes the exploitation that domestic workers were subjected to. He portrays them as prey to all sorts of human indignities such as having to enter and exit by the side door, receiving extremely low wages, and being subjected to the sexual exploitation of their employer. An example of the latter is cited by Dollard:

> An informant pointed out what it means to the Negro woman who gets two to four dollars a week as a cook to have the men of the house offer her five dollars for sexual intercourse. She probably has a family to support, certainly has bills to pay and needs the money.[9]

Because the Black masses enjoyed a more healthy sexual equality than was possible for Whites in the post-bellum era, a more permissive sexual code developed. Moreover, some of the controls on Euro-American sexuality did not exist in the same degree among Afro-Americans. Black males did not classify women into bad and good groups on the basis of their virginal status. White men did make these distinctions, and women were eligible for the respectability of marriage according to their classification in one group or the other. During an epoch in which the majority of White women were economically dependent on their men, this was an effective censor of their sexuality. Black women, in the main, were more economically and psychologically independent.

BODIES FOR SALE: THE PROSTITUTE

After emancipation, the flagrant sexual abuse of Black women by White men decreased. However, the amount of organized prostitution among Black women increased because it was the only means that some Black women had of supporting their families. And, these Black women met a need of White men. As one writer asserted,

> For the young White man, Negro or mulatto girls existed to initiate him into sexual experience. Later he might set up one such girl as a concubine and produce a family. Or he might continue to indulge himself throughout life whenever the opportunity presented itself. The point to bear in mind is that despite legislation, official sexual propriety, and Christianity itself the Southern White had embarked upon the systematic prostitution of Negro women.[10]

Although many factors compelled Black women to become prostitutes, the most important was the need for money. As an economically deprived group they were subject to enticement into sexual relations with White men of considerable means. While they may have disliked the idea of intercourse with the oppressor, their families could not be supported with high moral values. According to Hernton, ever since the Black woman has been in America, she has largely been forced into the role of a "whore"—not only sexually, but also as an economic and cultural "prostitute" in American society. When she has been made to escape having to surrender to sexual advances of the White man, she has not escaped having to "prostitute" her femininity, her sex, in the form of being a "domestic servant" in White people's homes, in their shops, restaurants, office buildings, and elsewhere,

where the qualities and labor of her sex were expropriated from her by having to nurture White babies and children, clean and take care of White homes, wash, iron, and cook for White people. And, she was not respected for these things, but was demeaned by them.[11]

Whatever monetary advantage the Black prostitute may have gained is canceled by the loss of social esteem. Women who "play for pay" are looked down upon everywhere. Although she often performed a service for chaste White women, by allowing White men to release their prenuptial sexual urges upon her, the Black woman receives opprobrium. Universally despised, she makes herself ineligible for marriage through her sale of passion.

Prostitution has arisen in Western society because of our hypocritical attitude toward sexual behavior. Theoretically, we have a single code of sexual conduct that sexual relations are to take place only between a man and a woman married to each other. In reality, men are permitted permissive sexual activity with women other than their wives. Since the male's violation of the sex code cannot take place without a female partner, prostitutes traditionally provided males with their illicit sexual pleasures. For performing this service, women usually receive money or its equivalent. In turn, they are denied respect and make themselves ineligible for "respectful" marriage.

Because these disadvantages attend the role of prostitute, most women reject the job. Women who become prostitutes have usually done so because of their impoverished circumstances or because they were forced to do so. Black women who became prostitutes originally did so for the latter reason. As slaves they had to submit to their masters and received no compensation. However, some White slavemasters saw the opportunity for commercial profit in peddling the bodies of their female slaves. As a result, there was in the South a considerable traffic in Black women for prostitution. Particularly desirable was the mulatto woman, herself a result of earlier miscegenation between a White man and a Black woman. In the antebellum South, large numbers of mulatto girls were carried to the cities and sold at enormous prices into private prostitution. Little respect was shown for kinship ties, as some White men even sold their Black daughters as prostitutes to other men.[12]

Men with perverted sexual tastes often seek out prostitutes to satisfy their tastes. Sadists and masochists form a part of the prostitute's clientele and their peculiar needs must be catered to. Beatings administered by the sadist are common for the prostitute, though sometimes the beating is purely symbolic and not carried to the extent of causing pain. A Black prostitute remarked that men only tried to hurt her once in a while and usually it was the White men who did it.[13]

Beatings bring a higher price, and some impoverished Black women are forced to undergo such treatment for their bread and butter. One Black hustler explained that White tricks pay a hundred dollars to beat a prostitute. Sometimes, she says, they hit you so hard you land in the hospital.[14] Other men who attain sexual gratification in bizarre ways that defy description usually have a need to degrade the woman before they can enjoy her. And it is probably easier for them to vent their pernicious sexual urges on Black women because they consider these women to be less than human. As one White man told a Black prostitute, "Gal, there's two places where niggers is as good as White folks—the bedroom and the graveyard."[15] One sociologist has even declared that prostitutes receive money not only for their sexual services but also for their loss of status in the community.[16] They fail to consider that prostitution is a crime punishable by imprisonment in this country and that in most cases only the woman is arrested.

The only open prostitution left in the United States is frequently found in the Black ghetto. Many hotels and brothels exist there, and it is a usual sight to see a dozen streetwalkers on every corner.

One reason for this situation is the dual standard of law enforcement in this country. The police maintain a much less rigorous standard of law enforcement in the Black community, tolerating there illegal activities such as drug sales, prostitution, and street violence that they would not tolerate elsewhere. Moreover, investigations of the police force in certain large cities have revealed a close collaboration between the men in blue and the peddlers of vice in ghetto communities.[17]

The recent increase in crime in the streets has made prostitution an unsafe trade. One woman who dropped out of the profession said that it had become a holy hell.[18] Many women have been mugged or killed by criminals who roam the streets at night. With the recent reluctance of ordinary citizens to venture into the inner cities at night, prostitutes have become the victims of muggings and killings. Sometimes the trick takes her money after the act of coitus, adding insult to injury.

Women who become prostitutes face a multitude of problems. Men have been known to say that females never face starvation because they can always sell sex if they cannot do anything else. Such statements ignore the realities of the prostitute's life. Not infrequently, it is the male pimp who gets the greatest monetary gain from the sale of the prostitute's body. And even though prostitution may be lucrative for a while, the passage of time takes its toll on the pulchritude of most prostitutes, as it does on that of all women. When she reaches a certain age, the prostitute becomes less desirable as a sex object to most men. If she stays in the hustler's underworld, she then resorts to performing degrading services for emotionally disturbed men that all other women refuse to perform.

What happens to the prostitute in her declining years? According to Iceberg Slim, many of them become lesbians, and some become the pimps of lesbians.[19] In some cases they become the operators of bordellos. But in too many cases prostitutes have become hooked on narcotics. Many of them wind up in mental institutions. Prostitutes have a very high suicide rate, and, in general, do not earn very much.[20]

A woman who shares her body with all types of men inevitably encounters the occupational hazards of promiscuity, venereal disease and AIDS.

Some 30 percent of the Black prison women in the Atlanta sample, most of whom were former prostitutes, had sexually transmitted infections.[21]

The more recent increase in venereal disease can hardly be attributed to prostitution. Indeed, most public health authorities agree that prostitutes are usually conscientious about avoiding venereal disease and seeking treatment if they do contract it. Prostitutes, also, are rarely the transmitter of AIDS to their male clients.

Racist oppression and problems of poverty have made prostitution more common among Black women than among White women. But differences in the degree of prostitution among Black and White women tend to be hidden by their different sphere of activity. With sufficient accuracy, we can designate the typical Black prostitute as a streetwalker and the White prostitute as a call girl.

Call girls are described by one writer as the "aristocrats of prostitution."[22] They live in the most expensive residential sections of our large cities, they dress in rich, good taste and charge a minimum of a hundred dollars per sexual contact. Unlike the streetwalker, they are selective about customers, entertain clients in their homes or apartments, and assiduously avoid bars and restaurants patronized by other prostitutes.

The low status of Black women generally prevents them from becoming call girls. The clients of call girls are usually White men who want the call girl to be a part of their social life. Often these clients require an entire night of a girl's time, maybe taking her out to a night club as part of the arrangement. Most call girls are found in the better cocktail lounges and restaurants where the presence of a Black woman would be suspect. Police officers have been known to arrest Black females solely because they find them in the company of White men. Ordinarily a White woman can approach White men without having her motives questioned.[23]

There is very little glamour in the Black prostitute's life. Prostitution is a miserable occupation that exposes the Black woman to every sordid side of the human personality and to all the social ills that exist in human society. Prostitutes are disproportionately prey to the problems of drug addiction, alcoholism, mental illness, venereal disease and AIDS. They are exploited sexually and economically by the pimp, the customer, and the police. Their entire lives are not the carefree and happy ones depicted in the motion pictures and books. Instead, they live in a constant state of insecurity and most of them wind up penniless. They represent the epitome of womanhood abused to the level of a thing.

SEXUAL AGGRESSION

Crimes of sexual attacks against women are pervasive and sharply increasing in this country. The typical rapist is a Black male and his victim is most often a Black female. However, the most severe penalties for rape are reserved for Black males accused of raping White women. Although 50 percent of those convicted for rape in the South were White males, over 90 percent of those executed for this crime in that region were Black. Most of their alleged victims were White. No White male has ever been executed for raping a Black women.[24]

As is probably true of White females, the incidence of rape of Black women is underreported. Ladner reported that an eight-year-old girl has a good chance of being exposed to rape and violence if she is a member of the Black underclass.[25] The examples of Black males who have "taken it" from Black women are probably known to us all. Widespread incidents of this kind are rooted in the sexist socialization of all men in this society. And, it is pronounced among Black men who have other symbols of manhood blocked to them. Various explanations have been put forth to explain why Black men rape their women. Poussaint attributes it to the tendency of Black men to adopt the attitudes of the majority group toward Black women. Because White men have historically raped Black women with impunity many Black males believe they can do the same.[26] They are often correct in that assumption, as depicted in the saying of Sapphire that she realizes that "it is useless to report being raped because no one will believe that she didn't just give it away."[27]

Sexual violence is also rooted in the dynamics of the Black dating game. The majority of Black rape victims are familiar with their attacker, who was a friend, relative, or neighbor. Many of the rapes occur after a date and are what some describe as date rape.[28] A typical pattern is for the Black male to seek sexual compliance from his date, encounter resistance which he thinks is feigned, and proceed to forcibly extract sexual gratification from her. Large numbers of Black men believe sexual relations to be their "right" after a certain amount of dating. A truly reluctant Black woman is often victimized by the tendency of many Black women to play a coquettish role in resisting male sexual demands, when they actually are willing to engage in sexual intercourse.[29]

Rape, however, is not regarded as the act of a sexually starved male but rather as an aggressive act toward females. Students of the subject suggest that it is a long-delayed reaction against authority and powerlessness. In the case of Black men, it is asserted that they grow up feeling emasculated and powerless before reaching manhood. They often encounter women as authority figures and teachers or as the head of their household. These men consequently act out their feeling of powerlessness against Black women in the form of sexual aggression.[30] While such a characterization of Black rapists may be fairly accurate, rape should be viewed as both a sexual and political act because it is a function of external social factors, such as racial oppression, which maintain the barriers to normal channels of manhood for Black males.

Manhood in American society is closely tied to the acquisition of wealth. Wealth is power—power to control others. Men of wealth are rarely required to rape women because they gain sexual access through other means. The secretary or other female employee who submits to the sexual demands of a male employer, in order to advance in her job, is as much an unwilling partner in this situation as is the rape victim. The rewards for her sexual compliance are normatively sanctioned, whereas the rapist does not often have the resources to induce such sexual compliance. Moreover, it is the concept of women as sexual property that is at the root of rape as a crime that is ipso facto a male transgression. This concept is peculiar to capitalistic, European societies rather than African nations, where the incidence of rape is much lower. For Black men, rape is often an act of aggression against women because the kinds of status men can acquire through success in a job is not available to them.

THE POLITICS OF AIDS

There can be hardly a person in the world who has not heard of the AIDS "epidemic." Surprisingly, the reason for its widespread fame lies as much in the media blitz this disease has received as in its importance. Rarely, if ever, has one particular subject—including wars, race riots, poverty, governmental scandals, nuclear fallout, and so on—gotten such media exposure. Statisticians began keeping records on AIDS cases in early 1981 and as of April 1991, there were 171,876 cases of full-blown AIDS infection in the United States, 44 percent of them Black and Latino. During this ten-year period the disease had killed 108,731 persons.[31] On the basis of those known figures, one poll showed that Americans rated AIDS, over all other diseases, as the nation's number one health problem.[32]

Around the 1980s the news media was reporting the end of the sexual revolution, that men and women were looking for commitment and marriage chances instead of casual sex. This new sexual conservatism coincided with the aging of baby boom women (those born between 1945 and 1960) and the election of a conservative president who supported the traditional sexual ideals. Because women were getting older and facing biological deadlines for bearing a child, they started looking for fathers instead of sexual partners.

Adding to the rising tide of conservatism has been the massive amount of media publicity around the largely sexual disease known as AIDS. Although originally thought of as a White male's disease, the Centers for Disease Control report that Blacks and Latinos constitute 25 percent of those diagnosed with AIDS, 70 percent of the heterosexual cases, 70 percent of the female cases and 75 percent of all pediatric cases in 1988.[33] When one talks to middle class Blacks, most of them heterosexual, the topic of AIDS is always mentioned whenever the subject of sex is raised. However, it seemed to be women who appeared to be most frightened of acquiring the disease. Such a fear is disproportionate to the risks they face. According to the Centers for Disease Control, of the documented AIDS cases as of April 1991, heterosexual transmission of AIDS is the cause of but 5 percent (9,191) of the cases and these heterosexual transmissions include sexual partners from the high risk pool: intravenous drug users account for 4,868 such infections, and partners born in Pattern 2 high-risk countries of Central Africa, South America and the Caribbean where transmission is predominately heterosexual account for another 2,143 cases. Thus, of the 5 percent portion of Americans who have acquired the disease through heterosexual contact, 76 percent of such infections come from high-risk partners; another 6 percent of this group, or 540 cases, come from a sexual partner who also has had homosexual experiences and about 3 percent, or 260 cases, come from blood transfusion activity. Thirteen percent of infections are from other causes. About 93 percent of the AIDS victims are men. When the other high risk group of intravenous drug users are excluded, the Centers for Disease Control found that fewer than 1,000 heterosexual Americans in 1987 had acquired the AIDS disease by intercourse with others who did not belong to one of the high risk groups.[34]

Emphasis on the very small portion of infections occurring through heterosexual contact among low-risk partners should not trivialize the seriousness of this disease—it is always fatal—nor discourage respect and care for one's self and others in sexual matters. But this analysis of the reality of AIDS serves to highlight the politics of AIDS, the particular media spin put upon this disease that orchestrates racism, homophobia and sexual anxiety. Interest groups inadvertently arise in response to the AIDS hysteria—or at least it appears so on the surface. Gays believe society will treat the disease as a serious threat if the country believes it will affect heterosexuals. Members of the people of color community may feel the government will make a serious effort to deal with the presence of drugs among their group if they regard drug addicts as a serious source of AIDS propagation. The politicians will exploit the issue of AIDS in whichever way it will appeal to their constituencies. Liberals will demand money for education, research and treatment of AIDS. Politicians of a conservative mode are demanding mandatory testing, an emphasis on sexual abstinence and confinement of infected individuals. For selected businesses, the AIDS hysteria has provided a number of commercial opportunities. They include manufacturers of condoms and blood testing kits.[35]

One has to be struck by the anomaly of White middle class women being the most frightened of acquiring AIDS. Not only are 93 percent of the AIDS victims men, but of the heterosexual women with AIDS, 70 percent are women of color from inner city neighborhoods.[36] Yet, the fear and the campaigns for safe sex and education efforts seem to target a group of middle class White women who probably number fewer than 1 percent of the 107,000 AIDS deaths in the United States. Understandably racial attitudes in this country would make it difficult to promote safe sex practices if the educational programs were aimed primarily at lower income Black and Hispanic women. The conventional wisdom is that sexual promiscuity and drug use are strongly ingrained parts of those cultures. This begs the question of why the condom commercials are not aimed at the White male population.

The AIDS hysteria will, and has, impacted negatively on other groups. Already the number of incidents of physical or verbal violence against homosexuals has more than doubled from 1985 to 1986.[37] Various forms of discrimination against gay men are on the increase. At least White male homosexuals have the option of hiding their sexual preference. If the number of AIDS cases among Blacks and Latinos grows, and they become strongly associated with the disease, their high visibility will add to the discriminatory treatment they already face in American society. Worst of all may be the treatment of AIDS victims. The hysteria surrounding this disease has led to the denial of civil liberties for many of them and proposals to isolate them from the rest of society. Any vulnerable group such as foreigners, many of them people of color, may be subject to mandatory testing procedures.

While AIDS is a serious disease and deserves to be fully researched and treated regardless of what groups it impacts, this country faces a number of problems that are more likely to weaken its social fabric and impair its ability to function. Bombarding us with fearful projections about a sexually transmitted disease that has barely touched 90 percent of the country's population may erode the credibility of the medical and journalistic professions, and weaken our resolve to respond to more serious and life threatening issues when they occur. Meanwhile, the society has put on the back burner the issues of racial and class division, poverty and unemployment, the homeless, and nuclear destruction, in order to inculcate sexual guilt in the population on the basis of the fear that anything less than sexual monogamy will lead to death. The real danger is that we will become so preoccupied with the sexual aspects of the problem that Americans will ignore the problems of drug addiction and its causes, social alienation and joblessness, that precipitate drug use, especially among peoples of color.

In the decade of the 1980s, the dominant issues before the body politic have been moral concerns dealing with the individual's use of drugs, alcohol, tobacco and sex. At the same time, a growing gap in the income of the poor and the rich, a society that is increasingly segregated by race, a foreign policy that contributes to the untold deaths of millions each year has been subordinated to the push to return Americans to an earlier era when people did not drink, smoke or enjoy sex. AIDS has become the source of such pervasive fear because it is a disease that is transmitted largely by sexual contact. The sexual aspect of the disease feeds into the puritanical and uncomfortable attitudes that many Americans hold toward this subject. And, the power structure has used it to divert our attention and energy away from the arsenal of serious problems that afflict this nation. As Gore Vidal has asserted, "Sex is politics. The sexual mores of a society are the result of political decisions. Not vice versa. You enslave people through prohibitions, preferably based on religion. Sexual guilt among the population is a good thing for those who rule. That, of course, doesn't mean the rulers take seriously what they impose on the ruled."[38]

AIDS certainly lends itself to a divide and conquer strategy. It will pit major groups in the society against each other. The homosexual victims of AIDS find themselves scorned, isolated and discriminated against by a heterosexual majority for forces largely beyond their control. People of color such as Blacks and Latinos have long used drugs as a form of coping with their systematic exclusion from mainstream activity. Now, they face a choice of early death from drug overdoses or AIDS. The issue of color in some nations has already been raised as many countries have singled out Africans as a target of immigration restrictions and mandatory testing procedures. In this country it only adds to the racial hostilities that lie just below the surface for Black and White Americans.[39] The concentration of AIDS in the highly visible Black and Latino populations only adds to the racial polarization in this country.

SUMMARY

Sexuality, in a historical and biological sense, was the tool by which Homo sapiens reproduced the species. There is evidence that in its original